Date Due

Analysis of Discrete Physical Systems

McGraw-Hill Electrical and Electronic Engineering Series

Herman E. Koenig

Professor of Electrical Engineering
and Systems Science
Michigan State University

Yılmaz Tokad

Associate Professor of Electrical Engineering
and Systems Science
Michigan State University

Hiremaglur K. Kesavan

Professor of Electrical Engineering
Indian Institute of Technology
Kanpur, India

With the collaboration of
Harry G. Hedges

Associate Professor
of Electrical Engineering
Michigan State University

Analysis of Discrete Physical Systems

McGraw-Hill Book Company
New York St. Louis San Francisco Toronto London Sydney

Analysis of Discrete Physical Systems

Preface

This book presents a discipline for the analysis of systems made up of a finite number of interacting components drawing primarily on examples of application from three types of physical processes—electrical, mechanical, and hydraulic. The analysis procedures presented are based primarily on state-space models and establish a foundation for advanced work in design, synthesis, and control.

The subjects included in the solid-line sections of the flow diagram of system theory on page viii are contained in this book and fall within the scope of analysis as defined here. The salient aspects of control, design, and synthesis are included in the dashed-line sections of the diagram and relate to analysis at the stages indicated.

The first step in analysis, identification of the system components and the variables, is considered in Chapter 1. Elementary mathematical forms useful in modeling the unconstrained terminal characteristics of typical two-terminal and multiterminal components are considered in Chapters 2 and 3, along with basic techniques for establishing the parameters in the models from controlled experiments. A laboratory program, embracing a broad spectrum of physical components and systems, is considered a very desirable, if not an essential complement to this phase of the development. It is in the laboratory that the constructional features and detailed performance characteristics of particular devices are appropriately considered.

The interconnection model is presented in Chapter 4 as a set of linear algebraic constraint equations formulated from a linear graph of the system. Operational procedures are given for constructing the graph of any system of components, and the basic properties of graphs are developed. It is shown that Kirchhoff's postulates, stated originally only in electrical network theory, are indeed equally fundamental to *all* types of physical processes. The "laws of mechanics" as given in this new context differ from the traditional statements both in substance and in philosophical orientation.

As implied by the flow diagram on page viii, a model of the system is generated by systematically combining the component models and the interconnection model. In the special case of linear systems, the system model may be developed as a set of first-order differential equations (called *state equations* or *time-domain models*) or as a set of algebraic equations in the complex variable s (called *complex-frequency models* or *s-domain models*). In view of the general utility of state models in both linear and nonlinear analysis and simulations and their position in modern design, synthesis, and control theory, they are emphasized throughout this book. State models of systems of relatively elementary components, both linear and nonlinear, and their machine solutions are considered in Chapter 5.

General analytical solutions and stability concepts of both continuous

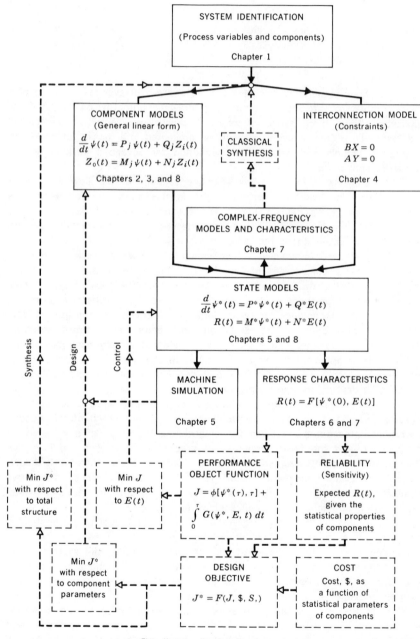

Flow diagram of system theory

and discrete-time models are developed in Chapter 6 in terms of functions of matrices (calculus of matrices). These developments provide the foundations for the more detailed study of important response characteristics presented in Chapter 7. Laplace- and z-transform methods are introduced as logical extensions of real frequency concepts and as alternative procedures for solving linear continuous and discrete-time models. Generalized forms of the more traditional mesh and node equations of electrical-network theory are introduced as methods for developing admittance, impedance, and transfer matrices of systems as explicit functions of the s-domain short-circuit, open-circuit, and mixed-parameter models of the components and the interconnection constraints.

Chapter 8 is devoted to the analysis of large-scale systems through models of subassemblies and in some respects represents a synthesis of many of the concepts presented in the first seven chapters. State models and complex-frequency models are used interchangeably and alternatively in the analysis of important two-port and other simple configurations. Single-variable feedback systems are considered in terms of both state models and s-domain and z-domain transfer functions. The book concludes with the development of the properties of systems of arbitrarily connected linear multiterminal components of the most general form as encountered in the analysis of large-scale systems through subassemblies.

This text has its origin in an educational development program in the electrical engineering department at Michigan State University. This program recognizes discrete physical systems, continuum theory (continuous systems), and materials science as three major scientific disciplines in electrical engineering. The book was developed to present the subject of analysis in the systems program.

The style of presentation is such that each important property is developed and stated as a theorem in the discipline and then demonstrated by at least one example. The book therefore can be used either as a beginning graduate or as an undergraduate text. At the undergraduate level the formal proofs of many theorems can be omitted with the emphasis on the concepts and procedures demonstrated by the many examples. At the graduate level, on the other hand, some examples can be omitted in favor of emphasizing the theoretical foundations and concepts inherent in the formal proofs of the theorems. Each chapter includes a large set of home problems from which selections can be made to emphasize either objective.

In general, the development assumes that the reader is familiar with differential equations and elementary matrix algebra. The more specialized properties of matrices required in the development are included in the Appendix.

The authors acknowledge the support by the National Science Foundation of the Curriculum Development Program under which the material in this book was developed. They are deeply indebted to the faculty of the Department of Electrical Engineering and to the administration of the College of Engineering for their support. Acknowledgment is made of suggestions of the faculty directly involved in teaching the material during its developments. The authors especially recognize the contributions of Dr. H. G. Hedges as an outstanding teacher and technical editor.

Finally, the authors recognize the contribution of the secretarial staff of the Department of Electrical Engineering and the Division of Engineering Research.

Herman E. Koenig
Yılmaz Tokad
Hiremaglur K. Kesavan

Contents

Analysis of Discrete Physical Systems

1

Systems Concepts
and the First Postulate

1.1 INTRODUCTION

This book presents a discipline for the analysis of systems of discrete physical components such as those shown in Figs. 1.1.1 to 1.1.3. Systems exemplified by the control system in Fig. 1.1.1 and the electronic network in Fig. 1.1.2 are referred to as *physical systems*, since they are clearly realized as an interconnected set of physical devices or components. The transportation system in Fig. 1.1.3, on the other hand, is somewhat more conceptual in nature, is concerned with one of the activities of a living society, and is sometimes referred to as a *socioeconomic system*.

The significant feature common to both types of systems is that they are viewed as collections of discrete components united at a finite number of interfaces.

Thus, a system as defined in the context of this book is a collection of interacting components, which in the most general case can be represented schematically as shown in Fig. 1.1.4. The closed regions represent components, and the points of contact $A, B, C, \ldots, G$ between the regions represent interfaces.

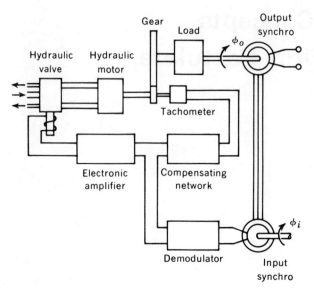

Fig. 1.1.1 Typical control system.

The development in the first several chapters is concerned primarily with a discipline for developing *mathematical models* of such systems of interacting components, i.e., a set of simultaneous algebraic and/or differential or difference equations showing the interdependence of a set of variables which characterize the observable behavior of the system. These models, as we shall see, are developed systematically from an identified system structure, i.e., from:

1.   *Mathematical models of the components themselves*
2.   *A mathematical model of their interconnection pattern*

In this sense the system model reflects a system structure explicitly— a feature which is absolutely essential to sensitivity, reliability, and other

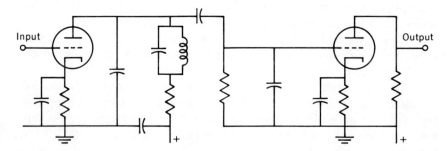

Fig. 1.1.2 Typical electronic system.

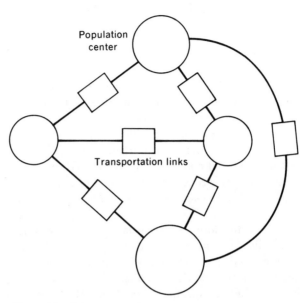

Fig. 1.1.3 A transportation system.

simulation studies as well as to all design and synthesis objectives. Indeed, it is only in the system structure that changes can be made in an effort to improve the system performance.

A fundamental axiom of the discipline is that *a mathematical model of a component characterizes the behavior of that component of the system as an entity and independently of how the component is interconnected with other components to form a system.* This implies that the various components can be "removed" either literally or conceptually from the remaining components and studied in "isolation" to establish models of their characteristics. It is precisely this feature that makes system theory

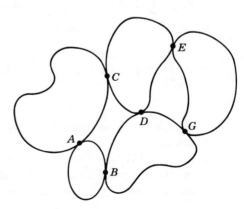

Fig. 1.1.4 Schematic representation of a system of interacting components.

a universal tool of science—the analyst can go as far as he wishes in breaking a system down in search of "building blocks" which are sufficiently simple to be modeled and which identify a structure upon which alterations can be made.   In the physical sciences the building blocks, generally speaking, are well defined.   There are many decades of experience in modeling, and a tremendous catalogue of component characteristics has been developed.   At least the *general form* of the mathematical model is known for essentially every component that goes into a guidance system, a control mechanism, or an electronic circuit.   In the area of economics, business, marketing, transportation, etc., the system components are as yet not well defined, and the accumulation of experience in modeling is short.   For this reason the examples of applications presented in this book are limited to physical systems of the electrical, mechanical, and hydraulic types.

The development in the last several chapters of the book is concerned primarily with the use of mathematical models in simulating the operating characteristics of systems of interacting components *as functions of a defined system structure*.   Thus, system theory can, in general, be divided into two broad aspects: (1) modeling theory—the process of generating a model of the system from a defined system structure; (2) behavioral theory—the process of analyzing the solution characteristics of the system model to simulate the physical behavior of the system as a function of a change in the structural features.

Machine simulations as well as recent advances in the theory of stability, control, optimization, design, and synthesis are all based on what are referred to as *state-space models*.   It is sufficient for the present to indicate that, in general, such a model is in the form of a set of simultaneous first-order differential or difference equations and a set of simultaneous algebraic equations, which for linear systems are typically of the form

$$\frac{d}{dt}\psi_i = \sum_{j=1}^{n} p_{ij}\psi_j + e_i \qquad i = 1, 2, \ldots, n$$

and

$$r_l = \sum_{j=1}^{n} m_{lj}\psi_j \qquad l = 1, 2, \ldots, k$$

where

p_{ij} and m_{lj} are constants that depend upon the identified system structure

ψ_i are called the *state variables*

e_i are the identified inputs or excitation variables

r_l are the identified output or response variables

The objective of this book is to present general methods for system analysis and simulations and to establish the foundations for system design and synthesis, control, optimization, and other areas of advanced system theory. Consequently, state-space models are considered almost exclusively.

1.2 THE FIRST POSTULATE OF SYSTEM THEORY

As already implied, the mathematical models of the components in the identified structure of a system serve as the building blocks of system theory and therefore represent the starting point of our development. In the case of the majority of physical systems, such as those shown in Figs. 1.1.1 and 1.1.2, the components can each be literally disjointed or uncoupled from the other components of the system, placed on a laboratory bench, and subjected to a series of arbitrary tests which will be considered in more detail in a later section. In the case of socioeconomic and some types of physical systems the uncoupling and isolation may be only conceptual.

Although physical components are usually easily enough disjointed, there may be various practical problems of isolation, such as induced voltages in certain classes of electronic circuits as a result of their proximity to other components or other systems. In such cases one is forced either to neglect these effects or to consider the isolation as conceptual rather than literal.

To establish a basis for identifying a useful system structure and the subsequent process of modeling, let the system be indicated conceptually by a set of regions joined at interfaces A, B, . . . , G as shown in Fig. 1.1.4. Each component (indicated as a region) is said to have a *terminal* corresponding to each of its interfaces with other components.

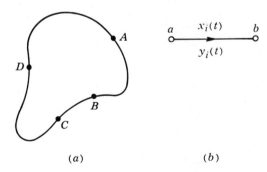

(a)   *(b)*

Fig. 1.2.1 A system component (a) and a mapping (b) identifying a pair of complementary variables x_i and y_i with an arbitrary pair of terminals A and B.

The question now is: What constitutes a mathematical model of each identified component, whether a piece of physical hardware or part of a socioeconomic process?   To answer this question, consider the four-terminal component shown in Fig. 1.2.1a.   Let a pair of complementary variables x_i and y_i [actually functions of time $x_i(t)$ and $y_i(t)$] be identified with the pair of component terminals A and B by the mapping shown in Fig. 1.2.1b.   The line segment in the mapping is called an *edge*.   The end points a and b corresponding to the component terminals A and B are called the *vertices* of the mapping, and the variables x and y are called *terminal variables*.

In general, if a component has n terminals, then, of course, it is possible to identify a pair of complementary variables $x_i(t)$ and $y_i(t)$ with each possible pair of terminals on the component by a mapping that includes exactly one vertex for each component terminal and one edge for each pair of terminals.   The edges of the mapping illustrated in Fig. 1.2.2 for a four-terminal component identify a pair of oriented complementary variables with every possible pair of terminals on the component.

However, not all these variables are required to model the characteristics of the component.   They can be modeled by the complementary variables identified by a *tree* of edges on the n vertices of the mapping, defined as follows:

Definition 1.2.1:   A set of $n - 1$ edges connecting n vertices but forming no closed paths is called a tree of edges (or simply a tree) on the n vertices. If the n vertices correspond to the terminals of an n-terminal component, then the tree of edges is called a *terminal graph* of the component.

Several terminal graphs for a four-terminal component are shown in Fig. 1.2.3.

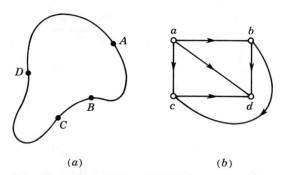

(a)   (b)

Fig. 1.2.2   A system component (*a*) and a mapping (*b*) identifying a pair of complementary variables with each possible pair of terminals.

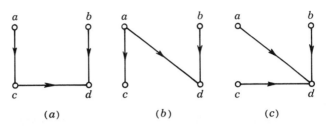

Fig. 1.2.3 Three distinct terminal graphs for a four-terminal component.

The first fundamental postulate of system theory is now stated as follows:

Postulate 1: The pertinent performance (behavioral) characteristics of each n-terminal component in an identified system structure are completely specified by a set of $n - 1$ equations in $n - 1$ pairs of oriented complementary variables $x_i(t)$ and $y_i(t)$ identified by an arbitrarily chosen terminal graph (the variables x_i and y_i may be vectors if necessary).

The identities of the complementary terminal variables $x(t)$ and $y(t)$ are shown in Table 1.2.1 for physical and socioeconomic processes. Following Firestone[2] and Trent[3], one variable, $x(t)$, is known as the *across variable* and the other, $y(t)$, the *through variable*. Although this terminology is used throughout this book, *propensity* and *flow rate* are also sometimes used, particularly in socioeconomic applications.

Conceptually, the pairs of complementary variables used to characterize each of the various processes are associated with a pair of component terminals and are oriented in one sense or another. In the physical sciences, each pair of complementary variables is also defined operationally; i.e., the variables are defined in terms of a specific set of operations (the instrumentation) for assigning a numerical value to the

Table 1.2.1 Complementary variables for typical processes

Process	Me-chanical	Hydraulic	Electrical	Traffic	Economic	General
$x(t)$	Velocity	Pressure	Voltage	Density	Unit price	Across variable (propensity)
$y(t)$	Force	Flow rate	Current	Flow rate	Flow of goods	Through variable (flow)

variables.   Through the efforts of the Bureau of Standards a volt and an ampere are operationally identical to all scientists, although conceptually they vary somewhat from one individual to another.   Unfortunately, operational definitions of the complementary variables identifying many of the socioeconomic processes have not been established, while others have not even been defined conceptually.

The first postulate of system theory is suggested in part by a generalization of Kirchhoff's laws of electrical network theory, considered in detail in Chap. 4.

Where the complementary variables characterizing a process have not as yet been defined, it can be said that they must be defined so as to be consistent with the first postulate if system theory is to serve as a scientific tool of investigation.

Insofar as the mathematical development of the discipline of system theory presented in this book is concerned, the pairs of complementary variables $x(t)$ and $y(t)$ characterizing each of the various physical and nonphysical processes are regarded as *mathematically undefined* (they are conceptually and operationally defined as the basis for characterizing a given process).   All other variables of system theory, including power and energy, are *mathematically defined* in terms of these complementary variables.

Definition 1.2.2:   Let the row vectors $\mathbf{X} = (x_1, x_2, \ldots, x_{n-1})$ and $\mathbf{Y} = (y_1, y_2, \ldots, y_{n-1})$ represent, respectively, the across and through variables of an n-terminal component identified by an arbitrarily selected terminal graph; then, the scalar function of time

$$P(t) = \mathbf{X}(t)\mathbf{Y}^T(t) = \mathbf{Y}(t)\mathbf{X}^T(t)$$
$$= x_1(t)y_1(t) + x_2(t)y_2(t) + \cdots + x_{n-1}(t)y_{n-1}(t)$$

is defined as the *power input* to the component.   The *energy* input to the component over the time interval $t_0 \leq t \leq t_1$ is defined as

$$W(t_1) = \int_{t_0}^{t_1} p(t)\, dt$$

It is, of course, possible in an alternative development to regard the components of power $p_i(t) = x_i(t)y_i(t)$ or energy $w_i(t)$ associated with the edges of the terminal graph along with either $x(t)$ *or* $y(t)$, but not both, as the basic complementary variables.

In the case where multiple processes are associated with a given component, a set of terminals is associated with each process, and the complementary variables of each process are identified by means of a tree of edges on the set of terminals associated with each process as shown in Fig. 1.2.4.   The terminal graph, in this case, forms a tree of edges on the set of vertices associated with each process, and we say that the terminal

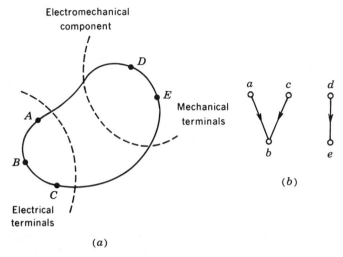

Fig. 1.2.4 Terminal graph identifying the variables in a multi-process component (electromechanical component).

graph for the component is in separate parts. Physical components involving two processes are called *transducers* and are considered in more detail in a later chapter.

1.3 ISOMORPHISM BETWEEN THE COMPONENT TERMINAL GRAPH AND PHYSICAL MEASUREMENTS

For quantitative analysis it is necessary to relate, unambiguously, the complementary through and across variables identified by the terminal graph of an n-terminal component to the measurements they represent. Such an identification is referred to as an *isomorphism* between the terminal graph and the physical measurements.

An effective scheme for identifying this isomorphism is evident when one considers the basic properties of physical measurements.

The properties of voltage and current measurements, for example, are reflected in the principle of operation of the D'Arsonval, or permanent-magnet, mechanism. This device consists of a movable coil of wire located in a magnetic field as shown in Fig. 1.3.1. The rotation of the coil of wire against a spring is proportional to the "electric current" flowing between the two terminals. There are various techniques for automatically recording the position of the coil as a function of time, the details of which are more appropriate to a laboratory activity than the development given here. Because of the nonzero mass of the moving element in the D'Arsonval mechanism, the rate of change in the measure-

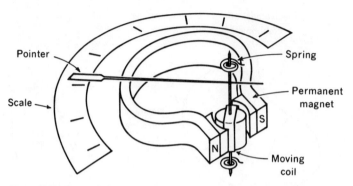

Fig. 1.3.1 D'Arsonval mechanism.

ment that can be recorded is quite low compared with what is required in an effective analysis of some electrical systems, such as radio, television, and other electronic systems. Such time-varying measurements can, however, be recorded with a cathode-ray oscilloscope. As an instrument to measure time-varying signals, this device has the same basic properties and serves precisely the same purpose as the D'Arsonval mechanism, but it uses the deflection of an electron beam rather than a rotating coil as an indicator.

The basic difference between a voltmeter and a current meter is only in the application and sensitivity (i.e., maximum deflection) of the D'Arsonval instrument or its equivalent. The D'Arsonval mechanism used for the voltage measurement may be connected in series with a resistor† as shown in Fig. 1.3.2a. When used for current measurement

---

† A resistor is defined later as an electrical component for which the voltage and current measurements are related by a constant. If it is not already evident, it will be at that time that the extent to which the current measurement is influenced by the voltmeter connection decreases as the magnitude of the resistance of the series resistor increases.

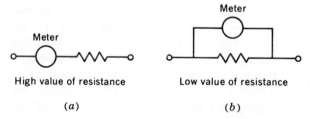

Fig. 1.3.2 (a) High-resistance voltmeter and (b) low-resistance ammeter.

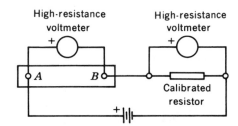

Fig. 1.3.3 Voltage and current measurements using two high-resistance meters and a calibrated resistor.

the same device may be paralleled by a resistor as shown in Fig. 1.3.2*b*. These resistors can be included as part of the instruments, as is frequently the case with manually read meters, or, alternatively, two high-resistance instruments can be used in conjunction with a calibrated resistor, as shown in Fig. 1.3.3, to realize both the voltage and current measurements. In modern instrumentation this latter technique is the more frequently used, since the oscilloscope and recording galvanometers, with the associated electronic amplifiers, are inherently very high-resistance devices.

The two important properties of both voltage and current measurements are that (1) they are both associated with a pair of points (the measuring device has two terminals) and (2) the indication of the instrument (the direction of deflection) reverses when the terminals of the meter are reversed with respect to a given pair of points. The meters are, therefore, polarized by affixing a standard mark, usually at "$+$", to one terminal of the instrument. In the case of the oscilloscope, one terminal is identified as "ground." The voltage measurement V at a pair of terminals A and B is always made by connecting the meter "across" the terminals, as shown in Fig. 1.3.4, and is therefore identified as the across variable $x(t)$ referred to in Table 1.2.1. In contrast, the current measurement I at a pair of terminals A and B is always made by connecting the instrument in series with the terminals (and an appropriate source of excitation if necessary), as shown in Fig. 1.3.4, and is therefore identi-

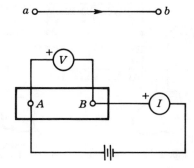

Fig. 1.3.4 Isomorphism between an edge in a component terminal graph and the corresponding electrical instrumentation.

fied as the through variable $y(t)$. The relative orientation of both the voltage and current meters with respect to the given pair of terminals is recorded in the terminal graph of the component by the correspondence indicated in Fig. 1.3.4 between the orientation of the edge of the terminal graph and the polarization of the instruments. This indicated correspondence or isomorphism, though arbitrary, is used consistently throughout this text. Note that the marked terminal of the voltmeter is connected to the point corresponding to the tail of the arrow. This isomorphism is sometimes described as representing the "potential" of point A with respect to B. In terms of the concept of electrical current as a movement of positive charge, it can be said that the current is in the direction of the arrow *when the number indicated by the instrument is greater than zero.*

Models of pneumatic and hydraulic systems are based on the complementary variables of *pressure* $p(t)$ and *flow* $g(t)$ or *flow rate* $\dot{g}(t)$. The operation of much of the practical instrumentation for measurement of pressure is based on detecting the displacement of a metallic membrane (or one of some other suitable material) located between the two points or regions in question, as shown schematically in Fig. 1.3.5. Time variations in pressure are frequently recorded by detecting the displacement of the metallic membrane by means of strain gauges cemented to the membrane. The voltage measurement at the terminal of an appropriate network of strain gauges is then directly proportional to the pressure measurement between regions A and B. The entire device is referred to as a *pressure transducer.*

When one of the regions A or B corresponds to free atmosphere, the measurement is referred to as *gauge pressure.* On the other hand, if A or B is an evacuated region, the measurement is called *absolute pressure.* When neither region A nor B corresponds to free atmosphere or an evacuated region, the measurement is referred to as *differential pressure.*

The numerical value of the measurement (whether positive or negative) depends, of course, on the orientation of the indicating instrument

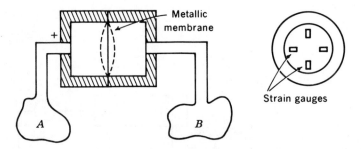

Fig. 1.3.5 Membrane used as a basis for pressure measurements.

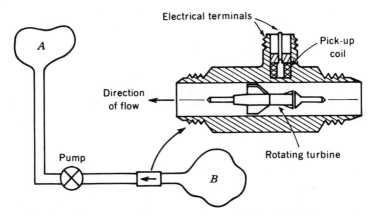

Fig. 1.3.6 Flow measurements using a turbine-type flowmeter.

with respect to the two regions.   From the manner in which the instrument is associated with the two regions, it is an across type of measurement.

The volume flow, or rate of flow, can be recorded as a function of
time either by means of a turbine type of instrument, shown schematically
in Fig. 1.3.6, or through the use of a pressure transducer and calibrated
"hydraulic resistor," shown in Fig. 1.3.7.

In the former technique, the number of revolutions is proportional
to the volume of flow, and the rotational velocity of the turbine is directly
proportional to the volume rate of flow.   To count automatically the
number of revolutions of the turbine, or to record the turbine speed as a
function of time, an appropriate electrical circuit is provided to give an
electrical measurement proportional to the speed.   The entire unit then
is referred to as a *flow transducer*.

Although the instrumentation shown in Fig. 1.3.7 is perhaps not
used as frequently in modern instrumentation as that shown in Fig. 1.3.6,

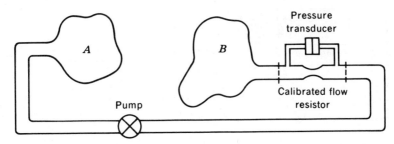

Fig. 1.3.7 Flowmeter using a pressure transducer in conjunction with a
calibrated resistor.

it nevertheless is a practical procedure and has an interesting parallel to the instrumentation shown in Figs. 1.3.2 and 1.3.3.

The isomorphism between the edges of component terminal graphs and hydraulic instrumentation is shown in Fig. 1.3.8. The pressure measurement is said to represent the relative pressure of region A with respect to region B; that is, the side of the pressure meter marked $+$ is the "high-pressure point" if the instrument indication is represented by a positive number. In making so-called "gauge-pressure" measurements this terminal or port is connected to the region in question, whereas the unmarked terminal is open to the atmosphere.

It is common practice to polarize the flowmeter by establishing an arrow on the meter so that the flow is in the direction of the arrow when the meter indicates a positive number. Note that the orientation of the terminal graph is consistent with the orientation on the flowmeter.

When the measurements are made with electromechanical or electro-hydraulic transducers, it is implied, of course, that the edges of the terminal graph are isomorphic to instrumentation equivalent to that shown in Fig. 1.3.8.

Since there are three directions in which a rigid body can translate and three axes about which it can rotate, the measurements involved in characterizing general mechanical motion are more complex than are electrical and hydraulic measurements. Consider first pure translation between fixed points A and B on two rigid bodies, as indicated in Fig. 1.3.9. The displacement between the two points A and B is said to represent the displacement between the bodies or regions.

Fundamentally, displacement measurements are realized by means of a calibrated scale, and in the case of three-dimensional translation, three such calibrated scales or lines are required. These lines, called

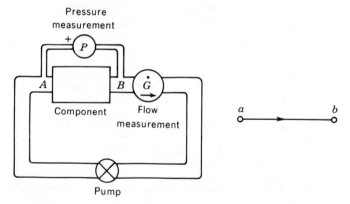

Fig. 1.3.8 Isomorphism between an edge of a component terminal graph and the corresponding hydraulic instrumentation.

coordinate axes, may be straight or curved in any manner. However, in practice, the three coordinate systems most frequently used are cartesian, cylindrical, and spherical, all of which are orthogonal systems. The system shown in Fig. 1.3.9 is called a *right-hand cartesian system.*

It is clear that three distinct numbers, usually arranged in the form of a vector $(\delta_x, \delta_y, \delta_z)$, are required to specify the translational displacement between two points at any instant of time. The coordinate system can be regarded as the "instrument." In the application of this instrument the origin of the three coordinate axes is located at either point A or point B. For the location of the origin indicated in Fig. 1.3.9, all position numbers δ_x, δ_y, and δ_z are positive. However, as an alternative procedure, the origin might just as well be located at point A, the new position of the coordinate axes being parallel to the original. In this case the displacement between the two bodies is represented by three negative numbers. Thus, like the electrical and hydraulic across measurements, the displacement measurement depends upon the orientation of the instrument. The isomorphism used throughout this book between the edges of the component graph and three-dimensional translation measurements is indicated in Fig. 1.3.9 and can be described as representing the position of point A with respect to B.

To measure the rotational displacement between two rigid bodies, a set of three reference lines, such as a right-hand cartesian-coordinate system, is associated with both bodies, as shown in Fig. 1.3.10. In this figure, body B is shown to have rotated about the y axis. The angle of rotation is specified by measuring the angle between x_a and x_b. It is common practice to calibrate the circular scale used to measure this angle with increasing scale in the direction in which a right-hand screw rotates when advancing in the positive direction of the axis of rotation. Thus,

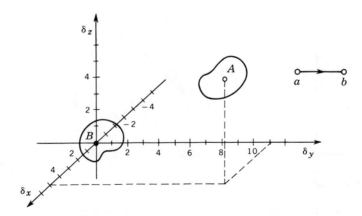

Fig. 1.3.9 Measurement of displacement between two bodies.

to measure the angle of rotation about the y axis in Fig. 1.3.10, a circular scale calibrated in a clockwise direction is used. This right-hand convention for calibrating the circular scales is adopted here for making rotational-displacement measurements. As in calibrating the coordinate axes, the direction of increasing scale is part of the instrument and must be standardized for a given system study.

As in the case of translational-displacement measurements, the sign of the number ϕ_y used to represent the rotation depends on the location of the origin of the measuring instrument, i.e., whether we consider the rotation of the coordinate axis on B with respect to that on A, or vice versa. Unfortunately, three-dimensional rotation between two bodies or regions cannot be represented simply by three independent numbers; the numerical values depend also on the sequence in which the three rotations occur. At present our discussion is limited to rotations about only one axis, in which case the concepts reflected in Fig. 1.3.10 are totally adequate.

In mechanical-system studies, as in any system study, we are interested in measurements that vary with time, and it is necessary to record automatically such displacement measurements. There are many practical techniques for recording both translational and rotational measurements using electromechanical transducers to generate voltages which are directly proportional to the displacements. It is not within the scope of this book to consider the details of these transducers.

Although the intuitive concept of force is usually described as "something pushing at a point," the instrumentation used in translating this concept to the real-number system involves two points, and, as in the case of the previous measurements, the results obtained depend upon an orientation of the instrument with respect to the points in question. To see that this is so, consider the measurements shown schematically in Fig. 1.3.11a.

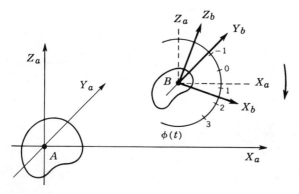

Fig. 1.3.10   Measurement of angle of rotation about the y axis.

The displacement measurement between the two ends of the calibrated spring is proportional to the force transmitted from point A to point B and is usually represented by the symbol f. When the standard spring, along with the calibrated scale, is regarded as the force meter, we see that the instrument is connected in series with the two points A and B through a source of mechanical excitation. In this respect the force measurement is similar to current and fluid-flow measurements and is appropriately referred to as a *through measurement* (it measures the transmitted force). In comparing the mechanical measurements in Fig. 1.3.11 with the electrical measurements shown in Fig. 1.3.2, we also see that in both cases the through-type measurement is realized by the use of the across meter and a calibrated device.

The nature of the oriented property of the force measurement is contained in a comparison between Figs. 1.3.11a and b. As the origin of the calibrated scale is transferred from one end of the calibrated spring to the other, the numerical value of the meter indication changes sign. This change in orientation is isomorphic to a change in the orientation of the edge in the terminal graph.

Although the simple force meter consisting of a spring and calibrated scale shows clearly the basic properties of force measurement, it is, of course, very primitive as a scientific instrument. Force measurements, like displacement measurements, are conveniently recorded as a function of time through the use of various transducers. In any event the isomorphism between the edges of the terminal graph and the instrumentation is equivalent to that shown by the primitive instruments in Fig. 1.3.11. Since force is usually not regarded as a "flow," it is difficult to describe this isomorphism adequately in words.

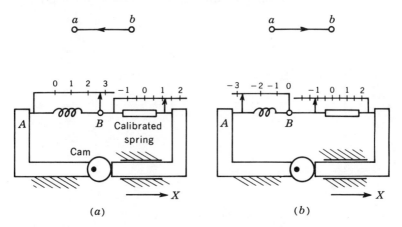

Fig. 1.3.11 Isomorphism between edges of component terminal graphs and mechanical measurements.

In general, it is always possible, even for various socioeconomic processes, to identify each pair of complementary terminal variables associated with the edges of a selected terminal graph with a unique pair of measurements at the terminals of the component. The isomorphism selected is, of course, somewhat arbitrary, but once defined it must be used consistently throughout a given system study. It can be regarded as establishing an unambiguous tie between the physical process and the mathematical model characterizing it.

1.4 COMPONENT MODELS

Beyond selecting a terminal graph on the n terminals of a component to identify the $2(n - 1)$ complementary terminal variables for the model, there remains the task of actually establishing the model. In general, one is required to select one set S_1 of $(n - 1)$-terminal variables as independent variable functions of time and the remaining set S_2 of $(n - 1)$-terminal variables as dependent variable functions of time. The only requirement on the sets S_1 and S_2 is that each contains $(n - 1)$-terminal variables. The model consists of a set of $n - 1$ relations or, more generally, a mapping showing the variable functions of time in S_2 as a function of the variable functions of time in set S_1. These relations can be given in the form of tables, curves, or mathematical functions, but, generally speaking, mathematical functions are required in all but the very simple system studies.

To be more specific, consider the simplest possible component—a component with only two terminals, such as a single rigid body with its inertial reference shown in Fig. 1.4.1. Upon using the terminal variables (x velocity, y force) identified by the terminal graph, a model requires that we establish an algebraic or differential equation which gives the time

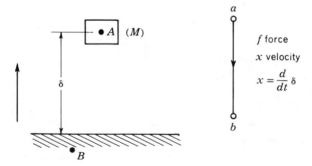

Fig. 1.4.1   A two-terminal rigid body (mass) free to move vertically only (one-dimensional motion).

variation in one terminal variable as a function of an *arbitrary* time variation in the complementary variable, i.e.,

$$y(t) = F[x(t)] \qquad \text{or} \qquad x(t) = G[y(t)]$$

Note that we are not looking simply for the magnitude of y as a function of the magnitude of x, but rather for a function F or mapping which tells us the time variation in $y(t)$ *given an arbitrary time variation in $x(t)$*. If, for example, we plot the measured value of $y(t)$ as a function of the particular *time function* $x(t)$ = const (constant velocity), we obtain, of course, $y(t) = 0$. On the other hand, if we take $x(t) = Kt$ (constant acceleration), then we find that $y(t)$ = const. The equation which establishes the time function $y(t)$ for both the given time variations in $x(t)$ is, of course, the differential equation

$$y(t) = M \frac{d}{dt} x(t) \qquad (1.4.1)$$

Accumulated empirical evidence shows that Eq. (1.4.1) does, in fact, apply for a very large class of time functions $x(t)$, and so a useful model of this component has been established.

The point to be emphasized is that in modeling the characteristics of an n-terminal component it is necessary to excite or subject the system to one set of $n - 1$ time-varying signals and observe the response or time variation in the other set of $n - 1$ variables. But what type of time functions should be used for excitation? Unfortunately there is no universal answer to this question, and rarely, if ever, is it possible to establish equations that model the behavior of the component for all classes of time variations. Any model is inherently limited to certain classes of functions as characterized by their magnitudes and time derivatives.

Several types of time functions, found to be useful in system studies, are discussed in detail in the next section, along with definitions of various features used to characterize them. It is shown that any function with a finite period can be expanded into a Fourier series of sinusoidal functions of time. Further, a pulse or square wave, theoretically at least, contains an infinite number of harmonics in its expansion. For these reasons sinusoidal time functions of variable frequency, pulse trains, and square-wave functions are effective test signals for modeling the terminal characteristics of a component.

Applications of these test signals in modeling the characteristics of typical components are considered in the following two chapters.

1.5   MATHEMATICAL REPRESENTATIONS OF TYPICAL SIGNALS

(A) CLOSED FORMS

Definition 1.5.1:   The function $x(t)$ is described as a *step function* if

$$x(t) = \begin{cases} X & \text{for } t \geq t_1 \\ 0 & \text{for } t < t_1 \end{cases} \tag{1.5.1}$$

where X is a real constant.

A plot of this function for $t_1 \neq 0$ is shown in Fig. 1.5.1a and for $t_1 = 0$ in Fig. 1.5.1b. At the point $t = t_1$, $x(t)$ "jumps" to the value X. In the special case where $X = 1$, $x(t)$ is called a *unit step function*. It is convenient to designate this unit step function by the special notation $u(t - t_1)$. That is, by definition,

$$u(t - t_1) = \begin{cases} 1 & t \geq t_1 \\ 0 & t < t_1 \end{cases} \tag{1.5.2}$$

so that Eq. (1.5.1) can be written alternatively as

$$x(t) = Xu(t - t_1)$$

Some further examples of the use of the unit step function are included in the remainder of this section.

Definition 1.5.2:   The function $x(t)$ is described as an *exponential function* if

$$x(t) = \begin{cases} Xe^{-\alpha t} & \text{for } t \geq 0 \\ 0 & \text{for } t < 0 \end{cases} \tag{1.5.3}$$

where α and X are real constants.

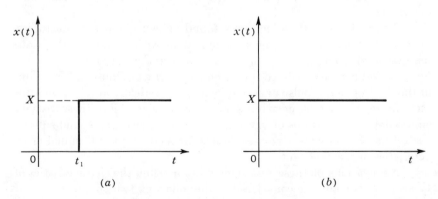

Fig. 1.5.1   Step function.   (a) $t_1 \neq 0$; (b) $t_1 = 0$.

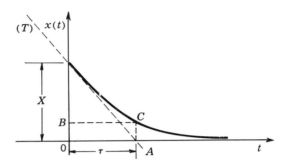

Fig. 1.5.2   Exponential function.

The plot of such a function for $X > 0$, $\alpha > 0$ is shown in Fig. 1.5.2. At $t = 0$ the function is discontinuous, with a discontinuity, or "jump," of the magnitude X.   As t takes on positive values, the function decays monotonically toward the asymptotic value of zero.   The number $1/\alpha$ is called the *time constant*.   It is usually denoted by the symbol τ and has the dimensions of time.   The time constant τ is very useful in measuring the rate of decrease of the function $x(t)$.   Two points on the curve are of special interest.

At $t = \tau$, Eq. (1.5.3) gives

$$x(t) = Xe^{-1} = 0.368X$$

and we see that $x(t)$ has been reduced to 36.8 percent of its original value.

At $t = 4\tau$, Eq. (1.5.3) gives

$$x(t) = Xe^{-4} = (0.368)^4 X$$
$$= 0.02X$$

and we see that $x(t)$ has been reduced to 2 percent of its original value. For most engineering purposes, the magnitude of the function after a period of $t = 5\tau$ is negligible compared with the original value.

Example 1.5.1:   Given the exponential curve of Fig. 1.5.2, graphically determine the time constant.

Solution: The function $x(t)$ is of the form

$$x(t) = Xe^{-t/\tau} \tag{1.5.4}$$

The value τ can be determined from either of the two following methods:

(a)   A tangent (T) to the curve at the point on the curve corresponding to $t = t_1$ intersects the time axis at the point t_A.   As shown below, the distance $t_A - t_1$ is equal to the time constant τ.   Since

$$x(t) = Xe^{-t/\tau}$$
$$\frac{d}{dt} x(t) = -\frac{X}{\tau} e^{-t/\tau}$$

and

$$\frac{d}{dt}x(t)\bigg|_{t=t_1} = -\frac{X}{\tau}e^{-t_1/\tau} = \text{slope of tangent } (T) \text{ at } t = t_1$$

Then, the equation of the tangent line (T) is

$$x = -\frac{X}{\tau}e^{-t_1/\tau}(t - t_1) + Xe^{-t_1/\tau} \tag{1.5.5}$$

At $t = t_A$, $x = 0$; so

$$0 = -\frac{X}{\tau}e^{-t_1/\tau}(t_A - t_1) + Xe^{-t_1/\tau}$$

$$\frac{t_A - t_1}{\tau} = 1$$

or

$$t_A - t_1 = \tau$$

In most cases, of course, it is convenient to make $t_1 = 0$, and then the tangent is drawn from the intersection of the exponential curve and the $x(t)$ axis.

An alternative method for determination of τ is as follows:

(b)   Again referring to Fig. 1.5.2, consider a point B on the $x(t)$ axis such that the distance $OB = 0.368X$. A line drawn from B parallel to the t axis intersects the curve at point C. Upon substituting $t = \tau$ in Eq. (1.5.4) we see that the distance BC is equal to the time constant τ.

Definition 1.5.3:   A function $x(t)$ is said to be *periodic* if there exists a T such that

$$x(t) = x(t \pm nT) \qquad n = 0, 1, 2, \ldots \tag{1.5.6}$$

In this functional notation, T is called the *period* of the periodic function (usually measured in seconds), and the functional variation of $x(t)$ is exactly repeated during each period T. The portion of the curve of $x(t)$ in any interval $t_1 \leq t < t_1 + T$ is called a *cycle*. The number of cycles per second is called the *frequency* and is usually denoted by the symbol f; that is, $f = 1/T$.

Definition 1.5.4:   A *sinusoidal function* is a periodic function of the form

$$x(t) = X_m \sin(\omega t - \phi) \tag{1.5.7}$$

where

X_m represents the maximum or peak value of the function and is considered positive

$\omega = 2\pi f$ is called the *angular frequency* and is measured in radians per second

ϕ is called the phase angle and is measured in radians

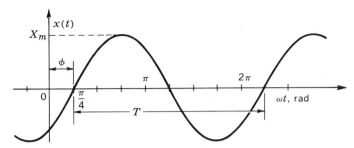

Fig. 1.5.3 Waveform of the function $x(t) = X_m \sin(\omega t - \pi/4)$.

A plot of this function for one period with $\phi = \pi/4$ is shown in Fig. 1.5.3. Such a plot is referred to as the *waveform* of the function. Note that the horizontal axis in this case is not the time axis but the ωt axis, that is, the time axis multiplied by the constant ω.

Example 1.5.2: Given the waveform in Fig. 1.5.4 for which the frequency is 1,000 cycles per second (cps), determine the periodic function.

Solution: From the figure, the maximum value is

$$X_m = 30$$

Since $AO = 2.5$ and $AB = 6$, we have

$$\phi = 2\pi \left(\frac{2.5}{6}\right) = 2.62 \text{ rad}$$

Therefore

$$x(t) = 30 \sin(2,000\pi t + 2.62)$$

Other periodic functions frequently encountered have waveforms which are square or triangular.

Definition 1.5.5: The periodic function $x(t)$ of period T is said to be a *rectangular wave* if, for $0 < k < 1$,

$$x(t) = \begin{cases} X & \text{for } t_1 \le t < (t_1 + kT) \\ -X & \text{for } (t_1 + kT) \le t < (t_1 + T) \end{cases} \tag{1.5.8}$$

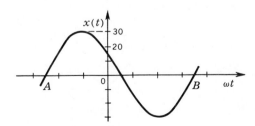

Fig. 1.5.4 Sinusoidal waveform.

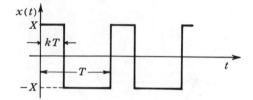

Fig. 1.5.5 Rectangular waveform.

A typical rectangular wave is shown in Fig. 1.5.5. In words, the function $x(t)$ assumes, alternately and at regular intervals of T, the values of $\pm X$. If the parameter k is equal to 0.5, the waveform is said to be square.

The rectangular wave of Eq. (1.5.8) can also be written, by use of the unit step function, as

$$x(t) = X[u(t) - u(t - kT)] - X[u(t - kT) - u(t - T)] \\ + X\{u(t - T) - u[t - (k + 1)T]\} - \cdots \quad (1.5.9)$$

or

$$x(t) = X\{u(t) - 2u(t - kT) + 2u(t - T) \\ - 2u[t - (k + 1)T] + \cdots \} \quad (1.5.10)$$

Definition 1.5.6: A periodic function $x(t)$ of period T is said to be a *triangular wave* if, when $x(t) = 0$ at $t = 0$,

$$x(t) = \begin{cases} \dfrac{4X}{T}\, t & \text{for } 0 \leq t < \dfrac{T}{4} \\[2ex] \dfrac{-4X}{T}\left(t - \dfrac{T}{2}\right) & \text{for } \dfrac{T}{4} \leq t < \dfrac{3T}{4} \\[2ex] \dfrac{4X}{T}\,(t - T) & \text{for } \tfrac{3}{4}T \leq t < T \end{cases} \quad (1.5.11)$$

A typical waveform is shown in Fig. 1.5.6.

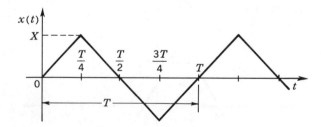

Fig. 1.5.6 Triangular waveform.

Alternatively, the triangular wave can be written, by use of the unit step function, as

$$x(t) = \frac{4X}{T} t \left[u(t) - u\left(t - \frac{T}{2}\right) \right] - \frac{4X}{T} \left(t - \frac{T}{2}\right) \left[u\left(t - \frac{T}{4}\right) \right.$$
$$\left. - u(t - \tfrac{3}{4}T) \right] + \frac{4X}{T} (t - T)[u(t - \tfrac{3}{4}T)$$
$$- u(t - \tfrac{5}{4}T)] - \cdots \quad (1.5.12)$$

or

$$x(t) = \frac{4X}{T} tu(t) - \frac{8X}{T} \left(t - \frac{T}{4}\right) u\left(t - \frac{T}{4}\right)$$
$$+ \frac{8X}{T} (t - \tfrac{3}{4}T)u(t - \tfrac{3}{4}T)$$
$$- \frac{8X}{T} (t - \tfrac{5}{4}T)u (t - \tfrac{5}{4}T) + \cdots \quad (1.5.13)$$

(B) FOURIER SERIES REPRESENTATIONS

Any periodic function or any function defined over a finite interval of time $t_1 < t < t_2$ can be represented by means of an infinite series of sinusoidal functions of time known as the *Fourier series*. To establish this series, it is convenient to consider first the notion of orthogonal functions defined as follows:

Definition 1.5.7: Two functions $\Phi_p(t)$ and $\Phi_q(t)$ are said to be *orthogonal*† over an interval (t_1,t_2) if the integral of the product $\Phi_p(t)\Phi_q(t)$ over that interval vanishes, i.e., if

$$\int_{t_1}^{t_2} \Phi_p(t)\Phi_q(t) \, dt = 0 \qquad (1.5.14)$$

Example 1.5.3: Show the orthogonality of the functions

$$\Phi_1(t) = A \sin \omega t$$
$$\Phi_2(t) = B \sin \omega t$$

over the time interval $(0, T = 2\pi/\omega)$.

Solution: For the integral in Eq. (1.5.14) we have

$$\int_0^T \Phi_1(t)\Phi_2(t) \, dt = AB \int_0^T \sin \omega t \sin 3\omega t \, dt = 0$$

and the two functions $\Phi_1(t)$ and $\Phi_2(t)$ are orthogonal over the given interval.

A *set* (finite or infinite) of functions such that every possible pair of distinct functions in the set satisfy Eq. (1.5.14) over a specified interval (t_1,t_2) is called a *set of orthogonal functions*.

† Orthogonality of these functions can be defined with respect to a weighting function. In the above definition the weighting function is taken equal to unity.

Example 1.5.4: Consider the infinite set of sinusoidal functions

$$\Phi_i(t) = A_i \sin i\omega t \qquad i = 1, 2, 3, \ldots \tag{1.5.15}$$

over the time interval $(0, T = 2\pi/\omega)$, and show that this set is orthogonal.

Solution: Let two distinct members of the set be designated as $\Phi_p(t)$ and $\Phi_q(t)$, where p and q are integers and $p \neq q$. For the integral in Eq. (1.5.14) we have

$$\int_{t_1}^{t_2} \Phi_p(t)\Phi_q(t)\,dt = A_p A_q \int_0^{2\pi/\omega} \sin p\omega t \sin q\omega t\,dt$$

$$= A_p A_q \left[\frac{\sin(p-q)\omega t}{2\omega(p-q)} - \frac{\sin(p+q)\omega t}{2\omega(p+q)} \right]\Big|_0^{2\pi/\omega}$$

$$= 0$$

Therefore, the infinite set of functions defined by Eq. (1.5.15) is orthogonal over the given interval.

It is easy to show by direct application of the definition of orthogonality that the functions

$$\Phi_i(t) = A_i \sin i\omega t$$
$$\Psi_i(t) = B_i \cos i\omega t \tag{1.5.16}$$
$$i = 0, 1, 2, \ldots$$

also comprise an orthogonal set over the interval $(0, T = 2\pi/\omega)$.

The sum of the orthogonal functions in Eqs. (1.5.16) is given by

$$f(t) = A_1 \sin \omega t + A_2 \sin 2\omega t + A_3 \sin 3\omega t + \cdots$$
$$+ B_0 + B_1 \cos \omega t + B_2 \cos 2\omega t + B_3 \cos 3\omega t + \cdots \tag{1.5.17}$$

and is called the *general Fourier series* representation of $f(t)$ in the interval $(0, T)$.

Given the function $f(t)$ in Eq. (1.5.17), the coefficients A_k and B_k $(k = 0, 1, 2, \ldots)$ in the series are evaluated by applying the properties of orthogonal functions.

The coefficient A_k may be evaluated by multiplying both sides of Eq. (1.5.17) by $\sin k\omega t$ and integrating over the interval $(0, T = 2\pi/\omega)$. The result is

$$\int_0^T f(t) \sin k\omega t\,dt = A_1 \int_0^T \sin \omega t \sin k\omega t\,dt + \cdots$$
$$+ A_k \int_0^T \sin^2 k\omega t\,dt + \cdots$$
$$+ B_0 \int_0^T \sin k\omega t\,dt + B_1 \int_0^T \cos \omega t \sin k\omega t\,dt + \cdots \tag{1.5.18}$$

Since the functions $\Phi_i(t)$ and $\Psi_i(t)$ in Eqs. (1.5.16) constitute an orthogonal set, all integrals on the right-hand side of Eq. (1.5.18) vanish except the one multiplied by A_k and we have

$$\int_0^T f(t) \sin k\omega t\,dt = A_k \int_0^T \sin^2 k\omega t\,dt = A_k \frac{\pi}{\omega} = \frac{T}{2} A_k$$

so that

$$A_k = \frac{2}{T} \int_0^T f(t) \sin k\omega t \, dt \qquad k = 1, 2, 3, \ldots \tag{1.5.19}$$

In a similar manner, the expression for B_k ($k = 1, 2, \ldots$) may be established by multiplying both sides of Eq. (1.5.17) by $\cos k\omega t$ and integrating over the interval $(0, T = 2\pi/\omega)$. The result is

$$B_k = \frac{2}{T} \int_0^T f(t) \cos k\omega t \, dt \qquad k = 1, 2, \ldots, n \tag{1.5.20}$$

The constant term B_0 in Eq. (1.5.17) is evaluated by simply integrating both sides of the equation over the interval $(0, T = 2\pi/\omega)$. The result is

$$\int_0^T f(t) \, dt = A_1 \int_0^T \sin \omega t \, dt + A_2 \int_0^T \sin 2\omega t \, dt + \cdots$$
$$+ B_0 \int_0^T dt + B_1 \int_0^T \cos \omega t \, dt + \cdots$$

or

$$B_0 = \frac{1}{T} \int_0^T f(t) \, dt \tag{1.5.21}$$

An alternative form of the Fourier series is obtained by combining the sine and cosine terms of like frequencies; i.e., let

$$A_k \sin k\omega t + B_k \cos k\omega t = C_k \sin (k\omega t + \Phi_k)$$

where

$$C_k = \sqrt{A_k{}^2 + B_k{}^2}$$

and

$$\Phi_k = \arctan \frac{B_k}{A_k} \tag{1.5.22}$$

Equation (1.5.17) can now be written in the form

$$f(t) = B_0 + C_1 \sin (\omega t + \Phi_1) + C_2 \sin (2\omega t + \Phi_2) + \cdots$$
$$= B_0 + \sum_{k=1}^{\infty} C_k \sin (k\omega t + \Phi_k) \tag{1.5.23}$$

The constant term B_0 is called the *average value* of $f(t)$ over the interval $(0,T)$.† The first sinusoidal term, namely, $C_1 \sin (\omega t + \Phi_1)$, is called the *fundamental*, since it has a period T equal to the interval over which the function $f(t)$ is to be represented. All other terms

$$C_k \sin (k\omega t + \Phi_k) \qquad k = 2, 3, \ldots$$

are called *harmonics* and are identified as the *second harmonic* if $k = 2$, as the *third harmonic* if $k = 3$, and so on.

† Equation (1.5.21) is exactly the definition of the average value given in Eq. (1.6.1).

It should be noted that if the given function $f(t)$ is periodic with period $T = 2\pi/\omega$ then the Fourier series expansion of $f(t)$ in the interval $(0,\ T = 2\pi/\omega)$ represents the function $f(t)$ over all t.

Example 1.5.5: Expand the square wave shown in Fig. 1.5.7 into a Fourier series of the form given in Eq. (1.5.17).

Solution: Since the given function is periodic, with period T, the coefficients in the Fourier series can be evaluated by expanding the given function over the interval $(0, T)$.

From Eq. (1.5.19), the coefficients A_k ($k = 1, 2, \ldots$) in the series expansion are

$$
\begin{aligned}
A_k &= \frac{2}{T} \int_0^T x(t) \sin k\omega t\, dt \\
&= \frac{2}{T} X \left(\int_0^{T/2} \sin k\omega t\, dt - \int_{T/2}^T \sin k\omega t\, dt \right) \\
&= \frac{2X}{\pi k} (1 - \cos k\pi)
\end{aligned}
$$

and

$$
A_k = \begin{cases} 0 & \text{if } k \text{ is even} \\ \dfrac{4X}{\pi k} & \text{if } k \text{ is odd} \end{cases}
$$

In a similar manner, it is easy to verify that the coefficients B_k ($k = 1, 2, \ldots$), as given by Eq. (1.5.20), and the constant coefficient B_0, as given by Eq. (1.5.23), are all zero. The Fourier series representation of the given square wave is therefore

$$
x(t) = \frac{4X}{\pi} \left(\sin \omega t + \frac{1}{3} \sin 3\omega t + \frac{1}{5} \sin 5\omega t + \cdots \right) \tag{1.5.24}
$$

It is important to note in the above example that at the points of discontinuity in the given function, i.e., at $t = T/2,\ T,\ 3T/2,\ \ldots$

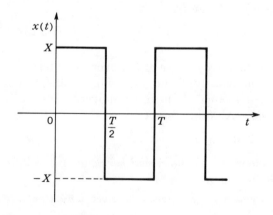

Fig. 1.5.7 A square wave with period T.

$(T = 2\pi/\omega)$, the right-hand side of Eq. (1.5.24) vanishes. That is, the expansion gives a unique value of the function at the points of discontinuity which is equal to the average of the values of the function just to the right and to the left of the discontinuity. It can be shown that, in general, the Fourier series expansion of any function which is bounded and contains at most a finite number of discontinuities in the interval $(0,T)$ converges to the function everywhere except at the points of discontinuity, and at these points it gives the average value of the function at the discontinuity.

In any practical application of a Fourier series representation of a recorded signal it is obviously necessary to truncate the series. The number of terms to be considered, in general, depends on the accuracy of the approximation required and the rate of convergence of the series. In the above example, for instance, the sum of the fundamental and third harmonic gives the approximation shown by the trace labeled (1) in Fig. 1.5.8. The sum of the fundamental, third, and fifth harmonics gives an even better approximation as indicated by the trace labeled (2) in the same figure.

It is also important to note that some of the harmonics in the Fourier series expansion of a given function $f(t)$ may not be present. In Example 1.5.4, for instance, $A_k \neq 0$ only for $k = 1, 3, 5, 7, \ldots$, and we say that the waveform in Fig. 1.5.7 contains only odd harmonics. In general, if $f(t)$ is an odd function, i.e., if $f(-t) = -f(t)$, then all cosine terms in Eq. (1.5.17) vanish identically. Similarly, if $f(t)$ is an even function, i.e., if $f(t) = f(-t)$, then all sine terms vanish identically in Eq. (1.5.17).

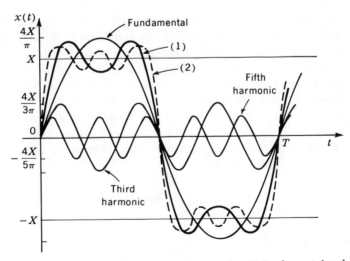

Fig. 1.5.8 Approximation of a square wave by (1) fundamental and third harmonics; (2) fundamental, third, and fifth harmonics.

Under other conditions of symmetry in the plot of $f(t)$, certain additional terms in the expansion may be absent.　The square wave in Fig. 1.5.7, for example, contains only odd sine terms.

1.6　AVERAGE AND ROOT-MEAN-SQUARE REPRESENTATION

In many engineering studies it is neither necessary nor desirable to consider the actual time variation of periodic waveforms; i.e., the measurement can be characterized in other ways.　Two such characterizations sometimes used are the average and the root-mean-square (rms) numbers as defined below.

Definition 1.6.1:　Let a function $x(t)$ be defined in the interval (t_1, t_2). The *average value* X_{avg} of $x(t)$ is defined as

$$X_{avg} = \frac{1}{t_2 - t_1} \int_{t_2}^{t_1} x(t)\, dt \tag{1.6.1}$$

Definition 1.6.2:　Let a function $x(t)$ be defined in the interval (t_1, t_2). The *rms value* X_{rms} of $x(t)$ is defined as

$$X_{rms} = \left[\frac{1}{t_2 - t_1} \int_{t_1}^{t_2} x^2(t)\, dt \right]^{1/2} \tag{1.6.2}$$

The rms value of a function is sometimes referred to as its *effective value*.

Table 1.6.1 lists the average and rms values (for $t_2 - t_1 = mT$, $m = 1, 2, 3, \ldots$) of some of the functions frequently encountered in the analysis of physical systems.　Note that, for the periodic functions in Figs. 1.5.3, 1.5.6, and 1.5.7, the average value is zero and so is not useful as a basis for characterizing the periodic function in these cases. However, when the function is squared before it is averaged, all negative sections also become positive and a nonzero result is obtained.　On this basis alone, we see why the rms number might be more effective in characterizing periodic functions than is the average value.　Other bases will become apparent later.

Example 1.6.1:　Find the average and rms values of the following function in the interval $(0,3)$:

$$x(t) = \begin{cases} \frac{5}{2}t & \text{for } t < 2 \\ 5(t-3)^2 & \text{for } t \geq 2 \end{cases} \tag{1.6.3}$$

The function is plotted in Fig. 1.6.1.

Table 1.6.1

Function $x(t)$	Signal $x(t)$	Average value	Rms value
1. Step function: $x(t) = X,\ t \geq 0$	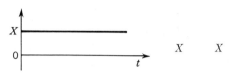	X	X
2. Sine function: $x(t) = X_m \sin \omega t$		0	$\dfrac{X_m}{\sqrt{2}}$
3. Half-wave sine function: $x(t) = X_m \sin \omega t$ for $0 \leq t < \frac{1}{2}T$ $x(t) = 0$ for $\frac{1}{2}T \leq t \leq T$	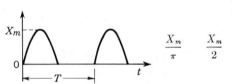	$\dfrac{X_m}{\pi}$	$\dfrac{X_m}{2}$
4. Rectified sine function: $x(t) = X_m|\sin \omega t|$	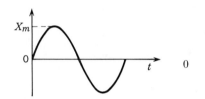	$\dfrac{2}{\pi} X_m$	$\dfrac{X_m}{\sqrt{2}}$
5. Triangular wave: $x(t) = \dfrac{2X_m}{T} t$ for $0 \leq t < \dfrac{T}{2}$ $x(t) = -\dfrac{2X_m}{T}(t - T)$ for $\dfrac{T}{2} \leq t < T$	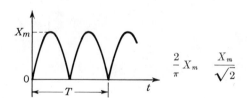	$\frac{1}{2}X_m$	$\dfrac{1}{\sqrt{3}} X_m$

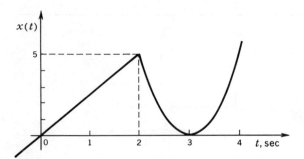

Fig. 1.6.1   Plot of Eq. (1.6.3).

Solution: The average value is given by

$$X_{avg} = \frac{1}{t_2 - t_1} \int_{t_1}^{t_2} x(t)\, dt = \tfrac{1}{3} \left[\int_0^2 \tfrac{5}{2}t\, dt + \int_2^3 5(t-3)^2\, dt \right]$$

$$= \tfrac{1}{3} \left[\tfrac{5}{4}t^2 \Big|_0^2 + \tfrac{5}{3}(t-3)^3 \Big|_2^3 \right] = \tfrac{20}{9}$$

The rms (effective) value is given by

$$X_{rms} = \left[\frac{1}{t_2 - t_1} \int_{t_1}^{t_2} x^2(t)\, dt \right]^{1/2}$$

Therefore

$$X^2_{rms} = \tfrac{1}{3} \left\{ \int_0^2 (\tfrac{5}{2}t)^2\, dt + \int_2^3 [5(t-3)^2]^2\, dt \right\}$$

$$= \tfrac{1}{3} \left[\tfrac{25}{12}t^3 \Big|_0^2 + 5(t-3)^5 \Big|_2^3 \right] = \tfrac{65}{9}$$

Hence

$$X_{rms} = (\tfrac{65}{9})^{1/2} = 2.69$$

The average power input to a given pair of terminals over a given interval of time (t_1, t_2) can, of course, be computed as

$$P_{avg} = \frac{1}{t_2 - t_1} \int_{t_1}^{t_2} P(t)\, dt \tag{1.6.4}$$

If $P(t)$ is a periodic function of period T, then the interval is frequently taken as one period and the expression for the average power for any integral number of periods is the same.

Example 1.6.2:   Let

$$v(t) = 10 \cos \omega t$$

$$i(t) = 5 \cos \left(\omega t - \frac{\pi}{2} \right) \tag{1.6.5}$$

Determine the instantaneous power function and the average power over an integral number of periods.

Solution: The instantaneous power is given by

$$P(t) = v(t)i(t) = 50 \cos \omega t \cos \left(\omega t - \frac{\pi}{2} \right)$$

$$= 25 \cos \left(2\omega t - \frac{\pi}{2} \right)$$

Since $P(t)$ is periodic with period $T = \pi/\omega$, the average power is given by

$$P_{\text{avg}} = \frac{1}{T} \int_0^T P(t) \, dt = \frac{25\omega}{\pi} \int_0^{\pi/\omega} \cos \left(2\omega t - \frac{\pi}{2} \right) dt = 0$$

Example 1.6.3: Evaluate the instantaneous power and the average power over an integral number of periods when

$$i(t) = A_1 \cos (\omega t + \phi_1)$$
$$v(t) = A_2 \cos (\omega t + \phi_2)$$

Solution: In this case we have

$$P(t) = i(t)v(t) = A_1 A_2 \cos (\omega t + \phi_1) \cos (\omega t + \phi_2)$$
$$= \tfrac{1}{2} A_1 A_2 [\cos (2\omega t + \phi_1 + \phi_2) + \cos (\phi_1 - \phi_2)]$$

Note that the function $P(t)$ contains a constant term plus a periodic time function of period $T = \pi/\omega$. It is easy to show that the time integral of the periodic term vanishes over an integral number of periods and that the expression for the average power reduces to

$$P_{\text{avg}} = \frac{A_1 A_2}{2nT} \cos (\phi_1 - \phi_2) \int_{t_1}^{t_1 + nT} dt = \frac{A_1 A_2}{2} \cos (\phi_1 - \phi_2)$$

Note that the average power is nonzero as long as $\phi_1 - \phi_2 \neq (2k + 1)\pi/2$, where k is an integer. Also, note that Example 1.6.2 is a special case of the above, obtained by taking $\phi_1 = 0$ and $\phi_2 = \pi/2$.

PROBLEMS

1.1   Three of the possible terminal graphs for a four-terminal component are given in Fig. 1.2.3. Give all other possible terminal graphs (13 in number) for this component.

1.2   A time-varying signal as recorded in the laboratory is shown in Fig. P1.2. The scale factors for the vertical and horizontal axes are, respectively, $k_x = 20$ volts/cm and $k_t = 10^{-2}$ sec/cm. Determine the analytical expression for this recorded signal, and identify the time constant. If the time scale k_t is multiplied by a constant β, what is the new time constant?

1.3   Sketch the curve

$$x(t) = X(1 - e^{-t/\tau}) \tag{P1.3}$$

and show that this function can be conveniently sketched by graphically adding two components, one of which is the exponential function shown in Fig. 1.5.2. If the sketch of Eq. (P1.3) is given, how could you determine graphically the constants X and τ?

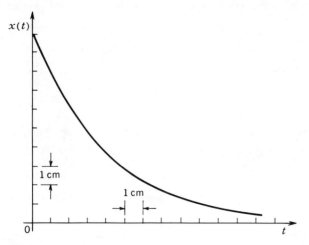

Fig. P1.2

1.4   Determine the average and rms values for one period of the rectangular wave given by Eq. (1.5.8).

1.5   Let a signal be defined by

$$x(t) = X_0 = \text{const}$$

for all values of t.   Show from the definition of a periodic function [Eq. (1.5.6)] that $x(t)$ is periodic.   What is the period of $x(t)$?

1.6   Verify the average and rms values of the signals given in Table 1.6.1.

1.7   Determine the average and rms values of the signals given in Fig. P1.7.

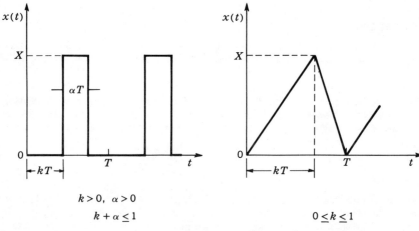

Fig. P1.7

1.8   Suppose that the following signals are applied to the input terminals of an xy recorder or an oscilloscope:

$v_x(t) = 10 \sin 3t$ volts
$v_y(t) = 2$ volts

If the scale constants of the axes are

$k_x = 0.2$ cm/volt
$k_y = 1.5$ cm/volt

determine the figure obtained on the screen, and give its exact location and *dimension* in the xy plane.

1.9   Let a periodic voltage $v_y(t)$ of period T be applied to the vertical input terminals of an xy recorder or an oscilloscope.   If a voltage having the waveform shown in Fig. P1.9 (a triangular wave) is applied to the horizontal input terminals, what kind of figure will be obtained on the screen of the instrument?   Discuss.

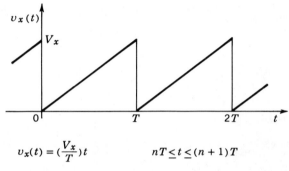

$$v_x(t) = (\frac{V_x}{T})t \qquad\qquad nT \le t \le (n+1)T$$

Fig. P1.9

1.10   In Prob. 1.9 assume that

$$v_y(t) = V_y \sin \frac{2\pi}{T} t$$

and $v_x(t)$ is given by Fig. P1.10.   Sketch the curve that will be observed on the screen.

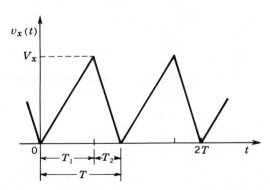

Fig. P1.10

1.11   When two sinusoidal signals (voltages)

$$v_x(t) = V_x \sin(\omega_1 t + \phi_1)$$
$$v_y(t) = V_y \sin(\omega_2 t + \phi_2)$$

are applied to the horizontal and vertical input terminals of an xy recorder or an oscilloscope, the trace as observed on the screen is usually called a *Lissajous figure*. If the scale factors of the horizontal and vertical axes are taken into account, the parametric equations of this figure are of the form

$$x = A \sin(\omega_1 t + \phi_1)$$
$$y = B \sin(\omega_2 t + \phi_2) \qquad \text{(P1.11.1)}$$

with $A = k_x V_x$, $B = k_y V_y$. From Eq. (P1.11.1) it is evident that x and y are always within the limits $(-A,A)$ and $(-B,B)$, respectively; i.e., a Lissajous figure lies in a rectangle of sides $2A$ and $2B$.

An alternative equation for a Lissajous figure, but one which is usually more difficult for plotting purposes, can be obtained by eliminating the parameter t in Eqs. (P1.11.1), i.e.,

$$\arcsin \frac{x}{A} = \omega_1 t + \phi_1$$

$$\arcsin \frac{y}{B} = \omega_2 t + \phi_2$$

Hence

$$\arcsin \frac{x}{A} - \frac{\omega_1}{\omega_2} \arcsin \frac{y}{B} = \phi_1 - \frac{\omega_1}{\omega_2} \phi_2 \qquad \text{(P1.11.2)}$$

(a)   Let $\omega_1 = \omega_2$ and $\phi - \phi_2 = \alpha$. By use of Eq. (P1.11.2), obtain the equation of the Lissajous figure in the form of $F(x,y) = 0$, and sketch this curve for $\alpha = 0$, $\alpha = \pi/4$, and $\alpha = \pi/2$.

(b)   By use of Eqs. (P1.11.1) show that if ω_1 and ω_2 are rational multiples of each other the Lissajous figure is closed.

(c)   For $\omega_1 = m\omega_2$, where m is a rational number, show that the maximum number of intersections of the figure and a horizontal line is n_x and the maximum number of intersections of the figure and a vertical line is n_y, where

$$\frac{n_y}{n_x} = m = \frac{\omega_1}{\omega_2}$$

(d)   Show that for a given Lissajous figure if $f_1 = \omega_1/2\pi$ is known then

$$f_2 = \frac{\omega_2}{2\pi}$$

can be determined from the relation in (c). This relation is used as a basis of measuring the frequency of a sinusoidal signal.

1.12   The Lissajous figure in Fig. P1.12 is obtained on an oscilloscope screen. If $f_1 = 1{,}000$ cps and $\phi_1 = 0$, determine ω_2 and ϕ_2.

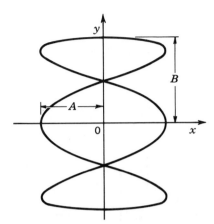

Fig. P1.12

1.13 Under what conditions will a Lissajous figure appear as a circle on the screen of an xy recorder?

1.14 Let across and through variables be given by

$$x(t) = E = 10 \text{ volts}$$
$$y(t) = 10^{-3}e^{-t/3} \quad \text{amp}$$

Calculate the average power if the interval is taken as $(0, \infty)$.

1.15 Let

$$\delta(t) = 2 \times 10^{-2} \sin 500t \quad \text{meters}$$
$$f(t) = 10 \sin\left(500t - \frac{\pi}{4}\right) \quad \text{newtons}$$

Calculate the mechanical average power and energy for one period of the signals.

1.16 Let the pulse function $f_{t_i}(t)$ be defined as

$$f_{t_i}(t) = \begin{cases} 0 & \text{for} \quad -\infty < t < t_i \\ 1 & \text{for} \quad t_i \leq t \leq t_{i+1} \\ 0 & \text{for} \quad t_{i+1} < t < +\infty \end{cases}$$

Consider the set of pulse functions

$$S = \{f_{t_i}(t) | i = 0, \mp 1, \mp 2, \ldots ; t_i < t_{i+1}\}$$

Show that S is an orthogonal set of functions in the time interval (t_1, t_2).

1.17 If a function $f(t)$ is defined in an interval (t_1, t_2) and if the set of functions $\{\Phi_1(t)\}$ is orthogonal in the given interval, then $f(t)$ can be expressed in terms of an infinite series of the form

$$f(t) = A_0\phi_0(t) + A_1\phi_1(t) + A_2\phi_2(t) + \cdots$$
$$= \sum_{i=0}^{\infty} A_i\phi_i(t)$$

provided that the series is uniformly convergent in the said interval. Apply a technique similar to that used in Fourier series to calculate the unknown coefficients A_i of the series.

1.18 In the orthogonal set of pulse functions defined in Prob. 1.16, let $t_i = i$; that is, $S = \{f_i(t) | i = 0, \mp 1, \mp 2, \ldots\}$.

Determine the series expansion of the functions represented by the curves given in Fig. P1.18a and b in terms of the functions in S in the indicated intervals (t_1, t_2).

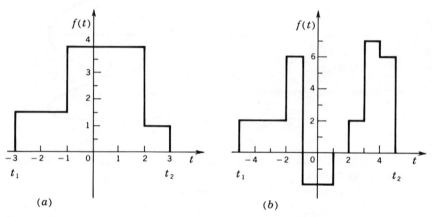

(a)   (b)

Fig. P1.18

1.19 Obtain the Fourier series coefficients for the triangular wave given in Fig. P1.19 over the interval $(0,T)$.

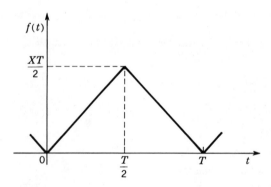

Fig. P1.19

1.20 Assuming that the derivative of a function is equal to the derivative of its Fourier series expansion, show that from the series in Prob. 1.19 the series expansion given in Example 1.5.4 can be deduced.

1.21 The Fourier series expansion of a periodic function in the interval $(0, T = 2\pi/\omega)$ is

$$f(t) = B_0 + \sum_{i=1}^{\infty} C_i \sin(i\omega t + \phi_i)$$

Show that the rms value of $f(t)$ in the given interval is given by

$$F_{\text{rms}} = \left(B_0{}^2 + \tfrac{1}{2} \sum_{i=1}^{\infty} C_i{}^2 \right)^{1/2}$$

1.22   Let the voltage $v(t)$ and current $i(t)$ be periodic functions with Fourier series representations

$$v(t) = V_0 + \sum_{k=1}^{\infty} V_k \sin (k\omega t + \phi_k)$$

$$i(t) = I_0 + \sum_{k=1}^{\infty} I_k \sin (k\omega t + \theta_k)$$

Show that the average electrical power is given by

$$P_{\text{avg}} = \tfrac{1}{2} \sum_{k=1}^{\infty} |V_k I_k| \cos (\phi_k - \theta_k) + V_0 I_0$$

FURTHER READING

1.   Poincaré, H.: "Science and Hypothesis," Dover Publications, Inc., New York, 1952.
2.   Firestone, F. A.: A New Analogy between Mechanical and Electrical Systems, *J. Acoust. Soc. Am.*, 1963, pp. 248–267.
3.   Trent, H. M.: Isomorphisms between Oriented Linear Graphs and Lumped Physical Systems, *J. Acoust. Soc. Am.*, 1955, pp. 500–527.
4.   Hildebrand, F. B.: "Advanced Calculus for Engineers," Prentice-Hall, Inc., Englewood Cliffs, N.J., 1949.

2
Mathematical Models of Typical Two-terminal Components

Mathematical models of the components identified in a system structure serve as the building blocks in the analysis and design of physical systems. These mathematical models must be established from empirical tests on the components or calculated from the constructional features of the components, such as their geometric dimensions and material composition. The problem of establishing a mathematical model of a component having four, five, or six terminals is by no means a simple task, since, as already indicated in the previous chapter, it involves finding the mathematical functions which give one set of time functions as functions of a second set. For this reason the models are taken to be as simple as possible. Either the components have only two or three terminals, or if the component contains many terminals, the form of the model must be relatively simple. This chapter considers typical forms of elementary models used to approximate the characteristics of typical two-terminal physical components and shows how these models are used as conceptual building blocks for generating models of somewhat more complex forms. The specific techniques involved in evaluating the coefficients from measurements at the component terminals are considered in detail.

2.1 ELEMENTARY TWO - TERMINAL - COMPONENT MODELS

The generic forms of a class of two-terminal-component models, which we shall refer to as the *elementary forms*, are shown in Table 2.1.1, along

Table 2.1.1   Elementary two-terminal components

	Dissipator	Delay	Accumulator	Generator
Generic form	$x(t) = a\,y(t)$	$b\dfrac{d}{dt}y(t) = x(t)$	$c\dfrac{d}{dt}x(t) = y(t)$	$x(t)$ known or $y(t)$ known
Electrical schematic	Resistance	Inductance	Capacitance	$i(t)$ Current gen. / $v(t)$ Voltage gen.
Rectilinear motion / Mechanical schematic	Dissipation	Elastance	Inertia	$\dot{\delta}(t)$ Velocity gen. / $f(t)$ Force gen.
Rotary motion / Mechanical schematic	Dissipation	Elastance	Inertia	$\dot{\phi}(t)$ Velocity gen. / $\tau(t)$ Torque gen.
Hydraulic and pneumatic	Resistance	Inertia	Capacitance	$p(t)$ Pressure gen. / $g(t)$ Flow gen.

with the accepted standard schematic representations of the various types of physical components and the associated names.

In the case of all linear passive-type components, the terminal equation is insensitive to the orientation of the edge of the terminal graph, i.e., a simultaneous change in orientation of *both* the through and across measurements does not alter the magnitude or sign of the equation. This, however, is not the case for generator-type or certain nonlinear-type components. The table includes the four generic types discussed briefly in the following paragraphs.

DISSIPATIVE COMPONENTS

The coefficient a in the simple linear algebraic model

$$x(t) = ay(t) \tag{2.1.1}$$

or

$$y(t) = \frac{1}{a} x(t) \tag{2.1.2}$$

of course, represents the slope of a straight-line approximation to a measured characteristic such as that shown in Fig. 2.1.1. This sketch is intended to emphasize once more that any model applies only to limited classes of signals, i.e., limited magnitudes and rates of change. The names of the component and the coefficient a or $1/a$ in the model unfortunately depend upon the process represented by the signals $x(t)$ and $y(t)$. The identifying names for electrical, mechanical, and hydraulic or pneumatic components are indicated in the table. For electrical processes the coefficient $1/a = G$ is called the *electrical conductance;* for mechanical processes $1/a = B$ is called the *damping coefficient;* and for hydraulic and

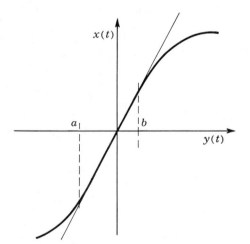

Fig. 2.1.1 A linear characteristic of a two-terminal component.

pneumatic processes $1/a = G_h$ is called the hydraulic or pneumatic conductance.

In many applications nonlinear characteristics can be adequately approximated by this very simple linear model by considering what is called a *small-signal approximation* about an operating point, as illustrated in the following example.

Example 2.1.1: The nonlinear pressure–flow-rate characteristics of some hydraulic valves are very closely approximated by the nonlinear equations

$$p(t) = \begin{cases} K\dot{g}^2(t) & \text{for } \dot{g}(t) > 0 \\ -K\dot{g}^2(t) & \text{for } \dot{g}(t) < 0 \end{cases}$$

or, for all $\dot{g}(t)$,

$$p(t) = K\dot{g}(t)|\dot{g}(t)|$$

where $|\dot{g}(t)|$ represents the magnitude of the flow rate. A sketch of this function is shown in Fig. 2.1.2. Determine a small-signal linear approximation about an operating point $\dot{g}(t) = \dot{g}_0 \geq 0$.

Solution: The required approximation for an operating point $\dot{g}(t) = \dot{g}_0 \geq 0$ is given as

$$\Delta p(t) = K_d \, \Delta\dot{g}(t)$$

where

$$K_d = \frac{dp}{d\dot{g}}\bigg|_{\dot{g}_0} = 2K\dot{g}\bigg|_{\dot{g}_0} = 2K\dot{g}_0$$

represents the slope of the line at $\dot{g}(t) = \dot{g}_0$ and Δp and $\Delta\dot{g}$ represent, respectively, the change in pressure and flow-rate variables from the indicated fixed operating point. It is common practice simply to write

$$p(t) = K_d\dot{g}(t)$$

with the understanding that the terminal variables represent changes about an operating point Q.

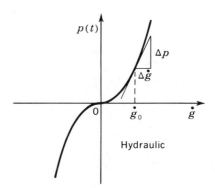

Fig. 2.1.2 A typical nonlinear pressure–flow-rate characteristic of a hydraulic valve.

It should be noted that for a small-signal approximation to exist it is necessary that the characteristic to be approximated have a derivative at the selected operating point. The following example demonstrates the difficulty that may arise in this respect.

Example 2.1.2: The characteristic of a typical silicon diode is shown in Fig. 2.1.3. Consider the establishment of a small-signal linear approximation to this characteristic about the origin. Note that the scale on the $i(t)$ axis differs by a factor of 1,000 on either side of the origin.

Solution: This characteristic can be regarded as two straight lines intersecting at the origin, one with a slope of 10 and the other with a slope of 10^4. Thus

$$v(t) = \begin{cases} 10i(t) & \text{for } i(t) > 0 \\ 10^4 i(t) & \text{for } i(t) < 0 \end{cases}$$

An attempt to use a small-signal approximation for an operating point at $i(t) = 0$ fails, since the derivative of the characteristic, dv/di, is not unique at this point: the right-hand derivative is 10, whereas the left-hand derivative is 10^4. We can also see from the characteristic in Fig. 2.1.3 that a small-signal approximation at this point is meaningless.

If a small-signal linear approximation does not exist or is not acceptable, then, of course, a nonlinear equation must be considered. The *thyrite resistor* shown in Fig. 2.1.4 is typical of a nonlinear characteristic that must be modeled by a nonlinear equation.

For positive values of $v(t)$ and $i(t)$ this characteristic is essentially the same as the plot of the function

$$i(t) = kv^n(t)$$

where k and n are positive constants with $1 < n < 3$.

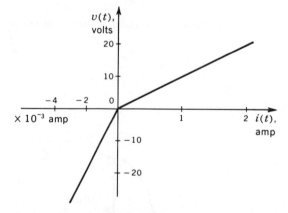

Fig. 2.1.3 Approximated $v(t)$-$i(t)$ characteristic of a silicon diode.

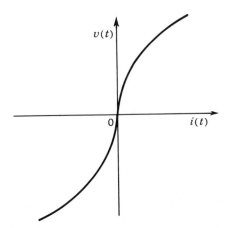

Fig. 2.1.4 A typical $v(t)$-$i(t)$ characteristic of a thyrite resistor, or varistor.

Almost any single-valued nonlinear curve can be approximated by a polynomial of the form

$$x(t) = R_0 + R_1 y(t) + R_2 y^2(t) + \cdots + R_n y^n(t)$$

However, the techniques involved in fitting a polynomial to a given characteristic are not considered here.

An alternative approximation to the type of nonlinear characteristic shown in Fig. 2.1.4 is provided by the use of sections of straight lines as shown in Fig. 2.1.5. The choice of the number of straight-line sections to be used depends upon the range of variation in the component terminal variables and the accuracy desired.

It is cumbersome to write, in analytical form, the equations for the sections of straight lines shown in Fig. 2.1.5. For this reason, this type of representation is not particularly attractive in analytical studies.

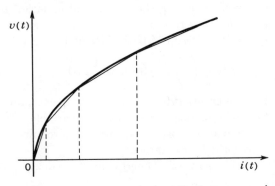

Fig. 2.1.5 Definition of piecewise-linear approximations.

It is, however, a very practical representation to use when an analog computer is used in the study of the system.

The name of a generic algebraic equation of the forms given in Eqs. (2.1.1) and (2.1.2) has its origin in the energy characteristics of the component. The power and energy inputs are

$$P_a(t) = ay^2(t) = \frac{1}{a} x^2(t) \tag{2.1.3}$$

and

$$W_a(t) = \int_{t_0}^{t} P(\tau) \, d\tau = a \int_{t_0}^{t} y^2(\tau) \, d\tau = \frac{1}{a} \int_{t_0}^{t} x^2(\tau) \, d\tau \tag{2.1.4}$$

Since the power and energy input functions $P(t)$ and $W(t)$ are always positive, components modeled by equations of this form are referred to as *dissipative passive* components. The electrical, mechanical, or hydraulic energy input to the component is "converted" to heat energy.

DELAY COMPONENTS

If the characteristic of a two-terminal component is modeled by a linear differential equation of the generic form

$$\frac{d}{dt} y(t) = \frac{1}{b} x(t) \tag{2.1.5}$$

or

$$x(t) = b \frac{d}{dt} y(t) \tag{2.1.6}$$

the component is referred to as a *delay* component. Since the through variable (flow) is proportional to the time integral of $x(t)$, the flow does not respond immediately to a step change in the across variable (the "driving force")—hence the name "delay" component.

The coefficient in the models of delay components can be evaluated by first converting the differential equation to algebraic form by use of the time integral of one terminal variable. Thus, upon taking the indefinite integral of both sides of Eq. (2.1.6) we have

$$y(t) = \left(\frac{1}{b} \right) \int_{t_0}^{t} x(t) \, dt = \frac{1}{b} \Gamma(t)$$

Instrumentation for automatically performing the required time integration of the measured terminal variable $x(t)$ is available as standard equipment in most laboratories; the required characteristic can therefore be recorded automatically.

The power and energy inputs to delay-type components are given by

$$P_b(t) = by(t) \frac{dy(t)}{dt} \tag{2.1.7}$$

and

$$W_b(t) = b \int_{t_0}^{t} y(\tau) \frac{dy(\tau)}{d\tau} d\tau$$

$$= \frac{b}{2} [y^2(t) - y^2(t_0)] \qquad (2.1.8)$$

To interpret these results, let us assume that $y(t)$ and $x(t)$ in Eqs. (2.1.7) and (2.1.8) are bounded periodic functions of time with period T. The average power input to the component over the interval $(t_0, t_0 + t)$ is

$$(P_b)_{\text{avg}} = \frac{b}{t} \int_{t_0}^{t_0+t} y(\tau) \frac{dy(\tau)}{d\tau} d\tau \qquad (2.1.9)$$

This integral vanishes at the points $t = T, 2T, \ldots, nT, \ldots$ and is finite for all other values of t. Therefore, in the limit as $t \to \infty$, the average power vanishes.

Two-terminal components of this type are also referred to as *nondissipative* passive components. The energy input to the component takes on both positive and negative values, but in the limit the average power is zero—i.e., there is no dissipation. Such components are said to be capable of storing and delivering energy without dissipation.

It can also be shown that, when the coefficient b in Eq. (2.1.6) is a function of y, the average power input to the component is zero as long as $b(y)$ is a single-valued function.

ACCUMULATIVE COMPONENTS

For the accumulative type of component, or simply accumulator, we have

$$\frac{d}{dt} x(t) = \frac{1}{c} y(t)$$

and we see that the across variable $x(t)$ is proportional to the time integral or "accumulation" of the through variable (flow or force). As with the delay components, the coefficients in these models are also obtained by converting the differential equation to algebraic form by use of the time integral of $y(t)$ as a variable.

The energy stored in an accumulator at any point in time is

$$W_c(t) = c \int_{t_0}^{t} x(\tau) \frac{d}{d\tau} x(\tau) d\tau$$

$$= \frac{c}{2} [x^2(t) - x^2(t_0)]$$

As in the case of the delay component, the long-term average power input to an accumulator is zero for periodic variations in the terminal variables, and this component, therefore, is also classified as nondissipative.

GENERATORS

Finally, if the complementary terminal variables of a two-terminal component are mutually independent and either

$x(t)$ = known function of time

or

$y(t)$ = known function of time

then the two-terminal component is referred to as an *ideal generator*, or *driver*. To cite an obvious example, the terminal voltage of a battery over some range of current of interest can frequently be taken as a constant.

In general, any component for which the across variable is considered independent of the through variable is referred to as an *ideal across driver*. For example, if the pressure at the two ports of a hydraulic pump is regarded as independent of the flow through the component, the pump is regarded an ideal pressure driver. Likewise the two ends of a rod or beam are frequently regarded as having no relative displacement between them, regardless of the applied forces. Such a beam or rod is regarded as a displacement driver of constant magnitude.

Similarly, if the through variable of a two-terminal component is independent of the across variable, the component is referred to as an *ideal through driver*. Positive-displacement (piston-type) hydraulic pumps, when driven at a constant speed, can be regarded as ideal through (flow) drivers. Most hydraulic pistons or motors when supplied from a constant-pressure hydraulic source produce ram forces or shaft torques that are independent of position, at least for a relatively wide range of ram velocities and shaft speeds.

The power input to a generator is, of course,

$$P(t) = x(t)y(t)$$

from which it follows that energy is being received by the component at any given point in time if both x and y are of the same algebraic sign. When they are of opposite sign the component is delivering energy from its terminals.

2.2 SOME BASIC COMPOUND - COMPONENT MODELS AND THEIR SOLUTION CHARACTERISTICS

Effective models of two-terminal components are frequently more complex than the elementary form given in Table 2.1.1. However, these more complex forms can usually be viewed as a combination of the elementary forms and are therefore referred to as *compound models*. The terminal characteristics of most batteries and other electrical sources, for example, are actually more nearly of the form shown in Fig. 2.2.1. If this characteristic can be approximated by a straight line of slope R, then the mathematical model is of the form

$$v(t) = Ri(t) + E_0 \tag{2.2.1}$$

and can be viewed as a series combination of two elementary forms. The intercept E_0 on the $v(t)$ axis obviously represents the magnitude of the terminal voltage for zero terminal current and therefore is referred to as the *open-circuit voltage*. Only in the event that one is willing to neglect R is the component regarded as an "ideal" voltage driver.

As a second example, the electrical terminal characteristics of a coil of wire can frequently be modeled by a differential equation of the form

$$v(t) = Ri(t) + L\frac{d}{dt}i(t) \tag{2.2.2}$$

or

$$\frac{d}{dt}i(t) = -\frac{R}{L}i(t) + \frac{1}{L}v(t) \tag{2.2.3}$$

and the component is viewed conceptually as a series combination of two elementary components—a resistor and inductor. Similarly, a rigid body operating in a semiclosed oil or pneumatic chamber can frequently be viewed conceptually as an elementary mass and damper operating in parallel, giving a two-terminal model of the form

$$f(t) = B\dot{\delta}(t) + M\frac{d}{dt}\dot{\delta}(t) \tag{2.2.4}$$

or

$$\frac{d}{dt}\dot{\delta}(t) = -\frac{B}{M}\dot{\delta}(t) + \frac{1}{M}f(t) \tag{2.2.5}$$

Both coefficients in these differential equations must be established from signals measured at the terminals of the component. Various techniques are available for making these measurements, all of which are based on the solution characteristics of the differential equation, considered next.

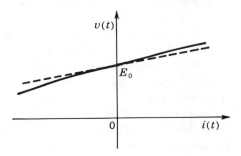

Fig. 2.2.1 A typical electrical voltage-generator characteristic.

For convenience, let the differential equation

$$x(t) = Ay(t) + B\frac{d}{dt}y(t)$$

be written in standard form

$$\frac{d}{dt}y(t) = -\frac{A}{B}y(t) + \frac{1}{B}x(t) \tag{2.2.6}$$

If $x(t)$ is a continuous function of time for all $t \geq 0$, then the solution can be written as the sum of two components, namely,

$$y(t) = y_h(t) + y_p(t)$$

where $y_h(t)$ is the *homogeneous solution*, i.e., the solution to Eq. (2.2.6) when $x(t) = 0$, and $y_p(t)$ is the *particular solution*, i.e., the solution introduced by the independent terminal variable $x(t)$.

By direct substitution, it is easy to see that when $x(t) = 0$ the homogeneous component of the solution is a decaying exponential function of time,

$$y_h(t) = Ke^{-t/\tau}$$

where

$\tau = B/A$ is called the *time constant*
K is an arbitrary constant

If $x(t)$ is a step function at $t = 0$,

$$x(t) = \begin{cases} X & t \geq 0 \\ 0 & t < 0 \end{cases}$$

then the given differential equation is satisfied by the particular solution

$$y_p(t) = \frac{X}{A}$$

Consequently, the complete solution is

$$y(t) = y_h(t) + y_p(t) = \frac{X}{A} + Ke^{-t/\tau} \tag{2.2.7}$$

This solution is indicated in Fig. 2.2.2 for various values of the arbitrary constant K and a given value of $\tau = B/A$.

From these sketches it is evident that the solution of the differential equation gives a family of solutions and the problem now is to select the one solution (i.e., the value of K) that corresponds to the actual terminal conditions. To select this one solution, we must know the value of $y(t)$ somewhere in the region of $t \geq 0$, that is, we must know one point on the solution curve. If, for example, $y(t)$ is known at $t = 0$, as is frequently the case, then the value of K in the solution is determined by setting $t = 0$ in Eq. (2.2.7), i.e.,

$$y(0) = \frac{X}{A} + K$$

or

$$K = y(0) - \frac{X}{A} \tag{2.2.8}$$

For the present, suppose that $y(0) = 0$. This corresponds to a physical condition wherein the current in a coil of wire, for example, is equal to zero at the time of application of the step function of voltage. The solution of interest is then

$$y(t) = \frac{X}{A} (1 - e^{-t/\tau}) \tag{2.2.9}$$

The complementary component of the solution,

$$y_h(t) = -\frac{X}{A} e^{-t/\tau}$$

vanishes as $t \to \infty$ and therefore is frequently referred to as the *transient* component of the solution. In contrast, the particular component

$$y_p(t) = \frac{X}{A}$$

does not vanish with increasing time and therefore is frequently called the *steady-state* component of the solution. It is also very important to

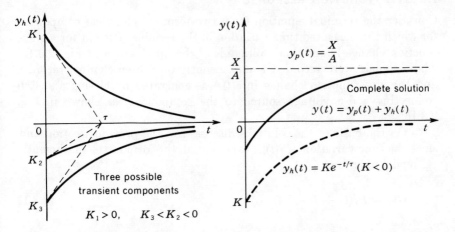

Fig. 2.2.2 Solution to the first-order differential equation [Eq. (2.2.6)] for a step-function variation in $x(t)$.

note that the transient term is a function of the value of $y(t)$ at $t = 0$, that is, $y(0)$. The steady-state term is completely independent of $y(0)$.

To obtain the solution to Eq. (2.2.6) for other time variations in $x(t)$, the same procedure as given above can be followed. If, for example,

$$x(t) = \begin{cases} X_m \sin \omega t & \text{for } t \geq 0 \\ 0 & \text{for } t < 0 \end{cases}$$

then the solution to Eq. (2.2.6) is found to be

$$y(t) = Y_c e^{-t/\tau} + \frac{X_m}{(A^2 + \omega^2 B^2)^{1/2}} \sin (\omega t + \Phi)$$

where

$$\tan \Phi = -\omega\tau \qquad Y_c = \frac{X_m K}{B} \qquad \tau = \frac{B}{A}$$

The coefficient K is a constant that must be determined from the known value of $y(t)$ at $t = 0$ or some other point on the solution curve. Again, by virtue of the fact that the first term in the solution vanishes as $t \to \infty$, it is called the transient component of the solution. On the other hand, the second component (the steady-state component) does not vanish with increasing t.

Both the step function and the sinusoidal steady-state response characteristics can be used effectively as bases for measuring the parameters in component models, as shown in the next two sections.

2.3 STEP-FUNCTION RESPONSE

Consider the terminal equation for a two-terminal electrical component for which the measured time variation in the terminal current for a step-function change in terminal voltage is of the form shown in Fig. 2.3.1a. These signals were recorded simultaneously on a dual-channel recorder and the step-function change in $v(t)$ was generated by closing a switch connecting a d-c voltage source to the component, as shown in Fig. 2.3.1b.

On the basis of the solutions discussed in the previous section and since the time variation of $i(t)$ is exponential, the form of the mathematical model must be

$$v(t) = Ri(t) + L\frac{d}{dt} i(t) \tag{2.3.1}$$

where R and L are constants to be determined. The solution to Eq. (2.3.1) for a step-function change in $v(t)$ at $t = 0$ has already been shown to be of the form

$$i(t) = \frac{V}{R} (1 - Ke^{-t/\tau}) \tag{2.3.2}$$

where

$$\tau = \frac{L}{R}$$

To determine the numerical values of the parameters R and L in the differential equation, we have only to fit the solution curve in Eq. (2.3.2) to the response curve in Fig. 2.3.1. This is accomplished by considering three critical values of t:

1.   From the response curve, $i(t) \to 3$ as $t \to \infty$. From the solution,

$$\lim_{t \to \infty} i(t) = \frac{V}{R}$$

Hence,

$$R = \tfrac{100}{3} = 33.3 \text{ ohms}$$

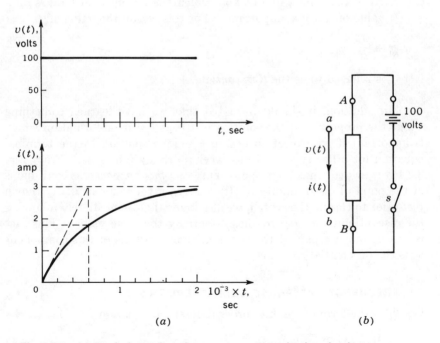

(a)   (b)

Fig. 2.3.1   (a) Typical step-function response; (b) excitation circuit.

2.　　　At $t = 0$, from the response curve, $i(0) = 0$, and $V = 100$ volts. From the solution,

$$i(0) = \frac{V}{R}(1 - K) = 0$$

Thus, $K = 1$, and we have established also the arbitrary constant associated with the general solution to the differential equation.

3.　　　At $t = \tau$, from the solution,

$$i(\tau) = \frac{V}{R}(1 - Ke^{-1}) = 3(1 - e^{-1})$$

$$= 3 \times 0.632 = 1.90 \text{ amp}$$

From the response curve, the time at which $i(t)$ takes on the value 1.90 amp is found to be

$$t = \tau = 0.6 \times 10^{-3} \text{ sec}$$

Therefore

$$\frac{L}{R} = \tau = 0.6 \times 10^{-3} \text{ sec}$$

$$L = 0.6 \times 33.3 \times 10^{-3} = 0.02 \text{ henry}$$

Note that the value of t at which the exponent of e takes on a value of unity is important. For this reason the value of

$$\tau = \frac{L}{R}$$

is referred to as the *time constant*.

In addition, it should be noted that we have learned something about the properties of the solution of $i(t)$ at $t = 0$—information which is important if we expect to obtain a unique solution to the terminal equation for other types of time-varying driving functions. From Fig. 2.3.1 it is evident that the response curve *for this component* is continuous at the point of discontinuity in $v(t)$. Thus, if the value of $i(t)$ is known just prior to closing the switch, we also know that, immediately following the discontinuity in $v(t)$, $i(t)$ has essentially the same value. This fact is just as much a part of the terminal characteristics of this component as is the differential equation.

2.4 FREQUENCY - RESPONSE CHARACTERISTICS

Consider the form of the first-order differential equation

$$x(t) = Ay(t) + B\frac{d}{dt}y(t) \tag{2.4.1}$$

when the time variation of $x(t)$ is a sinusoidal function of time with angular frequency ω, that is,

$$x(t) = X_m \sin \omega t \qquad (2.4.2)$$

In Sec. 2.2 it is shown that, under this mode of excitation, the steady-state component of the solution for $y(t)$ is also a sinusoidal function of the same frequency but of a different amplitude and phase angle, i.e.,

$$y_p(t) = Y_m \sin (\omega t + \Phi) \qquad (2.4.3)$$

where

$$Y_m = \frac{X_m}{(A^2 + \omega^2 B^2)^{1/2}} \qquad (2.4.4)$$

and

$$\Phi = -\arctan \frac{\omega B}{A} \qquad (2.4.5)$$

Clearly, both the magnitude Y_m and the phase angle Φ of the response function $y(t)$ are functions of the excitation frequency, ω. Plots of these variations with ω are shown in Fig. 2.4.1 and are called the *frequency-response* characteristics.

Note that, in Fig. 2.4.1a, the intercept on the Y_m axis represents X_m/A, where A represents one coefficient in the differential equation. Further, this intercept represents the limit of the magnitude of Y_m as $\omega \to 0$; that is, substituting $\omega = 0$ in Eq. (2.4.4) gives

$$Y_m(0) = \frac{X_m}{A}$$

At all other frequencies, the magnitude of Y_m is less than this value and, in fact, approaches zero as the frequency increases without bound.

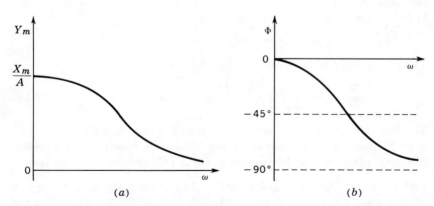

Fig. 2.4.1 Frequency-response characteristics showing variation in (*a*) magnitude Y_m and (*b*) phase angle Φ with frequency ω.

In reference to the plot of the phase angle Φ in Fig. 2.4.1b, note that at $\omega = 0$ the phase angle is zero and the two signals are in phase. On the other hand, as ω increases without bound, the phase angle approaches $-90°$ and the signals are out of phase by $90°$, with $y(t)$ *lagging* $x(t)$.

Although the plots of variation in the magnitude Y_m and phase angle Φ of the response function with frequency as given in Fig. 2.4.1 are acceptable, there are more convenient forms in which these plots can be made, forms which in fact make it possible to establish the value of the coefficients A and B in Eq. (2.4.1) directly from the plot. To provide this facility, Eq. (2.4.4) is first divided through by X_m to obtain

$$\frac{Y_m}{X_m} = \frac{1}{(A^2 + \omega^2 B^2)^{1/2}} = \frac{1}{A(1 + \omega^2 B^2/A^2)^{1/2}} \tag{2.4.6}$$

If Eq. (2.4.6) is then multiplied by A, a *normalized* form of the equation is obtained, i.e.,

$$\frac{Y_m}{X_m/A} = \frac{Y_m}{Y_m(0)} = \frac{1}{(1 + \omega^2 B^2/A^2)^{1/2}} = \frac{1}{(1 + \omega^2 \tau^2)^{1/2}} \tag{2.4.7}$$

The terminology "normalized form" arises from the fact that at zero frequency the magnitude of the function to be plotted has a value of unity, i.e.,

$$\frac{Y_m}{X_m/A} = \frac{Y_m}{Y_m(0)} = 1 \qquad \text{at } \omega = 0$$

As shown previously, the term $Y_m(0)$ represents the magnitude of Y_m at zero frequency. Consequently, Eq. (2.4.7) relates the ratio of the magnitude of the through variable as a function of frequency to the magnitude of the through variable at zero frequency.

Consider now the base-10 logarithm of Eq. (2.4.7). To shorten the notation and at the same time emphasize that a function of frequency is considered, let

$$|G(\omega)| = \frac{Y_m}{Y_m(0)} = \frac{1}{(1 + \omega^2 \tau^2)^{1/2}} \tag{2.4.8}$$

Taking the logarithm of Eq. (2.4.8), we have

$$\log |G(\omega)| = \log \frac{Y_m}{Y_m(0)} = -\frac{1}{2} \log (1 + \omega^2 \tau^2) \tag{2.4.9}$$

The function $20 \log |G(\omega)|$† is referred to as the *ratio* in *decibels.*†

To plot the magnitude of $20 \log |G(\omega)|$ as a function of frequency, it is convenient to consider two regions of ω, (1) the low-frequency region,

---

† When the base e (natural) logarithm of Eq. (2.4.7) is taken, the unit of $\log |G(\omega)|$ is called a *neper*. The units of neper and decibel are related by: db $= 20 \log e$ or db $= 8.686$ nepers. For example, if the ratio $|G(\omega)| = 100$, then it could also be expressed as $20 \log 100 = 40$ db or $40/8.686 = 4.61$ nepers.

where $\omega^2\tau^2 \ll 1$, and (2) the high-frequency region, where $\omega^2\tau^2 \gg 1$. In the low-frequency region, as a very good approximation,

$$20 \log |G(\omega)| \cong -10 \log 1 = 0 \qquad \omega^2\tau^2 \ll 1 \qquad (2.4.10)$$

and for the high-frequency region

$$20 \log |G(\omega)| \cong -10 \log \omega^2\tau^2 = -20 \log \omega\tau$$
$$\cong -20 \log \omega - 20 \log \tau \qquad \omega^2\tau^2 \gg 1 \qquad (2.4.11)$$

A plot of these approximating equations at the high and low frequencies is given in Fig. 2.4.2a, where the function $20 \log |G(\omega)|$ is plotted as a function of the argument $\Omega = \log \omega$, that is, the ω axis is a log scale.

These functions are, of course, straight lines and represent only the asymptotic behavior of the function $|G(\omega)|$; the actual plot of $20 \log |G(\omega)|$ only approaches these two lines in the limiting cases where $\omega \rightarrow 0$ and

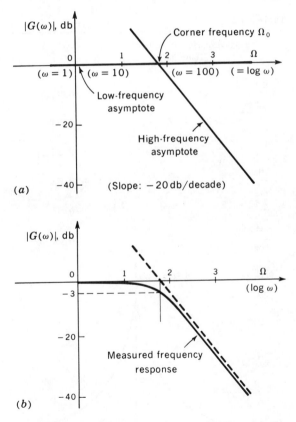

Fig. 2.4.2 Log-frequency response showing (a) the low- and high-frequency asymptotes and (b) the actual plot with the asymptote approximations.

$\omega \to \infty$. For this reason they are referred to as the *asymptotes* of the frequency response. Note that the low-frequency asymptotes intersect at the point for which

$$-20 \log \omega\tau = 0$$

or

$$\omega\tau = 1 \tag{2.4.12}$$

The frequency

$$\omega = \omega_0 = \frac{1}{\tau} \tag{2.4.13}$$

is called the *corner frequency* since the two asymptotes meet at this particular value.

The actual plot of $20 \log |G(\omega)|$ as determined from the set of points shown in Table 2.4.1 is given in Fig. 2.4.2b along with the two asymptotes.

Table 2.4.1

ω	Asymptotic value of $20 \log |G(\omega)|$	Actual value of $20 \log |G(\omega)|$	Error, db
$\dfrac{1}{\tau}$	0	-3.01	3.01
$\dfrac{2}{\tau}$	-6	-6.99	0.99
$\dfrac{4}{\tau}$	-12	-12.30	0.30
$\dfrac{10}{\tau}$	-20	-20.04	0.04
$\dfrac{1}{2\tau}$	0	-0.97	0.97
$\dfrac{1}{10\tau}$	0	0.04	0.04

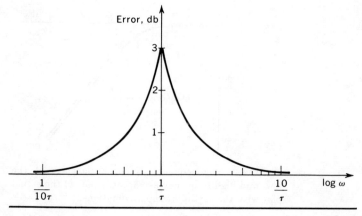

From either Table 2.4.1 or Fig. 2.4.2b it is seen that at the corner frequency the actual value of the frequency response is 3 db less than that given by the two asymptotes at this point. Consequently, the corner frequency can also be located by finding the point on the ω axis where the frequency-response curve is 3 db below the axis.

The way in which the frequency-response curve is used to determine the coefficients in a differential-equation model is shown in the following example.

Example 2.4.1: The frequency-response curve as measured for the two-terminal mechanical component in Fig. 2.4.3a is shown in Fig. 2.4.3b. What is the differential-equation model of the component if the spring constant (as measured at a very low frequency) is 10 mks units?

Solution: From the form of the measured frequency-response characteristic we expect a differential-equation model of the form

$$f(t) = K\delta(t) + B\frac{d}{dt}\delta(t)$$

To establish the time constant of the component, two tangents to the frequency-response curve are drawn as indicated by the dashed lines. Since the point of intersection of these two tangents is $\omega = 4\pi$, the ratio of the two coefficients in the differential equation is given by

$$\frac{B}{K} = \tau = \frac{1}{\omega_0} = \frac{1}{12.56} = 0.0796$$

From the value of the spring constant established by the low-frequency test, we have

$$B = 0.0796K = 0.796 \text{ mks unit}$$

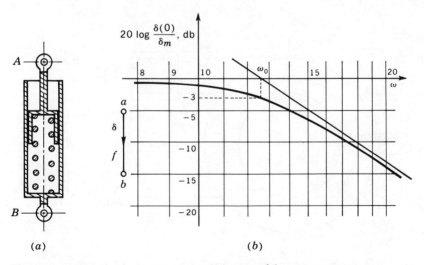

(a)   (b)

Fig. 2.4.3 (a) Mechanical component; (b) measured frequency response.

so that the numerical form of the mathematical model is

$$f(t) = 10\delta(t) + 0.796 \frac{d}{dt} \delta(t)$$

It should be noted in this example that, since the measured characteristic is down essentially 3 db at the corner frequency, it is certain that the resulting model represents the actual characteristics quite accurately.

The magnitude of the parameters in component models can sometimes be evaluated from the geometric configuration of the components and the material used in construction. Consider, for example, the coil of wire shown in Fig. 2.4.4. The linear model of this component is taken as a first-order differential equation of the form

$$v(t) = Ri(t) + L \frac{d}{dt} i(t)$$

For relatively slow time variations in $i(t)$ (low-frequency sinusoids, for example) the resistance coefficient R can be calculated if the length of wire l and its cross-sectional area A are known, along with a characteristic number σ for the material. Specifically

$$R = \frac{l}{\sigma A}$$

The constant σ is called the *electrical conductivity* of the material.

The inductance coefficient L is also related to the geometry and the properties of the material of construction by the relation

$$L = \frac{N^2 S \mu}{l_c}$$

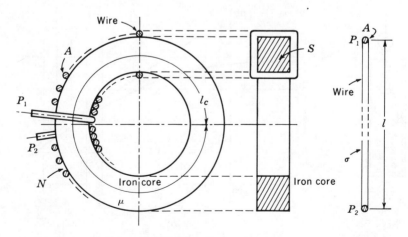

Fig. 2.4.4 A coil of wire, with its dimensions.

where (Fig. 2.4.4)

N is the number of turns on the iron core
S is the cross-sectional area of the iron core
l_c is the length of the core

The constant μ is called the magnetic *permeability* of the material from which the core is constructed.

Another example of a component for which the coefficients in the mathematical model can be easily evaluated from the component geometry and material properties is the cylindrical rigid body. When the cylinder is rotated about its axis, the differential equation relating the angular velocity and torque is

$$\tau(t) = J \frac{d}{dt} \dot{\Phi}(t)$$

The numerical value of J is found to be

$$J = \tfrac{1}{2}\pi\rho Lr^4$$

where the constants ρ, L, and r are, respectively, the *density*, the geometric length, and the radius of the cylinder.

Mathematical models of two-terminal components may, of course, take on more complex forms. Some of these will be considered in a later chapter after considering methods for developing models of subassemblies of components. The basic forms and examples given in this chapter, along with those given in the next chapter, represent only some of the most common building blocks of physical systems.

PROBLEMS

2.1 Let the mass component M be thrown upward from a point B on earth in a vertical direction with a speed equal to v_0. Find the maximum height that the mass component can reach and the time it will take for the component to reach that position. Sketch the curve $\delta(t)$, and determine the time that it will take for the mass component to return to the point B on earth.

The mathematical model of a mass component, as indicated in Table 2.1.1, is given in Fig. P2.1. The component is assumed to move along an axis δ, and its

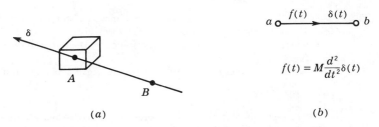

Fig. P2.1 (*a*) A mass component; (*b*) its terminal representation.

position at any instant of time is determined simply by the distance between the points A and B; point A is taken on the body and point B on the δ axis. The motion of the component AB is given by the terminal equation

$$f(t) = M \frac{d^2\delta(t)}{dt^2} \tag{P2.1}$$

Equation (P2.1) is valid when the motion of the mass component is considered in free space, i.e., when the motion of the body is considered in total isolation. In the practical case, the gravitational force has to be taken into consideration. For instance, in Fig. P2.1a, if the point B is taken as a point on the earth's surface and the δ axis is perpendicular to the earth's surface at B, then the gravitational force which brings the free-falling body to earth is given by the equation

$$W = Mg$$

where

> W denotes the weight of the body
> g is the gravitational constant of the earth

The constant $g = 9.81$ m/sec². The terminal equation for the mass component in this case is equal to

$$f(t) = M \frac{d^2}{dt^2} \delta(t) + W$$

2.2   A rigid body is moving along a δ axis on a horizontal plane with an initial velocity v_0 ($v = v_0$ at $t = 0$). The terminal equation for this component in terms of the mass M and the frictional force F is given below. Determine the distance traversed and the time taken before the body comes to rest.

Consider the mass component shown in Fig. P2.1 to be moving on a horizontal plane. When this component moves on the plane, there is friction between the surface of the plane and the component. Let the initial position of the component be at $\delta = 0$. It is assumed that when the body is slowly displaced along the δ axis with respect to the point B the force F as measured between the points A and B is constant and is given by

$$f(t) = F \frac{\delta(t)}{|\delta(t)|} = \begin{cases} F & \text{if } \delta(t) > 0 \\ -F & \text{if } \delta(t) < 0 \end{cases}$$

When the motion of the body is not slow, an additional force $f(t) = M\ddot{\delta}(t)$ must be taken into consideration. Hence, the terminal equation of this component is given by

$$f(t) = M\ddot{\delta}(t) + F \frac{\delta(t)}{|\delta(t)|}$$

2.3   In Fig. P2.3 the characteristics of a nonlinear resistor are plotted.

   (a) If the terminal voltage $v(t)$ has the form given in item 5, Table 1.6.1, where $X_m = 10$ volts, construct, graphically, the waveform for the current function $i(t)$.

   (b) Let the equation for the characteristic in Fig. P2.3 be given by

$$v(t) = 10 \sqrt{i(t)}$$

   Calculate, analytically, the expression for $i(t)$ when $v(t)$ is given as in (a), and determine the first four harmonics of $i(t)$.

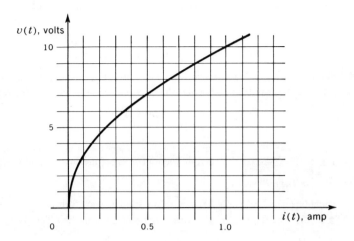

Fig. P2.3 $v\text{-}i$ characteristic of a nonlinear resistor.

2.4   Repeat Prob. 2.3b if $v(t)$ is given as in item 4, Table 1.6.1, with $X_m = 15$ volts.

2.5   Let the $\lambda\text{-}i$ characteristic of an inductor be given as in Fig. P2.5. If $i(t) = 0.5 \sin \omega t$, determine graphically the waveform of $\lambda(t)$, and then sketch the waveform for $v(t)$ from the curve of $\lambda(t)$. Note that the across variable $\lambda(t)$, called the *flux linkage*, is defined by $v(t) = (d/dt)\lambda(t)$.

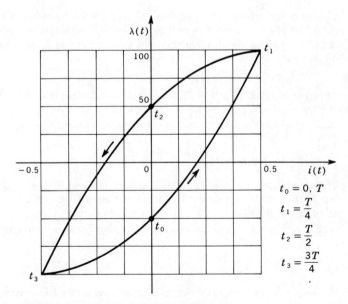

Fig. P2.5 $\lambda\text{-}i$ characteristic of an inductor.

2.6 Let the λ-i characteristic in Prob. 2.5 be approximated by the single-valued function

$$\lambda(t) = \begin{cases} 250i(t) & \text{for } |i(t)| \leq 0.2 \text{ amp} \\ \frac{500}{3} i(t) + \frac{50}{3} & \text{for } |i(t)| > 0.2 \text{ amp} \end{cases}$$

Sketch $v(t)$ when $i(t) = 0.5 \sin \omega t$. Give an analytical expression for $v(t)$.

2.7 Repeat Prob. 2.6 when the equations for the approximated characteristic are

$$\lambda(t) = \begin{cases} 150(1 - e^{-2i(t)}) & \text{for } i(t) > 0 \\ -150(1 - e^{2i(t)}) & \text{for } i(t) < 0 \end{cases}$$

2.8 Let the approximated v-i characteristic of a silicon diode be as given in Fig. 2.1.3. Sketch the current waveform as a function of time if $v(t)$ is given by

$$v(t) = 20 \sin \omega t$$

Calculate the first three harmonics for the $i(t)$ waveform.

2.9 Let the nonlinear characteristic of a spring be given by the equation

$$\frac{df}{d\delta} = k_1 - k_2\delta^2$$

where k_1 and k_2 are positive constants. Also, it is given that $f = 0$ at $\delta = 0$. When the terminal variable $f(t)$ is constant and equal to F_0, determine the displacement δ if the numerical values are given as follows:

$$F_0 = 0.3 \qquad k_1 = 2 \qquad k_2 = \tfrac{3}{2}$$

(Use a graphical method to determine the approximate solution.)

2.10 Let a hydraulic pipe have a terminal equation of the form

$$p(t) = R\dot{g}(t) + M\ddot{g}(t)$$

If a constant pressure P_0 is applied suddenly to the terminals of the pipe, find the fluid flow $\dot{g}(t)$ as the function of time. What is the value of $\dot{g}(t)$ as $t \to \infty$?

2.11 Let the terminal equation of a two-terminal hydraulic component be given by

$$p(t) = R\dot{g}(t) + Dg(t)$$

If $p(t)$ is specified as $p(t) = P_m \cos \omega t$, calculate the expression for $\dot{g}(t)$, and indicate the transient and steady-state components of the solution.

2.12 Consider a two-terminal mechanical component having the terminal equation of the form

$$T(t) = K\dot{\Phi}(t) + J\ddot{\Phi}(t)$$

If $T(t)$ is a step function, i.e., $T(t) = 0$ for $t < 0$ and $T(t) = T_0 > 0$ for $t \geq 0$, calculate the rotational velocity $\dot{\Phi}(t)$ as a function of time. What is the value of $\dot{\Phi}(t)$ as t tends to infinity?

2.13 For a two-terminal component having a terminal equation of the form

$$x(t) = Ay(t) + B\frac{dy(t)}{dt} \tag{P2.13}$$

the ellipse in Fig. P2.13 is obtained under a sinusoidal excitation. Calculate the numerical values of the coefficients A and B in Eq. (P2.13) by use of Fig. P2.13.

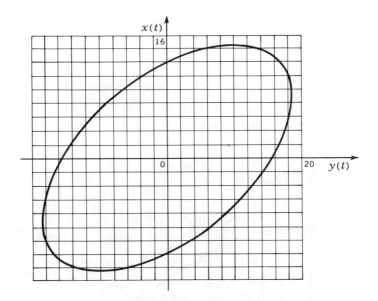

Fig. P2.13 $x(t)$-$y(t)$ characteristic under sinusoidal excitation.

2.14   The characteristic in Fig. P2.14 is obtained from a two-terminal mechanical component when excited from a sinusoidal driver of the form

$$\delta(t) = \tfrac{3}{100} \sin 10t$$

The through variable $h(t)$ in Fig. P2.14 is defined by

$$f(t) = \frac{dh(t)}{dt}$$

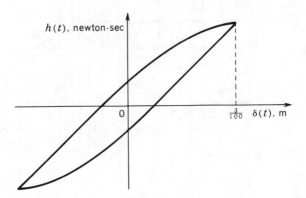

Fig. P2.14 $\delta(t)$-$h(t)$ characteristic of a two-terminal mechanical component.

Assume that the area of the closed curve in Fig. P2.14 is equal to 10^{-4} newton-m-sec. If the equation

$$\delta(t) = bh(t) + k \frac{dh(t)}{dt}$$

is to be taken as the approximated terminal equation for this component, determine the numerical value of b and k from an elliptical approximation of the area of the hysteresis curve in Fig. P2.14.

2.15   The frequency-response characteristic of a two-terminal component is given in Fig. P2.15.   Write the mathematical expression for $|G(\omega)|$.

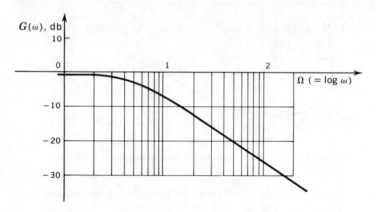

Fig. P2.15   Frequency-response characteristic.

2.16   Repeat Prob. 2.15 if the frequency responses are given by Fig. P2.16a and b.

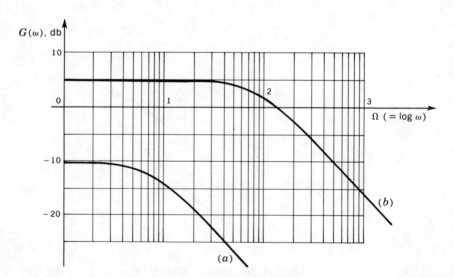

Fig. P2.16   Two different frequency-response characteristics.

2.17   The terminal characteristic of a nonlinear resistor (tunnel diode) is given in Fig. P2.17.

    (*a*)   Is it a passive or active component?

    (*b*)   Obtain a small-signal approximation to the given characteristics at the operating point described by $v = 0.15$ volt, $i = 0.3$ amp, and write the small-signal terminal equations.   Is the two-terminal component described by the small-signal terminal equation a passive or an active component?

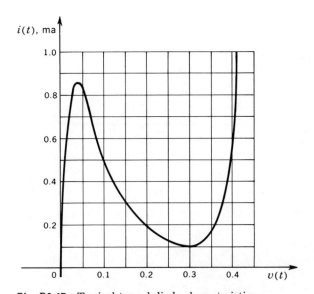

Fig. P2.17   Typical tunnel-diode characteristics.

FURTHER READING

1.   Koenig, H. E., and W. A. Blackwell: "Electromechanical System Theory," McGraw-Hill Book Company, New York, 1961.

3
Mathematical Models of Multiterminal Components

As in the case of two-terminal components, certain simple types of n-terminal-component models can be regarded as elementary forms. While these forms are more frequently than not unrealistic approximations to actual component characteristics, they nevertheless are conceptual tools useful in developing the more realistic forms. This chapter defines three such elementary linear forms and presents typical examples of realistic linear n-terminal-component models incorporating these basic forms. Finally, the concept of small-signal approximations to nonlinear characteristics of three-terminal components is developed and applied to important examples.

3.1 ELEMENTARY n-TERMINAL DISSIPATIVE COMPONENTS

If we let $\mathbf{X}(t)$ represent a column vector whose $n - 1$ components correspond to the across variables identified by the edges of a terminal graph of an n-terminal component and $\mathbf{Y}(t)$ the complementary vector of through variables, then a generalization of the two-terminal dissipative component is the n-terminal generic form

$$\mathbf{X}(t) = \mathbf{A}\mathbf{Y}(t) \tag{3.1.1}$$

where $\mathbf{A}$ is a real square matrix of order $n - 1$. The power input to such an n-terminal component is

$$P(t) = \mathbf{Y}^T(t)\mathbf{X}(t) = \mathbf{Y}^T(t)\mathbf{A}\mathbf{Y}(t)$$

By definition, the matrix $\mathbf{A}$ is positive definite if $P(t) > 0$ for all vectors $\mathbf{Y}(t) \neq 0$. It is shown in the Appendix that $\mathbf{A}$ is positive definite if and only if all principal minors of $\mathbf{A}$ are greater than zero. This implies, of course, that if $\mathbf{A}$ is positive definite then it is also nonsingular. Further, the component power input is *always* positive†—hence the name *dissipative component*.

Since the coefficient matrix of a dissipative component is always nonsingular, the model can be inverted to give

$$\mathbf{Y}(t) = \mathbf{G}\mathbf{X}(t) \tag{3.1.2}$$

where $\mathbf{G} = \mathbf{A}^{-1}$ is called the *conductance matrix* for electrical and hydraulic processes and the *damping matrix* for mechanical processes.

The entries in the matrices $\mathbf{A}$ and $\mathbf{G}$ in Eqs. (3.1.1) and (3.1.2) are referred to, respectively, as the *open-circuit* and *short-circuit* parameters of the component, for reasons demonstrated in the following example.

Example 3.1.1: With all transport delays and fluid compression or accumulation within the coupling neglected, the terminal characteristics of the three-terminal

---

† The case where $\mathbf{A}$ may be singular is not considered here.

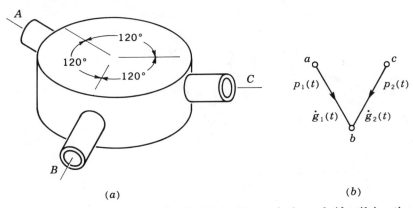

Fig. 3.1.1 (a) Symmetrical hydraulic joint; (b) terminal graph identifying the two sets of measurements to be used as a basis for modeling the component.

hydraulic coupling in Fig. 3.1.1a can be approximated by the elementary form

$$\begin{bmatrix} p_1(t) \\ p_2(t) \end{bmatrix} = \begin{bmatrix} a_{11} & a_{12} \\ a_{21} & a_{22} \end{bmatrix} \begin{bmatrix} \dot{g}_1(t) \\ \dot{g}_2(t) \end{bmatrix} \tag{3.1.3}$$

where the terminal variables $p_i(t)$ and $\dot{g}_i(t)$, $i = 1, 2$, are defined by the terminal graph shown in Fig. 3.1.1b. Determine the numerical values of the parameters in Eq. (3.1.3).

Solution: The edges of the selected terminal graph are isomorphic to the specific measurements indicated in the schematic diagram of Fig. 3.1.2. To realize nonzero values for the independent variables, it is, of course, necessary to excite the component by means of fluid pumps, as indicated.

The form of Eq. (3.1.3) suggests a definite procedure for determining the entries a_{11}, a_{12}, a_{21}, and a_{22} in the parameter matrix. Indeed, if $\dot{g}_2(t) = 0$, then Eq. (3.1.3) reduces to

$$\begin{bmatrix} p_1(t) \\ p_2(t) \end{bmatrix} = \begin{bmatrix} a_{11} \\ a_{21} \end{bmatrix} \dot{g}_1(t) \tag{3.1.4}$$

To impose the condition $\dot{g}_2(t) = 0$, hydraulic valve V_2 (shown in Fig. 3.1.2) is closed. Under this condition, terminal characteristics relating $p_1(t)$ to $\dot{g}_1(t)$ and $p_2(t)$ to $\dot{g}_1(t)$ are obtained and, for slow time variations, might typically be of the form given in Fig. 3.1.3.

The terminal characteristics of Fig. 3.1.3a and b are essentially linear in the region $-1 < \dot{g}_1(t) < 1$, and the slopes of the straight-line approximations represent the entries $a_{11} = 10$ and $a_{21} = 6$, respectively.

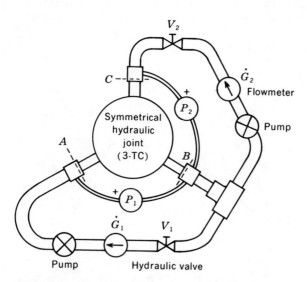

Fig. 3.1.2 Schematic diagram representing measurements as identified by the terminal graph of Fig. 3.1.1b.

Similarly, if $\dot{g}_1(t) = 0$, then Eq. (3.1.3) reduces to

$$\begin{bmatrix} p_1(t) \\ p_2(t) \end{bmatrix} = \begin{bmatrix} a_{12} \\ a_{22} \end{bmatrix} \dot{g}_2(t) \tag{3.1.5}$$

The entries a_{12} and a_{22} are obtained as the slope of the measured characteristics shown in Fig. 3.1.3c and d, respectively, and give entry values of $a_{12} = 6$ and $a_{22} = 10$.

The numerical form of the entries in the hydraulic-resistance matrix has been established, and the model is

$$\begin{bmatrix} p_1(t) \\ p_2(t) \end{bmatrix} = \begin{bmatrix} 10 & 6 \\ 6 & 10 \end{bmatrix} \begin{bmatrix} \dot{g}_1(t) \\ \dot{g}_2(t) \end{bmatrix}$$

Note that the coefficient matrix is symmetric and positive definite.

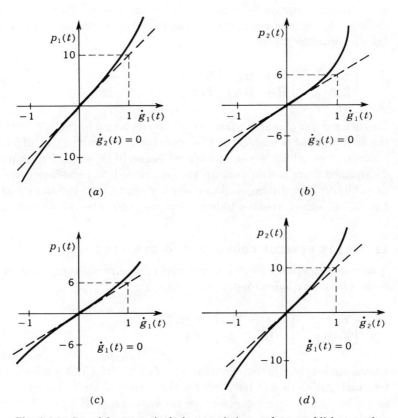

Fig. 3.1.3 Set of four terminal characteristics used to establish a mathematical model of the hydraulic component in Fig. 3.1.1.

Upon generalizing the test procedure demonstrated in the above example, it follows that the entries in the **A** matrix of Eq. (3.1.1) can be evaluated one column at a time from a sequence of controlled test conditions in which all but one of the independent variables are set equal to zero. Since these conditions are described as *open-circuit tests* (no flow), the entries in the model are called the *open-circuit parameters*.

It follows that the entries in the matrix $\mathbf{G} = \mathbf{A}^{-1}$ in Eq. (3.1.2) are determined from a sequence of controlled test conditions in which all but one *across variable* are set equal to zero. The entries in **G** are therefore called the *short-circuit parameters*.

A so-called hybrid-parameter model can be obtained by partitioning Eq. (3.1.1) into the form

$$\begin{bmatrix} \mathbf{X}_1(t) \\ \mathbf{X}_2(t) \end{bmatrix} = \begin{bmatrix} \mathbf{A}_{11} & \mathbf{A}_{12} \\ \mathbf{A}_{21} & \mathbf{A}_{22} \end{bmatrix} \begin{bmatrix} \mathbf{Y}_1(t) \\ \mathbf{Y}_2(t) \end{bmatrix}$$

where $\mathbf{A}_{11}$ is a square submatrix of arbitrary order. Since **A** is positive definite, $\mathbf{A}_{11}$ is nonsingular and the model can also be written in the *hybrid-parameter* form

$$\begin{bmatrix} \mathbf{Y}_1(t) \\ \mathbf{X}_2(t) \end{bmatrix} = \begin{bmatrix} \mathbf{H}_{11} & \mathbf{H}_{12} \\ \mathbf{H}_{21} & \mathbf{H}_{22} \end{bmatrix} \begin{bmatrix} \mathbf{X}_1(t) \\ \mathbf{Y}_2(t) \end{bmatrix} \qquad (3.1.6)$$

The designation "hybrid parameters" has its origin in the fact that, since the independent variables in the model are a combination of through and across variables, the entries (parameters) in the coefficient matrix are determined from a combination of open-circuit and short-circuit conditions (hybrid conditions). Since the inverse of the coefficient matrix of Eq. (3.1.6) exists, another hybrid form can, of course, be obtained.

3.2 LINEAR PERFECT COUPLERS AND GYRATORS

A second elementary form encountered in n-terminal-component models is the particular hybrid-parameter form

$$\begin{bmatrix} \mathbf{Y}_1(t) \\ \mathbf{X}_2(t) \end{bmatrix} = \begin{bmatrix} 0 & \mathbf{H}_{12} \\ -\mathbf{H}_{12}^T & 0 \end{bmatrix} \begin{bmatrix} \mathbf{X}_1(t) \\ \mathbf{Y}_2(t) \end{bmatrix} \qquad (3.2.1)$$

where, as before, the components of $(\mathbf{Y}_1, \mathbf{Y}_2)$ and $(\mathbf{X}_1, \mathbf{X}_2)$ represent the terminal variables as identified by the edges of an arbitrary terminal graph on the n-terminal component. In general, $\mathbf{H}_{12}$ is a rectangular matrix of arbitrary order but typically is either a row or a column matrix. In any case, the coefficient matrix in Eq. (3.2.1) is skew-symmetric, and the power input to the component vanishes, i.e.,

$$P(t) = [\mathbf{X}_1^T(t) \quad \mathbf{Y}_2^T(t)] \begin{bmatrix} \mathbf{Y}_1(t) \\ \mathbf{X}_2(t) \end{bmatrix}$$

$$= [\mathbf{X}_1^T(t) \quad \mathbf{Y}_2^T(t)] \begin{bmatrix} 0 & \mathbf{H}_{12} \\ -\mathbf{H}_{12}^T & 0 \end{bmatrix} \begin{bmatrix} \mathbf{X}_1(t) \\ \mathbf{Y}_2(t) \end{bmatrix} \equiv 0 \qquad (3.2.2)$$

The identifying name "perfect coupler" has its origin, of course, in the fact that there is no energy loss in the component and the fact that the coefficient matrix is skew-symmetric.

Note that it is not possible to characterize a perfect coupler in terms of open-circuit or short-circuit parameters.

Example 3.2.1: Develop the mathematical model of the common mechanical lever shown schematically in Fig. 3.2.1a. The terminals A_1 and A_2 refer to the end points of the lever, and A_3 is some point on the surface of the earth.

Solution: By use of the measurements identified by the terminal graph of Fig. 3.2.1b, it is easy to see that, upon neglecting the mass and spring effects of the lever, the terminal characteristics of the component for small-signal operation about the horizontal position can be modeled in hybrid-parameter form as

$$\begin{bmatrix} \dot{\delta}_1(t) \\ f_2(t) \end{bmatrix} = \begin{bmatrix} 0 & -l_1/l_2 \\ l_1/l_2 & 0 \end{bmatrix} \begin{bmatrix} f_1(t) \\ \dot{\delta}_2(t) \end{bmatrix} \qquad (3.2.3)$$

where l_1 and l_2 represent the lengths of the lever arms as indicated.

A more realistic model, of course, could include the equation relating $f_2(t)$ and $\dot{\delta}_2(t)$ under the controlled conditions for which $f_1(t) = 0$, that is, when A_1 is free. If we include the damping action of the atmosphere and bearing, then this equation is of the form

$$f_2(t) = \left(B + M \frac{d}{dt} \right) \dot{\delta}_2(t) \qquad \text{for } f_1(t) = 0 \qquad (3.2.4)$$

Procedures have already been given in Chap. 2 for establishing the magnitudes of the coefficients in a first-order differential equation of the above form.

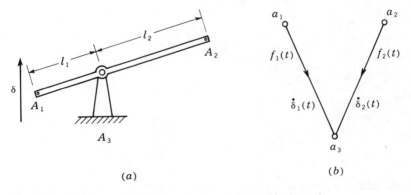

(a)

(b)

Fig. 3.2.1 (a) Schematic diagram of a lever; (b) terminal graph.

The complete model of the lever is obtained by compounding the perfect-coupler characteristics with the damping and inertia characteristics so as to form the model

$$\begin{bmatrix} \dot{\delta}_1(t) \\ f_2(t) \end{bmatrix} = \begin{bmatrix} 0 & -l_1/l_2 \\ l_1/l_2 & B + M(d/dt) \end{bmatrix} \begin{bmatrix} f_1(t) \\ \dot{\delta}_2(t) \end{bmatrix} \tag{3.2.5}$$

In a similar manner, it can be shown that, for small vertical displacements, the free lever in Fig. 3.2.2, as a five-terminal component, can be modeled by a system of four equations of the form

$$\begin{bmatrix} \dot{\delta}_1(t) \\ \dot{\delta}_2(t) \\ \hline f_3(t) \\ f_4(t) \end{bmatrix} = \left[\begin{array}{cc|cc} 0 & 0 & -l_1/l_3 & 1 \\ 0 & 0 & l_2/l_3 & 1 \\ \hline l_1/l_3 & -l_2/l_3 & B_3 + M_3(d/dt) & 0 \\ -1 & -1 & 0 & B_4 + M_4(d/dt) \end{array} \right] \begin{bmatrix} f_1(t) \\ f_2(t) \\ \hline \dot{\delta}_3(t) \\ \dot{\delta}_4(t) \end{bmatrix} \tag{3.2.6}$$

where the terminal variables are identified by the indicated terminal graph. The coefficients B_3 and M_3 represent, respectively, the damping and inertia coefficients for rotation about point B; B_4 and M_4, the corresponding coefficients for vertical translation with no rotation. When the damping and inertia effects are neglected, the model, of course, reduces to the perfect-coupler form.

In electrical-network studies, a perfect coupler is usually represented schematically as shown in Fig. 3.2.3a, and although the component actually has four terminals, only two pairs of complementary terminal variables are required to model its characteristics, i.e., the terminal graph in Fig. 3.2.3b identifies only "input" and "output" terminal pairs or ports. The characteristics of the component are such that the current variable identified by an edge between a and c (or between b and d) is identically zero, and all remaining terminal variables are independent of the voltage between either of these two pairs of terminals. A component having this special characteristic is sometimes referred to as an *isolation component* and is frequently used for just that purpose, to "electrically isolate" one section of a network from another.

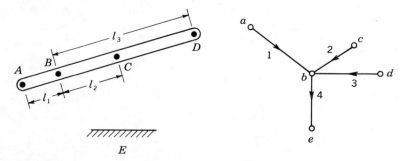

Fig. 3.2.2 Free lever and terminal graph identifying the complementary variables for the model shown in Eq. (3.2.6).

For iron-core transformers operating at frequencies between about 20 and 10,000 cps, the input-output characteristics are reasonably well represented by a model of the form

$$\begin{bmatrix} 1 & 0 \\ 0 & R_2 + L_2(d/dt) \end{bmatrix} \begin{bmatrix} v_1(t) \\ i_2(t) \end{bmatrix} = \begin{bmatrix} R_e + L_e(d/dt) & n \\ -n[R_2 + L_2(d/dt)] & 1 \end{bmatrix} \begin{bmatrix} i_1(t) \\ v_2(2) \end{bmatrix}$$
(3.2.7)

It is easy to see that the parameters in this model can be established from one open-circuit and one short-circuit test and that R_e and L_e represent the resistance and inductance as measured at port 1 with the terminals of port 2 short-circuited. The coefficient n represents the open-circuit voltage ratio, and R_2 and L_2 represent the resistance and inductance as measured at port 2 with port 1 open-circuited.

In the range of frequencies indicated earlier, the term $L_2(d/dt)i_2(t)$ is frequently quite large compared with other terms in the equations, and the characteristic is sometimes approximated by the somewhat less complex model

$$\begin{bmatrix} v_1(t) \\ i_2(t) \end{bmatrix} = \begin{bmatrix} R_e + L_e(d/dt) & n \\ -n & 0 \end{bmatrix} \begin{bmatrix} i_1(t) \\ v_2(t) \end{bmatrix}$$
(3.2.8)

If R_e and L_e are neglected, the model is then of the perfect-coupler form.

If the coefficient matrix of an open-circuit or short-circuit model is skew-symmetric, we have the *ideal-gyrator* form

$$\begin{bmatrix} \mathbf{Y}_1(t) \\ \mathbf{Y}_2(t) \end{bmatrix} = \begin{bmatrix} \mathbf{0} & \mathbf{G}_{12} \\ -\mathbf{G}_{12}^T & \mathbf{0} \end{bmatrix} \begin{bmatrix} \mathbf{X}_1(t) \\ \mathbf{X}_2(t) \end{bmatrix}$$
(3.2.9)

Simple algebra will establish that the power input to the component is zero as in the case of the perfect coupler. This type of model is encountered most frequently in connection with transducers, i.e., components which couple one physical process to another, such as the hydraulic ram of the next example.

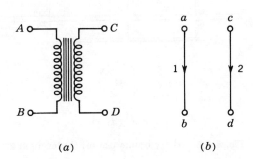

Fig. 3.2.3 (a) Schematic diagram and (b) terminal graph of a two-winding transformer.

(a) (b)

Example 3.2.2: Determine a mathematical model of the hydraulic ram shown schematically in Fig. 3.2.4 in terms of the force and velocity of the ram and the pressure and flow at the cylinder ports as indicated by the accompanying terminal graph.

Solution: Assuming that the cylinder is filled with an incompressible fluid and neglecting all leakage and inertia effects, one would expect to model the characteristics by a pair of algebraic equations of the form

$$\begin{bmatrix} f_1(g) \\ \dot{g}_2(t) \end{bmatrix} = \begin{bmatrix} G_{11} & G_{12} \\ G_{21} & G_{22} \end{bmatrix} \begin{bmatrix} \dot{\delta}_1(t) \\ p_2(t) \end{bmatrix} \tag{3.2.10}$$

The magnitudes of the coefficients in the first column, of course, are established by setting $p_2(t) = 0$, that is, with terminals D and C connected (short-circuited) by a "resistanceless" hose filled with the same fluid as the cylinder. Considering the isomorphism between the edges of the graph and the terminal measurements defined in Chap. 1, it is not difficult to establish that the flow rate $\dot{g}_2$ through the short-circuited hose is related to the velocity of the piston by

$$\dot{g}_2(t) = G_{21}\dot{\delta}_1(t) = -A\,\dot{\delta}_1(t) \qquad p_2(t) = 0$$

where $G_{21} = -A$ is proportional to the area of the piston (exclusive of the rod). In passing, let it be pointed out that under these same test conditions one would expect the force required to move the piston to be related to its velocity by a differential equation of the form

$$f_1(t) = \left(B_1 + M_1 \frac{d}{dt} \right) \dot{\delta}_1(t) \qquad \text{for } p_2(t) = 0 \tag{3.2.11}$$

To the extent that the coefficients in the indicated model are actually constants, they can be evaluated from a frequency-response characteristic taken under the indicated test conditions. The coefficient M_1 can also be calculated from the weight of the piston and the fluid in motion.

The coefficients in the second column of the coefficient matrix in Eq. (3.2.10) are evaluated under the conditions for which $\dot{\delta}_1(t) = 0$, i.e., the piston is stationary. Again taking into consideration the isomorphism between the edges of the terminal graph and the measurements, it is easy to see that, under this condition of operation, the force required to hold the piston in a stationary

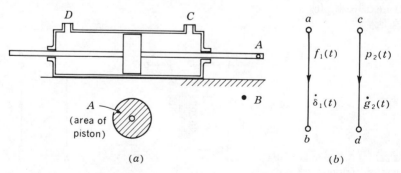

Fig. 3.2.4 (a) Hydraulic piston; (b) terminal graph.

position is related to the applied cylinder pressure by

$$f_1(t) = G_{12}p_2(t) = Ap_2(t) \qquad \dot{\delta}_1(t) = 0 \tag{3.2.12}$$

where A is again proportional to the area of the piston.

If, under this condition, there is appreciable leakage from one side of the piston to the other (as with a worn cylinder wall), and if we approximate this leakage characteristic by a linear function, then G_{22} is some nonzero constant.

Upon neglecting the leakage, mass, and damping coefficients, it follows that the model of the hydraulic ram is the simple gyrator form

$$\begin{bmatrix} f_1(t) \\ \dot{g}_2(t) \end{bmatrix} = \begin{bmatrix} 0 & A \\ -A & 0 \end{bmatrix} \begin{bmatrix} \dot{\delta}_1(t) \\ p_2(t) \end{bmatrix}$$

A more realistic model, of course, includes the damping, mass, and leakage effects on the main diagonal, to give a compound model of the form

$$\begin{bmatrix} f_1(t) \\ \dot{g}_2(t) \end{bmatrix} = \begin{bmatrix} B_1 + M_1(d/dt) & A \\ -A & G_{22} \end{bmatrix} \begin{bmatrix} \dot{\delta}_1(t) \\ p_2(t) \end{bmatrix}$$

It should also be pointed out, in conjunction with this example, that when the compressibility of the medium is not negligible, as in the case of pneumatic rams, the flow rates at ports C and D of the cylinder are no longer the same in magnitude at any given point in time. This differential flow is included in the model by the addition of an atmospheric reference and an additional pair of complementary variables, as indicated in Fig. 3.2.5. It is not too difficult to establish that a linear mathematical model for small displacements of the piston from the center of the cylinder and small changes in pressure is of the form

$$\begin{bmatrix} f_1(t) \\ \dot{g}_2(t) \\ p_3(t) \end{bmatrix} = \begin{bmatrix} B_1 + M_1(d/dt) & A & 0 \\ -A & G_{22} + (C/4)(d/dt) & \tfrac{1}{2}(d/dt) \\ 0 & -\tfrac{1}{2} & 1/C \end{bmatrix} \begin{bmatrix} \dot{\delta}_1(t) \\ p_2(t) \\ g_3(t) \end{bmatrix} \tag{3.2.13}$$

where the coefficients in the third column are determined from the measurements made under terminal conditions indicated in Fig. 3.2.6. From the geometry of this system it is evident that, for relatively small changes in pres-

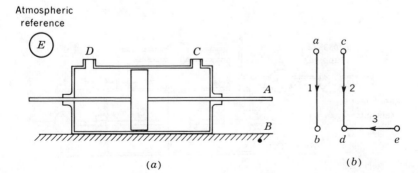

Fig. 3.2.5 (a) Pneumatic piston; (b) terminal graph.

sure, the total volume flow $g_3(t)$ into the system can be approximated by the linear equation

$$g_3(t) = Cp_3(t) \quad \text{for } \dot{\delta}_1(t) = 0,\ p_2(t) = 0$$

where the capacity coefficient C can be determined by simply multiplying the volume compressibility of the medium by the total volume of the cavity. Further, it is evident that, as long as the piston is located near the center of the cylinder, the volume flow $g_2(t)$ is approximately one-half the total volume flow $g_3(t)$.

The fact that the coefficient matrices in the gyrator and ideal-coupler models are not positive definite implies that only certain sets of terminal variables can be chosen as the independent variables for the model.

There is no such restriction, of course, for dissipative components where the coefficient matrix is positive definite. Unfortunately, there is no way to determine a priori which of the $2(n - 1)$-terminal variables identified by a terminal graph constitutes an independent set. This is part of the information that must be established from tests on the component under controlled conditions.

It is also not possible to determine a priori which one of the $n^{(n-2)}$ possible terminal graphs of an n-terminal component defines the "most convenient" variables as measured, for example, by the number of zeros contained in the coefficient matrix. While there are only 3 basically different terminal graphs for a three-terminal component, there are 1,296 possible graphs for a six-terminal component; i.e., there are 1,296 different sets of measurements that can be used in modeling the characteristics of a six-terminal component! It will be shown in a later chapter, however, that the model corresponding to one terminal graph can *always* be derived from the model corresponding to another terminal graph by a simple operation called a *tree transformation*, and that this transformation does not change the rank of the coefficient matrices in the model.

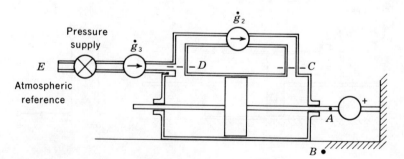

Fig. 3.2.6 Terminal conditions for measuring coefficients in third column of coefficient matrix in Eq. (3.2.13).

3.3 LOW - FREQUENCY NONLINEAR CHARACTERISTICS OF TYPICAL TWO - PORT COMPONENTS

If a component contains only two ports, then it is possible to display the steady-state or low-frequency terminal characteristics of this component in the form of a family of curves, as demonstrated in the following examples. In some cases, it is also possible to represent these displayed characteristics by mathematical functions and thereby develop an explicit mathematical model.

Example 3.3.1 (transistors): The transistor is a three-terminal electrical device made of semiconducting materials, i.e., materials having conductivity lower than that of metals but higher than that of insulators. The discipline of system analysis is not concerned with the theory of the mechanism by which conduction takes place within transistors or how they are constructed. These questions are rightfully subjects for the theory of the properties of materials. The concern here, as with all system components, is the terminal characteristics of the device, how these characteristics are represented mathematically, and, finally, what can be achieved by bringing this device together in combination with other discrete devices or components to form a system. To this end it is sufficient to say that most transistors are made up of a combination of two types of materials (i.e., materials having two distinct conduction properties), one called *p*-type, the other *n*-type material. Schematic diagrams of typical transistors, identified by their construction as *p-n-p* and *n-p-n* types, are shown in Fig. 3.3.1. The three terminals E, B, and C of the component are called *emitter*, *base*, and *collector*, respectively.

In modeling the low-frequency characteristics of the transistor, the variables identified by the terminal graph of Fig. 3.3.1c are found by experience to be the most convenient in many cases and are usually identified as the *base* and *collector voltages* and *currents*, without showing the terminal graph explicitly. If the base current $i_b(t)$ and collector voltage $v_c(t)$ are selected as the independent terminal variables, then the low-frequency model to be established is of the form

$$\begin{bmatrix} v_b(t) \\ i_c(t) \end{bmatrix} = \begin{bmatrix} f_1[i_b(t),v_c(t)] \\ f_2[i_b(t),v_c(t)] \end{bmatrix} \tag{3.3.1}$$

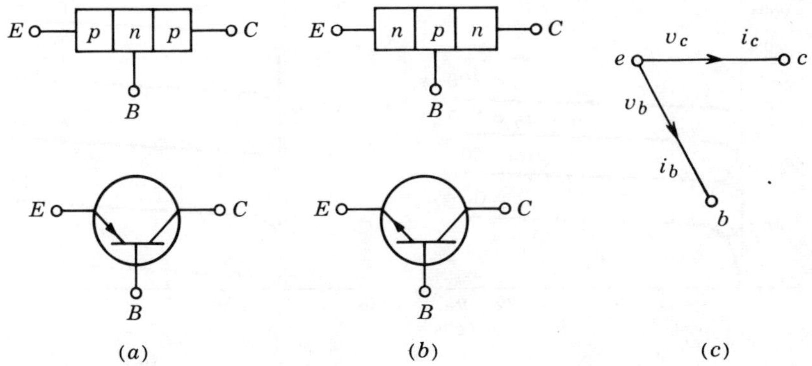

Fig. 3.3.1 Schematic diagrams of (a) *p-n-p* transistor; (b) *n-p-n* transistor; (c) most frequently used terminal graph.

Since each of the terminal variables $v_b(t)$ and $i_c(t)$ is a function of two variables, a three-dimensional surface is required to display the characteristic represented by each equation. However, if only discrete values of one of the independent variables are used, then the same information can be displayed in two dimensions in the form of families of curves such as those shown in Fig. 3.3.2.

These families of curves represent the measured characteristics of a typical transistor, with sets (a) and (c) showing the functional dependence among the three variables v_b, i_b, and v_c in two different forms. Sets (b) and (d) show the interdependence of i_c, i_b, and v_c in two different forms. Clearly, the function f_1 in the model can be determined from either set (a) or set (c) and the function f_2 from either set (b) or set (d); that is, only two families of curves are required to model the component. In general, the families of curves can only be approximated over limited regions by an analytical function in closed form, such as a polynomial in i_b and v_c.

Example 3.3.2 (triodes): The accepted standard schematic representation of a vacuum triode is shown in Fig. 3.3.3, along with an identified terminal graph and the

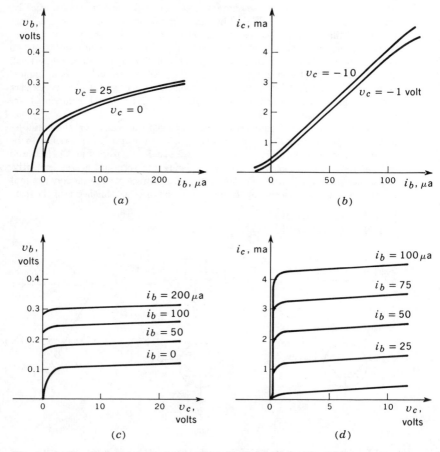

Fig. 3.3.2 Families of terminal characteristics for a typical transistor.

measured low-frequency characteristics presented in two forms. The filament, or heating element, along with its power supply, is considered as an integral part of the component, and since there are no other components of the system connected to the filament, its terminals are not identified in the model. The terminals of the device are usually identified by the letters G, P, and K, meaning *grid*, *plate*, and *cathode*, respectively. Almost invariably the terminal characteristics of the triode are presented in terms of the grid-to-cathode and plate-to-cathode terminal variables identified by the terminal graph. One of the unique and important features of the low-frequency characteristics of

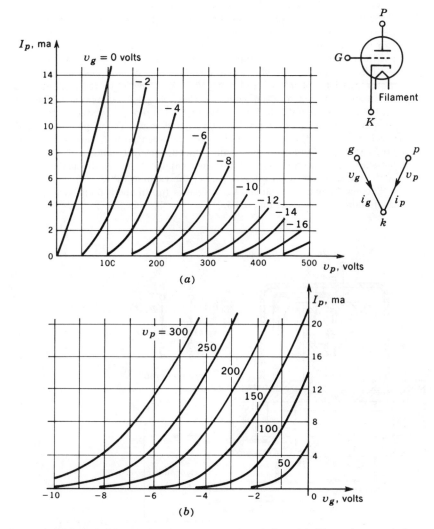

Fig. 3.3.3 Family of characteristics for a 6J6 triode. (*a*) Plate characteristics; (*b*) transfer characteristics.

this device is that the grid current $i_g(t)$ is essentially zero, so that the model is of the form

$$\begin{bmatrix} i_g(t) \\ i_p(t) \end{bmatrix} = \begin{bmatrix} 0 \\ G[v_g(t), v_p(t)] \end{bmatrix} \tag{3.3.2}$$

where the function $G[v_g(t), v_p(t)]$ is established from either of the two families of curves shown in Fig. 3.3.3.

Example 3.3.3 (hydraulic servo valve): A cross section of a typical electrically operated control valve is shown in Fig. 3.3.4. A qualitative description of the operation of the valve follows.

A very small amount of oil flows continuously out of the pressure cavity through the flexible pipe connected to the movable element (armature) of the electrical torque motor and out of the jet. The oil from the jet impinges on the two receiver pipes connected to each end of the spool. At the null, or zero, position, equal pressure is supplied to each end of the spool, and there is no resulting motion. However, when a voltage signal is applied to the torque motor, the jet is displaced and more oil is directed to one receiver pipe than the other. The net result, of course, is that the spool is displaced. The spool continues to move until the force on the end of the pipe jet created by the spring is equal to the force developed by the torque motor. The displacement of the spool, and hence the opening of the valve between ports C and D, is roughly proportional to the magnitude of the applied electrical signal. The constant-pressure supply is an integral part of the component, just as the heater element of the vacuum tube is an integral part of the vacuum tube.

The low-frequency terminal characteristics (up to about 5 cps) are given by the families of curves in Fig. 3.3.5.

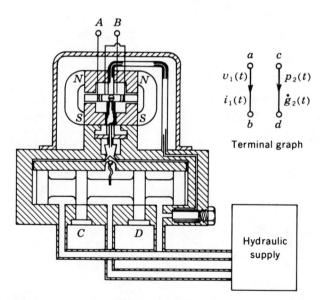

Terminal graph

Fig. 3.3.4 (*a*) A typical hydraulic control valve; (*b*) the terminal measurements of interest. (Model 415 servo valve.) (*Courtesy of Raymond Atchley Co.*)

Consider a mathematical model explicit in the through variables, i.e.,

$$\begin{bmatrix} i_1(t) \\ \dot{g}_2(t) \end{bmatrix} = \begin{bmatrix} Y_1[v_1(t),p_2(t)] \\ Y_2[v_1(t),p_2(t)] \end{bmatrix} \tag{3.3.3}$$

As might be expected from the construction of the component, the function $Y_1[v_1(t),p_2(t)]$ in Eq. (3.3.3) is independent of $p_2(t)$, and its value, from Fig.

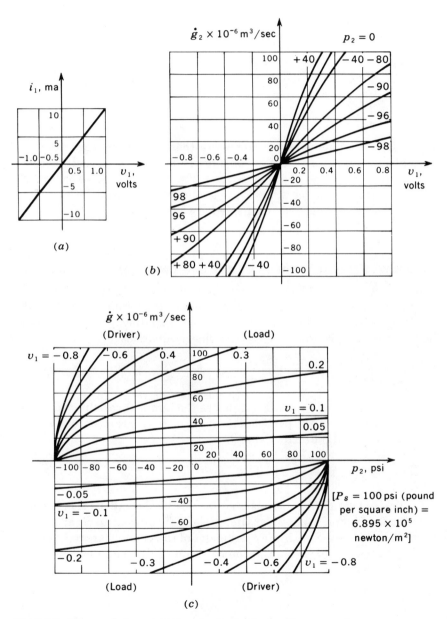

Fig. 3.3.5 Measured characteristics of a typical hydraulic servo valve.

3.3.5a, is $Y_1 = 0.01v_1(t)$.   The families of curves in Fig. 3.3.5b and c represent the same information in two different forms and are very closely approximated by the equation

$$\dot{g}_2(t) = Kv_1(t) \sqrt[+]{\left| p_2(t) + \frac{v_1(t)}{|v_1(t)|} P_s \right|} \tag{3.3.4}$$

where

$\sqrt[+]{}$ represents the positive square root

$P_s = 100$ psi represents the supply pressure and K is a constant

Therefore, the low-frequency nonlinear terminal characteristics for the servo valve are represented by

$$\begin{bmatrix} i_1(t) \\ \dot{g}_2(t) \end{bmatrix} = \begin{bmatrix} 0.01v_1(t) \\ Kv_1(t) \sqrt[+]{\left| p_2(t) + [v_1(t)/|v_1(t)|]P_s \right|} \end{bmatrix} \tag{3.3.5}$$

When a component contains more than two ports, each terminal variable, in general, is a function of three or more variables and the characteristics can no longer be recorded as a family of two-dimensional plots. There are at present no known ways of even recording the measured characteristics of nonlinear components when the number of variables exceeds four.

3.4 SMALL - SIGNAL MODELS OF TYPICAL TWO - PORT COMPONENTS

The terminal characteristics of two-port components can be approximated by linear functions if the magnitudes of the terminal variables are limited to "small" excursions about some operating point.   To show how this is done, consider the two nonlinear equations

$$\begin{aligned} U &= F(X,Y) \\ V &= G(X,Y) \end{aligned} \tag{3.4.1}$$

where U, V, X, and Y can be regarded as the terminal variables of a two-port component.   If the partial derivatives of F with respect to X and Y exist, then the total differential of U is

$$dU = \frac{\partial F}{\partial X} dX + \frac{\partial F}{\partial Y} dY \tag{3.4.2}$$

The function U represents a surface S_1 in three-dimensional space as indicated in Fig. 3.4.1.   Consider a plane P_1 tangent to S_1 at a point Q_1 on the surface of S_1.   If the coordinates of the point Q_1 are represented by X_0, Y_0, and $U_0 = F(X_0,Y_0)$, the equation of the tangent plane P_1 at Q_1 is given by

$$U - U_0 = \left(\frac{\partial F}{\partial X}\right)_{Q_1} (X - X_0) + \left(\frac{\partial F}{\partial Y}\right)_{Q_1} (Y - Y_0) \tag{3.4.3}$$

where $(\partial F/\partial X)_{Q_1}$ and $(\partial F/\partial Y)_{Q_1}$ are constants representing the partial derivatives evaluated at $Q_1 = (X_0, Y_0)$. In the vicinity of the operating point Q_1, let the surface S_1 be approximated by the plane P_1, and let the origin of the coordinate system be translated from 0 to Q_1; that is, let

$$
\begin{aligned}
u &= U - U_0 \\
x &= X - X_0 \\
y &= Y - Y_0
\end{aligned}
\tag{3.4.4}
$$

The equation of P_1 in the new coordinate system is the linear equation

$$
u = \left(\frac{\partial F}{\partial X}\right)_{Q_1} x + \left(\frac{\partial F}{\partial Y}\right)_{Q_1} y
\tag{3.4.5}
$$

Applying a similar approximation to Eq. (3.4.2) gives

$$
v = \left(\frac{\partial G}{\partial X}\right)_{Q_2} x + \left(\frac{\partial G}{\partial Y}\right)_{Q_2} y
\tag{3.4.6}
$$

which represents a plane P_2 passing through the operating point (X_0, Y_0) and $V_0 = G(X_0, Y_0)$.

Equations (3.4.5) and (3.4.6) can be written together as

$$
\begin{bmatrix} u \\ v \end{bmatrix} = \begin{bmatrix} (\partial F/\partial X)_{Q_1} & (\partial F/\partial Y)_{Q_1} \\ (\partial G/\partial X)_{Q_2} & (\partial G/\partial Y)_{Q_2} \end{bmatrix} \begin{bmatrix} x \\ y \end{bmatrix}
\tag{3.4.7}
$$

and represent a linear approximation to the given functions in a small region about operating points having coordinates X_0, Y_0, $U_0 = F(X_0, Y_0)$ and X_0, Y_0, $V_0 = G(X_0, Y_0)$.

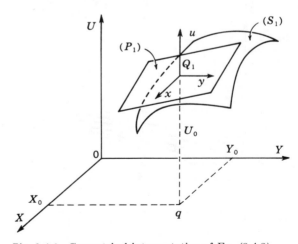

Fig. 3.4.1 Geometrical interpretation of Eq. (3.4.3).

Example 3.4.1:   The transistor whose terminal characteristics are shown in Fig. 3.4.2 is to be used as a component in a system wherein it is desired that the time-varying input and output signals are related by linear equations.   The operating point is given by

$$E_c = 4 \text{ volts}$$
$$I_b = 0.2 \text{ ma}$$

Show the regions, in terms of the magnitudes of the time-varying components of the terminal variables, in which linear approximations are valid, and establish the corresponding small-signal terminal equations.

Solution: The operating points Q_1 and Q_2, corresponding to the given bias variables $E_c = 4$ volts and $I_b = 0.2$ ma, are indicated on the given families of characteristics.   For the regions indicated by the shaded areas, $v_c(t)$ is less than 1 volt,

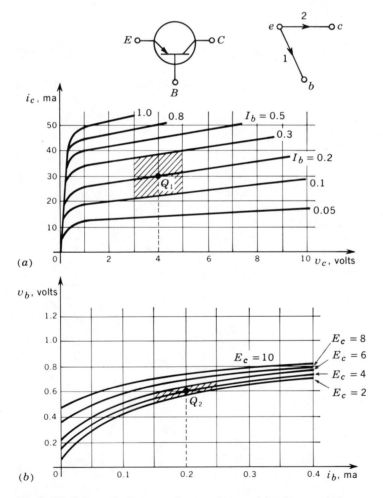

Fig. 3.4.2   Schematic diagram of a transistor and its characteristics.

and $i_b(t)$ is less than 0.1 ma. The small-signal terminal equations interrelating the terminal variables in these regions are

$$\begin{bmatrix} v_b(t) \\ i_c(t) \end{bmatrix} = \begin{bmatrix} h_{11}(I_b, E_c) & h_{12}(I_b, E_c) \\ h_{21}(I_b, E_c) & h_{22}(I_b, E_c) \end{bmatrix} \begin{bmatrix} i_b(t) \\ v_c(t) \end{bmatrix} \tag{3.4.8}$$

The coefficients h_{11} and h_{22} as determined from the slopes of the tangent to the curves in the shaded area indicated in Fig. 3.4.2b and a, respectively, are

$$h_{11} \cong \frac{\Delta v_b(t)}{\Delta i_b(t)} = \frac{0.4}{0.4 \times 10^{-3}} = 1{,}000 \text{ ohms} \qquad \text{for } E_c = 4$$

$$h_{22} \cong \frac{\Delta i_c(t)}{\Delta v_c(t)} = \frac{15}{11} = 1.36 \text{ ma/volt} \qquad \text{for } I_b = 0.2$$

The coefficients h_{12} and h_{21} as determined from incremental changes in Fig. 3.4.2b and a, respectively, are

$$h_{12} \cong \frac{\Delta v_b}{\Delta E_c} = \frac{0.1}{4} = 0.025 \qquad \text{for } I_b = 0.2$$

$$h_{21} \cong \frac{\Delta i_c}{\Delta I_b} = \frac{-5 \times 10^{-3}}{0.2 \times 10^{-3}} = 75 \qquad \text{for } E_c = 4$$

Therefore, the hybrid-parameter coefficient matrix at the specified operating point is

$$\begin{bmatrix} h_{11} & h_{12} \\ h_{21} & h_{22} \end{bmatrix} = \begin{bmatrix} 1{,}000 & 0.025 \\ 75 & 1.36 \end{bmatrix} \tag{3.4.9}$$

Example 3.4.2: An electrically operated servo valve is used to control a hydraulic motor as shown schematically in Fig. 3.4.3. In the design of many speed-control servomechanisms, such as the one under discussion, the objective is to vary the speed of the hydraulic motor over a relatively small range in the vicinity of the normal operating speed, say 1,000 rpm, for instance. In such a system the "normal," or bias, speed can be established by inserting a constant-voltage driver V_1 in series with the time-varying signal $v_1(t)$ as shown.

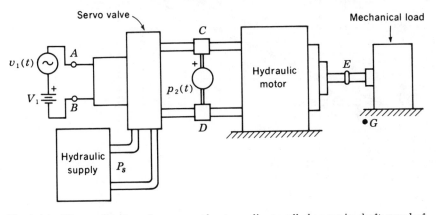

Fig. 3.4.3 The application of a servo valve to realize small changes in shaft speed of a hydraulic motor.

Consider that the terminal characteristics of the servo valve are as given in Fig. 3.3.5. Let the value of bias voltage corresponding to the constant shaft speed be $V_1 = 0.2$ volt, and let the pressure between the terminals C and D be $P_2 = -60$ psi. Under these conditions, obtain a small-signal linear model of the servo valve.

Solution: For convenience, the characteristics of the servo valve are redrawn in Fig. 3.4.4 with the operating point Q identified. For the shaded region, the small-signal equation is of the form

$$\dot{g}_2(t) = W_{21}v_1(t) + W_{22}p_2(t) \tag{3.4.10}$$

From the slope of the straight line, tangent to the $v_1 = 0.2$ curve at the point Q, the numerical value of W_{22} in mks units is

$$W_{22} = \frac{\Delta \dot{g}_2}{\Delta p_2} = \frac{26.5 \times 10^{-6}}{60 \times 6.895 \times 10^3} = 0.64 \times 10^{-10} \text{ m}^3/\text{newton-sec}$$

From the same characteristics, the numerical value of the coefficient W_{21} is

$$W_{21} = \frac{\Delta \dot{g}_2}{\Delta v_1} = \frac{18 \times 10^{-6}}{0.1} = 18 \times 10^{-5} \text{ m}^3/\text{volt-sec}$$

From Fig. 3.3.5a, the equation relating the terminal voltage and current is

$$i_1(t) = 0.01v_1(t)$$

Therefore the desired terminal equations of the component for the selected operating point are

$$\begin{bmatrix} i_1(t) \\ \dot{g}_2(t) \end{bmatrix} = \begin{bmatrix} 0.01 & 0 \\ 18 \times 10^{-5} & 0.64 \times 10^{-10} \end{bmatrix} \begin{bmatrix} v_1(t) \\ p_2(t) \end{bmatrix} \tag{3.4.11}$$

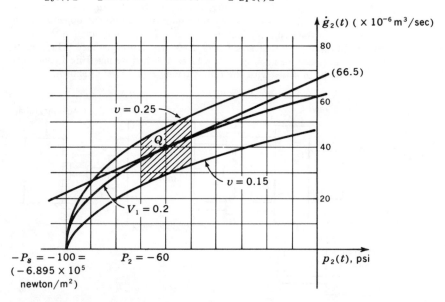

Fig. 3.4.4 Determination of the coefficients W_{21} and W_{22} in the small-signal terminal equation of a hydraulic valve.

Equation (3.4.11) can also be obtained analytically from the expression for the flow-pressure characteristics as given in Eq. (3.3.5). In the vicinity of the given operating point, $v_1(t)$ and $p_2(t)$ do not change signs, that is, $v_1(t)$ is always positive, and $p_2(t)$ is always negative; and since, in addition, $|p_2(t)| < P_s$, Eq. (3.3.5) can be written as

$$\dot{g}_2(t) = K v_1(t) \sqrt{p_2(t) + P_s} \qquad (3.4.12)$$

At the operating point Q in Fig. 3.4.4 we have $v_1(t) = 0.2$ volt, $p_2(t) = -60$ psi, $P_s = 100$ psi, and $\dot{g}_2(t) = 40 \times 10^{-6}$ m^3/sec. Substituting these values in Eq. (3.4.12) establishes the value of the parameter K as

$$K = 3.81 \times 10^{-7}$$

The numerical form of Eq. (3.4.12) is therefore

$$\dot{g}_2(t) = 3.81 \times 10^{-7} v_1(t) \sqrt{p_2(t) + 6.895 \times 10^5} \qquad (3.4.13)$$

The partial derivatives of $\dot{g}_2(t)$ with respect to $v_1(t)$ and $p_2(t)$, evaluated at the operating point, establish the coefficients in Eq. (3.4.10) as

$$W_{21} = 3.81 \times 10^{-7} \sqrt{p_2(t) + 6.895 \times 10^5} \Big|_Q = 20 \times 10^{-5}$$

and

$$W_{22} = \frac{3.81 \times 10^{-7} v_1(t)}{2 \sqrt{p_2(t) + 6.895 \times 10^5}} \Big|_Q = 0.725 \times 10^{-10}$$

3.5 TWO-PORT ACTIVE COMPONENTS

Referring to the examples in the previous section, we see that the hybrid-parameter coefficient matrix for the transistor and the conductance-parameter matrix for the servo valve are nonsymmetric. The power input to such components, as a function of arbitrary values of the terminal variables, can be investigated by expressing the nonsymmetric matrix as the sum of a skew-symmetric matrix and a symmetric matrix. Thus, if $\mathbf{K}$ is an arbitrary square matrix, then

$$\mathbf{K} = \mathbf{K}_1 + \mathbf{K}_2 \qquad (3.5.1)$$

where $\mathbf{K}_1 = \frac{1}{2}(\mathbf{K} + \mathbf{K}^T)$ is symmetric and $\mathbf{K} = \frac{1}{2}(\mathbf{K} - \mathbf{K}^T)$ is skew-symmetric. If $\mathbf{Z}_1$ and $\mathbf{Z}_2$ represent vectors of complementary terminal variables on the component with

$$\mathbf{Z}_1 = \mathbf{K}\mathbf{Z}_2$$

then it follows that the input power for arbitrary terminal conditions is

$$P(t) = \mathbf{Z}_2^T \mathbf{K}_1 \mathbf{Z}_2 + \mathbf{Z}_2^T \mathbf{K}_2 \mathbf{Z}_2$$

Since $\mathbf{K}_2$ is skew-symmetric, the last term in this expression is identically zero and the power input is determined entirely by the first term, i.e., by the symmetric part of the given matrix. If, for example, the coefficient matrix in Eq. (3.5.1) is of the special form

$$\mathbf{K} = \begin{bmatrix} 0 & k_{12} \\ k_{21} & 0 \end{bmatrix}$$

then the symmetric part of $\mathbf{K}$ is

$$\mathbf{K}_1 = \begin{bmatrix} 0 & (k_{12} + k_{21})/2 \\ (k_{12} + k_{21})/2 & 0 \end{bmatrix}$$

Since the coefficient matrix is neither a positive nor a negative definite matrix, it follows that the power input to the component may become *negative* for some nontrivial terminal conditions; i.e., the component sometimes acts as an energy source. Such components are called *active components.* Four possible elementary forms of active-component models are shown in Fig. 3.5.1, along with schematic diagrams frequently used to represent them in electrical-network diagrams. The same schematics can, of course, be used in schematic representations of mechanical and other systems if one so chooses. These components are gross

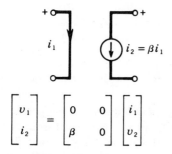

Current-dependent current source

Voltage-dependent voltage source

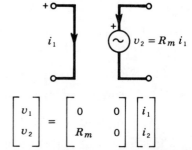

Voltage-dependent current source

Current-dependent voltage source

Fig. 3.5.1 Four possible elementary forms of two-port active components and their electrical schematic diagrams.

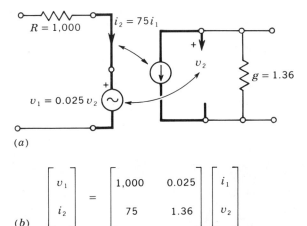

(a)

$$\begin{bmatrix} v_1 \\ \\ i_2 \end{bmatrix} = \begin{bmatrix} 1{,}000 & 0.025 \\ \\ 75 & 1.36 \end{bmatrix} \begin{bmatrix} i_1 \\ \\ v_2 \end{bmatrix}$$

(b)

Fig. 3.5.2 Combination of elementary forms representing the low-frequency small-signal model of the transistor given in Eq. (3.4.9).

idealizations of models encountered in practical application, but some investigators find it convenient to regard the more realistic forms as combinations of these elementary forms. For example, the low-frequency model of the transistor given in Eq. (3.4.9) can be regarded as a combination of a dependent current source, a dependent voltage source, and two resistors as shown in Fig. 3.5.2a. If the coefficient 0.025 is neglected, then the schematic diagram reduces to a combination of one dependent current source and two resistors.

It should be noted that the coefficient matrices in the models of the transistor and servo valve in Eqs. (3.4.9) and (3.4.11) are neither positive nor negative semidefinite. Indeed, the symmetric part of the servo-valve terminal matrix is

$$\begin{bmatrix} 0.01 & 9 \times 10^{-5} \\ 9 \times 10^{-5} & 0.64 \times 10^{-10} \end{bmatrix}$$

and we see that two of the principal minors are positive and the determinant is negative. This implies that the power input may be positive or negative, depending upon the magnitudes of the terminal variables; i.e., the power dissipation caused by the main diagonal coefficients can, under certain terminal conditions, exceed the power generated within the component.

PROBLEMS

3.1 In some of the early analyses of multiterminal electrical networks given in the literature, a fictitious reference point (see Fig. P3.1) is introduced, and the voltage and current measurements considered are those between the terminals of the network and the reference point.

For a general n-terminal component let the terminal variables indicated in Fig. P3.1b be related by a set of algebraic equations of the form

$$\begin{bmatrix} y_1(t) \\ y_2(t) \\ \cdots \\ y_n(t) \end{bmatrix} = \begin{bmatrix} b_{11} & b_{12} & \cdots & b_{1n} \\ b_{21} & b_{22} & \cdots & b_{2n} \\ \cdots\cdots\cdots\cdots\cdots \\ b_{n1} & b_{n2} & \cdots & b_{nn} \end{bmatrix} \begin{bmatrix} x_1(t) \\ x_2(t) \\ \cdots \\ x_n(t) \end{bmatrix} \tag{P3.1}$$

Show that the rank of the coefficient matrix cannot exceed $n - 1$.

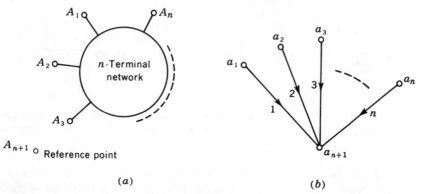

Fig. P3.1   (a) n-terminal network with a reference point A_{n+1}; (b) terminal graph.

3.2   In Prob. 3.1, if the reference point is chosen as one of the terminals of the n-terminal component, derive the form of the new terminal equations, and establish a relationship between these equations and those in Eq. (P3.1).

3.3   Two rigid bodies, (A) and (B) in Fig. P3.3, are free to rotate about an axis (D) which is fixed with respect to another body represented by a plane (P).   The

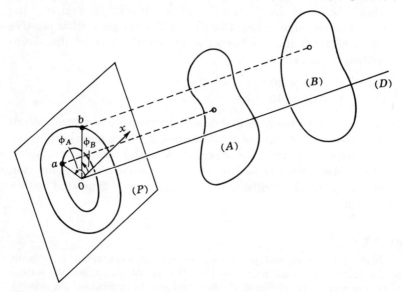

Fig. P3.3   Two rotating rigid bodies.

positions of these bodies can be described by the angles Φ_A and Φ_B shown in Fig. P3.3, where $0x$ is a fixed reference axis in (P).

Show that the position of the rigid body (B) with respect to the rigid body (A) can be expressed in terms of the angles Φ_A and Φ_B. (Draw the oriented line segments corresponding to the measurements Φ_A and Φ_B and give your answer on the basis of the resulting tree graph.)

3.4 For a three-terminal component the most general form of a linear algebraic model is

$$\begin{bmatrix} \alpha_{11} & \alpha_{12} & \vdots & -\beta_{11} & -\beta_{12} \\ \alpha_{21} & \alpha_{22} & \vdots & -\beta_{21} & -\beta_{22} \end{bmatrix} \begin{bmatrix} x_1(t) \\ x_2(t) \\ ----- \\ y_1(t) \\ y_2(t) \end{bmatrix} = 0 \qquad (P3.4a)$$

Apply the appropriate matrix operations on the coefficient matrix of Eq. (P3.4a) to obtain short-circuit, open-circuit, hybrid, another form of hybrid, and cascade parameter forms.

Hint: As an example, the hybrid parameters are obtained from Eq. (P3.4a) by first rearranging columns of the coefficient matrix of Eq. (P3.4a) to give

$$\begin{bmatrix} -\beta_{11} & \alpha_{12} & \vdots & \alpha_{11} & -\beta_{12} \\ -\beta_{21} & \alpha_{22} & \vdots & \alpha_{21} & -\beta_{22} \end{bmatrix} \begin{bmatrix} y_1(t) \\ x_2(t) \\ ------ \\ x_1(t) \\ y_2(t) \end{bmatrix} = 0 \qquad (P3.4b)$$

The required result is obtained by premultiplying Eq. (3.4b) by the matrix

$$\begin{bmatrix} -\beta_{11} & \alpha_{12} \\ -\beta_{21} & \alpha_{22} \end{bmatrix}^{-1}$$

3.5 Using a similar procedure to that described in Prob. 3.4, express the open-circuit, hybrid, and cascade parameters for a three-terminal component in terms of the short-circuit parameters.

Hint: As an example, the cascade parameters are obtained by first writing Eq. (3.3.2) in the form

$$\begin{bmatrix} -W_{11} & 1 & -W_{12} & 0 \\ -W_{21} & 0 & -W_{22} & -1 \end{bmatrix} \begin{bmatrix} x_1(t) \\ y_1(t) \\ x_2(t) \\ -y_2(t) \end{bmatrix} = 0 \qquad (P3.5)$$

The required result is realized by premultiplying Eq. (P3.5) by

$$\begin{bmatrix} -W_{11} & 1 \\ -W_{21} & 0 \end{bmatrix}^{-1}$$

Derive all other parameters from:
(a) The open-circuit parameters
(b) The h parameters
(c) The G parameters (the other form of h parameters)
(d) The cascade parameters

3.6 The terminal graph of a six-terminal component is given in Fig. P3.6. The terminal equations are algebraic and of the form

$$\mathbf{X}(t) = \mathbf{Z}\mathbf{Y}(t)$$

The component is to be used as a three-terminal component having the terminals A_1, A_2, and A_3. Terminals A_4, A_5, and A_6 are to be left free. Derive the terminal representation for this three-terminal component from the information given.

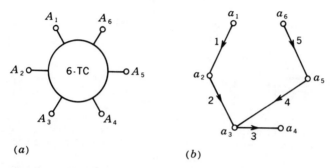

(a)   (b)

Fig. P3.6 (a) A six-terminal component; (b) terminal graph.

3.7   Repeat Prob. 3.6 when the terminal equations are given as

$$\mathbf{Y}(t) = \mathbf{W}\mathbf{X}(t)$$

where the entries in $\mathbf{W}$ are real numbers.

3.8   The terminal graph of a five-terminal component is given in Fig. P3.8. The terminal equations are algebraic and of the form

$$\mathbf{Y}(t) = \mathbf{W}\mathbf{X}(t)$$

This component is to be used as a three-terminal component having the terminals A_1, A_2, and A_3. Terminals A_4 and A_5 are connected to the terminals A_3 and A_1, respectively. Derive the terminal representation for this three-terminal component from the information given. Compare the algebra involved in this derivation with that involved in deriving a similar terminal representation when A_4 and A_5 are connected to the terminals A_2 and A_3.

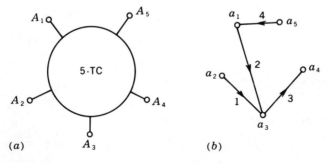

(a) A_3 (b)

Fig. P3.8 (a) A five-terminal component; (b) terminal graph.

3.9   Write the terminal equations for a three-terminal gearbox shown in Fig. P3.9a, using the variables indicated by the terminal graph in Fig. P3.9b.   The numbers of teeth of the gears are indicated as N_1 and N_2.   Include the inertia and damping characteristics, but neglect any spring action.

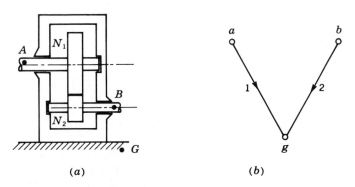

(a)   (b)

Fig. P3.9   (a) A simple gearbox; (b) a selected terminal graph.

3.10   The terminal equations of the four-terminal ideal gearbox shown in Fig. P3.10a, corresponding to the terminal graph in Fig. P3.10b, are given in the form

$$
\begin{bmatrix} \phi_1(t) \\ \phi_2(t) \\ \tau_3(t) \end{bmatrix} = \begin{bmatrix} 0 & 0 & \alpha \\ 0 & 0 & \beta \\ -\alpha & -\beta & 0 \end{bmatrix} \begin{bmatrix} \tau_1(t) \\ \tau_2(t) \\ \phi_3(t) \end{bmatrix}
$$

Determine the values of the constant α and β from the construction detail and the number of teeth N_1, N_2, N_3, and N_4.

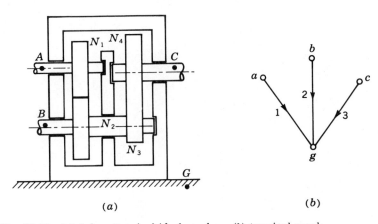

(a)   (b)

Fig. P3.10   (a) A four-terminal ideal gearbox; (b) terminal graph.

3.11   The terminal equations of a four-terminal nonlinear hydraulic component
are given as

$$\dot{g}_1(t) = F_1[p_1(t),p_2(t),p_3(t)]$$
$$\dot{g}_2(t) = F_2[p_1(t),p_2(t),p_3(t)]$$
$$\dot{g}_3(t) = F_3[p_1(t),p_2(t),p_3(t)]$$

Show the general form of the small-signal terminal equations for this component at an
operating point described by the pressures P_1, P_2, and P_3.

3.12   By use of the characteristics given in Fig. 3.3.3, calculate the small-signal
terminal equations of the triode for the operating point given by $v_g = -8$ volts and
$i_p = 6$ ma.

FURTHER READING

1.   Koenig, H. E., and W. A. Blackwell: "Electromechanical System Theory,"
         McGraw-Hill Book Company, New York, 1961.
2.   Shekel, J.: Two Theorems Concerning the Change of Reference Voltage
         Terminal, *Proc. IRE*, vol. 42, p. 1125, 1954.
3.   Shekel, J.: Voltage Reference Node, *Wireless Engr.*, vol. 31, pp. 6–10, 1954.
4.   Belevitch, V.: Four Dimensional Transformations of 4-pole Matrices with
         Applications to the Synthesis of Reactance 4-poles, *Trans. IRE Circuit Theory*,
         vol. 3, pp. 105–111, 1956.

4

The System Graph and
Associated Constraint Equations

We return now to the problem of developing mathematical models of systems of interconnected components, given a mathematical model of each component in the system and the pattern of interconnection by which the components are united. Recall that, in the model of each n-terminal component discussed in the previous chapters, exactly half the $2(n-1)$ complementary terminal variables are taken as independent variables. When components of a set are interconnected to form a system, these variables are no longer independent—they are constrained by the interconnections. The equations characterizing these constraints are derived from what is called the *system graph*. This chapter presents a simple operational procedure for generating the system graph, followed by a study of the properties of these graphs and the associated constraint equations.

4.1 THE SYSTEM GRAPH

Consider an arbitrary system of interconnected components represented schematically in Fig. 4.1.1a. Let the terminal variables in each compo-

nent model be identified by a tree of edges on the vertices corresponding
to the terminals of each component as indicated in Fig. 4.1.1b.   These
models, of course, are developed from controlled tests on the components
in isolation, as discussed in the previous chapters.

The system graph is defined operationally as the collection of edges
and vertices obtained by coalescing the vertices of the component terminal graphs in a one-to-one correspondence with the way in which the
terminals of the corresponding components are united to form the system.
The resulting graph appears as shown in Fig. 4.1.1c.   The graph can be
characterized as having one vertex for each interface and an edge corresponding to each edge in the terminal graphs of the components.   Unlike

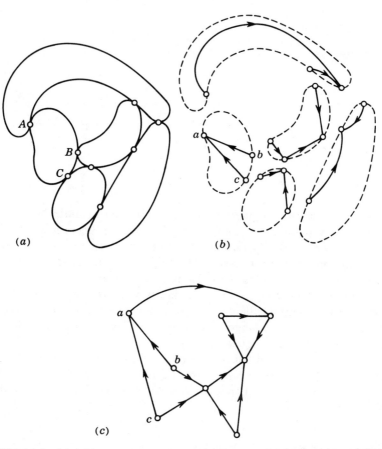

Fig. 4.1.1   (a) Arbitrary system of components; (b) selected terminal graphs
used in modeling the characteristics of each component as an isolated entity;
(c) the system graph obtained by coalescing the vertices of the component
terminal graphs according to the interconnection of their corresponding
components.

the component terminal graphs, the edges in the system graph may form closed paths, called *circuits*. These circuits, as we shall see, form the basis of one set of constraint equations which "bind" the component models together to form a model of the system.

It should be clear that the system graph is unique for any given set of component models and any given interconnection pattern. However, since any one of several terminal graphs can be used as a basis for modeling the characteristics of multiterminal components, the system graph is not unique until at least the terminal graph in each component model has been specified, i.e., the system graph depends upon the terminal graphs used in the component models.

Example 4.1.1: The system shown schematically in Fig. 4.1.2a contains three two-terminal components (the spring, mass, and dashpot), a three-terminal component (the lever), and a four-terminal component (the hydraulic piston, a transducer). The terminal graphs used in modeling the characteristics of each of these components are shown assembled in the form of a system graph in Fig. 4.1.2b.

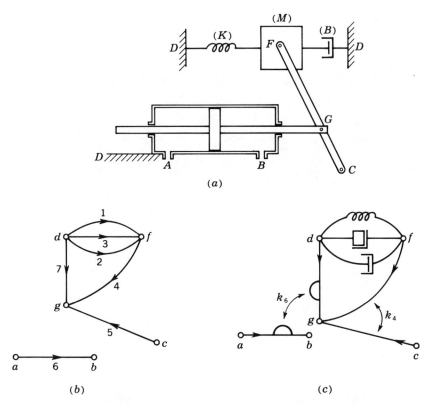

Fig. 4.1.2 (a) A hydromechanical system; (b) its system graph; (c) a coded system graph to indicate the form of the component models.

The models of the components might typically be taken as follows:

Spring: Edge 1 with

$$\frac{d}{dt} f_1(t) = K_1 \dot{\delta}_1(t)$$

Damper: Edge 2 with

$$f_2(t) = B_2 \dot{\delta}(t)$$

Mass: Edge 3 with

$$\frac{d}{dt} \dot{\delta}_3(t) = \frac{1}{M_3} f_3(t)$$

Lever: Edges 4 and 5 with

$$\begin{bmatrix} f_4(t) \\ \dot{\delta}_5(t) \end{bmatrix} = \begin{bmatrix} 0 & k_4 \\ -k_4 & 0 \end{bmatrix} \begin{bmatrix} \dot{\delta}_4(t) \\ f_5(t) \end{bmatrix}$$

Hydraulic ram (gyrator): Edges 6 and 7 with

$$\begin{bmatrix} \dot{g}_6(t) \\ f_7(t) \end{bmatrix} = \begin{bmatrix} 0 & k_6 \\ -k_6 & 0 \end{bmatrix} \begin{bmatrix} p_6(t) \\ \dot{\delta}_7(t) \end{bmatrix}$$

It is sometimes helpful conceptually to "code" the system graph as indicated in Fig. 4.1.2c to represent the forms of the component models.

In the special case in which the system contains only two-terminal electrical components as in Fig. 4.1.3, the system graph looks very much

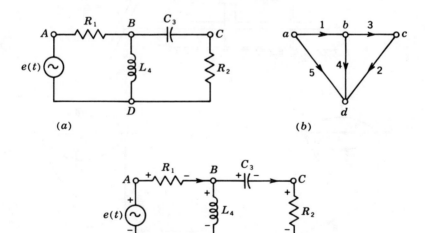

Fig. 4.1.3 Schematic diagrams and system graph of a network of two-terminal components.

like the network schematic diagram in that one line segment is included for each two-terminal component.

This obvious similarity is the primary reason why linear graphs found application first in the analysis of electrical systems. But even here, it has been only in recent years that the problem has been abstracted to the point of formally recognizing the graph as such. In earlier and less abstract developments of electrical-network theory, the information contained in the graph Fig. 4.1.3b is frequently included on the network schematic diagram as shown in Fig. 4.1.3c. The arrow is described as representing the "reference direction of electrical current" and the + and − marks are described as representing the "reference voltage polarity." The diagram in Fig. 4.1.3c, without the + and − marks, is a coded graph of the system as defined in this book.

4.2 BASIC DEFINITIONS AND ELEMENTARY PROPERTIES OF LINEAR GRAPHS

Linear graphs have many applications in engineering and science besides the applications to system modeling presented in this book, and there are many properties besides those presented in this chapter. In almost any problem wherein a collection of either oriented or nonoriented line segments is found to be a useful conceptual tool, some aspect of abstract linear-graph theory is useful.

Since the emphasis in this book is on applications of graph-theoretic concepts to the problem of system modeling rather than the development of an abstract theory, the basic definitions are stated in a semiformal manner. Most of the nontrivial properties of linear graphs important to the subject of system modeling are presented in the form of theorems with formal proofs. Some of the formal proofs are necessarily long and involved. For the uninitiated reader interested primarily in applications, it may be desirable to skip the proofs in the first reading. This is particularly true for those theorems which are intuitively obvious.

The following definitions are accompanied by examples from the graph in Fig. 4.2.1.

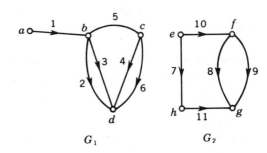

Fig. 4.2.1 A typical system graph.

G_1 G_2

Definition 4.2.1: Each of the oriented line segments 1 through 11 together with its two end points is called an *edge* (or element).

For instance, edge *ab* includes the line segment 1 together with its end points *a* and *b*.

Definition 4.2.2: The end point of an edge is called a *vertex*.

Vertices of the graph of Fig. 4.2.1 are *a*, *b*, . . . , *h*. Lowercase letters are used to indicate vertices of the graph so as to distinguish them from the terminals of the corresponding system components, the latter being identified by corresponding capital letters.

Definition 4.2.3: A graph containing a finite number of edges, and hence a finite number of vertices, is called a *finite graph*.

Only finite graphs are introduced in this text, since the systems considered are assumed to include a finite number of discrete components. The number of edges and vertices in a finite graph is denoted by e and v, respectively. In the graph of Fig. 4.2.1, $e = 11$, and $v = 8$.

Definition 4.2.4: In the study of linear graphs it is convenient to refer to a *subset* of the edges of the graph. Such a subset is called a *subgraph* of the graph.†

For instance, the subset containing edges 1, 5, 6, 7, and 9 is a subgraph of the given graph and is denoted by (1,5,6,7,9). It can be shown (see Prob. 4.15) that, for a graph having e edges, the number of subgraphs is equal to $2^e - 2$. Therefore, the number of subgraphs in the graph of Fig. 4.2.1 is equal to $2^{11} - 2 = 2,046$.

Definition 4.2.5: Edge k is said to be *incident* to vertex l if vertex l is an end point of edge k.

For instance, edge number 3 is incident to vertices *b* and *d* but is not incident to any other vertices.

Definition 4.2.6: Any vertex of the graph having only one edge incident to it is called an *end vertex*, and the edge incident to an end vertex is called an *end edge*.

---

† It is assumed that the given graph itself is not a subgraph. It is also assumed that a subgraph must contain at least one edge.

Vertex a in Fig. 4.2.1, for example, is an end vertex, and edge 1 is an end edge.

Definition 4.2.7: The particular subgraph (1,3,6) in Fig. 4.2.1 is called a *path*, since one can "proceed" from vertex a to vertex c, traversing the edges 1, 3, and 6 in a sequential manner.

In general a graph may contain many paths, each of which is identified by sequentially labeling the edges in the path. For example, in Fig. 4.2.1 the subgraphs (1,2,6), (1,3,6), (1,2,4), (1,3,4), and (1,5) constitute all the possible paths between the vertices a and c in the graph. Although subgraph (1,2,3,6) includes the two vertices a and c, it does not constitute a path, since the traverse from a to c could be either by 1, 2, and 6 or by 1, 3, and 6, neither of which includes all four edges in the subgraph. If two paths have no vertices in common that are not end vertices they are said to be *distinct paths*. Paths (5,6) and (2) in Fig. 4.2.2 are distinct paths.

Definition 4.2.8: If there exists a path between every pair of vertices of a graph, then the graph is said to be a *connected graph*.

The subgraph $G_1 = (1,2,3,4,5,6)$ in Fig. 4.2.1, for example, has at least one path between every pair of vertices a, b, c, and d. Therefore, this subgraph is connected. Similarly, the subgraph $G_2 = (7,8,9,10,11)$ is also connected. On the other hand, there is clearly no path between any of the vertices of subgraphs G_1 and G_2. Hence the complete graph is described as a *separated graph* consisting of two parts.

Definition 4.2.9: The notion of a circuit of a system graph has already been described intuitively as a closed path in the graph. More formally, a *circuit* is defined as a set of edges such that exactly two edges are incident to each of the vertices in the set.

The graph (2,4,5) in Fig. 4.2.1 is a circuit subgraph of the graph. A circuit is also characterized by the property that between any pair of its

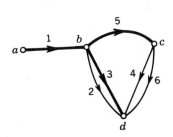

Fig. 4.2.2 A connected graph with a tree indicated by heavy lines.

vertices there are exactly two distinct paths. This immediately implies, of course, that a circuit is a connected graph.

Definition 4.2.10: A frequently used and simple concept of graph theory is that of a *tree*. A tree T of a connected graph G is defined as a set of edges which (1) is *connected*, (2) contains *all the vertices of G*, but (3) contains *no circuits*.

A tree T of the graph of Fig. 4.2.2 is identified by the heavy lines. Clearly, the subgraph $T = (1,3,5)$ (the heavy lines) contains all the vertices of the graph but no circuits; i.e., *there is one and only one path between any two vertices of T*. There are, of course, many other trees in the graph of Fig. 4.2.2 besides the one shown by the heavy lines. The remaining possible trees are $(1,3,4)$, $(1,3,6)$, $(1,5,2)$, $(1,5,4)$, $(1,5,6)$, $(1,2,4)$, and $(1,2,6)$, giving a total of eight. Although it is possible to develop a general expression for the total number of trees in a connected graph of v vertices and e edges, the expression is not particularly simple and is really of little interest here (see Prob. 4.14). It should be noted that the terminal graphs of all electrical, mechanical, and hydraulic components discussed in the preceding chapters have already been identified as tree graphs.

Another important property of a tree with v vertices is that it contains exactly v − 1 edges. This result can easily be verified for the trees enumerated for the connected graph in Fig. 4.2.2.

Definition 4.2.11: When a graph G contains more than one part, as in Fig. 4.2.1, a tree as defined above does not exist, since a tree by definition is connected. However, it is possible to select a tree in each connected part of G. The collection of such trees is called a *forest*.

Definition 4.2.12: The edges of a connected graph G that are included in a given tree T are referred to as *branches*. Those edges of G which are not in T constitute a subgraph T, called the *complement* of T, or the *cotree*. The edges of the cotree are called *chords* (or links). Further, when the graph contains p parts, a cotree is defined for each of the p parts. A set of p cotrees is called a *coforest*.

Thus, in Fig. 4.2.1, subgraph $(2,4,6)$ of graph $(1,2,3,4,5,6)$ is a cotree of tree $(1,3,5)$. Note that, unlike the tree, the cotree is not necessarily connected.

It has already been stated that the number of branches in a tree T of a connected graph G containing v vertices is $v - 1$. Consequently, if G contains a total of e edges, then the total number of chords in the cotree is $e - (v - 1) = e - v + 1$. If a graph G with v vertices and e

edges contains p connected parts, then the total number of branches in the p trees is $v - p$, leaving a total of $e - (v - p) = e - v + p$ chords.

One of the basic properties of a tree is that the addition of a chord between any two of its vertices establishes a circuit. For example, the tree (1,5,3) in Fig. 4.2.1 and the chord 4 form the circuit (4,5,3). Since, in a connected graph having v vertices and e edges, there are $e - v + 1$ chords for any given tree T, a set of $e - v + 1$ circuits is uniquely defined by the chords of T. In this set of $e - v + 1$ circuits no two circuits are identical, since each contains a chord not included in the other.

Definition 4.2.13: The set of $e - v + 1$ circuits formed by each of the defining chords of the given tree T is called a fundamental set of circuits or simply *fundamental circuits*.

Consider, for example, the connected graph G shown in Fig. 4.2.3. A tree T is indicated by the heavy lines. The number of edges and vertices in G are eight and five, respectively. Therefore the number of chords is $e - v + 1 = 4$. The four fundamental circuits defined by these chords and their tree paths are as given in the accompanying table.

Chord	Tree path	Fundamental circuit
(1)	(2,3,4,5)	(1,2,3,4,5)
(6)	(3,4,5)	(6,3,4,5)
(7)	(2,3)	(7,2,3)
(8)	(2,3,4)	(8,2,3,4)

This tabulation includes only the fundamental circuits for the tree $T_1 = (2,3,4,5)$. It can be established by the use of Theorem 4.2.1 that *any circuit in the graph can be made a fundamental circuit with respect to some tree.* For instance, circuit (1,6,3,7) in the graph of Fig. 4.2.4 is not a fundamental circuit for the tree $T_1 = (2,3,4,5)$. But this circuit is a fundamental circuit for trees $T_2 = (4,7,3,6)$, $T_3 = (1,8,7,3)$, and $T_4 = (1,6,3,8)$.

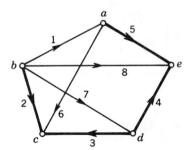

Fig. 4.2.3 A connected graph with a tree T indicated by the heavy lines.

One of the essential purposes of the system graph is that it serves to establish constraints on the across variables used in modeling the system components.   To establish these constraint equations, it is necessary to assign an *orientation* to each circuit.   This is defined as follows:

Definition 4.2.14:   *Circuit orientation* of a circuit is defined by an arrow r drawn parallel to the edges of the circuit.

In Fig. 4.2.4a, a circuit orientation is shown of circuit (4,8,7.) This arrow, of course, may be oriented in either direction around the circuit.   In the special case of the $e - v + 1$ fundamental circuits, the defining chord is used to establish the orientation of the circuit.   For instance, the orientation of circuit (6,3,4,5) in Fig. 4.2.4b is determined by the orientation of the defining edge 6.

Consider the connected graph as shown in Fig. 4.2.5a.   When the set of edges (4,6,7) is deleted from the graph, the resulting graph is in exactly two parts, i.e., part A and part B as indicated in the figure.   The set of edges (4,6,7) is called a *cut set*.   More formally, we have:

Definition 4.2.15:   A cut set of a connected graph G is defined as a set of edges C having such properties that (1) when set C is deleted the graph is in exactly two parts† and (2) no subset of C has the property 1.

The significance of the second part of the definition of a cut set is indicated by noting that, when the set of edges (4,6,7,8) in Fig. 4.2.5a is removed, the graph is in exactly two parts.   But the removal of a subset of these edges, namely, (4,6,7), also leaves the graph in two parts.   Consequently, the set (4,6,7,8) is not a cut set.

† An isolated vertex is also considered as a part.

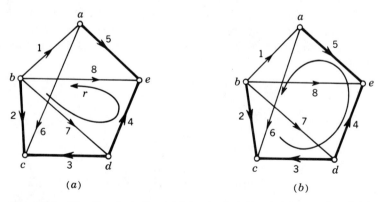

Fig. 4.2.4   Circuit orientation of (a) a typical circuit in general and (b) a typical fundamental circuit.

The implications of the first part of the cut-set definition are indicated by noting that, when the set of edges (3,4,5,6,7) is deleted, the graph of Fig. 4.2.5a is in three parts. Consequently, this set of edges is not a cut set. The second part of the definition is also not satisfied, since the subsets of edges (4,6,7), (3,5) are themselves cut sets. An operational procedure for selecting a cut set of edges as defined above is provided by the concept of a tree. Since there is one and only one path between any pair of vertices in a tree, it is intuitively obvious that removal of a branch from the tree leaves the tree subgraph disconnected and in exactly two parts. If the selected branch is an end edge of the tree, one of the parts contains an isolated vertex.

Consider now the graph G in Fig. 4.2.5b and the tree indicated by the set of heavy lines. Let C be any set of edges, such as (4,6,7), that divides the graph into exactly two parts and includes one and only one branch of the tree. Note that the one branch in C automatically divides the tree T of the graph into two parts T_1 and T_2. Consequently, a set of edges selected in this manner automatically satisfies the definition of a cut set; i.e., removal of C divides the graph into *exactly* two parts, and no proper subset of C so divides the graph.

The above procedure is implemented in practice by simply drawing a closed line, as shown dashed in Fig. 4.2.5b, which "cuts" exactly one branch of the tree. The set of edges cut by such a closed line then constitutes a cut set.†

† In order to obtain such a closed line, it may be necessary to redraw part of the graph in a different form. The modified graph is "isomorphic" topologically to the original. For example, for the cut set defined by branch 11 of the tree (2,5,11,7,9,10) in Fig. 4.2.5a, a closed line cannot be drawn unless the graph is isomorphically modified.

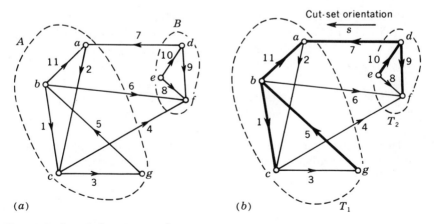

(a)   (b)

Fig. 4.2.5 A typical system graph.

Note that such a procedure does not present edges (3,5,4,6,7) in Fig. 4.2.5b as a cut set, since any tree must include at least one edge from the set (4,6,7) and at least one edge from the set (3,5) as branches. The subgraph (3,5,4,6,7) therefore contains at least two branches of any tree that can be selected.

Definition 4.2.16:   The set of $v - 1$ cut sets corresponding to any *one* tree T in G is defined as a *fundamental set of cut sets.*

Consider, for example, the connected graph G, as shown in Fig. 4.2.3. The tree indicated by the heavy lines has four edges.   Therefore, there are four fundamental cut sets defined by the four branches as in the accompanying tabulation.

Branch	Cut set
(2)	(2,7,8,1)
(3)	(3,1,8,6,7)
(4)	(4,1,8,6)
(5)	(5,6,1)

Definition 4.2.17:   *Cut-set orientation* of a cut set is defined by an arrow s drawn from one part of the graph to the other.

For example, a cut-set orientation s is indicated in Fig. 4.2.5b. Note that since every cut set C contains one and only one branch of some tree, the orientation of the cut set is uniquely defined by taking it coincident with the branch defining it.

Definition 4.2.18:   An *incidence* set is defined simply as the set of all edges incident to any given vertex of the graph.   The orientations of the edges of the incidence set are formally defined as positive when they are directed away from the vertex.

The following theorems pertaining to the properties of graphs are important and will be used extensively in later chapters.

Theorem 4.2.1:   If, in a connected graph G, G_s is a subgraph which contains no circuits, then G_s is a subgraph of a tree T in G.

Proof: Consider the union† of G_s and an arbitrary tree T in G. This union is indicated symbolically as $G_s \cup T$.   Of course, T may con-

† The union of subgraphs G_s and T is the set of edges in either G_s or T, or both.

tain some of the edges in G_s. The subgraph of $G_s \cup T$ is connected and contains all the vertices of G, since it includes T. If $G_s \cup T$ has a circuit, removal of one edge of T, which is in this circuit, leaves the remaining subgraph connected. If this process is continued until $G_s \cup T$ contains no circuits, the remaining subgraph, called $(G_s \cup T)'$, is connected and contains all the vertices of G. Further it contains no circuits, that is, $(G_s \cup T)'$ is a tree in G which contains G_s; hence the proof.

The above theorem applies to a separated graph with the word "tree" replaced by the word "forest."

An alternative statement of Theorem 4.2.1 is as follows.

Theorem 4.2.2: If a subgraph G_s of a connected (separated) graph G cannot be made a part of a tree (forest) in G, then G_s contains at least one circuit.

A corresponding theorem (Theorem 4.2.3) relating to cut sets and cotrees follows. However, it is first necessary to establish the following lemma.

Lemma 4.2.1: Let e_1 represent a branch of a tree T in a connected graph G, and let $(e_2, e_3, \ldots, e_n)$ represent the cut set defined by e_1. Then each of the fundamental circuits defined by the chords $e_2, e_3, \ldots, e_n$ includes e_1.

Proof of lemma: As shown in Fig. 4.2.6, let a and b be the vertices of e_1. First, it is clear that when e_1 is deleted from G there is no path in

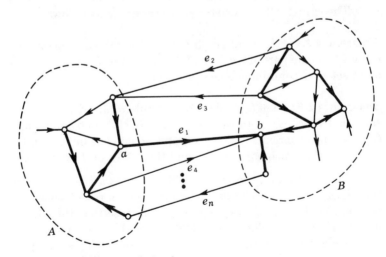

Fig. 4.2.6 Branch e_1 and chords $e_2, e_3, \ldots, e_n$ of a fundamental cut set.

T between a and b. Thus, we may construct two sets of vertices A and B, A containing vertex a and all vertices with a path in the tree to a and B containing vertex b and all vertices with a path in the tree to b. Since there is no branch of T other than e_1 with one vertex in A and the other in B, the fundamental circuits defined by e_2, e_3, . . . , e_n must contain e_1 as an edge.

Theorem 4.2.3: If, in a connected graph G, G_s is a subgraph containing no cut sets in G, then G_s is a subgraph of a cotree in G.

Proof: Consider the union of G_s and an arbitrary tree T in G. In general, T contains some of the edges of G_2. In the special case where it does not, the theorem is trivial. Consider the branches b_i of T which are also edges of G_s. The cut sets defined by each b_i must contain at least one edge e_j of G which is not contained in G_s. If this were not true, such a cut set would contain only edges in G_s—a contradiction to the hypothesis of the theorem.

Consider now the subgraph $T \cup e_j$. Since e_j is a chord in G, from Lemma 4.2.1 subgraph $T \cup e_j$ contains a circuit which includes b_i as an element. Therefore, deleting b_i from $T \cup e_j$ leaves a new tree in G. By this process all elements common to G_s and T can be removed to generate a tree T' having no elements in common with G_s, that is, the intersection† of T' and G_s is empty; symbolically we can write, $T' \cap G_s = 0$. This implies that G_s is in the cotree of T'.

The applicability of the above theorem to a separated graph is evident, since it is true for each "part" of the separated graph.

Theorem 4.2.3 can be stated alternatively as follows.

Theorem 4.2.4: If a subgraph G_s of a connected (separated) graph G cannot be made part of a cotree of T (coforest of F) in G, then there exists a cut set in G containing edges of G_s only.

Theorem 4.2.5: Let G_{s_1} and G_{s_2} be two subgraphs of a connected graph G such that $G_{s_1} \cap G_{s_2} = 0$; that is, G_{s_1} and G_{s_2} have no common edges. If G_{s_1} contains no circuits and G_{s_2} contains no cut sets in G, then there exists a tree T in G which contains G_{s_1} and the cotree of T contains G_{s_2}.

Proof: From Theorem 4.2.3 there exists a tree which includes all the edges of G_{s_2} as its chords. Consider such a tree T which, in general, may not contain all the edges of G_{s_1}. Suppose that the edge e_i in G_{s_1} is not included in T. The subgraph $T \cup e_i$ contains a circuit. Remove one of the edges b_j of T in this circuit. The remaining subgraph of $T \cup e_i$ is a tree in G. This new tree contains e_i and still includes the edges of

† The intersection of two subgraphs G_{s_1} and G_{s_2} is the set of edges in *both* G_{s_1} and G_{s_2}. Symbolically, the intersection is denoted by the symbol $\cap$.

G_{s_2} as its chords.   By repeating this process, if necessary, a tree which satisfies the requirement of the theorem is established.

4.3 CIRCUIT VECTORS AND MATRICES

If we let r_i and r_i' represent, respectively, the two possible orientations for any given circuit C_i in a system graph G, then each C_i is said to define two oppositely directed *circuit vectors* $\beta_i(r_i)$ and $\beta_i(r_i')$ each of order $1 \times e$ whose jth entries β_{ij} are

$$\beta_{ij}(r_i) = -\beta_{ij}(r_i') = \begin{cases} 1 & \text{if edge } j \text{ is in circuit } i, \text{ with orientation } r_i \\ -1 & \text{if edge } j \text{ is in circuit } i, \text{ with orientation } r_i' \\ 0 & \text{if edge } j \text{ is not in circuit } i \end{cases}$$

Example 4.3.1:   Circuits $\{1,2,3,4,5\}$ and $\{2,3,7\}$ in Fig. 4.2.3 define the respective circuit row vectors.

$$\begin{array}{ccccccccc} & 1 & 2 & 3 & 4 & 5 & 6 & 7 & 8 \\ \beta_1(r_1) = -\beta_1(r_1') = [1 & -1 & 1 & -1 & 1 & 0 & 0 & 0] \\ & 1 & 2 & 3 & 4 & 5 & 6 & 7 & 8 \\ \beta_2(r_2) = -\beta_2(r_2') = [0 & -1 & 1 & 0 & 0 & 0 & 1 & 0] \end{array}$$

The second basic postulate of system theory can now be stated as follows.

Postulate 2:   For any circuit row vector β and any arbitrary vector $\mathbf{X}$ of across variables identified by the e edges of a system graph G

$$\beta\mathbf{X} = 0 \tag{4.3.1}$$

Equation (4.3.1) is called a *circuit equation* of the system graph.

The set of $e - v + 1$ circuits, *each containing exactly one chord* of some cotree T' in a connected graph G, has already been defined as a fundamental set of circuits.   The orientation for the circuit is taken so that the component of the circuit vector corresponding to the defining chord is $+1$.

Example 4.3.2:   The cotree T' indicated by the light lines in Fig. 4.2.3 defines four fundamental circuits $\{1,2,3,4,5\}$, $\{6,3,4,5\}$, $\{7,2,3\}$, $\{8,4,3,2\}$.   These four fundamental circuits define four corresponding circuit equations that can be written in the following form:

$$\begin{array}{c} \text{Circuit} \\ (1,2,3,4,5) \\ (6,3,4,5) \\ (7,2,3) \\ (8,4,3,2) \end{array} \left[\begin{array}{cccc:cccc} -1 & 1 & -1 & 1 & 1 & 0 & 0 & 0 \\ 0 & -1 & 1 & -1 & 0 & 1 & 0 & 0 \\ -1 & 1 & 0 & 0 & 0 & 0 & 1 & 0 \\ -1 & 1 & -1 & 0 & 0 & 0 & 0 & 1 \end{array}\right] \begin{array}{l} \begin{bmatrix} x_2(t) \\ x_3(t) \\ x_4(t) \\ x_5(t) \\ \hdashline x_1(t) \\ x_6(t) \\ x_7(t) \\ x_8(t) \end{bmatrix} \begin{array}{l} \\ \\ \text{branches} \\ = 0 \\ \\ \text{chords} \\ \\ \end{array} \end{array}$$

$$\tag{4.3.2}$$

These equations are referred to as the *fundamental circuit equations*. They are obtained by summing the across variables around the fundamental circuits by considering the relative orientation of the edges in the circuits as follows: If the edge orientation is coincident with the circuit orientation (the orientation of the defining chord), then the across variable for that edge is entered with a positive sign, otherwise a negative sign.

For convenience, the variables in the column matrix have been arranged so that all branches appear first and then the chords.

In general, when the columns of the fundamental circuit vectors are arranged so as to include the chords of the defining cotree as the *last* $e - v + 1$ columns, the fundamental circuit vectors form a matrix of the form

$$
\begin{array}{cc}
\text{branches} & \text{chords} \\
(e - v + 1)\ [\quad \mathbf{B} & \mathbf{U} \quad] \\
(v - 1) & (e - v + 1)
\end{array}
$$

and the corresponding circuit equations, called fundamental circuit equations, are

$$
[\mathbf{B} \quad \mathbf{U}] \begin{bmatrix} \mathbf{X}_b \\ \mathbf{X}_c \end{bmatrix} = 0 \tag{4.3.3}
$$

where $\mathbf{X}_b$ and $\mathbf{X}_c$ represent, respectively, the $v - 1$ and $e - v + 1$ across variables identified by the branches and chords.

4.4   CUT-SET VECTORS AND MATRICES

If we let s_i and s_i' represent, respectively, the two possible orientations for any given cut set α_i in a system graph G, than α_i is said to define two oppositely directed cut-set vectors $\alpha_i(s_i)$ and $\alpha_i(s_i')$ each of order $1 \times e$ whose jth entries α_{ij} are

$$
\alpha_{ij}(s_i) = -\alpha_{ij}(s_i') = \begin{cases} 1 & \text{if edge } j \text{ is in cut set } i, \text{ with orientation } s_i \\ -1 & \text{if edge } j \text{ is in cut set } i, \text{ with orientation } s_i' \\ 0 & \text{if edge } j \text{ is not in cut set } i \end{cases}
$$

Example 4.4.1:   Cut sets $\{2,1,7,8\}$ and $\{3,6,7,8,1\}$ in Fig. 4.2.3 define the respective cut-set row vectors

$$
\begin{array}{ccccccccc}
& 1 & 2 & 3 & 4 & 5 & 6 & 7 & 8 \\
\alpha_1(s_1) = -\alpha_1(s_1') = [1 & 1 & 0 & 0 & 0 & 0 & 1 & 1]
\end{array}
$$

$$
\begin{array}{ccccccccc}
& 1 & 2 & 3 & 4 & 5 & 6 & 7 & 8 \\
\alpha_2(s_2) = -\alpha_2(s_2') = [-1 & 0 & 1 & 0 & 0 & 1 & -1 & -1]
\end{array}
$$

The third basic postulate of system theory can now be stated as follows.

Postulate 3:   For any cut-set row vector $\boldsymbol{\alpha}$ and any arbitrary vector $\mathbf{Y}$ of through variables identified by the e edges of the system graph

$$\boldsymbol{\alpha}\mathbf{Y} = 0 \tag{4.4.1}$$

Equation (4.4.1) is called a *cut-set equation* of the system graph. The set of $v - 1$ cut sets, *each containing exactly one branch* of some tree T in a connected graph G, has already been defined as a fundamental set of cut sets.   The orientations for the fundamental cut sets are taken so that the component of the cut-set vector corresponding to the defining branch of the tree is $+1$.

Example 4.4.2:   The tree indicated by the heavy lines in Fig. 4.2.3 defines the fundamental cut sets $\{2,1,7,8\}$, $\{3,1,6,7,8\}$, $\{4,1,6,8\}$, and $\{5,1,6\}$.   These four fundamental cut sets define four corresponding cut-set equations that can be written in the form

$$
\begin{array}{c}
\text{Cut set} \\
\begin{array}{l}
(2,1,7,8) \\
(3,1,6,7,8) \\
(4,1,6,8) \\
(5,1,6)
\end{array}
\left[
\begin{array}{cccc:cccc}
1 & 0 & 0 & 0 & 1 & 0 & 1 & 1 \\
0 & 1 & 0 & 0 & -1 & 1 & -1 & -1 \\
0 & 0 & 1 & 0 & 1 & -1 & 0 & 1 \\
0 & 0 & 0 & 1 & -1 & 1 & 0 & 0
\end{array}
\right]
\begin{bmatrix}
y_2(t) \\
y_3(t) \\
y_4(t) \\
y_5(t) \\
\hdashline
y_1(t) \\
y_6(t) \\
y_7(t) \\
y_8(t)
\end{bmatrix}
\begin{array}{l}
\text{branches} \\[4pt]
= 0 \\[4pt]
\text{chords}
\end{array}
\end{array}
$$

$$\tag{4.4.2}$$

These equations are referred to as the *fundamental cut-set equations*.   They are obtained by summing the through variables of the fundamental set of cut sets by considering the relative orientations of the edges in the cut sets as follows: If the edge orientation is coincident with that of the cut set (the orientation of the defining branch), then the through variable for that edge is entered into the cut-set equation with a positive sign, otherwise a negative sign.

Again, as in the circuit equations, it is convenient to arrange the through variables in a column matrix in order so that the variables associated with the branches appear first.

In general, when the columns of the fundamental cut-set vectors are arranged so as to include the branches of the defining tree T as the first $v - 1$ columns, the fundamental cut sets form a matrix of the form

$$
\begin{array}{c}
\text{branches} \;\vdots\; \text{chords} \\
(v - 1) \; [\quad \mathbf{U} \quad \vdots \quad \mathbf{A} \quad] \\
(v - 1) \quad \vdots \quad (e - v + 1)
\end{array}
$$

and the corresponding cut-set equations, called *fundamental cut-set equations*, are

$$[\mathbf{U} \quad \mathbf{A}]\begin{bmatrix} \mathbf{Y}_b \\ \mathbf{Y}_c \end{bmatrix} = 0 \tag{4.4.3}$$

where the vectors $\mathbf{Y}_b$ and $\mathbf{Y}_c$ are of order $v - 1$ and $e - v + 1$, respectively, and represent the through variables identified by the branches and chords.

4.5 INCIDENCE VECTORS AND MATRICES

Any given incidence set I_i in a connected graph G is said to define an incidence vector γ_i of order $1 \times e$ whose jth entry γ_{ij} is

$$\gamma_{ij} = \begin{cases} \ \ 1 & \text{if edge } j \text{ is incident to vertex } i \text{ and directed away from it} \\ -1 & \text{if edge } j \text{ is incident to vertex } i \text{ and directed toward it} \\ \ \ 0 & \text{if edge } j \text{ is not incident to vertex } i \end{cases}$$

Example 4.5.1: Incidence sets $\{5,8,7,4\}$ and $\{3,6,4\}$ at vertices e and d, respectively, in Fig. 4.5.1 define the incidence row vectors

$$\begin{array}{ccccccccc} & 1 & 2 & 3 & 4 & 5 & 6 & 7 & 8 \\ \gamma_e = [0 & 0 & 0 & -1 & -1 & 0 & 1 & -1] \\ & 1 & 2 & 3 & 4 & 5 & 6 & 7 & 8 \\ \gamma_d = [0 & 0 & 1 & 1 & 0 & -1 & 0 & 0] \end{array}$$

From Fig. 4.5.1, it is evident that, when the incidence set $\{5,8,7,4\}$ is removed, the resulting system graph is in three parts, rather than two. Consequently, an incidence set is not always a cut set—it may be a collection of *disjoint cut sets*. However, it is easy to see that the fundamental cut sets for a Lagrangian tree† are also incidence sets.

Since incidence sets are cut sets or collections of disjoint cut sets, it follows that the cut-set postulate also applies to the incidence set; i.e., for any incidence row vector γ and any arbitrary vector $\mathbf{Y}$ of through

† A Lagrangian tree T_e is a tree in the graph which has all its branches incident to a common vertex.

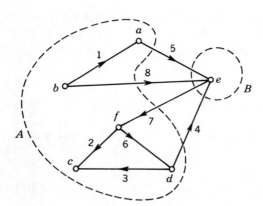

Fig. 4.5.1 Graph for incidence matrix in Eq. (4.5.2).

variables identified by the e edges of a system graph G

$$\gamma Y = 0 \tag{4.5.1}$$

Equation (4.5.1) is called an *incidence equation.*

The matrix $\bar{\Pi}$ of order $v \times e$ formed from the v incidence vectors, taken in any order, is called the *complete incidence matrix,* and the corresponding equations are called the *complete incidence equations.*

Example 4.5.2: The complete set of $v = 6$ incidence equations for the graph of Fig. 4.5.1 is

$$
\begin{array}{c}
\begin{array}{cccccccc}
1 & 2 & 3 & 4 & 5 & 6 & 7 & 8
\end{array} \\
\begin{array}{c}
a \\ b \\ c \\ d \\ e \\ f
\end{array}
\left[
\begin{array}{cccccccc}
-1 & 0 & 0 & 0 & 1 & 0 & 0 & 0 \\
1 & 0 & 0 & 0 & 0 & 0 & 0 & 1 \\
0 & -1 & -1 & 0 & 0 & 0 & 0 & 0 \\
0 & 0 & 1 & 1 & 0 & -1 & 0 & 0 \\
0 & 0 & 0 & -1 & -1 & 0 & 1 & -1 \\
0 & 1 & 0 & 0 & 0 & 1 & -1 & 0
\end{array}
\right]
\end{array}
\begin{bmatrix}
y_1 \\ y_2 \\ y_3 \\ y_4 \\ y_5 \\ y_6 \\ y_7 \\ y_8
\end{bmatrix}
= 0
\tag{4.5.2}
$$

Note that each column of $\bar{\Pi}$ in Eq. (4.5.2) contains exactly one $+1$ and one -1 entry. That this condition prevails in general follows from the definition of the matrix; i.e., each edge is directed toward one vertex and away from another. Therefore, the addition of all v rows in $\bar{\Pi}$ generates a row of zeros. Consequently, the rank of the incidence matrix is at most $v - 1$. The reader can show that the rank of the incidence matrix in Eq. (4.5.2) is not less than $v - 1$ by applying elementary row and column operations to reduce the matrix to normal form. In general, we have the following theorem.

Theorem 4.5.1: The rank of an incidence matrix $\bar{\Pi}$ of a connected graph G containing v vertices is exactly $v - 1$.

Proof: That the rank of $\bar{\Pi}$ is not more than $v - 1$ follows from the fact that each column contains exactly one $+1$ and one -1 entry. To prove that the rank is at least $v - 1$, we first establish the following lemma.

Lemma 4.5.1: Let $\bar{\Pi}$ represent the incidence matrix for a connected graph G. The sum of any r rows of $\bar{\Pi}$, $r < v$, contains at least one nonzero entry.

Proof of lemma: This lemma is established by contradiction. Suppose that r rows of $\bar{\Pi}$ add to a row of zeros. Let this set of r rows be arranged so as to form the first r rows in $\bar{\Pi}$. Since the first r rows of the rearranged vertex matrix (which is still an incidence matrix) add to zero, it follows that each column of these r rows must contain either all zeros or exactly two nonzero entries. Let the columns of $\bar{\Pi}$ be permuted so that the columns with zero entries in the first r rows appear last. The vertex matrix can now be partitioned as

$$\bar{\Pi} = \begin{bmatrix} \bar{\Pi}_{11} & 0 \\ 0 & \bar{\Pi}_{22} \end{bmatrix}$$

where $\bar{\Pi}_{11}$ contains r rows and $\bar{\Pi}_{22}$ contains $v - r$ rows. Consequently, any edges incident to the first r vertices are not incident to the last $v - r$ vertices. But this can be true only if the graph is not connected. Hence the lemma is proved by contradiction.

Continuing with the proof of the theorem, let the first $v - 1$ rows of $\bar{\Pi}$ be added to the last row. The last row is thereby reduced to a row of zeros. Since G is connected, each row has at least one nonzero entry. Consider a nonzero entry in the first row. Permute the columns so that this nonzero entry is brought to the 1×1 position. If there is any other nonzero entry, say in the kth row, first column ($k > 1$), add the first row to the kth row to reduce this entry to zero. By Lemma 4.5.1 the kth row still contains nonzero entries. There is a nonzero entry in the second row which is not in the first column. Interchange columns so that this nonzero entry is brought to the 2-2 position. If there is any nonzero entry in the second column below the 2-2 entry, use the second row to reduce it to zero. Again, fewer than v rows have been added, and so no row of zeros is produced thereby. By repeated application of this process, a triangular matrix of order $v - 1$ results, and the rank of $\bar{\Pi}$ is therefore $v - 1$.

Since the rank of the incidence matrix is always less than the number of vertices, one row is usually omitted. Indeed, given any $v - 1$ rows, the remaining row is obtained simply as the negative sum of the given $v - 1$ rows. The incidence matrix with $v - 1$ rows hereafter is represented by the symbol Π in contrast to the incidence matrix $\bar{\Pi}$ of v rows. Unless otherwise stated, hereafter in referring to the incidence matrix of a connected graph, the matrix is assumed to have $v - 1$ rows.

Since the incidence matrix Π is of maximum rank, it contains at least one square submatrix of order $v - 1$ that is nonsingular; i.e., at least one set of $v - 1$ columns of Π is linearly independent.

Consider, for example, the incidence matrix for the graph of Fig. 4.5.2. Considering the vertices a, b, and d and including the branches of the tree (1,2,3) as the first three columns, we have

$$\Pi = \begin{matrix} & 1 & 2 & 3 & 4 & 5 & 6 \\ a \\ b \\ d \end{matrix} \begin{bmatrix} 1 & 0 & 0 & 1 & 0 & 1 \\ -1 & 1 & 0 & 0 & 1 & 0 \\ 0 & 0 & -1 & -1 & -1 & 0 \end{bmatrix} = [\Pi_b \,\vdots\, \Pi_c] \qquad (4.5.3)$$

Note that the 3×3 submatrix $\mathbf{\Pi}_b$ in the leading position (columns corresponding to the branches of the indicated tree) is nonsingular. Direct investigation will show that any square submatrix made up of a set of columns corresponding to a tree in the graph is nonsingular. However, if the three columns selected do not correspond to the branches of some tree, then the resulting third-order matrix is singular. For example, the third-order matrix consisting of columns 3, 4, and 6 is singular, and the subgraph $(3,4,6)$ is not a tree.

A general statement of the property demonstrated above is given in the following theorem.

Theorem 4.5.2: Let $\mathbf{\Pi}$ represent an incidence matrix of order $v - 1$ for a connected graph G containing v vertices, and let $\mathbf{\Pi}_T$ represent any square submatrix of order $v - 1$ in $\mathbf{\Pi}$. The submatrix $\mathbf{\Pi}_T$ is nonsingular if and only if the edges corresponding to the $v - 1$ columns of $\mathbf{\Pi}_T$ constitute some tree T in G.

Proof: To establish sufficiency, consider a submatrix $\mathbf{\Pi}_T$ of $\mathbf{\Pi}$ corresponding to a tree T. Removal of all chords from G results in the tree T. The incidence matrix $\mathbf{\Pi}_T$ for T is square and has rank $v - 1$. Hence it is nonsingular.

To establish the necessity part of the theorem, consider a set of $v - 1$ columns, corresponding to edges $e_1, e_2, \ldots, e_{v-1}$ in $\mathbf{\Pi}$ such that these columns constitute a nonsingular submatrix. The subgraph G_s of G which contains the edges $e_1, e_2, \ldots, e_{v-1}$ cannot contain a circuit. Indeed, if it contains a circuit G_c with edges $e_{i_1}, e_{i_2}, \ldots, e_{i_k}$ then the rows and the columns of the matrix $\mathbf{\Pi}$ can be rearranged so that the matrix has the form

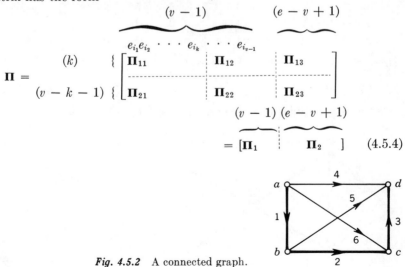

$$\mathbf{\Pi} = \begin{matrix} (k) \{ \\ (v-k-1) \{ \end{matrix} \begin{bmatrix} \mathbf{\Pi}_{11} & \mathbf{\Pi}_{12} & \mathbf{\Pi}_{13} \\ \mathbf{\Pi}_{21} & \mathbf{\Pi}_{22} & \mathbf{\Pi}_{23} \end{bmatrix}$$

$$= [\mathbf{\Pi}_1 \quad \mathbf{\Pi}_2] \qquad (4.5.4)$$

Fig. 4.5.2   A connected graph.

where it is assumed that the circuit G_c contains k vertices of the graph G_s and the edges $e_{i_1}, e_{i_2}, \ldots, e_{i_k}$ are incident to these vertices only. Hence the submatrix Π_{21} is empty.

To show that the columns of the submatrix Π_{11} are linearly dependent, i.e., that the whole submatrix Π_1 of order $v - 1$ of Π, indicated in Eq. (4.5.4), is singular, consider the sum of the k columns of the submatrix Π_{11}. From the definition of a circuit, in any row of Π_{11} there are exactly two nonzero entries. If necessary, the edges in circuit G_c are to be reoriented so that these edges all have the same relative orientation with respect to the circuit orientation. The rank of Π_{11} is, of course, not affected by this change. It follows that the two entries in any row of Π_{11} have opposite signs, and addition of the columns yields a column of zeros which implies the linear dependency of these columns (see Prob. 4.6).

From the above discussion it follows that since the submatrix Π_1 is *nonsingular*, edges $e_1, e_2, \ldots, e_{v-1}$ *cannot* form a circuit. Hence the subgraph G_s is a tree, since it contains v vertices, $v - 1$ edges, and no circuits and since it is connected (see Prob. 4.12).

4.6 ORTHOGONALITY OF CIRCUIT AND CUT-SET (OR INCIDENCE) VECTORS AND MATRICES

One of the most fundamental properties of graphs is that the circuit and cut-set (or incidence) vectors are orthogonal; i.e., the scalar product of the two vectors vanishes. Consider, for example, the cut set $\{2,3,4\}$ and the circuit $\{3,5,4\}$ in Fig. 4.6.1. The corresponding cut-set and circuit row vectors are

$$
\begin{array}{ccccccccc}
 & 1 & 2 & 3 & 4 & 5 & 6 & 7 & 8 \\
\alpha = [0 & -1 & 1 & 1 & 0 & 0 & 0 & 0] \\
\beta = [0 & 0 & 1 & -1 & 1 & 0 & 0 & 0]
\end{array}
$$

Direct computation establishes that

$$\alpha\beta^T = 0$$

This result is established in general by the following theorem.

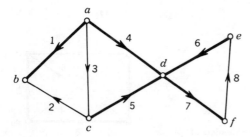

Fig. 4.6.1 A connected graph.

Theorem 4.6.1:   Each cut-set (or incidence) vector α_i of a connected graph G is orthogonal to each circuit vector β_j of G, that is,

$$\alpha_i\beta_j{}^T = \beta_j\alpha_i{}^T = 0$$

Proof: Let the vertices of the connected graph G be divided into two mutually exclusive sets A and B (Fig. 4.6.2).   The edges having one vertex in A and the other in B constitute cut set i.   It follows that any circuit j in the graph G includes an even number of edges from cut set i.

It is easy to see that, if edges α_{ik} and β_{jk} common to cut set i and circuit j are taken in the order in which they are traversed around the circuit in a given direction, then for consecutive common edges the products $\alpha_{ik}\beta_{jk}$ are alternatively 1 and -1.   Since cut set i and circuit j include an even number of common edges,

$$\sum_k \alpha_{ik}\beta_{jk} = 0$$

and the theorem is proved for α_i being a cut-set vector.   However, since an incidence vector is either a cut-set vector or the sum of cut-set vectors, the conclusion obtained is also valid for any incidence and any circuit vector.   This completes the proof.

From Theorem 4.6.1 it follows that in particular, each row vector of the fundamental cut-set matrix is orthogonal to each row vector of the fundamental circuit matrix, and we have the following important theorem relating the fundamental circuit and cut-set matrices defined by a given tree T in the system graph.

Theorem 4.6.2:   Let T be a tree of a connected graph G, and let $[\mathbf{U}\ \ \mathbf{A}]$ and $[\mathbf{B}\ \ \mathbf{U}]$ represent the fundamental cut-set and circuit matrices, respectively, for a tree T and its complement.   Then, if the edges are

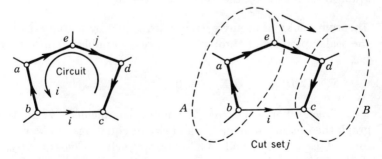

Fig. 4.6.2   Edges in cut set j and circuit i.

taken in the same order in each matrix,

$$[\mathbf{B} \quad \mathbf{U}] \begin{bmatrix} \mathbf{U} \\ \mathbf{A}^T \end{bmatrix} = 0 \quad \text{or} \quad [\mathbf{U} \quad \mathbf{A}] \begin{bmatrix} \mathbf{B}^T \\ \mathbf{U} \end{bmatrix} = 0$$

i.e.,

$$\mathbf{B} = -\mathbf{A}^T \quad \text{or} \quad \mathbf{A} = -\mathbf{B}^T$$

Example 4.6.1: The fundamental cut-set matrix corresponding to the tree indicated by the heavy lines in Fig. 4.6.1 is

$$
\begin{array}{c}
\\1\\4\\5\\6\\7
\end{array}
\begin{array}{c}
\begin{array}{cccccccc}
1 & 4 & 5 & 6 & 7 & 2 & 3 & 8
\end{array}\\
\begin{bmatrix}
1 & 0 & 0 & 0 & 0 & 1 & 0 & 0\\
0 & 1 & 0 & 0 & 0 & -1 & 1 & 0\\
0 & 0 & 1 & 0 & 0 & 1 & -1 & 0\\
0 & 0 & 0 & 1 & 0 & 0 & 0 & -1\\
0 & 0 & 0 & 0 & 1 & 0 & 0 & -1
\end{bmatrix}
\end{array} = [\mathbf{U} \;\vdots\; \mathbf{A}]
$$

where $\mathbf{U}$ and $\mathbf{A}$ are the submatrices indicated by the partitioning lines. The corresponding fundamental circuit matrix is

$$
\begin{array}{c}
\\2\\3\\8
\end{array}
\begin{array}{c}
\begin{array}{cccccccc}
1 & 4 & 5 & 6 & 7 & 2 & 3 & 8
\end{array}\\
\begin{bmatrix}
-1 & 1 & -1 & 0 & 0 & 1 & 0 & 0\\
0 & -1 & 1 & 0 & 0 & 0 & 1 & 0\\
0 & 0 & 0 & 1 & 1 & 0 & 0 & 1
\end{bmatrix}
\end{array} = [\mathbf{B} \;\vdots\; \mathbf{U}]
$$

where again $\mathbf{B}$ and $\mathbf{U}$ are the submatrices indicated by the partitioning lines. By direct comparison we see that $\mathbf{A} = -\mathbf{B}^T$, or

$$\mathbf{B} + \mathbf{A}^T = \begin{bmatrix} -1 & 1 & -1 & 0 \\ 0 & -1 & -1 & 0 \\ 0 & 0 & 0 & 1 \end{bmatrix} + \begin{bmatrix} 1 & -1 & 1 & 0 & 0 \\ 0 & 1 & -1 & 0 & 0 \\ 0 & 0 & 0 & -1 & -1 \end{bmatrix} \equiv 0$$

The second and third basic postulates of system theory together with the orthogonality property of the circuit and cut-set vectors imply the conservation of power and energy in *any* system characterized by a graph G, as stated by the following theorem.

Theorem 4.6.3: For any system represented by a graph G with e edges, the scalar product of through and across variables vanishes identically, i.e.,

$$\mathbf{X}_e^T(t)\mathbf{Y}_e(t) = \mathbf{Y}_e^T(t)\mathbf{X}_e(t) \equiv 0$$

Proof: For some tree T and its complement T' in the system graph the fundamental cut-set and circuit equations can be written in the form of Eqs. (4.4.3) and (4.3.3), respectively. Consequently, the sum of the scalar product of the across and through variables of the e edges in the system graph is

$$\sum_{i=1}^{e} x_i y_i = [\mathbf{X}_b{}^T \quad \mathbf{X}_c{}^T] \begin{bmatrix} \mathbf{Y}_b \\ \mathbf{Y}_c \end{bmatrix}$$

$$= \mathbf{X}_b{}^T [\mathbf{U} \quad -\mathbf{B}^T] \begin{bmatrix} -\mathbf{A} \\ \mathbf{U} \end{bmatrix} \mathbf{Y}_c$$

which vanishes identically since, by Theorem 4.6.2, $\mathbf{A} = -\mathbf{B}^T$.

The properties of the incidence matrix stated in Theorem 4.5.2 suggest that all cut-set matrices for a given graph G can be obtained from the incidence matrix of G by a nonsingular transformation. That this is the case is indicated by the following theorem.

Theorem 4.6.4: Let the incidence matrix for a connected graph G be written as

$$\mathbf{\Pi} = [\mathbf{\Pi}_b \quad \mathbf{\Pi}_c] \tag{4.6.1}$$

Then the matrix

$$\mathbf{A} = \mathbf{\Pi}_b{}^{-1}[\mathbf{\Pi}_b \quad \mathbf{\Pi}_c] = [\mathbf{U} \mid \mathbf{\Pi}_b{}^{-1} \quad \mathbf{\Pi}_c] \tag{4.6.2}$$

represents the cut-set matrix for a tree T in G.

Proof: Since the columns of $\mathbf{\Pi}_b$ correspond to a tree T in G, $\mathbf{\Pi}_b$ is nonsingular.

To show that the matrix in Eq. (4.6.2) is indeed a cut-set matrix corresponding to the tree T, consider the orthogonal product $\mathbf{C}$ of the incidence matrix $\mathbf{\Pi}$ and the fundamental circuit matrix $[\mathbf{B} \quad \mathbf{U}]$ corresponding to T.

$$\mathbf{C} = [\mathbf{\Pi}_b \quad \mathbf{\Pi}_c] \begin{bmatrix} \mathbf{B}^T \\ \mathbf{U} \end{bmatrix} \tag{4.6.3}$$

A typical entry c_{ij} of $\mathbf{C}$ is computed by multiplying row i (incidence row vector α_i) into column j of $[\mathbf{B} \quad \mathbf{U}]^T$ (circuit row vector β_j); that is,

$$c_{ij} = \alpha_i \beta_j{}^T = \sum_{k=1}^{e} \alpha_{ik} \beta_{jk}$$

To conclude that $c_{ij} = 0$, two cases must be considered: (1) If the edges in circuit j are not incident to vertex i, then $\alpha_{ik} = 0$ and it follows that $c_{ij} = 0$. (2) If $\alpha_{ik} \neq 0$, then in circuit j there are exactly two edges incident to vertex i and exactly two of the α_{ik} entries, say α_{im} and α_{in}, are nonzero, as shown in Fig. 4.6.3. Thus, in this latter case

$$c_{ij} = \alpha_{im}\beta_{jm} + \alpha_{in}\beta_{jn} \tag{4.6.4}$$

It is easily verified that c_{ij} in Eq. (4.6.3) is equal to zero for all possible orientations of edges m and n and of circuit j.

From Eqs. (4.6.3) and (4.6.4) it now follows that

$$\mathbf{C} = \mathbf{\Pi}_b \mathbf{B}^T + \mathbf{\Pi}_c = 0$$

or premultiplying by $\mathbf{\Pi}_b^{-1}$,

$$\mathbf{B}^T = -\mathbf{\Pi}_b^{-1}\mathbf{\Pi}_c \tag{4.6.5}$$

Substituting Eq. (4.6.5) into Eq. (4.6.2), we have

$$\mathbf{\Pi}_b^{-1}\mathbf{\Pi} = [\mathbf{U} \quad -\mathbf{B}^T] \tag{4.6.6}$$

and it follows from Theorem 4.6.2 that $\mathbf{\Pi}_b^{-1}\mathbf{\Pi} = [\mathbf{U} \quad \mathbf{A}]$ is indeed a fundamental cut-set matrix for the tree T in G.

Example 4.6.2: From the incidence matrix given by Eq. (4.5.3) for the graph in Fig. 4.5.2, determine the cut-set matrices for the tree (2,4,6).

Solution: To establish the cut-set equations for the tree (2,4,6), let the columns of the incidence matrix in Eq. (4.5.3) be rearranged as

$$\mathbf{\Pi} = \begin{matrix} a \\ b \\ d \end{matrix} \begin{bmatrix} \overset{2}{0} & \overset{4}{1} & \overset{6}{1} & \overset{1}{1} & \overset{3}{0} & \overset{5}{0} \\ 1 & 0 & 0 & -1 & 0 & 1 \\ 0 & -1 & 0 & 0 & -1 & -1 \end{bmatrix} = [\mathbf{\Pi}_b \quad \mathbf{\Pi}_c]$$

Then

$$\mathbf{\Pi}_b^{-1}[\mathbf{\Pi}_b \quad \mathbf{\Pi}_c] = \begin{matrix} 2 \\ 4 \\ 6 \end{matrix} \begin{bmatrix} \overset{2}{1} & \overset{4}{0} & \overset{6}{0} & \overset{1}{-1} & \overset{3}{0} & \overset{5}{1} \\ 0 & 1 & 0 & 0 & 1 & 1 \\ 0 & 0 & 1 & 1 & -1 & -1 \end{bmatrix} \tag{4.6.7}$$

By direct comparison, it can be seen that Eq. (4.6.7) is the cut-set matrix for the tree (2,4,6) in the graph of Fig. 4.5.2.

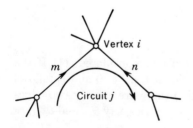

Fig. 4.6.3 Circuit j containing vertex i.

The fact that the cut-set matrices for a tree T_1 and a tree T_2 in a given graph can both be determined from the incidence matrix by a nonsingular transformation suggests that one should be able to establish the cut-set matrix for T_2 from the cut-set matrix for T_1 by a nonsingular transformation, and vice versa.   The existence of such a transformation is given without proof by the following theorem.

Theorem 4.6.5:   Let $[\mathbf{U} \quad \mathbf{A}_1]$ and $[\mathbf{U} \quad \mathbf{A}_2]$ represent any two fundamental cut-set matrices of a given connected graph G; then there exist nonsingular transformations relating $\mathbf{A}_1$ to $\mathbf{A}_2$.

The counterparts of Theorems 4.5.2 and 4.6.5 for the cut-set and the circuit matrices are also given below without proof.

Theorem 4.6.6:   Any square submatrix of maximum order in the cut-set and circuit matrices is of maximum rank if and only if the columns correspond to a tree and a cotree, respectively.

Theorem 4.6.7:   If $[\mathbf{B}_1 \quad \mathbf{U}]$ and $[\mathbf{B}_2 \quad \mathbf{U}]$ represent any two fundamental circuit matrices of a given connected graph G, then there exist nonsingular transformations relating $\mathbf{B}_1$ to $\mathbf{B}_2$.

4.7 PRACTICAL APPLICATION OF CIRCUIT AND CUT-SET EQUATIONS

The $e - v + p$ fundamental circuit and the $v - p$ fundamental cut-set equations of a system graph G having v vertices, e edges, and p parts are usually referred to as the *constraint equations* of the system.

Insofar as the practical applications of these constraint equations are concerned, it is important to recognize that the fundamental circuit equations for a cotree T' in G as given in Eq. (4.3.3) can also be written as

$$\mathbf{X}_c(t) \;=\; -\mathbf{B}\mathbf{X}_b(t)$$

which, in words, states that *the chord across variables are uniquely determined by the branch across variables;* i.e., only the $v - p$ across variables of the branches can be specified arbitrarily, and, once specified, they determine all remaining chord across variables.   Likewise, the fundamental cut-set equations for a tree T in G as given in Eq. (4.4.3) can always be written in the form

$$\mathbf{Y}_b(t) \;=\; -\mathbf{A}\mathbf{Y}_c(t)$$

which, in words, states that *the branch through variables are uniquely determined by the chord through variables;* i.e., only the $e - v + p$ through variables corresponding to a cotree can be specified arbitrarily.

In general, the cotree T' used to define the fundamental circuit equations need not be the complement of the tree T used to define the fundamental circuits. Further, the cut-set constraints for an arbitrary tree can be generated from the incidence matrix $\mathbf{\Pi}$ by reducing the latter to normal form by elementary row and column operations. Since these operations are easy to carry out in computing machines, the incidence equations, rather than fundamental cut-set or circuit equations, represent the most practical form in which to specify the system constraints when machine computation is involved.

We conclude this chapter with a final example demonstrating some specific techniques useful for generating the constraint equations directly or indirectly through the incidence matrix.

Example 4.7.1: Establish a fundamental set of circuit and cut-set equations for the system graph given in Fig. 4.7.1.

Solution: First select a tree such as that indicated by the heavy lines, and arrange the across variables in two columns, as indicated by the format of Eq. (4.7.1). The branch variables (in any order) are included as one column vector, and the chord variables (in any order) as a second column matrix. Since there is one and only one chord in each circuit, the coefficient matrix of the second vector is known to be unity and so need not be written. Since there is one equation for each chord, we know immediately that there are five equations. The variables having been arranged in a convenient format, the across variables are summed around each of the fundamental circuits identified by the chord variables, filling in one equation at a time. The result is the set of simul-

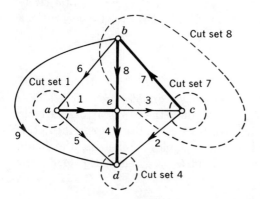

Fig. 4.7.1 System graph for Eqs. (4.7.1) and (4.7.2).

taneous equations

$$
\begin{bmatrix}
1 & 0 & -1 & 0 \\
0 & -1 & -1 & -1 \\
0 & 0 & 1 & 1 \\
-1 & -1 & 0 & 0 \\
0 & -1 & -1 & 0
\end{bmatrix}
\begin{bmatrix}
x_1(t) \\
x_4(t) \\
x_8(t) \\
x_7(t)
\end{bmatrix}
+
\begin{bmatrix}
x_6(t) \\
x_2(t) \\
x_3(t) \\
x_5(t) \\
x_9(t)
\end{bmatrix}
= 0
\tag{4.7.1}
$$

The through variables in the cut-set equations are arranged in a format similar to that of Eq. (4.7.2). Since there is one and only one branch in each cut set, the coefficient matrix for the branch through variables is unity and need not be written. Since there are four branches in the tree, there are, of course, four cut-set equations.

The summation of the through variables in each cut set is conveniently established by drawing a closed circular line that cuts exactly one branch of the tree, as shown dashed in Fig. 4.7.1. Filling in the cut-set equations one at a time gives

$$
\begin{bmatrix}
y_1(t) \\
y_4(t) \\
y_8(t) \\
y_7(t)
\end{bmatrix}
+
\begin{bmatrix}
-1 & 0 & 0 & 1 & 0 \\
0 & 1 & 0 & 1 & 1 \\
1 & 1 & -1 & 0 & 1 \\
0 & 1 & -1 & 0 & 0
\end{bmatrix}
\begin{bmatrix}
y_6(t) \\
y_2(t) \\
y_3(t) \\
y_5(t) \\
y_9(t)
\end{bmatrix}
= 0
\tag{4.7.2}
$$

As a check against error, the coefficient matrix in Eq. (4.7.1), of course, should be the negative transpose of that given in Eq. (4.7.2).

If we wish to generate the fundamental circuit and cut-set equations indirectly from the incidence matrix, the latter may be written initially in any form whatsoever. Consider, for example, the incidence equations with the vertices and edges arranged in natural order.

	1	2	3	4	5	6	7	8
a	1	0	0	0	1	-1	0	0
b	0	0	0	0	0	1	-1	1
c	0	1	-1	0	0	0	1	0
d	0	-1	0	-1	-1	0	0	0
check row e	-1	0	1	1	0	0	0	-1

The last row, of course, is not required but is included as a check on the column sum. Upon performing elementary row operations only, the given matrix reduces to

1	2	3	4	5	6	7	8
1	0	0	0	1	-1	0	0
0	1	0	1	1	0	0	0
0	0	1	1	1	0	-1	0
0	0	0	0	0	1	-1	1

The fact that the rank of the submatrix consisting of the first five columns is only 3 implies, of course, that edges 4 and 5 form circuits with edges 1, 2, and 3. Permuting columns 4 and 8, for example, establishes the fundamental cut-set equations for the tree $T = \{1,2,3,8\}$.

PROBLEMS

4.1   By means of a terminal graph identify the variables you would use in modeling the characteristics of each component in the systems of Fig. P4.1, and establish the resulting system graph.

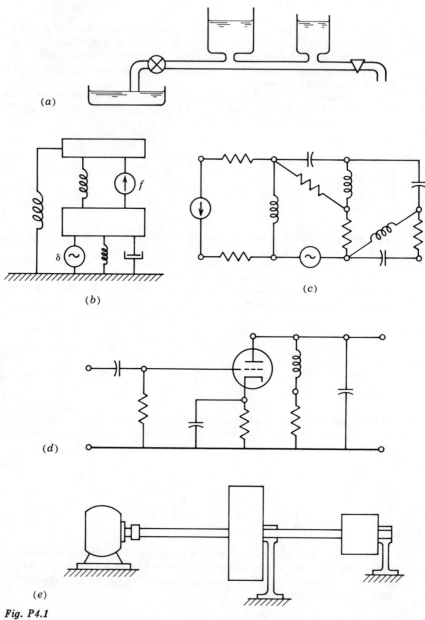

(a)

(b)

(c)

(d)

(e)

Fig. P4.1

4.2   Consider the graph G shown in Fig. P4.2.

   (a) Indicate a few (five or six) trees of G, and show the corresponding fundamental cut sets and circuits.

   (b) For the tree (1,5,3) write the fundamental cut-set and circuit equations, and check all the relations you know between the two matrices.

   (c) Write the incidence matrix for graph G, and check for the properties you know of. Demonstrate that any row of the fundamental cut-set matrix in (b) is a linear combination of some set of rows of $\mathbf{\Pi}$.

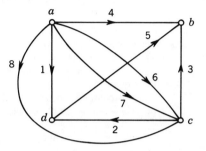

Fig. P4.2

4.3   For some graph G, an incidence matrix $\mathbf{\Pi}$ is given as

$$\mathbf{\Pi} = \begin{bmatrix} 0 & 1 & 0 & -1 & 0 & 1 & 0 & 0 \\ -1 & 0 & 0 & 0 & -1 & 0 & 0 & 1 \\ 0 & 0 & 1 & 0 & 0 & 0 & -1 & 0 \\ 0 & -1 & 0 & 0 & 0 & 0 & 0 & 0 \\ 0 & 0 & 0 & 0 & 0 & 0 & 0 & 0 \\ 1 & 0 & 0 & 0 & 0 & -1 & 0 & 0 \end{bmatrix}$$

   (a) Determine the graph.

   (b) Derive a fundamental cut-set and a fundamental circuit matrix using Theorems 4.6.2 and 4.6.4.

4.4   (a) Sketch the system graph G for the system shown in Fig. P4.4.

   (b) Indicate a tree of the graph G, and write the fundamental cut-set equations. Write the fundamental circuit equations from the fundamental cut-set equations, and check your results.

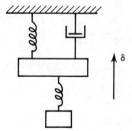

Fig. P4.4

4.5   Suppose that the incidence matrix of a graph G is of the form

$$\mathbf{\Pi} = \begin{bmatrix} \mathbf{\Pi}_1 & 0 & 0 \\ 0 & \mathbf{\Pi}_2 & 0 \\ 0 & 0 & \mathbf{\Pi}_3 \end{bmatrix}$$

What can you conclude about G?

4.6   Let a connected graph G contain the vertices $a_1, a_2, \ldots, a_v$ and the edges e_i, $i = 1, 2, \ldots, v$, such that e_i has the vertices a_i and a_{i+1} $[v + 1 \equiv 1 \pmod{v}]$ as its end points and is oriented from the vertex a_i to a_{i+1}.

    (a)   Show that graph G is a circuit.

    (b)   Write the incidence matrix $\mathbf{\Pi}$, and show that every column and row of $\mathbf{\Pi}$ contains exactly two nonzero entries with opposite signs.

    (c)   Show that $\mathbf{\Pi}_1 = \mathbf{\Pi}^T$ is an incidence matrix. Construct the graph G_1 corresponding to $\mathbf{\Pi}_1$. What could you say about this graph G_1?

    (d)   Show that, in the incidence matrix $\mathbf{\Pi}$, any submatrix of order $v - 1$ is nonsingular.

4.7   If every subgraph of a connected graph G has at least two vertices in common with its complement, the graph G is said to be *nonseparable*.

    (a)   Give examples to illustrate this definition. Is it always possible to select a tree for a separable graph? Consider a connected graph G which is separable. If C is the vertex common to a subgraph G_s of G and its complement, then C is called a *cut vertex*.

    (b)   Consider a graph G which is its own tree. Verify that every nonend vertex in G is a cut vertex.

    (c)   Can you construct a nonseparable graph G containing no circuits?

4.8   Let the graph G of a system be connected and contain e edges and v vertices.

    (a)   What is the maximum number of through variables that can be specified arbitrarily?

    (b)   What is the maximum number of across variables that can be specified arbitrarily?

    (c)   Why, out of all the possible circuit and cut-set equations, is it convenient to use the fundamental circuit and cut-set equations?

4.9   A system of two-terminal components is given in Fig. P4.9.

    (a)   Draw the system graph.

    (b)   Indicate a tree of the system graph. Write the fundamental cut-set and circuit equations for this tree. How many through variables and across variables can be specified arbitrarily?

    (c)   Verify all the relations between the fundamental cut-set and circuit matrices.

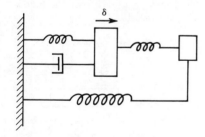

Fig. P4.9

4.10   Consider the system graph given in Fig. P4.10.

    (a)   Is this a separable or nonseparable graph?

    (b)   Are there separable and nonseparable subgraphs of the graph? If so, identify them.

    (c)   Choose a formulation forest (set of trees), and write the fundamental cut-set and circuit equations.

    (d)   Develop an expression for the number of independent circuit and cut-set equations as a function of the number of edges, the number of vertices, and the number of nonseparable and/or separable parts in the system graph.

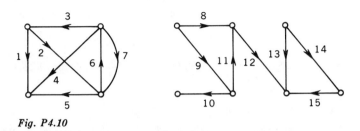

Fig. P4.10

4.11   Euler has given the following formula for a polyhedron (a solid with polygonal faces),

$$V - E + F = 2$$

where

V denotes the number of vertices
E denotes the number of edges
F denotes the number of faces

Consider a graph corresponding to a given polyhedron, and derive Euler's formula from the number of independent circuits of the graph.

4.12   A connected graph G with e edges and v vertices is said to have *rank* $v - 1$ and *nullity* $e - v + 1$. In this terminology, a graph containing no circuits has nullity zero. From the above definitions of rank and nullity prove that any three of the following statements imply the fourth:

(a)   A tree contains no circuits of G.
(b)   A tree is connected.
(c)   The number of edges in a tree is equal to $v - 1$.
(d)   A tree contains all the vertices of G.

4.13   Consider the graph G_1 corresponding to a nonsingular submatrix of an incidence matrix $\mathbf{\Pi} = [\mathbf{\Pi}_b \quad \mathbf{\Pi}_c]$. Let a be the reference vertex in G_1.

(a)   What can you say about the graph G_1?
(b)   Consider a Lagrangian tree T having the same vertices as G_1, with vertex a as its common vertex. Write the expression for the incidence matrix, $\mathbf{\Pi}_T$, of the graph $G_1 U T$ when a is taken as a reference.
(c)   If the fundamental cut-set matrix of $G_1 U T$ corresponding to T is written as

[$\mathbf{U}$ $\mathbf{A}_1$]

establish the relationship between A_1 and $\mathbf{\Pi}_T$.
(d)   From the result in (c) state a procedure for calculating the inverse of a nonsingular submatrix.

4.14   By use of the Binet-Cauchy formula calculate the determinant of $\mathbf{\Pi\Pi}^T$, where $\mathbf{\Pi}$ is an incidence matrix of a connected graph G. Show that this number is equal to the number of trees in G.

4.15   Prove that if a graph G contains e edges then the number of all possible subgraphs of G is $2^e - 2$.

Hint: Consider the combination of e elements taken p at a time, $p = 1, 2,$ $\ldots, e - 1$, and notice the fact that these combinations are the terms in the binomial formula for $(1 + 1)^e$.

4.16   Let $\mathbf{\Pi}$ and $\mathbf{B}_G$ be the incidence and circuit matrices of a graph.   Prove that

$$\mathbf{\Pi B}_G{}^T = 0$$

4.17   Extend Theorem 4.6.2 to a separated graph with p parts.

FURTHER READING

1.   Seshu, S., and M. B. Reed: "Linear Graphs and Electrical Networks," Addison-Wesley Publishing Company, Inc., Reading, Mass., 1961.

2.   Synge, J. L.: The Fundamental Theorem of Electrical Networks, *Quart. Appl. Math.*, vol. 9, no. 2, pp. 113-127, 1951.

3.   Saltzer, C.: The Second Fundamental Theorem of Electrical Networks, *Quart. Appl. Math.*, vol. 11, no. 1, pp. 119–121, 1953.

4.   Trent, H. M.: Isomorphisms between Oriented Linear Graphs and Lumped Physical Systems, *J. Acoust. Soc. Am.*, vol. 27, pp. 500–527, 1955.

5
State Models and Numerical Solutions

Within the context of the discipline presented in this book, the structural features of a system of discrete components are completely and uniquely specified by the component models and the system graph. The first objective of this chapter is to present a method for combining these two structural features to form what is called a *state model* of the system. Models of this form are ideally suited for solution by either digital or analog computers and constitute the basis of much of modern system theory. So that these models may serve a purpose beyond that of merely providing a basis for obtaining solutions to particular analysis problems, the development attempts to establish the general properties of the model as they relate to the structure of the system. These general properties are essential to any machine program for automatic analysis and supply the foundation for many system design and synthesis procedures.

The chapter includes sections devoted to numerical solutions of state models of linear and nonlinear systems. The uninitiated reader will find this discussion helpful before proceeding to the analytical solutions given in the later chapters.

5.1 SYSTEMS OF DIFFERENTIAL EQUATIONS IN NORMAL FORM

Let us consider a system of linear differential equations of the type

$$\frac{d\psi_{1i}(t)}{dt} = \sum_{j=1}^{n} p_{ij}\psi_{1j}(t) + \sum_{j=1}^{m} q_{ij}\psi_{0j}(t) \qquad i = 1, 2, \ldots, n \qquad (5.1.1)$$

where p_{ij} and q_{ij} are assumed as constants and $\psi_{0j}(t)$ is a continuous function of t in some interval $T_1 < t < T_2$. This system of differential equations is said to be written in *standard*, or *normal*, form, since the equations are explicit in the derivatives of the variables $\psi_{1i}(t)$. When written in matrix form, the system of Eqs. (5.1.1) reads

$$\frac{d}{dt} \mathbf{\Psi}_1(t) = \mathbf{P}\mathbf{\Psi}_1(t) + \mathbf{Q}\mathbf{\Psi}_0(t) \qquad (5.1.2)$$

and $(d/dt)\mathbf{\Psi}_1(t)$ is referred to as the *derivative vector*.

A special class of nonlinear differential equations results when the derivative vector is a nonlinear function of the vector $\mathbf{\Psi}(t)$. The differential equations in this case are still described as being in normal form and are represented symbolically as

$$\frac{d}{dt} \mathbf{\Psi}(t) = \mathbf{F}[\mathbf{\Psi}(t),t] \qquad (5.1.3)$$

where $\mathbf{F}[\mathbf{\Psi}(t),t]$ is a vector function of the vector $\mathbf{\Psi}$ and the scalar t, that is,

$$\mathbf{F}[\mathbf{\Psi}(t),t] = \begin{bmatrix} f_1[\psi_1(t),\psi_2(t), \ldots ,\psi_n(t),t] \\ f_2[\psi_1(t),\psi_2(t), \ldots ,\psi_n(t),t] \\ \cdots\cdots\cdots\cdots\cdots\cdots \\ f_n[\psi_1(t),\psi_2(t), \ldots ,\psi_n(t),t] \end{bmatrix}$$

Almost all known numerical methods for solving simultaneous, ordinary differential equations require the normal forms given above.

The next several sections present procedures for formulating mathematical models of linear and certain classes of nonlinear systems in normal form from the two structural features of the system. For reasons that will become apparent later, such models are referred to as *state models*.

5.2 STATE EQUATIONS FOR LINEAR SYSTEMS OF TWO-TERMINAL COMPONENTS†

The basic procedure for formulating state models is first demonstrated by means of a simple example.

† Methods for formulating state models for certain special cases in electrical networks have been considered by T. R. Bashkow[1] and in the more general case by P. R. Bryant.[2] General procedures for linear and nonlinear systems are given by J. L. Wirth.[3] (Superior numbers refer to the numbered items in Further Reading at the end of the chapter.)

Example 5.2.1: Formulate a state model of the mechanical system shown in Fig. 5.2.1.

Solution: The terminal graphs used as a basis of modeling each of the components in the system are shown assembled in the form of a system graph in Fig. 5.2.1b. The equations representing the terminal characteristics of the components in the system are written in the following forms:

Mass elements—edges 1 and 2:

$$\frac{d}{dt}\begin{bmatrix} \dot{\delta}_1(t) \\ \dot{\delta}_2(t) \end{bmatrix} = \begin{bmatrix} 1/M_1 & 0 \\ 0 & 1/M_2 \end{bmatrix} \begin{bmatrix} f_1(t) \\ f_2(t) \end{bmatrix} \tag{5.2.1}$$

Spring elements—edges 4 and 5:

$$\frac{d}{dt}\begin{bmatrix} f_4(t) \\ f_5(t) \end{bmatrix} = \begin{bmatrix} K_4 & 0 \\ 0 & K_5 \end{bmatrix} \begin{bmatrix} \dot{\delta}_4(t) \\ \dot{\delta}_5(t) \end{bmatrix} \tag{5.2.2}$$

Damper—edge 3:

$$f_3(t) = B_3\dot{\delta}_3(t) \tag{5.2.3}$$

Force driver—edge 6:

$$f_6(t) = \text{specified function of time} \tag{5.2.4}$$

Note that we have used $\dot{\delta}$ rather than δ as the variable in characterizing the components, thereby avoiding second-order differential equations. Note further that Eq. (5.2.1) is written explicitly in the derivative of the across variables, while Eq. (5.2.2) is written explicitly in the derivative of the through variables.

In selecting a tree in the system graph to use as a basis for writing the circuit and cut-set equations, it is in the interest of maximum simplicity to include edges 1 and 2 as branches and edges 4 and 5 as chords. The corresponding tree

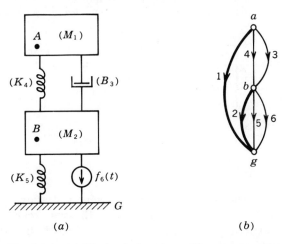

(a)   *(b)*

Fig. 5.2.1 *(a)* Mechanical system; *(b)* system graph.

is identified by the heavy lines in Fig. 5.2.1b, and the cut-set and circuit equations are

$$\begin{bmatrix} f_1(t) \\ f_2(t) \end{bmatrix} = \begin{bmatrix} -1 & -1 & 0 & 0 \\ 1 & 1 & -1 & -1 \end{bmatrix} \begin{bmatrix} f_3(t) \\ f_4(t) \\ f_5(t) \\ f_6(t) \end{bmatrix} \tag{5.2.5}$$

$$\begin{bmatrix} \dot{\delta}_4(t) \\ \dot{\delta}_5(t) \end{bmatrix} = \begin{bmatrix} 1 & -1 \\ 0 & 1 \end{bmatrix} \begin{bmatrix} \dot{\delta}_1(t) \\ \dot{\delta}_2(t) \end{bmatrix} \tag{5.2.6}$$

and

$$\dot{\delta}_3(t) = \dot{\delta}_1(t) - \dot{\delta}_2(t) \tag{5.2.7}$$
$$\dot{\delta}_6(t) = \dot{\delta}_2(t) \tag{5.2.8}$$

The component terminal equations in Eqs. (5.2.1) to (5.2.4) and the graph equations in Eqs. (5.2.5) to (5.2.8) constitute 12 equations in 12 variables. The number of equations and variables can immediately be reduced to 6 by substituting Eqs. (5.2.5), (5.2.6), and (5.2.7), respectively, into Eqs. (5.2.1), (5.2.2), and (5.2.3), to obtain

$$\frac{d}{dt}\begin{bmatrix} \dot{\delta}_1(t) \\ \dot{\delta}_2(t) \end{bmatrix} = \begin{bmatrix} -1/M_1 \\ 1/M_2 \end{bmatrix} f_3(t) + \begin{bmatrix} -1/M_1 & 0 \\ 1/M_2 & -1/M_2 \end{bmatrix} \begin{bmatrix} f_4(t) \\ f_5(t) \end{bmatrix}$$
$$+ \begin{bmatrix} 0 \\ -1/M_2 \end{bmatrix} f_6(t) \quad (5.2.9)$$

$$\frac{d}{dt}\begin{bmatrix} f_4(t) \\ f_5(t) \end{bmatrix} = \begin{bmatrix} K_4 & -K_4 \\ 0 & K_5 \end{bmatrix} \begin{bmatrix} \dot{\delta}_1(t) \\ \dot{\delta}_2(t) \end{bmatrix} \tag{5.2.10}$$

$$f_3(t) = B_3[\dot{\delta}_1(t) - \dot{\delta}_2(t)] \tag{5.2.11}$$

$f_6(t) = $ specified function of time

Now note that $f_3(t)$ is the only variable, other than the specified variable $f_6(t)$, appearing to the right of the equality signs that is not also included in the derivative vector of Eq. (5.2.9) or (5.2.10). Substituting the algebraic equation for $f_3(t)$ in Eq. (5.2.11) into Eq. (5.2.9) and combining the results with Eq. (5.2.10) gives the system of four simultaneous first-order differential equations,

$$\frac{d}{dt}\begin{bmatrix} \dot{\delta}_1(t) \\ \dot{\delta}_2(t) \\ \hdashline f_4(t) \\ f_5(t) \end{bmatrix} = \begin{bmatrix} -B_3/M_1 & B_3/M_1 & -1/M_1 & 0 \\ B_3/M_2 & -B_3/M_2 & 1/M_2 & -1/M_2 \\ \hdashline K_4 & -K_4 & 0 & 0 \\ 0 & K_5 & 0 & 0 \end{bmatrix} \begin{bmatrix} \dot{\delta}_1(t) \\ \dot{\delta}_2(t) \\ \hdashline f_4(t) \\ f_5(t) \end{bmatrix}$$
$$+ \begin{bmatrix} 0 \\ -f_6(t)/M_2 \\ \hdashline 0 \\ 0 \end{bmatrix} \quad (5.2.12)$$

The differential equations in the above example as given in the form of Eq. (5.2.12) are called the *state equations* of the system. The fourth-order column vector with entries $\dot{\delta}_1(t)$, $\dot{\delta}_2(t)$, $f_4(t)$, $f_5(t)$ is called the *state vector* and its components the *state variables*. This terminology comes from the fact that a solution to this final system of four differential equations for the four unknown state variables establishes all remaining variables in the system. Specifically, Eq. (5.2.11) shows $f_3(t)$ as an explicit function of two of the state variables. All other variables in the system are shown as explicit functions of the state variables and $f_3(t)$ by the graph equations. Thus, the dynamic performance of the mechanical system is completely determined by the properties of the solution to the state equations. The state equations, along with the algebraic equations showing other variables in the system as functions of the state vector, are called a *state model* of the system.

Numerical methods for realizing solutions to the state equations of the general form given in the above example and interpretation of the solutions in terms of the dynamic performance of the system are considered systematically in a later section. Analytical procedures are considered in the next chapter. Our concern for the present is the relationship between the state equations and the structure of relatively simple systems. More complex systems are considered in Chap. 8.

To describe the methodology used in developing the state equations of the mechanical system in Example 5.2.1, let the set of $v - 1$ across variables associated with the edges of a tree T and the set of $e - v + 1$ through variables associated with a cotree T' of a system graph be identified as a set of *primary variables* of the system graph, and their complement as *secondary* variables. By use of this terminology, it can be said that the tree T and its complement T' in the system graph were selected in such a way that:

1.   The terminal equations for the components with algebraic equations show primary variables as explicit functions of secondary variables and/or the independent variable t.
2.   The terminal equations for the remaining (dynamic) components show the time derivatives of primary variables as explicit functions of secondary variables.

It is to be noted that, since an algebraic terminal equation can be inverted, one may, if the topology of the graph permits, classify the corresponding edge of the system graph as either a branch or a chord. On the other hand, if the component is an ideal driver (for which the through or across variable is given as an explicit function of time only), the corresponding edge will, as a part of this development, be classified exclusively in one way, depending on the type of driver the edge represents. That is, every cotree T' selected in the system graph will include all edges corresponding to the through drivers, and every tree T will include all edges corresponding to the across drivers.

It should be noted that, if the edges corresponding to the through drivers cannot be included in a cotree, then from Theorem 4.2.4 it follows that they from a cut set. Also if the edges corresponding to across drivers cannot be included in a tree, then from Theorem 4.2.2 they form a circuit. Since the driving functions are independently specified functions of time, cut sets of through drivers and circuits of across drivers are, in general, in direct violation of the cut-set and circuit postulates. If a system of two-terminal components contains no cut sets of through drivers and no circuits of across drivers, then it is said to be a *consistent system.*

If the topology of the system graph is such that it is possible to find a tree and cotree in the system graph for which the terminal equations can be written explicitly in the primary variables or their time derivatives as indicated above, then the system is consistent and the simple procedure for developing the state equations demonstrated in the above example is applicable. However, as the following example demonstrates, the structure of the system may be such that a tree having the above properties does not exist.

Example 5.2.2: Derive a set of state equations for the electrical network given in Fig. 5.2.2.

Solution: The given network contains a circuit of edges (1,4,7) corresponding to a voltage driver and two capacitors and a cut set of edges (3,6,8) corresponding to a current driver and two inductors. Therefore, with the across driver in the tree and the through driver in the cotree, all capacitors cannot be included in a tree and all inductors cannot be included in a cotree; i.e., it is not possible to find a tree and cotree in the graph for which the dynamic equations can be written explicitly in the time derivatives of the primary variables. In this case, a formulation tree is selected which contains the edges corresponding to the voltage source and one capacitor as branches and the edges corresponding to the current source and one inductor as chords. Such a tree is indicated in heavy lines in Fig. 5.2.2b.

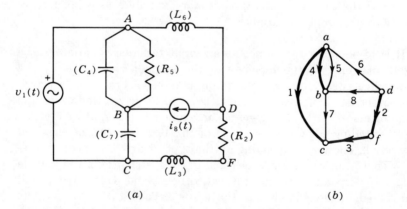

(a)   (b)

Fig. 5.2.2 (a) An electrical network; (b) system graph with a formulation tree.

The component equations can be written in the form

$$\frac{d}{dt}\begin{bmatrix} v_4(t) \\ i_6(t) \end{bmatrix} = \begin{bmatrix} 1/C_4 & 0 \\ 0 & 1/L_6 \end{bmatrix}\begin{bmatrix} i_4(t) \\ v_6(t) \end{bmatrix} \tag{5.2.13}$$

$$\begin{bmatrix} i_7(t) \\ v_3(t) \\ v_2(t) \\ i_5(t) \end{bmatrix} = \begin{bmatrix} C_7(d/dt) & 0 & 0 & 0 \\ 0 & L_3(d/dt) & 0 & 0 \\ 0 & 0 & R_2 & 0 \\ 0 & 0 & 0 & G_5 \end{bmatrix}\begin{bmatrix} v_7(t) \\ i_3(t) \\ i_2(t) \\ v_5(t) \end{bmatrix} \tag{5.2.14}$$

$$\begin{aligned} v_1(t) &= \text{specified function of time} \\ i_8(t) &= \text{specified function of time} \end{aligned} \tag{5.2.15}$$

Note that these equations are again explicit in the primary variables or their time derivatives. Following the same procedure used in the previous example, we first eliminate all secondary variables (branch through and chord across variables) from the component terminal equations using the appropriate circuit and cutset equations for the indicated tree. The required relations are, of course, conveniently obtained by direct reference to the graph. Referring to Eq. (5.2.13), for example, we have immediately from the graph

$$i_4(t) = -i_8(t) - i_5(t) + i_7(t)$$

Upon applying the constraint equations of the system graph to the terminal equations there results

$$\frac{d}{dt}\begin{bmatrix} v_4(t) \\ i_6(t) \end{bmatrix} = \begin{bmatrix} 1/C_4 & 0 & 0 & -1/C_4 \\ 0 & 1/L_6 & 1/L_6 & 0 \end{bmatrix}\begin{bmatrix} i_7(t) \\ v_3(t) \\ v_2(t) \\ i_5(t) \end{bmatrix}$$

$$+ \begin{bmatrix} 0 & -1/C_4 \\ -1/L_6 & 0 \end{bmatrix}\begin{bmatrix} v_1(t) \\ i_8(t) \end{bmatrix} \tag{5.2.16}$$

and

$$\begin{bmatrix} i_7(t) \\ v_3(t) \\ v_2(t) \\ i_5(t) \end{bmatrix} = \begin{bmatrix} -C_7(d/dt) & 0 \\ 0 & -L_3(d/dt) \\ 0 & -R_2 \\ G_5 & 0 \end{bmatrix}\begin{bmatrix} v_4(t) \\ i_6(t) \end{bmatrix}$$

$$+ \begin{bmatrix} C_7(d/dt) & 0 \\ 0 & -L_3(d/dt) \\ 0 & -R_2 \\ 0 & 0 \end{bmatrix}\begin{bmatrix} v_i(t) \\ i_8(t) \end{bmatrix} \tag{5.2.17}$$

The state equations for the system are obtained by substituting Eq. (5.2.17) into Eq. (5.2.16) and solving for the state vector. The result of the first operation is

$$\begin{bmatrix} 1 + C_7/C_4 & 0 \\ 0 & 1 + L_3/L_6 \end{bmatrix}\frac{d}{dt}\begin{bmatrix} v_4(t) \\ i_6(t) \end{bmatrix} = \begin{bmatrix} -G_5/C_4 & 0 \\ 0 & -R_2/L_6 \end{bmatrix}\begin{bmatrix} v_4(t) \\ i_6(t) \end{bmatrix}$$

$$+ \begin{bmatrix} 0 & -1/C_4 \\ -1/L_6 & -R_2/L_6 \end{bmatrix}\begin{bmatrix} v_1(t) \\ i_8(t) \end{bmatrix} - \begin{bmatrix} C_7/C_4 & 0 \\ 0 & -L_3/L_6 \end{bmatrix}\begin{bmatrix} (d/dt)\ v_1(t) \\ (d/dt)\ i_8(t) \end{bmatrix} \tag{5.2.18}$$

Solving for the state vector $[v_4(t), i_6(t)]$ gives

$$\frac{d}{dt} \begin{bmatrix} v_4(t) \\ i_6(t) \end{bmatrix} = \begin{bmatrix} -G_5/(C_4 + C_7) & 0 \\ 0 & -R_2/(L_3 + L_6) \end{bmatrix} \begin{bmatrix} v_4(t) \\ i_6(t) \end{bmatrix}$$

$$+ \begin{bmatrix} 0 & -1/(C_4 + C_7) \\ -1/(L_3 + L_6) & -R_2/(L_3 + L_6) \end{bmatrix} \begin{bmatrix} v_1(t) \\ i_8(t) \end{bmatrix}$$

$$+ \begin{bmatrix} C_7/(C_4 + C_7) & 0 \\ 0 & -L_3/(L_3 + L_6) \end{bmatrix} \frac{d}{dt} \begin{bmatrix} v_1(t) \\ i_8(t) \end{bmatrix} \quad (5.2.19)$$

Several points are to be noted in conjunction with the above:

1. The state vector contains a subset of the primary variables corresponding to the chosen tree. All other unknown variables, including those of the capacitor and inductor which would not go, respectively, into the tree and its complement, are eliminated by the graph equations.

2. The resulting state equations call for the driving functions and their derivatives. Among other things, this implies that the driving functions must be differentiable in the interval of time over which the system model applies. This point is discussed in more detail in Sec. 6.1.

3. The inverse of a coefficient matrix is required in the final step in the development of the state equations. Although, in the example given, the inverse obviously exists for all finite values of C_7 and L_3, the question arises as to whether or not this inverse exists in all cases. The existence of this inverse is established by a general theorem, to be given subsequently.

The tree T and its complement T' selected as a basis for developing the state equations in this second example can be described as satisfying the following two simple conditions:

1. In the algebraic component equations, the primary variables are expressed as explicit functions of secondary variables and/or the independent variable t.

2. In a *maximum number* of the terminal equations for the dynamic components, the time derivatives of primary variables are expressed as explicit functions of secondary variables.

A tree T and cotree T' satisfying these two conditions are hereafter referred to as a *maximally selected* tree and cotree. The tree selected in Example 5.2.1 is, by this definition, a maximally selected tree, since both mass components are included as branches and both spring components are included as chords.

It is entirely possible for the structure of the system to be such that a maximally selected tree and cotree contain *no dynamic* elements for which the equations are written explicitly in the derivatives of the primary variables. It follows from a development similar to that in the two examples given so far that the state vector for such a system is of zero order, i.e., the system is characterized by algebraic equations only.

If a system of two-terminal components is consistent, i.e., if it contains no circuits of across drivers or cut sets of through drivers, it is always possible to find a *tree* and *cotree*† for which the algebraic equations can be written explicitly in the primary variables and the system can be characterized by a set of state equations (possibly of zero order) as established by the following theorem.

Theorem 5.2.1: Let a system contain only two-terminal components each of which is either a specified driver or is a passive component modeled by a linear algebraic or differential equation of one of the three types

$$x(t) = ay(t)$$
$$x(t) = b\frac{dy(t)}{dt}$$

(5.2.20)

or

$$y(t) = c\frac{dx(t)}{dt}$$

where

$x(t)$ and $y(t)$ represent across and through variables, respectively
a, b, and c represent positive real constants

If the edges in the system graph corresponding to the across drivers do not form circuits and the edges corresponding to through drivers do not form cut sets, then the system state is characterized by a set of differential equations in normal form.

Proof: For general reference, we shall refer to these components as a elements, b elements, and c elements, with the understanding, of course, that each corresponds to a specific kind of element in electrical, mechanical, and hydraulic systems.

Let the across and through variables associated with the edges of an arbitrary tree T be designated by the vectors $\mathbf{X}_T$ and $\mathbf{Y}_T$. If the vectors $\mathbf{\Psi}_p = (\mathbf{X}_T, \mathbf{Y}_T')$ and $\mathbf{\Psi}_s = (\mathbf{X}_T', \mathbf{Y}_T)$ represent, respectively, the primary and the secondary variables corresponding to the tree T and the cotree T', it is possible, by proper partitioning of these vectors, to write the direct sum of the terminal equations for the components in the form

$$\mathbf{\Psi}_{p_0} = \text{specified functions of time} \tag{5.2.21}$$

$$\frac{d}{dt}\mathbf{\Psi}_{p_1} = \mathbf{D}_1\mathbf{\Psi}_{s_1} \tag{5.2.22}$$

† A system of two-terminal components of necessity has a connected system graph.

and

$$\begin{bmatrix} \boldsymbol{\Psi}_{p_2} \\ \boldsymbol{\Psi}_{p_3} \end{bmatrix} = \begin{bmatrix} \mathbf{D}_2(d/dt) & \mathbf{0} \\ \mathbf{0} & \mathbf{D}_3 \end{bmatrix} \begin{bmatrix} \boldsymbol{\Psi}_{s_2} \\ \boldsymbol{\Psi}_{s_3} \end{bmatrix} \tag{5.2.23}$$

Although it is not evident from the development so far, we shall see later that the vector $\boldsymbol{\Psi}_{p_1}$ represents the state vector of the system. The matrices $\mathbf{D}_i$ ($i = 1, 2, 3$) in Eqs. (5.2.22) and (5.2.23) are all diagonal, with positive diagonal entries, and $\mathbf{D}_3$ corresponds to the type a elements.

The vectors of primary variables $\boldsymbol{\Psi}_{p_i}$, $i = 0, 1, 2, 3$, contain exactly one variable for each edge of the graph and are identified with the across and through variables of the various components. The vectors of secondary variables $\boldsymbol{\Psi}_{s_i}$, $i = 0, 1, 2, 3$, likewise contain exactly one variable for each edge of the graph and represent the complementary variables of the respective primary vectors. The circuit and cut-set equations of the system graph for any tree T' can be written in the form

$$\begin{bmatrix} \boldsymbol{\Psi}_{s_0} \\ \boldsymbol{\Psi}_{s_1} \\ \boldsymbol{\Psi}_{s_2} \\ \boldsymbol{\Psi}_{s_3} \end{bmatrix} + \begin{bmatrix} \boldsymbol{\Phi}_{01} & \boldsymbol{\Phi}_{02} & \boldsymbol{\Phi}_{03} \\ \boldsymbol{\Phi}_{11} & \boldsymbol{\Phi}_{12} & \boldsymbol{\Phi}_{13} \\ \boldsymbol{\Phi}_{21} & \boldsymbol{\Phi}_{22} & \boldsymbol{\Phi}_{23} \\ \boldsymbol{\Phi}_{31} & \boldsymbol{\Phi}_{32} & \boldsymbol{\Phi}_{33} \end{bmatrix} \begin{bmatrix} \boldsymbol{\Psi}_{p_1} \\ \boldsymbol{\Psi}_{p_2} \\ \boldsymbol{\Psi}_{p_3} \end{bmatrix} + \begin{bmatrix} \boldsymbol{\Phi}_{00} \\ \boldsymbol{\Phi}_{10} \\ \boldsymbol{\Phi}_{20} \\ \boldsymbol{\Phi}_{30} \end{bmatrix} \boldsymbol{\Psi}_{p_0} = \mathbf{0} \tag{5.2.24}$$

where each one of the submatrices $\boldsymbol{\Phi}_{ij}$ has the form

$$\boldsymbol{\Phi}_{ij} = \begin{bmatrix} \mathbf{0} & \mathbf{A}_{ij} \\ \mathbf{B}_{ij} & \mathbf{0} \end{bmatrix} \qquad i, j = 0, 1, 2, 3$$

A maximally selected tree and cotree by definition include a maximum number of edges corresponding to c-type elements in T and a maximum number of edges corresponding to b-type elements in T'. We shall now show that, for such a tree, certain of the submatrices in Eq. (5.2.24) are identically zero and that the vector of primary variables $\boldsymbol{\Psi}_{p_1}$ identified with the tree and cotree represents the state vector of the system.

A systematic procedure for identifying a maximally selected tree in the system graph G is based on a sequence of subgraphs of the system graph selected as follows:

1.　　Consider a subgraph G_1 of G consisting of all the edges corresponding to across drivers. Select a tree T_1 in G_1.† By a hypothesis of the theorem, the across drivers form no circuits. Consequently, in G_1 the complement T_1' of T_1 contains no edges.

2.　　Consider a subgraph G_2 of G consisting of all the edges in G_1 and the edges corresponding to type c elements. Select a tree T_2 in G_2 containing T_1. In G_2, the complement of T_2 contains at most

† If a subgraph G_i ($i = 1, 2, 3, 4$) is not connected, a tree T_i in G_i, of course, does not exist; in this case, a forest T_i is selected.

edges corresponding to type c elements, i.e., the edges associated with the across variables in Ψ_{s_2} or the through variables in Ψ_{p_2}.

3. Consider a subgraph G_3 of G consisting of all the edges in G_2 and the edges corresponding to the type a elements, i.e., the edges corresponding to the variables in Ψ_{p_3}. Select a tree T_3 in G_3 containing T_2. In G_3 the complement T_3' of T_3 contains at most edges corresponding to type c and type a elements, i.e., the edges corresponding to the across variables in Ψ_{s_2} and Ψ_{p_3}, respectively.

4. Consider a subgraph G_4 of G consisting of all the edges in G_3 and the edges corresponding to type b elements. Select a tree T_4 in G_4 which includes T_3. In G_4, the complement T_4' includes, at most, edges corresponding to type c, a, and b elements, i.e., edges corresponding to the across variables in Ψ_{s_2}, Ψ_{s_3}, and Ψ_{s_1}, respectively.

5. Consider the entire graph G. Select a tree $T_5 = T$ which includes T_4. Since, by hypothesis, the graph contains no cut sets of edges corresponding only to through drivers, $T_5' = T_4' = T'$ and the maximally selected tree and cotree have been identified.

From the second step in selecting the tree, it is evident that the fundamental circuits defined by T_2' span only those edges of the graph that are contained in T_2. It thus follows that the fundamental circuit equations introduce only zero entries in Φ_{22} and Φ_{23}, that is, $\mathbf{B}_{22} = 0$, $\mathbf{B}_{23} = 0$. Likewise the circuits defined by the edges of T_3' span only those edges of the graph contained in T_3, and the fundamental circuit equations can introduce only zero entries in Φ_{32}, that is, $\mathbf{B}_{32} = 0$.

From step 4, it follows that the cut sets defined by the edges of T_4 corresponding to type b elements contain only those edges corresponding to type b elements and specified through drivers. It follows, therefore, that the fundamental cut-set equations introduce only zero entries in Φ_{22} and Φ_{23}, that is, $\mathbf{A}_{22} = 0$, $\mathbf{A}_{23} = 0$, and we conclude that $\Phi_{22} = 0$ and $\Phi_{23} = 0$. Likewise, since the cut sets defined by the edges of T_3 do not include edges corresponding to through variables in Ψ_{p_1}, it follows that $\Phi_{32} = 0$.

The state equations for the system are developed by substituting Eq. (5.2.24) into Eqs. (5.2.22) and (5.2.23) with $\Phi_{22} = 0$, $\Phi_{23} = 0$, and $\Phi_{32} = 0$. The results are

$$\frac{d}{dt}\Psi_{p_1} = -\mathbf{D}_1[\Phi_{12} \quad \Phi_{13}]\begin{bmatrix} \Psi_{p_2} \\ \Psi_{p_3} \end{bmatrix} - \mathbf{D}_1\Phi_{11}\Psi_{p_1} - \mathbf{D}_1\Phi_{10}\Psi_{p_0} \quad (5.2.25)$$

and

$$\begin{bmatrix} \mathbf{U} & 0 \\ 0 & \mathbf{U} + \mathbf{D}_3\Phi_{33} \end{bmatrix}\begin{bmatrix} \Psi_{p_2} \\ \Psi_{p_3} \end{bmatrix} = -\begin{bmatrix} \mathbf{D}_2\Phi_{21}(d/dt) \\ \mathbf{D}_3\Phi_{31} \end{bmatrix}\Psi_{p_1} - \begin{bmatrix} \mathbf{D}_2\Phi_{20}(d/dt) \\ \mathbf{D}_3\Phi_{30} \end{bmatrix}\Psi_{p_0} \quad (5.2.26)$$

If the coefficient matrix to the left of the equality sign in Eq. (5.2.26) is nonsingular, then Eq. (5.2.26) can be solved explicitly for $\mathbf{\Psi}_{p_2}$ and $\mathbf{\Psi}_{p_3}$. The result is

$$\begin{bmatrix} \mathbf{\Psi}_{p_2} \\ \mathbf{\Psi}_{p_3} \end{bmatrix} = - \begin{bmatrix} \mathbf{D}_2\mathbf{\Phi}_{21}(d/dt) & \mathbf{D}_2\mathbf{\Phi}_{20}(d/dt) \\ \mathbf{M}_{21} & \mathbf{M}_{22} \end{bmatrix} \begin{bmatrix} \mathbf{\Psi}_{p_1} \\ \mathbf{\Psi}_{p_0} \end{bmatrix} \tag{5.2.27}$$

where

$$\mathbf{M}_{21} = (\mathbf{U} + \mathbf{D}_3\mathbf{\Phi}_{33})^{-1}\mathbf{D}_3\mathbf{\Phi}_{31} \tag{5.2.28}$$
$$\mathbf{M}_{22} = (\mathbf{U} + \mathbf{D}_3\mathbf{\Phi}_{33})^{-1}\mathbf{D}_3\mathbf{\Phi}_{30} \tag{5.2.29}$$

Substituting the indicated solution in Eq. (5.2.27) into Eq. (5.2.25) gives a system of differential equations of the form

$$(\mathbf{U} - \mathbf{D}_1\mathbf{\Phi}_{12}\mathbf{D}_2\mathbf{\Phi}_{21})\frac{d}{dt}\mathbf{\Psi}_{p_1} = \mathbf{N}_1\mathbf{\Psi}_{p_1} + \mathbf{N}_2\mathbf{\Psi}_{p_0} + \mathbf{N}_3\frac{d}{dt}\mathbf{\Psi}_{p_0} \tag{5.2.30}$$

These equations can be reduced to normal form if the coefficient matrix on the vector $(d/dt)\mathbf{\Psi}_{p_1}$ is nonsingular. Thus, a set of state equations is obtainable if and only if the coefficient matrices to the left of the equality signs in Eqs. (5.2.26) and (5.2.30) are nonsingular. That these coefficient matrices are indeed nonsingular is established by use of the following lemma from matrix algebra, the proof of which is given in the Appendix.

Lemma 5.2.1:   Let $\mathbf{D}_1$ and $\mathbf{D}_2$ be diagonal matrices of order m and n, respectively, with all positive diagonal entries, and let $\mathbf{P}$ be a rectangular matrix of order $m \times n$; then the matrix

$$\mathbf{D}_1 + \mathbf{P}\mathbf{D}_2\mathbf{P}^T$$

is nonsingular.

To show that $\mathbf{U} + \mathbf{D}_3\mathbf{\Phi}_{33}$ is nonsingular, observe that $\mathbf{D}_{33}$ is a diagonal matrix and

$$\mathbf{\Phi}_{33} = \begin{bmatrix} \mathbf{0} & \mathbf{A}_{33} \\ \mathbf{B}_{33} & \mathbf{0} \end{bmatrix}$$

where $\mathbf{A}_{33}$ and $\mathbf{B}_{33}$ are submatrices of the fundamental cut set and circuit matrices and $\mathbf{B}_{33} = -\mathbf{A}_{33}^T$. The coefficient matrix under consideration after the partitioning can therefore be written as

$$\begin{aligned}
\mathbf{U} + \mathbf{D}_3\mathbf{\Phi}_{33} &= \begin{bmatrix} \mathbf{U} & \mathbf{0} \\ \mathbf{0} & \mathbf{U} \end{bmatrix} + \begin{bmatrix} \mathbf{D}_3' & \mathbf{0} \\ \mathbf{0} & \mathbf{D}_3'' \end{bmatrix}\begin{bmatrix} \mathbf{0} & \mathbf{A}_{33} \\ -\mathbf{A}_{33}^T & \mathbf{0} \end{bmatrix} \\
&= \begin{bmatrix} \mathbf{U} & \mathbf{D}_3'\mathbf{A}_{33} \\ -\mathbf{D}_3''\mathbf{A}_{33}^T & \mathbf{U} \end{bmatrix} \\
&= \begin{bmatrix} \mathbf{D}_3' & \mathbf{0} \\ \mathbf{0} & \mathbf{D}_3'' \end{bmatrix}\begin{bmatrix} \mathbf{D}_3'^{-1} & \mathbf{A}_{33} \\ -\mathbf{A}_{33}^T & \mathbf{D}_3''^{-1} \end{bmatrix} \tag{5.2.31}
\end{aligned}$$

The first matrix to the right of the equality sign in Eq. (5.2.31) is non-singular, since it is a diagonal matrix with all positive diagonal entries. Let the second matrix be premultiplied by a nonsingular matrix, as shown in Eq. (5.2.32) below.

$$\begin{bmatrix} \mathbf{U} & \mathbf{0} \\ \mathbf{A}_{33}^T\mathbf{D}_3' & \mathbf{U} \end{bmatrix} \begin{bmatrix} \mathbf{D}_3'^{-1} & \mathbf{A}_{33} \\ -\mathbf{A}_{33}^T & \mathbf{D}_3''^{-1} \end{bmatrix} = \begin{bmatrix} \mathbf{D}_3'^{-1} & \mathbf{A}_{33} \\ \mathbf{0} & \mathbf{D}_3''^{-1} + \mathbf{A}_{33}^T\mathbf{D}_3'\mathbf{A}_{33} \end{bmatrix} \quad (5.2.32)$$

From Lemma 5.2.1, it follows that the coefficient matrix $\mathbf{D}_3''^{-1} + \mathbf{A}_{33}^T\mathbf{D}_3'\mathbf{A}_{33}$ is nonsingular and the inverse indicated in Eqs. (5.2.28) and (5.2.29) exists.

Consider now the coefficient matrix $\mathbf{U} - \mathbf{D}_1\mathbf{\Phi}_{12}\mathbf{D}_2\mathbf{\Phi}_{21}$ in Eq. (5.2.30). From the properties of the fundamental circuit and cut-set equations of the system graph, it follows that

$$\mathbf{\Phi}_{12}^T = \begin{bmatrix} \mathbf{0} & \mathbf{A}_{12} \\ \mathbf{B}_{12} & \mathbf{0} \end{bmatrix}^T = \begin{bmatrix} \mathbf{0} & \mathbf{B}_{12}^T \\ \mathbf{A}_{12}^T & \mathbf{0} \end{bmatrix} = -\begin{bmatrix} \mathbf{0} & \mathbf{A}_{21} \\ \mathbf{B}_{21} & \mathbf{0} \end{bmatrix} = -\mathbf{\Phi}_{21}$$

and the coefficient matrix takes on the form

$$\mathbf{D}_1[\mathbf{D}_1^{-1} + \mathbf{\Phi}_{12}\mathbf{D}_2\mathbf{\Phi}_{12}^T]$$

Since $\mathbf{D}_1$ and $\mathbf{D}_2$ are diagonal, it follows from Lemma 5.2.1 that the inverse of the coefficient matrix required to reduce Eq. (5.2.30) to normal form exists. The resulting normal form is

$$\frac{d}{dt}\mathbf{\Psi}_{p_1} = \mathbf{P}\mathbf{\Psi}_{p_1} + \mathbf{Q}_1\mathbf{\Psi}_{p_0} + \mathbf{Q}_2\frac{d}{dt}\mathbf{\Psi}_{p_0} \quad (5.2.33)$$

and the theorem is proved.

The proof of Theorem 5.2.1 also gives a general procedure for generating the state model. The techniques demonstrated in Examples 5.2.1 and 5.2.2 represent special cases of this general procedure.

If the driving functions and their derivatives in Eq. (5.2.33) are continuous over some interval $T_1 < t < T_2$, then the system of first-order differential equations has a unique solution for any given set of initial conditions on the state vector $\mathbf{\Psi}_{p_1}$. Consequently, it can also be concluded that any system of two-terminal components has a unique solution under these same conditions. Note that the number of state equations given as Eq. (5.2.33) is identical in number to the number of component equations in Eq. (5.2.22) and that the state vector represents a subset of the primary variables defined by the maximally selected tree and cotree. It follows, therefore, that the choice of tree determines the variables that will appear in the state vector.

5.3 MORE ON STATE EQUATIONS

As the following two examples show, the procedures for developing the state equations for systems containing multiterminal components are fundamentally the same as those given in the previous section for systems of two-terminal components.

Example 5.3.1: Derive the state equations for the electronic amplifier shown schematically in Fig. 5.3.1a. The characteristics of the output transformer are to be modeled by terminal equations of the form

$$\begin{bmatrix} v_4(t) \\ i_5(t) \end{bmatrix} = \begin{bmatrix} R_4 + L_4(d/dt) & n_{45} \\ -n_{45} & 0 \end{bmatrix} \begin{bmatrix} i_4(t) \\ v_5(t) \end{bmatrix}$$

where L_4 is called the leakage inductance, since it represents the input inductance, with the output short-circuited.

Solution: The system graph is shown in Fig. 5.3.1b. The characteristics of the components in the system are represented by linear equations written as follows:

Source of excitation—edge 1:

$v_1(t)$ = specified function of time

Capacitors—edges 2 and 3:

$$\frac{d}{dt}\begin{bmatrix} v_2(t) \\ v_3(t) \end{bmatrix} = \begin{bmatrix} 1/C_2 & 0 \\ 0 & 1/C_3 \end{bmatrix}\begin{bmatrix} i_2(t) \\ i_3(t) \end{bmatrix} \tag{5.3.1}$$

Transformer—edges 4 and 5:

$$\frac{d}{dt}i_4(t) = \frac{1}{L_4}v_4(t) - \frac{R_4}{L_4}i_4(t) - \frac{n_{45}}{L_4}v_5(t) \tag{5.3.2}$$

$$i_5(t) = -n_{45}i_4(t) \tag{5.3.3}$$

Resistors—edges 6, 7, and 8:

$$\begin{bmatrix} v_6(t) \\ v_7(t) \\ i_8(t) \end{bmatrix} = \begin{bmatrix} R_6 i_6(t) \\ R_7 i_7(t) \\ G_8 v_8(t) \end{bmatrix} \tag{5.3.4}$$

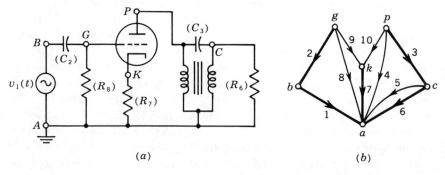

(a)   *(b)*

Fig. 5.3.1 (a) An electronic amplifier circuit; (b) system graph with formulation tree.

Triode—edges 9 and 10:

$$\begin{bmatrix} i_9(t) \\ i_{10}(t) \end{bmatrix} = \begin{bmatrix} 0 & 0 \\ g_m & g_p \end{bmatrix} \begin{bmatrix} v_9(t) \\ v_{10}(t) \end{bmatrix} \tag{5.3.5}$$

Note that, as in the case of systems of two-terminal components, the tree and cotree as identified in Fig. 5.3.1b for formulating the state equations are maximally selected; i.e., all the algebraic terminal equations for the components are explicit in the primary variables, and as many as possible (in this case all) differential equations are explicit in the derivatives.

The circuit and cut-set equations of the system graph are now used to eliminate all secondary variables from the component terminal equations. The direct sum of the resulting equations is

$$\frac{d}{dt}\begin{bmatrix} v_2(t) \\ v_3(t) \\ i_4(t) \end{bmatrix} = \begin{bmatrix} 0 & 0 \\ 0 & -1/C_3 \\ 1/L_4 & -R_4/L_4 \end{bmatrix}\begin{bmatrix} v_3(t) \\ i_4(t) \end{bmatrix}$$

$$+ \begin{bmatrix} 0 & -1/C_2 & -1/C_2 & 0 \\ 0 & 0 & 0 & -1/C_3 \\ (1-n_{45})/L_4 & 0 & 0 & 0 \end{bmatrix}\begin{bmatrix} v_6(t) \\ i_8(t) \\ i_9(t) \\ i_{10}(t) \end{bmatrix} \tag{5.3.6}$$

$$i_5(t) = -n_{45}i_4(t) \tag{5.3.7}$$

$$\begin{bmatrix} 1 & 0 & \vdots & 0 & 0 & R_6 \\ 0 & 1 & \vdots & 0 & -R_7 & -R_7 \\ \cdots & & & & & \\ 0 & 0 & \vdots & 1 & 0 & 0 \\ 0 & 0 & \vdots & 0 & 1 & 0 \\ -g_p & g_m+g_p & \vdots & 0 & 0 & 1 \end{bmatrix}\begin{bmatrix} v_6(t) \\ v_7(t) \\ \cdots \\ i_8(t) \\ i_9(t) \\ i_{10}(t) \end{bmatrix}$$

$$= \begin{bmatrix} 0 \\ 0 \\ \cdots \\ G_8 \\ 0 \\ g_m \end{bmatrix}v_1(t) + \begin{bmatrix} 0 & 0 & \vdots & -R_6 & -R_6 \\ 0 & 0 & \vdots & 0 & 0 \\ \cdots & & & & \\ G_8 & 0 & \vdots & 0 & 0 \\ 0 & 0 & \vdots & 0 & 0 \\ g_m & g_p & \vdots & 0 & 0 \end{bmatrix}\begin{bmatrix} v_2(t) \\ v_3(t) \\ \cdots \\ i_4(t) \\ i_5(t) \end{bmatrix} \tag{5.3.8}$$

This system of equations, of course, involves only the primary variables for the selected tree and cotree. The required state equations are realized when the algebraic equations are eliminated from this set.

The coefficient matrix of order 5 to the left of Eq. (5.3.8) is nonsingular, and the solution as obtained by premultiplying both sides by the inverse of this coefficient matrix is

$$\begin{bmatrix} v_6(t) \\ v_7(t) \\ i_8(t) \\ i_9(t) \\ i_{10}(t) \end{bmatrix} = \begin{bmatrix} -g_m R_6 \alpha \\ g_m R_7 \alpha \\ G_8 \\ 0 \\ g_m \alpha \end{bmatrix}v_1(t)$$

$$+ \begin{bmatrix} -g_m R_6 \alpha & -g_p R_6 \alpha & -R_6(1-g_p R_6 \alpha) & -R_6(1-g_p R_6 \alpha) \\ g_m R_7 \alpha & g_p R_7 \alpha & -g_p R_6 R_7 \alpha & -g_p R_6 R_7 \alpha \\ G_8 & 0 & 0 & 0 \\ 0 & 0 & 0 & 0 \\ g_m \alpha & g_p \alpha & -g_p R_6 \alpha & -g_p R_6 \alpha \end{bmatrix}\begin{bmatrix} v_2(t) \\ v_3(t) \\ i_4(t) \\ i_5(t) \end{bmatrix} \tag{5.3.9}$$

where $\alpha = [g_p R_6 + (g_m + g_p) R_7]^{-1}$ and $i_5(t)$ is given as a function of the state variable, $i_4(t)$, by Eq. (5.3.7). Substituting Eq. (5.3.7) into Eq. (5.3.9) and this result into Eq. (5.3.6) establishes the state equations of the system. The result is

$$\frac{d}{dt} \begin{bmatrix} v_2(t) \\ v_3(t) \\ i_4(t) \end{bmatrix} =$$

$$\begin{bmatrix} -G_8/C_2 & 0 & 0 \\ -g_m\alpha/C_3 & -g_p\alpha/C_3 & -(1 - Kg_p R_6\alpha)/C_3 \\ -Kg_m R_6\alpha/L_4 & [(1 - Kg_p R_6\alpha)/L_4](-R_6/L_4) & [-R_4 - K^2 R_6(1 - g_p R_6\alpha)]/L_4 \end{bmatrix}$$

$$\times \begin{bmatrix} v_2(t) \\ v_3(t) \\ i_4(t) \end{bmatrix} - \begin{bmatrix} G_8/C_2 \\ g_m\alpha/C_3 \\ Kg_m R_6\alpha/L_4 \end{bmatrix} v_1(t) \quad (5.3.10)$$

where $K = 1 - n_{45}$.

In the above example, it was relatively easy to find a tree and cotree such that all the algebraic equations could be written explicitly in the primary variables and all the dynamic equations explicitly in the time derivatives of the primary variables. As soon as such a tree and cotree are found, the tree is known to be maximal. However, if the selected tree and cotree do not include all the edges with appropriate dynamic equations, then many combinations of proposed trees and forms of component equations may have to be considered before one can be sure that a maximally selected tree has been identified. For example, if the topology of the system graph in Fig. 5.3.1 is such that edges 9 and 10 cannot both be included in the same cotree, then from the form of Eq. (5.3.5) it is evident that the second equation can be inverted and edge 10 can, correspondingly, be included as an edge of the tree. Since $i_9(t) \equiv 0$, edge 9, as a part of this development, would be included as an edge in a cotree. Similarly, we see from the given form of Eq. (5.3.3) that *either* edge 4 *or* edge 5 would be included in every candidate cotree. From Eq. (5.3.2) *either* edge 4 *or* edge 5 can be included in a tree, if the topology demands, since it is possible to express the equation explicitly in either $v_4(t)$ or $v_5(t)$ as well as in the form given. Note, however, that, if the topology is such that a tree containing either of these edges is *maximal* in the sense defined earlier, then $i_4(t)$ will not appear in the state vector.

In the case of systems of two-terminal components, a maximally selected tree and cotree can be obtained systematically by following the procedure given in the proof of Theorem 5.2.1. In the case of systems of multiterminal components there is at present no such simple and systematic procedure available. A fundamental theorem presented in Chap. 8 does, however, establish the existence of a maximally selected tree, and its associated corollaries provide direction for identifying a maximally selected tree and cotree for large classes of systems. Further discussion of this subject falls within the realm of advanced modeling theory and accordingly is deferred to a later chapter.

Before proceeding to the subject of solution of state equations, we demonstrate, by means of an example, the application of the concepts discussed so far in this chapter to developing state equations for nonlinear systems.

Example 5.3.2: The network shown in Fig. 5.3.2 represents a basic configuration used in d-c power-supply design. The sinusoidal output signal of the transformer is rectified and then "smoothed" by means of the filter connected between the output of the rectifier and the load conductance g_7. In the design of such a power supply, it is required to predict the values of the maximum voltages that occur across the diodes if, for example, the load resistance suddenly goes to zero as in the case of an accidental short circuit at the load terminals. This information, of course, must be obtained from a solution to the mathematical model of the system, which we shall now develop.

Solution: The mathematical models of the system components are taken as follows:

Transformer—edges 0, 1, and 2:

$$\begin{bmatrix} i_0 \\ v_1 \\ v_2 \end{bmatrix} = \begin{bmatrix} 0 & -n & -n \\ n & R_{11} & R_{12} \\ n & R_{12} & R_{22} \end{bmatrix} \begin{bmatrix} v_0 \\ i_1 \\ i_2 \end{bmatrix} + \begin{bmatrix} 0 & 0 \\ L_{11} & L_{12} \\ L_{12} & L_{22} \end{bmatrix} \frac{d}{dt} \begin{bmatrix} i_1 \\ i_2 \end{bmatrix}$$

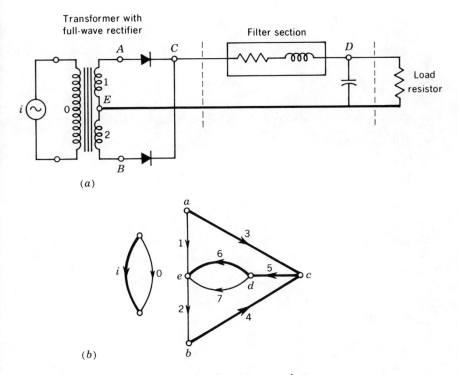

Fig. 5.3.2 (a) Typical power supply; (b) system graph.

where hereafter it is assumed that $R_{11} = R_{22} = R_1$ and that $L_{11} = L_{22} = L_1$. In normal form the equations are

$$\frac{d}{dt}\begin{bmatrix} i_1 \\ i_2 \end{bmatrix} = \begin{bmatrix} \tau_1 & \tau_{12} \\ \tau_{12} & \tau_1 \end{bmatrix}\begin{bmatrix} i_1 \\ i_2 \end{bmatrix} + \begin{bmatrix} n(\Gamma_{11} + \Gamma_{12}) & -\Gamma_{11} & -\Gamma_{12} \\ n(\Gamma_{11} + \Gamma_{12}) & -\Gamma_{12} & -\Gamma_{11} \end{bmatrix}\begin{bmatrix} v_0 \\ v_1 \\ v_2 \end{bmatrix}$$

$$i_0 = -[n \quad n]\begin{bmatrix} i_1 \\ i_2 \end{bmatrix}$$

where

$$\begin{bmatrix} \Gamma_{11} & \Gamma_{12} \\ \Gamma_{12} & \Gamma_{11} \end{bmatrix} = -\begin{bmatrix} L_1 & L_{12} \\ L_{12} & L_1 \end{bmatrix}^{-1} \quad \text{and} \quad \begin{bmatrix} \tau_1 & \tau_{12} \\ \tau_{12} & \tau_1 \end{bmatrix} = \begin{bmatrix} \Gamma_{11} & \Gamma_{12} \\ \Gamma_{12} & \Gamma_{11} \end{bmatrix}\begin{bmatrix} R_1 & R_{12} \\ R_{12} & R_1 \end{bmatrix}$$

or, more explicitly,

$$\Gamma_{11} = \frac{-L_1}{L_1^2 - L_{12}^2}$$

$$\Gamma_{12} = \frac{L_{12}}{L_1^2 - L_{12}^2}$$

$$\tau_1 = \Gamma_{11}R_1 + \Gamma_{12}R_{12}$$

$$\tau_{12} = \Gamma_{11}R_{12} + \Gamma_{12}R_1$$

Diodes—edges 3 and 4:

$$i_j = G_j(v_j) = I_j(e^{k_j v_j} - 1) \qquad j = 3, 4$$

or, inverting,

$$v_j = f_j(i_j) = \frac{1}{k_j} \ln \frac{i_j + I_j}{I_j} \qquad j = 3, 4$$

where I_j and k_j are constants, depending on the particular diode used.

Inductor—edge 5:

$$\frac{d}{dt} i_5 = \tau_5 i_5 + \Gamma_5 v_5$$

where

$$\tau_5 = -\frac{R_5}{L_5} \qquad \Gamma_5 = \frac{1}{L_5}$$

Capacitor—edge 6:

$$\frac{d}{dt} v_6 = \frac{1}{C_6} i_6$$

Load resistor—edge 7:

$$i_7 = g_7 v_7$$

For reference in developing the state equations of the system, let the component equations be compiled into two sets as follows:

$$\frac{d}{dt}\begin{bmatrix} i_1 \\ i_2 \\ v_6 \end{bmatrix} = \begin{bmatrix} \tau_1 & \tau_{12} \\ \tau_{12} & \tau_1 \\ 0 & 0 \end{bmatrix}\begin{bmatrix} i_1 \\ i_2 \end{bmatrix} + \begin{bmatrix} -\Gamma_{11} & -\Gamma_{12} & 0 \\ -\Gamma_{12} & -\Gamma_{11} & 0 \\ 0 & 0 & 1/C_6 \end{bmatrix}\begin{bmatrix} v_1 \\ v_2 \\ i_6 \end{bmatrix}$$
$$+ \begin{bmatrix} (\Gamma_{11}+\Gamma_{12})n \\ (\Gamma_{11}+\Gamma_{12})n \\ 0 \end{bmatrix} v_0 \quad (5.3.11)$$

and

$$\begin{bmatrix} i_0 \\ i_7 \\ v_3 \\ v_4 \\ v_5 \end{bmatrix} = \begin{bmatrix} -n(i_1+i_2) \\ g_7 v_7 \\ (1/k_3)\ln[(i_3+I_3)/I_3] \\ (1/k_4)\ln[(i_4+I_4)/I_4] \\ [R_5+L_5(d/dt)]i_5 \end{bmatrix} \quad (5.3.12)$$

These equations are explicit in the primary variables of the maximally selected tree and cotree indicated in Fig. 5.3.2. Note that it is not possible to find a cotree which includes all edges corresponding to the inductor-type elements. It is therefore established that the order of the state vector is 3.

Applying the constraint equations of the system graph to the component equations given in Eqs. (5.3.11) and (5.3.12) gives

$$\frac{d}{dt}\begin{bmatrix} i_1 \\ i_2 \\ v_6 \end{bmatrix} = \begin{bmatrix} \tau_1 & \tau_{12} & -(\Gamma_{11}-\Gamma_{12}) \\ \tau_{12} & \tau_1 & \Gamma_{11}-\Gamma_{12} \\ -1/C_6 & 1/C_6 & 0 \end{bmatrix}\begin{bmatrix} i_1 \\ i_2 \\ v_6 \end{bmatrix}$$
$$+ \begin{bmatrix} 0 & -\Gamma_{11} & \Gamma_{12} & -(\Gamma_{11}-\Gamma_{12}) \\ 0 & -\Gamma_{12} & \Gamma_{11} & \Gamma_{11}-\Gamma_{12} \\ -1/C_6 & 0 & 0 & 0 \end{bmatrix}\begin{bmatrix} i_7 \\ v_3 \\ v_4 \\ v_5 \end{bmatrix} + \begin{bmatrix} n(\Gamma_{11}+\Gamma_{12}) \\ n(\Gamma_{11}+\Gamma_{12}) \\ 0 \end{bmatrix} v_0 \quad (5.3.13)$$

and

$$\begin{bmatrix} i_0 \\ i_7 \\ v_3 \\ v_4 \\ v_5 \end{bmatrix} = \begin{bmatrix} -n(i_1+i_2) \\ g_7 v_6 \\ (1/k_3)\ln[(-i_1+I_3)/I_3] \\ (1/k_4)\ln[(i_2+I_4)/I_4] \\ [R_5+L_5(d/dt)](i_2-i_1) \end{bmatrix} \quad (5.3.14)$$

The state equations are obtained by substituting Eq. (5.3.14) into Eq. (5.3.13). The result is

$$\begin{bmatrix} 1-\Gamma_s L_5 & \Gamma_s L_5 & 0 \\ \Gamma_s L_5 & 1-\Gamma_s L_5 & 0 \\ 0 & 0 & 1 \end{bmatrix}\frac{d}{dt}\begin{bmatrix} i_1 \\ i_2 \\ v_6 \end{bmatrix} = \begin{bmatrix} n(\Gamma_{11}+\Gamma_{12}) \\ n(\Gamma_{11}+\Gamma_{12}) \\ 0 \end{bmatrix} v_i$$
$$+ \begin{bmatrix} \tau_1+\Gamma_s R_5 & \tau_{12}-\Gamma_s R_5 & -\Gamma_s \\ \tau_{12}-\Gamma_s R_5 & \tau_1+\Gamma_s R_5 & \Gamma_s \\ -1/C_6 & 1/C_6 & -g_7/C_6 \end{bmatrix}\begin{bmatrix} i_1 \\ i_2 \\ v_6 \end{bmatrix} + \begin{bmatrix} -\Gamma_{11} & \Gamma_{12} \\ -\Gamma_{12} & \Gamma_{11} \\ 0 & 0 \end{bmatrix}\begin{bmatrix} f_3(-i_1) \\ f_4(i_2) \end{bmatrix}$$
$$(5.3.15)$$

where

$$\Gamma_s = \Gamma_{11} - \Gamma_{12}$$

$$f_3(-i_1) = \frac{1}{k_3} \ln \frac{-i_1 + I_3}{I_3}$$

$$f_4(i_2) = \frac{1}{k_4} \ln \frac{i_2 + I_4}{I_4}$$

Multiplying both sides of Eq. (5.3.15) by the inverse of the coefficient matrix on the state vector gives the state equations explicitly as

$$\frac{d}{dt} \begin{bmatrix} i_1 \\ i_2 \\ v_6 \end{bmatrix} = \begin{bmatrix} \alpha_{11} & \alpha_{12} & \alpha_{13} \\ \alpha_{21} & \alpha_{22} & \alpha_{23} \\ -1/C_6 & 1/C_6 & -g_7/C_6 \end{bmatrix} \begin{bmatrix} i_1 \\ i_2 \\ v_6 \end{bmatrix} + \begin{bmatrix} \delta_{11} & \delta_{12} \\ \delta_{21} & \delta_{22} \\ 0 & 0 \end{bmatrix} \begin{bmatrix} f_3(-i_1) \\ f_4(i_2) \end{bmatrix} + \begin{bmatrix} \beta_1 \\ \beta_2 \\ 0 \end{bmatrix} v_i$$

$$(5.3.16)$$

where

$$\alpha_{11} = \frac{\tau_1(1 - \Gamma_s L_5) + \Gamma_s(R_5 - \tau_{12}L_5)}{1 - 2\Gamma_s L_5}$$

$$\alpha_{12} = \frac{\tau_{12}(1 - \Gamma_s L_5) + \Gamma_s(-R_5 - \tau_1 L_5)}{1 - 2\Gamma_s L_5}$$

$$\alpha_{13} = \frac{-\Gamma_s}{1 - 2\Gamma_s L_5}$$

$$\alpha_{21} = \frac{\tau_{12}(1 - \Gamma_s L_5) - \Gamma_s(R_5 + \tau_1 L_5)}{1 - 2\Gamma_s L_5 \cdot} = \alpha_{12}$$

$$\alpha_{22} = \frac{\tau_1(1 - \Gamma_s L_5) - \Gamma_s(-R_5 + \tau_{12}L_5)}{1 - 2\Gamma_s L_5} = \alpha_{11}$$

$$\alpha_{23} = \frac{\Gamma_s}{1 - 2\Gamma_s L_5} = -\alpha_{13}$$

$$\delta_{11} = \frac{\Gamma_{11}(-1 + \Gamma_s L_5) + \Gamma_{12}\Gamma_s L_5}{1 - 2\Gamma_s L_5}$$

$$\delta_{12} = \frac{-\Gamma_{12}(-1 + \Gamma_s L_5) - \Gamma_{11}\Gamma_s L_5}{1 - 2\Gamma_s L_5}$$

$$\delta_{21} = -\frac{\Gamma_{12}(1 - \Gamma_s L_5) - \Gamma_{11}\Gamma_s L_5}{1 - 2\Gamma_s L_5} = -\delta_{12}$$

$$\delta_{22} = \frac{\Gamma_{11}(1 - \Gamma_s L_5) - \Gamma_{12}\Gamma_s L_5}{1 - 2\Gamma_s L_5} = -\delta_{11}$$

$$\beta_1 = n(\Gamma_{11} + \Gamma_{12})$$
$$\beta_2 = n(\Gamma_{11} + \Gamma_{12}) = \beta_1$$

In the above example, it is to be noted that the procedure used in developing the state equations is identical to that used in the case of linear systems. In this particular example, it was possible to eliminate the algebraic equations after applying the constraint equations of the graph [see Eqs. (5.3.11) and (5.3.12)]; in fact, it was not necessary even to take an inverse at this point. This, of course, is not the situation in general. Depending on the structure of the system, it may not be possible, in the case of nonlinear systems, to solve the algebraic equations corresponding to Eq. (5.3.14) explicitly for the required variables. If this is the case, reduction beyond the forms in Eqs. (5.3.13) and (5.3.14) is not possible and one is forced into considering a model of the system that is in the general form

$$\frac{d}{dt}\,\mathbf{\Psi}_1 = \mathbf{F}_1(\mathbf{\Psi}_1,\mathbf{\Psi}_2,t)$$

$$0 = \mathbf{F}_2(\mathbf{\Psi}_1,\mathbf{\Psi}_2,t)$$

That is, one must consider a system of simultaneous differential *and* algebraic equations.

5.4 THE TRANSITION MATRIX AND THE CONCEPT OF STATE

The simplest of all possible forms of state equations is the linear homogeneous time-invariant form

$$\frac{d}{dt}\,\mathbf{\Psi}(t) = \mathbf{P}\mathbf{\Psi}(t) \tag{5.4.1}$$

with initial conditions

$$\mathbf{\Psi}(0) = \mathbf{\Psi}_0$$

If $\mathbf{\Psi}(t)$ is a scalar, i.e., a vector of order 1, then the solution to the scalar differential equation can be obtained by expanding $\psi(t)$ in a Maclaurin series in powers of t. The result is

$$\psi(t) = \psi_0 + \dot{\psi}_0 t + \ddot{\psi}_0 \frac{t^2}{2!} + \cdots + \psi_0^{(n)} \frac{t^n}{n!} + \cdots \tag{5.4.2}$$

where

$$\dot{\psi}_0 = \frac{d}{dt}\,\psi(t)\,\Big|_{t=0}$$

$$\ddot{\psi}_0 = \frac{d^2}{dt^2}\,\psi(t)\,\Big|_{t=0}$$

$$\cdots \cdots \cdots \cdots$$

$$\psi_0^{(n)} = \frac{d^n}{dt^n}\,\psi(t)\,\Big|_{t=0}$$

$$\cdots \cdots \cdots \cdots$$

Since the vector $\mathbf{\Psi}(t)$ is simply an ordered set of scalar functions, the Maclaurin expansion of the vector $\mathbf{\Psi}(t)$ is obtained from Eq. (5.4.2) by replacing the scalar ψ by the vector $\mathbf{\Psi}$, that is,

$$\mathbf{\Psi}(t) = \mathbf{\Psi}_0 + \dot{\mathbf{\Psi}}_0 t + \ddot{\mathbf{\Psi}}_0 \frac{t^2}{2!} + \cdots + \mathbf{\Psi}_0^{(n)} \frac{t^n}{n!} + \cdots \tag{5.4.3}$$

The vector coefficients of the powers of t in this expansion are obtained from the given state vector and the given differential equations and their successive time derivatives evaluated at $t = 0$. The results are

$$\dot{\Psi}_0 = \mathbf{P}\Psi_0$$
$$\ddot{\Psi}_0 = \mathbf{P}\dot{\Psi}_0 = \mathbf{P}^2\Psi_0$$
$$\cdot \cdot \cdot \cdot \cdot \cdot \cdot \cdot \cdot \cdot \cdot \cdot$$
$$\Psi_0^{(n)} = \mathbf{P}^n\Psi_0 \qquad (5.4.4)$$
$$\cdot \cdot \cdot \cdot \cdot \cdot \cdot \cdot \cdot$$

Substituting these coefficients into the series expansion for the state vector given in Eq. (5.4.3) establishes the solution to the system of differential equations as

$$\Psi(t) = \left(\mathbf{U} + \mathbf{P}t + \mathbf{P}^2\frac{t^2}{2!} + \cdot \cdot \cdot + \mathbf{P}^n\frac{t^n}{n!} + \cdot \cdot \cdot\right)\Psi_0 \qquad (5.4.5)$$

When the coefficients of the powers of t in Eq. (5.4.5) are scalars, i.e., when $\mathbf{P}$ is a 1×1 matrix, the series is defined as the exponential function e^{pt}. Extending this definition to matrices, $e^{\mathbf{P}t}$ is defined as the *infinite series of matrices*

$$e^{\mathbf{P}t} = \mathbf{U} + \mathbf{P}t + \mathbf{P}^2\frac{t^2}{2!} + \cdot \cdot \cdot + \mathbf{P}^n\frac{t^n}{n!} + \cdot \cdot \cdot \qquad (5.4.6)$$

and the solution to the differential equations is

$$\Psi(t) = e^{\mathbf{P}t}\Psi_0 \qquad (5.4.7)$$

It should be noted that since $e^{\mathbf{P}t}$ is an infinite polynomial in powers of the matrix $\mathbf{P}$, it *is itself a matrix;* that is, $e^{\mathbf{P}t}$ is a matrix whose value is a *function of* the matrix $\mathbf{P}$ and the scalar t.

The matrix function $e^{\mathbf{P}t}$ has several properties essential to the ensuing development. First of all, it is defined as an infinite series of matrices. By definition, the matrix series

$$\sum_{k=1}^{\infty} \mathbf{C}_k = \sum_{k=1}^{\infty} [c_{ij}^{(k)}]$$

where $\mathbf{C}_k$ is of order n, converges if each of the entries in the summation converges, i.e., if the series

$$\sum_{k=1}^{\infty} c_{ij}^{(k)} \qquad i, j = 1, 2, \ldots, n$$

converges for every pair of indices i and j. As in the case of infinite series of scalars, two infinite series of matrices can be multiplied term by term and summed in any order if each series is absolutely convergent.

Thus, if

$$C = \sum_{k=1}^{\infty} C_k \quad \text{and} \quad D = \sum_{k=1}^{\infty} D_k$$

are absolutely convergent, then the product can, for example, be given in the form of the Cauchy product

$$CD = \sum_{k=1}^{\infty} C_k \sum_{l=1}^{\infty} D_l = (C_1 + C_2 + C_3 + \cdots)(D_1 + D_2 + D_3 + \cdots)$$
$$= C_1D_1 + (C_1D_2 + C_2D_1) + (C_1D_3 + C_2D_2 + C_3D_1) + \cdots \quad (5.4.8)$$

It is to be noted that if *every term* in C is commutative with *every term* in D, that is, if

$$C_kD_l = D_lC_k \quad k, l = 1, 2, 3, \ldots$$

then it follows from the product that

$$CD = DC \quad (5.4.9)$$

If C is a real square matrix, it can be shown that the infinite series

$$e^C = U + C + \frac{C^2}{2!} + \frac{C^3}{3!} + \cdots$$

is absolutely convergent. Consequently, if C and D are commutative matrices, then the Cauchy product is

$$e^Ce^D = \left(U + C + \frac{C^2}{2!} + \cdots\right)\left(U + D + \frac{D^2}{2!} + \cdots\right)$$
$$= U + (D + C) + \left(\frac{D^2}{2!} + CD + \frac{C^2}{2!}\right) + \cdots$$
$$= U + (D + C) + \frac{1}{2!}(D + C)^2 + \cdots$$
$$= e^{(D+C)} \quad (5.4.10)$$

In a similar manner

$$e^De^C = e^{(C+D)} \quad (5.4.11)$$

Since $C + D = D + C$, it follows that

$$e^Ce^D = e^De^C = e^{C+D} \quad (5.4.12)$$

If $D = -C$, then from the above result it follows that

$$e^Ce^{-C} = e^{-C}e^C = e^0 = U \quad (5.4.13)$$

where e^0 by definition is the unit matrix. But the above result also defines the inverse, i.e., by definition,

$$(e^C)^{-1} = e^{-C} = U - C + \frac{C^2}{2!} - \frac{C^3}{3!} + \cdots \quad (5.4.14)$$

Returning now to the solution of Eq. (5.4.1) as given in Eq. (5.4.7), we note that the solution, of course, is not complete until the matrix e^{Pt} is evaluated explicitly as a function of time. Analytical procedures for evaluating e^{Pt} are given in the next chapter. If digital-computing facilities are available, the solution indicated in Eq. (5.4.7) can be evaluated numerically by considering a sequence of uniformly spaced points $t = 0$, h, $2h$, $\ldots$, nh, $\ldots$ on the time scale, where h is a suitably chosen small increment. Substituting $t = h$ in Eq. (5.4.7) gives

$$\mathbf{\Psi}(h) = e^{Ph}\mathbf{\Psi}(0) \tag{5.4.15}$$

Note that, since h is a constant, the state vector at $t = h$ is obtained by simply multiplying the initial state vector by a matrix of constants. Then, substituting $t = 2h$ in Eq. (5.4.7) and making use of Eq. (5.4.15) gives

$$\begin{aligned} \mathbf{\Psi}(2h) &= e^{2Ph}\mathbf{\Psi}(0) = e^{Ph}[e^{Ph}\mathbf{\Psi}(0)] \\ &= e^{Ph}\mathbf{\Psi}(h) \end{aligned}$$

That is, the state vector at $t = 2h$ is obtained by multiplying the state vector at $t = h$ by the same coefficient matrix e^{Ph}. In general, the numerical value of the state vector at the point $t = nh$ can be obtained from the numerical value of the state vector at the point $t = (n - 1)h$ by the recursion formula

$$\mathbf{\Psi}(nh) = \mathbf{\Phi}\mathbf{\Psi}[(n - 1)h] \tag{5.4.16}$$

where $\mathbf{\Phi} = e^{Ph}$ is a matrix of constants.

If one elects to evaluate e^{Ph} accurately by the methods presented in the next chapter, then the increment h can be as large or as small as one likes, depending only on how many points on the solution curve are desired. However, if h is taken sufficiently small, then the matrix $\mathbf{\Phi}$ can be approximated by the first several terms in the series expansion

$$\mathbf{\Phi} = e^{Ph} = \mathbf{U} + \mathbf{P}h + \mathbf{P}^2\frac{h^2}{2!} + \mathbf{P}^3\frac{h^3}{3!} + \mathbf{P}^4\frac{h^4}{4!} + \cdots \tag{5.4.17}$$

Such approximations are the basis of all numerical solutions to differential equations. Given numerical values for the coefficients in the matrix $\mathbf{P}$ and the increment h, it should be evident that the solution to the state equations can be generated by first evaluating the matrix $\mathbf{\Phi} = e^{Ph}$ and then simply forming the product of a square matrix into a sequence of vectors starting with the given initial state vector. For this reason, the matrix $\mathbf{\Phi} = e^{Ph}$ is called the *discrete-state transition matrix* for the increment h. In contrast, the matrix e^{Pt} is, in general, a function of time and relates the state vector at any arbitrary time to the initial state, and for this reason it is called the *continuous-state transition matrix*.

Clearly, the matrix operations required to evaluate a numerical solution can be carried out on digital-computing machines, and the numerical accuracy realized depends upon (1) the magnitude of the increment h, (2) the number of terms taken in the series approximation of e^{Ph}, and (3) the properties of the matrix $\mathbf{P}$. A given accuracy can be realized by taking small increments and using, for example, the first four terms in the series expansion of e^{Ph}. Alternatively, for the same accuracy, the magnitude of the increment h can be increased at the expense of more time needed to evaluate e^{Ph} because of the additional terms required. The fact that the error in evaluating $\mathbf{\Phi} = e^{Ph}$ is cumulative is immediately evident when Eq. (5.4.16) is substituted into itself recursively, starting with $n = 1$. The result is

$$\mathbf{\Psi}(nh) = \mathbf{\Phi}^n \mathbf{\Psi}(0)$$

and we see that the error in the state vector is a function of the error in evaluating the nth power of the transition matrix.

5.5 NONHOMOGENEOUS LINEAR SYSTEMS

The most general form of the linear state equations considered so far in this chapter is the nonhomogeneous form

$$\frac{d}{dt}\,\mathbf{\Psi}(t) = \mathbf{P}\mathbf{\Psi}(t) + \mathbf{Q}_1\mathbf{E}(t) + \mathbf{Q}_2\frac{d}{dt}\,\mathbf{E}(t) \tag{5.5.1}$$

where

$\mathbf{\Psi}(t)$ represents a vector of unknown through and across variables
$\mathbf{E}(t)$ represents a vector of known time functions, called *excitation functions*

In the special cases wherein the coefficient matrix $\mathbf{Q}_2$ is identically zero, Eq. (5.5.1) reduces to

$$\frac{d}{dt}\,\mathbf{\Psi}(t) = \mathbf{P}\mathbf{\Psi}(t) + \mathbf{Q}\mathbf{E}(t) \qquad \mathbf{Q} \equiv \mathbf{Q}_1 \tag{5.5.2}$$

The system in Eq. (5.5.1) can always be reduced to the form given in Eq. (5.5.2) by a simple change of state variables. If we let

$$\bar{\mathbf{\Psi}}(t) = \mathbf{\Psi}(t) - \mathbf{Q}_2\mathbf{E}(t) \tag{5.5.3}$$

represent a new state vector, then Eq. (5.5.1) can be written as

$$\frac{d}{dt}\,\bar{\mathbf{\Psi}}(t) = \mathbf{P}\bar{\mathbf{\Psi}}(t) + (\mathbf{Q}_1 + \mathbf{P}\mathbf{Q}_2)\mathbf{E}(t) \tag{5.5.4}$$

which clearly is of the same general form as Eq. (5.5.2). In the succeeding development, it is assumed that a system of state equations of the form given in Eq. (5.5.1) is first reduced to the form given in Eq. (5.5.2).

Consider now the solution to the nonhomogeneous linear system in Eq. (5.5.2) when each entry in the excitation vector $\mathbf{E}(t)$ is given as a continuous function of time in the time interval $0 \le t \le t_1$ and the initial state vector is given as

$$\boldsymbol{\Psi}(0) = \boldsymbol{\Psi}_0$$

To establish the general form of the solution to this system of equations, let $\boldsymbol{\Omega}(t)$ be a vector of unknown time functions related to the state vector $\boldsymbol{\Psi}(t)$ by the equation

$$\boldsymbol{\Psi}(t) = e^{\mathbf{P}t}\boldsymbol{\Omega}(t) \tag{5.5.5}$$

The time derivative of $\boldsymbol{\Psi}(t)$ is symbolized as

$$\frac{d}{dt}\boldsymbol{\Psi}(t) = (e^{\mathbf{P}t})\frac{d}{dt}\boldsymbol{\Omega}(t) + \left(\frac{d}{dt}e^{\mathbf{P}t}\right)\boldsymbol{\Omega}(t) \tag{5.5.6}$$

The time derivative of $e^{\mathbf{P}t}$ as evaluated by differentiating the series definition of $e^{\mathbf{P}t}$ given in Eq. (5.4.6), term by term, is

$$\frac{d}{dt}e^{\mathbf{P}t} = \mathbf{P} + \mathbf{P}^2 t + \mathbf{P}^3\frac{t^2}{2!} + \cdots + \mathbf{P}^n\frac{t^{n-1}}{(n-1)!} + \cdots$$
$$= \mathbf{P}e^{\mathbf{P}t}$$

and Eq. (5.5.6) takes on the form

$$\frac{d}{dt}\boldsymbol{\Psi}(t) = e^{\mathbf{P}t}\frac{d}{dt}\boldsymbol{\Omega}(t) + \mathbf{P}e^{\mathbf{P}t}\boldsymbol{\Omega}(t)$$
$$= e^{\mathbf{P}t}\frac{d}{dt}\boldsymbol{\Omega}(t) + \mathbf{P}\boldsymbol{\Psi}(t) \tag{5.5.7}$$

Substituting Eq. (5.5.7) into Eq. (5.5.2) gives

$$e^{\mathbf{P}t}\frac{d}{dt}\boldsymbol{\Omega}(t) = \mathbf{Q}\mathbf{E}(t) \tag{5.5.8}$$

Since the inverse of the square matrix $e^{\mathbf{P}t}$ is $e^{-\mathbf{P}t}$ [see Eq. (5.4.14)], Eq. (5.5.8) can be written as

$$\frac{d}{dt}\boldsymbol{\Omega}(t) = e^{-\mathbf{P}t}\mathbf{Q}\mathbf{E}(t)$$

The solution to this differential equation is

$$\boldsymbol{\Omega}(t) = \int_0^t e^{-\mathbf{P}\tau}\mathbf{Q}\mathbf{E}(\tau)\,d\tau + \mathbf{C} \tag{5.5.9}$$

where, by the integral of the vector $e^{-\mathbf{P}\tau}\mathbf{Q}\mathbf{E}(\tau)$, is meant, of course, the integral of each term in the vector and $\mathbf{C}$ is a vector of constants yet to be determined. This constant vector is evaluated by substituting the solution from Eq. (5.5.9) into Eq. (5.5.5), whereupon we have

$$\boldsymbol{\Psi}(t) = e^{\mathbf{P}t} \left[\int_0^t e^{-\mathbf{P}\tau} \mathbf{Q} \mathbf{E}(\tau) \, d\tau + \mathbf{C} \right]$$
$$= e^{\mathbf{P}t} \mathbf{C} + \int_0^t e^{\mathbf{P}(t-\tau)} \mathbf{Q} \mathbf{E}(\tau) \, d\tau$$

Setting $\boldsymbol{\Psi}(t) = \boldsymbol{\Psi}_0$ at $t = 0$ gives

$$\boldsymbol{\Psi}(0) = \mathbf{C} + \int_0^0 e^{\mathbf{P}(0-\tau)} \mathbf{Q} \mathbf{E}(\tau) \, d\tau = \mathbf{C} = \boldsymbol{\Psi}_0$$

The constant vector $\mathbf{C}$ therefore represents the initial value of the state vector, and the solution to Eq. (5.5.2) for the interval $0 \le t \le t_1$ is established as

$$\boldsymbol{\Psi}(t) = e^{\mathbf{P}t} \boldsymbol{\Psi}_0 + \int_0^t e^{\mathbf{P}(t-\tau)} \mathbf{Q} \mathbf{E}(\tau) \, d\tau$$
$$= e^{\mathbf{P}t} \boldsymbol{\Psi}_0 + e^{\mathbf{P}t} \int_0^t e^{-\mathbf{P}\tau} \mathbf{Q} \mathbf{E}(\tau) \, d\tau \qquad (5.5.10)$$

By a simple change in the time variable it is easy to show that when the excitation vector $\mathbf{E}(t)$ is continuous over some arbitrary interval $t_0 \le t \le t_1$ the solution is

$$\boldsymbol{\Psi}(t) = e^{\mathbf{P}(t-t_0)} \boldsymbol{\Psi}_0 + \int_{t_0}^t e^{\mathbf{P}(t-\tau)} \mathbf{Q} \mathbf{E}(\tau) \, d\tau \qquad (5.5.11)$$

where $\boldsymbol{\Psi}_0 = \boldsymbol{\Psi}(t_0)$ represents the value of the state vector at $t = t_0$.

If the excitation vector $\mathbf{E}(t)$ is identically zero, then, of course, the solution given above in Eq. (5.5.10) reduces to the solution to the homogeneous system given in the previous section. The integral term in Eq. (5.5.10) can therefore be regarded as the contribution of the excitation vector to the solution of the state equations. Analytical procedures for evaluating this integral are given in the next chapter.

Given the numerical values of the coefficients in the matrices $\mathbf{P}$ and $\mathbf{Q}$ and the time variation in each of the variables in $\mathbf{E}(t)$, the solution indicated in Eq. (5.5.10) can be evaluated numerically by again considering the value of the state vector at discrete points $t = 0, h, 2h, \ldots, nh, \ldots$ on the time scale.

Setting $t = h$ in Eq. (5.5.10) gives

$$\boldsymbol{\Psi}(h) = e^{\mathbf{P}h} \boldsymbol{\Psi}(0) + e^{\mathbf{P}h} \int_0^h e^{-\mathbf{P}\tau} \mathbf{Q} \mathbf{E}(\tau) \, d\tau \qquad (5.5.12)$$

As in the numerical solution of homogeneous equations, the matrix $e^{\mathbf{P}h}$ is approximated as the first few terms in its series expansion. The integral can be approximated by any one of several numerical integration formulas. The very simplest of such formulas, but one which may require an excessively small increment h, is obtained by simply assuming that $e^{\mathbf{P}t}$ is constant over each successive interval and equal to its value at the beginning of the interval; i.e., for $0 \leq t < h$, $e^{-\mathbf{P}t} \cong \mathbf{U}$ and $\mathbf{E}(\tau) \cong \mathbf{E}(0)$. On the basis of this simple approximation, Eq. (5.5.12) becomes

$$\mathbf{\Psi}(h) \cong e^{\mathbf{P}h}\mathbf{\Psi}(0) + he^{\mathbf{P}h}\mathbf{Q}\mathbf{E}(0) = \mathbf{\Phi}\mathbf{\Psi}(0) + \mathbf{\Delta}\mathbf{E}(0) \qquad (5.5.13)$$

where $\mathbf{\Phi} = e^{\mathbf{P}h}$ and $\mathbf{\Delta} = he^{\mathbf{P}h}\mathbf{Q}$ are constant matrices.

In a similar manner, the state vector at $t = 2h$ is given by

$$\mathbf{\Psi}(2h) = e^{\mathbf{P}2h}\mathbf{\Psi}(0) + e^{\mathbf{P}2h}\left[\int_0^h e^{-\mathbf{P}\tau}\mathbf{Q}\mathbf{E}(\tau)\,d\tau + \int_h^{2h} e^{-\mathbf{P}\tau}\mathbf{Q}\mathbf{E}(\tau)\,d\tau\right]$$

$$(5.5.14)$$

If it is assumed that, over the interval $h \leq t < 2h$, $e^{-\mathbf{P}\tau} \cong e^{-\mathbf{P}h}$ and $\mathbf{E}(\tau) \cong \mathbf{E}(h)$, then Eq. (5.5.14) is approximated as

$$\mathbf{\Psi}(2h) \cong e^{\mathbf{P}h}[e^{\mathbf{P}h}\mathbf{\Psi}(0) + he^{\mathbf{P}h}\mathbf{Q}\mathbf{E}(0)] + e^{\mathbf{P}h}h\mathbf{Q}\mathbf{E}(h)$$

or, using Eq. (5.5.13),

$$\mathbf{\Psi}(2h) = \mathbf{\Phi}\mathbf{\Psi}(h) + \mathbf{\Delta}\mathbf{E}(h) \qquad (5.5.15)$$

If, for notational purposes, we denote $\mathbf{\Psi}(nh)$ simply as $\mathbf{\Psi}(n)$ and $\mathbf{\Psi}(nh + h)$ as $\mathbf{\Psi}(n + 1)$, then, by repeated application of the above procedure, it is easy to show that, as an approximation, the state vector at the nth point on the time scale is related to the state vector and the excitation vector at the previous point by the simple recursion formula

$$\mathbf{\Psi}(n) = \mathbf{\Phi}\mathbf{\Psi}(n - 1) + \mathbf{\Delta}\mathbf{E}(n - 1) \qquad n = 1, 2, \ldots \qquad (5.5.16)$$

where $\mathbf{\Phi}$ and $\mathbf{\Delta}$ are constant matrices already defined as

$$\mathbf{\Phi} = e^{\mathbf{P}h} = \mathbf{U} + \mathbf{P}h + \mathbf{P}^2\frac{h^2}{2!} + \cdots$$

and

$$\mathbf{\Delta} = he^{\mathbf{P}h}\mathbf{Q} = \left(h\mathbf{U} + \mathbf{P}h^2 + \mathbf{P}^2\frac{h^3}{2!} + \cdots\right)\mathbf{Q}$$

Given the matrices $\mathbf{P}$ and $\mathbf{Q}$, the initial state vector $\mathbf{\Psi}(0)$, and the time variation in the excitation vector, a numerical solution is realized by first evaluating the constant matrices $\mathbf{\Phi}$ and $\mathbf{\Delta}$ as truncated series and then evaluating Eq. (5.5.16) recursively, starting at $n = 1$. The numerical accuracy of the solution depends upon both the accuracy with which $e^{\mathbf{P}h}$ is evaluated and the accuracy with which the integral in Eq. (5.5.10) is approximated. Although the very simple integration formula used above gives results that are conceptually simple, it requires, in general, an increment that is much too small for practical application. Although this limitation can be avoided by the use of more sophisticated integration formulas, the basic procedure suffers from one additional practical consideration. The value of the excitation vector $\mathbf{E}(t)$ at each point $t = nh$ is required as an input (a known vector) to the calculation of the state vector at $t = (n + 1)h$. This means that the functions in the excitation vector must be generated within the computing machine. In view of this consideration it is usually more expedient, in realizing numerical solutions to nonhomogeneous differential equations, first to transform them to an equivalent system of homogeneous equations. The restrictions on the excitation vector under which such a transformation can be made are considered next, along with the techniques involved in making the transformation.

Consider first the linear system in Eq. (5.5.2) when the initial state is given as $\boldsymbol{\Psi}(0) = \boldsymbol{\Psi}_0$ and the excitation vector is given as

$$\mathbf{E}(t) = \begin{cases} \mathbf{0} & \text{for } t < 0 \\ \mathbf{E}, \text{ a constant vector} & \text{for } t \geq 0 \end{cases}$$

Let this excitation vector be written as

$$\mathbf{E}(t) = \mathbf{E}u(t)$$

where $u(t)$ is the unit step function. For all $t \geq 0$, $u(t)$ represents the solution to the simple differential equation

$$\frac{d}{dt} u(t) = 0 \qquad \text{with } u(0) = 1$$

Consequently, the nonhomogeneous system

$$\frac{d}{dt} \boldsymbol{\Psi}(t) = \mathbf{P}\boldsymbol{\Psi}(t) + \mathbf{Q}\mathbf{E}u(t) \qquad \boldsymbol{\Psi}(0) = \boldsymbol{\Psi}_0$$

is equivalent to the augmented homogeneous system

$$\frac{d}{dt} \begin{bmatrix} \boldsymbol{\Psi}(t) \\ u(t) \end{bmatrix} = \begin{bmatrix} \mathbf{P} & \mathbf{Q}\mathbf{E} \\ \mathbf{0} & 0 \end{bmatrix} \begin{bmatrix} \boldsymbol{\Psi}(t) \\ u(t) \end{bmatrix} \qquad \begin{bmatrix} \boldsymbol{\Psi}(0) \\ u(0) \end{bmatrix} = \begin{bmatrix} \boldsymbol{\Psi}_0 \\ 1 \end{bmatrix} \qquad (5.5.17)$$

If $\boldsymbol{\Psi}'$ and $\mathbf{P}'$ represent, respectively, the augmented state vector and coefficient matrix, then Eq. (5.5.17) can be represented symbolically as

$$\frac{d}{dt} \boldsymbol{\Psi}'(t) = \mathbf{P}'\boldsymbol{\Psi}'(t) \qquad \boldsymbol{\Psi}'(0) = \boldsymbol{\Psi}_0'$$

which has the solution

$$\boldsymbol{\Psi}'(t) = e^{\mathbf{P}'t}\boldsymbol{\Psi}'(0)$$

It is to be noted that, in the homogeneous equivalent, the excitation function $u(t)$ is generated as the solution to an auxiliary differential equation. Evidently, then, any system of nonhomogeneous equations can be transformed into an equivalent system of homogeneous equations, provided only that the excitation functions represent solutions to differential equations over finite intervals of time. More specifically, let the excitation vector $\mathbf{E}(t)$ in Eq. (5.5.2) be a vector of functions of the independent variable t, these functions having at most a finite number of first-order discontinuities over the interval I ($t_1 < t < t_2$). Such a vector of time functions can be represented everywhere on I, except at the finite number of discontinuities, by the infinite series of vectors of time functions

$$\mathbf{E}(t) = \mathbf{E}_1(t) + \mathbf{E}_2(t) + \cdots + \mathbf{E}_j(t) + \cdots \tag{5.5.18}$$

where each vector is of the form

$$\mathbf{E}_j(t) = \mathbf{K}_j \begin{bmatrix} 1 \\ t \\ \cdot \\ \cdot \\ \cdot \\ t^{m_j} \end{bmatrix} e^{\alpha_j t} = \mathbf{K}_j \mathbf{F}_j(t) \tag{5.5.19}$$

$\mathbf{K}_j$ is a rectangular matrix of constants, and $\mathbf{F}_j(t)$ is a vector of time functions of order $m_j + 1$, as indicated. The coefficients in $\mathbf{K}_j$ and the exponents α_j in $\mathbf{F}_j(t)$ may be real or complex.

It should be noted that the infinite series in Eq. (5.5.18) includes the Fourier series as a special case. Indeed, if all the columns in $\mathbf{K}_j$ except the first are identically zero, then Eq. (5.5.18) reduces to an infinite series of exponentials which includes the Fourier series as a special case. Likewise if all the exponential coefficients α_j are identically zero, the series reduces to a finite power series in t.

By direct differentiation it is easy to show that the time derivative of the vector $\mathbf{F}_j(t)$ in Eq. (5.5.19) is

$$\frac{d}{dt} \mathbf{F}_j(t) = \mathbf{T}_j \mathbf{F}_j(t) \tag{5.5.20}$$

where

$$\mathbf{T}_j = \begin{bmatrix} \alpha_j & 0 & 0 & \cdots & 0 & 0 \\ 1 & \alpha_j & 0 & \cdots & 0 & 0 \\ 0 & 2 & \alpha_j & \cdots & 0 & 0 \\ \cdot & \cdot & \cdot & \cdots & \cdot & \cdot \\ 0 & 0 & 0 & \cdots & \alpha_j & 0 \\ 0 & 0 & 0 & \cdots & m_j & \alpha_j \end{bmatrix} \tag{5.5.21}$$

The initial value of the vector $\mathbf{F}_j(t)$ as obtained from Eq. (5.5.19) by setting $t = 0$ is

$$\mathbf{F}_j(0) = \begin{bmatrix} 1 \\ 0 \\ \cdot \\ \cdot \\ \cdot \\ 0 \end{bmatrix} \tag{5.5.22}$$

It follows, therefore, that $\mathbf{F}_j(t)$ represents the solution to the system of differential equations in Eq. (5.5.20) with initial conditions given by Eq. (5.5.22).

Upon using the series expansion for $\mathbf{E}(t)$ given in Eq. (5.5.18), the nonhomogeneous system of equations in Eq. (5.5.2) becomes

$$\frac{d}{dt}\,\mathbf{\Psi}(t) = \mathbf{P}\mathbf{\Psi}(t) + [\mathbf{QK}_1 \quad \mathbf{QK}_2 \quad \cdots]\begin{bmatrix} \mathbf{F}_1(t) \\ \mathbf{F}_2(t) \\ \cdot \\ \cdot \\ \cdot \end{bmatrix} \qquad (5.5.23)$$

When each of the vector functions $\mathbf{F}_j(t)$ is taken as the solution to a system of differential equations of the form given in Eq. (5.5.20), this system of nonhomogeneous equations reduces to the augmented homogeneous equivalent

$$\frac{d}{dt}\begin{bmatrix} \mathbf{\Psi}(t) \\ \mathbf{F}_1(t) \\ \mathbf{F}_2(t) \\ \cdots \\ \mathbf{F}_r(t) \\ \cdots \end{bmatrix} = \begin{bmatrix} \mathbf{P} & \mathbf{QK}_1 & \mathbf{QK}_2 & \cdots & \mathbf{QK}_r & \cdots \\ 0 & \mathbf{T}_1 & 0 & \cdots & 0 & \cdots \\ 0 & 0 & \mathbf{T}_2 & \cdots & 0 & \cdots \\ \cdots & \cdots & \cdots & \cdots & \cdots & \cdots \\ 0 & 0 & 0 & \cdots & \mathbf{T}_r & \cdots \\ \cdots & \cdots & \cdots & \cdots & \cdots & \cdots \end{bmatrix}\begin{bmatrix} \mathbf{\Psi}(t) \\ \mathbf{F}_1(t) \\ \mathbf{F}_2(t) \\ \cdots \\ \mathbf{F}_r(t) \\ \cdots \end{bmatrix}$$

$$(5.5.24)$$

Example 5.5.1: Develop the homogeneous equivalent of Eq. (5.5.2) when

$$\mathbf{E}(t) = \begin{bmatrix} E_1 \cos\,(\omega t + \theta_1) \\ E_2 \cos\,(\omega t + \theta_2) \\ \cdots\cdots\cdots\cdots \\ E_m \cos\,(\omega t + \theta_m) \end{bmatrix} \qquad (5.5.25)$$

Solution: Let Eq. (5.5.25) be written as

$$\mathbf{E}(t) = \tfrac{1}{2}\bar{\mathbf{E}}e^{j\omega t} + \tfrac{1}{2}\hat{\bar{\mathbf{E}}}e^{-j\omega t} \qquad (5.5.26)$$

where the kth entry in the vector $\bar{\mathbf{E}}$ is the complex number

$$\bar{E}_k = E_k e^{j\theta_k}$$

Since $e^{\pm j\omega t}$ is realized as a solution to the scalar equation

$$\frac{d}{dt}f(t) = \pm j\omega f(t) \qquad f(0) = 1$$

it follows that the augmented system of homogeneous equations is

$$\frac{d}{dt}\begin{bmatrix} \mathbf{\Psi}(t) \\ \hline f_1(t) \\ f_2(t) \end{bmatrix} = \begin{bmatrix} \mathbf{P} & \tfrac{1}{2}\mathbf{Q}\bar{\mathbf{E}} & \tfrac{1}{2}\mathbf{Q}\hat{\bar{\mathbf{E}}} \\ \hline 0 & j\omega & 0 \\ 0 & 0 & -j\omega \end{bmatrix}\begin{bmatrix} \mathbf{\Psi}(t) \\ \hline f_1(t) \\ f_2(t) \end{bmatrix} \qquad \begin{bmatrix} \mathbf{\Psi}(0) \\ \hline f_1(0) \\ f_2(0) \end{bmatrix} = \begin{bmatrix} \mathbf{\Psi}_0 \\ \hline 1 \\ 1 \end{bmatrix} \qquad (5.5.27)$$

Note that the resulting augmented coefficient matrix contains complex coefficients. Complex numbers can be avoided by the use of orthogonal functions; i.e., let the sinusoidal excitation vector in Eq. (5.5.25) be written as the sum of two orthogonal functions,

$$\mathbf{E}(t) = [\mathbf{E}_a \quad \mathbf{E}_b] \begin{bmatrix} \cos \omega t \\ \sin \omega t \end{bmatrix} \tag{5.5.28}$$

where $\mathbf{E}_a$ and $\mathbf{E}_b$ are vectors of real numbers.

The time derivative of the vector at the right in Eq. (5.5.28) is

$$\frac{d}{dt} \mathbf{F}(t) = \frac{d}{dt} \begin{bmatrix} \cos \omega t \\ \sin \omega t \end{bmatrix} = \begin{bmatrix} 0 & -\omega \\ \omega & 0 \end{bmatrix} \begin{bmatrix} \cos \omega t \\ \sin \omega t \end{bmatrix}$$

and its $t = 0$ value is

$$\mathbf{F}(0) = \begin{bmatrix} 1 \\ 0 \end{bmatrix}$$

It follows, therefore, that the required time functions can be generated as the solution of the system of differential equations

$$\frac{d}{dt} \begin{bmatrix} f_a(t) \\ f_b(t) \end{bmatrix} = \begin{bmatrix} 0 & -\omega \\ \omega & 0 \end{bmatrix} \begin{bmatrix} f_a(t) \\ f_b(t) \end{bmatrix} \qquad \begin{bmatrix} f_a(0) \\ f_b(0) \end{bmatrix} = \begin{bmatrix} 1 \\ 0 \end{bmatrix}$$

and an alternative homogeneous equivalent of the nonhomogeneous system in Eq. (5.5.2) for the excitation vector given in Eq. (5.5.25) is

$$\frac{d}{dt} \begin{bmatrix} \mathbf{\Psi}(t) \\ f_a(t) \\ f_b(t) \end{bmatrix} = \begin{bmatrix} \mathbf{P} & \mathbf{QE}_a & \mathbf{QE}_b \\ \mathbf{0} & 0 & -\omega \\ \mathbf{0} & \omega & 0 \end{bmatrix} \begin{bmatrix} \mathbf{\Psi}(t) \\ f_a(t) \\ f_b(t) \end{bmatrix} \qquad \begin{bmatrix} \mathbf{\Psi}(0) \\ f_a(0) \\ f_b(0) \end{bmatrix} = \begin{bmatrix} \mathbf{\Psi}_0 \\ 1 \\ 0 \end{bmatrix} \tag{5.5.29}$$

Since the vector $\mathbf{E}(t)$ is a real function of time, any complex functions of time appearing in the expansion of $\mathbf{E}(t)$ given in Eq. (5.5.18) must occur in conjugate pairs. These terms can be grouped together to form real orthogonal functions as in the above example. Thus, it is possible to develop homogeneous equivalents of nonhomogeneous systems that contain only real coefficients.

Application of homogeneous equivalents in generating numerical solutions to linear systems is demonstrated by the following example.

Example 5.5.2: The electrical network given in Fig. 5.5.1 is referred to as a *bandpass filter*.

(a) Write the augmented state equations for this network when

$$v_7(t) = 20 \cos \omega t$$

where $\omega = 2\pi f$ and $f = 2$, 5, and 8 kc.

(b) From a numerical solution to the system of differential equations established in (a), sketch the form of the results for $i_8(t)$ and $i_9(t)$. Assume all initial conditions equal to zero, and take the element values as

$L_1 = L_2 = 39.9$ mhenrys
$L_3 = 3.32$ mhenrys
$C_4 = C_5 = 0.0264$ μf
$C_6 = 0.319$ μf
$R_8 = R_9 = 500$ ohms

Solution

(a) Following the development introduced in this section, the augmented state equations corresponding to Eq. (5.5.29) are

$$\frac{d}{dt}\begin{bmatrix} i_1(t) \\ i_2(t) \\ i_3(t) \\ v_4(t) \\ v_5(t) \\ v_6(t) \\ \hline f_a(t) \\ f_b(t) \end{bmatrix} =$$

$$\begin{bmatrix} -R_8/L_1 & 0 & 0 & -1/L_1 & 0 & -1/L_1 & 1/L_1 & 0 \\ 0 & -R_9/L_2 & 0 & 0 & -1/L_2 & 1/L_2 & 0 & 0 \\ 0 & 0 & 0 & 0 & 0 & 1/L_3 & 0 & 0 \\ 1/C_4 & 0 & 0 & 0 & 0 & 0 & 0 & 0 \\ 0 & 1/C_5 & 0 & 0 & 0 & 0 & 0 & 0 \\ 1/C_6 & -1/C_6 & -1/C_6 & 0 & 0 & 0 & 0 & 0 \\ \hline 0 & 0 & 0 & 0 & 0 & 0 & 0 & -\omega \\ 0 & 0 & 0 & 0 & 0 & 0 & \omega & 0 \end{bmatrix}\begin{bmatrix} i_1(t) \\ i_2(t) \\ i_3(t) \\ v_4(t) \\ v_5(t) \\ v_6(t) \\ \hline f_a(t) \\ f_b(t) \end{bmatrix}$$

where $\begin{bmatrix} f_a(0) \\ f_b(0) \end{bmatrix} = \begin{bmatrix} 20 \\ 0 \end{bmatrix}$.

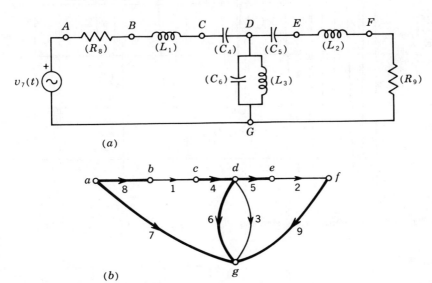

Fig. 5.5.1 (a) An electrical network; (b) system graph.

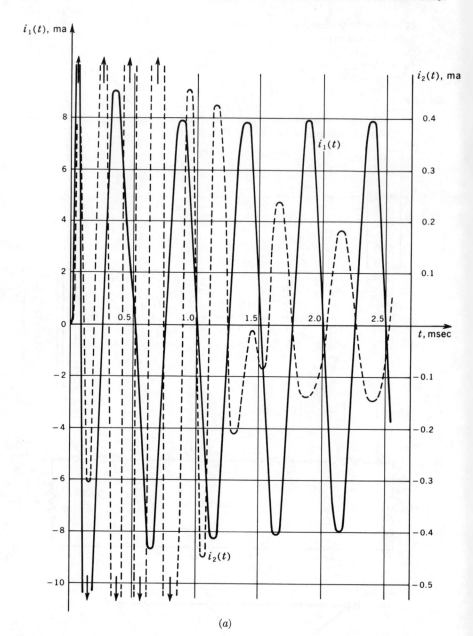

(a)

Fig. 5.5.2 *(a)* Solution for systems of Fig. 5.5.1, with signal frequency of 2 kc.

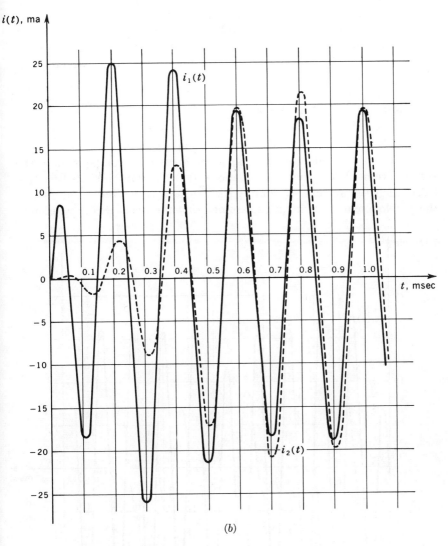

Fig. 5.5.2 (b) Solution for system of Fig. 5.5.1, with signal frequency of 5 kc.

(b) After substitution of the given element values in the above state equations, a numerical solution obtained by use of digital computer gave the value of each state variable corresponding to each of the three different frequencies. From these results the desired solutions for $i_8(t) = i_1(t)$ and $i_9(t) = i_2(t)$ are sketched in Fig. 5.5.2a to c.

5.6 TIME - VARYING AND NONLINEAR SYSTEMS

If the terminal equations characterizing the components in the system are linear in the complementary terminal variables, but the coefficients

in these equations are explicit functions of time, then the system is
described as a *linear time-varying* system or a *nonstationary linear system*.
In the subsequent development it is assumed that the structure of such a
system permits the differential and algebraic equations characterizing
the system to be reduced to the form

$$\frac{d}{dt}\,\boldsymbol{\Psi}(t) = \mathbf{P}(t)\boldsymbol{\Psi}(t) + \mathbf{QE}(t) \qquad (5.6.1)$$

where the entries in $\mathbf{P}(t)$ are known functions of time.

When the terminal equations characterizing the components in the
system are nonlinear functions of the terminal variables, as in Example
5.3.1, then the system, of course, is described as *nonlinear*. Again, in
the development following, it is assumed that the structure of a nonlinear

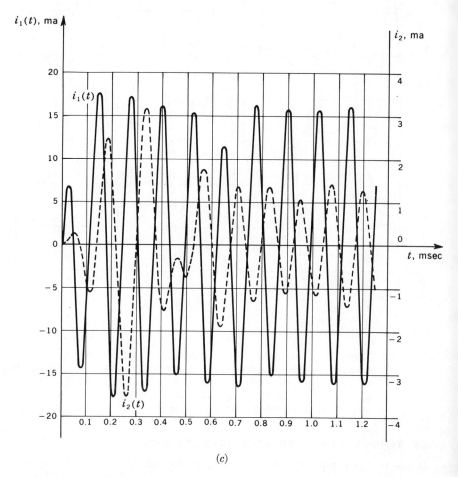

Fig. 5.5.2   (c) Solution for system of Fig. 5.5.1, with signal frequency of 8 kc.

system is such that the equations characterizing the system can be reduced to the form

$$\frac{d}{dt}\, \mathbf{\Psi}(t) = \mathbf{F}[\mathbf{\Psi}(t), t] \tag{5.6.2}$$

where $\mathbf{F}$ is a vector function of the vector $\mathbf{\Psi}$ and the scalar t. It has already been pointed out in an earlier section of this chapter that system equations are not necessarily always reducible to this form. However, we shall not here be concerned with the solution of such nonreducible systems.

The problem is to generate the vector function of time, $\mathbf{\Psi}(t)$, that satisfies Eq. (5.6.2) and passes through the initial point $\mathbf{\Psi}(t_0) = \mathbf{\Psi}_0$ at $t = t_0$. As in the solution of linear differential equations, we assume that $\mathbf{\Psi}(t)$ has a Taylor series expansion about the point $t = t_0$; that is, let

$$\mathbf{\Psi}(t) = \mathbf{\Psi}(t_0) + \mathbf{\Psi}^{(1)}(t_0)t + \mathbf{\Psi}^{(2)}(t_0)\frac{t^2}{2!} + \cdots$$
$$+ \mathbf{\Psi}^{(n)}(t_0)\frac{t^n}{n!} + \cdots \tag{5.6.3}$$

The coefficients in this expression are evaluated from the given initial state vector, the vector function to the right of Eq. (5.6.2), and its higher-order derivatives as follows:

$$\mathbf{\Psi}(t_0) = \mathbf{\Psi}_0$$
$$\mathbf{\Psi}^{(1)}(t_0) = \mathbf{F}[\mathbf{\Psi}(t), t]\Big|_{t=t_0} = \mathbf{F}(\mathbf{\Psi}_0, t_0)$$
$$\mathbf{\Psi}^{(2)}(t_0) = \frac{d}{dt}\mathbf{F}[\mathbf{\Psi}(t), t]\Big|_{t=t_0} = \mathbf{F}^{(1)}(\mathbf{\Psi}_0, t_0)$$
$$\cdots \cdots \cdots \cdots \cdots \cdots \cdots \cdots$$
$$\mathbf{\Psi}^{(n)}(t_0) = \frac{d^{n-1}}{dt^{n-1}}\mathbf{F}[\mathbf{\Psi}(t), t]\Big|_{t=t_0} = \mathbf{F}^{(n-1)}(\mathbf{\Psi}_0, t_0)$$
$$\cdots \cdots \cdots \cdots \cdots \cdots \cdots \cdots$$

On the assumption for the present that these vectors can be evaluated numerically, the solution at a point $t = h$, where h is a suitably small increment, can be approximated as the first $m + 1$ terms in the series expansion given as Eq. (5.6.3). That is,

$$\mathbf{\Psi}(h) = \mathbf{\Psi}_0 + \mathbf{F}(\mathbf{\Psi}_0, t_0)h + \mathbf{F}^{(1)}(\mathbf{\Psi}_0, t_0)\frac{h^2}{2!} + \mathbf{F}^{(2)}(\mathbf{\Psi}_0, t_0)\frac{h^3}{3!} + \cdots$$
$$+ \mathbf{F}^{(m)}(\mathbf{\Psi}_0, t_0)\frac{h^{m+1}}{(m+1)!} \tag{5.6.4}$$

To evaluate the solution at the point $t = 2h$, $\Psi(t)$ is first expanded about the point $t = h$ to obtain

$$\Psi(h + \tau) = \Psi(h) + \Psi^{(1)}(h)\tau + \Psi^{(2)}(h)\frac{\tau^2}{2!} + \cdots$$

$$+ \Psi^{(n)}(h)\frac{\tau^n}{n!} + \cdots \quad (5.6.5)$$

where $t = h + \tau$.

The coefficients are now evaluated from the solution at $t = h$, already constructed, and the value of $\mathbf{F}$ and its higher-order derivatives as follows:

$$\Psi(h) = \Psi_h$$
$$\Psi^{(1)}(h) = \mathbf{F}(\Psi_h, h)$$
$$\cdots \cdots \cdots \cdots \cdots$$
$$\Psi^{(n)}(h) = \mathbf{F}^{(n-1)}(\Psi_h, h)$$
$$\cdots \cdots \cdots \cdots \cdots$$

The solution at $t = 2h$ is then obtained by setting $\tau = h$ in Eq. (5.6.5) and again truncating the series after the first $m + 1$ terms as

$$\Psi(2h) = \Psi(h) + \mathbf{F}(\Psi_h, h)h + \mathbf{F}^{(1)}(\Psi_h, h)\frac{h^2}{2!} + \cdots$$

$$+ \mathbf{F}^{(m)}(\Psi_h, h)\frac{h^{m+1}}{(m+1)!} \quad (5.6.6)$$

It should be noted that the method of construction used above is identical to that used in Sec. 5.4 for the linear system. Indeed, if the system is linear and time-invariant, then

$$\mathbf{F}[\Psi(t), t] = \Psi^{(1)}(t) = \mathbf{P}\Psi(t)$$
$$\mathbf{F}^{(1)}[\Psi(t), t] = \mathbf{P}\Psi^{(1)}(t) = \mathbf{P}^2\Psi(t)$$
$$\cdots \cdots \cdots \cdots \cdots \cdots \cdots \cdots$$
$$\mathbf{F}^{(m)}[\Psi(t), t] = \mathbf{P}^{m+1}\Psi(t)$$

Substituting these expressions into Eq. (5.6.6) with $t = n$ (actually $t = hn$) gives exactly the recursion formula given in Eq. (5.4.16). The only difference between the numerical solutions of the linear and nonlinear differential equations is in the evaluation of the coefficients in the series expansion of Eq. (5.6.6)—but this difference is significant. In the case of linear time-invariant systems, $\mathbf{F}[\Psi(t), t]$ and its higher-order derivatives can be evaluated easily and explicitly as general functions of the coefficient matrix $\mathbf{P}$. In the case of nonlinear and time-varying systems, however, the required time derivatives of the vector function may be very difficult indeed to evaluate. In fact in many cases such evaluation may be so difficult as to be totally impractical.

Runge and Kutta developed formulas for approximating the time derivatives of $\mathbf{F}(\boldsymbol{\Psi},t)$ in terms of $\mathbf{F}(\boldsymbol{\Psi},t)$ and $\boldsymbol{\Psi}$ and established what is now known as the *Runge-Kutta method*. The most commonly used recursion formula for realizing the solution to a system of differential equations of the form given in Eq. (5.6.2) is

$$\boldsymbol{\Psi}[(n+1)h] = \boldsymbol{\Psi}(nh) + \frac{h}{6}(\mathbf{K}_1 + 2\mathbf{K}_2 + 2\mathbf{K}_3 + \mathbf{K}_4) \qquad (5.6.7)$$

where $\mathbf{K}_i$, $i = 1, 2, 3, 4$, are vectors evaluated as follows:

$$\mathbf{K}_1 = \mathbf{F}(\boldsymbol{\Psi}_n, nh)$$
$$\mathbf{K}_2 = \mathbf{F}(\boldsymbol{\Psi}_n + \tfrac{1}{2}h\mathbf{K}_1, nh + \tfrac{1}{2}h)$$
$$\mathbf{K}_3 = \mathbf{F}(\boldsymbol{\Psi}_n + \tfrac{1}{2}h\mathbf{K}_2, nh + \tfrac{1}{2}h)$$
$$\mathbf{K}_4 = \mathbf{F}(\boldsymbol{\Psi}_n + h\mathbf{K}_3, nh + h)$$

It is to be noted that in the expression for $\mathbf{K}_2$, for example, the numerical value of the vector $\boldsymbol{\Psi}$ used in evaluating the vector $\mathbf{F}$ is taken as $\boldsymbol{\Psi}_n + \tfrac{1}{2}h\mathbf{K}_1$ and the numerical value of t is $nh + \tfrac{1}{2}h$. This notation should be clear from the following example.

Example 5.6.1: Evaluate the first term in the Runge-Kutta recursion formula for the nonlinear differential equations given below:

$$\frac{d}{dt}\begin{bmatrix} \psi_1(t) \\ \psi_2(t) \end{bmatrix} = \begin{bmatrix} f_1(\psi_1,\psi_2,t) \\ f_2(\psi_1,\psi_2,t) \end{bmatrix} = \begin{bmatrix} 2\psi_1 + \psi_2{}^2 + t \\ \psi_1{}^2 t + \psi_2 \end{bmatrix} \qquad \begin{bmatrix} \psi_1(0) \\ \psi_2(0) \end{bmatrix} = \begin{bmatrix} 1 \\ 1 \end{bmatrix}$$

Solution: For $n = 0$, $t = 0$, we have

$$\boldsymbol{\Psi}_0 = \boldsymbol{\Psi}(0) = \begin{bmatrix} 1 \\ 1 \end{bmatrix} \qquad \mathbf{F}(\boldsymbol{\Psi}_0,0) = \begin{bmatrix} 3 \\ 1 \end{bmatrix}$$

and

$$\mathbf{K}_1 = \begin{bmatrix} k_{11} \\ k_{12} \end{bmatrix} = \mathbf{F}(\boldsymbol{\Psi}_0,0) = \begin{bmatrix} 3 \\ 1 \end{bmatrix}$$

$$\mathbf{K}_2 = \begin{bmatrix} k_{21} \\ k_{22} \end{bmatrix} = \begin{bmatrix} 2[1 + (k_{11}/2)h] + (1 + \tfrac{1}{2}k_{12}h)^2 + \tfrac{1}{2}h \\ [1 + (k_{11}/2)h]^2\tfrac{1}{2}h + (1 + \tfrac{1}{2}k_{12}h) \end{bmatrix}$$

$$\mathbf{K}_3 = \begin{bmatrix} k_{31} \\ k_{32} \end{bmatrix} = \begin{bmatrix} 2[1 + (k_{21}/2)h] + (1 + \tfrac{1}{2}k_{22}h)^2 + \tfrac{1}{2}h \\ [1 + (k_{21}/2)h]^2\tfrac{1}{2}h + (1 + \tfrac{1}{2}k_{22}h) \end{bmatrix}$$

$$\mathbf{K}_4 = \begin{bmatrix} k_{41} \\ k_{42} \end{bmatrix} = \begin{bmatrix} 2(1 + k_{31}h) + (1 + k_{32}h)^2 + h \\ (1 + k_{31}h)^2 h + (1 + k_{32}h) \end{bmatrix}$$

from which the solution at the first point is

$$\boldsymbol{\Psi}(1) = \begin{bmatrix} 1 \\ 1 \end{bmatrix} + \frac{h}{6}\begin{bmatrix} k_{11} + 2k_{21} + 2k_{31} + k_{41} \\ k_{12} + 2k_{22} + 2k_{32} + k_{42} \end{bmatrix}$$

$$= \begin{bmatrix} 1 \\ 1 \end{bmatrix} + \frac{h}{6}\begin{bmatrix} 18 + 27h + 24h^2 + 22h^3 + 22h^4 + \tfrac{493}{16}h^5 + \cdots \\ 6 + 6h + 23h^2 + 46h^3 + \tfrac{157}{2}h^4 + \tfrac{297}{4}h^5 + \cdots \end{bmatrix}$$

$$(5.6.8)$$

It should be noted that the actual polynomials in Eq. (5.6.8) contain terms through h^{18}; only the first six terms are shown explicitly.

The second point is calculated in exactly the same way but with $n = 1$, $t = h$, and $\Psi_1 = \Psi(1)$.

Most computer libraries have standard routines for the numerical integration of nonlinear differential equations as described above, and most of these routines have built-in subroutines which automatically select the increment h. The basis for such a subroutine is very simple and can be seen by referring to Eq. (5.6.8). If, for any initially selected value of h, the change in magnitude of either component of the state vector at $t = h$ over the values at $t = 0$ is excessive, then it is necessary only to have the machine decrease h progressively until the change is acceptable. Likewise, if the change is too small, then h can be increased progressively until an acceptable change is realized. The value of h selected by this process is carried over and used to calculate the state vector at $t = 2h$. If the changes in the magnitudes of the variables in the state vector from $t = h$ to $t = 2h$ are acceptable, the program proceeds. If not, h is increased or decreased until the change is acceptable.

Example 5.6.2:   In Fig. 5.3.2, let the network parameters be given as

$R_1 = R_{12} = R_5 = 10$ ohms
$L_1 = L_{12} = L_5 = 1$ henry
$n = 1$
$g_7 = 10^{-3}$ mho
$C_6 = 0.2 \times 10^{-4}$ farad
$\dfrac{1}{k_3} = \dfrac{1}{k_4} = 0.0257$
$I_3 = I_4 = 10^{-8}$ amp

Let $v_i(t) = 155.6 \cos 377t$. Then, using the state model in Eq. (5.3.16), obtain the augmented state model for the full-wave rectifier circuit. Plot the solution curves for the state variables, utilizing a computer program (Runge-Kutta method) already available.

Solution: The entries in the coefficient matrices appearing in Eq. (5.3.16) can also be written as

$$\alpha_{11} = \alpha_{22} = \frac{L_{12}R_{12} - L_1R_1 - L_5(R_1 + R_{12}) - R_5(L_1 + L_{12})}{(L_1 + L_{12})(L_1 - L_{12} + 2L_5)}$$

$$\alpha_{12} = \alpha_{21} = \frac{L_{12}R_1 - L_1R_{12} - L_5(R_1 + R_{12}) + R_5(L_1 + L_{12})}{(L_1 + L_{12})(L_1 - L_{12} + 2L_5)}$$

$$\alpha_{13} = -\alpha_{23} = \frac{1}{L_1 - L_{12} + 2L_5}$$

$$\delta_{11} = -\delta_{22} = \frac{L_1 + L_5}{(L_1 + L_{12})(L_1 - L_{12} + 2L_5)}$$

$$\delta_{12} = -\delta_{21} = \frac{L_{12} - L_5}{(L_1 + L_{12})(L_1 - L_{12} + 2L_5)}$$

$$\beta_1 = \beta_2 = \frac{-n}{L_1 + L_{12}}$$

After substituting the given numerical values we have

$$\alpha_{11} = \alpha_{22} = -10 \qquad \alpha_{12} = \alpha_{21} = 0$$
$$\alpha_{13} = -\alpha_{23} = 0.5 \qquad \delta_{11} = -\delta_{22} = 0.5$$
$$\delta_{12} = -\delta_{21} = 0 \qquad \beta_1 = \beta_2 = -0.5$$

and Eq. (5.3.16) becomes

$$\frac{d}{dt}\begin{bmatrix} i_1 \\ i_2 \\ V_6 \end{bmatrix} = \begin{bmatrix} -10 & 0 & 0.5 \\ 0 & -10 & -0.5 \\ -5 \times 10^4 & 5 \times 10^4 & -50 \end{bmatrix}\begin{bmatrix} i_1 \\ i_2 \\ v_6 \end{bmatrix} + \begin{bmatrix} 0.5 & 0 \\ 0 & -0.5 \\ 0 & 0 \end{bmatrix}\begin{bmatrix} f_3(-i_1) \\ f_4(i_2) \end{bmatrix}$$
$$+ \begin{bmatrix} -0.5 \\ -0.5 \\ 0 \end{bmatrix} v_i$$

$$f_3(-i_1) = 0.0257 \ln (-10^8 i_1 + 1)$$
$$f_4(i_2) = 0.0257 \ln (10^8 i_2 + 1)$$

The augmented system of state equations is

$$\frac{d}{dt}\begin{bmatrix} i_1 \\ i_2 \\ v_6 \\ -- \\ v_i \\ f_i \end{bmatrix} = \left[\begin{array}{ccc:cc} -10 & 0 & 0.5 & 0.5 & 0 \\ 0 & -10 & -0.5 & -0.5 & 0 \\ -5 \times 10^4 & 5 \times 10^4 & -50 & 0 & 0 \\ \hdashline 0 & 0 & 0 & 0 & -377 \\ 0 & 0 & 0 & 377 & 0 \end{array}\right]\begin{bmatrix} i_1 \\ i_2 \\ v_6 \\ -- \\ v_i \\ f_i \end{bmatrix}$$
$$+ \begin{bmatrix} 0.5 f_3(-i_1) \\ -0.5 f_4(i_2) \\ 0 \\ \hdashline 0 \\ 0 \end{bmatrix}$$

The solution curves for the state variables are plotted in Fig. 5.6.1.

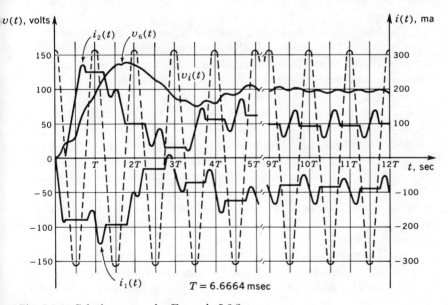

$T = 6.6664 \text{ msec}$

Fig. 5.6.1   Solution curves for Example 5.6.2.

5.7 ANALOG - COMPUTER SOLUTIONS

It is not our purpose here to enter into a detailed discussion of the design features of analog computers.   Rather, our purpose is to show how state equations are programmed for solution on such a machine, considering only the problem of scaling and the appropriate interconnection of the various basic operational components of the machines.

Consider the system of linear constant-coefficient differential equations

$$\frac{d}{dt} \begin{bmatrix} x_1(t) \\ x_2(t) \\ x_3(t) \end{bmatrix} = \begin{bmatrix} a_{11} & a_{12} & a_{13} \\ a_{21} & a_{22} & a_{23} \\ a_{31} & a_{32} & a_{33} \end{bmatrix} \begin{bmatrix} x_1(t) \\ x_2(t) \\ x_3(t) \end{bmatrix} + \begin{bmatrix} e_1(t) \\ e_2(t) \\ e_3(t) \end{bmatrix} \qquad (5.7.1)$$

In an analog-computer solution of these equations, the state variables $x_1(t)$, $x_2(t)$, $x_3(t)$ and the excitation variables $e_1(t)$, $e_2(t)$, $e_3(t)$ are represented as voltages in a system of interconnected electronic components.   Each of the electronic components is designed so that the input and output voltages are related by an equation which corresponds to one of the several mathematical operations represented in the given equations.   An analog computer, then, is basically a collection of such components, with a convenient and flexible interconnection scheme, from which it is possible to construct an electronic system whose performance is represented by the given differential equations.

The measured performance of this system so constructed then represents, within a degree of approximation, the solution to the system of equations.

The basic operational components of a linear analog computer are shown in Fig. 5.7.1, along with the schematic diagram we shall use to represent them.   First a few words about the operational components themselves and then the schematic diagrams representing them.

In each case the terminal pairs on the left of the components in Fig. 5.7.1 are called *inputs* and the terminal pair on the right the *output*. The components labeled A are described as very high-gain low-frequency electronic amplifiers.   With appropriate selection and use of the amplifiers and the other elements in the operational units, the input-output characteristics of the units involve only the input and output terminal voltages.   Further, the operational components are always interconnected so that the output port of one component is connected to the input ports of other components with one terminal (ground) common to each component.

For this restricted class of components and interconnection patterns, the *signal-flow graph* is a useful tool for characterizing the system.   To show the basis for constructing a signal-flow graph, consider the algebraic

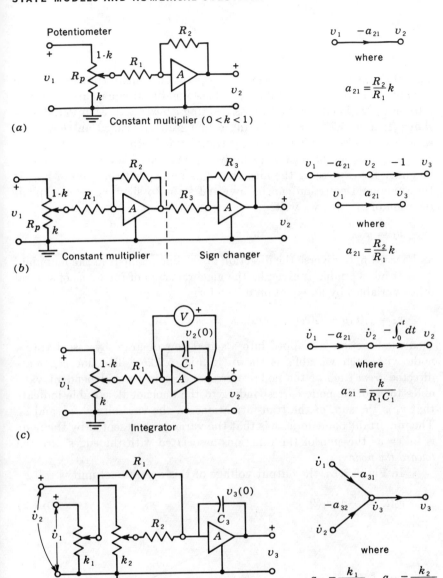

Fig. 5.7.1 Basic analog-computer operational components, along with signal-flow graph representations. (*a*) Constant multiplier; (*b*) constant multiplier with sign changer; (*c*) integrator; (*d*) integrator with multiple inputs.

equation

$$v_2 = f(v_1)$$

The function f can be regarded as an operation which "transforms" the variable v_1 into a new variable v_2. This functional equation is mapped into an operational diagram by associating a *node* with each variable as shown in Fig. 5.7.2a and directing a line segment, called an *element* or *edge, from v_1 to v_2* to signify that v_1 is transformed into v_2 by the function f. This mapping can be regarded simply as an alternative way of or another language for expressing the idea that v_2 is an explicit function of v_1. If the functional equation can be inverted so as to show v_1 as an explicit function of v_2, then we write

$$v_1 = g(v_2)$$

and accordingly reverse the direction of the line segment in the mapping.

If one variable is given as the algebraic sum of functions of several other variables by an equation of the form

$$v_4 = f_1(v_1) + f_2(v_2) + f_3(v_3)$$

then the function is mapped into a signal-flow diagram by associating a node with each variable as shown in Fig. 5.7.2b. The line segments directed *from* each of the nodes corresponding to the independent variables toward the node corresponding to the dependent variable indicate that v_4 is the sum of the transformations on the variables v_1, v_2, and v_3. The important point to note is that the variable represented by the node is taken as the sum of the functions associated with the edges directed *toward the node*.

In Fig. 5.7.1a, the output voltage of this operational unit is

$$v_2(t) = -a_{21}v_1(t) \tag{5.7.2}$$

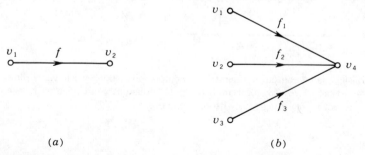

(a)   (b)

Fig. 5.7.2   (a) Mapping of the equation $v_2 = f(v_1)$; (b) mapping of the equation $v_4 = f_1(v_1) + f_2(v_2) + f_3(v_3)$ into a signal-flow graph.

where a_{21} is a positive constant, and therefore this unit is called a *constant multiplier*. The input to this component, like the inputs to all other components in the same figure, is shown as being across a continuously variable potentiometer in order to provide a continuously variable positive constant a_{21}. If a_{21} can be realized by the ratio R_2/R_1 of two fixed resistors, then, of course, the potentiometer can be omitted. The mapping of the function in Eq. (5.7.2) is shown in the diagram accompanying Fig. 5.7.1*a*. Note that the nodes in the mapping of this function can also be associated directly with the input and output ports of the components. Consequently, when two constant multipliers are cascaded as shown in Fig. 5.7.1*b* to realize a positive multiplier, the corresponding nodes in the mappings are united as one. The overall input-output characteristic of the assembly is given by

$$v_3(t) = a_{21}v_1(t)$$

and the mapping accordingly can be reduced to the alternative form shown.

The input-output characteristic of the integrator in Fig. 5.7.1*c* is given by

$$v_2(t) = -a_{21}\left[\int_0^t \dot{v}_1(\tau)\, d\tau + v_1(0) \right]$$

which, for convenience, is usually written in the form

$$v_2(t) = \int_0^t \dot{v}_2(\tau)\, d\tau + v_2(0) \tag{5.7.3}$$

where

$$\dot{v}_2(t) = -a_{21}v_1(t) \tag{5.7.4}$$

The signal-flow graph shown corresponds to this latter form with the use of the simple integral symbol to indicate integration. The initial value of the output voltage $v_2(0)$ is established as an initial voltage on the capacitor in the sense indicated by the meter shown.

The basic operation of summation is realized operationally by providing multiple inputs to the basic constant multipliers and integrators as shown in Fig. 5.7.1*d* for an integrator with two inputs. The same concept applies to constant multipliers having an arbitrary number of inputs. For the two inputs indicated, the output is given by

$$v_3(t) = \int_0^t \dot{v}_3(\tau)\, d\tau + v_3(0) \tag{5.7.5}$$

with

$$\dot{v}_3(t) = -a_{31}v_1(t) - a_{32}v_2(t) \tag{5.7.6}$$

The corresponding signal-flow graph accompanies the operational component.

Example 5.7.1: Establish an analog-computer circuit for the solution of the differential equation

$$\frac{d}{dt} x(t) = -ax(t) + be(t) = -0.9x(t) + e(t) \qquad x(0) = x_0$$

Solution: The signal-flow graph for this equation is shown in Fig. 5.7.3a and is established by simply associating a node with each variable in the equation and interconnecting these nodes with directed line segments consistent with the functional dependences indicated by the equation. In the analog-computer circuit, the magnitude of $x(t)$ corresponds to the negative of the voltage measured between the point labeled $-x$ and the ground point. The initial value of $x(t)$ is established as the initial voltage on the capacitor. Note the correspondence between the general appearance of the signal-flow graph and the computer

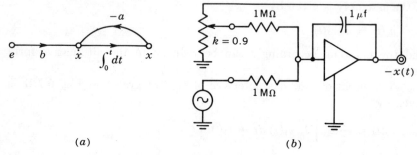

(a)   (b)

Fig. 5.7.3 (a) Signal-flow graph; (b) corresponding analog-computer setup for the solution of the equation $\dot{x}(t) = -ax(t) + be(t)$, with $a = 0.9$ and $b = 1$.

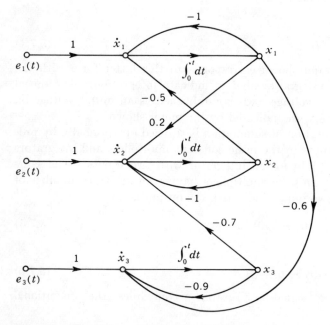

Fig. 5.7.4 Signal-flow graph for Eq. (5.7.7).

circuit. Both suggest the idea that the output of the integrator is multiplied by -0.9 and fed back into the input. This concept of "feedback" is used extensively in the study of certain classes of control systems and will be considered again in a later chapter.

Example 5.7.2: Establish an analog-computer circuit for the solution of the system of first-order differential equations

$$\frac{d}{dt}\begin{bmatrix} x_1(t) \\ x_2(t) \\ x_3(t) \end{bmatrix} = \begin{bmatrix} -1 & -0.5 & 0 \\ 0.2 & -1 & -0.7 \\ -0.6 & 0 & -0.9 \end{bmatrix}\begin{bmatrix} x_1(t) \\ x_2(t) \\ x_3(t) \end{bmatrix} + \begin{bmatrix} e_1(t) \\ e_2(t) \\ e_3(t) \end{bmatrix} \qquad (5.7.7)$$

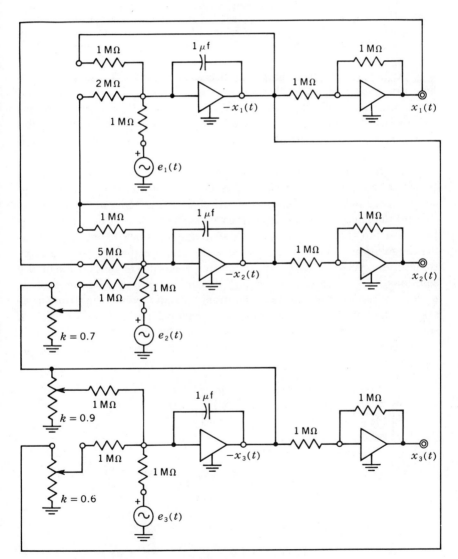

Fig. 5.7.5 Analog-computer representation of Eq. (5.7.7).

Solution: The given system of differential equations is mapped into a signal-flow graph by simply identifying a node with each excitation variable, each state variable, and the time derivative of each state variable as indicated in Fig. 5.7.4. The functional dependence of each of the dependent variables on the independent variables is indicated by directed edges between appropriate nodes. The fact that the state variables are obtained as time integrals of their derivatives is indicated by the edges with the associated integral signs. Note that the entries in the coefficient matrix appear as feedback elements, or edges, between the output nodes and the nodes of the various edges whose functional operation is integration.

The analog-computer network is established as shown in Fig. 5.7.5. The operational amplifiers are interconnected as indicated by the signal-flow graph. The excitation signals are supplied by appropriate signal generators. The numerical values of the various resistors in the operational components correspond to the numerical values of the coefficients in the given equations.

Although the linear graph as discussed in Chap. 4 and the signal-flow graph as defined in this section both contain directed edges and vertices, or nodes, the two should not be confused. The operational procedures used in developing the two graphs are entirely different, and they serve entirely different purposes, each having its own algebra and basic properties.

There is, of course, an upper bound on the magnitude of signals that can be tolerated in the analog computer, and for this reason it may be necessary to scale the equations so that the magnitudes of the state vector and their derivatives do not exceed certain bounds. It may sometimes be difficult to give an estimate of these magnitudes before actually realizing the solution. A knowledge of the system represented by the equations sometimes serves as a basis for estimating the order of magnitude of the solutions. In other cases one may obtain the necessary scale factors only after repeated attempts at solution. In any event, the problem of scaling the equations is an important practical problem in realizing a solution to a system of differential equations by an analog machine and one which can be approached systematically. Consider the system of equations

$$\frac{d}{dt}\begin{bmatrix} x_1(t) \\ x_2(t) \\ \cdots \\ x_n(t) \end{bmatrix} = \begin{bmatrix} p_{11} & p_{12} & \cdots & p_{1n} \\ p_{21} & p_{22} & \cdots & p_{2n} \\ \cdots & \cdots & \cdots & \cdots \\ p_{n1} & p_{n2} & \cdots & p_{nn} \end{bmatrix} \begin{bmatrix} x_1(t) \\ x_2(t) \\ \cdots \\ x_n(t) \end{bmatrix}$$

$$+ \begin{bmatrix} q_{11} & q_{12} & \cdots & q_{1k} \\ q_{21} & q_{22} & \cdots & q_{2k} \\ \cdots & \cdots & \cdots & \cdots \\ q_{n1} & q_{n2} & \cdots & q_{nk} \end{bmatrix} \begin{bmatrix} e_1(t) \\ e_2(t) \\ \cdots \\ e_k(t) \end{bmatrix}$$

The state variable x_i can be altered by simply substituting

$$x_i = \alpha_i x_i' \qquad i = 1, 2, \ldots, n$$

Applying this change to the state variable x_2, for example, gives

$$\frac{d}{dt} \begin{bmatrix} x_1(t) \\ x_2'(t) \\ x_3(t) \\ \cdots \\ x_n(t) \end{bmatrix} = \begin{bmatrix} p_{11} & \alpha_2 p_{12} & p_{13} & \cdots & p_{1n} \\ (1/\alpha_2)p_{21} & p_{22} & (1/\alpha_2)p_{23} & \cdots & (1/\alpha_2)p_{2n} \\ p_{31} & \alpha_2 p_{32} & p_{33} & \cdots & p_{3n} \\ \cdots & \cdots & \cdots & \cdots & \cdots \\ p_{n1} & \alpha_2 p_{n2} & p_{n3} & \cdots & p_{nn} \end{bmatrix}$$

$$\times \begin{bmatrix} x_1(t) \\ x_2'(t) \\ x_3(t) \\ \cdots \\ x_n(t) \end{bmatrix} + \begin{bmatrix} q_{11} & q_{12} & \cdots & q_{1k} \\ (1/\alpha_2)q_{21} & (1/\alpha_2)q_{22} & \cdots & (1/\alpha_2)q_{2k} \\ \cdots & \cdots & \cdots & \cdots \\ q_{n1} & q_{n2} & \cdots & q_{nk} \end{bmatrix} \begin{bmatrix} e_1(t) \\ e_2(t) \\ \cdots \\ e_k(t) \end{bmatrix}$$

Note that a change in the magnitude of a variable in the state vector results in a change in the magnitude of all coefficients in the corresponding row and column of the coefficient matrix except the term on the diagonal. It also alters the magnitude of the coefficients in the corresponding $\mathbf{Q}$ matrix. The magnitude of the excitation signals can likewise be scaled to any size by simply setting

$$e_i(t) = \beta_i e_i'(t)$$

To alter the magnitude of the time derivative of the state variables, it is necessary to make a substitution of variables on t. Thus, if we let

$$t = c\tau$$

then

$$\frac{d}{dt} x_i(t) = \frac{1}{c} \frac{d}{d\tau} x_i(c\tau) \qquad e_i(t) = e_i(c\tau)$$

and we see that such a change in time scale affects the magnitude of the derivatives of all state variables alike and changes the argument of all time-varying excitation functions.

Most analog computers also contain a limited number of nonlinear operational components such as multipliers, as well as function generators, etc. These components, along with the basic linear operational components discussed above, provide the capability for solving at least certain classes of nonlinear differential equations. The basic procedure for solution, however, is identical to that described above for linear systems.

5.8 SYSTEMS OF DISCRETE - STATE COMPONENTS AND NUMERICAL SOLUTIONS

In the previous sections of this chapter, the characteristics of the system components considered have been assumed to be represented by ordinary

differential and/or algebraic equations.   When some or all of the components in the system are characterized by ordinary *difference* equations,
rather than differential equations, the system is referred to as a *discrete-
state system*.   Notable examples of discrete-state systems occur in the
areas of socioeconomic system studies, where accounting records are
maintained at regular intervals of time, and in digital feedback control
systems, where correction signals are applied at discrete intervals of time,
as shown in Fig. 5.8.1.

The techniques and concepts for analyzing discrete-state systems
closely parallel those of continuous systems.   This section develops the
counterpart of each important concept developed in the previous sections
as it applies to discrete-state systems.

Although it is possible to represent the terminal characteristics
of each physical component in a system in a discrete-state form before
applying the constraint equations resulting from interconnections, such
a procedure does not, in general, lead to a satisfactory discrete-state model
of the system unless the sampling interval is very small.

General methods for realizing numerical solutions to discrete-state
equations of the form

$$\mathbf{\Psi}(n + 1) = \mathbf{\Phi}\mathbf{\Psi}(n) + \mathbf{\Delta}\mathbf{E}(n) \qquad n = 0, 1, 2, \ldots \tag{5.8.1}$$

have already been discussed in Sec. 5.5 in connection with the solution
of the continuous-state equations of the form

$$\frac{d}{dt}\,\mathbf{\Psi}(t) = \mathbf{P}\mathbf{\Psi}(t) + \mathbf{Q}\mathbf{E}(t) \tag{5.8.2}$$

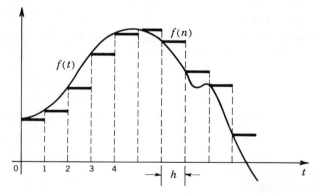

Fig. 5.8.1   Time variation of terminal variables implied in a
discrete-state model.

One of the techniques discussed there is first to transform Eq. (5.8.2) to a homogeneous equivalent form before representing the differential equations in a discrete form for numerical solution. When all component models are discrete-state forms, a system of nonhomogeneous discrete-state equations of the general form given in Eq. (5.8.1) is developed directly from the structure of the system. Numerical solutions and certain theoretical studies of such discrete-state systems are greatly simplified when the system of nonhomogeneous difference equations is first transformed to an equivalent homogeneous form. The techniques involved in making such a transformation are similar to those used in Sec. 5.5 to transform nonhomogeneous differential equations to the homogeneous equivalent form.

Consider, for example, the homogeneous equivalent of Eq. (5.8.1) when $\mathbf{\Psi}(0) = \mathbf{\Psi}_0$ and

$$\mathbf{E}(n) = \mathbf{E}u(n)$$

where

$$u(n) = \begin{cases} 0 & n < 0 \\ 1 & n \geq 0 \end{cases}$$

The sequence of numbers $u(n) = 1$, $n = 0, 1, \ldots$, can be considered as the magnitudes of a unit step function $u(t)$ sampled at regularly spaced intervals of time, and represents the solution to the difference equation

$$u(n + 1) = u(n) \qquad u(0) = 1$$

Consequently, the nonhomogeneous system

$$\mathbf{\Psi}(n + 1) = \mathbf{\Phi}\mathbf{\Psi}(n) + \mathbf{\Delta E}u(n) \qquad \mathbf{\Psi}(0) = \mathbf{\Psi}_0$$

is equivalent to the homogeneous system

$$\begin{bmatrix} \mathbf{\Psi}(n + 1) \\ u(n + 1) \end{bmatrix} = \begin{bmatrix} \mathbf{\Phi} & \mathbf{\Delta E} \\ 0 & 1 \end{bmatrix} \begin{bmatrix} \mathbf{\Psi}(n) \\ u(n) \end{bmatrix} \qquad \begin{bmatrix} \mathbf{\Psi}(0) \\ u(0) \end{bmatrix} = \begin{bmatrix} \mathbf{\Psi}_0 \\ 1 \end{bmatrix}$$

Any system of nonhomogeneous difference equations can be transformed into a homogeneous equivalent system provided only that the excitation vector represents the solution to difference equations.

Following a development very similar to that beginning with Eq. (5.5.18), let the excitation vector $\mathbf{E}(n)$ in Eq. (5.8.1) be an mth-order vector defined on the interval I ($n_1 < n < n_2$). Such a vector sequence of numbers can be represented by the infinite series of vectors in n,

$$\mathbf{E}(n) = \mathbf{E}_1(n) + \mathbf{E}_2(n) + \cdots + \mathbf{E}_r(n) + \cdots \qquad (5.8.3)$$

where each vector sequence in n is of the form

$$\mathbf{E}_i(n) = \mathbf{K}_i \begin{bmatrix} 1 \\ n \\ n(n-1) \\ \cdot \\ \cdot \\ \cdot \\ \prod_{j=0}^{m_i} (n-j) \end{bmatrix} \gamma_i^n = \mathbf{K}_i \mathbf{F}_i(n) \tag{5.8.4}$$

and where

$\mathbf{K}_i$ is a rectangular matrix of constants
$\mathbf{F}_i(n)$ is a vector sequence of order $m_i + 1$ as indicated

The coefficients in $\mathbf{K}_i$ and the constants γ_i may be real or complex numbers. In the special case where $\mathbf{K}_i$ is a column vector $\mathbf{K}_i$, $\mathbf{E}(n)$ in Eq. (5.8.3) reduces to

$$\mathbf{E}(n) = \mathbf{K}_1 \gamma_1^n + \mathbf{K}_2 \gamma_2^n + \cdots \tag{5.8.5}$$

Upon setting $\gamma_1^n = e^{a_i h n}$ we see that, when $a_i = j\omega_i$, Eq. (5.8.5) can be regarded as a sequence of numbers obtained by sampling a Fourier series at regular intervals $t = hn$, and $\gamma_i = e^{j\omega_i h}$ is a complex number. Likewise, if $\gamma_i = 1$ ($i = 1, 2, 3, \ldots$), then Eq. (5.8.4) reduces to a sampled power series in t.

Upon replacing the argument n by $n + 1$ in Eq. (5.8.4) it is easy to show that in general

$$\mathbf{F}_i(n+1) = \mathbf{T}_i \mathbf{F}_i(n) \tag{5.8.6}$$

where

$$\mathbf{T}_i = \gamma_i \begin{bmatrix} 1 & 0 & 0 & \cdots & 0 & 0 \\ 1 & 1 & 0 & \cdots & 0 & 0 \\ 0 & 2 & 1 & \cdots & 0 & 0 \\ \cdot & \cdot & \cdot & \cdots & \cdot & \cdot \\ 0 & 0 & & \cdots & 1 & 0 \\ 0 & 0 & & \cdots & m_i & 1 \end{bmatrix}$$

The initial value of the vector $\mathbf{F}_i(n)$ as obtained by setting $n = 0$ in Eq. (5.8.4) is

$$\mathbf{F}_i(0) = \begin{bmatrix} 1 \\ 0 \\ \cdot \\ \cdot \\ \cdot \\ 0 \end{bmatrix} \tag{5.8.7}$$

It follows that $F_i(n)$ represents the solution to the difference equations in Eq. (5.8.6) with initial conditions given by Eq. (5.8.7), and the homogeneous equivalent of Eq. (5.8.1) for the excitation vector given in Eq. (5.8.3) is

$$
\begin{bmatrix}
\Psi(n+1) \\
F_1(n+1) \\
F_2(n+1) \\
\cdots \\
F_r(n+1)
\end{bmatrix}
=
\begin{bmatrix}
\Phi & \Delta K_1 & \Delta K_2 & \cdots & \Delta K_r \\
0 & T_1 & 0 & \cdots & 0 \\
0 & 0 & T_2 & \cdots & 0 \\
\cdots & & & & \\
0 & 0 & 0 & \cdots & T_r
\end{bmatrix}
\begin{bmatrix}
\Psi(n) \\
F_1(n) \\
F_2(n) \\
\cdots \\
F_r(n)
\end{bmatrix}
\tag{5.8.8}
$$

Example 5.8.1: Establish the homogeneous equivalent of the discrete-state equations

$$\Psi(n+1) = \Phi\Psi(n) + \Delta E(n)$$

when

$$E(n) = E_0 + E_1 n + E_2 n^2$$

Solution: The given function can be represented by the series

$$
E(n) = K_1 + K_2 n + K_3 n(n-1) = \begin{bmatrix} K_1 & K_2 & K_3 \end{bmatrix}
\begin{bmatrix}
1 \\
n \\
n(n-1)
\end{bmatrix}
$$

where $K_1 = E_0$, $K_2 = E_1 + E_2$, and $K_3 = E_2$ are column vectors. Upon setting $f_1(n) = 1$, $f_2(n) = n$, and $f_3(n) = n(n-1)$, it follows that

$$
\begin{bmatrix}
f_1(n+1) \\
f_2(n+1) \\
f_3(n+1)
\end{bmatrix}
=
\begin{bmatrix}
1 & 0 & 0 \\
1 & 1 & 0 \\
0 & 2 & 1
\end{bmatrix}
\begin{bmatrix}
f_1(n) \\
f_2(n) \\
f_3(n)
\end{bmatrix}
$$

and the homogeneous equivalent is

$$
\begin{bmatrix}
\Psi(n+1) \\
\hline
f_1(n+1) \\
f_2(n+1) \\
f_3(n+1)
\end{bmatrix}
=
\left[
\begin{array}{c|ccc}
\Phi & \Delta K_1 & \Delta K_2 & \Delta K_3 \\
\hline
0 & 1 & 0 & 0 \\
0 & 1 & 1 & 0 \\
0 & 0 & 2 & 1
\end{array}
\right]
\begin{bmatrix}
\Psi(n) \\
\hline
f_1(n) \\
f_2(n) \\
f_3(n)
\end{bmatrix}
$$

With initial conditions $f_1(0) = 1$ and $f_2(0) = f_3(0) = 0$.

Given a system of homogeneous discrete-state equations of the form

$$\Psi(n+1) = \Phi\Psi(n) \qquad \Psi(0) = \Psi_0$$

it follows, of course, that the analytical solution is simply

$$\Psi(n) = \Phi^n \Psi(0)$$

where Φ^n is a matrix whose entries are a function of n. Φ^n can be evaluated through the properties of functions of a matrix, as discussed in Chap. 6.

PROBLEMS

5.1   Draw the system graphs for the systems shown schematically in Fig. P5.1, and identify a maximally selected tree in each graph.

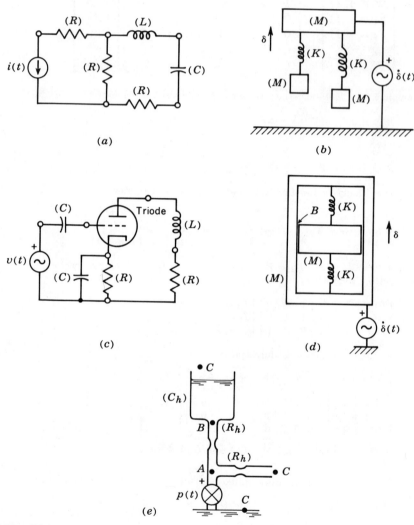

Fig. P5.1

5.2   Terminal equations for the two-winding transformer shown schematically in Fig. P5.2 are given as

$$\begin{bmatrix} v_1(t) \\ v_2(t) \end{bmatrix} = \begin{bmatrix} L_1 & M \\ M & L_2 \end{bmatrix} \frac{d}{dt} \begin{bmatrix} i_1(t) \\ i_2(t) \end{bmatrix} + \begin{bmatrix} R_1 & 0 \\ 0 & R_2 \end{bmatrix} \begin{bmatrix} i_1(t) \\ i_2(t) \end{bmatrix}$$

(a)   Assuming that the coefficient matrix

$$L = \begin{bmatrix} L_1 & M \\ M & L_2 \end{bmatrix}$$

is nonsingular, arrange these terminal equations in a state-model form.

(b)   Let **L** be singular, and repeat part a. Show that only one state equation (which also involves the derivative of the terminal voltages) must be considered.

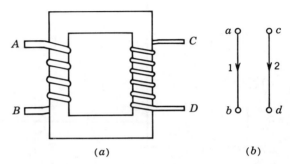

Fig. P5.2   (a) A two-winding transformer; (b) terminal graph.

5.3   Obtain a state model for the systems of two-terminal components indicated in Fig. P5.3.

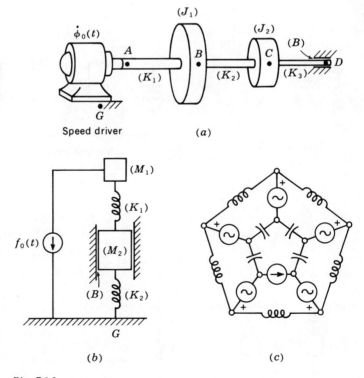

Fig. P5.3

5.4   Derive state models for the systems in Fig. P5.4.   In each case, explain
how the tree is selected, and discuss any problems encountered.

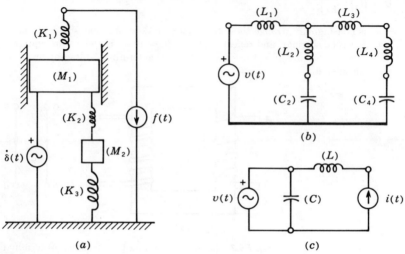

Fig. P5.4

5.5   Derive state-model equations for the systems of multiterminal components
shown in Fig. P5.5.

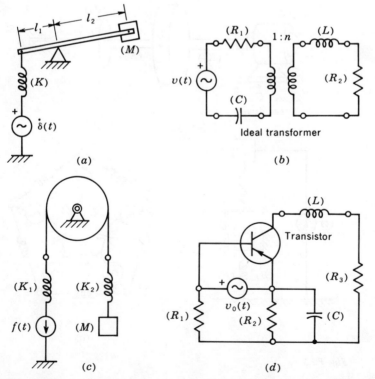

Fig. P5.5

5.6   For the matrix

$$\mathbf{P} = \begin{bmatrix} 1 & 1 \\ -1 & -1 \end{bmatrix}$$

calculate $e^{\mathbf{P}t}$ from Eq. (5.4.6).

5.7   If

$$\mathbf{P} = \begin{bmatrix} 1 & -1 \\ -1 & 1 \end{bmatrix}$$

calculate the general term of the infinite series $e^{\mathbf{P}t}$ given in Eq. (5.4.6).

5.8   Calculate $e^{\mathbf{P}t}$ and $e^{-\mathbf{P}t}$ if

$$\mathbf{P} = \begin{bmatrix} 1 & -1 & 1 \\ 1 & -1 & 1 \\ 0 & 0 & 0 \end{bmatrix}$$

5.9   Determine a numerical solution of the following state-model equations for $t = h, 2h, 3h, \ldots, 10h$:

$$\frac{d}{dt}\begin{bmatrix} \psi_1(t) \\ \psi_2(t) \\ \psi_3(t) \end{bmatrix} = \begin{bmatrix} 1 & -1 & 1 \\ 1 & -1 & 1 \\ 0 & 0 & 0 \end{bmatrix}\begin{bmatrix} \psi_1(t) \\ \psi_2(t) \\ \psi_3(t) \end{bmatrix} \qquad \psi_0 = \begin{bmatrix} 1 \\ 1 \\ 1 \end{bmatrix}$$

Note that the coefficient matrix is the same as that given in Prob. 5.8. Make a sketch indicating the discrete values of each of the state variables.

5.10   Determine the solution of the following nonhomogeneous state equations by the method leading to Eq. (5.5.10),

$$\frac{d}{dt}\mathbf{\Psi}(t) = \mathbf{P}\mathbf{\Psi}(t) + \mathbf{Q}\mathbf{E}(t)$$

where

$$\mathbf{P} = \begin{bmatrix} 6 & -4 \\ 9 & -6 \end{bmatrix} \qquad \mathbf{Q} = \begin{bmatrix} 1 & 0 \\ 0 & 1 \end{bmatrix} \qquad \mathbf{E}(t) = \begin{bmatrix} 1 \\ 1 \end{bmatrix} \qquad \mathbf{\Psi}_0 = \begin{bmatrix} 2 \\ 3 \end{bmatrix}$$

5.11   Write a homogeneous equivalent to the nonhomogeneous state equations in Prob. 5.10 by augmenting the coefficient matrix, and obtain the solution for the augmented homogeneous equations. Compare your result with that obtained in Prob. 5.10.

5.12   For the following state equations, first draw the corresponding signal-flow graphs, and then determine an analog-computer setup corresponding to each set of equations.

(a) $\dfrac{d}{dt}\psi(t) = 5\psi(t) - 2e(t)$

(b) $\dfrac{d}{dt}\begin{bmatrix} \psi_1(t) \\ \psi_2(t) \end{bmatrix} = \begin{bmatrix} 0.5 & 3 \\ -2 & 1.5 \end{bmatrix}\begin{bmatrix} \psi_1(t) \\ \psi_2(t) \end{bmatrix} + \begin{bmatrix} 1 & -1 \\ 0 & 1 \end{bmatrix}\begin{bmatrix} e_1(t) \\ e_2(t) \end{bmatrix}$

(c) $\dfrac{d}{dt}\begin{bmatrix} \psi_1(t) \\ \psi_2(t) \\ \psi_3(t) \end{bmatrix} = \begin{bmatrix} 0 & -1 & -1 \\ 1 & 0 & 0 \\ -0.5 & 1 & 0 \end{bmatrix}\begin{bmatrix} \psi_1(t) \\ \psi_2(t) \\ \psi_3(t) \end{bmatrix} + \begin{bmatrix} 1 & 0 \\ 1 & -1 \\ 1 & 1 \end{bmatrix}\begin{bmatrix} e_1(t) \\ e_2(t) \end{bmatrix}$

5.13   An nth-order differential equation of the form

$$\frac{d^n}{dt^n}\psi(t) + a_1 \frac{d^{n-1}}{dt^{n-1}}\psi(t) + \cdots + a_{n-1}\frac{d}{dt}\psi(t) + a_n\psi(t) = 0$$

with the initial conditions

$$\psi(0) = \psi_0$$
$$\psi'(0) = \psi_0'$$
$$\cdots\cdots\cdots\cdots$$
$$\psi^{(n-1)}(0) = \psi_0^{(n-1)}$$

can be put in a normal form by defining a new set of variables. Indeed if

$$\psi_1 = \psi$$
$$\psi_2 = \psi_1' = \psi'$$
$$\psi_3 = \psi_2' = \psi''$$
$$\cdots\cdots\cdots$$
$$\psi_n = \psi_{n-1}' = \psi^{(n-1)}$$

then

$$\frac{d}{dt}\begin{bmatrix} \psi_1 \\ \psi_2 \\ \psi_3 \\ \cdots \\ \psi_{n-1} \\ \psi_n \end{bmatrix} = \begin{bmatrix} 0 & 1 & 0 & 0 & \cdots & 0 & 0 \\ 0 & 0 & 1 & 0 & \cdots & 0 & 0 \\ 0 & 0 & 0 & 1 & \cdots & 0 & 0 \\ \cdots\cdots\cdots\cdots\cdots\cdots\cdots\cdots \\ 0 & 0 & 0 & 0 & \cdots & 0 & 1 \\ -a_n & -a_{n-1} & -a_{n-2} & -a_{n-3} & \cdots & a_2 & a_1 \end{bmatrix} \begin{bmatrix} \psi_1 \\ \psi_2 \\ \psi_3 \\ \cdots \\ \psi_{n-1} \\ \psi_n \end{bmatrix}$$

$$\begin{bmatrix} \psi_1(0) \\ \psi_2(0) \\ \psi_3(0) \\ \cdots \\ \psi_{n-1}(0) \\ \psi_n(0) \end{bmatrix} = \begin{bmatrix} \psi(0) \\ \psi'(0) \\ \psi''(0) \\ \cdots \\ \psi^{(n-2)}(0) \\ \psi^{(n-1)}(0) \end{bmatrix}$$

Following a similar procedure, put the following higher-order differential equations into a normal form, and set up the analog-computer diagram for each of these normal-form equations:

(a) $3\dfrac{d^2}{dt^2}\psi(t) - \dfrac{d}{dt}\psi(t) + 2\psi(t) = 0$

      $\psi(0) = 0 \qquad \psi'(0) = 1$

(b) $2\dfrac{d^3}{dt^3}\psi(t) + 4\dfrac{d^2}{dt^2}\psi(t) - 2\dfrac{d}{dt}\psi(t) + 3\psi(t) = e(t)$

      $\psi(0) = 1 \qquad \psi'(0) = -1 \qquad \psi''(0) = 0$
      $e(t)$ is a known function of time

(c) $-\dfrac{d^2}{dt^2}\psi(t) + 7\dfrac{d}{dt}\psi(t) = 2e(t)$

      $\psi(0) = 1 \qquad \psi'(0) = 2$
      $e(t)$ is a known function of time

5.14   Obtain the homogeneous equivalent to the nonhomogeneous discrete-state equations

$$\Psi(n+1) = \Phi\Psi(n) + \Delta E(n)$$

$$E(n) = \begin{bmatrix} 1 \\ 1 \end{bmatrix} + \begin{bmatrix} 0 \\ 2 \end{bmatrix} n + \begin{bmatrix} -1 \\ 0 \end{bmatrix} n^3$$

FURTHER READING

1.   Bashkow, T. R.: The A Matrix, New Network Description, *IRE Trans. Circuit Theory*, vol. CT-4, pp. 117–120, September, 1957.

2.   Bryant, P. R.: The Order of Complexity of Electrical Networks, *Proc. IEE*, Monograph 335E, vol. 106C, pp. 174–188, June, 1959.

3.   Wirth, J. L.: Time Domain Models of Physical Systems and Existence of Solutions, *Tech. Rept.* 1, NSF G-20949, Division of Engineering Research, College of Engineering, Michigan State University, May, 1962.

4.   Hildebrand, F. B.: "Introduction to Numerical Analysis," McGraw-Hill Book Company, New York, 1956.

5.   Mason, S. J.: Feedback Theory; Some Properties of Signal-flow-graphs, *Proc. IRE*, vol. 41, pp. 1144–1156, September, 1954.

6.   Mason, S. J.: Feedback Theory; Further Properties of Signal-flow-graphs, *Proc. IRE*, vol. 44, pp. 920–926, July, 1956.

6
Analytical Solutions
of Linear Systems

Although solutions of state equations on digital and analog computers are effective in realizing answers to given numerical problems, they give little insight as to the general properties of the solutions. In the case of nonlinear state equations, little can be said about the general properties of solutions. However, the general properties of the solutions of linear constant-coefficient state equations are well established. It is the specific objective of this chapter to explore these properties and relate them to the performance characteristics of the system represented by the state equations. This development introduces such important concepts as stability, transient and steady-state response characteristics, and frequency response.

6.1 INITIAL CONDITIONS AND CONTINUITY OF SOLUTIONS

It was shown in the previous chapter that the general form of the state equations for linear time-invariant systems is

$$\frac{d}{dt}\,\mathbf{\Psi}(t) = \mathbf{P\Psi}(t) + \mathbf{Q}_1\mathbf{E}(t) + \mathbf{Q}_2\frac{d}{dt}\,\mathbf{E}(t) \tag{6.1.1}$$

and that, to realize a solution, it is necessary to know the initial value of the state vector $\mathbf{\Psi}^{\cdot}(t)$. From a purely mathematical point of view, the initial value of the state vector represents a boundary condition that must be specified. From a practical application point of view, this boundary condition must be obtained from the system modeled by the state equations.

It was shown in Sec. 5.5 that by a change in the state vector the system in Eq. (6.1.1) can always be reduced to the form

$$\frac{d}{dt}\,\overline{\mathbf{\Psi}}^{\cdot}(t) = \mathbf{P}\overline{\mathbf{\Psi}}^{\cdot}(t) + (\mathbf{Q}_1 + \mathbf{P}\mathbf{Q}_2)\mathbf{E}(t) \qquad (6.1.2)$$

where

$$\overline{\mathbf{\Psi}}^{\cdot}(t) = \mathbf{\Psi}^{\cdot}(t) - \mathbf{Q}_2\mathbf{E}(t)$$

and that for solution purposes the state equations are always reduced to this form. Let the excitation vector $\mathbf{E}(t)$ be a finite and continuous function of time except for a finite number of jump discontinuities at $t = t_0, t_1, t_2, \ldots, t_n$.

To investigate the properties of the solution at the points of discontinuity, consider the integral of both sides of Eq. (6.1.2) with respect to t over the interval $t_0 - \epsilon \le t \le t_0 + \epsilon$, where ϵ is an arbitrary positive number. If we assume that the state vector $\mathbf{\Psi}^{\cdot}(t)$ is bounded in the neighborhood of $t = t_0$, then $\overline{\mathbf{\Psi}}^{\cdot}(t)$ is also bounded, and in the limit as $\epsilon \to 0$ the integral of the right-hand side of Eq. (6.1.2) vanishes and we have

$$\lim_{\epsilon \to 0} \int_{t_0-\epsilon}^{t_0+\epsilon} \frac{d}{dt}\,\overline{\mathbf{\Psi}}^{\cdot}(t)\,dt = \lim_{\epsilon \to 0} [\overline{\mathbf{\Psi}}^{\cdot}(t_0 + \epsilon) - \overline{\mathbf{\Psi}}^{\cdot}(t_0 - \epsilon)]$$
$$= \overline{\mathbf{\Psi}}^{\cdot}(t_0+) - \overline{\mathbf{\Psi}}^{\cdot}(t_0-) = 0$$

and it is established that the solution $\overline{\mathbf{\Psi}}^{\cdot}(t)$ to Eq. (6.1.2) is continuous if only the original state vector $\mathbf{\Psi}^{\cdot}(t)$ and the excitation vector are both bounded everywhere. The proposition that the state vector $\mathbf{\Psi}^{\cdot}(t)$ for physical systems is bounded is consistent with the observed properties of physical systems and is taken as the fourth basic postulate of system theory. This postulate is worth stating formally.

Postulate 4: If the excitation vector in the state equations for a linear time-invariant physical system consists of defined and bounded functions of time, then the state vector is also a bounded function of time in the neighborhood of any point $t = t_i$ on the finite time scale.

It is to be noted that this postulate makes no assertions about the behavior of the state vector as $t \to \infty$. It does, however, assert that the state variables do not increase without bound in any finite time interval. For example, in an electrical network, capacitor voltages and inductor currents may be discontinuous at points of discontinuity in the driving functions, but the variables are always finite. It is possible for the capacitor currents and the inductor voltages to be unbounded at certain points on the time scale, but these variables never appear in the state vector.

The really important consequence of the fourth basic postulate is, of course, that $\boldsymbol{\bar{\Psi}}(t)$ in Eq. (6.1.2) is continuous for any bounded excitation vector. Since

$$\boldsymbol{\Psi}(t) = \boldsymbol{\bar{\Psi}}(t) + \mathbf{Q}_2\mathbf{E}(t)$$

it follows that any discontinuities in the state vector are introduced directly by the term $\mathbf{Q}_2\mathbf{E}(t)$. Thus, if $\mathbf{E}(t)$ is discontinuous at $t = t_0$, then the corresponding discontinuity in the state vector is

$$\boldsymbol{\Psi}(t_0+) - \boldsymbol{\Psi}(t_0-) = \mathbf{Q}_2[\mathbf{E}(t_0+) - \mathbf{E}(t_0-)] \tag{6.1.3}$$

From Eq. (6.1.3) it follows that:

1. The state vector is always continuous if the excitation vector is continuous. This, however, is not a necessary condition for continuity, since $\mathbf{Q}_2$ is not necessarily of maximum rank.

2. If $\mathbf{Q}_2$ is a zero matrix, the state vector is continuous at $t = t_0$. In a system of two-terminal components, $\mathbf{Q}_2$ is a zero matrix if the edges in the system graph corresponding to the across drivers form no circuits with those components whose terminal equations are explicit in the derivative of across variables (that is, c-type components) and if the edges corresponding to the through drivers form no cut sets with those components whose terminal equations are explicit in the derivative of the through variables, that is, b-type components. This statement can be verified easily from the expressions derived in the previous chapter. Note that, in the system graph, circuits of edges corresponding to c-type components only and cut sets of edges corresponding to b-type components only are also allowed, but the existence of such circuits and cut sets in the system graph will not alter the situation; $\mathbf{Q}_2$ is still zero.

3. Since $\boldsymbol{\bar{\Psi}}(t) = \boldsymbol{\Psi}(t) - \mathbf{Q}_2\mathbf{E}(t)$ is continuous, the initial value of the transformed state vector can be evaluated from the $t = 0-$ values of the state vector and the excitation vector; i.e.,

$$\boldsymbol{\bar{\Psi}}(0+) = \boldsymbol{\bar{\Psi}}(0-) = \boldsymbol{\Psi}(0-) - \mathbf{Q}_2\mathbf{E}(0-)$$

and, insofar as the solution to the state equations is concerned, $t = 0-$ values can be used for the initial conditions.

Example 6.1.1: The electrical network in Fig. 5.2.2 was considered in Chap. 5 and the state equations developed as

$$\frac{d}{dt}\begin{bmatrix} v_4(t) \\ i_6(t) \end{bmatrix} = \begin{bmatrix} -G_5/(C_4 + C_7) & 0 \\ 0 & -R_2/(L_3 + L_6) \end{bmatrix} \begin{bmatrix} v_4(t) \\ i_6(t) \end{bmatrix}$$
$$+ \begin{bmatrix} 0 & -1/(C_4 + C_7) \\ -1/(L_3 + L_6) & -R_2/(L_3 + L_6) \end{bmatrix} \begin{bmatrix} v_1(t) \\ i_8(t) \end{bmatrix}$$
$$+ \begin{bmatrix} C_7/(C_4 + C_7) & 0 \\ 0 & -L_3/(L_3 + L_6) \end{bmatrix} \frac{d}{dt}\begin{bmatrix} v_1(t) \\ i_8(t) \end{bmatrix} \quad (6.1.4)$$

Determine the initial value of the state vector required to realize a solution to these state equations, and calculate explicitly the voltages of the capacitors and currents of the inductors at $t = 0-$ and $t = 0+$ when the driving functions are discontinuous at $t = 0$ with

$$v_1(t) = \begin{cases} 0 & t < 0 \\ E \cos \omega t & t \geq 0 \end{cases}$$
$$i_8(t) = \begin{cases} I & t < 0 \\ 0 & t \geq 0 \end{cases}$$

Solution: First of all, since in the system the voltage and current sources with discontinuous driving functions form circuits and cut sets, respectively, with capacitors and inductors, it follows that the solution is not continuous at $t = 0$. The $t = 0-$ values of the capacitor voltages and inductor currents can be found by solving the system for the time interval $t < 0$.

Since for $t < 0$ all voltage and current variables are of constant value, it follows from the terminal equations that all capacitor currents and all inductor voltages are identically equal to zero. Therefore, for the time region $t < 0$ all capacitors can be removed and all inductors can be replaced by short circuits in the original network. A solution of the resulting simple network gives

$$v_4(0-) = v_5(0-) = -R_5 I$$
$$i_6(0-) = -I \quad\quad\quad (6.1.5)$$
$$i_3(0-) = 0$$

To obtain a solution to the system model for the region $t > 0$, let the given state equations be transformed into the form of Eq. (6.1.2) by defining the new state vector

$$\begin{bmatrix} \psi_1(t) \\ \psi_2(t) \end{bmatrix} = \begin{bmatrix} v_4(t) - [C_1/(C_4 + C_7)]v_1(t) \\ i_6(t) + [L_3/(L_3 + L_6)]i_8(t) \end{bmatrix}$$

This vector is continuous at the discontinuities in $v_1(t)$ and $i_8(t)$ and therefore can be evaluated from the $t = 0-$ values as

$$\begin{bmatrix} \psi_1(0+) \\ \psi_2(0+) \end{bmatrix} = \begin{bmatrix} \psi_1(0-) \\ \psi_2(0-) \end{bmatrix} = \begin{bmatrix} -R_5 I \\ -I + [L_3/(L_3 + L_6)]I \end{bmatrix}$$

The values of the state variables at $t = 0+$ are given explicitly by

$$\begin{bmatrix} v_4(0+) \\ i_6(0+) \end{bmatrix} = \begin{bmatrix} v_4(0-) \\ i_6(0-) \end{bmatrix}$$
$$+ \begin{bmatrix} C_7/(C_4 + C_7) & 0 \\ 0 & -L_3/(L_3 + L_6) \end{bmatrix} \begin{bmatrix} v_1(0+) - v_1(0-) \\ i_8(0+) - i_8(0-) \end{bmatrix} \quad (6.1.6)$$

From the given driving functions and Eq. (6.1.5) we have

$$
\begin{bmatrix} v_4(0+) \\ i_6(0+) \end{bmatrix} = \begin{bmatrix} -R_5 I \\ -I \end{bmatrix} + \begin{bmatrix} C_7/(C_4 + C_7) & 0 \\ 0 & -L_3/(L_3 + L_6) \end{bmatrix} \begin{bmatrix} E \cos (0+) \\ -I \end{bmatrix}
$$

$$
= \begin{bmatrix} C_7/(C_4 + C_7) & -R_5 \\ 0 & -L_6/(L_3 + L_6) \end{bmatrix} \begin{bmatrix} E \\ I \end{bmatrix} \quad (6.1.7)
$$

Example 6.1.2: The cam used to derive the mechanical system in Fig. 6.1.1a is an "Archimedes spiral." The cam is at rest for $t < 0$, and it starts to rotate with a constant speed at $t = 0$. The displacement and velocity characteristics of the pin driven by the cam are shown in Fig. 6.1.1b; that is, the pin is assumed to follow the surface of the drive cam. Show that the state vector is continuous at $t = 0$ but is discontinuous at $t = t_1$.

Solution: The maximally selected tree and cotree identified in Fig. 6.1.1c include all dynamic components. Consequently, the state variables f_1, f_2, δ_3, and $\dot{\delta}_4$ are all continuous if the excitation velocity $\dot{\delta}_0(t)$ is bounded. However, from the given characteristics it is clear that $\dot{\delta}_0(t)$ is not defined at $t = t_1$, since $\delta_0(t)$ is discontinuous at this point. The velocity function is sometimes described as having an "impulse" at $t = t_1$. In any event $\dot{\delta}_0(t)$ does not satisfy the hypothesis of Postulate 4. The displacement as a function of time, however, is bounded. To show the properties of the solution at the points $t = 0$ and $t = t_1$, consider the state equations of the system, which are easily derived as

$$
\frac{d}{dt} \begin{bmatrix} f_1(t) \\ f_2(t) \\ \dot{\delta}_3(t) \\ \dot{\delta}_4(t) \end{bmatrix} = \begin{bmatrix} 0 & 0 & -K_1 & 0 \\ 0 & 0 & K_2 & -K_2 \\ 1/M_3 & -1/M_3 & 0 & 0 \\ 0 & 1/M_4 & 0 & 0 \end{bmatrix} \begin{bmatrix} f_1(t) \\ f_2(t) \\ \dot{\delta}_3(t) \\ \dot{\delta}_4(t) \end{bmatrix} + \begin{bmatrix} K_1 \\ 0 \\ 0 \\ 0 \end{bmatrix} \dot{\delta}_0(t)
$$

By setting $\dot{\delta}_0(t) = (d/dt)\delta_0(t)$ and defining a new state variable

$$
\psi_1(t) = f_1(t) - K_1 \delta_0(t)
$$

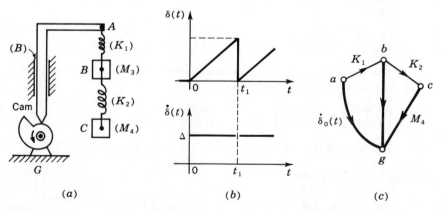

     (a)   (b)   (c)

Fig. 6.1.1 (a) A mechanical system; (b) cam characteristics; (c) system graph.

this system is transformed into the equivalent system

$$
\frac{d}{dt}\begin{bmatrix} \psi_1(t) \\ f_2(t) \\ \delta_3(t) \\ \delta_4(t) \end{bmatrix} = \begin{bmatrix} 0 & 0 & -K_1 & 0 \\ 0 & 0 & K_2 & -K_2 \\ 1/M_3 & -1/M_3 & 0 & 0 \\ 0 & 1/M_4 & 0 & 0 \end{bmatrix} \begin{bmatrix} \psi_1(t) \\ f_2(t) \\ \delta_3(t) \\ \delta_4(t) \end{bmatrix}
$$

$$
+ \begin{bmatrix} 0 \\ 0 \\ K_1/M_3 \\ 0 \end{bmatrix} \delta_0(t) \quad (6.1.8)
$$

for which the transformed state variable

$$
\psi_1(t) = f_1(t) - K_1\delta_0(t)
$$

is a continuous function of time. It follows, therefore, that $f_1(t)$ is continuous at $t = 0$ since $\delta_0(t)$ is continuous at this point. However, at $t = t_1$, $f_1(t)$ is discontinuous since $\delta_0(t)$ is discontinuous at this point. The magnitude of the discontinuity is, of course,

$$
f_1(t_1+) - f_1(t_1-) = K_1[\delta_0(t_1+) - \delta_0(t_1-)]
$$

6.2 ANALYTICAL EVALUATION OF THE TRANSITION MATRIX

It is shown in Sec. 5.4 that the solution of the linear state equations

$$
\frac{d}{dt}\mathbf{\Psi}(t) = \mathbf{P}\mathbf{\Psi}(t) \qquad \mathbf{\Psi}(0) = \mathbf{\Psi}_0
$$

is of the form

$$
\mathbf{\Psi}(t) = e^{\mathbf{P}t}\mathbf{\Psi}(0)
$$

where by definition

$$
e^{\mathbf{P}t} = \mathbf{U} + \mathbf{P}t + \mathbf{P}^2\frac{t^2}{2!} + \cdots
$$

The matrix function $f(\mathbf{P}) = e^{\mathbf{P}t}$ has already been identified as the transition matrix, and it is obtained by replacing the scalar λ in the infinite-series representation of $e^{\lambda t}$ by the matrix $\mathbf{P}$. Let this function be represented as

$$
f(\lambda) = e^{\lambda t} = 1 + t\lambda + \frac{t^2}{2!}\lambda^2 + \cdots
$$

There are, of course, other functions of a matrix $\mathbf{P}$ that one might be interested in evaluating, such as $\mathbf{P}^n$, $\cos \mathbf{P}$, $\mathbf{P}^{1/2}$, etc. This concept is extended to any analytic function of a complex variable λ defined by the series

$$
f(\lambda) = k_0 + k_1\lambda + k_2\lambda^2 + \cdots + k_m\lambda^m + \cdots \qquad (6.2.1)
$$

having a radius of convergence ρ, that is, a series which for $|\lambda| > \rho$ diverges. Upon substituting the matrix $\mathbf{P}$ for λ, we obtain the series

$$f(\mathbf{P}) = k_0\mathbf{U} + k_1\mathbf{P} + k_2\mathbf{P}^2 + \cdots k_m\mathbf{P}^m + \cdots \qquad (6.2.2)$$

The matrix series in Eq. (6.2.2) and the function $f(\mathbf{P})$ defined on the matrix $\mathbf{P}$ are said to converge if the numerical series consisting of the elements in the i, j position of $\mathbf{P}$ converge. It is shown in the Appendix that if the roots of the determinant $|\lambda\mathbf{U} - \mathbf{P}|$ are within the circle of convergence of Eq. (6.2.1) then the matrix series in Eq. (6.2.2) converges.

As we shall see, it is possible to evaluate any such function of a matrix $f(\mathbf{P})$ in closed form by finding another function $g(\lambda)$, in fact a finite polynomial, such that when we replace λ by the matrix $\mathbf{P}$ we have

$$f(\mathbf{P}) = g(\mathbf{P})$$

or

$$f(\mathbf{P}) - g(\mathbf{P}) = 0$$

This implies that the difference polynomial

$$d(\lambda) = f(\lambda) - g(\lambda) \qquad (6.2.3)$$

must have the property such that upon replacing λ by $\mathbf{P}$

$$d(\mathbf{P}) \equiv 0$$

The objective now is to find a polynomial $d(\lambda)$ for which $d(\mathbf{P}) \equiv 0$. With this polynomial and $f(\lambda)$ known, the finite polynomial $g(\lambda)$ which is to be used as a basis for evaluating $e^{\mathbf{P}t}$ is determined by Eq. (6.2.3).

In general, if a polynomial in λ vanishes when λ is replaced by a matrix $\mathbf{P}$, it is called an *annihilating polynomial* of $\mathbf{P}$. It is shown in the Appendix, Sec. A.2, that the *characteristic polynomial* $D(\lambda)$ obtained from the expansion of the determinant of the matrix $\lambda\mathbf{U} - \mathbf{P}$ is an annihilating polynomial of $\mathbf{P}$; that is, if

$$D(\lambda) = |\lambda\mathbf{U} - \mathbf{P}|$$

then

$$D(\mathbf{P}) \equiv 0$$

There may, of course, be other annihilating polynomials for a given square matrix $\mathbf{P}$. The monic† annihilating polynomial $m(\lambda)$ of *least degree* in λ is called the *minimal polynomial* of the matrix $\mathbf{P}$ and is the one used as a basis for evaluating the transition matrix $e^{\mathbf{P}t}$ and other functions of $\mathbf{P}$.

† A monic polynomial, by definition, has unity as the coefficient of the highest power of λ.

It is also shown in the Appendix that the minimal polynomial $m(\lambda)$ of a given square matrix $\mathbf{A}$ is determined from the relation

$$m(\lambda) = \frac{D(\lambda)}{D_{n-1}(\lambda)} \qquad (6.2.4)$$

where $D(\lambda)$ is the determinant of $\lambda\mathbf{U} - \mathbf{P}$ and $D_{n-1}(\lambda)$ consists of the greatest common divisors of all the minors of order $n - 1$ of $\lambda\mathbf{U} - \mathbf{P}$.

Example 6.2.1:   Calculate the characteristic and minimal polynomials of the matrix

$$\mathbf{P} = \begin{bmatrix} 2 & 1 & 0 \\ 0 & 2 & 0 \\ 0 & 0 & 2 \end{bmatrix}$$

and show that they are both annihilating polynomials.

Solution: Consider the inverse of $\lambda\mathbf{U} - \mathbf{P}$,

$$(\lambda\mathbf{U} - \mathbf{P})^{-1} = \frac{1}{D(\lambda)} \text{ adj } (\lambda\mathbf{U} - \mathbf{P}) = \frac{1}{D(\lambda)} \begin{bmatrix} (\lambda - 2)^2 & \lambda - 2 & 0 \\ 0 & (\lambda - 2)^2 & 0 \\ 0 & 0 & (\lambda - 2)^2 \end{bmatrix}$$

where

$$D(\lambda) = |\lambda\mathbf{U} - \mathbf{P}| = (\lambda - 2)^3$$

The entries in adj $(\lambda\mathbf{U} - \mathbf{P})$ represent the minors of order $n - 1$ of $\lambda\mathbf{U} - \mathbf{P}$. The highest common factor among these entries is

$$D_{n-1}(\lambda) = \lambda - 2$$

Therefore, the minimal polynomial is

$$m(\lambda) = \frac{D(\lambda)}{D_{n-1}(\lambda)} = (\lambda - 2)^2$$

To show that $m(\lambda)$ is an annihilating polynomial, replace λ by the matrix $\mathbf{P}$ to obtain

$$m(\mathbf{P}) = (\mathbf{P} - 2\mathbf{U})^2 = \begin{bmatrix} 0 & 1 & 0 \\ 0 & 0 & 0 \\ 0 & 0 & 0 \end{bmatrix}^2 = 0$$

Since

$$D(\lambda) = m(\lambda)D_{n-1}(\lambda) = (\lambda - 2)^2(\lambda - 2)$$

it follows that

$$D(\mathbf{P}) = (\mathbf{P} - 2\mathbf{U})^2(\mathbf{P} - 2\mathbf{U}) = 0$$

Return now to Eq. (6.2.3) and the problem of evaluating the finite polynomial $g(\lambda)$. The minimal polynomial $m(\lambda)$ defined in Eq. (6.2.4) serves as the annihilating polynomial $d(\lambda)$, that is,

$$d(\lambda) = m(\lambda) = f(\lambda) - g(\lambda) \qquad (6.2.5)$$

with

$$0 = f(\mathbf{P}) - g(\mathbf{P})$$

To establish the polynomial $g(\lambda)$, let $m(\lambda)$ be expressed in the general factored form

$$m(\lambda) = (\lambda - \lambda_1)^{r_1}(\lambda - \lambda_2)^{r_2} \cdots (\lambda - \lambda_k)^{r_k} \qquad (6.2.6)$$

where $\lambda_1, \lambda_2, \ldots, \lambda_k$ are all distinct. Substituting Eq. (6.2.6) into Eq. (6.2.5), we have

$$m(\lambda) = (\lambda - \lambda_1)^{r_1}(\lambda - \lambda_2)^{r_2} \cdots (\lambda - \lambda_k)^{r_k} = f(\lambda) - g(\lambda)$$

Since $m(\lambda)$ and its r_i derivative vanishes at $\lambda = \lambda_i$, the polynomials $f(\lambda)$ and $g(\lambda)$ are equal at these points, i.e.,

$$f(\lambda_i) = g(\lambda_i) \qquad f'(\lambda_i) = g'(\lambda_i) \cdots f^{(r_i-1)}(\lambda_i) = g^{(r_i-1)}(\lambda_i)$$
$$i = 1, 2, \ldots, k \quad (6.2.7)$$

The numerical values of the given function

$$f(\lambda_i), f'(\lambda_i), \ldots, f^{(r_i-1)}(\lambda_i) \qquad i = 1, 2, \ldots, k$$

in Eq. (6.2.7) are called the values of $f(\lambda)$ on the *spectrum of* $\mathbf{P}$, and by the relations in Eq. (6.2.7) the functions $f(\lambda)$ and $g(\lambda)$ are said to have the same values on the spectrum of $\mathbf{P}$. Thus, it has been established that two functions of a matrix $f(\mathbf{P})$ and $g(\mathbf{P})$ are equal if their corresponding scalar functions $f(\lambda)$ and $g(\lambda)$ are equal on the spectrum of the matrix $\mathbf{P}$.

The problem of analytically evaluating $e^{\mathbf{P}t}$ has been reduced to that of finding a polynomial $g(\lambda)$ which has the same values on the spectrum of $\mathbf{P}$ as the function $f(\lambda) = e^{\lambda t}$. This procedure is demonstrated in the following example.

Example 6.2.2: Evaluate the matrix $e^{\mathbf{P}t}$ when

$$\mathbf{P} = \begin{bmatrix} 2 & -1 \\ -1 & 4 \end{bmatrix}$$

Solution: The minimal polynomial is evaluated by considering the inverse of the characteristic matrix

$$\lambda\mathbf{U} - \mathbf{P} = \begin{bmatrix} \lambda - 2 & 1 \\ 1 & \lambda - 4 \end{bmatrix}$$

This inverse is

$$(\lambda\mathbf{U} - \mathbf{P})^{-1} = \frac{1}{D(\lambda)}\begin{bmatrix} \lambda - 4 & -1 \\ -1 & \lambda - 2 \end{bmatrix}$$

where

$$D(\lambda) = (\lambda - 4)(\lambda - 2) - 1 = \lambda^2 - 6\lambda + 7 = (\lambda - \lambda_1)(\lambda - \lambda_2)$$

and

$$\lambda_1 = 3 + \sqrt{2} \quad \text{and} \quad \lambda_2 = 3 - \sqrt{2}$$

Since for the given matrix **P** there are no common factors among the entries of the adjoint matrix, the characteristic polynomial is also the minimal polynomial.

To evaluate e^{Pt}, it is necessary to find a polynomial $g(\lambda)$ which has the same value as

$$f(\lambda) = e^{\lambda t}$$

on the spectrum of **P**, that is, a polynomial $g(\lambda)$ such that

$$g(\lambda_1) = f(\lambda_1) = e^{\lambda_1 t}$$

and   (6.2.8)

$$g(\lambda_2) = f(\lambda_2) = e^{\lambda_2 t}$$

Any polynomial $g(\lambda)$ passing through the two points in Eq. (6.2.8) is acceptable. The polynomial of least degree is a straight line passing through the points $[\lambda_1, f(\lambda_1)]$ and $[\lambda_2, f(\lambda_2)]$ as indicated in Fig. 6.2.1. The equations for this straight line as established by the Lagrange interpolation formula† are

$$g(\lambda) = \frac{\lambda - \lambda_2}{\lambda_1 - \lambda_2} f(\lambda_1) + \frac{\lambda - \lambda_1}{\lambda_2 - \lambda_1} f(\lambda_2)$$

or   (6.2.9)

$$g(\lambda) = \frac{\lambda - 3 + \sqrt{2}}{2\sqrt{2}} e^{\lambda_1 t} + \frac{\lambda - 3 - \sqrt{2}}{-2\sqrt{2}} e^{\lambda_2 t}$$

† A general discussion of the Lagrange interpolation formula is given in the Appendix.

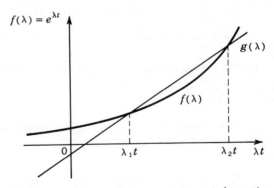

Fig. 6.2.1 Polynomial representation of $e^{\lambda t}$ on the spectrum of the matrix P.

The required matrix function $e^{\mathbf{P}t}$ is evaluated by simply replacing λ by $\mathbf{P}$ in Eqs. (6.2.9). The result is

$$g(\mathbf{P}) = f(\mathbf{P}) = e^{\mathbf{P}t} = (\mathbf{P} - \lambda_2\mathbf{U}) \frac{e^{\lambda_1 t}}{\lambda_1 - \lambda_2} - (\mathbf{P} - \lambda_1\mathbf{U}) \frac{e^{\lambda_2 t}}{\lambda_2 - \lambda_1}$$

$$= \begin{bmatrix} 2 - \lambda_2 & -1 \\ -1 & 4 - \lambda_2 \end{bmatrix} \frac{e^{\lambda_1 t}}{\lambda_1 - \lambda_2} + \begin{bmatrix} 2 - \lambda_1 & -1 \\ -1 & 4 - \lambda_1 \end{bmatrix} \frac{e^{\lambda_2 t}}{\lambda_2 - \lambda_1}$$

or, numerically,

$$e^{\mathbf{P}t} = \begin{bmatrix} 0.414 & -1 \\ -1 & 2.414 \end{bmatrix} \frac{e^{4.414t}}{2.828} + \begin{bmatrix} 2.414 & 1 \\ 1 & 0.414 \end{bmatrix} \frac{e^{1.586t}}{2.828}$$

In the above example it is to be noted that the polynomial given in Eqs. (6.2.9) is of degree 1; i.e., it is of one degree lower than the degree of the minimal polynomial $m(\lambda)$. This is a direct consequence of the fact that an $(n - 1)$-degree polynomial can be passed through n arbitrary points. Such a polynomial is referred to as an *interpolation polynomial*, and is hereafter indicated as $h(\lambda)$. The interpolation polynomial is unique and can be obtained from any other higher-order interpolation polynomial $g(\lambda)$ by simply dividing $g(\lambda)$ by the minimal polynomial $m(\lambda)$ and taking the remainder as $h(\lambda)$, that is,

$$g(\lambda) = q(\lambda)m(\lambda) + h(\lambda)$$

where $h(\lambda)$ is the remainder of degree less than both $g(\lambda)$ and $m(\lambda)$. Since $m(\mathbf{P}) \equiv 0$, it follows that

$$h(\mathbf{P}) = g(\mathbf{P})$$

The interpolation polynomial $h(\lambda)$ can also be obtained directly from the given $f(\lambda)$ by use of the Lagrange interpolation formula developed in the Appendix. If the n zeros of the minimal polynomial $m(\lambda)$ are distinct, then $m(\lambda)$ can be factored in the form

$$m(\lambda) = D(\lambda) = (\lambda - \lambda_1)(\lambda - \lambda_2) \cdots (\lambda - \lambda_n)$$

and the values of the function $f(\lambda)$ on the spectrum of $\mathbf{P}$ are given by

$$f(\lambda_1), f(\lambda_2), \ldots, f(\lambda_n)$$

The Lagrange interpolation polynomial in this case is of degree $n - 1$ and of the form

$$h(\lambda) = \sum_{j=1}^{n} \frac{(\lambda - \lambda_1) \cdots (\lambda - \lambda_{j-1})(\lambda - \lambda_{j+1}) \cdots (\lambda - \lambda_n)}{(\lambda_j - \lambda_1) \cdots (\lambda_j - \lambda_{j-1})(\lambda_j - \lambda_{j+1}) \cdots (\lambda_j - \lambda_n)}$$
$$\times f(\lambda_j) \quad (6.2.10)$$

Note that this expression gives $h(\lambda_j) = f(\lambda_j)$ as required. Upon replacing λ by $\mathbf{P}$ any function of the matrix $\mathbf{P}$ is evaluated as

$$f(\mathbf{P}) = h(\mathbf{P})$$

$$= \sum_{j=1}^{n} \frac{(\mathbf{P} - \lambda_1\mathbf{U}) \cdots (\mathbf{P} - \lambda_{j-1}\mathbf{U})(\mathbf{P} - \lambda_{j+1}\mathbf{U}) \cdots (\mathbf{P} - \lambda_n\mathbf{U})}{(\lambda_j - \lambda_1) \cdots (\lambda_j - \lambda_j - 1)(\lambda_j - \lambda_{j+1}) \cdots (\lambda_j - \lambda_n)}$$

$$\times f(\lambda_j) \quad (6.2.11)$$

The particular function of interest in the solution of linear differential equations is, of course, the function

$$f(\mathbf{P}) = e^{\mathbf{P}t}$$

although other functions can also be evaluated by means of the Lagrange interpolation polynomial, as shown in the following example.

Example 6.2.3: Evaluate the matrix function $\mathbf{P}^n$ when

$$\mathbf{P} = \begin{bmatrix} 2 & 1 & 1 \\ 0 & 3 & 0 \\ 3 & 0 & 4 \end{bmatrix}$$

Solution: The minimal polynomial is

$$m(\lambda) = D(\lambda) = (\lambda^2 - 6\lambda + 5)(\lambda - 3) = (\lambda - \lambda_1)(\lambda - \lambda_2)(\lambda - \lambda_3)$$

where

$$\lambda_1 = 1 \qquad \lambda_2 = 3 \qquad \lambda_3 = 5$$

Using the Lagrange interpolation polynomial as given in Eq. (6.2.10), we have

$$h(\lambda) = \frac{(\lambda - \lambda_2)(\lambda - \lambda_3)}{(\lambda_1 - \lambda_2)(\lambda_1 - \lambda_3)} f(\lambda_1) + \frac{(\lambda - \lambda_1)(\lambda - \lambda_3)}{(\lambda_2 - \lambda_1)(\lambda_2 - \lambda_3)} f(\lambda_2)$$

$$+ \frac{(\lambda - \lambda_1)(\lambda - \lambda_2)}{(\lambda_3 - \lambda_1)(\lambda_3 - \lambda_2)} f(\lambda_3) \quad (6.2.12)$$

where

$$f(\lambda) = \lambda^n$$

Replacing λ by $\mathbf{P}$ in Eq. (6.2.12) gives

$$h(\mathbf{P}) = f(\mathbf{P}) = \mathbf{P}^n = \frac{(\mathbf{P} - \lambda_2\mathbf{U})(\mathbf{P} - \lambda_3\mathbf{U})}{(\lambda_1 - \lambda_2)(\lambda_1 - \lambda_3)} \lambda_1{}^n + \frac{(\mathbf{P} - \lambda_1\mathbf{U})(\mathbf{P} - \lambda_3\mathbf{U})}{(\lambda_2 - \lambda_1)(\lambda_2 - \lambda_3)} \lambda_2{}^n$$

$$+ \frac{(\mathbf{P} - \lambda_1\mathbf{U})(\mathbf{P} - \lambda_2\mathbf{U})}{(\lambda_3 - \lambda_1)(\lambda_3 - \lambda_2)} \lambda_3{}^n$$

or, numerically,

$$\mathbf{P}^n = \frac{1}{8}(\mathbf{P} - 3\mathbf{U})(\mathbf{P} - 5\mathbf{U}) - \frac{3^n}{4}(\mathbf{P} - \mathbf{U})(\mathbf{P} - 5\mathbf{U}) + \frac{5^n}{8}(\mathbf{P} - \mathbf{U})(\mathbf{P} - 3\mathbf{U})$$

$$= \frac{1}{8}\begin{bmatrix} 6 & -3 & -2 \\ 0 & 0 & 0 \\ -6 & 3 & 2 \end{bmatrix} - \frac{3^n}{4}\begin{bmatrix} 0 & -1 & 0 \\ 0 & -4 & 0 \\ 0 & 3 & 0 \end{bmatrix} + \frac{5^n}{8}\begin{bmatrix} 2 & 1 & 2 \\ 0 & 0 & 0 \\ 6 & 3 & 6 \end{bmatrix}$$

In the more general case where the zeros of the minimal polynomial are repeated, we have

$$m(\lambda) = (\lambda - \lambda_1)^{r_1}(\lambda - \lambda_2)^{r_2} \cdots (\lambda - \lambda_k)^{r_k}$$

where $n = r_1 + r_2 + \cdots + r_k$ represents the degree of $m(\lambda)$. In this case the interpolation polynomial $h(\lambda)$ can be evaluated by expanding the ratio of polynomials $h(\lambda)/m(\lambda)$ into partial fractions, as illustrated in the following example.

Example 6.2.4:   Compute e^{Pt} when

$$\mathbf{P} = \begin{bmatrix} 2 & 3 & -4 \\ 0 & 10 & -12 \\ 0 & 6 & -7 \end{bmatrix}$$

Solution: The minimal polynomial of **P** is

$$m(\lambda) = (\lambda - \lambda_1)(\lambda - \lambda_2)^2$$

where $\lambda_1 = 1$, $\lambda_2 = 2$.

To construct the Lagrange interpolation polynomial $h(\lambda)$, consider the partial-fraction expansion of the rational function

$$\frac{h(\lambda)}{m(\lambda)} = \frac{\alpha_{11}}{(\lambda - \lambda_2)^2} + \frac{\alpha_{12}}{\lambda - \lambda_2} + \frac{\alpha_{21}}{\lambda - \lambda_1} \tag{6.2.13}$$

Evaluating the coefficients in the partial-fraction expansion, we have

$$\alpha_{11} = \frac{h(\lambda)}{m(\lambda)} (\lambda - \lambda_2)^2 \Big|_{\lambda = \lambda_2} = \frac{h(\lambda_2)}{\lambda_2 - \lambda_1} = h(2)$$

but on the spectrum of **P** we have $h(2) = f(2) = e^{2t}$ and

$$\alpha_{11} = e^{2t}$$

In a similar manner

$$\alpha_{12} = \frac{d}{d\lambda}\left[\frac{h(\lambda)}{m(\lambda)}(\lambda - \lambda_2)^2\right]\Big|_{\lambda = \lambda_2} = h(\lambda)\frac{d}{d\lambda}\left[\frac{(\lambda - \lambda_2)^2}{m(\lambda)}\right]\Big|_{\lambda = \lambda_2}$$
$$+ \frac{(\lambda - \lambda_2)^2}{m(\lambda)} h'(\lambda)\Big|_{\lambda = \lambda_2}$$

$$= -\frac{h(\lambda_2)}{(\lambda_2 - \lambda_1)^2} + \frac{h'(\lambda_2)}{\lambda_2 - \lambda_1} = -h(2) + h'(2)$$

but since $f'(\lambda) = te^{\lambda t}$, then $h'(2) = f'(2) = te^{2t}$ and we have

$$\alpha_{12} = -e^{2t} + te^{2t}$$

For α_{21} we have

$$\alpha_{21} = \frac{h(\lambda)}{m(\lambda)}(\lambda - \lambda_1)\Big|_{\lambda = \lambda_1} = \frac{h(\lambda_1)}{(\lambda_1 - \lambda_2)^2} = h(1) = f(1) = e^t$$

and the partial-fraction expansion in Eq. (6.2.13) becomes

$$\frac{h(\lambda)}{m(\lambda)} = \frac{e^{2t}}{(\lambda - 2)^2} + \frac{-e^{2t} + te^{2t}}{\lambda - 2} + \frac{e^t}{\lambda - 1}$$

Multiplication of both sides by $m(\lambda) = (\lambda - 2)^2(\lambda - 1)$ establishes the interpolation polynomial $h(\lambda)$ as

$$h(\lambda) = (\lambda - 1)(3 - \lambda)e^{2t} + (\lambda - 2)(\lambda - 1)te^{2t} + (\lambda - 2)^2 e^t \qquad (6.2.14)$$

Replacing λ by $\mathbf{P}$ gives $e^{\mathbf{P}t}$ as

$$f(\mathbf{P}) = e^{\mathbf{P}t} = h(\mathbf{P}) = (\mathbf{P} - \mathbf{U})(3\mathbf{U} - \mathbf{P})e^{2t} + (\mathbf{P} - 2\mathbf{U})(\mathbf{P} - \mathbf{U})te^{2t}$$
$$+ (\mathbf{P} - 2\mathbf{U})^2 e^t$$

$$= \begin{bmatrix} 1 & 0 & 0 \\ 0 & 9 & -12 \\ 0 & 6 & -8 \end{bmatrix} e^{2t} + \begin{bmatrix} 0 & 3 & -4 \\ 0 & 0 & 0 \\ 0 & 0 & 0 \end{bmatrix} te^{2t} + \begin{bmatrix} 0 & 0 & 0 \\ 0 & -8 & 12 \\ 0 & -6 & 9 \end{bmatrix} e^t$$

The matrices appearing as the coefficients in this section are called the *constituent* or *component* matrices of the given matrix $\mathbf{P}$. *Note that these constituent matrices are completely independent of the function $f(\mathbf{P})$. They depend only on the matrix $\mathbf{P}$.*

It is always possible to evaluate the Lagrange interpolation polynomial $h(\lambda)$ in terms of the constituent matrices using the partial-fraction expansion demonstrated in Example 6.2.4. To show this, let the minimal polynomial of $\mathbf{P}$ be written in the form

$$m(\lambda) = (\lambda - \lambda_1)^{r_1}(\lambda - \lambda_2)^{r_2} \cdots (\lambda - \lambda_k)^{r_k} \qquad (6.2.15)$$

Then expansion of $h(\lambda)/m(\lambda)$ in partial fractions gives an expression for $f(\mathbf{P})$ in which the coefficients in the expansion are independent of the function f. This important result is summarized in the following theorem.

Theorem 6.2.1: Let $\mathbf{P}$ be a square matrix of order n with a minimal polynomial of the form given in Eq. (6.2.15). If $f(\lambda)$ is an analytic function, then any analytic matrix function $f(\mathbf{P})$ is expressible in the form

$$f(\mathbf{P}) = \mathbf{Z}_{11}f(\lambda_1) + \mathbf{Z}_{12}\frac{f^{(1)}(\lambda_1)}{1!} + \cdots + \mathbf{Z}_{1r_1}\frac{f^{(r_1 - 1)}(\lambda_1)}{(r_1 - 1)!}$$
$$+ \mathbf{Z}_{21}f(\lambda_2) + \mathbf{Z}_{22}\frac{f^{(1)}(\lambda_2)}{1!} + \cdots + \mathbf{Z}_{2r_2}\frac{f^{(r_2 - 1)}(\lambda_2)}{(r_2 - 1)!}$$
$$+ \cdots \cdots \cdots \cdots \cdots \cdots \cdots$$
$$+ \mathbf{Z}_{k1}f(\lambda_k) + \mathbf{Z}_{k2}\frac{f^{(1)}(\lambda_k)}{1!} + \cdots + \mathbf{Z}_{kr_k}\frac{f^{(r_k - 1)}(\lambda_k)}{(r_k - 1)!} \qquad (6.2.16)$$

where the matrices

$$\mathbf{Z}_{ij} \qquad i = 1, 2, \ldots, k; j = 1, 2, \ldots, r$$

called *constituent matrices*, are independent of the function $f(\lambda)$.

Proof: Consider the minimal polynomial given in Eq. (6.2.15), and expand $h(\lambda)/m(\lambda)$ into partial fractions to obtain

$$
\begin{aligned}
\frac{h(\lambda)}{m(\lambda)} =\ & \frac{\alpha_{11}}{(\lambda - \lambda_1)^{r_1}} + \frac{\alpha_{12}}{(\lambda - \lambda_1)^{r_1-1}} + \cdots + \frac{\alpha_{1r_1}}{\lambda - \lambda_1} \\
& + \frac{\alpha_{21}}{(\lambda - \lambda_2)^{r_2}} + \frac{\alpha_{22}}{(\lambda - \lambda_2)^{r_2-1}} + \cdots + \frac{\alpha_{2r_2}}{\lambda - \lambda_2} \\
& + \cdots \cdots \cdots \cdots \cdots \cdots \cdots \cdots \cdots \\
& + \frac{\alpha_{k1}}{(\lambda - \lambda_k)^{r_k}} + \frac{\alpha_{k2}}{(\lambda - \lambda_k)^{r_k-1}} + \cdots + \frac{\alpha_{kr_k}}{\lambda - \lambda_k}
\end{aligned}
$$

If we let $m_i(\lambda) = m(\lambda)/(\lambda - \lambda_i)^{r_i}$, then the coefficients in the expansion are

$$
\alpha_{i1} = \frac{f(\lambda_i)}{m_i(\lambda_i)} \qquad\qquad i = 1, 2, \ldots, k
$$

$$
\alpha_{i2} = \left[\frac{f(\lambda)}{m_i(\lambda)} \right]^{(1)}_{\lambda=\lambda_i} = f(\lambda_i) \left[\frac{1}{m_i(\lambda)} \right]^{(1)}_{\lambda=\lambda_i} + f^{(1)}(\lambda_i) \frac{1}{m_i(\lambda_i)}
$$

$$
i = 1, 2, \ldots, k
$$

or, in general,

$$
\alpha_{ij} = \frac{1}{(j-1)!} \left[\frac{f(\lambda)}{m_i(\lambda)} \right]^{(j-1)}_{\lambda=\lambda_i} \qquad i = 1, 2, \ldots, k;\ j = 1, 2, \ldots, r_i
$$

Substituting the expressions for α_{ij} into the expansion and multiplying by $m(\lambda)$ gives a polynomial of the form

$$
\begin{aligned}
h(\lambda) =\ & \phi_{11}(\lambda)f(\lambda_1) + \phi_{12}(\lambda) \frac{f^{(1)}(\lambda_1)}{1!} + \cdots + \phi_{1r_1}(\lambda) \frac{f^{(r_1-1)}(\lambda_1)}{(r_1-1)!} \\
& + \phi_{21}(\lambda)f(\lambda_2) + \phi_{22}(\lambda) \frac{f^{(1)}(\lambda_2)}{1!} + \cdots + \phi_{2r_2}(\lambda) \frac{f^{(r_2-1)}(\lambda_2)}{(r_2-1)!} \\
& + \cdots \cdots \cdots \cdots \cdots \cdots \cdots \cdots \cdots \cdots \cdots \\
& + \phi_{k1}(\lambda)f(\lambda_k) + \phi_{k2}(\lambda) \frac{f^{(1)}(\lambda_k)}{1!} + \cdots + \phi_{kr_k}(\lambda) \frac{f^{(r_k-1)}(\lambda_k)}{(r_k-1)!}
\end{aligned}
$$

where the $\phi_{ij}(\lambda)$ are polynomials in λ with degree less than that of $m(\lambda)$, are uniquely determined directly from the minimal polynomial, and hence are independent of $f(\lambda)$. The theorem follows upon replacing λ by the matrix $\mathbf{P}$ and setting $\phi_{ij}(\mathbf{P}) = \mathbf{Z}_{ij}$.

This theorem is fundamental to the solution of linear-state models and will be used extensively. Once the constituent matrices of a matrix $\mathbf{P}$ are known, any analytic function of that matrix is easily evaluated, as the following example shows.

Example 6.2.5: For the matrix $\mathbf{P}$ given in Example 6.2.4 evaluate the following functions of $\mathbf{P}$.

(a) $f_1(\mathbf{P}) = \mathbf{P}^n$
(b) $f_2(\mathbf{P}) = \mathbf{P}^{-1}$
(c) $f_3(\mathbf{P}) = (s\mathbf{U} - \mathbf{P})^{-1}$

Solution: The partial fraction of $h(\lambda)/m(\lambda)$ is given in Eq. (6.2.13) as

$$\frac{h(\lambda)}{m(\lambda)} = \frac{\alpha_{11}}{(\lambda - \lambda_2)^2} + \frac{\alpha_{12}}{\lambda - \lambda_2} + \frac{\alpha_{21}}{\lambda - \lambda_1} \tag{6.2.17}$$

where

$$\lambda_1 = 1 \qquad \lambda_2 = 2$$
$$\alpha_{11} = f(2) \qquad \alpha_{12} = -f(2) + f'(2) \qquad \alpha_{21} = f(1)$$

and

$$m(\lambda) = (\lambda - \lambda_1)(\lambda - \lambda_2)^2$$

Multiplying Eq. (6.2.17) by $m(\lambda)$ gives as the interpolation polynomial

$$h(\lambda) = -(\lambda - 1)(\lambda - 3)f(2) + (\lambda - 1)(\lambda - 2)f'(2) + (\lambda - 2)^2 f(1) \tag{6.2.18}$$

which, of course, is the general form of Eq. (6.2.14). The general form of any function $f(\mathbf{P})$ of the given matrix is obtained by simply replacing λ by $\mathbf{P}$ in Eq. (6.2.18), to obtain

$$h(\mathbf{P}) = f(\mathbf{P}) = \begin{bmatrix} 1 & 0 & 0 \\ 0 & 9 & -12 \\ 0 & 6 & -8 \end{bmatrix} f(2)$$

$$+ \begin{bmatrix} 0 & 3 & -4 \\ 0 & 0 & 0 \\ 0 & 0 & 0 \end{bmatrix} f'(2) + \begin{bmatrix} 0 & 0 & 0 \\ 0 & -8 & 12 \\ 0 & -6 & 9 \end{bmatrix} f(1) \tag{6.2.19}$$

or, symbolically,

$$f(\mathbf{P}) = \mathbf{Z}_{11} f(2) + \mathbf{Z}_{12} f'(2) + \mathbf{Z}_{21} f(1) \tag{6.2.20}$$

(a) To evaluate $f_1(\mathbf{P}) = \mathbf{P}^n$, consider the corresponding scalar functions

$$f(\lambda) = \lambda^n \qquad \text{and} \qquad f'(\lambda) = n\lambda^{n-1}$$

Evaluating these functions at $\lambda = 1$ and $\lambda = 2$ and substituting them into Eq. (6.2.20) gives

$$\mathbf{P}^n = \mathbf{Z}_{11} 2^n + \mathbf{Z}_{12} n 2^{n-1} + \mathbf{Z}_{21}$$

(b) Setting $f(\lambda) = \dfrac{1}{\lambda}$ and $f'(\lambda) = -\dfrac{1}{\lambda^2}$ the inverse of $\mathbf{P}$ is

$$\mathbf{P}^{-1} = \tfrac{1}{2}\mathbf{Z}_{11} - \tfrac{1}{4}\mathbf{Z}_{12} + \mathbf{Z}_{21}$$

(c) Finally, setting $f(\lambda) = (s - \lambda)^{-1}$ and $f'(\lambda) = (s - \lambda)^{-2}$, the inverse of $(s\mathbf{U} - \mathbf{P})$ is

$$(s\mathbf{U} - \mathbf{P})^{-1} = \frac{1}{(s - 2)} \mathbf{Z}_{11} + \frac{1}{(s - 2)^2} \mathbf{Z}_{12} + \frac{1}{(s - 1)} \mathbf{Z}_{21}$$

or, upon rationalizing the denominators, we have

$$(s\mathbf{U} - \mathbf{P})^{-1} = \frac{1}{m(s)}[(s - 2)(s - 1)\mathbf{Z}_{11} + (s - 1)\mathbf{Z}_{12} + (s - 2)^2\mathbf{Z}_{21}]$$

where

$$m(s) = (s - 2)^2(s - 1)$$

In addition to being independent of the function being evaluated, the constituent matrices also have the fundamental properties stated in the following theorems.

Theorem 6.2.2:   The constituent matrices of a square matrix $\mathbf{P}$ are linearly independent.

Proof: It is necessary to show that no linear sum of the constituent matrices in Eq. (6.2.16) vanishes.   Consider, therefore, the summation

$$\sigma(\mathbf{P}) = \sum_{i=1}^{k} \sum_{j=1}^{r_i} c_{ij}\mathbf{Z}_{ij}$$

where the constant c_{ij} is arbitrary except that not all $c_{ij} = 0$.

Since $\mathbf{Z}_{ij} = \phi_{ij}(\mathbf{P})$ and $\phi_{ij}(\lambda)$ is a polynomial of degree lower than that of the minimal polynomial $m(\lambda)$, it follows that the degree of the polynomial

$$\sigma(\lambda) = \sum_{i=1}^{k} \sum_{j=1}^{r_i} c_{ij}\phi_{ij}(\lambda)$$

is also less than that of $m(\lambda)$.   The polynomial $\sigma(\mathbf{P})$ cannot vanish, (unless all $c_{ij} = 0$), for if it did, it would be an annihilating polynomial of lower degree than $m(\lambda)$.   But this is not possible, since by definition $m(\lambda)$ is the annihilating polynomial of lowest degree.   It follows, therefore, that $\sigma(\mathbf{P}) = 0$ only if $c_{ij} = 0$ and hence the constituent matrices are linearly independent.

Theorem 6.2.3:   The constituent matrices $\mathbf{Z}_{i1}$ $(i = 1, 2, \ldots, k)$ in Eq. (6.2.16) are idempotent and sum to unity, i.e.,

$$\mathbf{Z}_{i1}^2 = \mathbf{Z}_{i1}$$

and

$$\mathbf{Z}_{11} + \mathbf{Z}_{21} + \cdots + \mathbf{Z}_{k1} = \mathbf{U}$$

Proof: To show that the indicated matrix sum is the unit matrix, let $f(\lambda) = 1$ in Eq. (6.2.16), to obtain

$$f(\mathbf{P}) = \mathbf{U} = \mathbf{Z}_{11} + \mathbf{Z}_{21} + \cdots + \mathbf{Z}_{k1}$$

To show that the matrices $\mathbf{Z}_{i1}$ are idempotent, expand $1/m(\lambda)$ in partial fractions, to obtain

$$\frac{1}{m(\lambda)} = \frac{1}{(\lambda - \lambda_1)^{r_1}(\lambda - \lambda_2)^{r_2} \cdots (\lambda - \lambda_k)^{r_k}} = \sum_{i=1}^{k} \frac{d_i(\lambda)}{(\lambda - \lambda_i)^{r_i}}$$

(6.2.21)

where the degree of $\alpha_i(\lambda)$ is less than r_i.

Consider now the polynomials

$$\begin{aligned}
g_i(\lambda) &= \frac{\alpha_i(\lambda)m(\lambda)}{(\lambda - \lambda_i)^{r_i}} \\
&= \frac{\alpha_i(\lambda)(\lambda - \lambda_1)^{r_1}(\lambda - \lambda_2)^{r_2} \cdots (\lambda - \lambda_k)^{r_k}}{(\lambda - \lambda_i)^{r_i}}
\end{aligned}$$

$$i = 1, 2, \ldots, k \quad (6.2.22)$$

From the form of the numerator and denominator of Eq. (6.2.22) it is clear that the polynomials $g_i(\lambda)$ $(i = 1, 2, \ldots, k)$ have the following values when evaluated at the eigenvalues of $\mathbf{P}$,

$$\begin{aligned}
g_i(\lambda_i) &= 1 \\
g_i(\lambda_j) &= 0 \qquad i \neq j
\end{aligned}$$

(6.2.23)

and the derivatives of $g_i(\lambda)$ have the properties

$$\begin{aligned}
g_i^{(l)}(\lambda_i) &= 0 \qquad l > 1 \\
g_i^{(l)}(\lambda_j) &= 0 \qquad l > 1
\end{aligned}$$

(6.2.24)

Upon multiplying Eq. (6.2.21) by $m(\lambda)$ we see further that

$$\sum_{i=1}^{k} g_i(\lambda) = 1$$

(6.2.25)

Setting $f(\lambda) = g_i(\lambda)$ in Eq. (6.2.16) gives

$$g_i(\mathbf{P}) = \mathbf{Z}_{i1} \qquad i = 1, 2, \ldots, k$$

(6.2.26)

Consider now the polynomials $g_i(\lambda)g_i(\lambda)$, $i = 1, 2, \ldots, k$. From Eqs. (6.2.23) and (6.2.24) it follows that these polynomials vanish at all the eigenvalues of $\mathbf{P}$ except $\lambda = \lambda_i$, and their derivatives vanish at all the eigenvalues. Therefore, upon taking $f(\lambda) = g_i(\lambda)g_i(\lambda)$ in Eq. (6.2.16) we have

$$g_i(\mathbf{P})g_i(\mathbf{P}) = \mathbf{Z}_{i1}\mathbf{Z}_{i1} = \mathbf{Z}_{i1} \qquad i = 1, 2, \ldots, k$$

and the theorem is proved.

Theorem 6.2.4: The product of the constituent matrices $\mathbf{Z}_{il}$ and $\mathbf{Z}_{jq}$ $(i \neq j)$ vanishes, i.e.,

$$\mathbf{Z}_{il}\mathbf{Z}_{jq} = 0$$

Further

$$\mathbf{Z}_{il} = \begin{cases} (\mathbf{P} - \lambda_i\mathbf{U})^{l-1}\mathbf{Z}_{i1} & \text{for } l \leq r_i \\ 0 & \text{for } l > r_i \end{cases}$$

Proof: To establish the first part, let $f(\lambda)$ in Eq. (6.2.16) be taken as $g_i(\lambda)g_j(\lambda)$, $i \neq j$, where $g_i(\lambda)$ is defined in Eq. (6.2.22). From Eqs. (6.2.23) and (6.2.24) these polynomials and their derivatives vanish at all the eigenvalues of $\mathbf{P}$, and we have

$$g_i(\mathbf{P})g_j(\mathbf{P}) = \mathbf{Z}_{i1}\mathbf{Z}_{j1} = 0 \qquad i \neq j$$

and it has been established that the product of the idempotent constituent matrices vanishes.

To show that the remaining constituent matrices have the same property, consider the general expansion of an arbitrary function of $\mathbf{P}$, which, by applying Theorem 6.2.3, can be written as

$$f(\mathbf{P}) = f(\mathbf{P})\mathbf{U} = f(\mathbf{P}) \sum_{i=1}^{k} \mathbf{Z}_{i1} = \sum_{i=1}^{k} f(\mathbf{P})\mathbf{Z}_{i1} \tag{6.2.27}$$

But from Eq. (6.2.26) $\mathbf{Z}_{i1} = g_i(\mathbf{P})$, and $f(\mathbf{P})$ in Eq. (6.2.27) corresponds to the scalar polynomial

$$f(\lambda) = \sum_{i=1}^{k} f(\lambda)g_i(\lambda) \tag{6.2.28}$$

Let $f(\lambda)$ in each term of the summation in Eq. (6.2.28) be expanded in a Taylor series about the point $\lambda = \lambda_i$, to obtain

$$f(\lambda) = \sum_{i=1}^{k} \left[f(\lambda_i) + (\lambda - \lambda_i)f'(\lambda_i) + (\lambda - \lambda_i)^2 \frac{f^{(2)}(\lambda_i)}{2!} + \cdots \right] g_i(\lambda) \tag{6.2.29}$$

Upon replacing λ by $\mathbf{P}$ in Eq. (6.2.29), the corresponding matrix polynomial is

$$f(\mathbf{P}) = \sum_{i=1}^{k} \left[\mathbf{U}f(\lambda_i) + (\mathbf{P} - \lambda_i\mathbf{U})f'(\lambda_i) + (\mathbf{P} - \lambda_i\mathbf{U})^2 \frac{f^{(2)}(\lambda_i)}{2!} \right.$$
$$\left. + \cdots \right] \mathbf{Z}_{i1} \tag{6.2.30}$$

Comparing the expansion in Eq. (6.2.30) with that in Eq. (6.2.16), we have

$$\mathbf{Z}_{il} = \begin{cases} (\mathbf{P} - \lambda_i\mathbf{U})^{l-1}\mathbf{Z}_{i1} & \text{for } l \leq r_i \\ 0 & \text{for } l > r_i \end{cases} \tag{6.2.31}$$

From this result it follows that

$$Z_{il}Z_{jq} = (P - \lambda_i U)^{l-1}Z_{i1}(P - \lambda_j U)^{q-1}Z_{j1} \qquad i \neq j \qquad (6.2.32)$$

But since Z_{i1} and $(P - \lambda_j U)^{q-1}$ are both polynomials in the matrix P, they are commutative. Also, it has already been established that $Z_{i1}Z_{j1} = 0$. Therefore, Eq. (6.2.32) reduces to

$$Z_{il}Z_{jq} = (P - \lambda_i U)^{l-1}(P - \lambda_j U)^{q-1}Z_{i1}Z_{j1} = 0$$

and the theorem is established.

Theorem 6.2.5: The constituent matrices Z_{il}, $i = 1, 2, \ldots, k$, $l = 2, 3, \ldots, k$, in Eq. (6.2.16) are nilpotent of order† $s = [r_i/(l - 1)]$, that is, $Z_{il}^s = 0$.

$Proof:$ Let Z_{il} in Eq. (6.2.31) be multiplied by itself s times. Since Z_{i1} is idempotent, the result is

$$Z_{il}^s = (P - \lambda_i U)^{(l-1)s}Z_{i1}^s = (P - \lambda_i U)^{(l-1)s}Z_{i1}$$

But Eq. (6.2.31) also shows that the right-hand side vanishes when the exponent exceeds $r_i - 1$, that is, if $(l - 1)s \geq r_i - 1$. Consequently if $s = [r_i/(l - 1)]$, then $Z_{il}^s = 0$ $(l \neq 1)$ and the theorem is proved.

Example 6.2.6: Show that the constituent matrices in Example 6.2.5 satisfy Theorems 6.2.2 to 6.2.5.

Solution
Independence: The constituent matrices in Eq. (6.2.19) are independent, since one cannot be obtained as a linear combination of the other two.
Idempotent:

$$Z_{11}^2 = \begin{bmatrix} 1 & 0 & 0 \\ 0 & 9 & -12 \\ 0 & 6 & -8 \end{bmatrix} \begin{bmatrix} 1 & 0 & 0 \\ 0 & 9 & -12 \\ 0 & 6 & -8 \end{bmatrix} = \begin{bmatrix} 1 & 0 & 0 \\ 0 & 9 & -12 \\ 0 & 6 & -8 \end{bmatrix}$$

$$Z_{21}^2 = \begin{bmatrix} 0 & 0 & 0 \\ 0 & -8 & 12 \\ 0 & -6 & 9 \end{bmatrix} \begin{bmatrix} 0 & 0 & 0 \\ 0 & -8 & 12 \\ 0 & -6 & 9 \end{bmatrix} = \begin{bmatrix} 0 & 0 & 0 \\ 0 & -8 & 12 \\ 0 & -6 & 9 \end{bmatrix}$$

Sum to unity:

$$Z_{11} + Z_{21} = \begin{bmatrix} 1 & 0 & 0 \\ 0 & 9 & -12 \\ 0 & 6 & -8 \end{bmatrix} + \begin{bmatrix} 0 & 0 & 0 \\ 0 & -8 & 12 \\ 0 & -6 & 9 \end{bmatrix} = U$$

† In the notation used here, if n is a real number then $[n]$ represents the least integer which is greater than or equal to n.

Products:

$$Z_{11}Z_{21} = 0$$
$$Z_{12}Z_{21} = 0$$

$$Z_{12} = (\mathbf{P} - 2\mathbf{U})Z_{11} = \begin{bmatrix} 0 & 3 & -4 \\ 0 & 8 & -12 \\ 0 & 6 & -9 \end{bmatrix} \begin{bmatrix} 1 & 0 & 0 \\ 0 & 9 & -12 \\ 0 & 6 & -8 \end{bmatrix} = \begin{bmatrix} 0 & 3 & -4 \\ 0 & 0 & 0 \\ 0 & 0 & 0 \end{bmatrix}$$

It should be noted that, in general, Theorem 6.2.4 indicates that, if the idempotent matrices Z_{i1} are known, then all other constituent matrices can be calculated.

Nilpotent:

$$Z_{12}^2 = (\mathbf{P} - 2\mathbf{U})^2 Z_{11} = \begin{bmatrix} 0 & 3 & -4 \\ 0 & 0 & 0 \\ 0 & 0 & 0 \end{bmatrix} \begin{bmatrix} 0 & 3 & -4 \\ 0 & 0 & 0 \\ 0 & 0 & 0 \end{bmatrix} = \mathbf{0}$$

6.3 EVALUATING THE CONSTITUENT MATRICES

The problem of solving analytically linear time-invariant state equations finally reduces to that of evaluating the constituent matrices in the general expansion formula given by Theorem 6.2.1. Although the Lagrange interpolation polynomial was used to establish this result, it is not necessarily the most effective procedure to use in actually evaluating the constituent matrices in the solution of a given systems problem. The two basic procedures and several techniques given in this section are based on the properties of the constituent matrices given in Theorems 6.2.1 to 6.2.5. Some techniques are particularly effective in the solution of relatively low-order systems by manual computation; others are particularly suited for machine computation.

METHOD OF THE RESOLVENT MATRIX

Consider the square matrix $\mathbf{P}$ with minimal polynomial

$$m(\lambda) = (\lambda - \lambda_1)^{r_1}(\lambda - \lambda_2)^{r_2} \cdots (\lambda - \lambda_k)^{r_k} \tag{6.3.1}$$

The matrix function $f(\mathbf{P}) = (s\mathbf{U} - \mathbf{P})^{-1}$, where s is an arbitrary constant, corresponds to the scalar function $f(\lambda) = (s - \lambda)^{-1}$. From Theorem 6.2.1 this function has an expansion of the form

$$\begin{aligned}
(s\mathbf{U} - \mathbf{P})^{-1} = {}&Z_{11}\frac{1}{s - \lambda_1} + Z_{12}\frac{1}{(s - \lambda_1)^2} + \cdots + Z_{1r_1}\frac{1}{(s - \lambda_1)^{r_1}} \\
&+ Z_{21}\frac{1}{s - \lambda_2} + Z_{22}\frac{1}{(s - \lambda_2)^2} + \cdots + Z_{2r_2}\frac{1}{(s - \lambda_2)^{r_2}} \\
&+ \cdots \cdots \cdots \cdots \cdots \cdots \cdots \cdots \cdots \cdots \cdots \cdots \\
&+ Z_{k1}\frac{1}{s - \lambda_k} + Z_{k2}\frac{1}{(s - \lambda_k)^2} + \cdots + Z_{kr_k}\frac{1}{(s - \lambda_k)^{r_k}}
\end{aligned} \tag{6.3.2}$$

But the inverse of $s\mathbf{U} - \mathbf{P}$ is also given as

$$(s\mathbf{U} - \mathbf{P})^{-1} = \frac{1}{D(s)} \operatorname{adj} (s\mathbf{U} - \mathbf{P}) = \frac{1}{m(s)} \mathbf{C}(s) \tag{6.3.3}$$

where $\mathbf{C}(s)$ is the reduced adjoint matrix of $s\mathbf{U} - \mathbf{P}$, that is, the adjoint after canceling the common factors with $D(s)$, and $m(s)$ is given by Eq. (6.3.1) with λ replaced by s. When the right-hand side of Eq. (6.3.3) is expanded in partial fractions, the result is a form identical to that appearing on the right-hand side of Eq. (6.3.2). Consequently, the *constituent matrices are identified as the coefficient matrices in the partial-fraction expansion of* $(s\mathbf{U} - \mathbf{P})^{-1}$. For this reason $(s\mathbf{U} - \mathbf{P})^{-1}$ is referred to as the *resolvent matrix* of $\mathbf{P}$.

Example 6.3.1: Evaluate $e^{\mathbf{P}t}$ when

$$\mathbf{P} = \begin{bmatrix} 1 & -1 & -1 \\ -1 & 1 & -1 \\ -1 & -1 & 1 \end{bmatrix}$$

Solution: The adjoint matrix of $s\mathbf{U} - \mathbf{P}$ is

$$\operatorname{adj} (s\mathbf{U} - \mathbf{P}) = \begin{bmatrix} s(s-2) & -(s-2) & -(s-2) \\ -(s-2) & s(s-2) & -(s-2) \\ -(s-2) & -(s-2) & s(s-2) \end{bmatrix}$$

The characteristic polynomial is easily calculated from the relation

$$D(s)\mathbf{U} = (s\mathbf{U} - \mathbf{P}) \operatorname{adj} (s\mathbf{U} - \mathbf{P})$$

and is

$$D(s) = (s+1)(s-2)^2$$

For the resolvent matrix we have then

$$(s\mathbf{U} - \mathbf{P})^{-1} = \frac{1}{(s+1)(s-2)} \begin{bmatrix} s & -1 & -1 \\ -1 & s & -1 \\ -1 & -1 & s \end{bmatrix} \tag{6.3.4}$$

which has the partial-fraction expansion

$$(s\mathbf{U} - \mathbf{P})^{-1} = \mathbf{Z}_{11} \frac{1}{s+1} + \mathbf{Z}_{21} \frac{1}{s-2}$$

where

$$\mathbf{Z}_{11} = \lim_{s \to -1} (s+1)(s\mathbf{U} - \mathbf{P})^{-1} = \frac{1}{3} \begin{bmatrix} 1 & 1 & 1 \\ 1 & 1 & 1 \\ 1 & 1 & 1 \end{bmatrix}$$

and

$$\mathbf{Z}_{21} = \lim_{s \to 2} (s-2)(s\mathbf{U} - \mathbf{P})^{-1} = \frac{1}{3} \begin{bmatrix} 2 & -1 & -1 \\ -1 & 2 & -1 \\ -1 & -1 & 2 \end{bmatrix}$$

As a check it is noted that the computed constituent matrices have the properties

$$\mathbf{Z}_{11}^2 = \mathbf{Z}_{11} \qquad \mathbf{Z}_{21}^2 = \mathbf{Z}_{21} \qquad \mathbf{Z}_{11} + \mathbf{Z}_{21} = \mathbf{U}$$

The required evaluation is therefore

$$e^{\mathbf{P}t} = \mathbf{Z}_{11}e^{-t} + \mathbf{Z}_{21}e^{2t}$$

In this first procedure it is necessary to evaluate both the determinant and the adjoint matrix of the matrix $s\mathbf{U} - \mathbf{P}$. Because of the special form of $s\mathbf{U} - \mathbf{P}$, the required determinant and adjoint matrix can be evaluated by an algorithm discovered independently by several mathematicians, including Souriau,[1] Faddeev,[2] Fettis,[3] and Frame.[4]

This algorithm is given in terms of the trace of a sequence of matrices and requires that the characteristic polynomial and adjoint matrix be written in the following forms:

$$D(s) = |s\mathbf{U} - \mathbf{P}| = s^n + d_1 s^{n-1} + \cdots + d_{n-1}s + d_n \qquad (6.3.5)$$
$$\text{adj } (s\mathbf{U} - \mathbf{P}) = \mathbf{F}(s) = \mathbf{F}_0 s^{n-1} + \mathbf{F}_1 s^{n-2} + \cdots$$
$$+ \mathbf{F}_{n-2}s + \mathbf{F}_{n-1} \qquad (6.3.6)$$

From the form of the expansion of the determinants $|s\mathbf{U} - \mathbf{P}|$ it is noted that the characteristic polynomial is a monic polynomial. The entries in adj $(s\mathbf{U} - \mathbf{P})$ are, in general, polynomials in s of at most degree $n - 1$. Consequently, the adjoint matrix can always be written as a polynomial in s with matrix coefficients. Further, since

$$(s\mathbf{U} - \mathbf{P}) \text{ adj } (s\mathbf{U} - \mathbf{P}) = D(s)\mathbf{U}$$

it follows that $\mathbf{F}_0 = \mathbf{U}$.

The algorithm as stated by Frame[5] is given in the following theorem.

Theorem 6.3.1: The scalar coefficients d_i in the characteristic polynomial of Eq. (6.3.5) and the matrix coefficients $\mathbf{F}_i$ in adj $(s\mathbf{U} - \mathbf{P})$ of Eq. (6.3.6) are given recursively by the following formulas:

$$\mathbf{F}_1 = \mathbf{P} + d_1\mathbf{U} \qquad\qquad d_1 = -\text{tr } \mathbf{P}$$
$$\mathbf{F}_2 = \mathbf{P}\mathbf{F}_1 + d_2\mathbf{U} \qquad\quad d_2 = -\tfrac{1}{2}\text{tr } \mathbf{P}\mathbf{F}_1$$
$$\mathbf{F}_3 = \mathbf{P}\mathbf{F}_2 + d_3\mathbf{U} \qquad\quad d_3 = -\tfrac{1}{3}\text{tr } \mathbf{P}\mathbf{F}_2$$
$$\cdots\cdots\cdots\cdots\qquad\qquad \cdots\cdots\cdots\cdots$$

$$\mathbf{F}_{n-1} = \mathbf{P}\mathbf{F}_{n-2} + d_{n-1}\mathbf{U} \qquad d_n = -\frac{1}{n}\text{tr } \mathbf{P}\mathbf{F}_{n-1}$$

$$\mathbf{F}_n = \mathbf{P}\mathbf{F}_{n-1} + d_n\mathbf{U} = \mathbf{0}$$

Proof (after Frame): Consider the identity

$$(s\mathbf{U} - \mathbf{P})\mathbf{F}(s) = D(s)\mathbf{U}$$

Taking the trace of both sides gives

$$\text{tr } s\mathbf{F}(s) - \text{tr } \mathbf{P}\mathbf{F}(s) = nD(s) \tag{6.3.7}$$

where, of course, the trace of a matrix whose entries are polynomials is a polynomial.

Lemma 6.3.1: The trace of $\mathbf{F}(s) = \text{adj } (s\mathbf{U} - \mathbf{P})$ is equal to the derivative of the characteristic polynomial

$$\text{tr } \mathbf{F}(s) = D'(s) = \frac{d}{ds} D(s)$$

Proof of lemma: Consider the derivative of the determinant $|s\mathbf{U} - \mathbf{P}|$. We have

$$\frac{d}{ds} D(s) = \frac{d}{ds}
\begin{bmatrix}
s - p_{11} & -p_{12} & \cdots & -p_{1n} \\
-p_{21} & s - p_{22} & \cdots & -p_{2n} \\
\cdots\cdots\cdots\cdots\cdots\cdots\cdots\cdots\cdots \\
-p_{n1} & -p_{n2} & \cdots & s - p_{nn}
\end{bmatrix}$$

$$=
\begin{bmatrix}
1 & -p_{12} & \cdots & -p_{1n} \\
0 & s - p_{22} & \cdots & -p_{2n} \\
\cdots\cdots\cdots\cdots\cdots\cdots\cdots \\
0 & -p_{n2} & \cdots & s - p_{nn}
\end{bmatrix}
+
\begin{bmatrix}
s - p_{11} & 0 & \cdots & -p_{1n} \\
-p_{21} & 1 & \cdots & -p_{2n} \\
\cdots\cdots\cdots\cdots\cdots\cdots\cdots\cdots \\
-p_{n1} & 0 & \cdots & s - p_{nn}
\end{bmatrix}$$

$$+ \cdots +
\begin{bmatrix}
s - p_{11} & -p_{12} & \cdots & 0 \\
-p_{21} & s - p_{22} & \cdots & 0 \\
\cdots\cdots\cdots\cdots\cdots\cdots\cdots \\
-p_{n1} & -p_{n2} & \cdots & 1
\end{bmatrix}$$

Upon expanding each of the determinants in the summation by the respective columns 1, 2, . . . , n, we have

$$\frac{d}{ds} D(s) = c_{11}(s) + c_{22}(s) + \cdots + c_{nn}(s)$$

where $c_{ii}(s)$ represents the cofactor of the (i,i) entry in the determinant

$$|s\mathbf{U} - \mathbf{P}| =
\begin{bmatrix}
s - p_{11} & -p_{12} & \cdots & -p_{1n} \\
-p_{21} & s - p_{22} & \cdots & -p_{2n} \\
-p_{n1} & -p_{n2} & \cdots & s - p_{nn}
\end{bmatrix}$$

But the diagonal entries of adj $(s\mathbf{U} - \mathbf{P})$ are also given as the cofactors of $|s\mathbf{U} - \mathbf{P}|$, and the lemma is proved.

To return to the main theorem, Eq. (6.3.7) can now be written as

$$sD'(s) - \text{tr } \mathbf{P}\mathbf{F}(s) = nD(s) \tag{6.3.8}$$

where

$$F(s) = F_0 s^{n-1} + F_1 s^{n-2} + \cdots + F_{k-1} s^{n-k} + \cdots + F_n \quad (6.3.9)$$
$$nD(s) = ns^n + nd_1 s^{n-1} + \cdots + nd_k s^{n-k} + \cdots + nd_n \quad (6.3.10)$$

and

$$sD'(s) = sc_{11}(s) + sc_{22}(s) + \cdots + sc_{kk}(s) + \cdots + sc_{nn}(s) \quad (6.3.11)$$

But since

$$(s - p_{ii})c_{ii}(s) = D(s)$$

the expression for $sD'(s)$ can also be written as

$$sD'(s) = ns^n + (n-1)d_1 s^{n-1} + \cdots + (n-k)d_k s^{n-k}$$
$$+ \cdots + d_{n-1}s \quad (6.3.12)$$

Upon substituting Eqs. (6.3.9), (6.3.10), and (6.3.12) into Eq. (6.3.8) and equating coefficients in the resulting polynomials in s, the recursion formulas given by the theorem result.

The expression for F_n in the recursion formula of Theorem 6.3.1 can be used to evaluate the inverse of P, that is, since $F_n = 0$,

$$P^{-1} = \frac{-1}{d_n} F_{n-1} \qquad \text{if } |P| \neq 0 \tag{6.3.13}$$

Any discrepancy between F_n and the zero matrix can also be used as an indicator of the numerical accuracy of the calculation. Note, in addition, that, if $d_n = 0$, the inverse of P does not exist.

Example 6.3.2 (after Frame[5]): Evaluate the inverse of $sU - P$, and evaluate the constituent matrices when

$$P = \begin{bmatrix} -13 & -21 & -11 \\ 5 & 8 & 5 \\ 5 & 11 & 4 \end{bmatrix}$$

Solution

$$d_1 = -\operatorname{tr} P = 1$$

$$F_1 = P + U = \begin{bmatrix} -12 & -21 & -11 \\ 5 & 9 & 5 \\ 6 & 11 & 5 \end{bmatrix}$$

$$d_2 = -\tfrac{1}{2}\operatorname{tr} PF_1 = -8$$

$$F_2 = PF_1 - 8U = \begin{bmatrix} -23 & -37 & -17 \\ 10 & 14 & 10 \\ 7 & 17 & 1 \end{bmatrix}$$

$$d_3 = -\tfrac{1}{3}\operatorname{tr} PF_2 = -12$$

$$F_3 = PF_2 - 12U = \begin{bmatrix} 0 & 0 & 0 \\ 0 & 0 & 0 \\ 0 & 0 & 0 \end{bmatrix} \qquad \text{(Check)}$$

The inverse of $s\mathbf{U} - \mathbf{P}$ is therefore

$$(s\mathbf{U} - \mathbf{P})^{-1} = \frac{\mathbf{F}(s)}{D(s)}$$

where

$$\mathbf{F}(s) = \mathbf{U}s^2 + \mathbf{F}_1 s + \mathbf{F}_2 \tag{6.3.14}$$

and

$$D(s) = s^3 + s^2 - 8s - 12 \tag{6.3.15}$$

As a further check, the lemma used in the proof of Theorem 6.3.1 gives

$$\begin{aligned} D'(s) &= 3s^2 + 2s - 8 = (\text{tr } \mathbf{U})s^2 + (\text{tr } \mathbf{F}_1)s + \text{tr } \mathbf{F}_2 \\ &= 3s^2 + 2s - 8 \quad \text{(Check)} \end{aligned}$$

To evaluate the constituent matrices, it is necessary to know the roots of $D(s)$ so that $(s\mathbf{U} - \mathbf{P})^{-1}$ can be expanded into partial fractions. The polynomial in Eq. (6.3.15) can be factored in the form

$$D(s) = (s - 3)(s + 2)^2$$

The partial-fraction expansion of $(s\mathbf{U} - \mathbf{P})^{-1}$ is therefore

$$(s\mathbf{U} - \mathbf{P})^{-1} = \mathbf{Z}_{11} \frac{1}{s - 3} + \mathbf{Z}_{21} \frac{1}{s + 2} + \mathbf{Z}_{22} \frac{1}{(s + 2)^2}$$

where

$$\begin{aligned} \mathbf{Z}_{11} &= \lim_{s \to 3} (s - 3)(s\mathbf{U} - \mathbf{P})^{-1} = \frac{1}{(s + 2)^2} (\mathbf{U}s^2 + \mathbf{F}_1 s + \mathbf{F}_2)\Big|_{s=3} \\ &= \begin{bmatrix} -2 & -4 & -2 \\ 1 & 2 & 1 \\ 1 & 2 & 1 \end{bmatrix} \end{aligned}$$

$$\begin{aligned} \mathbf{Z}_{22} &= \lim_{s \to -2} (s + 2)^2 (s\mathbf{U} - \mathbf{P})^{-1} = \frac{1}{s - 3} (\mathbf{U}s^2 + \mathbf{F}_1 s + \mathbf{F}_2)\Big|_{s=-2} \\ &= \begin{bmatrix} -1 & -1 & -1 \\ 0 & 0 & 0 \\ 1 & 1 & 1 \end{bmatrix} \end{aligned}$$

and

$$\begin{aligned} \mathbf{Z}_{21} &= \lim_{s \to -2} \frac{d}{ds} (s + 2)^2 (s\mathbf{U} - \mathbf{P})^{-1} = \frac{1}{s - 3} (2s\mathbf{U} + \mathbf{F}_1) \\ &\qquad - \frac{1}{(s - 3)^2} (\mathbf{U}s^2 + \mathbf{F}_1 s + \mathbf{F}_2)\Big|_{s=-2} \\ &= \begin{bmatrix} 3 & 4 & 2 \\ -1 & -1 & -1 \\ -1 & -2 & 0 \end{bmatrix} \end{aligned}$$

The algorithm given in Theorem 6.3.1 and demonstrated in the above example is ideally suited for computer evaluation of $(s\mathbf{U} - \mathbf{P})^{-1}$. In fact, such an algorithm is critical to a computer program that attempts to evaluate the constituent matrices by partial-fraction expansion of the resolvent matrix. The inverse of $(s\mathbf{U} - \mathbf{P})^{-1}$ must be known as a matrix polynomial in s. Since it is not a matrix of numbers, the standard machine routines for inverting matrices cannot be applied.

Beyond evaluating the inverse of $s\mathbf{U} - \mathbf{P}$ it is necessary to know the zeros of the characteristic polynomial $D(\lambda)$ before the partial-fraction expansion can be carried out. Standard routines are available in practically every computer library for carrying out this operation. There are no general methods, short of numerical iteration, for evaluating the zeros of polynomials of higher degree. The general properties of the characteristic polynomial $D(\lambda)$ are discussed in Sec. 6.5.

METHOD OF RESOLVING POLYNOMIALS

Another method for evaluating the constituent matrices that is effective in both hand and machine computation is based on establishing a sequence of matrix functions from which the constituent matrices can be evaluated. To demonstrate the basic procedure, let us consider the general expansion of a matrix $\mathbf{P}$ of order 6 for which $m(\lambda)$ is of the form

$$m(\lambda) = (\lambda - \lambda_1)^3(\lambda - \lambda_2)^2(\lambda - \lambda_3) \tag{6.3.16}$$

From Theorem 6.3.1, $f(\mathbf{P})$ is of the general form

$$f(\mathbf{P}) = \mathbf{Z}_{11}f(\lambda_1) + \mathbf{Z}_{12}\frac{f^{(1)}(\lambda_1)}{1!} + \mathbf{Z}_{13}\frac{f^{(2)}(\lambda_1)}{2!}$$

$$+ \mathbf{Z}_{21}f(\lambda_2) + \mathbf{Z}_{22}\frac{f^{(1)}(\lambda_2)}{1!}$$

$$+ \mathbf{Z}_{31}f(\lambda_3) \tag{6.3.17}$$

Since there are six unknown constituent matrices, a sequence of six functions $f_i(\mathbf{P})$, $i = 1, 2, \ldots, 6$, are considered, and six matrix functions are generated as follows:

$$
\begin{bmatrix} f_1(\mathbf{P}) \\ f_2(\mathbf{P}) \\ \cdots \\ f_6(\mathbf{P}) \end{bmatrix}
=
\begin{bmatrix}
f_1(\lambda_1) & f_1^{(1)}(\lambda_1) & \dfrac{f_1^{(2)}(\lambda_1)}{2!} & f_1(\lambda_2) & f_1^{(1)}(\lambda_2) & f_1(\lambda_3) \\
f_2(\lambda_1) & f_2^{(1)}(\lambda_1) & \dfrac{f_2^{(2)}(\lambda_1)}{2!} & f_2(\lambda_2) & f_2^{(1)}(\lambda_2) & f_2(\lambda_3) \\
\cdots & \cdots & \cdots & \cdots & \cdots & \cdots \\
f_6(\lambda_1) & f_6^{(1)}(\lambda_1) & \dfrac{f_6^{(2)}(\lambda_1)}{2!} & f_6(\lambda_2) & f_6^{(1)}(\lambda_2) & f_6(\lambda_3)
\end{bmatrix}
\begin{bmatrix} \mathbf{Z}_{11} \\ \mathbf{Z}_{12} \\ \mathbf{Z}_{13} \\ \mathbf{Z}_{21} \\ \mathbf{Z}_{22} \\ \mathbf{Z}_{31} \end{bmatrix}
$$

$$\tag{6.3.18}$$

where in this special notation it is to be understood that the scalar entries in the coefficient matrix are multiplied into the constituent matrices. To be conformable in the usual sense, each entry in the coefficient matrix should be followed by a unit matrix of order 6. For simplicity in notation this unit matrix is omitted in the context of the present problem only.

The objective now is to select a sequence of six functions f_i such that the matrix of scalar coefficients in Eq. (6.3.18) is nonsingular and can easily be inverted. A triangular matrix is both nonsingular and relatively easy to invert. It can be generated easily for the minimal polynomial given in Eq. (6.3.16) by selecting a sequence of polynomials of increasing orders,

$$f_1(\lambda) = 1 \qquad\qquad f_4(\lambda) = (\lambda - \lambda_1)^3$$
$$f_2(\lambda) = \lambda - \lambda_1 \qquad f_5(\lambda) = (\lambda - \lambda_1)^3(\lambda - \lambda_2)$$
$$f_3(\lambda) = (\lambda - \lambda_1)^2 \quad f_6(\lambda) = (\lambda - \lambda_1)^3(\lambda - \lambda_2)^2$$

For these functions, Eq. (6.3.18) takes on the form

$$
\begin{bmatrix}
\mathbf{U} \\
\mathbf{P} - \lambda_1\mathbf{U} \\
(\mathbf{P} - \lambda_1\mathbf{U})^2 \\
(\mathbf{P} - \lambda_1\mathbf{U})^3 \\
(\mathbf{P} - \lambda_1\mathbf{U})^3(\mathbf{P} - \lambda_2\mathbf{U}) \\
(\mathbf{P} - \lambda_1\mathbf{U})^3(\mathbf{P} - \lambda_2\mathbf{U})^2
\end{bmatrix}
$$

$$
=
\begin{bmatrix}
1 & 0 & 0 & 1 & 0 & 1 \\
0 & 1 & 0 & \lambda_2 - \lambda_1 & 0 & \lambda_3 - \lambda_1 \\
0 & 0 & 1 & (\lambda_2 - \lambda_1)^2 & \lambda_2 - \lambda_1 & (\lambda_3 - \lambda_1)^2 \\
0 & 0 & 0 & (\lambda_2 - \lambda_1)^3 & (\lambda_2 - \lambda_1)^2 & (\lambda_3 - \lambda_1)^3 \\
0 & 0 & 0 & 0 & (\lambda_2 - \lambda_1)^3 & (\lambda_3 - \lambda_1)^3(\lambda_3 - \lambda_2) \\
0 & 0 & 0 & 0 & 0 & (\lambda_3 - \lambda_1)^3(\lambda_3 - \lambda)^2
\end{bmatrix}
\begin{bmatrix}
\mathbf{Z}_{11} \\
\mathbf{Z}_{12} \\
\mathbf{Z}_{13} \\
\mathbf{Z}_{21} \\
\mathbf{Z}_{22} \\
\mathbf{Z}_{31}
\end{bmatrix}
$$

The constituent matrices are evaluated by taking the inverse of the coefficient matrix and are clearly polynomials in $\mathbf{P} - \lambda_i\mathbf{U}$. For example, from the last expression

$$\mathbf{Z}_{31} = \frac{1}{(\lambda_3 - \lambda_1)^3(\lambda_3 - \lambda_2)^2}(\mathbf{P} - \lambda_1\mathbf{U})^3(\mathbf{P} - \lambda_2\mathbf{U})^2$$

and from the next to the last equation

$$\mathbf{Z}_{22} = \frac{1}{(\lambda_2 - \lambda_1)^3}(\mathbf{P} - \lambda_1\mathbf{U})^3(\mathbf{P} - \lambda_2\mathbf{U}) - \frac{\lambda_3 - \lambda_2}{(\lambda_2 - \lambda_1)^3}(\lambda_3 - \lambda_1)^3\mathbf{Z}_{31}$$

Example 6.3.3: Evaluate the constituent matrices for the matrix

$$\mathbf{P} = \begin{bmatrix} 1 & -1 & -1 \\ -1 & 1 & -1 \\ -1 & -1 & 1 \end{bmatrix}$$

Solution: The characteristic polynomial is

$$D(\lambda) = (\lambda + 1)(\lambda - 2)^2$$

It is not known, without evaluating the adjoint of $\lambda U - P$, whether the minimal polynomial is equal to the characteristic polynomial or not. In the absence of this information one simply uses the characteristic polynomial, and as we shall see, the results of the calculations will provide the missing information. Assuming that the minimal polynomial is equal to the characteristic polynomial,

$$f(\mathbf{P}) = \mathbf{Z}_{11}f(-1) + \mathbf{Z}_{21}f(2) + \mathbf{Z}_{22}f^{(1)}(2)$$

The sequence of resolving polynomials

$$f_1(\lambda) = 1 \qquad f_2(\lambda) = \lambda + 1 \qquad f_3(\lambda) = (\lambda + 1)(\lambda - 2)$$

generates the system of equations

$$\begin{bmatrix} \mathbf{U} \\ \mathbf{P} + \mathbf{U} \\ (\mathbf{P} + \mathbf{U})(\mathbf{P} - 2\mathbf{U}) \end{bmatrix} = \begin{bmatrix} 1 & 1 & 0 \\ 0 & 3 & 1 \\ 0 & 0 & 3 \end{bmatrix} \begin{bmatrix} \mathbf{Z}_{11} \\ \mathbf{Z}_{21} \\ \mathbf{Z}_{22} \end{bmatrix}$$

The constituent matrices are

$$\mathbf{Z}_{22} = \frac{1}{3}(\mathbf{P} + \mathbf{U})(\mathbf{P} - 2\mathbf{U}) = \begin{bmatrix} 2 & -1 & -1 \\ -1 & 2 & -1 \\ -1 & -1 & 2 \end{bmatrix} \begin{bmatrix} -1 & -1 & -1 \\ -1 & -1 & -1 \\ -1 & -1 & -1 \end{bmatrix}$$

$$= \begin{bmatrix} 0 & 0 & 0 \\ 0 & 0 & 0 \\ 0 & 0 & 0 \end{bmatrix}$$

$$\mathbf{Z}_{21} = \frac{1}{3}(\mathbf{P} + \mathbf{U}) = \frac{1}{3}\begin{bmatrix} 2 & -1 & -1 \\ -1 & 2 & -1 \\ -1 & -1 & 2 \end{bmatrix}$$

$$\mathbf{Z}_{11} = \mathbf{U} - \mathbf{Z}_{21} = \frac{1}{3}\begin{bmatrix} 1 & 1 & 1 \\ 1 & 1 & 1 \\ 1 & 1 & 1 \end{bmatrix}$$

Since $\mathbf{Z}_{22}$ as calculated is zero, we conclude that $f(\mathbf{P})$ is of the form

$$f(\mathbf{P}) = \mathbf{Z}_{11}f(\lambda_1) + \mathbf{Z}_{21}f(\lambda_2)$$

and that the minimal polynomial is actually

$$m(\lambda) = (\lambda + 1)(\lambda - 2)$$

This result agrees with the result already obtained in Example 6.3.1 by another method.

The constituent matrices of $\mathbf{P}$ can also be obtained as an explicit function of powers of $\mathbf{P}$ by using as the resolving polynomials a sequence of increasing powers of λ, that is,

$$f_1(\lambda) = 1 \qquad f_2(\lambda) = \lambda \qquad f_3(\lambda) = \lambda^2 \qquad \cdots \qquad f_n(\lambda) = \lambda^{n-1}$$

The resulting matrix functions for a matrix having a minimal polynomial of the form given in Eq. (6.3.16) are

$$\begin{bmatrix} \mathbf{U} \\ \mathbf{P} \\ \mathbf{P}^2 \\ \mathbf{P}^3 \\ \mathbf{P}^4 \\ \mathbf{P}^5 \end{bmatrix} = \begin{bmatrix} 1 & 0 & 0 & 1 & 0 & 1 \\ \lambda_1 & 1 & 0 & \lambda_2 & 1 & \lambda_3 \\ \lambda_1^2 & 2\lambda_1 & 1 & \lambda_2^2 & 2\lambda_2 & \lambda_3^2 \\ \lambda_1^3 & 3\lambda_1^2 & 3\lambda_1 & \lambda_2^3 & 3\lambda_2^2 & \lambda_3^3 \\ \lambda_1^4 & 4\lambda_1^3 & 6\lambda_1^2 & \lambda_2^4 & 4\lambda_2^3 & \lambda_3^4 \\ \lambda_1^5 & 5\lambda_1^4 & 10\lambda_1^3 & \lambda_2^5 & 5\lambda_2^4 & \lambda_3^5 \end{bmatrix} \begin{bmatrix} \mathbf{Z}_{11} \\ \mathbf{Z}_{12} \\ \mathbf{Z}_{13} \\ \mathbf{Z}_{21} \\ \mathbf{Z}_{22} \\ \mathbf{Z}_{31} \end{bmatrix} \qquad (6.3.19)$$

The coefficient matrix is the transpose of the (generalized) Vandermonde matrix and is therefore nonsingular. The solution, of course, gives the constituent matrices in terms of powers of the given matrix $\mathbf{P}$.

Example 6.3.4 (after Frame[5]): Evaluate the constituent matrices of the matrix $\mathbf{P}$ in Example 6.3.2 in terms of powers of $\mathbf{P}$.

Solution: The characteristic polynomial of the given matrix is

$$D(\lambda) = \lambda^3 + \lambda^2 - 8\lambda - 12 = (\lambda - 3)(\lambda + 2)^2$$

Taking $f_1(\lambda) = 1$, $f_2(\lambda) = \lambda$, $f_3(\lambda) = \lambda^2$ and using a form similar to that of Eq. (6.3.19),

$$\begin{bmatrix} \mathbf{U} \\ \mathbf{P} \\ \mathbf{P}^2 \end{bmatrix} = \begin{bmatrix} 1 & 1 & 0 \\ 3 & -2 & 1 \\ 9 & 4 & -4 \end{bmatrix} \begin{bmatrix} \mathbf{Z}_{11} \\ \mathbf{Z}_{21} \\ \mathbf{Z}_{22} \end{bmatrix}$$

Inverting the coefficient matrix gives

$$\mathbf{Z}_{11} = \tfrac{1}{25}(4\mathbf{U} + 4\mathbf{P} + \mathbf{P}^2)$$
$$\mathbf{Z}_{21} = \tfrac{1}{25}(21\mathbf{U} - 4\mathbf{P} - \mathbf{P}^2)$$
$$\mathbf{Z}_{22} = \tfrac{1}{25}(30\mathbf{U} + 5\mathbf{P} - 5\mathbf{P}^2)$$

where

$$\mathbf{P} = \begin{bmatrix} -13 & -21 & -11 \\ 5 & 8 & 5 \\ 6 & 11 & 4 \end{bmatrix} \quad \text{and} \quad \mathbf{P}^2 = \begin{bmatrix} -2 & -16 & -6 \\ 5 & 14 & 5 \\ 1 & 6 & 5 \end{bmatrix}$$

The numerical values of the resulting constituent matrices are, of course, the same as those given in Example 6.3.2.

In the special case in which the eigenvalues of the given matrix are distinct, it is possible to select the resolving polynomials in such a way that the coefficient matrix of the column of constituent matrices is diagonal. Indeed, if

$$D(\lambda) = (\lambda - \lambda_1)(\lambda - \lambda_2) \cdots (\lambda - \lambda_n)$$

then upon taking

$$f_1(\lambda) = \frac{D(\lambda)}{\lambda - \lambda_1} \qquad f_2(\lambda) = \frac{D(\lambda)}{\lambda - \lambda_2} \qquad \cdots \qquad f_n(\lambda) = \frac{D(\lambda)}{\lambda - \lambda_n}$$

we find immediately that

$$\mathbf{Z}_{11} = \frac{1}{f_1(\lambda_1)} f_1(\mathbf{P}) = \frac{1}{f_1(\lambda_1)} (\mathbf{P} - \lambda_2\mathbf{U})(\mathbf{P} - \lambda_3\mathbf{U}) \cdots (\mathbf{P} - \lambda_n\mathbf{U})$$

$$\mathbf{Z}_{21} = \frac{1}{f_2(\lambda_2)} f_2(\mathbf{P}) = \frac{1}{f_2(\lambda_2)} (\mathbf{P} - \lambda_1\mathbf{U})(\mathbf{P} - \lambda_3\mathbf{U}) \cdots (\mathbf{P} - \lambda_n\mathbf{U})$$

$$\cdots \cdots \cdots \cdots \cdots \cdots \cdots \cdots \cdots \cdots \cdots \cdots \cdots$$

$$\mathbf{Z}_{n1} = \frac{1}{f_n(\lambda_n)} f_n(\mathbf{P}) = \frac{1}{f_n(\lambda_n)} (\mathbf{P} - \lambda_1\mathbf{U})(\mathbf{P} - \lambda_2\mathbf{U}) \cdots (\mathbf{P} - \lambda_{n-1}\mathbf{U})$$

Although the resulting expressions are appealing from the standpoint of requiring no matrix inverse, the technique suffers from the disadvantage that it may require the numerical evaluation of many matrix products.

Example 6.3.5:   Evaluate the constituent matrices of the matrix

$$\mathbf{P} = \begin{bmatrix} 0 & 0 & -1 & 1 \\ 0 & 0 & 0 & -1 \\ 1 & 0 & 0 & 0 \\ -1 & 1 & 0 & 0 \end{bmatrix}$$

Solution: The matrix is skew-symmetric with characteristic polynomial

$$D(\lambda) = |\lambda\mathbf{U} - \mathbf{P}| = \lambda^4 + 3\lambda^2 + 1 = (\lambda - \lambda_1)(\lambda - \lambda_2)(\lambda - \lambda_3)(\lambda - \lambda_4)$$

where the eigenvalues are pure imaginary numbers and occur in conjugate pairs, i.e.,

$$\lambda_1 = j\left(\frac{3 + \sqrt{5}}{2}\right)^{1/2} \qquad \lambda_2 = \hat{\lambda}_1 = -j\left(\frac{3 + \sqrt{5}}{2}\right)^{1/2}$$

$$\lambda_3 = j\left(\frac{3 - \sqrt{5}}{2}\right)^{1/2} \qquad \lambda_4 = \hat{\lambda}_3 = -j\left(\frac{3 - \sqrt{3}}{2}\right)^{1/2}$$

The circumflex ^ indicates the conjugate.

In general, since the eigenvalues are distinct, $f(P)$ is of the form

$$f(\mathbf{P}) = \mathbf{Z}_{11}f(\lambda_1) + \mathbf{Z}_{21}f(\lambda_2) + \mathbf{Z}_{31}f(\lambda_3) + \mathbf{Z}_{41}f(\lambda_4)$$

Upon taking $f_1(\lambda) = (\lambda - \lambda_2)(\lambda - \lambda_3)(\lambda - \lambda_4)$ we find that

$$\mathbf{Z}_{11} = \frac{1}{(\lambda_1 - \lambda_2)(\lambda_1 - \lambda_3)(\lambda_1 - \lambda_4)} [(\mathbf{P} - \lambda_2\mathbf{U})(\mathbf{P} - \lambda_3\mathbf{U})(\mathbf{P} - \lambda_4\mathbf{U})]$$

For the matrix **P** given above and by use of the numerical values of the eigenvalues, $\mathbf{Z}_{11}$ is

$$\mathbf{Z}_{11} = \frac{j}{6.474} \begin{bmatrix} j3.854 & -j1.618 & 1.618 & -2.618 \\ -j1.618 & j2.236 & -1 & 1.618 \\ -1.618 & 1 & j2.236 & -j1.618 \\ 2.618 & -1.618 & -1.618 & j3.854 \end{bmatrix}$$

The constituent matrix $\mathbf{Z}_{21}$ is obtained by taking

$$f_2(\lambda) = (\lambda - \lambda_1)(\lambda - \lambda_3)(\lambda - \lambda_4)$$

from which it is found that

$$\mathbf{Z}_{21} = \hat{\mathbf{Z}}_{11}$$

where the circumflex ^ indicates that the entries of $\mathbf{Z}_{21}$ are complex conjugates of the corresponding entries in $\mathbf{Z}_{11}$; that is, all coefficients j in $\mathbf{Z}_{11}$ are replaced by $-j$.

The numerical values of the remaining constituent matrices are evaluated in a similar way.   The details are left to the reader, who should find that $\mathbf{Z}_{41} = \hat{\mathbf{Z}}_{31}$.

It should be evident that either of the basic methods discussed in this section can be programmed for machine execution. Of the various resolving polynomials that might be used in the second of the basic procedures, the sequence of polynomials in λ is perhaps the most expedient, particularly if the method for inverting the Vandermonde matrix suggested by Frame[5] is used. However, it should be recognized that all procedures require knowledge of both the characteristic polynomial $D(\lambda)$ and the zeros of this characteristic polynomial. In any systems-analysis problem the characteristic polynomial is obtainable only through the expansion of $|\lambda \mathbf{U} - \mathbf{P}|$, and, for this reason, the algorithm for generating adj $(\lambda \mathbf{U} - \mathbf{P})$ and $D(\lambda)$, given as part of the first basic method, is actually essential to a practical application of the second method. Therefore, this algorithm must be included as part of any general-purpose program for evaluating the constituent matrices. Such programs extend the capabilities of computing machines beyond the realm of generating only numerical solutions of the form described in Chap. 5 into the realm of generating solutions in the form of explicit functions of time.

Indeed, once the zeros of the characteristic polynomial and the constituent matrices are known numerically, the matrix $e^{\mathbf{P}t}$ is given as an explicit function of time by Theorem 6.2.1. If the state equations characterizing the system are reduced to the equivalent homogeneous form

$$\frac{d}{dt}\,\mathbf{\Psi}(t) = \mathbf{P}\mathbf{\Psi}(t) \qquad \mathbf{\Psi}(0) = \mathbf{\Psi}_0$$

and if the characteristic polynomial of P is of the form

$$m(\lambda) = |\lambda \mathbf{U} - \mathbf{P}| = (\lambda - \lambda_1)^{r_1}(\lambda - \lambda_2)^{r_2} \cdots (\lambda - \lambda_k)^{r_k} \qquad (6.3.20)$$

then the general form of the solution is specifically

$$\begin{aligned}
\mathbf{\Psi}(t) = {} & \left[\mathbf{Z}_{11}\mathbf{\Psi}(0) + \mathbf{Z}_{12}\mathbf{\Psi}(0)t + \cdots + \mathbf{Z}_{1r_1}\frac{\mathbf{\Psi}(0)t^{(r_1-1)}}{(r_1-1)!} \right] e^{\lambda_1 t} \\
& + \left[\mathbf{Z}_{21}\mathbf{\Psi}(0) + \mathbf{Z}_{22}\mathbf{\Psi}(0)t + \cdots + \mathbf{Z}_{2r_2}\frac{\mathbf{\Psi}(0)t^{(r_2-1)}}{(r_2-1)!} \right] e^{\lambda_2 t} \\
& + \cdots \cdots \cdots \cdots \cdots \cdots \cdots \cdots \cdots \cdots \cdots \\
& + \left[\mathbf{Z}_{k1}\mathbf{\Psi}(0) + \mathbf{Z}_{k2}\mathbf{\Psi}(0)t + \cdots + \mathbf{Z}_{kr_k}\frac{\mathbf{\Psi}(0)t^{(r_k-1)}}{(r_k-1)!} \right] e^{\lambda_k t}
\end{aligned}$$

$$(6.3.21)$$

From this general form it is evident that, in addition to the numerical values of the entries in the constituent matrices $\mathbf{Z}_{ij}$ and the initial conditions $\mathbf{\Psi}(0)$, the time variation of the state vector depends critically upon the numerical values of the eigenvalues λ_i. If, for example, one of the eigenvalues is a positive real number, then the solution increases without bound as $t \to \infty$. On the other hand, if all the eigenvalues are negative real numbers, then the solution goes to zero as $t \to \infty$. These general properties of the solution as $t \to \infty$ lead to the important concept of *stability*.

6.4 STABILITY IN THE SENSE OF LYAPUNOV

There are several ways in which stability of linear time-invariant systems can be defined mathematically. A fundamental requirement is that the mathematical definition be descriptive of the operational characteristic one wishes to represent mathematically. The definition of stability given originally by Lyapunov[6] applies to both linear and nonlinear systems and includes essentially all the useful definitions of stability in linear systems as special cases. These general conditions, which apply to all types of systems, both linear and nonlinear, are considered in this section.

Stability in the Lyapunov sense is based on the behavior of the state vector relative to an *equilibrium state*, defined as any constant vector $\boldsymbol{\Psi}_e$ for which the right-hand side of the equation

$$\frac{d}{dt} \boldsymbol{\Psi}(t) = \mathbf{F}(\boldsymbol{\Psi}, t) \tag{6.4.1}$$

vanishes. That is, if $\boldsymbol{\Psi}_e$ is an equilibrium state, then

$$\mathbf{F}(\boldsymbol{\Psi}_e, t) = 0$$

and the differential equation is satisfied.

In the special case of linear homogeneous systems, Eq. (6.4.1) is of the form

$$\frac{d}{dt} \boldsymbol{\Psi}(t) = \mathbf{P}(t)\boldsymbol{\Psi}(t) \tag{6.4.2}$$

and if $\mathbf{P}(t)$ is nonsingular, the right-hand side of the state equations vanishes only if

$$\boldsymbol{\Psi} = \boldsymbol{\Psi}_e = 0$$

If the right-hand side of Eq. (6.4.1) does not depend explicitly on time, the equations are said to be *autonomous* and the solution of $\mathbf{F}(\boldsymbol{\Psi}) = 0$ is a constant vector, if a solution exists at all. In the more general case of a nonautonomous system, such as the linear form

$$\frac{d}{dt} \boldsymbol{\Psi}(t) = \mathbf{P}(t)\boldsymbol{\Psi}(t) + \mathbf{Q}\mathbf{E}(t) = \mathbf{F}(\boldsymbol{\Psi}, t) \tag{6.4.3}$$

the solution to $\mathbf{F}(\boldsymbol{\Psi}, t) = 0$ may be a function of time, and the system accordingly may not have an equilibrium state but has instead a particular, or *equilibrium, solution* $\boldsymbol{\Psi}_e(t)$. For such systems, stability is defined in terms of the equilibrium points of an equivalent system obtained by setting

$$\mathbf{\Psi}'(t) = \mathbf{\Psi}(t) - \mathbf{\Xi}(t) \tag{6.4.4}$$

where $\mathbf{\Xi}(t)$ is a particular solution to Eq. (6.4.1); that is, $\mathbf{\Xi}(t)$ satisfies the equation

$$\frac{d}{dt}\mathbf{\Xi}(t) = \mathbf{F}(\mathbf{\Xi},t) \tag{6.4.5}$$

Substituting Eq. (6.4.4) into Eq. (6.4.1) gives

$$\frac{d}{dt}\mathbf{\Psi}'(t) + \frac{d}{dt}\mathbf{\Xi}(t) = \mathbf{F}(\mathbf{\Psi}' + \mathbf{\Xi}, t)$$

Or, upon using Eq. (6.4.5), we have the equivalent system

$$\frac{d}{dt}\mathbf{\Psi}'(t) = \mathbf{F}(\mathbf{\Psi}' + \mathbf{\Xi}, t) - \mathbf{F}(\mathbf{\Xi},t)$$
$$= \mathbf{F}'(\mathbf{\Psi}',t) \tag{6.4.6}$$

for which the equilibrium state is $\mathbf{\Psi}' = 0$; that is, the right-hand side of Eq. (6.4.6) vanishes at $\mathbf{\Psi}' = 0$.

It is important to note that, when applied to the linear system in Eq. (6.4.3), the transformation of variables in Eq. (6.4.4) gives

$$\frac{d}{dt}\mathbf{\Psi}'(t) = \mathbf{P}(t)(\mathbf{\Psi}' + \mathbf{\Xi}) + \mathbf{QE}(t) - \mathbf{P}(t)\mathbf{\Xi}(t) - \mathbf{QE}(t)$$
$$= \mathbf{P}(t)\mathbf{\Psi}'(t) \tag{6.4.7}$$

which is identical *in form* to the homogeneous part of the original system. Therefore, *the stability characteristics of linear time-varying or constant-coefficient state equations are based on only the equilibrium state $\mathbf{\Psi}_e$ of the homogeneous part of the equations.* Since any nonzero equilibrium solution can be translated to the origin by the simple transformation given in Eq. (6.4.4), only equilibrium states about the origin are considered in the subsequent developments.

Example 6.4.1: Establish the equilibrium state of the nonautonomous differential equation

$$\frac{d}{dt}\psi(t) = a[\psi(t) + t]^2 - 1$$

Solution: A particular solution to this differential equation is $\xi(t) = -t$; indeed

$$\frac{d}{dt}\xi(t) = -1 = a(-t + t)^2 - 1 = -1$$

Applying the transformation of variables

$$\psi'(t) = \psi(t) - \xi(t) = \psi(t) + t$$

yields

$$\frac{d}{dt} \psi'(t) - 1 = a[\psi'(t)]^2 - 1$$

or

$$\frac{d}{dt} \psi'(t) = a[\psi'(t)]^2$$

The state $\psi' = 0$ is clearly an equilibrium point of the equivalent equation. It should be noted that $\psi'(t) = \psi(t) - \xi(t)$ represents the difference between the actual solution and a particular solution. Thus, basing the stability characteristics on the transformed system of equations corresponds to investigating how the complete solution to the original differential equation departs from a particular solution.

Example 6.4.2: Establish equivalent systems for which the origin is an equilibrium point for the nonlinear autonomous system

$$\frac{d}{dt} \begin{bmatrix} \psi_1(t) \\ \psi_2(t) \end{bmatrix} = \begin{bmatrix} [\psi_1(t) + 2][\psi_2(t) + 3] \\ a\psi_2(t)[\psi_1(t) + 4] \end{bmatrix}$$

Solution: The particular solutions

$$\xi_1 = \begin{bmatrix} -2 \\ 0 \end{bmatrix} \qquad \xi_2 = \begin{bmatrix} -4 \\ -3 \end{bmatrix}$$

are also equilibrium states. The first equilibrium state is transferred to the origin by setting

$$\begin{bmatrix} \psi_1'(t) \\ \psi_2'(t) \end{bmatrix} = \begin{bmatrix} \psi_1(t) \\ \psi_2(t) \end{bmatrix} - \begin{bmatrix} -2 \\ 0 \end{bmatrix}$$

Applying this transformation of variables to the given state equations yields

$$\frac{d}{dt} \begin{bmatrix} \psi_1'(t) \\ \psi_2'(t) \end{bmatrix} = \begin{bmatrix} \psi_1'(t)[\psi_2'(t) + 3] \\ a\psi_2'(t)[\psi_1'(t) + 2] \end{bmatrix} \tag{6.4.8}$$

for which the origin is an equilibrium point.

The second equilibrium point is transferred to the origin by setting

$$\begin{bmatrix} \psi_1''(t) \\ \psi_2''(t) \end{bmatrix} = \begin{bmatrix} \psi_1(t) \\ \psi_2(t) \end{bmatrix} - \begin{bmatrix} -4 \\ -3 \end{bmatrix}$$

The state equations resulting from this transformation are

$$\frac{d}{dt} \begin{bmatrix} \psi_1''(t) \\ \psi_2''(t) \end{bmatrix} = \begin{bmatrix} [\psi_1''(t) - 2]\psi_2''(t) \\ a[\psi_2''(t) - 3]\psi_1''(t) \end{bmatrix} \tag{6.4.9}$$

for which the origin is an equilibrium point. The stability of the first equilibrium point is therefore investigated in terms of Eq. (6.4.8) and the second in terms of Eq. (6.4.9).

Lyapunov's definition of stability is based on the concept that if a stable system is disturbed a small amount from an equilibrium state it should either return to that state or stay within some preassigned finite region of the equilibrium state.   A vertical pendulum, for example, has two states—the stable state, wherein the pendulum hangs downward, and the unstable state, wherein the pendulum is "balanced" in an upward position.   In this latter position, if the pendulum is displaced a small amount from the balanced position, it will not return to any preassigned small region of this position.   On the other hand, if it is displaced when in the downward position, it will return eventually to an ϵ neighborhood of the equilibrium state.

To establish a basis for a mathematical definition of stability, consider the state equations

$$\frac{d}{dt} \mathbf{\Psi}(t) = \mathbf{F}(\mathbf{\Psi},t) \tag{6.4.10}$$

for which $\mathbf{\Psi}_e = 0$ is an equilibrium state.   Let the initial state of the system at some time $t = t_0$ be designated as $\mathbf{\Psi}(t_0) = \mathbf{\Psi}_0$, and let $\mathbf{\Psi}(t)$ represent the solution corresponding to this initial state for $t \geq t_0$.   A formal definition of stability of an equilibrium state as stated originally by Lyapunov is as follows:

Definition 6.4.1:   *Stability in the sense of Lyapunov*

(a)   The equilibrium state $\mathbf{\Psi}_e = 0$ of Eq. (6.4.10) is said to be *stable* if for each $\epsilon > 0$ there exists a $\delta > 0$ such that the norm of the state vector $\|\mathbf{\Psi}(t)\| = [\mathbf{\Psi}^T(t)\mathbf{\Psi}(t)]^{1/2}$ is such that $\|\mathbf{\Psi}(t)\| \leq \epsilon$ for all $t \geq t_0$ and

$$\|\mathbf{\Psi}_0\| < \delta$$

(b)   If, in addition, the solution $\mathbf{\Psi}(t)$ has the property that

$$\lim_{t \to \infty} \mathbf{\Psi}(t) = 0$$

then the system is said to be *asymptotically stable*.

(c)   If for some $\epsilon > 0$ it is not possible to find a δ, no matter how small, such that $\|\mathbf{\Psi}(t)\| \leq \epsilon$ for all $t \geq t_0$, then the equilibrium state $\mathbf{\Psi}_e = 0$ is said to be *unstable*.

Note that

$$\|\mathbf{\Psi}\|^2 = \mathbf{\Psi}^T\mathbf{\Psi} = \psi_1{}^2 + \psi_2{}^2 + \cdots + \psi_n{}^2$$

Consequently, the fact that the norm of the state vector remains bounded with time implies that the magnitude of *each entry* in the state vector remains bounded.   Also, note that the definition of stability requires that the ϵ, δ relations in (a) and (b) be satisfied for *every* $\epsilon > 0$.   While this point is unimportant in the stability of linear systems, it is important in nonlinear systems.

In the case of second-order systems it is possible to plot the two state variables $\psi_1(t)$ and $\psi_2(t)$ as functions of the parameter t, as shown in Fig. 6.4.1. Such a plot is called a *trajectory* of the state vector, and the line segment drawn from the origin to the trajectory represents the norm $\|\Psi\| = (\psi_1{}^2 + \psi_2{}^2)^{1/2}$ of the second-order state vector at the corresponding instant of time. The definition of stability states that, in the case of a stable system, the trajectory will remain inside some circular region of radius ϵ if it starts within a circular region of radius δ about the origin, as indicated in Fig. 6.4.1a. In the case of an asymptotically stable system, the trajectory stays within a radius ϵ of the origin *and* goes to zero as $t \to \infty$, as shown in Fig. 6.4.1b.

If the solution to a system of state equations is known as an explicit function of time or as a numerical solution, then one can easily enough ascertain in most cases whether or not the system is stable according to Definition 6.4.1. But this is not the primary objective of stability studies. The objective is to determine the stability characteristics without actually generating the solution and to discover, insofar as possible, how these stability characteristics are related to the structure of the system, i.e., to the component characteristics and the topology. An exhaustive study of the stability characteristics of nonlinear and time-varying state equations is outside the scope of this book—entire volumes are written on these subjects alone. The development given here, with a statement of the main theorem of Lyapunov and its application, is to be regarded only as an introduction to the subject and only autonomous

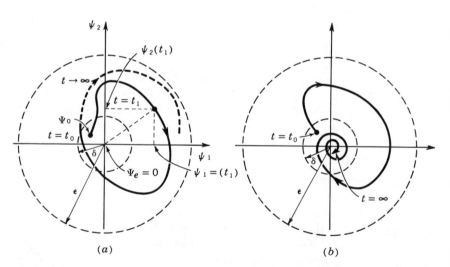

Fig. 6.4.1 Stable trajectories for second-order systems. (*a*) Stable; (*b*) asymptotically stable.

systems are considered, the specific form being

$$\frac{d}{dt}\,\mathbf{\Psi}(t) = \mathbf{F}(\mathbf{\Psi}) \qquad\qquad (6.4.11)$$

where $\mathbf{F}(\mathbf{\Psi})$ is continuous and $\mathbf{F}(0) \equiv 0$ is an equilibrium state.

It is important to recognize that the solution $\mathbf{\Psi}(t)$ to the differential equations in Eq. (6.4.11) depends upon the initial state $\mathbf{\Psi}(0) = \mathbf{\Psi}_0$ of the system at $t = t_0 = 0$.† This fact is emphasized by representing the solution to Eq. (6.4.11) by $\mathbf{\Psi}(\mathbf{\Psi}_0,t)$. It is assumed that the function $\mathbf{F}(\mathbf{\Psi})$ in Eq. (6.4.11) is such that the solution $\mathbf{\Psi}(\mathbf{\Psi}_0,t)$ is a continuous function of the initial state $\mathbf{\Psi}_0$.

The norm of the state vector $\|\mathbf{\Psi}(\mathbf{\Psi}_0,t)\| = [\mathbf{\Psi}^T(\mathbf{\Psi}_0,t)\,\mathbf{\Psi}(\mathbf{\Psi}_0,t)]^{1/2}$ used in the definition of stability is, of course, a scalar function of time. More importantly, it never assumes negative values, since, at any time t, it is the square root of the sum of the squares of its components. It has already been pointed out that if this scalar function is bounded with increasing time then the solution is stable. There are, of course, other scalar functions of the components of the state vector that can be used as a measure of the boundedness of the components $\psi_i(t)$ $(i = 1, 2, \ldots, n)$ of the state vector. The only requirement is that such a function, like the norm of a vector, must be positive for $\mathbf{\Psi} \neq 0$ and must be zero at $\mathbf{\Psi} = 0$. Any scalar function which satisfies these two conditions and at the same time has continuous partial derivatives with respect to the components of $\mathbf{\Psi}$ is called a *V function* and is hereafter represented as $V(\mathbf{\Psi})$. In the case of a second-order system, the scalar function $V(\mathbf{\Psi})$ can be regarded as a "generalized" measure of the "distance" of the trajectory from the origin and includes the norm of $\mathbf{\Psi}$ as a special case.

Suppose that the scalar function $V(\mathbf{\Psi})$ is evaluated for successive values of the state vector $\mathbf{\Psi}(\mathbf{\Psi}_0,t)$ as obtained from the solution of the differential equation. If $V[\mathbf{\Psi}(\mathbf{\Psi}_0,t)]$ increases without bound as $t \to \infty$, then we conclude that at least one of the state variables is also increasing without bound. Conversely, if $V[\mathbf{\Psi}(\mathbf{\Psi}_0,t)]$ goes to zero as $t \to \infty$, *all* the state variables approach zero with increasing t. Whether V is increasing or decreasing at any particular time t can, of course, be determined by evaluating its time derivative. The above considerations form the basis of Lyapunov's theorem on stability.

Theorem 6.4.1: Consider the system described by $(d/dt)\,\mathbf{\Psi}(t) = \mathbf{F}(\mathbf{\Psi})$. If in a neighborhood of the origin there exists a scalar function $V(\mathbf{\Psi})$ such that $V(\mathbf{\Psi}) > 0$ for $\mathbf{\Psi} \neq 0$, $V(0) = 0$, and $V(\mathbf{\Psi})$ has continuous

---

† For autonomous systems there is no loss in generality by taking $t = 0$ as the initial point on the time scale.

partial derivatives with respect to the components of $\mathbf{\Psi}$, then

(a)   The origin is stable if

$$\frac{d}{dt} V(\mathbf{\Psi}) \leq 0$$

for values of $\mathbf{\Psi}$ along the solution curves $\mathbf{\Psi} = \mathbf{\Psi}(\mathbf{\Psi}_0, t)$.

(b)   The system is asymptotically stable if $(d/dt)V(\mathbf{\Psi}) < 0$ for values of $\mathbf{\Psi}$ on the solution curves.

(c)   The system is unstable if

$$\frac{d}{dt} V(\mathbf{\Psi}) > 0$$

for values of $\mathbf{\Psi}$ on the solution curves.

Further,

$$\frac{d}{dt} V(\mathbf{\Psi}) = [\mathbf{F}(\mathbf{\Psi})]^T \text{ grad } V = (\text{grad } V)^T F(\mathbf{\Psi}) \tag{6.4.12}$$

where

$$(\text{grad } V)^T = \left[\frac{\partial V}{\partial \psi_1} \frac{\partial V}{\partial \psi_2} \cdots \frac{\partial V}{\partial \psi_n}\right]$$

Proof

(a)   To establish the first part of the theorem, it is necessary to show that there exists a $\delta > 0$ such that, when the norm of the initial state $\|\mathbf{\Psi}_0\| < \delta$, the solution $\mathbf{\Psi}(\mathbf{\Psi}_0, t)$ remains always within an arbitrarily selected region $\|\mathbf{\Psi}(\mathbf{\Psi}_0, t)\| < \epsilon$.

The constraint $\|\mathbf{\Psi}(\mathbf{\Psi}_0, t)\| < \epsilon$ defines an open region R_ϵ in the n-dimensional state space. If $n = 2$, as shown in Fig. 6.4.2, R_ϵ contains those states interior to the circle C of radius $\epsilon = (\psi_1{}^2 + \psi_2{}^2)^{1/2}$.

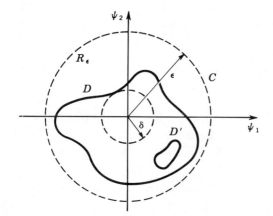

Fig. 6.4.2 Two-dimensional state space.

By hypothesis, $V(\Psi)$ is a positive definite function which vanishes only at $\Psi = 0$ and has continuous partial derivatives in some neighborhood, Ω, of the origin. Thus, given any $\epsilon > 0$, it is always possible to find a positive constant m such that every state satisfying $V(\Psi) < m$ is contained in the region R_ϵ. In Fig. 6.4.2, this implies that there exists at least one closed curve D, contained entirely within C, which defines the locus of all states $\Psi = (\psi_1, \psi_2)$ satisfying $V(\Psi) = m$.

There may exist other closed curves, like D', for example, which occur because of local maximums in $V(\Psi)$. Such curves enclose states for which $V(\Psi) > m$. It is clear that, in the general case, the n-dimensional surfaces defined by the constraint $V(\Psi) = m$ cannot pass through the origin, provided that $m > 0$. Thus, there exists a positive constant δ, such that

$$\|\Psi_0\| < \delta \qquad V(\Psi_0) < m \tag{6.4.13}$$

are simultaneously satisfied in Ω. That is, with reference to Fig. 6.4.2, one can always pick a δ neighborhood of the origin which contains only points within D but no points on or within D'. Since $\dot{V}(\Psi) \leq 0$, it follows that for all $t \geq t_0$

$$V(\Psi) - V(\Psi_0) = \int_{t_0}^{t} \dot{V}(\Psi)d\tau \leq 0 \tag{6.4.14}$$

or

$$V(\Psi) \leq V(\Psi_0) \tag{6.4.15}$$

Since $V(\Psi)$ is nonincreasing along the solution curves, $V(\Psi) < m$ for all $t \geq t_0$. Therefore, the solution curves do not leave the region R_ϵ in the state space, i.e.,

$$\|\Psi(\Psi_0, t)\| \leq \|\Psi_0\| < \epsilon \tag{6.4.16}$$

and the first part of the theorem is established.

(b) To establish asymptotic stability when $\dot{V} < 0$, it is necessary to show that, in addition to the conditions of part a,

$$\lim_{t \to \infty} \|\Psi(\Psi_0, t)\| = 0$$

By hypothesis, $V(\Psi) = 0$ only when $\|\Psi\| = 0$. Further, since $\dot{V}(\Psi) < 0$ for all values of Ψ on the solution curves and $V(\Psi) > 0$ for $\|\Psi\| \neq 0$, it follows that $\lim_{t \to \infty} V[\Psi(\Psi_0, t)] = 0$. Since this function approaches zero only as $\|\Psi(\Psi_0, t)\| \to 0$, it follows that the system is asymptotically stable.

(c)   To establish instability, it is necessary to show that it is not possible to select the norm of the initial state vector $\|\Psi_0\|$ sufficiently small so that the norm of the solution $\|\Psi(\Psi_0,t)\| < \epsilon$ for all $t > 0$. Consider

$$V[\Psi(\Psi_0,t)] = \int_0^t \dot{V}[\Psi(\Psi_0,\tau)] \, d\tau \tag{6.4.17}$$

By hypothesis, the integrand is positive, and therefore the integral increases without bound as $t \to \infty$. This implies that V is not bounded on the solution curves. But, by hypothesis, $V(\Psi)$ is continuous and is therefore a bounded function of Ψ in any finite region $\|\Psi\| < \epsilon$. It follows, therefore, that in this case the solution curves must leave this region.

That $\dot{V}(\Psi) = (\text{grad } V)^T F(\Psi)$ as given in Eq. (6.4.12) follows directly from the chain rule of differentiation,

$$\frac{d}{dt} V(\Psi) = \frac{\partial V}{\partial \psi_1} \frac{d\psi_1}{dt} + \frac{\partial V}{\partial \psi_2} \frac{d\psi_2}{dt} + \cdots + \frac{\partial V}{\partial \psi_n} \frac{d\psi_n}{dt}$$

$$= \left[\frac{\partial V}{\partial \psi_1} \frac{\partial V}{\partial \psi_2} \cdots \frac{\partial V}{\partial \psi_n} \right] \frac{d}{dt} \Psi(t)$$

$$= (\text{grad } V)^T F(\Psi) \tag{6.4.18}$$

This completes the proof of the theorem.

Example 6.4.3: Investigate the stability characteristics of the equilibrium state of the system characterized by the state equations

$$\frac{d}{dt} \begin{bmatrix} \psi_1(t) \\ \psi_2(t) \end{bmatrix} = \begin{bmatrix} 0 & 1 \\ -1 & 0 \end{bmatrix} \begin{bmatrix} \psi_1(t) \\ \psi_2(t) \end{bmatrix} - K \begin{bmatrix} \psi_1(t) & \psi_1(t) \\ \psi_2(t) & \psi_2(t) \end{bmatrix} \begin{bmatrix} \psi_1^2(t) \\ \psi_2^2(t) \end{bmatrix} \qquad K > 0 \tag{6.4.19}$$

Solution: The origin $\Psi = 0$ is an equilibrium state. To show that this system is stable with respect to this state, it is necessary to construct a scalar function of ψ_1 and ψ_2 satisfying the conditions of the theorem. Consider the quadratic form

$$V(\Psi) = \|\Psi\|^2 = \psi_1^2 + \psi_2^2$$

This function is clearly greater than zero for $\Psi \neq 0$ and vanishes at $\Psi = 0$. The time derivative of $V(\Psi)$ is

$$V(\Psi) = \frac{\partial V}{\partial \psi_1} \frac{d}{dt} + \frac{\partial V}{\partial \psi_2} \frac{d}{dt} = 2\psi_1(t) \frac{d}{dt} \psi_1(t) + 2\psi_2(t) \frac{d}{dt} \psi_2(t)$$

$$= 2[\psi_1(t) \quad \psi_2(t)] \begin{bmatrix} \psi_1(t) \\ \psi_2(t) \end{bmatrix} \tag{6.4.20}$$

Substituting Eq. (6.4.19) into Eq. (6.4.20) gives

$$\dot{V}(\Psi) = -2K(\psi_1^2 + \psi_2^2)^2$$

Since $V(\Psi)$ is negative definite (i.e., negative for *all* values of ψ_1 and ψ_2), the equilibrium point $\Psi = 0$ is asymptotically stable; i.e., any solution starting sufficiently close to the origin will eventually go to zero.

Example 6.4.4: Investigate the stability of one of the equilibrium points of the system characterized by the state equations

$$\frac{d}{dt}\begin{bmatrix} \psi_1(t) \\ \psi_2(t) \\ \psi_3(t) \end{bmatrix} = \begin{bmatrix} -(\psi_1 + \psi_2) \\ A(\psi_1 + \psi_2) \\ -\psi_3 \end{bmatrix}$$

The equilibrium state is

$$\begin{bmatrix} \psi_{1e} \\ \psi_{2e} \\ \psi_{3e} \end{bmatrix} = \begin{bmatrix} \alpha \\ -\alpha \\ 0 \end{bmatrix}$$

where α is an arbitrary constant.

To investigate the stability of the first equilibrium state, it is translated to the origin by setting

$$\psi_1'(t) = \psi_1(t) - \alpha \qquad \psi_2'(t) = \psi_2(t) + \alpha \qquad \psi_3'(t) = \psi_3$$

and thereby establishing the equivalent system

$$\frac{d}{dt}\begin{bmatrix} \psi_1'(t) \\ \psi_2'(t) \\ \psi_3'(t) \end{bmatrix} = \begin{bmatrix} -(\psi_1' + \psi_2') \\ A(\psi_1' + \psi_2') \\ -\psi_3' \end{bmatrix} \tag{6.4.21}$$

A suitable Lyapunov function for this system is found as

$$V(\Psi') = \psi_2'^2 - A(\psi_1'^2 + \psi_3'^2)$$

for which

$$\dot{V}(\Psi') = [-2A\psi_1' \;\vdots\; 2\psi_2' \;\vdots\; -2A\psi_3'] \begin{bmatrix} \psi_1'(t) \\ \psi_2'(t) \\ \psi_3'(t) \end{bmatrix} \tag{6.4.22}$$

If $A < 0$, then $V(\Psi')$ is positive definite. And, upon substituting Eq. (6.4.21) into Eq. (6.4.22), we find that

$$\dot{V}(\Psi') = 2A[\psi_3'^2 + (\psi_1' + \psi_2')^2] \leq 0$$

Therefore, from Theorem 6.4.1, the system is stable.

Example 6.4.5: Determine the stability characteristics of the linear system represented by the state equations

$$\frac{d}{dt}\begin{bmatrix} \psi_1(t) \\ \psi_2(t) \end{bmatrix} = \begin{bmatrix} 0 & 1 \\ -K_{21} & -K_{22} \end{bmatrix} \begin{bmatrix} \psi_1(t) \\ \psi_2(t) \end{bmatrix} + \begin{bmatrix} 1 \\ 0 \end{bmatrix} e(t) \tag{6.4.23}$$

Solution: Since the system is linear, the origin is the equilibrium point and the stability characteristics are determined entirely by the homogeneous part of the solution. As a possible Lyapunov function, consider the positive definite quadratic form

$$V(\Psi) = \psi_1^2 + \psi_2^2$$

for which

$$\dot{V}(\mathbf{\Psi}) = [2\psi_1(t) \quad 2\psi_2(t)] \begin{bmatrix} \dot{\psi}_1(t) \\ \dot{\psi}_2(t) \end{bmatrix} = 2\psi_1(t)\psi_2(t)(1 - K_{21}) - 2K_{22}[\psi_2(t)]^2$$

This is *not* an acceptable scalar function, since $\dot{V}(\mathbf{\Psi})$ may or may not be negative definite in the neighborhood of the origin. The sign of $\dot{V}(\mathbf{\Psi})$ depends upon the relative signs and magnitudes of $\psi_1(t)$ and $\psi_2(t)$, regardless of how small either variable is. The positive definite function

$$V(\mathbf{\Psi}) = K_{21}[\psi_1(t)]^2 + [\psi_2(t) + K_{22}\psi_1(t)]^2$$

has a time derivative

$$\dot{V}(\mathbf{\Psi}) = \left[2K_{21}\psi_1(t) + 2[\psi_2(t) + K_{22}\psi_1(t)]K_{22} \quad \vdots \quad 2[\psi_2(t) + K_{22}\psi_1(t)] \right] \begin{bmatrix} \dot{\psi}_1(t) \\ \dot{\psi}_2(t) \end{bmatrix}$$
$$= -2K_{21}K_{22}[\psi_1(t)]^2$$

and is therefore a Lyapunov function for this system. If $K_{21}K_{22} > 0$, the system is stable, whereas it is unstable if $K_{21}K_{22} < 0$.

As the above examples demonstrate, the critical step in applying Lyapunov's theorem is the generation of a positive definite scalar function of the state variables which has a negative definite or negative semi-definite time derivative on the solution curves. Unfortunately, there are no explicit procedures available for generating such functions for general nonlinear systems. For linear time-invariant systems and for certain special classes of nonlinear systems, there are well-defined procedures that are sometimes very effective. For example, if the system is linear of the form

$$\frac{d}{dt} \mathbf{\Psi}(t) = \mathbf{P}\mathbf{\Psi}(t)$$

then a suitable scalar function is the positive definite quadratic form

$$V(\mathbf{\Psi}) = \mathbf{\Psi}^T \mathbf{C} \mathbf{\Psi} \tag{6.4.24}$$

where $\mathbf{C}$ is a symmetric positive definite matrix.

The time derivative of this function as evaluated along the solution curves is

$$\dot{V}(\mathbf{\Psi}) = \mathbf{\Psi}^T \mathbf{C} \frac{d}{dt} \mathbf{\Psi} + \left(\frac{d}{dt} \mathbf{\Psi}^T \right) \mathbf{C} \mathbf{\Psi}$$
$$= \mathbf{\Psi}^T (\mathbf{C}\mathbf{P} + \mathbf{P}^T\mathbf{C}) \mathbf{\Psi}$$

It follows, therefore, that the system is stable if the symmetric matrix

$$\mathbf{D} = \mathbf{C}\mathbf{P} + \mathbf{P}^T\mathbf{C} \tag{6.4.25}$$

is negative definite or negative semidefinite and unstable if $\mathbf{D}$ is positive definite. It can be shown[7] that, for any given matrix $\mathbf{P}$ having no symmetrical eigenvalues with respect to the origin and a symmetric matrix $\mathbf{D}$, Eq. (6.4.25) uniquely defines the symmetric matrix $\mathbf{C}$ as a solution to the $n(n+1)/2$ linear equations obtained by equating the coefficients in the matrices on the two sides of the equation.† Since $\mathbf{D}$ is arbitrary, it can be taken as $\pm \mathbf{U}$. Furthermore, it can also be shown that, if the system is stable and $\mathbf{D}$ is negative definite, the solution $\mathbf{C}$ to Eq. (6.4.25) is a positive definite matrix. Conversely, if the system is unstable, then for the same $\mathbf{D}$ the solution $\mathbf{C}$ is a negative definite matrix. Thus, a Lyapunov function and the stability characteristics of an nth-order linear system can always be obtained by solving at most $n(n+1)/2$ simultaneous linear equations.

Example 6.4.6: Determine the stability characteristics of the system represented by the state equations

$$\begin{bmatrix} \psi_1(t) \\ \psi_2(t) \end{bmatrix} = \begin{bmatrix} p_{11} & p_{12} \\ p_{21} & p_{22} \end{bmatrix} \begin{bmatrix} \psi_1(t) \\ \psi_2(t) \end{bmatrix}$$

Solution: By taking $\mathbf{D} = -\mathbf{U}$, Eq. (6.4.25) gives

$$\begin{bmatrix} -1 & 0 \\ 0 & -1 \end{bmatrix} = \begin{bmatrix} c_{11} & c_{12} \\ c_{12} & c_{22} \end{bmatrix} \begin{bmatrix} p_{11} & p_{12} \\ p_{21} & p_{22} \end{bmatrix} + \begin{bmatrix} p_{11} & p_{21} \\ p_{12} & p_{22} \end{bmatrix} \begin{bmatrix} c_{11} & c_{12} \\ c_{12} & c_{22} \end{bmatrix}$$

which, after multiplication and rearrangement, gives the following three equations in three unknowns:

$$\begin{bmatrix} 2p_{11} & 2p_{21} & 0 \\ p_{12} & p_{11}+p_{22} & p_{21} \\ 0 & 2p_{12} & 2p_{22} \end{bmatrix} \begin{bmatrix} c_{11} \\ c_{12} \\ c_{22} \end{bmatrix} = \begin{bmatrix} -1 \\ 0 \\ -1 \end{bmatrix}$$

Solution of these equations gives

$$c_{11} = -\frac{|\mathbf{P}| + p_{21}^2 + p_{22}^2}{2(p_{11}+p_{22})|\mathbf{P}|}$$

$$c_{12} = \frac{p_{12}p_{22} + p_{21}p_{11}}{2(p_{11}+p_{22})|\mathbf{P}|}$$

$$c_{22} = -\frac{|\mathbf{P}| + p_{12}^2 + p_{11}^2}{2(p_{11}+p_{22})|\mathbf{P}|}$$

where

$$|\mathbf{P}| = p_{11}p_{22} - p_{12}p_{21}$$

The symmetric matrix $\mathbf{C} = [c_{ij}]$ is positive definite if $c_{11} > 0$, $c_{22} > 0$, and

$$|\mathbf{C}| = \frac{(p_{11}+p_{22})^2 + (p_{12}-p_{21})^2}{4(p_{11}+p_{22})^2|\mathbf{P}|} > 0$$

† In general, the equation $\mathbf{AC} - \mathbf{CB} = \mathbf{D}$, where $\mathbf{A}$ and $\mathbf{B}$ are square matrices of different order and the matrices $\mathbf{C}$ (unknown) and $\mathbf{D}$ have the same order, has a unique solution if and only if the matrices $\mathbf{A}$ and $\mathbf{B}$ have no common eigenvalues.[8] In the case under consideration $-\mathbf{P} = \mathbf{B}$, and $\mathbf{P}^T = \mathbf{A}$. It is evident that the eigenvalues of $\mathbf{P}$ and $\mathbf{P}^T$ are identical, whereas the eigenvalues of $-\mathbf{P}$ and $\mathbf{P}^T$ are opposite, i.e., they are located symmetrically with respect to origin. Therefore, $-\mathbf{P}$ and $\mathbf{P}^T$ have no eigenvalues in common only if the eigenvalues of $\mathbf{P}$ are not located symmetrically about the origin.

These inequalities are satisfied, and the system is stable, if

$$|\mathbf{P}| = p_{11}p_{22} - p_{12}p_{22} > 0$$

and

$$p_{11} + p_{22} < 0$$

The quadratic form in Eq. (6.4.24) frequently serves as a starting point in constructing Lyapunov functions for certain classes of nonlinear systems. Consider, for example, the nonlinear form

$$\frac{d}{dt}\, \boldsymbol{\Psi}(t) = \mathbf{F}(\boldsymbol{\Psi},t) = \mathbf{P}\boldsymbol{\Psi}(t) + \mathbf{G}(\boldsymbol{\Psi})$$

where $\mathbf{P}\boldsymbol{\Psi}(t)$ represents the linear portion of the equations and $\mathbf{G}(\boldsymbol{\Psi})$ is such that it has a power series expansion of the form

$$\mathbf{G}(\boldsymbol{\Psi}) = \mathbf{G}_2 \begin{bmatrix} \psi_1{}^2 \\ \psi_2{}^2 \\ \cdot \\ \cdot \\ \cdot \\ \psi_n{}^2 \end{bmatrix} + \mathbf{G}_3 \begin{bmatrix} \psi_1{}^3 \\ \psi_3{}^3 \\ \cdot \\ \cdot \\ \cdot \\ \psi_n{}^3 \end{bmatrix}$$

and $\mathbf{G}_2$ and $\mathbf{G}_3$ are square matrices.

Consider now the scalar function

$$V(\boldsymbol{\Psi}) = \boldsymbol{\Psi}^T \mathbf{C} \boldsymbol{\Psi}$$

where $\mathbf{C}$ is symmetric and positive definite. The time derivative of $V(\boldsymbol{\Psi})$ evaluated on the solution curves gives

$$\dot{V}(\boldsymbol{\Psi}) = \boldsymbol{\Psi}^T \mathbf{C} \frac{d\boldsymbol{\Psi}}{dt} + \left(\frac{d}{dt}\, \boldsymbol{\Psi}^T\right) \mathbf{C}\boldsymbol{\Psi}$$
$$= \boldsymbol{\Psi}^T(\mathbf{CP} + \mathbf{P}^T\mathbf{C})\boldsymbol{\Psi} + \boldsymbol{\Psi}^T\mathbf{CG}(\boldsymbol{\Psi}) + \mathbf{G}^T(\boldsymbol{\Psi})\mathbf{C}\boldsymbol{\Psi}$$

Since, by hypothesis, each function in the vector $\mathbf{G}(\boldsymbol{\Psi})$ is of order 2 or greater, the last two terms are of order 3 or greater. The first term, on the other hand, is a quadratic in the state vector. Consequently, there exists a neighborhood of the origin, $\|\boldsymbol{\Psi}\| < \delta$, where all but the first term in $\dot{V}(\boldsymbol{\Psi})$ can be neglected. Since the first term involves only the linear portion of the given state equations, we can conclude that *the stability of such a system is completely determined by only the linear part of the equations.*

For a more extensive discussion of the stability characteristics of nonlinear systems and methods for finding Lyapunov functions, the reader is referred to such books on the subject as those by Hahn[9] and LaSalle and Lefschetz.[7]

6.5 STABILITY CHARACTERISTICS
OF LINEAR CONTINUOUS - STATE SYSTEMS

It has already been pointed out in Sec. 6.4 that if the coefficient matrix $\mathbf{P}$ is nonsingular in the homogeneous system

$$\frac{d}{dt}\,\mathbf{\Psi}(t) = \mathbf{P}\mathbf{\Psi}(t)$$

then $\mathbf{\Psi}_e = \mathbf{0}$ is the only equilibrium state.   However, if $\mathbf{P}$ is singular, then nontrivial equilibrium states are obtained from the solutions of the equation

$$\mathbf{P}\mathbf{\Psi}(t) = \mathbf{0}$$

The stability characteristics of all equilibrium points, however, are the same and are related to the eigenvalues of the coefficient matrix $\mathbf{P}$ as stated in the following theorem:

Theorem 6.5.1:   The equilibrium states of the linear system

$$\frac{d}{dt}\,\mathbf{\Psi}(t) = \mathbf{P}\mathbf{\Psi}(t) \tag{6.5.1}$$

are stable in the sense of Lyapunov if:

(a)   The real parts of all the zeros of the minimal polynomial $m(\lambda)$ of $\mathbf{P}$ are negative or zero.

(b)   All imaginary zeros (including $\lambda = 0$) of the minimal polynomial $m(\lambda)$, if any, are simple.

If either condition a or condition b is violated, the system is unstable. The solution is asymptotically stable if and only if all the eigenvalues of $\mathbf{P}$ have negative real parts.

Proof: The general form of the minimal polynomial $m(\lambda)$ of $\mathbf{P}$ is given in Eq. (6.3.20) and the general form of the solution in Eq. (6.3.21). Each term in the summation to the right of this equation is a time-varying vector of the form

$$(\mathbf{Z}_{il}\mathbf{\Psi}_0)t^{l-1}e^{\lambda_i t} = \mathbf{Z}_{il}(t)\mathbf{\Psi}_0 \tag{6.5.2}$$

where, in general, λ_i $(i = 1, 2, \ldots, k)$ is a complex constant $\lambda_i = \alpha_i + j\beta_i$. Under the hypothesis of the theorem $\alpha_i \leq 0$.   If $r_i = 0$, the zero is a simple one.   Therefore, the entries in each of the matrices $\mathbf{Z}_{il}(t)$ are bounded functions of time in the entire interval $0 < t$.   Let m represent the maximum modulus of any one of the entries in the matrices $\mathbf{Z}_{il}(t)$, and let the maximum value of any of the state variables be γ.

Since the state vector as a function of time is given as the sum of $q = r_1 + r_2 + \cdots + r_k$ vectors of the form given in Eq. (6.5.2), it follows that the modulus of any given state variable cannot exceed $qm\gamma$, that is,

$$|\psi_i| \leq qm\gamma$$

The norm of the state vector at any instant of time $t = t_1$ and for an arbitrary initial state Ψ_0 therefore satisfies the inequality

$$\|\Psi(\Psi_0, t_1)\|^2 = \sum_{i=1}^{n} |\psi_i|^2 \leq nq^2 m^2 \gamma^2$$

but since

$$\|\Psi_0\|^2 \leq n\gamma^2$$

it follows that if the initial state Ψ_0 is selected inside the region

$$\|\Psi_0\| \leq \frac{\epsilon}{qm}$$

then the solution vector remains inside the circular region $\|\Psi(t)\| < \epsilon$. By Definition 6.4.1, the system is stable.

From Eq. (6.5.2) it follows that each of the vectors $Z_{il}(t) \Psi_0$ vanishes if and only if all the eigenvalues of P have negative real parts, and the conditions for asymptotic stability are established.

Example 6.5.1: Determine the stability characteristics of the system represented by the state equations

$$\frac{d}{dt} \begin{bmatrix} \psi_1(t) \\ \psi_2(t) \end{bmatrix} = \begin{bmatrix} 1 & -1 \\ -1 & 1 \end{bmatrix} \begin{bmatrix} \psi_1(t) \\ \psi_2(t) \end{bmatrix} + \begin{bmatrix} f_1(t) \\ 0 \end{bmatrix}$$

Solution: The characteristic polynomial is

$$D(\lambda) = m(\lambda) = \begin{bmatrix} \lambda - 1 & 1 \\ 1 & \lambda - 1 \end{bmatrix} = (\lambda - 1)^2 - 1 = \lambda(\lambda - 2)$$

and the system is unstable, since $\lambda = 2$ is a real positive zero of $m(\lambda)$.

In general, the stability characteristics of linear constant-parameter systems are more easily evaluated in terms of the eigenvalues of the coefficient matrix P than in terms of Lyapunov functions. In this respect it is important to recognize that the minimal polynomial of the matrix P has the same zeros as the characteristic polynomial, but perhaps with lower degrees of multiplicities. Consequently, stability studies might just as well be based on the characteristic polynomial, with special attention to the fact that, if it has multiple zeros on the imaginary axis, then the system may still be stable. Stability studies in linear systems finally reduce, then, to a study of the zeros of the characteristic polynomial and their relation to the properties of the coefficient matrix $\mathbf{P}$ in the state equations.

In general, the characteristic polynomial of any real matrix $\mathbf{P}$ of order n is of the form

$$D(\lambda) = |\lambda\mathbf{U} - \mathbf{P}| = \lambda^n + p_1\lambda^{n-1} + p_2\lambda^{n-2} + \cdots + p_n \qquad (6.5.3)$$

Since the coefficients $p_1, p_2, \ldots, p_n$ are all real numbers, it follows that the zeros of $D(\lambda)$ either are real or occur in complex conjugate pairs. Thus if $\lambda_1 = \alpha_1 + j\beta_1$ is known to be a zero of $D(\lambda)$, then

$$\lambda_2 = \hat{\lambda}_1 = \alpha_1 - j\beta_1$$

is also a zero.

In certain system studies the coefficient matrix $\mathbf{P}$ may have particular properties such as skew symmetry or symmetry, or it might be expressible as the product of a positive definite matrix and a skew-symmetric matrix. Such forms are encountered, for example, in the state equations of electrical networks that are composed entirely of inductors and capacitors (no resistors) or mechanical systems of masses and springs (no damping components). Such systems are sometimes called "lossless" or "undamped" systems, since, as we shall see, the real parts of the eigenvalues are all zero.

The following theorems summarize the important relationships between the various symmetric characteristics of a real matrix $\mathbf{P}$ and the zeros of its characteristic polynomial.

Theorem 6.5.2: The eigenvalues of a positive definite matrix $\mathbf{P}$ are all real and positive. If $\mathbf{P}$ is positive semidefinite, then the eigenvalues are all real and nonnegative.

Proof: Consider the solution, for the vector $\mathbf{X}$, to the equation

$$\mathbf{PX} = \lambda\mathbf{X} \qquad (6.5.4)$$

It is shown in Sec. A.2 that this equation has a nontrivial solution if the constant λ is equal to one of the eigenvalues of $\mathbf{P}$. The corresponding solution $\mathbf{X}_i$ for $\lambda = \lambda_i$ is called an eigenvector of $\mathbf{P}$.

In general, if λ_i is complex, then the corresponding eigenvector $\mathbf{X}_i$ is also complex, and if λ_i is real, the corresponding eigenvector is also real.

Let both sides of Eq. (6.5.4) be multiplied by $\mathbf{X}^*$ to obtain

$$\lambda_i = \frac{\mathbf{X}_i^*\mathbf{PX}_i}{\mathbf{X}_i^*\mathbf{X}_i} \qquad (6.5.5)$$

where $\mathbf{X}^*$ represents the transpose conjugate of $\mathbf{X}$ and

$$\mathbf{X}^*\mathbf{X} = |x_1|^2 + |x_2|^2 + \cdots + |x_n|^2$$

represents the sum of squares of the magnitudes of the entries in $\mathbf{X}$ and is therefore real and positive.

The quadratic form $\mathbf{X^*PX}$ is real and positive if $\mathbf{P}$ is positive definite and nonnegative if $\mathbf{P}$ is semidefinite. Hence the proof.

It should be noted that, if $\mathbf{P}$ is negative definite, then from the proof of Theorem 6.5.1 it follows immediately that the eigenvalues of $\mathbf{P}$ are all real and negative.

Theorem 6.5.3: The eigenvalues of a real symmetric matrix $\mathbf{P}$ are all real.

Proof: Any real symmetric matrix can be reduced to diagonal form by elementary row and column operations, with the use of column operations identical to row operations. This implies that $\mathbf{P}$ can be written as the triple product

$$\mathbf{P} = \mathbf{E}^T\mathbf{DE} \tag{6.5.6}$$

where $\mathbf{E}$ is a nonsingular transformation matrix and $\mathbf{D}$ is diagonal with real diagonal entries. Substituting Eq. (6.5.6) into Eq. (6.5.5) gives

$$\lambda_i = \frac{\mathbf{X}_i^*\mathbf{E}^T\mathbf{DEX}_i}{\mathbf{X}_i^*\mathbf{X}_i} = \frac{\beta_i^*\mathbf{D}\beta_i}{\mathbf{X}_i^*\mathbf{X}_i}$$

where $\beta_i = \mathbf{EX}_i$ is a new vector. Since the quadratic form $\beta_i^*\mathbf{D}\beta_i$ is real (but not necessarily positive definite), all eigenvalues $\lambda = \lambda_i$ of $\mathbf{P}$ are real.

Theorem 6.5.4: The eigenvalues of a real skew-symmetric matrix $\mathbf{P}$ are all imaginary and occur in conjugate pairs.

Proof: When $\mathbf{P}$ is skew-symmetric, $\mathbf{P} = -\mathbf{P}^T$ and Eq. (6.5.5) becomes

$$\begin{aligned}
\lambda_i\mathbf{X}_i^*\mathbf{X}_i = \mathbf{X}_i^*\mathbf{PX}_i &= -\mathbf{X}_i^*\mathbf{P}^T\mathbf{X}_i \\
&= -(\mathbf{P}\hat{\mathbf{X}}_i)^T\mathbf{X}_i \\
&= -(\hat{\lambda}_i\hat{\mathbf{X}}_i)^T\mathbf{X}_i \\
&= -\mathbf{X}_i^*\hat{\lambda}_i\mathbf{X}_i = -\hat{\lambda}_i\mathbf{X}_i^*\mathbf{X}_i
\end{aligned} \tag{6.5.6a}$$

where the circumflex $\wedge$ indicates the complex conjugate. Since $\mathbf{X}_i^*\mathbf{X}_i \neq 0$, from Eq. (6.5.6a) we have

$$\lambda_i = -\hat{\lambda}_i \tag{6.5.7}$$

But Eq. (6.5.7) is valid for nonzero values of λ_i only if λ_i is an imaginary number, and the theorem is proved.

Theorem 6.5.5: If a real symmetric (or a skew-symmetric) matrix $\mathbf{P}$ is premultiplied by a positive definite diagonal matrix $\mathbf{C}$, then the eigenvalues of the resulting matrix have the same properties as the eigenvalues of $\mathbf{P}$.

Proof: Let $\mathbf{C}^{1/2}$ represent the positive definite root of $\mathbf{C}$; that is, $\mathbf{C}^{1/2}$ is a diagonal positive definite matrix such that

$$\mathbf{C}^{1/2}\mathbf{C}^{1/2} = \mathbf{C}$$

Since $\mathbf{C}$ is positive definite, $(\mathbf{C}^{1/2})^{-1} = \mathbf{C}^{-1/2}$ exists. The characteristic polynomial of $\mathbf{CP}$ can now be written as

$$\begin{aligned} D(\lambda) &= |\lambda\mathbf{U} - \mathbf{CP}| = |\mathbf{C}^{1/2}|\,|\lambda\mathbf{C}^{-1/2} - \mathbf{C}^{1/2}\mathbf{P}| \\ &= |\mathbf{C}^{1/2}|\,|\lambda\mathbf{U} - \mathbf{C}^{1/2}\mathbf{P}\mathbf{C}^{1/2}|\,|\mathbf{C}^{-1/2}| \\ &= |\lambda\mathbf{U} - \mathbf{C}^{1/2}\mathbf{P}\mathbf{C}^{1/2}| \end{aligned}$$

Since $\mathbf{C}^{1/2}$ is a diagonal matrix, $\mathbf{C}^{1/2}\mathbf{P}\mathbf{C}^{1/2}$ has the same symmetric properties as $\mathbf{P}$ and therefore its eigenvalues have the same properties as the eigenvalues of $\mathbf{P}$.

Example 6.5.2: Determine the properties of the eigenvalues of the coefficient matrix of the state equations for the RC network in Fig. 6.5.1.

Solution: The state model is

$$\frac{d}{dt}\begin{bmatrix} v_1(t) \\ v_2(t) \end{bmatrix} = -\begin{bmatrix} C_1 & 0 \\ 0 & C_2 \end{bmatrix}^{-1}\begin{bmatrix} G_3 + G_4 & -G_4 \\ -G_4 & G_4 \end{bmatrix}\begin{bmatrix} v_1(t) \\ v_2(t) \end{bmatrix} + \begin{bmatrix} G_0/C_1 \\ 0 \end{bmatrix} v_0(t)$$

The coefficient matrix

$$\mathbf{P} = -\begin{bmatrix} 1/C_1 & 0 \\ 0 & 1/C_2 \end{bmatrix}\begin{bmatrix} G_3 + G_4 & -G_4 \\ -G_4 & G_4 \end{bmatrix}$$

is the product of a positive definite diagonal matrix and a negative definite matrix. Therefore, the eigenvalues of the matrix $\mathbf{P}$ have the same properties as those of a negative definite matrix; i.e., they are real and negative.

Example 6.5.3: Determine the properties of the eigenvalues of the coefficient matrix of the state equations for the simple mechanical system shown in Fig. 6.5.2.

Solution: The state equations for this system are

$$\frac{d}{dt}\begin{bmatrix} \dot{\delta}_1(t) \\ f_2(t) \end{bmatrix} = \begin{bmatrix} 1/M & 0 \\ 0 & K \end{bmatrix}\begin{bmatrix} 0 & 1 \\ -1 & 0 \end{bmatrix}\begin{bmatrix} \dot{\delta}_1(t) \\ f_2(t) \end{bmatrix} + \begin{bmatrix} 0 \\ K \end{bmatrix}\dot{\delta}_0(t)$$

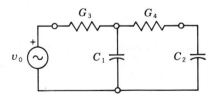

Fig. 6.5.1 An electrical network.

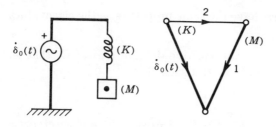

Fig. 6.5.2   A simple mechanical system.

Since the coefficient matrix is the product of a positive definite diagonal matrix and a skew-symmetric matrix, the eigenvalues have the properties of a skew-symmetric matrix; i.e., they are all imaginary.

When the coefficient matrix in the state equations has the properties of symmetry given in the above theorems, the stability characteristics of the system are immediately evident.   However, the bulk of the state equations encountered in system analysis and design do not fall into these categories, and one has no choice but to evaluate the characteristic polynomial either from the expansion of the determinant $|\lambda\mathbf{U} - \mathbf{P}|$ or by the algorithm given in Sec. 6.3.   If the minimal polynomial is the same as the characteristic polynomial, as it is for the vast majority of physical systems encountered in application, then the information as to the stability of the system can be determined without actually evaluating the zeros explicitly, by an algorithm known as the *Routh stability criterion.*[10]

Let the minimal polynomial of the system be written as

$$m(\lambda) = a_0\lambda^n + b_0\lambda^{n-1} + a_1\lambda^{n-2} + b_1\lambda^{n-3} + a_2\lambda^{n-4} + \cdots \quad (6.5.7a)$$

and let the coefficients be arranged as follows:

$$
\begin{array}{llll}
a_0 & a_1 & a_2 & a_3 \quad \cdots \\
b_0 & b_1 & b_2 & b_3 \quad \cdots \\
c_0 & c_1 & c_2 & c_3 \quad \cdots \\
d_0 & d_1 & d_2 & d_3 \quad \cdots \\
\multicolumn{4}{c}{\cdots\cdots\cdots\cdots\cdots} \\
m_0 & m_1 \\
n_0
\end{array}
\qquad (6.5.8)
$$

Note that the first row contains the first, third, fifth, . . . coefficients in the given polynomial and the second row contains the second, fourth, sixth, . . . coefficients.   The third row is generated from the first two by a series of cross products defined as

$$c_0 = \frac{b_0a_1 - a_0b_1}{b_0} \qquad c_1 = \frac{b_0a_2 - a_0b_2}{b_0} \qquad c_2 = \frac{b_0a_3 - a_0b_3}{b_0} \qquad \cdots$$

The fourth row is generated from the second and third rows by a similar cross product

$$d_0 = \frac{c_0 b_1 - b_0 c_1}{c_0} \qquad d_1 = \frac{c_0 b_2 - b_0 c_2}{c_0} \qquad d_3 = \frac{c_0 b_3 - b_0 c_3}{c_0} \qquad \cdots$$

Continuing in this way, all successive rows are generated. Note that in each new row the number of nonzero entries is less than or equal to the number in the previous row. Therefore, the number of rows generated is bounded; i.e., the procedure terminates after a finite number of rows are generated. The set of coefficients in Eq. (6.5.8) is called the *Routh array*, and the operation of getting this array is called the *Routh algorithm*.

Example 6.5.4: Determine the Routh array corresponding to

$$m(\lambda) = \lambda^4 + 7\lambda^3 + 17\lambda^2 + 17\lambda + 6$$

Solution: The Routh array is

$$
\begin{array}{c|ccc}
\lambda^4 & 1 & 17 & 6 \\
\lambda^3 & 7 & 17 & \\
\lambda^2 & \dfrac{(6)(17)}{7} & 6 & \\
\lambda^1 & \frac{1}{17}[(17)^2 - 49] & & \\
\lambda^0 & 6 & &
\end{array}
\qquad (6.5.9)
$$

where in front of each row the degree of the polynomials which could be written by use of the entries in that row is indicated; e.g., for the third row a polynomial of degree 2 could be written as $[(6)(17)/7]\lambda^2 + 6$. Note that each of these polynomials has only alternate terms.

It can be shown that if any one of the rows in the Routh array is multiplied by a *positive* constant, before generating the succeeding rows, the significance of the Routh scheme is not lost; i.e., the properties to be used later are not altered. This property makes it possible to realize some numerical simplification in calculating the entries in the rows. For example, we can multiply the third row in Eq. (6.5.9) by $\frac{7}{6}$ to obtain the entries (17,7). The fourth row could then be calculated more easily, being equal to $\frac{1}{17}[(17)^2 - 49]$. Then, this row can be multiplied by $[17/(17)^2 - 49]$ to give unity for the next to the last row. This new and equivalent Routh's array is

$$
\begin{array}{c|ccc}
\lambda^4 & 1 & 17 & 6 \\
\lambda^3 & 7 & 17 & \\
\lambda^2 & 17 & 7 & \\
\lambda^1 & 1 & & \\
\lambda^0 & 6 & &
\end{array}
$$

The following theorem due to Routh is stated here without proof.

Theorem 6.5.6 (Routh):   Let the Routh array in Eq. (6.5.8) be established for a polynomial $m(\lambda)$ which has no zeros on the imaginary axis. The number of zeros of $m(\lambda)$ in the right half of the λ plane ($\lambda = \sigma + j\omega$) is equal to the number of changes in the signs of the coefficients in the first column of the Routh array.

According to this theorem, the polynomial $m(\lambda)$ in Example 6.5.4 has no zeros in the right half plane, since all the entries in the first column of the corresponding Routh array are positive; i.e., there are no changes in sign.

Example 6.5.5:   Use the Routh criterion as stated in Theorem 6.5.6 to determine whether or not the following polynomial has zeros in the right half of the λ plane:

$$m(\lambda) = \lambda^8 + 2\lambda^7 + 4\lambda^6 + 4\lambda^5 + 6\lambda^4 + 10\lambda^3 + 7\lambda^2 + 4\lambda + 2$$

Solution: The Routh array is

λ^8	1	4	6	7	2
λ^7	2	4	10	4	
λ^6	2	1	5	2	
λ^5	3	5	2		
λ^4	-7	11	6	(multiplied by 3)	
λ^3	17	8		(multiplied by $\frac{7}{4}$)	
λ^2	81	2		(multiplied by $\frac{17}{3}$)	
λ^1	1			(multiplied by $\frac{81}{614}$)	
λ^0	2				

Since there are two changes in sign in the first column, $m(\lambda)$ has two zeros in the right half of the λ plane.

In certain cases, the first entry in one of the rows of the array vanishes.   In such a case, the succeeding rows cannot be generated by the same procedure.   This condition indicates that at least one root of $m(\lambda) = 0$ is in the right half plane, but, in general, unless additional information is available, we cannot determine how many roots lie in the right half plane.   This difficulty can be eliminated by multiplying the given polynomial $m(\lambda)$ by a selected known factor $\lambda + a$, with $a > 0$, to obtain a new polynomial $m_1(\lambda)$ having exactly the same zeros in the right half plane as $m(\lambda)$.   If the Routh array for $m_1(\lambda)$ contains no zeros in the first column, the Routh theorem can be applied.

An alternative procedure is to apply a change of variables by setting $\lambda = 1/x$.   After clearing the denominator, a new polynomial in x of the same degree is obtained for which the coefficients are the same as that of the original, but with reversed order.   It can be shown that the new polynomial has exactly the same number of zeros as the original polynomial in both the right and left halves of the λ plane.

Example 6.5.6: Determine the number of zeros in the right half plane of the polynomial

$$m(\lambda) = \lambda^4 + \lambda^3 + 2\lambda^2 + 2\lambda - 14$$

Solution: The first three rows of the Routh array are

$$
\begin{array}{c|ccc}
\lambda^4 & 1 & 2 & -14 \\
\lambda^3 & 1 & 2 & \\
\lambda^2 & 0 & -14 &
\end{array}
$$

Since the third row contains a zero entry in the leading position, $m(\lambda)$ contains at least one zero in the right half plane. To determine the number of these zeros, $m(\lambda)$ is multiplied by the factor $\lambda + 1$, to obtain

$$m_1(\lambda) = (\lambda + 1)m(\lambda) = \lambda^5 + 2\lambda^4 + 3\lambda^3 + 4\lambda^2 - 12\lambda - 14$$

The Routh array for $m_1(\lambda)$ is

$$
\begin{array}{c|ccc}
\lambda^5 & 1 & 3 & -12 \\
\lambda^4 & 1 & 2 & -7 \quad \text{(multiplied by } \tfrac{1}{2}) \\
\lambda^3 & 1 & -5 & \\
\lambda^2 & 7 & -7 & \\
\lambda^1 & -1 & & \text{(multiplied by } \tfrac{7}{28}) \\
\lambda^0 & -7 & &
\end{array}
$$

and we conclude that $m_1(\lambda)$ and $m(\lambda)$ each contain only one zero in the right half plane.

The alternative procedure is to substitute $\lambda = 1/x$ in $m(\lambda)$. The new polynomial having the same number of zeros as $m(\lambda)$ in both right and left half planes is

$$\bar{m}(x) = -14x^4 + 2x^3 + 2x^2 + x + 1$$

The Routh array for this new polynomial is

$$
\begin{array}{c|ccc}
x^4 & -14 & 2 & 1 \\
x^3 & 2 & 1 & \\
x^2 & 9 & 1 & \\
x^1 & 1 & & \text{(multiplied by } \tfrac{9}{7}) \\
x^0 & 1 & &
\end{array}
$$

which indicates again one zero of $\bar{m}(x)$ and $m(\lambda)$ in the right half plane.

It can be shown that, when $m(\lambda)$ contains zeros that are symmetrically located with respect to the origin of the λ plane ($\lambda = \sigma + j\omega$), the Routh array contains a complete row of zeros. Such zeros are shown explicitly in Fig. 6.5.3.

The fact that the coefficients of $m(\lambda)$ are real implies that zeros always occur in complex conjugate pairs. Consequently, any polynomial containing symmetrically located zeros contains one or more factors of the form $\lambda^2 - a$, $\lambda^2 + b$, or $\lambda^4 + a\lambda^2 + b$ ($a^2 - 4b < 0$). Note that each of these factors is a simple even polynomial. It can be shown that when $m(\lambda)$ contains any one or more of such factors the even and odd parts (i.e., the polynomials corresponding to the first and second rows in the Routh array) will also contain these factors. Routh's algorithm can be shown to be equivalent to finding the greatest common divisor of the even and odd parts of $m(\lambda)$. Consequently, when this scheme generates a row which vanishes completely, the last nonvanishing row corresponds to the common factor and hence can be detected. This common factor can be investigated separately or one can take the derivative of the polynomial corresponding to the last nonvanishing row with respect to λ and continue the scheme, using the coefficients in the differentiated polynomial.

Example 6.5.7: Determine the number of zeros in the right half plane of the polynomial

$$m(\lambda) = \lambda^6 + \lambda^5 - \lambda^3 + \lambda + 1$$

Solution: For the first four rows of the Routh array we have

$$
\begin{array}{c|cccc}
\lambda^6 & 1 & 0 & 0 & 1 \\
\lambda^5 & 1 & -1 & 1 & \\
\lambda^4 & 1 & -1 & 1 & \\
\lambda^3 & 0 & 0 & &
\end{array}
$$

Since the fourth row vanishes, the polynomial $\lambda^4 - \lambda^2 + 1$ corresponding to the third row is a factor in $m(\lambda)$ and its zeros are symmetrically located with respect to origin. The derivative of $\lambda^4 - \lambda^2 + 1$ is $4\lambda^3 - 2\lambda$, and the scheme is continued as follows:

$$
\begin{array}{c|ccl}
\lambda^4 & 1 & -1 & 1 \\
\lambda^3 & 2 & -1 & \text{(multiplied by } \tfrac{1}{2}) \\
\lambda^2 & -1 & 4 & \text{(multiplied by 2)} \\
\lambda^1 & 7 & & \\
\lambda^0 & 4 & &
\end{array}
$$

Since there are two changes in sign in the first column, two zeros of $m(\lambda)$ lie in the right half plane. These zeros are actually the right-half-plane zeros of $\lambda^4 - \lambda^2 + 1$, a fact that can easily be shown.

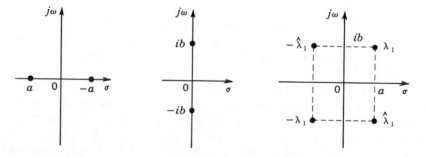

Fig. 6.5.3 The symmetrical zeros of $m(\lambda)$.

The above results are summarized in the following theorem, which is known as *Routh's stability criterion*.

Theorem 6.5.7 (Routh's stability criterion): All the zeros of the minimal polynomial $m(\lambda)$ have nonpositive real parts if and only if the entries of the first column in the Routh array corresponding to $m(\lambda)$ have the same sign.

Note that, to ensure stability, the imaginary zeros of $m(\lambda)$ must be simple. This implies that during the generation of Routh's array one should not have a vanishing row more than once.

A polynomial having zeros in the left half plane and possibly also on the imaginary axis is called a *Hurwitz polynomial*. If a polynomial has zeros *only* in the left half plane, it is referred to as a *strictly* Hurwitz polynomial.

6.6 ANALYTICAL SOLUTIONS AND STABILITY CHARACTERISTICS OF LINEAR DISCRETE-STATE SYSTEMS

For each major development in the study of the stability and solution characteristics of continuous systems there is a counterpart for discrete-state systems. A brief presentation of these counterparts follows.

The general form of the difference equations characterizing linear discrete-state time-invariant systems is

$$\begin{aligned}
\boldsymbol{\Psi}(n+1) &= \mathbf{P}\boldsymbol{\Psi}(n) + \mathbf{Q}\mathbf{E}(n) \qquad n = 0, 1, 2, \ldots \\
\mathbf{R}(n) &= \mathbf{M}\boldsymbol{\Psi}(n) + \mathbf{N}\mathbf{E}(n)
\end{aligned} \tag{6.6.1}$$

By recursive substitution, starting with $n = 0$, the solution is found as

$$\boldsymbol{\Psi}(n) = \mathbf{P}^n \boldsymbol{\Psi}(0) + [\mathbf{P}^{n-1}\mathbf{Q} \quad \mathbf{P}^{n-2}\mathbf{Q} \quad \cdots \quad \mathbf{Q}] \begin{bmatrix} \mathbf{E}(0) \\ \mathbf{E}(1) \\ \cdot \\ \cdot \\ \cdot \\ \mathbf{E}(n-1) \end{bmatrix}$$

$$= \mathbf{P}^n \boldsymbol{\Psi}(0) + \sum_{j=0}^{n-1} \mathbf{P}^j \mathbf{Q} \mathbf{E}(n - j - 1) \tag{6.6.2}$$

The analytical solution is complete upon evaluating the matrix $\mathbf{P}^n$ and the indicated summation. The various powers of $\mathbf{P}$ in Eq. (6.6.1) can, of course, be evaluated by expanding $\mathbf{P}$ into its constituent matrices. If $\mathbf{P}$ has k distinct eigenvalues, each of multiplicity m_j ($j = 1, 2, \ldots, k$), the expression for $\mathbf{P}^n$ is

$$
\begin{aligned}
\mathbf{P}^n = {}& \mathbf{Z}_{11}\lambda_1{}^n + \mathbf{Z}_{12}n\lambda_1{}^{n-1} + \cdots + \mathbf{Z}_{1m_1}\left[\prod_{i=0}^{m_1-2}(n-i)\right]\lambda_1{}^{n-m_1+1} \\
& + \mathbf{Z}_{21}\lambda_2{}^n + \mathbf{Z}_{22}n\lambda_2{}^{n-1} + \cdots + \mathbf{Z}_{2m_2}\left[\prod_{i=0}^{m_2-2}(n-i)\right]\lambda_2{}^{n-m_2+1} \\
& + \cdots\cdots\cdots\cdots\cdots\cdots\cdots\cdots\cdots\cdots\cdots\cdots \\
& + \mathbf{Z}_{k1}\lambda_k{}^n + \mathbf{Z}_{k2}n\lambda_k{}^{n-1} + \cdots + \mathbf{Z}_{km_k}\left[\prod_{i=0}^{m_k-2}(n-i)\right]\lambda_k{}^{n-m_k+1}
\end{aligned}
$$

$$(6.6.3)$$

If the sequences of numbers represented by the vectors $\mathbf{E}(0)$, $\mathbf{E}(1)$, $\ldots$, $\mathbf{E}(n-1)$ are known as explicit functions of n, the summation in Eq. (6.6.2) can usually be evaluated in closed form. Consider, for example, the case where $\mathbf{E}(i) = \mathbf{K}$; that is, the input is a constant. In this special case the summation reduces to

$$
\sum_{j=0}^{n-1}\mathbf{P}^j\mathbf{Q}\mathbf{K} = (\mathbf{P}^{n-1} + \mathbf{P}^{n-2} + \cdots + \mathbf{U})\mathbf{Q}\mathbf{K}
$$

If $\lambda \neq 1$, the sum of the finite scalar power series $\lambda^{n-1} + \lambda^{n-2} + \cdots + 1$ is given by $(\lambda^n - 1)/(\lambda - 1)$. Consequently, if $(\mathbf{P} - \mathbf{U})^{-1}$ exists, the finite power series of matrices is given by

$$
\sum_{j=0}^{n-1}\mathbf{P}^j = (\mathbf{P} - \mathbf{U})^{-1}(\mathbf{P}^n - \mathbf{U}) = (\mathbf{P}^n - \mathbf{U})(\mathbf{P} - \mathbf{U})^{-1}
$$

The required inverse exists, of course, if $\mathbf{P}$ has no unity eigenvalues.

A more general procedure for evaluating the required summations requires expressing the powers of $\mathbf{P}$ in terms of the constituent matrices of $\mathbf{P}$. If, for example, the k eigenvalues of $\mathbf{P}$ are simple, then the summation in Eq. (6.6.2) takes on the form

$$
\begin{aligned}
\sum_{j=0}^{n-1}\mathbf{P}^j\mathbf{Q}\mathbf{E}(n-j-1) = {}& (\mathbf{Z}_{11}\lambda_1{}^{n-1} + \mathbf{Z}_{21}\lambda_2{}^{n-1} + \cdots + \mathbf{Z}_{k1}\lambda_1{}^{n-1}) \\
& \times \mathbf{Q}\mathbf{E}(0) \\
& + (\mathbf{Z}_{11}\lambda_1{}^{n-2} + \mathbf{Z}_{21}\lambda_2{}^{n-2} + \cdots + \mathbf{Z}_{k1}\lambda_k{}^{n-2}) \\
& \times \mathbf{Q}\mathbf{E}(1) \\
& + \cdots\cdots\cdots\cdots\cdots\cdots\cdots\cdots \\
& + (\mathbf{Z}_{11}\lambda_1 + \mathbf{Z}_{21}\lambda_2 + \cdots + \mathbf{Z}_{k1}\lambda_k)\mathbf{Q}\mathbf{E}(n-2) \\
& + (\mathbf{Z}_{11} + \mathbf{Z}_{21} + \cdots + \mathbf{Z}_{k1})\mathbf{Q}\mathbf{E}(n-1)
\end{aligned}
$$

$$(6.6.4)$$

If the input vector is a constant, then $\mathbf{E}(i) = \mathbf{K}$ and Eq. (6.6.4) reduces to

$$\sum_{j=0}^{n-1} \mathbf{P}^j \mathbf{QK} = \mathbf{Z}_{11}\mathbf{QK}(\lambda_1{}^{n-1} + \lambda_1{}^{n-2} + \cdots + 1)$$
$$+ \mathbf{Z}_{21}\mathbf{QK}(\lambda_2{}^{n-1} + \lambda_2{}^{n-2} + \cdots + 1)$$
$$+ \cdots \cdots \cdots \cdots \cdots \cdots \cdots$$
$$+ \mathbf{Z}_{k1}\mathbf{QK}(\lambda_k{}^{n-1} + \lambda_k{}^{n-2} + \cdots + 1)$$

If $\lambda_i \neq 1$ for $i = 1, 2, \ldots, k$, then each finite power series in λ_i can be represented in closed form, to give

$$\sum_{j=0}^{n-1} \mathbf{P}^j \mathbf{QK} = \mathbf{Z}_{11}\mathbf{QK}\frac{\lambda_1{}^n - 1}{\lambda_1 - 1} + \mathbf{Z}_{21}\mathbf{QK}\frac{\lambda_2{}^n - 1}{\lambda_2 - 1}$$
$$+ \cdots + \mathbf{Z}_{k1}\mathbf{QK}\frac{\lambda_k{}^n - 1}{\lambda_k - 1} \quad (6.6.5)$$

If the input vector is a "ramp" sequence, then $\mathbf{E}(n) = n\mathbf{K}$, and if $\lambda_i \neq 1$, then Eq. (6.6.4) becomes

$$\sum_{j=0}^{n-1} \mathbf{P}^j \mathbf{Q}j\mathbf{K} = \mathbf{Z}_{11}\mathbf{QK}[(n-1) + (n-2)\lambda_1 + \cdots + 2\lambda_1{}^{n-3} + \lambda_1{}^{n-2}]$$
$$+ \cdots \cdots \cdots \cdots \cdots \cdots \cdots \cdots \cdots \cdots \cdots$$
$$+ \mathbf{Z}_{k1}\mathbf{QK}[(n-1) + (n-2)\lambda_k + \cdots + 2\lambda_2{}^{n-3} + \lambda_2{}^{n-2}]$$
$$= \sum_{i=1}^{k} \mathbf{Z}_{i1}\mathbf{QK}\left[n\frac{\lambda_i{}^{n-1} - 1}{\lambda_i - 1} - \frac{d}{d\lambda_i}\left(\lambda_i \frac{\lambda_i{}^{n-1} - 1}{\lambda_i - 1} \right) \right] \quad (6.6.6)$$

The summation in the solution given in Eq. (6.6.2) can be avoided by replacing the original system of nonhomogeneous equations by an equivalent homogeneous system, as discussed in Sec. 5.8. The definition of stability in the sense of Lyapunov, given in Sec. 6.4 for continuous systems, carries over directly to discrete-state systems by simply considering the time sequence of vectors $\mathbf{\Psi}(t_0 + nh)$, $n = 0, 1, \ldots$, generated from the continuous time function by replacing the argument t by the sequence of discrete points $t = nh$. As in linear constant-coefficient differential equations, the stability of linear constant-coefficient difference equations is determined by the eigenvalues of the coefficient matrix $\mathbf{P}$ in the homogeneous system. From the expansion of $\mathbf{P}^n$ given in Eq. (6.6.3) it is evident that the homogeneous to the solution system of difference equations given in Eq. (6.6.2) is bounded, i.e., stable, if and only if the modulus of each eigenvalue of *multiplicity 1 is less than or equal to* 1 and the modulus of each eigenvalue of multiplicity 2 or greater *is less than* 1.

If the modulus of each eigenvalue is less than 1 (regardless of multiplicity), then the state vector goes to zero in the limit as $n \to \infty$ and the solution is *asymptotically* stable.

It is apparent, then, that the basic theorem on stability of time-stationary linear systems given as Theorem 6.5.1 carries over directly to discrete-state systems if we replace the word "eigenvalues" by "logarithm of the eigenvalues." Thus, a discrete-state system is stable if:

1.   The real parts of the logarithms of the zeros of the minimal polynomial $m(\lambda)$ of $\mathbf{P}$ are negative or zero.
2.   Those zeros for which this real part vanishes, if any, are simple.

The solution is asymptotically stable if and only if the logarithms of the eigenvalues of $\mathbf{P}$ have negative real parts.

It is evident, then, that the unit circle forms the boundary between the stable and unstable regions of the λ plane for discrete-state systems just as the imaginary axis divides the stable and unstable regions of the λ plane for continuous-state systems. In fact, if λ_i' represents the eigenvalues for the discrete-state system, then the function $\lambda = \log \lambda'$ maps the unit circle in the λ' plane into the imaginary axis of the λ plane, as shown in Fig. 6.6.1. Simple zeros on the unit circle of the λ' plane correspond to sustained oscillations in discrete-state systems, just as simple zeros on the imaginary axis of the λ plane correspond to sustained oscillations in the continuous systems.

Example 6.6.1: Determine whether or not the system described by the following equations is stable:

$$\begin{bmatrix} \psi_1(n+1) \\ \psi_2(n+1) \end{bmatrix} = \begin{bmatrix} 0.5 & -0.25 \\ -1 & 0.5 \end{bmatrix} \begin{bmatrix} \psi_1(n) \\ \psi_2(n) \end{bmatrix} + \begin{bmatrix} f_1(n) \\ 0 \end{bmatrix}$$

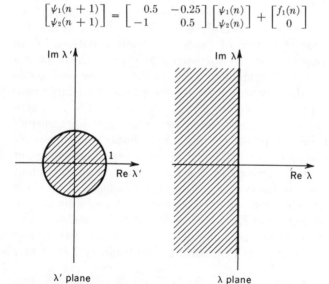

Fig. 6.6.1   Mapping of unit circle in λ' plane into imaginary axis of λ plane by function $\lambda = \log \lambda'$.

Solution: The characteristic polynomial is

$$D(\lambda) = \begin{vmatrix} \lambda - 0.5 & 0.25 \\ 1 & \lambda - 0.5 \end{vmatrix} = (\lambda - 0.5)^2 - 0.25 = \lambda^2 - \lambda = \lambda(\lambda - 1)$$

The system is stable, but not asymptotically stable, since one eigenvalue is on the unit circle.

An analytical test for stability of discrete-state systems depends upon a criterion for determining the number of zeros of the characteristic polynomial

$$D(\lambda) = |\lambda \mathbf{U} - \mathbf{P}| = \lambda^n + a_1\lambda^{n-1} + \cdots + a_n \qquad (6.6.7)$$

within the unit circle. Several such tests are available, but in general they are much more complex and difficult to apply than the Routh algorithm given in Sec. 6.5 for establishing the number of zeros of a polynomial in the right half plane.

It is also possible to map the region of the unit circle in the λ plane into the left half of the w plane by replacing λ in the polynomial by

$$\lambda = \frac{1 + w}{1 - w} \qquad (6.6.8)$$

Indeed, the polynomial

$$F(w) = (1 - w)^n D\left(\frac{1 + w}{1 - w}\right) \qquad (6.6.9)$$

and $D(\lambda)$ in Eq. (6.6.7) are corresponding polynomials; i.e., all zeros of $D(\lambda)$ are within the unit circle if all the zeros of $F(w)$ in Eq. (6.6.9) lie in the left half of the w plane.

Example 6.6.2: Investigate the stability of the discrete-state system

$$\begin{bmatrix} \Psi_1(n+1) \\ \Psi_2(n+1) \\ \Psi_3(n+1) \end{bmatrix} = \begin{bmatrix} 1 & 0 & 3 \\ 1 & 2 & -1 \\ 0 & 1 & 4 \end{bmatrix} \begin{bmatrix} \Psi_1(n) \\ \Psi_2(n) \\ \Psi_3(n) \end{bmatrix} + \begin{bmatrix} 1 & 0 \\ 0 & 2 \\ 2 & 1 \end{bmatrix} \begin{bmatrix} f_1(n) \\ f_2(n) \end{bmatrix}$$

Solution: Since

$$D(\lambda) = \lambda^3 - 7\lambda^2 + 15\lambda - 12$$

the transformation in Eq. (6.6.8) gives

$$D\left(\frac{1 + w}{1 - w}\right) = \frac{1}{(1 - w)^3}(35w^3 - 41w^2 + 17w - 3)$$

Therefore

$$F(w) = 35w^3 - 41w^2 + 17w - 3$$

Routh's algorithm applied to $F(w)$ yields

35	17
−41	−3
1	(multiplied by $\frac{41}{592}$)
−1	(multiplied by $\frac{1}{3}$)

From the Routh array, all the zeros of $F(w)$ lie in the right half of the w plane. Hence the modulus of each of the zeros of $D(\lambda)$ is greater than unity, and the system is unstable.

PROBLEMS

6.1   For the capacitor network shown in Fig. P6.1:

(a)   Write the state equations; then modify these equations by using a new state vector $\bar{\Psi}$ as defined in Eq. (6.1.6).

(b)   Determine the values of the capacitor voltages for $t > t_0$ if

$$e(t) = \begin{cases} 0 & t < t_0 \\ E & t \geq t_0 \end{cases}$$

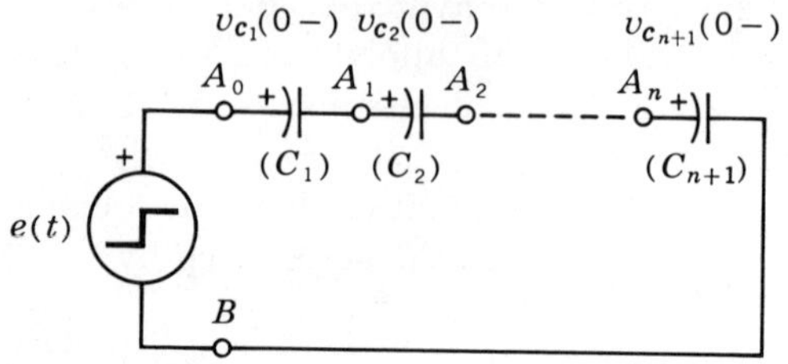

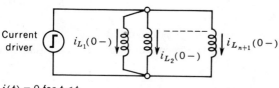

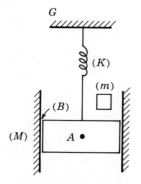

Fig. P6.1

6.2   Repeat Prob. 6.1 for the currents of the inductor circuit given in Fig. P6.2. Compare the results in the two cases.

Current driver

$i(t) = 0$ for $t < t_0$
$i(t) = I$ for $t \geq t_0$

Fig. P6.2

6.3   The mechanical system in Fig. P6.3 is at rest.   A small mass m is suddenly added to the system.   Draw the system graph, and determine whether or not the velocity of the point A is a continuous function of time.

Fig. P6.3

6.4   Determine $0+$ values of all the system variables (across and through) for the systems given in Fig. P6.4.

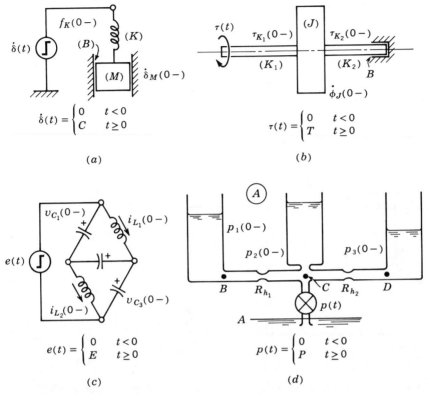

$$\dot{\delta}(t) = \begin{cases} 0 & t < 0 \\ C & t \geq 0 \end{cases}$$

$$\tau(t) = \begin{cases} 0 & t < 0 \\ T & t \geq 0 \end{cases}$$

(a)   (b)

$$e(t) = \begin{cases} 0 & t < 0 \\ E & t \geq 0 \end{cases}$$

$$p(t) = \begin{cases} 0 & t < 0 \\ P & t \geq 0 \end{cases}$$

(c)   (d)

Fig. P6.4

6.5   The terminal equations of the mechanical system (Attwood machine), in Fig. P6.5a, corresponding to the terminal graph in Fig. P6.5b, are given by

$$\frac{d}{dt} \begin{bmatrix} f_1(t) \\ \delta_2(t) \end{bmatrix} = \begin{bmatrix} M(d/dt) + B & 1 \\ -1 & 0 \end{bmatrix} \begin{bmatrix} \dot{\delta}_1(t) \\ f_2(t) \end{bmatrix}$$

The system is at rest, and, at $t = 0$, a small mass component m is suddenly attached to the system at point B. Derive the state equations for the system when $t > 0$, and determine the velocity of the points A and B of the system.

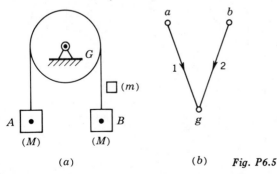

(a)   (b)   **Fig. P6.5**

6.6   In the RL network shown in Fig. P6.6 switch S is normally closed and then is opened suddenly at $t = 0$. Determine the inductor currents when $t > 0$. Note that the following necessary information can be obtained directly from the given network:

$$i_L(0-) = \frac{E}{R_1}$$

$$i_{L_2}(0-) = \frac{E}{R_2}$$

$$v_s(t) = 0$$

                       when $t < 0$

$$i_s(t) = \frac{E}{R_1} + \frac{E}{R_2}$$

$$i_s(t) = 0 \qquad \text{when } t \geq 0$$

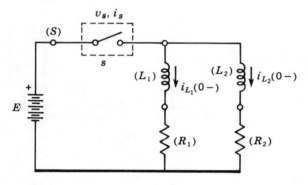

Fig. P6.6

6.7   The RC network in Fig. P6.7a contains a three-terminal switch S whose terminal graph is indicated in Fig. P6.7b. The switch is normally open and then is closed at $t = 0$.

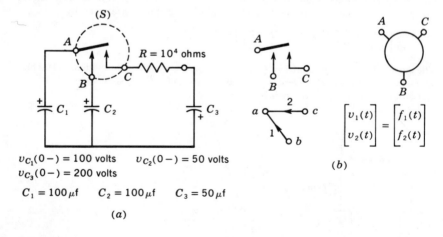

$v_{C_1}(0-) = 100$ volts $v_{C_2}(0-) = 50$ volts
$v_{C_3}(0-) = 200$ volts

$C_1 = 100 \, \mu f$ $C_2 = 100 \, \mu f$ $C_3 = 50 \, \mu f$

(a)

(b)

Fig. P6.7

(a) Write the terminal equations of the three-terminal switch in the form

$$\begin{bmatrix} v_1(t) \\ v_2(t) \end{bmatrix} = \begin{bmatrix} f_1(t) \\ f_2(t) \end{bmatrix}$$

from inspection of the given network.

(b) Derive the state model equations for the RC network (S is assumed to be a three-terminal voltage driver).

(c) From the state equations calculate the $0+$ values of all the capacitor voltages.

6.8 Determine the eigenvalues and the minimal polynomials of the following matrices.

(a) $\begin{bmatrix} 3 & 0 \\ 2 & -1 \end{bmatrix}$

(b) $\begin{bmatrix} 1 & 0 & 0 & 0 \\ 0 & 1 & 0 & 0 \\ 0 & 0 & 1 & 0 \\ 0 & 0 & 0 & 1 \end{bmatrix}$

(c) $\begin{bmatrix} 2 & 1 & 0 & 0 \\ 0 & 2 & 0 & 0 \\ 0 & 0 & 1 & 3 \\ 0 & 0 & 0 & 2 \end{bmatrix}$

(d) $\begin{bmatrix} 1 & -1 & 0 \\ 0 & 2 & 3 \\ 0 & 1 & 4 \end{bmatrix}$

6.9 Let

$$\mathbf{P} = \begin{bmatrix} 1 & -1 & -1 \\ -1 & 1 & -1 \\ -1 & -1 & 1 \end{bmatrix}$$

(a) Calculate the eigenvalues and the minimal polynomial of $\mathbf{P}$.

(b) Determine the expression of the polynomial $g(\lambda)$ which has the same values as $f(\lambda) = e^\lambda$ on the spectrum of $\mathbf{P}$.

(c) Calculate $f(\mathbf{P}) = e^{\mathbf{P}}$.

(d) Repeat parts b and c for

$$f(\lambda) = e^{-\lambda}$$
$$f(\lambda) = \lambda^2$$
$$f(\lambda) = \frac{1}{\lambda} = \lambda^{-1}$$

6.10 Considering the partial-fraction expansion of the rational function $h(\lambda)/m(\lambda)$, where $h(\lambda)$ is the interpolation polynomial and $m(\lambda)$ is the minimal polynomial, calculate the constituent matrices of each of the following matrices:

(a) $\mathbf{P} = \begin{bmatrix} 1 & 2 \\ 0 & 3 \end{bmatrix}$

(b) $\mathbf{P} = \begin{bmatrix} 0 & -1 \\ 1 & 0 \end{bmatrix}$

(c) $\mathbf{P} = \begin{bmatrix} 2 & -1 & 0 \\ -1 & 2 & -1 \\ 0 & -1 & 2 \end{bmatrix}$

(d) $\mathbf{P} = \begin{bmatrix} 1 & 0 & 0 & 0 \\ 0 & 0 & 0 & -96 \\ 0 & 1 & 0 & 32 \\ 0 & 0 & 1 & 2 \end{bmatrix}$

6.11   By using the algorithm described in Sec. 6.3, calculate the inverse of $s\mathbf{U} - \mathbf{P}$ when

(a) $\mathbf{P} = \begin{bmatrix} 2 & 1 \\ 3 & 4 \end{bmatrix}$

(b) $\mathbf{P} = \begin{bmatrix} 3 & -3 & 2 \\ -1 & 5 & -2 \\ -1 & 3 & 6 \end{bmatrix}$

(c) $\mathbf{P} = \begin{bmatrix} 3 & -1 & 1 \\ 2 & 0 & 1 \\ 1 & -1 & 2 \end{bmatrix}$

6.12   Using the results of Prob. 6.11, calculate the constituent matrices for each matrix $\mathbf{P}$ given in Prob. 6.11.

6.13   Repeat Prob. 6.12 by using the method of resolving polynomials.

6.14   Repeat Prob. 6.12, and calculate the constituent matrices in terms of the powers of the given matrices.

6.15   Determine the values of the voltages and currents as functions of time of each component of the network shown in Fig. P6.15. The initial conditions for the capacitor voltage and for the inductor current are indicated on the figure.

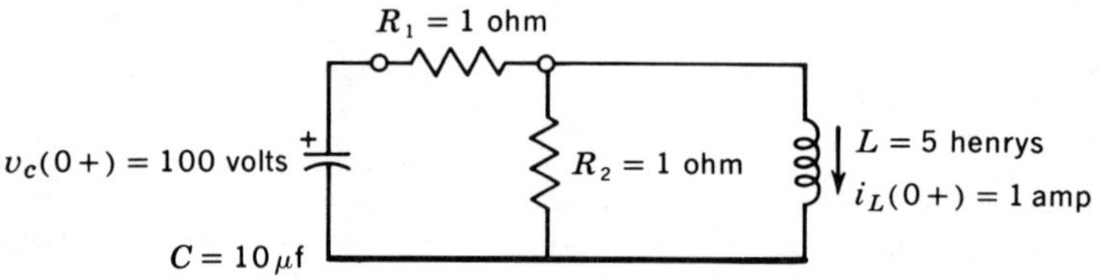

Fig. P6.15

6.16   Determine the equilibrium states $\mathbf{\Psi}_e$ of the following state equations, and carry these points to the origin by means of transformation of variables:

(a) $\dfrac{d}{dt}\begin{bmatrix} \psi_1(t) \\ \psi_2(t) \end{bmatrix} = \begin{bmatrix} \psi_1(t)[\psi_2(t) + 1] \\ [\psi_1(t) - 1][\psi_2(t) - 1] \end{bmatrix}$

(b) $\dfrac{d}{dt}\begin{bmatrix} \psi_1(t) \\ \psi_2(t) \\ \psi_3(t) \end{bmatrix} = \begin{bmatrix} \psi_1(t) + \frac{1}{2}\psi_3(t) \\ \psi_1(t) + 3\psi_2(t) + 2\psi_3(t) \\ 2\psi_2(t) + \psi_3(t) \end{bmatrix}$

(c) $\dfrac{d}{dt}\begin{bmatrix} \psi_1(t) \\ \psi_2(t) \end{bmatrix} = \begin{bmatrix} 3\psi_1(t) + 2\psi_2(t) \\ -\psi_1(t) + \psi_2(t) \end{bmatrix}$

(d) $\dfrac{d}{dt}\begin{bmatrix} \psi_1(t) \\ \psi_2(t) \end{bmatrix} = \begin{bmatrix} \psi_1{}^2(t) + \psi_2{}^2(t) - 1 \\ \psi_1(t) - \psi_2(t) \end{bmatrix}$

6.17   Determine the solution of the state equations

$$\frac{d}{dt}\begin{bmatrix} \psi_1(t) \\ \psi_2(t) \end{bmatrix} = \begin{bmatrix} 0 & 21 \\ -1 & -10 \end{bmatrix}\begin{bmatrix} \psi_1(t) \\ \psi_2(t) \end{bmatrix} \qquad \begin{bmatrix} \psi_1(0) \\ \psi_2(0) \end{bmatrix} = \begin{bmatrix} 1 \\ 0 \end{bmatrix}$$

Sketch the curves $\psi_1(t)$ and $\psi_2(t)$, and then obtain a sketch of the trajectory of the state vector $\mathbf{\Psi}(t)$ in the $\psi_1 - \psi_2$ plane.

6.18   Repeat Prob. 6.17 for the state equations

(a) $\dfrac{d}{dt}\begin{bmatrix} \psi_1(t) \\ \psi_2(t) \end{bmatrix} = \begin{bmatrix} 0 & \frac{1}{8} \\ -\frac{1}{2} & 0 \end{bmatrix}\begin{bmatrix} \psi_1(t) \\ \psi_2(t) \end{bmatrix} \qquad \begin{bmatrix} \psi_1(0) \\ \psi_2(0) \end{bmatrix} = \begin{bmatrix} 10 \\ 0 \end{bmatrix}$

(b) $\dfrac{d}{dt}\begin{bmatrix} \psi_1(t) \\ \psi_2(t) \end{bmatrix} = \begin{bmatrix} 0 & \frac{25}{4} \\ -1 & 4 \end{bmatrix}\begin{bmatrix} \psi_1(t) \\ \psi_2(t) \end{bmatrix} \qquad \begin{bmatrix} \psi_1(0) \\ \psi_2(0) \end{bmatrix} = \begin{bmatrix} 0 \\ 10 \end{bmatrix}$

(c) $\dfrac{d}{dt}\begin{bmatrix} \psi_1(t) \\ \psi_2(t) \end{bmatrix} = \begin{bmatrix} 0 & 1 \\ -1 & -\zeta \end{bmatrix}\begin{bmatrix} \psi_1(t) \\ \psi_2(t) \end{bmatrix} \qquad \begin{bmatrix} \psi_1(0) \\ \psi_2(0) \end{bmatrix} = \begin{bmatrix} 1 \\ 0 \end{bmatrix}$

for $\zeta = 0, 0.1, 0.5, 1$, and 2.

6.19   Investigate the stability characteristics of the equilibrium state of the system whose state equations are of the form

$$\frac{d}{dt}\begin{bmatrix} \psi_1(t) \\ \psi_2(t) \end{bmatrix} = \begin{bmatrix} \psi_2(t) \\ -3\psi_2(t) - \psi_2^3(t) - \psi_1(t) \end{bmatrix}$$

Select the function

$$V(\mathbf{\Psi}) = \psi_1^2(t) + \psi_2^2(t)$$

as a possible Lyapunov function.

6.20   Repeat Prob. 6.19 for

$$\frac{d}{dt}\begin{bmatrix} \psi_1(t) \\ \psi_2(t) \end{bmatrix} = \begin{bmatrix} 2 & -4 \\ 3 & -5 \end{bmatrix}\begin{bmatrix} \psi_1(t) \\ \psi_2(t) \end{bmatrix}$$

with

$$V(\mathbf{\Psi}) = 3\psi_1^2(t) - \tfrac{13}{3}\psi_1(t)\psi_2(t) + \tfrac{11}{6}\psi_2^2(t)$$

6.21   Applying Routh's algorithm, determine the number of zeros of the given polynomials in the right half plane.

(a) $\lambda^4 + 10\lambda^3 + 35\lambda^2 + 50\lambda + 24$
(b) $\lambda^5 - 8\lambda^4 + 2\lambda^3 + 34\lambda^2 + \lambda + 42$
(c) $\lambda^7 - 2\lambda^6 - \lambda^5 + 2\lambda^4 - 56\lambda^3 + 112\lambda^2 - 144\lambda + 228$

6.22   Investigate the stability of the system described by the equations

$$\begin{bmatrix} \psi_1(n+1) \\ \psi_2(n+1) \\ \psi_3(n+1) \end{bmatrix} = \begin{bmatrix} 1 & \frac{1}{2} & 0 \\ \frac{1}{4} & 1 & \frac{1}{2} \\ 0 & 0 & 1 \end{bmatrix}\begin{bmatrix} \psi_1(n) \\ \psi_2(n) \\ \psi_3(n) \end{bmatrix} + \begin{bmatrix} f_1(n) \\ f_2(n) \\ f_3(n) \end{bmatrix}$$

Note: First determine the zeros of the characteristic polynomial of the coefficient matrix; then by making the substitution

$$\lambda = \frac{1 + w}{1 - w}$$

in the characteristic polynomial apply Routh's criterion to the polynomial in w. Compare the results.

FURTHER READING

1. Souriau, Jean-Marie: Une Méthode pour la décomposition spectrale à l'inversion des matrices, *Compt. Rend.*, vol. 227, pp. 1010–1011, 1948.
2. Faddeev, D. K., and I. S. Sominskii: "Collection of Problems on Higher Algebra," 2d ed. (in Russian), Gostekhizdat, Moscow, 1949.
3. Fettis, H. E.: A Method for Obtaining the Characteristic Equation of a Matrix and Computing the Associated Model Columns, *Quart. Appl. Math.*, vol. 8, pp. 206–212, 1950.
4. Frame, J. S.: A Simple Recursion Formula for Inverting a Matrix (abstract), *Bull. Am. Math. Soc.*, vol. 55, p. 1045, 1949.
5. Frame, J. S.: Matrix Functions and Applications, *IEEE Spectrum*, vol. 1, no. 6, June, 1964.
6. Lyapunov, M. A.: Problème générale de la stabilité du mouvement, "Annals of Mathematical Studies," vol. 17, Princeton University Press, Princeton, N.J., 1947.
7. LaSalle, J., and S. Lefschetz: "Stability by Lyapunov's Direct Method with Applications," Academic Press Inc., New York, 1961.
8. Gantmacher, F. R.: "The Theory of Matrices," vol. I, Chelsea Publishing Company, New York, 1959.
9. Hahn, W.: "Theory and Application of Lyapunov's Direct Method," translated by S. H. Lehnigk and H. H. Hosenthien, Prentice-Hall, Inc., Englewood Cliffs, N.J., 1963.
10. Routh, E.: "Dynamics of a System of Rigid Bodies," The Macmillan Company, New York, 1877.

7
Response Characteristics
of Linear Systems

The relative merits of alternative systems in performing a given function must finally be evaluated in terms of their respective output responses to a given input signal or excitation signal. Certain types of excitation signals have become standards for such comparisons. This chapter presents a comprehensive study of the response characteristics of linear systems to several of the more common excitation signals and identifies important measures of performance.

7.1 POLYNOMIAL AND PULSE - RESPONSE CHARACTERISTICS OF LINEAR SYSTEMS

It was shown in Sec. 5.5 that the solution to the linear time-invariant system

$$\frac{d}{dt}\,\mathbf{\Psi}(t) = \mathbf{P}\mathbf{\Psi}(t) + \mathbf{Q}\mathbf{E}(t) \qquad \mathbf{\Psi}(0) = \mathbf{\Psi}_0 \tag{7.1.1}$$

can be evaluated in terms of a semidefinite time integral of the transition matrix and the excitation vector by the expression

$$\mathbf{\Psi}(t) = e^{\mathbf{P}t}\mathbf{\Psi}_0 + \int_0^t e^{\mathbf{P}(t-\tau)}\mathbf{QE}(\tau) \, d\tau \qquad (7.1.2)$$

Alternatively, it was shown that the nonhomogeneous system can be transformed into an equivalent homogeneous system by generating the given excitation vector as a solution to an auxiliary system of differential equations

$$\frac{d}{dt}\mathbf{F}(t) = \mathbf{TF}(t) \qquad \mathbf{F}(0) = \mathbf{F}_0 \qquad (7.1.3)$$

where $\mathbf{E}(t) = \mathbf{KF}(t)$, $\mathbf{K}$ and $\mathbf{T}$ are matrices with constant coefficients, and $\mathbf{F}_0$ is such that $\mathbf{E}(0) = \mathbf{KF}_0$. The augmented homogeneous equivalent of Eq. (7.1.1) is therefore of the form

$$\frac{d}{dt}\begin{bmatrix} \mathbf{\Psi}(t) \\ \mathbf{F}(t) \end{bmatrix} = \begin{bmatrix} \mathbf{P} & \mathbf{QK} \\ \mathbf{0} & \mathbf{T} \end{bmatrix}\begin{bmatrix} \mathbf{\Psi}(t) \\ \mathbf{F}(t) \end{bmatrix} \qquad (7.1.4)$$

or

$$\frac{d}{dt}\mathbf{\Psi}'(t) = \mathbf{P}'\mathbf{\Psi}'(t)$$

and the solution is

$$\mathbf{\Psi}'(t) = e^{\mathbf{P}'t}\mathbf{\Psi}_0' \qquad (7.1.5)$$

Since $\mathbf{P}$ is always of lower order than $\mathbf{P}'$, the form of the solution given in Eq. (7.1.2) requires the evaluation of fewer constituent matrices than does the equivalent homogeneous form. However, it also requires the evaluation of a time integral, whereas the homogeneous form does not.

Still a third form of the solution can be obtained when Eq. (7.1.1) is transformed into an equivalent homogeneous form by setting

$$\mathbf{\Xi}(t) = \mathbf{\Psi}(t) - \mathbf{WF}(t) \qquad (7.1.6)$$

where $\mathbf{W}$ is an as yet unknown real matrix of the same dimension as $\mathbf{Q}$ and $\mathbf{F}(t)$ satisfies the system of differential equations in Eq. (7.1.3). By substituting Eq. (7.1.6) into Eq. (7.1.1) and applying Eq. (7.1.3) there results

$$\frac{d}{dt}\mathbf{\Xi}(t) = \mathbf{P}\mathbf{\Xi}(t) + (\mathbf{PW} + \mathbf{QK} - \mathbf{WT})\mathbf{F}(t) \qquad (7.1.7)$$

If the matrix $\mathbf{W}$ can be selected such that

$$\mathbf{PW} + \mathbf{QK} - \mathbf{WT} = \mathbf{0} \qquad (7.1.8)$$

then the given system has been reduced to a homogeneous equivalent system for which the solution is

$$\Xi(t) = e^{Pt}\Xi_0 \qquad \Xi_0 = \Psi_0 - WF_0$$

Note that this homogeneous equivalent *is of exactly the same order* as the nonhomogeneous system and that the solution for the state vector $\Psi(t)$ is given simply as

$$\begin{aligned}\Psi(t) &= \Xi(t) + WF(t) = e^{Pt}\Xi_0 + WF(t) \\ &= e^{Pt}(\Psi_0 - WF_0) + WF(t)\end{aligned} \qquad (7.1.9)$$

The critical step in the transformation is, of course, that of finding the matrix W satisfying Eq. (7.1.8), if, indeed, such a matrix exists.

From the theory of functions of a matrix it is known that[1] the matrix equation

$$PW - WT = -QK \qquad (7.1.10)$$

has a unique solution for W if and only if the matrices P and T do not have common eigenvalues. If some of the eigenvalues of P and T are the same, either Eq. (7.1.10) is inconsistent or it has an infinite number of solutions.

If T and P have no common eigenvalues, then the matrix W can be evaluated by simply equating coefficients in the matrices on the two sides of Eq. (7.1.10). Furthermore, it is evident from the general form of the solution given in Eq. (7.1.9) that, if the eigenvalues of P all have negative real parts, then the system is asymptotically stable and $e^{Pt} \to 0$ in the limit as $t \to \infty$. For this reason, the vector $\Xi(t) = e^{Pt}(\Psi_0 - WF_0)$ in Eq. (7.1.9) is frequently referred to as the *transient* component of the solution and the second term, $WF(t)$, as the *steady-state* component of the solution, or ultimate response of the system. Note that these concepts have no meaning, i.e., they are not defined, unless (1) the system is asymptotically stable and (2) the eigenvalues of P are distinct from the eigenvalues of T. Further, when defined, the steady-state solution is obtained as the product $WF(t)$, where W is the solution to the transformation equations given as Eq. (7.1.10). The new state vector $\Xi(t)$ in Eq. (7.1.6) represents the difference between the complete solution and the steady-state solution. Thus, it should be evident that if only the steady-state component of the response characteristics is desired, and is known to exist, then it can be obtained without having to evaluate either the constituent matrices or the eigenvalues.

Since the latter technique of solution places the transient and steady-state solutions of asymptotically stable systems in direct evidence, it is usually, but not always, the more expedient of the three techniques to use in generating response characteristics. The following example demonstrates the application of all three techniques in realizing the complete solution to a simple electrical network.

Example 7.1.1: Consider the RC network in Fig. 7.1.1, where the excitation signal is a unit step function, as indicated. Determine the solution of this network for $t > 0$.

Solution: The state equations for the system are

$$\frac{d}{dt}\begin{bmatrix} v_1(t) \\ v_2(t) \end{bmatrix} = \begin{bmatrix} -2 & 1 \\ 1 & -1 \end{bmatrix}\begin{bmatrix} v_1(t) \\ v_2(t) \end{bmatrix} + \begin{bmatrix} 1 \\ 0 \end{bmatrix}v_0(t) \tag{7.1.11}$$

with

$$\mathbf{\Psi}_0 = \begin{bmatrix} v_1(0+) \\ v_2(0+) \end{bmatrix} = \begin{bmatrix} v_1(0-) \\ v_2(0-) \end{bmatrix} = \begin{bmatrix} 1 \\ 2 \end{bmatrix}$$

Note that the coefficient matrix is symmetric. The zeros of the characteristic polynomial of the coefficient matrix are therefore real and negative. Indeed,

$$D(\lambda) = \lambda^2 + 3\lambda + 1 = (\lambda - \lambda_1)(\lambda - \lambda_2)$$

where

$$\lambda_1 = \frac{-3}{2} - \frac{\sqrt{5}}{2} \quad \text{and} \quad \lambda_2 = \frac{-3}{2} + \frac{\sqrt{5}}{2}$$

(a) Consider first the solution as evaluated from the form given in Eq. (7.1.2). The transition matrix $e^{\mathbf{P}t}$ is

$$e^{\mathbf{P}t} = \mathbf{Z}_{11}e^{\lambda_1 t} + \mathbf{Z}_{21}e^{\lambda_2 t} \tag{7.1.12}$$

where

$$\mathbf{Z}_{11} = \frac{1}{\lambda_2 - \lambda_1}(\lambda_2\mathbf{U} - \mathbf{P}) = \frac{1}{2\sqrt{5}}\begin{bmatrix} 1 + \sqrt{5} & -2 \\ -2 & -1 + \sqrt{5} \end{bmatrix}$$

$$\mathbf{Z}_{21} = \frac{1}{\lambda_1 - \lambda_2}(\lambda_1\mathbf{U} - \mathbf{P}) = \frac{1}{2\sqrt{5}}\begin{bmatrix} -(1 - \sqrt{5}) & 2 \\ 2 & 1 + \sqrt{5} \end{bmatrix}$$

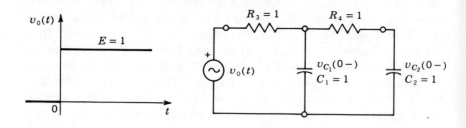

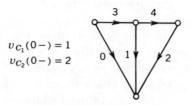

$$v_{C_1}(0-) = 1$$
$$v_{C_2}(0-) = 2$$

Fig. 7.1.1 An RC network and system graph.

The solution is therefore

$$\mathbf{\Psi}(t) = \mathbf{Z}_{11}\mathbf{\Psi}_0 e^{\lambda_1 t} + \mathbf{Z}_{21}\mathbf{\Psi}_0 e^{\lambda_2 t} + \mathbf{Z}_{11}e^{\lambda_1 t}\int_0^t e^{-\lambda_1 \tau}\mathbf{Q}v_0\,d\tau + \mathbf{Z}_{21}e^{\lambda_2 t}\int_0^t e^{-\lambda_2 \tau}\mathbf{Q}v_0\,d\tau$$

$$= \mathbf{Z}_{11}\left(\mathbf{\Psi}_0 + \frac{1}{\lambda_1}\mathbf{Q}v_0\right)e^{\lambda_1 t} + \mathbf{Z}_{21}\left(\mathbf{\Psi}_0 + \frac{1}{\lambda_2}\mathbf{Q}v_0\right)e^{\lambda_2 t}$$

$$- \left(\frac{1}{\lambda_1}\mathbf{Z}_{11} + \frac{1}{\lambda_2}\mathbf{Z}_{21}\right)\mathbf{Q}v_0$$

and since

$$\mathbf{\Psi}_0 = \begin{bmatrix} 1 \\ 2 \end{bmatrix} \qquad \mathbf{Q}v_0 = \begin{bmatrix} 1 \\ 0 \end{bmatrix}$$

then finally

$$\mathbf{\Psi}(t) = \frac{1}{2\sqrt{5}}\begin{bmatrix} -2 \\ -1 + \sqrt{5} \end{bmatrix}e^{\lambda_1 t} + \frac{1}{2\sqrt{5}}\begin{bmatrix} 2 \\ 1 + \sqrt{5} \end{bmatrix}e^{\lambda_2 t} + \begin{bmatrix} 1 \\ 1 \end{bmatrix} \qquad (7.1.13)$$

(b) The augmented homogeneous equivalent of Eq. (7.1.11) is

$$\frac{d}{dt}\begin{bmatrix} v_1(t) \\ v_2(t) \\ \hline f(t) \end{bmatrix} = \begin{bmatrix} -2 & 1 & 1 \\ 1 & -1 & 0 \\ \hline 0 & 0 & 0 \end{bmatrix}\begin{bmatrix} v_1(t) \\ v_2(t) \\ \hline f(t) \end{bmatrix} \qquad \mathbf{\Psi}_0 = \begin{bmatrix} v_1(0) \\ v_2(0) \\ \hline f(0) \end{bmatrix} = \begin{bmatrix} 1 \\ 2 \\ \hline 1 \end{bmatrix}$$

where the eigenvalues of the coefficient matrix $\mathbf{P}'$ are $\lambda_1 = -\frac{3}{2} - \sqrt{5}/2$, $\lambda_2 = -\frac{3}{2} + \sqrt{5}/2$, and $\lambda_3 = 0$.

The solution, therefore, is

$$\mathbf{\Psi}(t) = \mathbf{Z}'_{11}\mathbf{\Psi}_0 e^{\lambda_1 t} + \mathbf{Z}'_{21}\mathbf{\Psi}_0 e^{\lambda_2 t} + \mathbf{Z}'_{31}\mathbf{\Psi}_0 \qquad (7.1.14)$$

where

$$\mathbf{Z}'_{31} = \frac{1}{\lambda_1\lambda_2}[\lambda_1\mathbf{U} - \mathbf{P}'][\lambda_2\mathbf{U} - \mathbf{P}'] = \begin{bmatrix} 0 & 0 & 1 \\ 0 & 0 & 1 \\ \hline 0 & 0 & 1 \end{bmatrix}$$

$$\mathbf{Z}'_{21} = \frac{-1}{(\lambda_2 - \lambda_1)\lambda_2}[\lambda_1\mathbf{U} - \mathbf{P}']\mathbf{P}'$$

$$= \frac{1}{\sqrt{5}\,(3 - \sqrt{5})}\begin{bmatrix} -2(2 - \sqrt{5}) & 3 - \sqrt{5} & 1 - \sqrt{5} \\ 3 - \sqrt{5} & -1 + \sqrt{5} & -2 \\ \hline 0 & 0 & 0 \end{bmatrix}$$

$$\mathbf{Z}'_{11} = \mathbf{U} - \mathbf{Z}'_{21} - \mathbf{Z}'_{31}$$

$$= \frac{1}{\sqrt{5}\,(3 + \sqrt{5})}\begin{bmatrix} 2(2 + \sqrt{5}) & -(3 + \sqrt{5}) & -(1 + \sqrt{5}) \\ -(3 + \sqrt{5}) & 1 + \sqrt{5} & 2 \\ \hline 0 & 0 & 0 \end{bmatrix}$$

(c) To reduce the nonhomogeneous form in Eq. (7.1.11) to a homogeneous form of the same order, let the step function be generated as a solution to the differential equation

$$\frac{d}{dt}f(t) = 0 \qquad f(0) = 1$$

and consider the transformation

$$\begin{bmatrix} v_1'(t) \\ v_2'(t) \end{bmatrix} = \begin{bmatrix} v_1(t) \\ v_2(t) \end{bmatrix} - \begin{bmatrix} w_1 \\ w_2 \end{bmatrix} f(t) \tag{7.1.15}$$

The homogeneous equivalent system as obtained by substituting Eq. (7.1.15) into Eq. (7.1.11) is

$$\frac{d}{dt} \begin{bmatrix} v_1'(t) \\ v_2'(t) \end{bmatrix} = \begin{bmatrix} -2 & 1 \\ 1 & -1 \end{bmatrix} \begin{bmatrix} v_1'(t) \\ v_2'(t) \end{bmatrix} \qquad \begin{bmatrix} v_1'(0) \\ v_2'(0) \end{bmatrix} = \begin{bmatrix} 1 \\ 2 \end{bmatrix} - \begin{bmatrix} w_1 \\ w_2 \end{bmatrix}$$

where w_1 and w_2 satisfy Eq. (7.1.8), i.e., by using the form of Eq. (7.1.10),

$$\begin{bmatrix} -2 & 1 \\ 1 & -1 \end{bmatrix} \begin{bmatrix} w_1 \\ w_2 \end{bmatrix} - \begin{bmatrix} w_1 \\ w_2 \end{bmatrix} (0) = - \begin{bmatrix} 1 \\ 0 \end{bmatrix} \tag{7.1.16}$$

The solution to Eq. (7.1.16) is

$$\begin{bmatrix} w_1 \\ w_2 \end{bmatrix} = \begin{bmatrix} 1 \\ 1 \end{bmatrix} \tag{7.1.17}$$

and initial conditions for the equivalent homogeneous system are therefore

$$\begin{bmatrix} v_1'(0) \\ v_2'(0) \end{bmatrix} = \begin{bmatrix} 1 \\ 2 \end{bmatrix} - \begin{bmatrix} 1 \\ 1 \end{bmatrix} 1 = \begin{bmatrix} 0 \\ 1 \end{bmatrix}$$

and the solution is

$$\begin{bmatrix} v_1'(t) \\ v_2'(t) \end{bmatrix} = \mathbf{Z}_{11} \begin{bmatrix} v_1'(0) \\ v_2'(0) \end{bmatrix} e^{\lambda_1 t} + \mathbf{Z}_{21} \begin{bmatrix} v_1'(0) \\ v_2'(0) \end{bmatrix} e^{\lambda_2 t}$$

It follows therefore that the solution for the state variables is

$$\begin{bmatrix} v_1(t) \\ v_2(t) \end{bmatrix} = \begin{bmatrix} v_1'(t) \\ v_2'(t) \end{bmatrix} + \begin{bmatrix} w_1 \\ w_2 \end{bmatrix} f(t) = \mathbf{Z}_{11} \begin{bmatrix} v_1'(0) \\ v_2'(0) \end{bmatrix} e^{\lambda_1 t} + \mathbf{Z}_{21} \begin{bmatrix} v_1'(0) \\ v_2'(0) \end{bmatrix} e^{\lambda_2 t} + \begin{bmatrix} 1 \\ 1 \end{bmatrix} \tag{7.1.18}$$

where the constituent matrices have already been evaluated and are given after Eq. (7.1.12).

Since the eigenvalues λ_1 and λ_2 of $\mathbf{P}$ are both negative, the first two terms on the right-hand side of Eq. (7.1.18) vanish with increasing time, while the last term remains constant. The last term, therefore, is the steady-state solution, and it is evaluated simply as the product of the matrix $\mathbf{W}$ in Eq. (7.1.17) into the function $f = 1$. It should be noted in contrast that, although the steady-state component of the solution is clearly in evidence in the first two techniques of solution, it cannot be evaluated without evaluating the constituent matrices.

POLYNOMIAL EXCITATION

If the excitation vector $\mathbf{E}(t)$ in Eq. (7.1.1) is of the general form

$$\mathbf{E}(t) = \begin{cases} 0 & \text{for } t < 0 \\ \mathbf{K}_0 + \mathbf{K}_1 t + \mathbf{K}_2 t^2 + \cdots + \mathbf{K}_l t^l & \text{for } t \geq 0 \end{cases} \tag{7.1.19}$$

then the system is said to be excited by a polynomial input. It follows immediately from the properties of linear constant-coefficient differential equations that, if $\mathbf{\Psi}_1(t)$, $\mathbf{\Psi}_2(t)$, . . . , $\mathbf{\Psi}_l(t)$ represent, respectively, the solutions to Eq. (7.1.1) corresponding to each term in the polynomial $K_0, K_1t, \ldots, K_lt^l$, then the complete solution to the equations for $E(t)$ given in Eq. (7.1.19) is

$$\Psi_t(t) = \Psi_1(t) + \Psi_2(t) + \cdots + \Psi_l(t)$$

That is, the solution to a sum of excitation functions is equal to the sum of the solutions to each of the excitation functions. This property is sometimes referred to as the *superposition* property of linear time-invariant systems.

Since any nonperiodic excitation signal can be approximated by a polynomial in t, it has become common practice to evaluate the performance characteristics of physical systems in terms of the response to each of the first several terms in the power series in Eq. (7.1.19). The response of a typical system to a step function, i.e., to the first term in Eq. (7.1.19), has already been considered in Example 7.1.1. The response characteristics of a typical system to a "parabolic function," $E(t) = K_2t^2$, is considered in the following example.

Example 7.1.2: Establish the steady-state and transient solutions to the system

$$\frac{d}{dt}\begin{bmatrix} \psi_1(t) \\ \psi_2(t) \end{bmatrix} = \begin{bmatrix} -3 & 1 \\ 0 & -2 \end{bmatrix}\begin{bmatrix} \psi_1(t) \\ \psi_2(t) \end{bmatrix} + \begin{bmatrix} -1 \\ 1 \end{bmatrix}e(t) \qquad (7.1.20)$$

where

$$e(t) = 5t^2 \qquad \text{and} \qquad \begin{bmatrix} \psi_1(0) \\ \psi_2(0) \end{bmatrix} = \begin{bmatrix} 0 \\ 0 \end{bmatrix}$$

Solution: The given excitation function can be generated as a solution to a system of differential equations, developed systematically by considering the following sequence of functions in increasing powers of t:

$$f_0(t) = 1$$
$$f_1(t) = t$$
$$f_2(t) = t^2$$

By direct differentiation it follows that

$$\frac{d}{dt}\begin{bmatrix} f_2(t) \\ f_1(t) \\ f_0(t) \end{bmatrix} = \begin{bmatrix} 0 & 2 & 0 \\ 0 & 0 & 1 \\ 0 & 0 & 0 \end{bmatrix}\begin{bmatrix} f_2(t) \\ f_1(t) \\ f_0(t) \end{bmatrix} \qquad \begin{bmatrix} f_2(0) \\ f_1(0) \\ f_0(0) \end{bmatrix} = \begin{bmatrix} 0 \\ 0 \\ 1 \end{bmatrix} \qquad (7.1.21)$$

and the given excitation function is

$$e(t) = [5 \quad 0 \quad 0]\begin{bmatrix} f_2(t) \\ f_1(t) \\ f_0(t) \end{bmatrix} \qquad (7.1.22)$$

Substituting Eq. (7.1.22) into Eq. (7.1.20) gives

$$\frac{d}{dt}\begin{bmatrix} \psi_1(t) \\ \psi_2(t) \end{bmatrix} = \begin{bmatrix} -3 & 1 \\ 0 & -2 \end{bmatrix}\begin{bmatrix} \psi_1(t) \\ \psi_2(t) \end{bmatrix} + \begin{bmatrix} -5 & 0 & 0 \\ 5 & 0 & 0 \end{bmatrix}\begin{bmatrix} f_2(t) \\ f_1(t) \\ f_0(t) \end{bmatrix} \qquad (7.1.23)$$

Since the eigenvalues of the coefficient matrix $\mathbf{P}$ in Eq. (7.1.20) are $\lambda_1 = -3$ and $\lambda_2 = -2$ and the eigenvalues of the coefficient matrix $\mathbf{T}$ in Eq. (7.1.21) are $\lambda_1' = \lambda_2' = \lambda_3' = 0$, the steady-state solution is given by

$$\mathbf{WF}(t) = \begin{bmatrix} w_{11} & w_{12} & w_{13} \\ w_{21} & w_{22} & w_{23} \end{bmatrix} \begin{bmatrix} f_2(t) \\ f_1(t) \\ f_0(t) \end{bmatrix} \tag{7.1.24}$$

where $\mathbf{W}$ is the solution to the matrix equation

$$\mathbf{PW} - \mathbf{WT} = -\mathbf{QK}$$

or, in detail,

$$\begin{bmatrix} -3 & 1 \\ 0 & -2 \end{bmatrix} \begin{bmatrix} w_{11} & w_{12} & w_{13} \\ w_{21} & w_{22} & w_{23} \end{bmatrix} - \begin{bmatrix} w_{11} & w_{12} & w_{13} \\ w_{21} & w_{22} & w_{23} \end{bmatrix} \begin{bmatrix} 0 & 2 & 0 \\ 0 & 0 & 1 \\ 0 & 0 & 0 \end{bmatrix}$$
$$= -\begin{bmatrix} -1 \\ 1 \end{bmatrix} \begin{bmatrix} 5 & 0 & 0 \end{bmatrix}$$

This system of equations can be easily solved for the matrix $\mathbf{W}$ by considering recursively the following systems of equations:

$$\begin{bmatrix} -3 & 1 \\ 0 & -2 \end{bmatrix} \begin{bmatrix} w_{11} \\ w_{21} \end{bmatrix} = \begin{bmatrix} 5 \\ -5 \end{bmatrix}$$

$$\begin{bmatrix} -3 & 1 \\ 0 & -2 \end{bmatrix} \begin{bmatrix} w_{12} \\ w_{22} \end{bmatrix} - 2 \begin{bmatrix} w_{11} \\ w_{21} \end{bmatrix} = 0$$

$$\begin{bmatrix} -3 & 1 \\ 0 & -2 \end{bmatrix} \begin{bmatrix} w_{13} \\ w_{23} \end{bmatrix} - \begin{bmatrix} w_{12} \\ w_{22} \end{bmatrix} = 0$$

Note that only the inverse of the given matrix $\mathbf{P}$ is required in this solution. Solving these equations and substituting the result into Eq. (7.1.24) gives as the steady-state solution

$$\mathbf{WF}(t) = \begin{bmatrix} -\frac{5}{6} & -\frac{5}{18} & \frac{55}{108} \\ \frac{5}{2} & -\frac{5}{2} & \frac{5}{4} \end{bmatrix} \begin{bmatrix} t^2 \\ t \\ 1 \end{bmatrix} \tag{7.1.25}$$

To establish the transient solution, consider the homogeneous system

$$\frac{d}{dt} \, \boldsymbol{\Xi}(t) = \mathbf{P}\boldsymbol{\Xi}(t) \tag{7.1.26}$$

where $\boldsymbol{\Xi}(t) = \boldsymbol{\Psi}(t) - \mathbf{WF}(t)$. From the steady-state solution in Eq. (7.1.25) it follows that the initial conditions for the transient solution are given by

$$\boldsymbol{\Xi}_0 = \boldsymbol{\Psi}(0) - \mathbf{WF}(0) = -\begin{bmatrix} \frac{55}{108} \\ \frac{5}{4} \end{bmatrix}$$

The constituent matrices for $\mathbf{P}$ are

$$\mathbf{Z}_{21} = \frac{1}{\lambda_1 - \lambda_2} (\lambda_1 \mathbf{U} - \mathbf{P}) = \begin{bmatrix} 0 & 1 \\ 0 & 1 \end{bmatrix}$$

$$\mathbf{Z}_{11} = \frac{1}{\lambda_2 - \lambda_1} (\lambda_2 \mathbf{U} - \mathbf{P}) = \begin{bmatrix} 1 & -1 \\ 0 & 0 \end{bmatrix}$$

and it follows that the transient solution is

$$\Xi(t) = e^{Pt}\Xi_0$$

or, numerically,

$$\Xi(t) = \begin{bmatrix} \xi_1(t) \\ \xi_2(t) \end{bmatrix} = -\begin{bmatrix} \frac{5}{4} \\ \frac{5}{4} \end{bmatrix} e^{-2t} + \begin{bmatrix} \frac{20}{27} \\ 0 \end{bmatrix} e^{-3t} \qquad (7.1.27)$$

In general, the functions required to generate an excitation vector of the form $\mathbf{E}(t) = \mathbf{K}_l t^l$ are

$$f_0(t) = 1$$
$$f_1(t) = t$$
$$\cdot \ \cdot \ \cdot \ \cdot \ \cdot$$
$$f_l(t) = t^l$$

and the corresponding differential equations are

$$\frac{d}{dt}\begin{bmatrix} f_l(t) \\ f_{l-1}(t) \\ \cdot \ \cdot \ \cdot \\ f_1(t) \\ f_0(t) \end{bmatrix} = \begin{bmatrix} 0 & l & 0 & \cdots & 0 \\ 0 & 0 & l-1 & \cdots & 0 \\ \cdot & \cdot & \cdot & \cdot & \cdot & \cdot & \cdot & \cdot \\ 0 & 0 & 0 & \cdots & 1 \\ 0 & 0 & 0 & \cdots & 0 \end{bmatrix}\begin{bmatrix} f_l(t) \\ f_{l-1}(t) \\ \cdot \ \cdot \ \cdot \\ f_1(t) \\ f_0(t) \end{bmatrix}$$

$$\begin{bmatrix} f_l(0) \\ f_{l-1}(0) \\ \cdot \ \cdot \ \cdot \\ f_1(0) \\ f_0(0) \end{bmatrix} = \begin{bmatrix} 0 \\ 0 \\ \cdot \ \cdot \ \cdot \\ 0 \\ 1 \end{bmatrix}$$

$$(7.1.28)$$

Since all the eigenvalues of the coefficient matrix $\mathbf{T}$ are zero, it follows that the given system

$$\Psi'(t) = \mathbf{P}\Psi(t) + \mathbf{Q}\mathbf{E}(t) \qquad (7.1.29)$$

has a steady-state response to a polynomial input if and only if all the eigenvalues of $\mathbf{P}$ are nonvanishing. This, of course, implies that $\mathbf{P}$ must be a nonsingular matrix. Further, from the form of the coefficient matrix $\mathbf{T}$ in Eqs. (7.1.28) it follows that the solution to the matrix equation

$$\mathbf{PW} - \mathbf{WT} = -\mathbf{QK} = \mathbf{Q}' \qquad (7.1.30)$$

is obtained from a set of l recursion equations of the form

$$\mathbf{W}_1 = \mathbf{P}^{-1}\mathbf{Q}_1'$$
$$\mathbf{W}_2 = \mathbf{P}^{-1}(\mathbf{Q}_2' + l\mathbf{W}_1)$$
$$\mathbf{W}_3 = \mathbf{P}^{-1}[\mathbf{Q}_3' + (l-1)\mathbf{W}_2] \qquad (7.1.31)$$
$$\cdot \ \cdot \ \cdot \ \cdot \ \cdot \ \cdot \ \cdot \ \cdot \ \cdot \ \cdot \ \cdot \ \cdot \ \cdot \ \cdot \ \cdot$$
$$\mathbf{W}_l = \mathbf{P}^{-1}(\mathbf{Q}_l' + \mathbf{W}_{l-1})$$

where $\mathbf{W}_i$ and $\mathbf{Q}_i'$ represent, respectively, the ith column of the matrices $\mathbf{W}$ and $\mathbf{Q}' = -\mathbf{QK}$.

PULSE RESPONSE

The pulse function in Fig. 7.1.2a can be viewed as the sum of two step functions as shown in Fig. 7.1.2b. The equation of this pulse is, of course,

$$e(t) = \begin{cases} 0 & \text{when } t < t_1 \text{ and } t > t_2 \\ k & \text{when } t_1 \leq t \leq t_2 \end{cases} \tag{7.1.32}$$

In most pulse-response studies, the width of the pulse is substantially less than some of the time constants, $1/\lambda_i$. Consequently, there is nothing to be gained by attempting to separate the transient and steady-state components of the solution. In fact it is more expedient to consider the solution in the form

$$\boldsymbol{\Psi}(t) = e^{\mathbf{P}t}\boldsymbol{\Psi}(0) + e^{\mathbf{P}t}\int_0^t e^{-\mathbf{P}\tau}\mathbf{Q}e(\tau)\,d\tau \tag{7.1.33}$$

If $\mathbf{P}$ is nonsingular, the integral can be evaluated explicitly for the $e(t)$ given in Eq. (7.1.32) and the solution is

(a)   For $0 \leq t \leq t_1$

$$\boldsymbol{\Psi}(t) = e^{\mathbf{P}t}\boldsymbol{\Psi}_0 \tag{7.1.34}$$

(b)   For $t_1 \leq t \leq t_2$

$$\boldsymbol{\Psi}(t) = e^{\mathbf{P}t}\boldsymbol{\Psi}_0 - k\mathbf{P}^{-1}(\mathbf{U} - e^{\mathbf{P}(t-t_1)})\mathbf{Q} \tag{7.1.35}\dagger$$

(c)   For $t \geq t_2$

$$\begin{aligned} \boldsymbol{\Psi}(t) &= e^{\mathbf{P}t}[\boldsymbol{\Psi}_0 - k\mathbf{P}^{-1}(e^{-\mathbf{P}t_2} - e^{-\mathbf{P}t_1})\mathbf{Q}] \\ &= e^{\mathbf{P}(t-t_2)}\boldsymbol{\Psi}(t_2) \end{aligned} \tag{7.1.36}$$

where

$$\boldsymbol{\Psi}(t_2) = e^{\mathbf{P}t_2}\boldsymbol{\Psi}_0 - k\mathbf{P}^{-1}(\mathbf{U} - e^{\mathbf{P}(t_2-t_1)})\mathbf{Q}$$

$\dagger$ Using the series expansion for $e^{\mathbf{P}t}$, the integral in Eq. (7.1.33) for $t_1 \leq t \leq t_2$ can be shown to be equal to $k\mathbf{P}^{-1}(e^{-\mathbf{P}t_1} - e^{-\mathbf{P}t})\mathbf{Q}$.

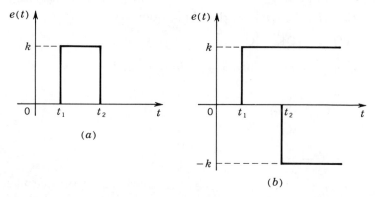

Fig. 7.1.2   (a) Pulse function; (b) pulse function as the sum of two step functions.

Example 7.1.3: Determine the current $i(t)$ in a series RL circuit as a function of time when excited by a voltage pulse of magnitude E and width $t_2 - t_1$. The initial value of the current $i(t)$ at $t = 0$ is zero.

Solution: The state equation is

$$\frac{d}{dt} i(t) = -\frac{R}{L} i(t) + \frac{1}{L} e(t)$$

and the solution is

(a) For $0 \leq t \leq t_1$

$$i(t) = 0$$

(b) For $t_1 \leq t \leq t_2$

$$i(t) = \frac{E}{R} (1 - e^{-(R/L)(t-t_1)}) \tag{7.1.37}$$

(c) For $t_2 \leq t$

$$i(t) = \frac{E}{R} e^{-(R/L)t} (e^{(R/L)t_2} - e^{(R/L)t_1}) \tag{7.1.38}$$

This solution is plotted in Fig. 7.1.3.

UNIT PULSE

In the special case where the area $k(t_2 - t_1)$ of the pulse in Fig. 7.1.2a is taken equal to unity, the pulse is called a *unit pulse*. If the width of the pulse is represented as $\delta = t_2 - t_1$ and the magnitude as $k = 1/\delta$, the pulse has unit area for any δ, t_2, and t_1. Further, if $\mathbf{\Psi}(0)$ is taken as zero and $t_1 = 0$, that is, the pulse occurs at $t = 0$, then the response characteristic given in Eq. (7.1.36) for $t_2 \leq t$ reduces to

$$\mathbf{\Psi}(t) = e^{\mathbf{P}(t-\delta)} \mathbf{\Psi}(\delta)$$

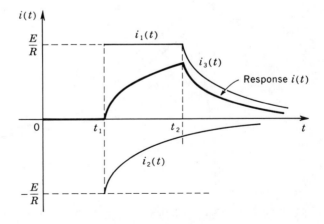

Fig. 7.1.3 Pulse response of the RL network.

where

$$\mathbf{\Psi}(\delta) = -\frac{1}{\delta}\mathbf{P}^{-1}(\mathbf{U} - e^{\mathbf{P}\delta})\mathbf{Q}$$

$$= -\frac{1}{\delta}\mathbf{P}^{-1}\left(\mathbf{U} - \mathbf{U} - \mathbf{P}\delta - \frac{\mathbf{P}^2\delta^2}{2!} - \cdots\right)\mathbf{Q}$$

$$= \left(\mathbf{U} + \frac{\mathbf{P}\delta}{2!} + \frac{\mathbf{P}^2\delta^2}{3!} + \cdots\right)\mathbf{Q} \qquad (7.1.39)$$

For δ sufficiently small, the expression for $\mathbf{\Psi}(\delta)$ in Eq. (7.1.39) can be approximated by the first term, and the solution is, approximately,

$$\mathbf{\Psi}(t) = e^{\mathbf{P}(t-\delta)}\mathbf{\Psi}(\delta) \approx e^{\mathbf{P}t}\mathbf{\Psi}(\delta) \approx e^{\mathbf{P}t}\mathbf{Q} \qquad (7.1.40)$$

When the width of the pulse is sufficiently small so that the approximation given in Eq. (7.1.40) is acceptable, the pulse is usually referred to as an "impulse" and the corresponding response as the "impulse response." By expanding $e^{\mathbf{P}t}$ in an infinite series before evaluating the integral in Eq. (7.1.33) it is possible to arrive at the approximation given in Eq. (7.1.40) even in the case where $\mathbf{P}$ is singular, i.e., if $\mathbf{P}$ has a zero eigenvalue.

Example 7.1.4: Let the amplitude and width of the pulse in Example 7.1.3 be $E = 1/\delta$ and $t_2 - t_1 = \delta$, respectively. Also, assume that the pulse occurs at the point $t = t_1 = 0$ and $i(0) = 0$. Consider the limit of the time solution as δ becomes progressively smaller.

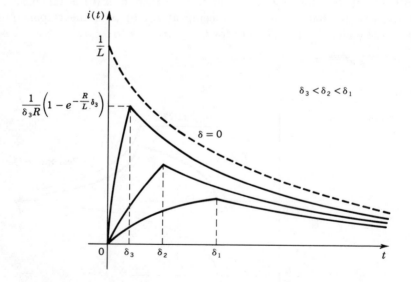

Fig. 7.1.4 Variation of solution in Eq. (7.1.42) with δ.

Solution: From Eq. (7.1.37) it follows that for $0 \leq t \leq \delta$

$$i(t) = \frac{1}{\delta R} (1 - e^{-(R/L)t})$$

from which

$$i(\delta) = \frac{1}{\delta R} (1 - e^{-(R/L)\delta}) \tag{7.1.41}$$

From Eq. (7.1.38) the solution for $\delta \leq t$ is

$$i(t) = \frac{1}{\delta R} (e^{-(R/L)(t-\delta)} - e^{-(R/L)t}) \tag{7.1.42}$$

This solution is sketched in Fig. 7.1.4 for various values of δ. Note that, in the limit as $\delta \to 0$, $i(\delta) \to 1/L$ and the solution for $t > 0$, in this limiting case, is

$$i(t) = \frac{1}{L} e^{-(R/L)t} \tag{7.1.43}$$

7.2 SINUSOIDAL - RESPONSE CHARACTERISTICS OF LINEAR SYSTEMS

The effectiveness of the sinusoidal excitation in performance studies is evident at least partially when it is recognized that, as shown in Chap. 1, any function $e(t)$ defined on a finite interval $-T/2 < t < T/2$ can be expanded in a Fourier series. Thus, because of the superposition property of linear time-invariant systems already cited, the response characteristics of any excitation function defined over a finite interval can be evaluated as the sum of the response characteristics to a set of sinusoidal signals.

For a general study of the sinusoidal response characteristics of linear systems, consider the system

$$\frac{d}{dt} \Psi(t) = \mathbf{P}\Psi(t) + \mathbf{Q}\mathbf{E}(t) \qquad \Psi(0) = \Psi_0 \tag{7.2.1}$$

$$\mathbf{R}(t) = \mathbf{M}\Psi(t) + \mathbf{N}\mathbf{E}(t) \tag{7.2.2}$$

where $\mathbf{R}(t)$ is a vector of signals measured somewhere in the system and is hereafter called the *output vector*. We shall consider the response of the state vector and the output vector to an input, or excitation, vector $\mathbf{E}(t)$ of order m with components $E_i \cos(\omega t + \theta_i)$, $i = 1, 2, \ldots, m$ [see Eq. (5.5.25)]. Note that each component in this vector is a cosine function of arbitrary magnitude E_i and phase angle θ_i but all are of the same frequency ω. This vector can be written as the sum of two complex functions of the form

$$\mathbf{E}(t) = \bar{\mathbf{E}}e^{j\omega t} + \hat{\bar{\mathbf{E}}}e^{-j\omega t} \tag{7.2.3}$$

where $\bar{\mathbf{E}}$ and $\hat{\mathbf{E}}$ are vectors of complex numbers $i = 1, 2, \ldots, m$ of $\bar{\mathbf{E}}$, with $\hat{\mathbf{E}}$ the complex conjugate of $\bar{\mathbf{E}}$. The components $E_i e^{j\theta_i}$ represent the magnitude and phase angle of the excitation signals. Alternatively, $\mathbf{E}(t)$ can be expanded as the sum of two orthogonal real functions

$$\mathbf{E}(t) = \mathbf{E}_1 \cos \omega t - \mathbf{E}_2 \sin \omega t \tag{7.2.4}$$

where the components of $\mathbf{E}_1$ and $\mathbf{E}_2$ are, respectively, $E_i \cos \theta_i$ and $E_i \sin \theta_i$, $i = 1, 2, \ldots, m$. The response characteristics to both these forms will be considered, the former being particularly useful and convenient in theoretical studies, the latter in machine computation, where complex algebra is usually inconvenient to work with.

Consider first the response of the system to the vector $\mathbf{E}(t)$ as given in Eq. (7.2.3). When this expression is substituted into Eq. (7.2.1), there results

$$\frac{d}{dt} \boldsymbol{\Psi}(t) = \mathbf{P}\boldsymbol{\Psi}(t) + \mathbf{Q}\bar{\mathbf{E}}e^{j\omega t} + \mathbf{Q}\hat{\mathbf{E}}e^{-j\omega t}$$

which we shall write simply as

$$\frac{d}{dt} \boldsymbol{\Psi}(t) = \mathbf{P}\boldsymbol{\Psi}(t) + \bar{\mathbf{Q}}_1 e^{j\omega t} + \hat{\mathbf{Q}}_1 e^{-j\omega t} \tag{7.2.5}$$

where $\bar{\mathbf{Q}}_1$ and $\hat{\mathbf{Q}}_1$ are complex conjugate vectors. The functions $f_1(t) = e^{j\omega t}$ and $f_2(t) = e^{-j\omega t}$ can be generated as solutions to the differential equations

$$\frac{d}{dt} \begin{bmatrix} f_1(t) \\ f_2(t) \end{bmatrix} = \begin{bmatrix} j\omega & 0 \\ 0 & -j\omega \end{bmatrix} \begin{bmatrix} f_1(t) \\ f_2(t) \end{bmatrix} \qquad \begin{bmatrix} f_1(0) \\ f_2(0) \end{bmatrix} = \begin{bmatrix} 1 \\ 1 \end{bmatrix}$$

or

$$\frac{d}{dt} \mathbf{F}(t) = \mathbf{T}\mathbf{F}(t) \qquad \mathbf{F}(0) = \mathbf{F}_0 \tag{7.2.6}$$

The given system of nonhomogeneous differential equations in Eq. (7.2.5) are therefore transformed to a homogeneous equivalent by the transformation

$$\boldsymbol{\Xi}(t) = \boldsymbol{\Psi}(t) - \mathbf{W}\mathbf{F}(t) \tag{7.2.7}$$

where $\mathbf{W}$ is a solution to the matrix equation

$$\mathbf{P}\mathbf{W} - \mathbf{W}\mathbf{T} = -[\bar{\mathbf{Q}}_1 \;\vdots\; \hat{\mathbf{Q}}_1] \tag{7.2.8}$$

and the homogeneous equivalent system is

$$\frac{d}{dt} \boldsymbol{\Xi}(t) = \mathbf{P}\boldsymbol{\Xi}(t) \qquad \boldsymbol{\Xi}_0 = \boldsymbol{\Psi}_0 - \mathbf{W}\mathbf{F}_0 \tag{7.2.9}$$

Since $\mathbf{T}$ is diagonal and $\mathbf{W}$ contains only two columns $\mathbf{W}_1$ and $\mathbf{W}_2$, Eq. (7.2.8) reduces to two systems of equations

$$\mathbf{PW}_1 - j\omega\mathbf{W}_1 = -\bar{\mathbf{Q}}_1$$

or

$$(j\omega\mathbf{U} - \mathbf{P})\mathbf{W}_1 = \bar{\mathbf{Q}}_1 \tag{7.2.10}$$

and

$$\mathbf{PW}_2 + j\omega\mathbf{W}_2 = -\hat{\mathbf{Q}}_1$$

or

$$(-j\omega\mathbf{U} - \mathbf{P})\mathbf{W}_2 = \hat{\mathbf{Q}}_1 \tag{7.2.11}$$

If $\pm j\omega$ are not eigenvalues of $\mathbf{P}$, then Eqs. (7.2.10) and (7.2.11) have the solutions

$$\mathbf{W}_1 = \bar{\boldsymbol{\Psi}} = (j\omega\mathbf{U} - \mathbf{P})^{-1}\bar{\mathbf{Q}}_1 \tag{7.2.12}$$

and

$$\mathbf{W}_2 = \hat{\boldsymbol{\Psi}} = (-j\omega\mathbf{U} - \mathbf{P})^{-1}\hat{\mathbf{Q}}_1 \tag{7.2.13}$$

where $\bar{\boldsymbol{\Psi}}$ and $\hat{\boldsymbol{\Psi}}$ are complex conjugate vectors and the steady-state solution has been established as

$$\boldsymbol{\Psi}_s(t) = \mathbf{WF}(t) = \bar{\boldsymbol{\Psi}}e^{j\omega t} + \hat{\boldsymbol{\Psi}}e^{-j\omega t} = \begin{bmatrix} \psi_1 e^{j\phi_1} \\ \psi_2 e^{j\phi_2} \\ \cdot \\ \cdot \\ \cdot \\ \psi_n e^{j\phi_n} \end{bmatrix} e^{j\omega t} + \begin{bmatrix} \psi_1 e^{-j\phi_1} \\ \psi_2 e^{-j\phi_2} \\ \cdot \\ \cdot \\ \cdot \\ \psi_n e^{-j\phi_n} \end{bmatrix} e^{-j\omega t} \tag{7.2.14}$$

The vector of complex numbers $\bar{\boldsymbol{\Psi}} = \mathbf{W}_1$ *obtained from the solution of Eq. (7.2.10) establishes the magnitudes and phase angles of the sinusoidally time-varying state variables.* Once this vector with complex number entries $\bar{\psi}_i = \psi_i e^{j\phi_i}$ is established, the steady-state solution for each of the state variables is known—each is a cosine function with magnitude ψ_i and phase angle ϕ_i.

Since the output, or response, variables $\mathbf{R}(t)$ are linear combinations of the state variables, it follows immediately that the entries of $\mathbf{R}(t)$ are also cosine functions with magnitudes and phase angles represented by the vector of complex numbers

$$\begin{aligned} \bar{\mathbf{R}} = \mathbf{M}\bar{\boldsymbol{\Psi}} &= \mathbf{N}\bar{\mathbf{E}} + \mathbf{M}(j\omega\mathbf{U} - \mathbf{P})^{-1}\bar{\mathbf{Q}}_1 + \mathbf{N}\bar{\mathbf{E}} \\ &= \mathbf{M}(j\omega\mathbf{U} - \mathbf{P})^{-1}\mathbf{Q}\bar{\mathbf{E}} + \mathbf{N}\bar{\mathbf{E}} \end{aligned} \tag{7.2.15}$$

Note finally that the inverse required to establish the sinusoidal steady-state solution is the inverse of $\lambda\mathbf{U} - \mathbf{P}$, with λ replaced by $j\omega$. These results are of such fundamental and extensive importance that they are worth summarizing in the form of a theorem.

Theorem 7.2.1:   Let the state equations of a linear time-invariant system be given in the form of Eq. (7.2.1), with the excitation vector given in the form of Eq. (7.2.3).   A sinusoidal steady-state solution exists for all frequencies ω if and only if the eigenvalues of $\mathbf{P}$ are in the left half of the λ plane.   The steady-state values of the magnitude and phase angle of each of the state variables are given by Eq. (7.2.14), where the complex state vector $\bar{\mathbf{\Psi}}$ is related to the complex excitation vector $\bar{\mathbf{E}}$ by the solution of the matrix equation†

$$(\lambda \mathbf{U} - \mathbf{P})\bar{\mathbf{\Psi}} = \mathbf{Q}\bar{\mathbf{E}} \qquad \text{with } \lambda = j\omega \tag{7.2.16}$$

Further, the steady-state characteristics for the response vector

$$\mathbf{R}(t) = \mathbf{M}\mathbf{\Psi}(t) + \mathbf{N}\mathbf{E}(t)$$

are given in the form

$$\mathbf{R}(t) = \bar{\mathbf{R}}e^{j\omega t} + \hat{\mathbf{R}}e^{-j\omega t}$$

where

$$\bar{\mathbf{R}} = \mathbf{M}(\lambda \mathbf{U} - \mathbf{P})^{-1}\mathbf{Q}\bar{\mathbf{E}} + \mathbf{N}\bar{\mathbf{E}} \qquad \text{with } \lambda = j\omega \tag{7.2.17}$$

Example 7.2.1:   Determine the steady-state displacement of the spring in the mechanical system shown in Fig. 7.2.1 when excited by a sinusoidal displacement driver $\delta_0(t) = 0.1 \cos(\omega t + 30°)$, where $\omega = 2\pi$.   The system parameters are $M_1 = 0.1$, $K_2 = 5$, and $B_3 = 1$.   Determine also the transient component of the state vector corresponding to zero initial state.

† Note that this equation is obtained operationally from the state equations by replacing the derivative operator d/dt by $\lambda = j\omega$ and also the excitation and state vectors by complex-number vectors $\bar{\mathbf{E}}$ and $\bar{\mathbf{\Psi}}$, respectively.

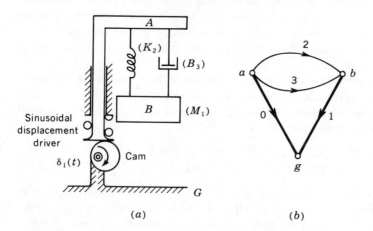

Fig. 7.2.1   (a) Mechanical system; b) system graph.

Solution: The state equations are

$$\frac{d}{dt}\begin{bmatrix} \dot\delta_1(t) \\ f_2(t) \end{bmatrix} = \begin{bmatrix} -B_3/M_1 & 1/M_1 \\ -K_2 & 0 \end{bmatrix}\begin{bmatrix} \dot\delta_1(t) \\ f_2(t) \end{bmatrix} + \begin{bmatrix} B_3/M_1 \\ K_2 \end{bmatrix}\dot\delta_0(t) \qquad (7.2.18)$$

The displacement of the spring in terms of the state variable is obtained directly from the system graph as

$$\delta_2(t) = \delta_0(t) - \delta_1(t) \qquad (7.2.19)$$

The excitation function is

$$\dot\delta_0(t) = -0.1\omega \sin (\omega t + 30°) = \bar E_0 e^{j\omega t} + \bar E_0 e^{-j\omega t}$$

where

$$\bar E_0 = j\omega 0.05 e^{j\,30°} \qquad (7.2.20)$$

From Theorem 7.2.1 the magnitude and phase angle of the steady-state solution is given by

$$\overline{\boldsymbol\Psi} = \begin{bmatrix} \bar E_1 \\ \bar F_2 \end{bmatrix} = \begin{bmatrix} j\omega + B_3/M_1 & -1/M_1 \\ +K_2 & j\omega \end{bmatrix}^{-1}\begin{bmatrix} B_3/M_1 \\ K_2 \end{bmatrix}\bar E_0$$

$$= \frac{\bar E_0}{D(j\omega)}\begin{bmatrix} B_3 j\omega + K_2 \\ M_1 K_2 j\omega \end{bmatrix} = \begin{bmatrix} 0.217 e^{j\,91°27'} \\ 0.156 e^{j\,129°27'} \end{bmatrix}$$

where

$$D(j\omega) = M_1(j\omega)^2 + B_3 j\omega + K_2$$

The steady-state solution for the velocity of the mass is

$$\dot\delta_1(t) = \bar E_1 e^{j\omega t} + \hat{\bar E}_1 e^{-j\omega t}$$

and the steady-state displacement is

$$\delta_1(t) = \frac{\bar E_1}{j\omega}e^{j\omega t} + \frac{\hat{\bar E}_1}{-j\omega}e^{-j\omega t}$$

The spring displacement as obtained by substituting this solution in Eq. (7.2.19) is

$$\delta_2(t) = \frac{\bar E_2}{j\omega}e^{j\omega t} + \frac{\hat{\bar E}_2}{-j\omega}$$

where

$$\bar E_2 = \bar E_0 - \bar E_1 = j\omega 0.05 e^{j\,30°} - 0.217 e^{j\,91°27'} = 0.0312 e^{j\,129°27'}$$

It follows, therefore, that the solution in sinusoidal form is

$$\delta_2(t) = 0.0624 \cos (\omega t + 129°27') \qquad \omega = 2\pi$$

and

$$f_2(t) = 0.312 \cos (\omega t + 129°27')$$

The transient component of the solution is obtained from the solution of the homogeneous system

$$\frac{d}{dt}\begin{bmatrix} \xi_1(t) \\ \xi_2(t) \end{bmatrix} = \begin{bmatrix} -B_3/M_1 & 1/M_1 \\ -K_2 & 0 \end{bmatrix}\begin{bmatrix} \xi_1(t) \\ \xi_2(t) \end{bmatrix}$$

with

$$\begin{bmatrix} \xi_1(0) \\ \xi_2(0) \end{bmatrix} = \begin{bmatrix} \dot{\delta}_1(0) \\ f_2(0) \end{bmatrix} - \begin{bmatrix} 0.217 \cos 91°27' \\ 0.312 \cos 129°27' \end{bmatrix} \cong \begin{bmatrix} 0.0004 \\ 0.198 \end{bmatrix}$$

The characteristic polynomial is

$$D(\lambda) = M_1\lambda^1 + B_3\lambda + K_2 = 0.1\lambda^2 + \lambda + 5$$
$$= (\lambda - \lambda_1)(\lambda - \lambda_2)$$

where

$$\lambda_1 = -5 + j5$$
$$\lambda_2 = \hat{\lambda}_1 = -5 - j5$$

The constituent matrices are

$$\mathbf{Z}_{11} = \hat{\mathbf{Z}}_{21} = \frac{1}{-2j}\begin{bmatrix} 1 - j & -2 \\ 1 & -(1 + j) \end{bmatrix}$$

The transient component of the solution is therefore

$$\boldsymbol{\Xi}(t) = \mathbf{Z}_{11}\boldsymbol{\Xi}_0 e^{\lambda_1 t} + \hat{\mathbf{Z}}_{11}\boldsymbol{\Xi}_0 e^{\hat{\lambda}_1 t}$$
$$= \begin{bmatrix} 0.392e^{-5t} & \cos(5t - 90°) \\ 0.2e^{-5t} & \cos(5t - 45°) \end{bmatrix}$$

Consider now the form of the response of the system when the vector $\mathbf{E}(t)$ is written in the form given in Eq. (7.2.4). When this expression is substituted into Eq. (7.2.1), there results

$$\frac{d}{dt}\boldsymbol{\Psi}(t) = \mathbf{P}\boldsymbol{\Psi}(t) + [\mathbf{QE}_1 \vdots -\mathbf{QE}_2]\begin{bmatrix} \cos \omega t \\ \sin \omega t \end{bmatrix} \qquad (7.2.21)$$

From the time derivatives of the excitation functions it follows that they are generated as the solutions to the differential equations

$$\begin{bmatrix} f_1(t) \\ f_2(t) \end{bmatrix} = \begin{bmatrix} 0 & -\omega \\ \omega & 0 \end{bmatrix}\begin{bmatrix} f_1(t) \\ f_2(t) \end{bmatrix} \qquad \begin{bmatrix} f_1(0) \\ f_2(0) \end{bmatrix} = \begin{bmatrix} 1 \\ 0 \end{bmatrix}$$

or

$$\frac{d}{dt}\mathbf{F}(t) = \mathbf{TF}(t)$$

and the given system is transformed to a homogeneous system by setting

$$\boldsymbol{\Xi}(t) = \boldsymbol{\Psi}(t) - \mathbf{WF}(t) \qquad (7.2.22)$$

where now $\mathbf{W}$ is the solution to the system of equations

$$\mathbf{PW} - \mathbf{WT} = -[\mathbf{QE}_1 \vdots -\mathbf{QE}_2] \qquad (7.2.23)$$

Since $\mathbf{T}$ is skew-symmetric and $\mathbf{W}$ contains only two columns, a solution of Eq. (7.2.23) reduces to the solution of the two systems of equations

$$\mathbf{PW}_1 - \omega\mathbf{W}_2 = -\mathbf{QE}_1 \tag{7.2.24}$$
$$\mathbf{PW}_2 - \omega\mathbf{W}_1 = \mathbf{QE}_2 \tag{7.2.25}$$

where $\mathbf{W}_1$ and $\mathbf{W}_2$ represent, respectively, the first and second columns of the matrix $\mathbf{W}$. Solving Eq. (7.2.25) for $\mathbf{W}_1$ and substituting the result into Eq. (7.2.24) gives

$$(\omega^2\mathbf{U} + \mathbf{P}^2)\mathbf{W}_2 = \omega\mathbf{QE}_1 + \mathbf{PQE}_2 \tag{7.2.26}$$

Similarly, solving Eq. (7.2.24) for $\mathbf{W}_2$ and substituting the result into Eq. (7.2.25) gives

$$(\omega^2\mathbf{U} + \mathbf{P}^2)\mathbf{W}_1 = \omega\mathbf{QE}_2 - \mathbf{PQE}_1 \tag{7.2.27}$$

Again, if $\pm j\omega$ are not eigenvalues of $\mathbf{P}$, then Eqs. (7.2.26) and (7.2.27) have solutions

$$\mathbf{W}_2 = (\omega^2\mathbf{U} + \mathbf{P}^2)^{-1}(\omega\mathbf{QE}_1 + \mathbf{PQE}_2) \tag{7.2.28}$$

and

$$\mathbf{W}_1 = (\omega^2\mathbf{U} + \mathbf{P}^2)^{-1}(\omega\mathbf{QE}_2 - \mathbf{PQE}_1) \tag{7.2.29}$$

and the steady-state solution is established as

$$\mathbf{\Psi}_s(t) = \mathbf{WF}(t) = \mathbf{W}_1 \cos \omega t + \mathbf{W}_2 \sin \omega t \tag{7.2.30}$$

The fundamental advantage of this latter technique over the former, of course, is that the algebra involves only real numbers and is therefore more suited to machine implementation than is the technique involving the complex-number forms. It is to be noted that the order of the inverse required to evaluate the steady-state solution in either technique is the same.

7.3 FREQUENCY - RESPONSE CHARACTERISTICS

The coefficient matrix

$$\mathbf{M}(\lambda\mathbf{U} - \mathbf{P})^{-1}\mathbf{Q} + \mathbf{N} \qquad \lambda = j\omega$$

in Eq. (7.2.17), relating the complex response vector $\bar{\mathbf{R}}$ to the complex excitation vector $\bar{\mathbf{E}}$, is called the *complex transfer matrix*. This coefficient matrix relates directly the magnitude and phase angle of the response variables to the magnitude, phase angle, and frequency of the excitation vector, and therefore performs a central role in the study of sinusoidal steady-state frequency-response characteristics. In the special case where the response and excitation vectors consist of only one entry each, the ratio of the response to the excitation is the scalar

$$\frac{\bar{R}}{\bar{E}} = \mathbf{M}(\lambda\mathbf{U} - \mathbf{P})^{-1}\mathbf{Q} + N$$

$$= \frac{1}{m(\lambda)}\mathbf{M}\mathbf{C}(\lambda)\mathbf{Q} + N \tag{7.3.1}$$

Since the entries in the reduced adjoint matrix $\mathbf{C}(\lambda)$ of $\lambda\mathbf{U} - \mathbf{P}$ are polynomials in λ, $\mathbf{M}$ and $\mathbf{Q}$ are row and column matrices, respectively, and $m(\lambda)$ is the minimal polynomial of $\mathbf{P}$, it follows that the ratio $\bar{R}/\bar{E}$ is a rational function of $\lambda = j\omega$, that is, a ratio of polynomials in λ. A plot of the magnitude and angle of this ratio as a function of $\lambda = j\omega$ is called a *frequency-response* characteristic of the system.

To show an important feature of frequency-response characteristics, consider the simple second-order systems shown in Fig. 7.3.1. The state-model equations for these systems are

$$\frac{d}{dt}\begin{bmatrix} v_C(t) \\ i_L(t) \end{bmatrix} = \begin{bmatrix} 0 & 1/C \\ -1/L & -R/L \end{bmatrix}\begin{bmatrix} v_C(t) \\ i_L(t) \end{bmatrix} + \begin{bmatrix} 0 \\ 1/L \end{bmatrix}v(t)$$
$$i(t) = i_L(t) \tag{7.3.2}$$

$$\frac{d}{dt}\begin{bmatrix} f_K(t) \\ \dot{\delta}_M(t) \end{bmatrix} = \begin{bmatrix} 0 & K \\ -1/M & -B/M \end{bmatrix}\begin{bmatrix} f_K(t) \\ \dot{\delta}_M(t) \end{bmatrix} + \begin{bmatrix} 0 \\ 1/M \end{bmatrix}f(t)$$
$$\dot{\delta}(t) = \dot{\delta}_M(t) \tag{7.3.3}$$

and

$$\frac{dt}{dt}\begin{bmatrix} p_C(t) \\ \dot{g}_M(t) \end{bmatrix} = \begin{bmatrix} 0 & 1/C_h \\ -1/M_h & -R_h/M_h \end{bmatrix}\begin{bmatrix} p_C(t) \\ \dot{g}_M(t) \end{bmatrix} + \begin{bmatrix} 0 \\ 1/M_h \end{bmatrix}p(t)$$
$$\dot{g}(t) = \dot{g}_M(t) \tag{7.3.4}$$

When the driving functions $v(t)$, $f(t)$, and $p(t)$ between terminals A and B are sinusoidal functions of angular frequency ω, the corresponding steady-

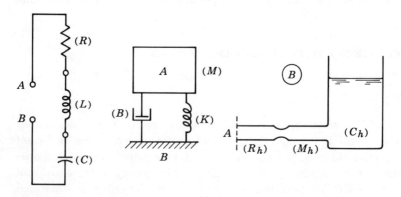

Fig. 7.3.1 Electrical, mechanical, and hydraulic systems possessing resonant characteristics.

state response characteristics are given by the complex functions

$$\bar{I} = \frac{\bar{V}}{R + j(\omega L - 1/\omega C)}$$
$$\dot{\bar{\Delta}} = \frac{\bar{F}}{B + j(\omega M - K/\omega)} \tag{7.3.5}$$
$$\dot{\bar{G}} = \frac{\bar{P}}{R_h + j(\omega M_h - 1/\omega C_h)}$$

In the cases of the electrical and hydraulic systems the complex numbers $R + j(\omega_L - 1/\omega C)$ and $R_h + j(\omega M_h - 1/\omega C_h)$ are called the *complex impedances* of the two-terminal component, since they represent the ratios of the complex numbers $\bar{V}/\bar{I}$ and $\bar{P}/\dot{\bar{G}}$. The complex number $B + j(\omega M - k/\omega)$ is called the *complex admittance* of the two-terminal mechanical component.

In general, if the scalar response variable $\bar{R}$ is an across variable and the scalar excitation variable $\bar{E}$ a through variable, the ratio is called the *complex impedance* of the system. The ratio is further classified as a *driving-point*, or *transfer*, impedance, depending upon whether $\bar{R}$ and $\bar{E}$ are associated with the same pair of terminals or distinct pairs. On the other hand, if $\bar{R}$ is a through variable and $\bar{E}$ an across variable, then the ratio is called an *admittance*, with the similar designations driving-point and transfer admittances, depending upon whether $\bar{R}$ and $\bar{E}$ are associated with the same or distinct terminal pairs.

At certain frequencies the complex admittance and impedance coefficients become real; i.e., the imaginary component vanishes. The frequency at which this occurs is called the *resonant frequency* and is represented by the symbol ω_0. Thus, the resonant frequencies of the three systems characterized by Eqs. (7.3.2) to (7.3.4) are, respectively,

$$\omega_0 = \frac{1}{\sqrt{LC}}$$
$$\omega_0 = \sqrt{\frac{K}{M}} \tag{7.3.6}$$
$$\omega_0 = \frac{1}{\sqrt{M_h C_h}}$$

Since the magnitudes of the denominators in Eqs. (7.3.5) are minimum at resonant frequency, the resonant point is also characterized as the frequency at which the magnitude of the response function is maximum.

To study more carefully the properties of the response functions at and near the resonant frequency, let the relations in Eqs. (7.3.5) be represented by an equation of the form

$$\bar{R}(\omega) = \frac{\bar{E}}{a + j(\omega b - 1/\omega c)} \tag{7.3.7}$$

where a, b, and c are positive real constants. This implies, of course, that the coefficient matrix in the corresponding state model is of the form

$$\begin{bmatrix} 0 & 1/c \\ -1/b & -a/b \end{bmatrix} \tag{7.3.8}$$

In discussing the properties of $\bar{R}(\omega)$ it is convenient to take $\bar{E}$ as a real number† E and to define the *normalized complex response function* as

$$\bar{R}_N(\omega) = \frac{\bar{R}(\omega)a}{E} \tag{7.3.9}$$

and the *normalized frequency* as

$$u = \frac{\omega}{\omega_0} \tag{7.3.10}$$

where $\omega_0 = 1/\sqrt{bc}$ is the resonant frequency. When normalized in this manner, the response function in Eq. (7.3.7) becomes

$$\bar{R}_N(u) = \frac{1}{1 + jQ(u - 1/u)} \tag{7.3.11}$$

where

$$Q = \omega_0 \frac{b}{a} \quad \text{or} \quad Q = \frac{1}{ac\omega_0}$$

The magnitude of the normalized response function is

$$R_N(u) = |\bar{R}_N(u)| = \frac{1}{\sqrt{1 + Q^2(u - 1/u)^2}} \tag{7.3.12}$$

and the phase angle is

$$\theta(u) = -\arctan Q\left(u - \frac{1}{u}\right) \tag{7.3.13}$$

These response functions are plotted in Fig. 7.3.2b. However, a more generally useful plot is obtained when we first define a change of variable on the normalized frequency by setting

$$u = e^{\Omega} \tag{7.3.14}$$

or

$$\Omega = \ln u \tag{7.3.15}$$

and consider Ω as the independent variable for the plots.

† Since, in general, $e(t) = E \cos(\omega t + \Phi)$, to take $\bar{E}$ as a real number is identical to taking $\Phi = 0$.

Since in Eqs. (7.3.12) and (7.3.13)

$$u - \frac{1}{u} = e^{\Omega} - e^{-\Omega} = 2 \sinh \Omega \qquad (7.3.16)$$

the response functions with Ω as the argument take on the form

$$R_N(\Omega) = \frac{1}{\sqrt{1 + 4Q^2 \sinh^2 \Omega}} \qquad (7.3.17)$$

and

$$\theta(\Omega) = -\arctan (2Q \sinh \Omega) \qquad (7.3.18)$$

The corresponding plots are shown in Fig. 7.3.2a. Note that the plot of $\theta(\Omega)$ is symmetric with respect to the origin and also that the plot of $R_N(\Omega)$ is symmetric about the vertical axis. Consequently, if we draw a horizontal line at *any* level to intersect the $R_N(\Omega)$ curves, as indicated, the points of intersection Ω_1 and Ω_2 are related by

$$\Omega_1 = -\Omega_2$$

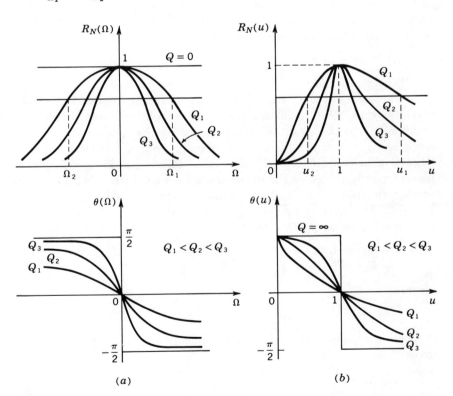

Fig. 7.3.2 Normalized response functions in Eqs. (7.3.12) and (7.3.13) as a function of (a) $\Omega = \ln u$ and (b) $u = \omega/\omega_0$.

Since $\Omega = \ln u$, we have

$$\ln u_1 = -\ln u_2$$

or

$$\ln u_2 u_1 = 0$$

which implies that the product of the normalized frequencies corresponding to these points is unity, i.e.,

$$u_2 u_1 = 1 \tag{7.3.19}$$

Also, since the normalized frequency is defined as $u = \omega/\omega_0$, the geometric mean of the angular frequencies at these two points is equal to the resonant frequency, i.e.,

$$\omega_1 \omega_2 = \omega_0{}^2 \tag{7.3.20}$$

Let it be emphasized that these relations apply to every pair of points defined by a horizontal intersection of $R_N(\Omega)$. However, the points of intersection between $R_N(\Omega)$ and the horizontal line drawn at a height equal to $1/\sqrt{2} = 0.707$ takes on special significance in characterizing frequency-response characteristics. If we let these intersection points be ω_1 and ω_2, then the difference

$$\Delta\omega = \omega_1 - \omega_2 = (u_1 - u_2)\omega_0 \tag{7.3.21}$$

is called the *bandwidth*.

The values of the bandwidth and the resonant frequency are used extensively as measures of the frequency-response characteristics of a system. These two quantities uniquely specify the complete frequency-response characteristics of any second-order system of the type under discussion in this section. To show that this is indeed the case, it is necessary only to derive the expression showing Q in Eq. (7.3.11) as an explicit function of $\Delta\omega$ and ω_0. This relation can be developed from Eq. (7.3.17). Letting Ω_1 and $\Omega_2 = -\Omega_1$ represent the points of intersection of the curve $R_N(\Omega)$ with the horizontal line $R_N = 1/\sqrt{2}$, we have

$$1 + 4Q^2 \sinh^2 \Omega_1 = 2$$
$$1 + 4Q^2 \sinh^2 \Omega_2 = 2 \tag{7.3.22}$$

where

$$\Omega_1 = -\Omega_2$$

A solution to these two simultaneous equations for $\sinh \Omega_1$ and $\sinh \Omega_2$ gives

$$\sinh \Omega_1 = \frac{1}{2Q}$$
$$\sinh \Omega_2 = -\frac{1}{2Q} \tag{7.3.23}$$

But, by definition,

$$u_1 = \frac{\omega_1}{\omega_0} = e^{\Omega_1} \quad \text{and} \quad u_2 = \frac{\omega_2}{\omega_0} = e^{\Omega_2}$$

and Eqs. (7.3.23) reduce to

$$u_1 = \frac{1}{2Q} + \sqrt{1 + \left(\frac{1}{2Q}\right)^2}$$

$$u_2 = -\frac{1}{2Q} + \sqrt{1 + \left(\frac{1}{2Q}\right)^2}$$

(7.3.24)

Therefore, the bandwidth as a function of Q is

$$\Delta\omega = \omega_1 - \omega_2 = \omega_0(u_1 - u_2) = \frac{\omega_0}{Q}$$

(7.3.25)

from which

$$Q = \frac{\omega_0}{\Delta\omega}$$

(7.3.26)

The curious reader should inquire as to why the line drawn at the level of $1/\sqrt{2}$ in Fig. 7.3.2, rather than any one of several other lines, should be used to define the bandwidth. Certainly any other line could have been used. The reason for selecting the horizontal line at the level $R_N = 1/\sqrt{2}$ is because it describes the half-power points. To show this, consider the average power at any angular frequency ω. From the definition of average power we have

$$P_{\text{avg}}(\omega) = R(\omega)E \cos\theta = \frac{E^2}{a} R_N(\omega) \cos\theta$$

$$= \frac{E^2}{a} \frac{\cos\theta}{\sqrt{1 + 4Q^2 \sinh^2 \Omega}}$$

(7.3.27)

But, since

$$\cos\theta = \frac{1}{\sqrt{1 + \tan^2\theta}} = \frac{1}{\sqrt{1 + 4Q^2 \sinh^2 \Omega}}$$

(7.3.28)

then

$$P_{\text{avg}}(\omega) = \frac{E^2/a}{1 + 4Q^2 \sinh^2 \Omega}$$

(7.3.29)

For $\omega = \omega_0$, we have $u - 1/u = 0$ or $\sinh\Omega = 0$, and therefore

$$P_{\text{avg}}(\omega_0) = \frac{E^2}{a}$$

Hence, Eq. (7.3.29) can be written as

$$P_{\text{avg}}(\omega) = \frac{P_{\text{avg}}(\omega_0)}{1 + 4Q^2 \sinh^2 \Omega}$$

(7.3.30)

From the above equations the average power $P_{avg}(\omega)$ will be half of $P_{avg}(\omega_0)$ when

$$1 + 4Q^2 \sinh^2 \Omega = 2 \tag{7.3.31}$$

which is identical with Eqs. (7.3.22). Therefore, the solution of Eq. (7.3.31) corresponds to the intersection of the resonance curve with a horizontal line with the height $1/\sqrt{2}$.

Note that at the frequencies corresponding to the half-power points, from Eq. (7.3.28),

$$\cos \theta = \frac{1}{\sqrt{2}}$$

or

$$\theta = \pm 45°$$

i.e., there is a phase shift of $\pm 45°$ between the excitation function and response function at the half-power points.[†] From Eq. (7.3.25) it is evident that the bandwidth decreases as the value of $Q = \omega_0(b/a)$ increases. From Fig. 7.3.2 it is again evident that a low value for the bandwidth implies a "sharp" resonance curve. For this reason Q is also a useful parameter in discussing the characteristics of resonant systems and is called the *quality factor*, or *selectivity*, of the system.

From the definition of Q and the expression for the bandwidth, it follows that in terms of the coefficients a and b in Eq. (7.3.7) the bandwidth is in general

$$\Delta\omega = \frac{a}{b}$$

or for the electrical network of Fig. 7.3.1 $\Delta\omega = R/L$, for the mechanical system $\Delta\omega = B/M$, and for the hydraulic system $\Delta\omega = R_h/M_h$.

To show how the frequency-response characteristic varies with the bandwidth $\Delta\omega = a/b$, consider the actual (nonnormalized) magnitude of the response function. From Eqs. (7.3.7) and (7.3.11), we have

$$R(u) = |\bar{R}(u)| = \frac{(1/a)E}{\sqrt{1 + (\omega_0^2 b^2/a^2)(u - 1/u)^2}} \tag{7.3.32}$$

This curve as a function of the normalized frequency u and as a function of $\Omega = \ln u$ is plotted in Fig. 7.3.3 for several values of $a = \omega_0(b/Q)$. From these plots we see that, as $a \to 0$ $(Q \to \infty)$, the magnitude of the unnormalized response function increases without bound at the resonance point. The condition $a = 0$ corresponds to:

1. $R = 0$ for electrical systems.
2. $B = 0$ for mechanical systems.
3. $R_h = 0$ for hydraulic systems.

[†] $\theta = -45°$ corresponds to u_1, whereas $\theta = +45°$ corresponds to u_2.

Such systems are called *lossless*, or *conservative*, systems, since the expression for the average power in Eq. (7.3.29) vanishes identically.   Note that in this case, since the eigenvalues of the matrix in Eq. (7.3.8) are $\mp j(1/\sqrt{bc}) = \mp j\omega_0$, Eqs. (7.2.24) and (7.2.25) have no solutions; i.e., the response is not defined at this frequency.   Therefore, lossless systems (systems containing only L and C, M and K, or M_h and C_h components) always have discontinuous frequency-response characteristics; i.e., at certain frequencies the magnitude of the response function increases without bound, and the phase characteristic "jumps" from one value to another.

Example 7.3.1:   The element values in the electric circuit of Fig. 7.3.1 are given as $R = 0.1$ ohm, $L = 1$ μhenry, and $C = 25$ $\mu\mu$f.   Determine the resonance frequency and bandwidth for this circuit.

Solution: Since

$$\omega_0 = \frac{1}{\sqrt{LC}} = \frac{1}{\sqrt{10^{-6} \times 25 \times 10^{-12}}} = \frac{10^9}{5}$$

then the resonance frequency is

$$f_0 = \frac{\omega_0}{2\pi} = \frac{10^9}{10\pi} \cong 31.8 \times 10^6 \text{ cps}$$

$$= 31.8 \text{ Mc}$$

The quality factor of the circuit is

$$Q = \frac{L\omega_0}{R} = \frac{10^{-6} \times \frac{1}{5} \times 10^9}{0.1} = 2,000$$

which represents a very *selective* circuit.   From Eq. (7.3.25), the bandwidth in radians per second is

$$\Delta\omega = \frac{\omega_0}{Q} = \frac{\frac{1}{5} \times 10^9}{2 \times 10^3} = 10^5 \text{ rps}$$

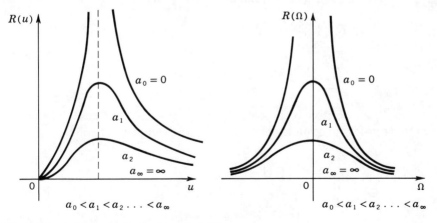

Fig. 7.3.3 Actual magnitude characteristics.

or, in cycles per second, is

$$\Delta f = \frac{\Delta \omega}{2\pi} = 15.92 \times 10^3 \text{ cps}$$

$$\cong 16 \text{ kc}$$

For other than simple second-order systems, frequency-response characteristics are usually plotted in terms of the logarithm of the magnitude of the ratio of the response function to the excitation function and as a function of the logarithm of the frequency (log ω). As we shall see, this technique allows one to sketch rapidly the form of the response characteristics for even high-order systems. Such logarithmic plots are often called *Bode plots* after their originator and were previously introduced in Sec. 2.4 in conjunction with the measured frequency-response characteristics of two-terminal components described by first-order differential equations. The techniques discussed here represent extensions of those concepts.

Consider a transfer function of the general form

$$G(\lambda) = \frac{\bar{R}}{\bar{E}} = \frac{P_m(\lambda)}{Q_n(\lambda)} = \frac{a_0 \lambda^m + a_1 \lambda^{m-1} + \cdots + a_m}{b_0 \lambda^n + b_1 \lambda^{n-1} + \cdots + b_n} \qquad (7.3.33)$$

where it is assumed that $P_m(\lambda)$ and $Q_n(\lambda)$ have no common factors.

REAL POLES AND ZEROS

Let us first suppose that the zeros of the polynomials $P_m(\lambda)$ and $Q_n(\lambda)$ in Eq. (7.3.33) are all simple and real and that $a_m \neq 0$ and $b_n \neq 0$. When this is the case, the transfer function $G(\lambda)$ can be written in the factored form

$$G(\lambda) = \frac{K(1 + \lambda \tau_1)(1 + \lambda \tau_2) \cdots (1 + \lambda \tau_m)}{(1 + \lambda \tau_a)(1 + \lambda \tau_b) \cdots (1 + \lambda \tau_n)}$$

$$= \frac{K \prod_{p=1}^{m} (1 + \lambda \tau_p)}{\prod_{q=a}^{n} (1 + \lambda \tau_q)} \qquad (7.3.34)$$

where K is a positive real constant. Since $\lambda = j\omega$, the sinusoidal steady-state transfer function is determined by the complex function

$$G(j\omega) = \frac{\bar{R}}{\bar{E}} = \frac{K \prod_{p=1}^{m} (1 + j\omega \tau_p)}{\prod_{q=a}^{n} (1 + j\omega \tau_q)} \qquad (7.3.35)$$

The ratio of the magnitude of the sinusoidal response signal $|\bar{R}|$ to the magnitude of the sinusoidal excitation signal $|\bar{E}|$ is therefore

$$\frac{|\bar{R}|}{|\bar{E}|} = |G(j\omega)| = \frac{K \prod\limits_{p=1}^{m} |1 + j\omega\tau_p|}{\prod\limits_{q=a}^{n} |1 + j\omega\tau_q|} \tag{7.3.36}$$

and the phase angle between them is

$$\theta(\omega) = \arg G(j\omega) = \sum_{p=1}^{n} \arg (1 + j\omega\tau_p) - \sum_{q=a}^{n} \arg (1 + j\omega\tau_q)$$

$$= \sum_{p=1}^{n} \arctan \omega\tau_p - \sum_{q=a}^{n} \arctan \omega\tau_q \tag{7.3.37}$$

If we let

$$G = 20 \log |G(j\omega)| \tag{7.3.38}$$

represent the gain characteristic in decibels, then from Eq. (7.3.36) we have

$$G = 20 \log K + \sum_{p=1}^{m} 20 \log |1 + j\omega\tau_p| - \sum_{q=1}^{n} 20 \log |1 + j\omega\tau_q| \tag{7.3.39}$$

The first term in the summation is, of course, a constant, whereas the remaining terms are functions of the excitation frequency. Each frequency-dependent term in the summation can be written in the form

$$g = \pm 20 \log |1 + j\omega\tau| = \pm 20 \log (1 + \omega^2\tau^2)^{1/2}$$
$$= \pm 10 \log (1 + \omega^2\tau^2) \tag{7.3.40}$$

where the $+$ sign is used if $-1/\tau$ represents a zero of $G(\lambda)$ and the $-$ sign is used if $-1/\tau$ represents a pole. The phase angle of this typical term as obtained from Eq. (7.3.37) is

$$\theta = \pm \arctan \omega \tag{7.3.41}$$

where again the $+$ sign and $-$ sign correspond, respectively, to zeros and poles.

The gain and phase characteristics in Eqs. (7.3.40) and (7.3.41) are plotted in Fig. 7.3.4 for both the $+$ and $-$ signs, i.e., for a zero and a pole. Techniques for sketching these curves in terms of the asymptotes and corner frequency are discussed in Sec. 2.4 and are not repeated here.

A similar sketch corresponds to each term in Eq. (7.3.35). The complete gain and phase plots are then obtained by simply adding these individual plots, point by point.   The following example illustrates this technique.

Example 7.3.2:   Sketch the gain and phase plots corresponding to

$$G(\lambda) = \frac{\lambda + 100}{\lambda^2 + 11\lambda + 10} \qquad \lambda = j\omega$$

Solution: $G(\lambda)$ is first written in the factored form

$$G(\lambda) = \frac{10(1 + \lambda/100)}{(1 + \lambda)(1 + \lambda/10)} = \frac{K(1 + \lambda\tau_1)}{(1 + \lambda\tau_a)(1 + \lambda\tau_b)} \tag{7.3.42}$$

where $\tau_1 = \frac{1}{100}$, $\tau_a = 1$, $\tau_b = \frac{1}{10}$, and $K = 10$.   The magnitude and phase angle of $G(j\omega)$ are, respectively,

$$|G(j\omega)| = \left| \frac{K(1 + j\omega\tau_1)}{(1 + j\omega\tau_a)(1 + j\omega\tau_b)} \right| \tag{7.3.43}$$

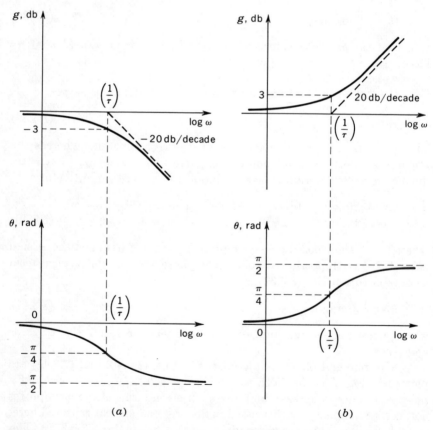

Fig. 7.3.4   Gain and phase characteristics for (a) a pole and (b) zero of $G(\lambda)$ at $\lambda = 1/\tau$.

and

$$\theta = \arctan \omega \tau_1 - \arctan \omega \tau_a - \arctan \omega \tau_b$$

The gain in decibels is found by taking the logarithm (base 10) of Eq. (7.3.43) and multiplying it by 20. The result is

$$\begin{aligned} G = 20 \log |G(j\omega)| &= 20 \log K + 10 \log (1 + \tau_1{}^2\omega^2) - 10 \log (1 + \tau_a{}^2\omega^2) \\ &\qquad - 10 \log (1 + \tau_b{}^2\omega^2) \\ &= 20 + 10 \log (1 + 10^{-4}\omega^2) - 10 \log (1 + \omega^2) - 10 \log (1 + 10^{-2}\omega^2) \end{aligned}$$

Sketches of G and θ as a function of log ω are given in Fig. 7.3.5. Note how the shape of the characteristic is related to the values of the zero, $-1/\tau_1$, and poles, $-1/\tau_a$ and $-1/\tau_b$, of the transfer function $G(\lambda)$.

Let us now consider, for further discussion, a rational function $G(\lambda)$ of the form

$$\begin{aligned} G(\lambda) = \frac{\bar{R}}{\bar{E}} &= \frac{a_0\lambda^m + a_1\lambda^{m-1} + \cdots + a_m}{\lambda^k(b_0\lambda^n + b_1\lambda^{n-1} + \cdots + b_n)} \\ &= \frac{K(1 + \lambda\tau_1) \cdots (1 + \lambda\tau_m)}{\lambda^k(1 + \lambda\tau_a) \cdots (1 + \lambda\tau_n)} \end{aligned} \qquad (7.3.44)$$

where $k + n \geq m$ and K is a positive integer. In addition to the terms in the summation in Eq. (7.3.39), the decibel gain characteristic G now clearly contains a term of the form

$$\begin{aligned} g &= -20 \log |j\omega|^k = -k\, 20 \log |j\omega| \\ &= -k\, 20 \log \omega \end{aligned}$$

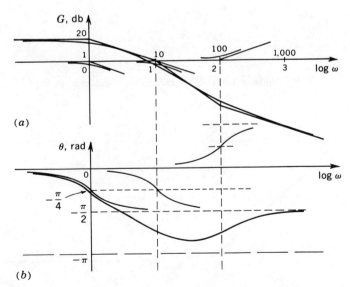

Fig. 7.3.5 (a) Gain and (b) phase characteristics for $G(s)$ given in Eq. (7.3.42).

When this term is plotted as a function of log ω, a straight line with a slope of $-20k$ db/decade results, as shown in Fig. 7.3.6. Note that this line crosses the log ω axis at the point

$$\log \omega = 0 \quad \text{or} \quad \omega = 1$$

The phase angle for the term λ^{-k} is simply

$$\theta = -k\,\frac{\pi}{2}$$

and is also shown plotted in Fig. 7.3.6.

Example 7.3.3: Sketch the frequency-response curves for

$$G(\lambda) = \frac{\lambda^2 + 3\lambda + 2}{2\lambda(\lambda + 1)} \qquad \lambda = j\omega$$

Solution: Factoring the numerator, we have

$$G(\lambda) = \frac{(\lambda + 1)(\lambda + 2)}{2\lambda(\lambda + 1)} = \frac{\lambda + 2}{2\lambda} = \frac{1 + \lambda/2}{\lambda}$$

Then

$$G = 20 \log |G(j\omega)| = 20 \log \left(1 + \frac{\omega^2}{4}\right)^{1/2} - 20 \log |\omega|$$

and

$$\theta(\omega) = \arctan \frac{\omega}{2} - \frac{\pi}{2}$$

This frequency-response characteristic is sketched in Fig. 7.3.7.

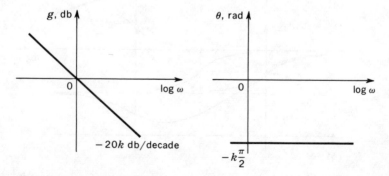

Fig. 7.3.6 The gain and phase plot for λ^{-k}.

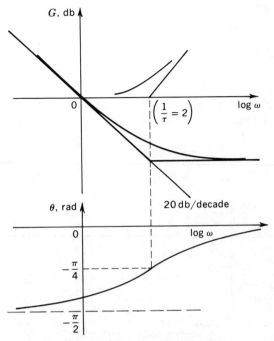

Fig. 7.3.7 Gain and phase characteristics for

$$G(\lambda) = \frac{\lambda^2 + 3\lambda + 2}{2\lambda(\lambda + 1)} \qquad \lambda = j\omega$$

COMPLEX POLES AND ZEROS

In general, some of the poles and zeros of $G(\lambda)$ may be complex. Of course, complex poles and zeros always appear in conjugate pairs so that the numerator and the denominator of $G(\lambda)$ can be factored in the form

$$G(\lambda) = \frac{K \prod\limits_{p} (1 + \lambda_p) \prod\limits_{p'} [1 + 2\zeta_{p'}(\lambda/\omega_{p'}) + (\lambda^2/\omega_{p'}^2)]}{\prod\limits_{q} (1 + \lambda_q) \prod\limits_{q'} [1 + 2\zeta_{q'}(\lambda/\omega_{q'}) + (\lambda^2/\omega_{q'}^2)]} \qquad (7.3.45)$$

where $\zeta_{p'}$ and $\zeta_{q'}$ represent *damping constants*† with $|\zeta_p| < 1$ and $|\zeta_q| < 1$. As a result of the complex zeros, the magnitude and phase characteristics have, in addition to the various terms discussed so far, terms of the form

$$
\begin{aligned}
g_{p'} &= 20 \log \left| 1 + j2\zeta_{p'}\frac{\omega}{\omega_{p'}} + \frac{-\omega^2}{\omega_{p'}^2} \right| \\
&= 20 \log \left[(1 - u^2)^2 + 4\zeta_{p'}^2 u^2\right]^{1/2}
\end{aligned} \qquad (7.3.46)
$$

† The damping constant ζ is defined in Prob. 7.1.

and

$$\theta_{p'} = \arctan \frac{2\zeta_{p'}u}{1 - u^2} \qquad (7.3.47)$$

where

$$u = \frac{\omega}{\omega_{p'}}$$

Similar terms, but of opposite sign, are introduced by complex poles. To establish the asymptotes of the magnitude characteristic $g_{p'}$, observe that $g_{p'}$ approaches zero as $\omega \to 0$. Therefore, the log ω axis represents the low-frequency asymptote. In the limit as $\omega \to \infty$, we have

$$\lim_{\omega \to \infty} g_{p'} = 20 \log u^2 = 40 \log u = 40(\log \omega - \log \omega_{p'}) \qquad (7.3.48)$$

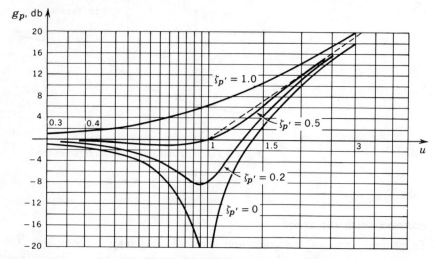

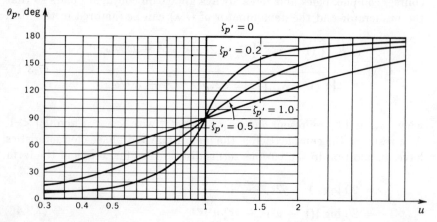

Fig. 7.3.8 Gain and phase characteristics for Eqs. (7.3.46) and (7.3.47). Phase characteristics are symmetrical with respect to point ($u = 1$, $\theta_p = 90°$).

which represents a straight line passing through the point log ω = log $\omega_{p'}$ of the log ω axis. The slope of this high-frequency asymptote is 40 db/ decade.

The actual curve for $g_{p'}$ depends only on the damping constant $\zeta_{p'}$. In the extreme case where $\zeta_{p'}$ = 1 we have

$$1 + 2\zeta_{p'} \frac{\lambda}{\omega_{p'}} + \frac{\lambda^2}{\omega_{p'}^2} = \left(1 + \frac{\lambda}{\omega_{p'}}\right)^2$$

$$= \left(1 + \frac{\lambda}{\omega_{p'}}\right)\left(1 + \frac{\lambda}{\omega_{p'}}\right)$$

That is, when the damping constant is equal to unity, there are no complex zeros. In the other extreme case where $\zeta_{p'}$ = 0, we have, from Eqs. (7.3.46) and (7.3.47),

$$g_{p'} = 20 \log\left(1 - \frac{\omega^2}{\omega_{p'}^2}\right) = 20 \log (1 - u^2) \qquad \text{for } \zeta_{p'} = 0$$

and

$$\theta_p = \begin{cases} 0 & \text{for } u < 1 \\ \pi & \text{for } u > 1 \end{cases} \tag{7.3.49}$$

Therefore, the magnitude characteristic for $\zeta_{p'}$ = 0 has another asymptote which is vertical and intersects the log ω axis at the point

$$\log \omega = \log \omega_{p'}$$

This asymptote, along with a family of response and phase characteristics for Eqs. (7.3.46) and (7.3.47), is given in Fig. 7.3.8 for several values of damping constant $\zeta_{p'}$.

Example 7.3.4: A rotational mechanical system is driven at the terminal pair CG by a torque driver $\tau_1(t)$, as shown in Fig. 7.3.9. The gearbox used in this system is assumed ideal, and the gear ratio is equal to unity.

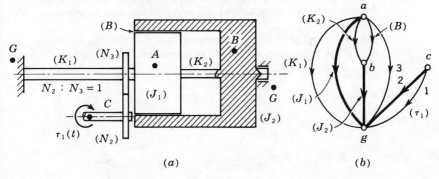

Fig. 7.3.9 (a) A rotational mechanical system; (b) the system graph.

(a)   Determine the transfer function

$$G(\lambda) = \frac{\Phi_1(\lambda)}{T_1(\lambda)} \qquad \lambda = j\omega$$

(b)   Sketch the gain and phase characteristics for $G(\lambda)$ in (a) by using the following numerical values:

$K_1 = 1 \qquad K_2 = 1 \qquad J_1 = 1 \qquad J_2 = 2$
B = variable

Solution

(a)   Since the gearbox (represented by edges 2 and 3 in the system graph) is ideal and the gear ratio is equal to unity, we have $\tau_3(t) = \tau_1(t)$, which is specified. Therefore, edges 1 and 2 in the system graph can be omitted. The state equations of the system are

$$\frac{d}{dt}\begin{bmatrix} \tau_{K_1}(t) \\ \tau_{K_2}(t) \\ \hline \phi_{J_1}(t) \\ \phi_{J_2}(t) \end{bmatrix} = \begin{bmatrix} 0 & 0 & K_1 & 0 \\ 0 & 0 & K_2 & -K_2 \\ \hline -1/J_1 & -1/J_1 & -B/J_1 & B/J_1 \\ 0 & 1/J_2 & B/J_2 & -B/J_2 \end{bmatrix}\begin{bmatrix} \tau_{K_1}(t) \\ \tau_{K_2}(t) \\ \hline \phi_{J_1}(t) \\ \phi_{J_2}(t) \end{bmatrix} + \begin{bmatrix} 0 \\ 0 \\ \hline -1 \\ 0 \end{bmatrix}\tau_3(t)$$

$$(7.3.50)$$

From Theorem 7.2.1, the system graph, and Eq. (7.3.50) the transfer function of interest is

$$G(\lambda) = \frac{\bar{\phi}_1}{\bar{T}_1} = \frac{-\bar{\phi}_3}{\bar{T}_3} = \frac{-J\bar{\phi}_1}{\bar{T}_3} = \frac{-\bar{\phi}_{J_1}}{\lambda\bar{T}_3} \qquad (7.3.51)$$

or

$$G(\lambda) = \frac{K_2 + B\lambda + J_2\lambda^2}{(K_1 + K_2 + B\lambda + J_1\lambda^2)(K_2 + B\lambda + J_2\lambda^2) - (K_2 + B\lambda)^2} \qquad (7.3.52)$$

(b)   Substituting the given numerical values into Eq. (7.3.52) we have

$$G(\lambda) = \frac{1 + B\lambda + 2\lambda^2}{2\lambda^4 + 5\lambda^2 + 1 + (3\lambda^2 + 1)B\lambda} \qquad (7.3.53)$$

It can be shown that, as long as B remains positive, the four zeros of the denominator polynomial are always in the left half plane.[†] On the other hand, if B is sufficiently large (for example, $B \geq 2$), two of the zeros of the denominator polynomial become real and the remaining zeros are complex conjugates.

If $B = 7/\sqrt{20} \cong 1.565$, it can be shown that the denominator polynomial has all complex zeros and can be written in the form

$$2(\lambda^2 + 2\zeta_1\omega_1\lambda + \omega_1^2)(\lambda^2 + 2\zeta_2\omega_2\lambda + \omega_2^2) \qquad (7.3.54)$$

where

$$\omega_1 = \sqrt{2} \cong 1.414 \qquad \omega_2 = \frac{1}{2} = 0.5$$

$$\zeta_1 = \frac{\sqrt{10}}{4} \cong 0.79 \qquad \zeta_2 = \frac{1}{2\sqrt{20}} \cong 0.1$$

[†] Polynomials having such property are called *Hurwitz polynomials* (see Sec. 6.5).

The transfer function in this case is

$$G(\lambda) = \frac{\lambda^2 + 0.7825 + 0.5}{(\lambda^2 + 0.2236\lambda + 2)(\lambda^2 + 0.118\lambda + 0.25)} \qquad (7.3.55)$$

Since the numerator and denominator of Eq. (7.3.55) contain only second-degree factors, the required frequency-response characteristics are obtained by adding the curves in Fig. 7.3.8, which correspond to the identified factors. The results are given in Fig. 7.3.10.

If $B = 0$, $G(\lambda)$ in Eq. (7.3.53) takes on the form

$$G(\lambda) = \frac{\lambda^2 + 0.5}{\lambda^4 + 2.5\lambda^2 + 0.5}$$

$$= \frac{\lambda^2 + 0.5}{(\lambda^2 + 2.2805)(\lambda^2 + 0.2195)}$$

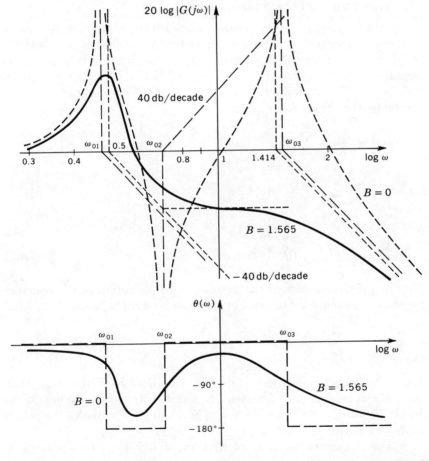

Fig. 7.3.10 Gain and phase characteristics for $G(\lambda)$ in Eq. (7.3.53) for $B = 0$ and $B = 1.565$.

Since the damping coefficients are zero, the gain characteristic has three vertical asymptotes at the resonance points $\omega = \omega_{01}$, ω_{02}, and ω_{03} and the phase characteristic is discontinuous, at these angular frequencies, as shown by the dashed lines in Fig. 7.3.10.

From Fig. 7.3.9 it follows that as $B \to \infty$ the two inertia components become rigidly connected, and Eq. (7.3.53) gives

$$G(\lambda) = \frac{1}{1 + 3\lambda^2}$$

The system is in this case resonant at

$$f_r = \frac{1}{2\pi\sqrt{3}}$$

7.4 REAL AND COMPLEX FREQUENCY SPECTRA (FOURIER AND LAPLACE TRANSFORMS)

Given the frequency-response characteristics of any given output variable in a physical system, it is at least theoretically possible to construct the steady-state response of this output variable to any arbitrary excitation signal defined on a finite interval. Indeed, if the excitation signal $e(t)$ is defined on the interval $T/2 < t < T/2$, then its Fourier series expansion can be written in the form

$$e(t) = \frac{E_0}{2} + \sum_{k=1}^{\infty} E_k \cos\left(k\omega t + \theta_k\right) \qquad \omega = \frac{2\pi}{T}$$

$$= \sum_{k=-\infty}^{\infty} \frac{\bar{E}_k}{2} e^{jk\omega t} \tag{7.4.1}$$

where $\bar{E}_k = E_k e^{j\theta k}$, $\bar{E}_i = \hat{\bar{E}}_{-i}$, $i = 1, 2, \ldots, \infty$, and

$$\frac{\bar{E}_k}{2} = \frac{1}{T} \int_{-T/2}^{T/2} e(t) e^{-jk\omega t}\, dt \tag{7.4.2}$$

By using similar notation, the Fourier series expansion of the response function over the same interval of time can be written as

$$r(t) = \sum_{k=-\infty}^{\infty} \frac{\bar{R}_k}{2} e^{jk\omega t} \qquad \bar{R}_k = R_k e^{j\phi_k}$$

From the frequency-response plots, the ratio R_k/E_k and the phase shift $\phi_k - \theta_k$ can be evaluated for each frequency component $k\omega$ in the expansions. Consequently, given E_k and θ_k in the expansion of $e(t)$, the values of R_k and ϕ_k can be determined.

The important point is not that one would use such a procedure, so much as the fact that it is possible to do so and that the frequency-response characteristic contains all the necessary information.

By means of the real and complex frequency spectra defined in this section it is also possible, under certain conditions, to construct the frequency-response characteristics from the transient response, and vice versa. The real frequency spectrum of a function $f(t)$ is defined in terms of the *Fourier transform* of $f(t)$ as given in the following theorem, stated here without proof.[2]

Theorem 7.4.1 (Fourier transform pairs): If $f(t)$ is a bounded function and the infinite integral

$$\int_{-\infty}^{\infty} |f(t)| \, dt$$

exists and has a finite value, then $f(t)$ is given uniquely by

$$f(t) = \frac{1}{2\pi} \int_{-\infty}^{+\infty} F(j\omega) e^{j\omega t} \, d\omega \tag{7.4.3}$$

where

$$F(j\omega) = \int_{-\infty}^{\infty} f(t) e^{-j\omega t} \, dt \tag{7.4.4}$$

Equations (7.4.3) and (7.4.4) are called a *Fourier transform pair* and are obtainable from the Fourier series pair in Eqs. (7.4.1) and (7.4.2) by allowing the interval $-T/2 < t < T/2$ to increase without bound.[2] The function $F(j\omega)$ in Eq. (7.4.4) is called the *Fourier transform* of the function $f(t)$ and the integral in Eq. (7.4.3) the *Fourier integral*, or the *inverse Fourier transform*. A plot of the magnitude and phase angle of the function $F(j\omega)$ as a function of ω is called the *frequency spectrum* of the function $f(t)$.

Example 7.4.1: Determine the Fourier transform of the function

$$f(t) = \begin{cases} 0 & t < 0 \\ e^{-kt} & t \geq 0, k > 0 \end{cases} \tag{7.4.5}$$

Solution: The Fourier transform of this function as given by Eq. (7.4.4) is

$$F(j\omega) = \int_{-\infty}^{\infty} f(t) e^{-j\omega t} \, dt = \int_{-\infty}^{0} 0 \, dt + \int_{0}^{\infty} e^{-(k+j\omega)t} \, dt$$

$$= \frac{1}{k + j\omega} = \frac{1}{k} \frac{1}{1 + j\omega/k} \tag{7.4.6}$$

It is, of course, possible to return from the frequency-spectrum function $F(j\omega)$ to the given time function $f(t)$ by means of the infinite integral in Eq. (7.4.3).

As we shall see, the frequency-spectrum functions of particular interest in the analysis of linear systems are the rational functions of the form

$$F(j\omega) = \frac{p(j\omega)}{q(j\omega)} \tag{7.4.7}$$

where $p(j\omega)$ and $q(j\omega)$ are polynomials in $j\omega$ and the degree of $p(j\omega)$ is less than that of $q(j\omega)$. For this class of functions the inverse Fourier integral in Eq. (7.4.3) is easily evaluated by expanding $F(j\omega)$ into partial fractions. If the poles of $F(j\omega)$ [the zeros of $q(j\omega)$] are all simple, then the expansion is of the form

$$F(j\omega) = \frac{c_1}{\alpha_1 + j\omega} + \frac{c_2}{\alpha_2 + j\omega} + \cdots + \frac{c_n}{\alpha_n + j\omega}$$

The inverse Fourier transform of each term is an exponential function, and, from the results of Example 7.4.1, it follows that

$$f(t) = c_1 e^{-\alpha_1 t} + c_2 e^{-\alpha_2 t} + \cdots + c_n e^{-\alpha_n t}$$

When the poles of $F(j\omega)$ are not simple, the partial-fraction expansion, of course, contains terms of the form

$$F_i(j\omega) = \frac{c_i}{(\alpha_i + j\omega)^{r_i}} \tag{7.4.8}$$

It is easy to verify that this function is the Fourier transform of the time function

$$f_i(t) = c_i \frac{t^{r_i-1}}{(r_i - 1)!} e^{-\alpha_i t} \tag{7.4.9}$$

Thus, by means of the partial-fraction expansion and the Fourier transform pairs given in Eqs. (7.4.8) and (7.4.9), the inverse Fourier transform of any rational function of $j\omega$ can be readily evaluated.

Example 7.4.2: Evaluate the time function $f(t)$ corresponding to the frequency spectrum

$$f(j\omega) = \frac{j\omega}{(j\omega + 1)(j\omega + 2)^2}$$

Solution: Expanding $F(j\omega)$ into partial fractions gives

$$F(j\omega) = \frac{-1}{j\omega + 1} + \frac{\frac{1}{2}}{(j\omega + 2)^2} + \frac{2}{j\omega + 2}$$

The inverse Fourier transform of each term gives

$$f(t) = -1 e^{-t} + \frac{t}{2} e^{-2t} + 2 e^{-2t}$$

It is to be noted that the Fourier transform of a function $f(t)$ exists only if it satisfies the hypothesis of Theorem 7.4.1. In general, if $f(t) = 0$ for $t < 0$ and if $f(t) \to 0$ as $t \to \infty$, that is, if $f(t)$ is asymptotically stable for $t > 0$, then the integral in Eq. (7.4.4) converges and the real frequency spectrum is defined. This integral, however, does *not* converge, for example, when $f(t)$ is a unit step function, a sinusoidal function, or an exponential function with a positive exponent. Consequently, one can consider the frequency spectrum, as defined so far, only for response functions which can be described as being *asymptotically stable*.

The concept of frequency spectrum can be extended to the analysis of other than asymptotically stable functions by multiplying the given function by an appropriate convergence factor. If $f(t) = 0$ for $t < 0$, then for $t > 0$ there exists a positive constant σ such that

$$\int_0^\infty |f(t)|e^{-\sigma t}\,dt < \infty$$

From Theorem 7.4.1, the Fourier transform of the function $f_1(t) = f(t)e^{-\sigma t}$ exists and is

$$\begin{aligned}F_1(j\omega) &= \int_0^\infty f_1(t)e^{-j\omega t}\,dt \\ &= \int_0^\infty f(t)e^{-\sigma t}e^{-j\omega t}\,dt \end{aligned} \qquad (7.4.10)$$

and the inverse transform is

$$f_1(t) = e^{-\sigma t}f(t) = \frac{1}{2\pi}\int_{-\infty}^\infty e^{j\omega t}F_1(j\omega)\,d\omega \qquad (7.4.11)$$

If we set $s = \sigma + j\omega$, then the transformation in Eq. (7.4.10) becomes

$$F_1(j\omega) = \mathbf{f}(s) = \int_0^\infty f(t)e^{-st}\,dt \qquad (7.4.12)$$

and, from the inverse transform integral in Eq. (7.4.11), we find

$$\begin{aligned}f(t) &= \frac{1}{2\pi} e^{\sigma t}\int_{-\infty}^\infty e^{j\omega t}\mathbf{f}(s)\,d\omega \\ &= \frac{1}{2\pi j}\int_{\sigma-j\infty}^{\sigma+j\infty} e^{st}\mathbf{f}(s)\,ds \end{aligned} \qquad (7.4.13)$$

The function $\mathbf{f}(s)$ of the complex variable s is called the *Laplace transform* of the function $f(t)$. By extending the concepts and terminology used in the case of the Fourier transform, the variable $s = \sigma + j\omega$ is called the *complex frequency* and the function $\mathbf{f}(s)$ the *complex frequency spectrum* of the function $f(t)$. The transform pair in Eqs. (7.4.12) and (7.4.13) is called a *Laplace transform pair* and, of course, includes the Fourier transform pair as the special case wherein $\sigma = 0$.

The Laplace transform is used extensively as a basis for interrelating the frequency-response and transient-response characteristics of linear time-invariant systems. The above results are therefore summarized in the form of a theorem.

Theorem 7.4.2 (Laplace transform pairs): Let $f(t) = 0$ for $t < 0$, and let σ be any finite positive constant. If $f(t)e^{-\sigma t}$ is a bounded integrable function such that, for some finite value of $\sigma > 0$, the integral

$$\int_0^\infty |f(t)|e^{-\sigma t}\,dt$$

exists and has a finite value, then $f(t)$ is given uniquely by

$$f(t) = \frac{1}{2\pi j} \int_{\sigma-j\infty}^{\sigma+j\infty} \mathbf{f}(s)e^{st}\,ds \tag{7.4.14}$$

where

$$\mathbf{f}(s) = \int_0^\infty f(t)e^{-st}\,dt$$

and

$$s = \sigma + j\omega$$

As in the case of the real frequency spectrum, we shall see that the complex-frequency-spectrum functions of primary interest in the analysis of linear time-invariant systems are the rational functions of s of the form

$$\mathbf{f}(s) = \frac{p(s)}{q(s)}$$

where $p(s)$ is of lower degree than $q(s)$. For such functions the inverse Laplace transform is easily evaluated by expanding $\mathbf{f}(s)$ into partial fractions. If $s = -\alpha_i$ is a zero of $q(s)$ of order r, then the corresponding terms in the partial-fraction expansion are of the general form

$$\mathbf{f}_i(s) = \frac{k_i}{(\alpha_i + s)^{r_i}}$$

By direct integration it is easy to show that this term is the Laplace transform of the function

$$f_i(t) = k_i \frac{t^{r_i-1}}{(r_i - 1)!}\, e^{-\alpha_i t}$$

This and other simple functions along with their Laplace transforms are listed in Table 7.4.1, for ready reference.

Example 7.4.3: Evaluate the time function $f(t)$ corresponding to the complex-frequency-spectrum function

$$\mathbf{f}_1(s) = \frac{s}{(s + 1)(s + 2)^2}$$

Table 7.4.1   Laplace transform pairs

$f(t)$ $t \geq 0$ $[f(t) = 0 \text{ for } t < 0]$	*Laplace transform* $\mathbf{f}(s)$
$f(t)$	$\int_0^\infty f(t)e^{-st}\,dt$
$u(t)$	$\dfrac{1}{s}$
$\dfrac{t^{n-1}}{(n-1)!}$	$\dfrac{1}{s^n}$
$e^{\alpha t}$	$\dfrac{1}{s-\alpha}$
$\dfrac{t^{n-1}}{(n-1)!}\,e^{\alpha t}$	$\dfrac{1}{(s-\alpha)^n}$
$\sin \omega t$	$\dfrac{\omega}{s^2 + \omega^2}$
$\cos \omega t$	$\dfrac{s}{s^2 + \omega^2}$

Solution: Expanding $f_1(s)$ into partial fractions gives

$$\mathbf{f}_1(s) = \frac{-1}{s+1} + \frac{1}{2}\frac{1}{(s+2)^2} + \frac{2}{s+2}$$

Taking the inverse Laplace transform of each term gives

$$f_1(t) = -1e^{-t} + \frac{t}{2}e^{-2t} + 2e^{-2t}$$

Note that this example is identical to Example 7.4.2 with $j\omega$ replaced by s.   Note, however, that in the function

$$\mathbf{f}_2(s) = \frac{s}{(s-1)(s+2)^2}$$

one of the poles is positive and the corresponding time function is

$$f_2(t) = \tfrac{1}{9}e^t + \tfrac{2}{3}te^{-2t} + \tfrac{1}{9}e^{-2t}$$

This time function is unstable and it does not have a Fourier transform. Consequently one cannot characterize the latter function in terms of the real frequency spectrum.   It can, however, be characterized in terms of the complex frequency spectrum $\mathbf{f}(s)$.

7.5   NUMERICAL EVALUATION OF FREQUENCY - RESPONSE CHARACTERISTICS

Techniques for numerical evaluation of frequency-response characteristics are developed in this section.   First, it is shown that the sinusoidal steady-state response characteristics can be evaluated in terms of the

Fourier transform of the transient component of the solution to the state equations for a particular set of initial conditions.

Consider the linear time-invariant system of the form

$$\frac{d}{dt}\mathbf{\Psi}(t) = \mathbf{P}\mathbf{\Psi}(t) + \mathbf{Q}\mathbf{E}(t) \qquad (7.5.1)$$

$$\mathbf{R}(t) = \mathbf{M}\mathbf{\Psi}(t) + \mathbf{N}\mathbf{E}(t) \qquad (7.5.2)$$

with excitation vector

$$\mathbf{E}(t) = \bar{\mathbf{E}}e^{j\omega t} + \hat{\mathbf{E}}e^{-j\omega t} \qquad (7.5.3)$$

It has already been shown that, if the system is asymptotically stable, then the sinusoidal steady-state response is

$$\mathbf{R}(t) = \bar{\mathbf{R}}e^{j\omega t} + \hat{\mathbf{R}}e^{-j\omega t}$$

with

$$\bar{\mathbf{R}} = [\mathbf{M}(j\omega\mathbf{U} - \mathbf{P})^{-1}\mathbf{Q} + \mathbf{N}]\bar{\mathbf{E}} = \mathbf{M}\bar{\mathbf{\Psi}} + \mathbf{N}\bar{\mathbf{E}} \qquad (7.5.4)$$

where the vector

$$\bar{\mathbf{\Psi}} = \bar{\mathbf{\Psi}}(\omega) = (j\omega\mathbf{U} - \mathbf{P})^{-1}\mathbf{Q}\bar{\mathbf{E}} \qquad (7.5.5)$$

represents the frequency response of the state vector. The vector $\mathbf{N}\bar{\mathbf{E}}$ is, of course, a constant, and the constant matrix $\mathbf{M}$ relates the frequency-response characteristics of the response variables to the frequency-response characteristics of the state variables.

If the system is asymptotically stable, the frequency response of the state vector $\bar{\mathbf{\Psi}}(\omega)$, as given in Eq. (7.5.5), can be evaluated as the Fourier transform of the solution to the homogeneous system

$$\frac{d}{dt}\mathbf{\Psi}(t) = \mathbf{P}\mathbf{\Psi}(t) \qquad (7.5.6)$$

with initial conditions $\mathbf{\Psi}(0) = \mathbf{Q}\bar{\mathbf{E}}$. To show that this is the case, we note first that the solution to Eq. (7.5.6) is

$$\mathbf{\Psi}(t) = e^{\mathbf{P}t}\mathbf{Q}\bar{\mathbf{E}} \qquad (7.5.7)$$

If $\mathbf{\Psi}(t) = 0$ for $t < 0$, and if all the eigenvalues of $\mathbf{P}$ have negative real parts (i.e., if the system is asymptotically stable), the Fourier transform of the vector $\mathbf{\Psi}(t)$ exists and is

$$\mathbf{\Psi}(j\omega) = \int_0^\infty e^{-j\omega u}\mathbf{\Psi}(u)\,dt = \int_0^\infty e^{-j\omega u}e^{\mathbf{P}u}\mathbf{Q}\bar{\mathbf{E}}\,du$$

$$= \int_0^\infty e^{-(j\omega\mathbf{U}-\mathbf{P})u}\mathbf{Q}\bar{\mathbf{E}}\,du = (j\omega\mathbf{U} - \mathbf{P})^{-1}\mathbf{Q}\bar{\mathbf{E}} \qquad (7.5.8)\dagger$$

Upon comparing this result with the right-hand side of Eq. (7.5.5) it is apparent that the vector $\bar{\mathbf{\Psi}}(\omega)$, which specifies the frequency-response

† See Eq. (7.1.35).

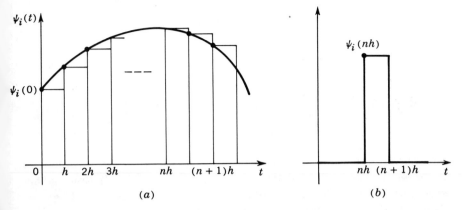

Fig. 7.5.1 Approximation by a sequence of rectangular pulses.

characteristics of the state vector, can be evaluated by multiplying the solution to the homogeneous system in Eq. (7.5.6) by

$$e^{-j\omega t} = \cos \omega t - j \sin \omega t$$

and integrating the result over a long time interval. Several methods are available for carrying out this integration numerically, by using only the solution points resulting from the numerical solution of the simple homogeneous system in Eq. (7.5.6). An effective procedure, and one which can be used for variable-increment solutions, is based on approximating each function $\psi_i(t)$ in the state vector by a sequence of rectangular pulses, as shown in Fig. 7.5.1a, or as a sequence of straight lines, shown in Fig. 7.5.2. Consider first the sequence of pulse approximations shown in Fig. 7.5.1b.

If the nth pulse is defined as

$$f_n(t) = \begin{cases} 0 & t < nh \text{ and } t > (n+1)h \\ \psi_i(nh) & nh \leq t \leq (n+1)h \end{cases} \qquad (7.5.9)$$

then

$$\psi_i \cong \sum_{n=0}^{\infty} f_n(t) \qquad (7.5.10)$$

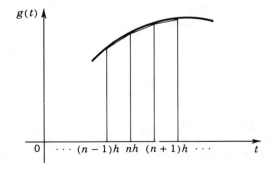

Fig. 7.5.2 Approximation by a series of straight lines.

and the Fourier transform of the state vector $\Psi(t)$ is

$$\bar{\Psi}(j\omega) = \int_{-\infty}^{\infty} \Psi(t)e^{-j\omega t}\,dt \cong \sum_{n=0}^{\infty} \Psi(nh) \int_{nh}^{(n+1)h} e^{-j\omega t}\,dt \qquad (7.5.11)$$

$$\bar{\Psi}(j\omega) \cong \sum_{n=0}^{\infty} \frac{\Psi(nh)}{\omega} [\sin \omega(n+1)h - \sin \omega nh]$$
$$+ j[\cos \omega(n+1)h - \cos n\omega h] \qquad (7.5.12)$$

where $\Psi(nh)$ represents the numerical value of the state vector evaluated at $t = nh$ as obtained from the solution of Eq. (7.5.7). If the system is asymptotically stable, then $\psi_i(nh) \to 0$ as $n \to \infty$ and the infinite series in Eq. (7.5.12) can be approximated by a truncated series and also evaluated numerically. The frequency-response characteristics of the output variables, of course, are evaluated numerically by simply substituting Eq. (7.5.12) into Eq. (7.5.4), to obtain

$$\bar{R}(j\omega) = M\bar{\Psi}(j\omega) + N\bar{E}(j\omega) \qquad (7.5.13)$$

The accuracy of the numerical results for any given increment h can be improved by approximating the solution curves between the solution points by the sequence of straight lines† shown in Fig. 7.5.2. By simple integration by parts, one can show (Prob. 7.38) that if each function $\psi_i(t)$ of the state vector is such that

$$\psi_i(t) = 0 \qquad \text{for } t < 0$$

and $(d/dt)\psi_i(t) = \dot{\psi}_i(t)$ is defined for $t > 0$, then the Fourier transform of $\Psi(t)$ is related to the Fourier transform of $\dot{\Psi}(t)$ by

$$\bar{\Psi}(j\omega) = \frac{1}{j\omega} \Psi(0) + \frac{1}{j\omega} \int_0^{\infty} \dot{\Psi}(t)e^{-j\omega t}\,dt \qquad (7.5.14)$$

When each function $\psi_i(t)$ in the state vector is approximated by a sequence of straight lines, as shown in Fig. 7.5.2, $\dot{\Psi}(t)$ in Eq. (7.5.14) is piecewise constant and the integral can be evaluated directly from the numerical values of the state vector at the solution points $\Psi(0)$, $\Psi(1)$, $\ldots$, $\Psi(n)$, $\ldots$. Indeed, if $f_i(n)$ represents the slope of the straight line between $\psi_i(n+1)$ and $\psi_i(n)$, then we have simply

$$f_i(n) = \frac{\psi_i(n+1) - \psi_i(n)}{h} \qquad (7.5.15)$$

---

† It is, of course, possible to use second-, third-, or even higher-order polynomials. The results given here for first-order polynomials can be extended to such approximations, but such results are more complex and difficult to apply.

Over the interval $0 < t < kh$, the integral in Eq. (7.5.14) can be approximated by a finite summation,† to give

$$\boldsymbol{\Psi}(j\omega) \cong \frac{1}{j\omega}\, \boldsymbol{\Psi}(0) + \frac{1}{\omega^2}\left\{ -\mathbf{F}(1) + \sum_{n=2}^{k} [\mathbf{F}(n-1) \right.$$
$$\left. - \mathbf{F}(n)]e^{-j\omega(n-1)h} + \mathbf{F}(k)e^{-j\omega kh} \right\} \quad (7.5.16)$$

where it is assumed that $\boldsymbol{\Psi}(t) \to 0$ as $t \to \infty$ and k is sufficiently large that the integral beyond $t = kh$ can be neglected. The vector $F(n)$ is, of course, related numerically to the state vector $\boldsymbol{\Psi}(n)$ by

$$\mathbf{F}(n) = \frac{1}{h}[\boldsymbol{\Psi}(n+1) - \boldsymbol{\Psi}(n)] \quad (7.5.17)$$

The magnitude and phase angle of the frequency response are easily evaluated when Eq. (7.5.16) is written as

$$\boldsymbol{\Psi}(j\omega) \cong \mathbf{A}(\omega) + j\mathbf{B}(\omega) \quad (7.5.18)$$

where

$$\mathbf{A}(\omega) = \frac{1}{\omega^2}\left\{ -\mathbf{F}(1) + \sum_{n=2}^{k} [\mathbf{F}(n-1) - \mathbf{F}(n)]\cos(n-1)\omega h \right.$$
$$\left. + \mathbf{F}(k)\cos\omega hk \right\}$$

and

$$\mathbf{B}(\omega) = -\frac{1}{\omega^2}\left\{ \omega\boldsymbol{\Psi}(0) + \sum_{n=2}^{k} [\mathbf{F}(n-1) - \mathbf{F}(n)]\sin(n-1)\omega h \right.$$
$$\left. + \mathbf{F}(k)\sin\omega hk \right\}$$

and the vector $\mathbf{F}(n)$ is evaluated in terms of the solution points $\boldsymbol{\Psi}(n)$ by Eq. (7.5.17).

Example 7.5.1: Determine the frequency-response characteristics of $i_6(t)$ and the time variation in $i_6(t)$ in the electrical network shown in Fig. 7.5.3, with parameters and excitation signal given by

$$L_2 = L_3 = \frac{R}{\omega_0} \quad \text{henrys} \quad C_1 = \frac{2}{\omega_0 R} \quad \mu\text{f} \quad R_6 = R_5 = R = 500 \text{ ohms}$$

$$\omega_0 = 2\pi f_0 = 8\pi \text{ kc} \quad v_4(t) = 20\cos\omega t$$

Solution: The state model of the network for the tree indicated in Fig. 7.5.3b is

$$\frac{d}{dt}\begin{bmatrix} v_1(t) \\ i_2(t) \\ i_3(t) \end{bmatrix} = \begin{bmatrix} 0 & -1/C_1 & 1/C_1 \\ 1/L_2 & -R_6/L_2 & 0 \\ -1/L_3 & 0 & -R_5/L_3 \end{bmatrix}\begin{bmatrix} v_1(t) \\ i_2(t) \\ i_3(t) \end{bmatrix} + \begin{bmatrix} 0 \\ 0 \\ 1/L_3 \end{bmatrix} 20\cos\omega t$$

$$i_6(t) = i_2(t)$$

† The form shown results after appropriate grouping of the terms.

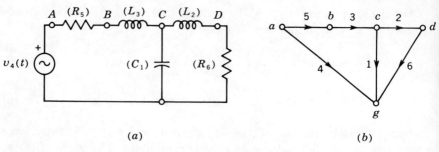

(a)   (b)

Fig. 7.5.3 An *RLC* network.

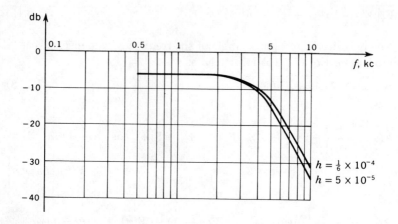

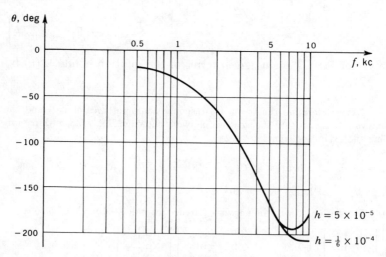

Fig. 7.5.4 Frequency-response characteristics for Example 7.5.1.

The frequency-response characteristics of $i_6(t) = i_2(t)$ can be obtained as the Fourier transform of the numerical solution to the system of homogeneous equations

$$\frac{d}{dt}\begin{bmatrix} v_1(t) \\ i_2(t) \\ i_3(t) \end{bmatrix} = \begin{bmatrix} 0 & -1/C_1 & 1/C_1 \\ 1/L_2 & -R_6/L_2 & 0 \\ -1/L_3 & 0 & -R_5/L_3 \end{bmatrix} \begin{bmatrix} v_1(t) \\ i_2(t) \\ i_3(t) \end{bmatrix}$$

with initial conditions

$$\begin{bmatrix} v_1(0) \\ i_2(0) \\ i_3(0) \end{bmatrix} = \begin{bmatrix} 0 \\ 0 \\ 1/L_3 \end{bmatrix} \frac{20}{2} = \begin{bmatrix} 0 \\ 0 \\ 10/L_3 \end{bmatrix}$$

The magnitude and phase frequency-response curves for i_6 as evaluated from this numerical solution, by using the development given in Eq. (7.5.18), are shown in Fig. 7.5.4. The response characteristics shown correspond to increments $h = 5 \times 10^{-5}$ sec and $h = \frac{10}{6} \times 10^{-5}$ sec.

It is to be noted from the frequency-response characteristic shown in Fig. 7.5.4 that, in the range $0 \le f \le 4$ kc, the magnitude of the output current is nearly constant, but that beyond $f = 4$ kc the magnitude becomes negligible. It is for this reason that the given network is called a *low-pass filter*—transmission of sinusoidal signals is limited to those of low frequency only.

7.6 FREQUENCY-RESPONSE CHARACTERISTICS AND z-TRANSFORM CONCEPTS IN DISCRETE-STATE SYSTEMS

The general form of the state model for a time-independent discrete-state system has been shown to be

$$\begin{aligned} \mathbf{\Psi}(n+1) &= \mathbf{P}\mathbf{\Psi}(n) + \mathbf{Q}E(n) \\ \mathbf{R}(n) &= \mathbf{M}\mathbf{\Psi}(n) + \mathbf{N}E(n) \end{aligned} \tag{7.6.1}$$

If the eigenvalues of $\mathbf{P}$ are all *within* the unit circle, the solution is asymptotically stable and the steady-state solution is obtained as the particular solution to the difference equations. If, for example, the excitation vector in Eqs. (7.6.1) is a constant sequence, then $E(n) = E$ and the steady-state (particular) solution is

$$\mathbf{\Psi}(n+1) = \mathbf{\Psi}(n) = \mathbf{\Psi}$$

where the constant vector $\mathbf{\Psi}$ satisfies the equation

$$\mathbf{\Psi} = \mathbf{P}\mathbf{\Psi} + \mathbf{Q}E$$

or

$$\mathbf{\Psi} = (\mathbf{U} - \mathbf{P})^{-1}\mathbf{Q}E \tag{7.6.2}$$

The steady-state response vector is, of course,

$$\mathbf{R} = \mathbf{M}(\mathbf{U} - \mathbf{P})^{-1}\mathbf{Q}E + \mathbf{N}E$$

The indicated inverse exists, since it is assumed that the eigenvalues of $\mathbf{P}$ are all *inside* the unit circle.

To obtain the steady-state response to a vector sinusoidal sequence, let the excitation vector be written as

$$\begin{aligned}
\mathbf{E}(n) &= \bar{\mathbf{E}}e^{j\beta n} + \hat{\mathbf{E}}e^{-j\beta n} \\
&= \bar{\mathbf{E}}\alpha^n + \hat{\mathbf{E}}\hat{\alpha}^n
\end{aligned} \tag{7.6.3}$$

where $\beta = \omega h$ if the sequence corresponds to the value of the function $f(t) = \cos \omega t$ at the discrete points $t = nh$, as shown in Fig. 7.6.1. As with differential equations, the particular solution to Eqs. (7.6.1) for the sinusoidal input vector in Eq. (7.6.3) is

$$\mathbf{\Psi}(n) = \bar{\mathbf{\Psi}}\alpha^n + \hat{\mathbf{\Psi}}\hat{\alpha}^n$$

where the vector of complex numbers $\mathbf{\Psi}$ satisfies the algebraic equations

$$(\bar{\mathbf{\Psi}}\alpha)\alpha^n = \mathbf{P}\bar{\mathbf{\Psi}}\alpha^n + \mathbf{Q}\bar{\mathbf{E}}\alpha^n$$

or

$$\mathbf{\Psi} = \mathbf{\Psi}(\lambda) = (\lambda\mathbf{U} - \mathbf{P})^{-1}\mathbf{Q}\bar{\mathbf{E}} \qquad \lambda = \alpha = e^{j\beta} \tag{7.6.4}$$

The magnitude and phase angle of the response vector are given by the complex vector

$$\begin{aligned}
\bar{\mathbf{R}} = \bar{\mathbf{R}}(\lambda) &= \mathbf{M}\bar{\mathbf{\Psi}}(\lambda) + \mathbf{N}\bar{\mathbf{E}} \\
&= \mathbf{M}(\lambda\mathbf{U} - \mathbf{P})^{-1}\mathbf{Q}\bar{\mathbf{E}} + \mathbf{N}\bar{\mathbf{E}} \qquad \lambda = \alpha = e^{j\beta}
\end{aligned} \tag{7.6.5}$$

The indicated inverse in Eqs. (7.6.4) and (7.6.5) exists if the eigenvalues of $\mathbf{P}$ are all different from $\alpha = e^{j\beta}$. Upon comparing Eq. (7.6.5) with Eq. (7.3.3), it is evident that the complex-variable equations characterizing the sinusoidal steady-state frequency response of linear continuous and discrete-state systems are identical except that $\lambda = j\omega$ for

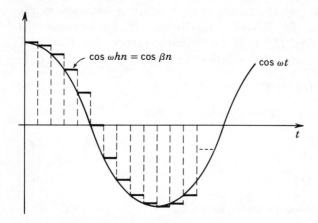

Fig. 7.6.1 Discrete-level signal for $f(t) = \cos \omega t$.

continuous systems, whereas $\lambda = \alpha = e^{j\beta} = e^{j\omega h}$ for the discrete-state system.

In general, if the sequence $f(n)$ represents the values of a periodic function $f(t)$ at the discrete points $t = nh$, as shown in Fig. 7.6.2, then from the Fourier series representation of $f(t)$ it follows that the sequence $f(n)$ can be represented by a power series of the general form

$$f(n) = a_0 + \sum_{i=1}^{\infty} a_i \cos(\omega_i nh + \theta_i)$$

$$= a_0 + \frac{1}{2} \sum_{i=1}^{\infty} \bar{A}_i \alpha_i^{\,n} + \frac{1}{2} \sum_{i=1}^{\infty} \hat{\bar{A}}_i \hat{\alpha}_i^{\,n}$$

$$= \frac{1}{2} \sum_{i=-\infty}^{\infty} \bar{A}_i \alpha_i^{\,n} \tag{7.6.6}$$

where

$$\alpha_i = e^{j\beta_i} = e^{j\omega_i h} \qquad \omega_i = i\,\frac{2\pi}{T_0}$$

and T_0 represents the period of $f(t)$.

It is evident, then, that the power series in α_i in Eq. (7.6.6) plays the same role in the representation of an arbitrary periodic sequence $f(n)$ as does the exponential series in representing an arbitrary periodic function $f(t)$. The coefficients α_i, of course, represent uniformly spaced points on the unit circle (rather than the imaginary axis) of the complex λ plane. The complex response vector $\bar{R}$ is given as a function of the magnitude and phase characteristics of an arbitrary excitation vector

$$E(n) = \bar{E}\alpha^n + \hat{\bar{E}}\hat{\alpha}^n$$

by Eq. (7.6.5). By using superposition, the steady-state response characteristics of the system to any periodic sequence $f(n)$ can be obtained

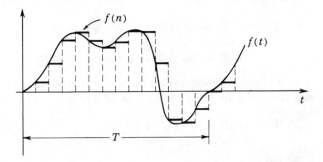

Fig. 7.6.2 Discrete-level signal resulting from "sampling" and "holding" a general periodic function at regular intervals.

by summing the solutions corresponding to the points α_i (on the unit circle) in the series expansion of $f(n)$.

Since $(\lambda U - P)^{-1} = [1/D(\lambda)] \text{ adj } (\lambda U - P)$, it is evident from Eq. (7.6.5) that the magnitude and phase of any component of the response vector r_k as a function of $\alpha = e^{j\beta}$ are given by a rational function of $\lambda = \alpha$ of the form

$$\bar{r}_k(\lambda) = \frac{p(\lambda)}{q(\lambda)}$$
$$= \frac{a_0 + a_1\lambda + a_2\lambda^2 + \cdots + a_m\lambda^m}{b_0 + b_1\lambda + b_2\lambda^2 + \cdots + b_n\lambda^n} \qquad m < n \qquad (7.6.7)$$

A plot of the magnitude and phase angle of this ratio of polynomials as a function of λ on the unit circle gives a response characteristic for discrete-state systems that is the exact counterpart of the frequency-response plot for continuous systems. However, since $\lambda = \alpha = e^{j\beta}$ rather than $j\omega$, the techniques for making Bode plots do not apply here.

The response characteristic, of course, can still be plotted analytically from Eq. (7.6.7), or it can be computed numerically as the solution of the homogeneous part of the state equations, as shown next.

The solution to the homogeneous part of Eqs. (7.6.1) for an arbitrary initial state $\Psi(0)$ is

$$\Psi(n) = P^n \Psi(0) \qquad (7.6.8)$$

The discrete-state counterpart of the Fourier transform of a sequence $f(n)$ is defined as

$$F(a) = \sum_{n=-\infty}^{\infty} f(n)\alpha^{-n} \qquad (7.6.9)$$

provided, of course, that the summation converges. If the vector sequence $\Psi(n)$ in Eq. (7.6.8) is zero for $n < 0$ and if it is asymptotically stable, then the series in Eq. (7.6.9) converges and the Fourier transform of the state vector is

$$\Psi(\alpha) = \sum_{n=0}^{\infty} P^n \Psi(0)\alpha^{-n} = \sum_{n=0}^{\infty} \Psi(n)\alpha^{-n}$$
$$= (U + P\alpha^{-1} + P^2\alpha^{-2} + \cdots)\Psi(0) \qquad (7.6.10)$$

If P contains no eigenvalues on the unit circle, then $(U - \alpha^{-1}P)^{-1}$ exists and the series in Eq. (7.6.10) can be written in the closed form

$$\Psi(\alpha) = (U - \alpha^{-1}P)^{-1}\Psi(0)$$
$$= (\alpha U - P)^{-1}\alpha \Psi(0) \qquad (7.6.11)$$

If we set

$$\Psi(0) = \alpha^{-1}Q\bar{E}$$

then the Fourier transform of the solution to the homogeneous equation (7.6.8) is identical to the steady-state response characteristics given in Eq. (7.6.4).

The summation in Eq. (7.6.10) can be evaluated numerically in terms of the recursion formula

$$\Psi(n + 1) = \mathbf{P}\Psi(n) \tag{7.6.12}$$

by expanding α into its real and imaginary parts, to give

$$\alpha^{-n} = e^{-j\beta n} = \cos \beta n - j \sin \beta n$$
$$\Psi(\beta) = [\Psi(0) + \Psi(1) \cos \beta + \Psi(2) \cos 2\beta + \cdot \cdot \cdot]$$
$$- j[0 + \Psi(1) \sin \beta + \Psi(2) \sin 2\beta + \cdot \cdot \cdot] \tag{7.6.13}$$

The vector coefficients $\Psi(n)$, of course, are obtained from the recursive application of Eq. (7.6.12), and the summation is continued until the successive terms are insignificant. If the system is asymptotically stable, then such a point will eventually be reached. The plot of any component $\psi_k(\beta)$ of $\Psi(\beta)$, of course, can be given in terms of its real and imaginary parts or in terms of magnitude $|\psi_k(\beta)|$ and phase angle $\phi_k(\beta)$ of

$$\psi_k(\beta) = |\psi_k(\beta)|e^{\phi_k(\beta)}$$

If the sequence $f(n)$ is not asymptotically stable, the Fourier transform does not exist, since the infinite summation in Eq. (7.6.9) does not converge. The transformation is extended to include such functions by introducing a convergence factor similar to that used to extend the Fourier transform to nonasymptotically stable functions. The resulting transformation is known as the z *transform* and is defined as follows.

Definition 7.6.1: In the sequence $\{f(n)\}$ let $f(n) = 0$ for $n < 0$ and be bounded for $n > 0$, and let γ be any finite positive constant such that the series

$$\sum_{n=0}^{\infty} \frac{1}{\gamma} f(n)$$

converges. The z transform of the sequence $\{f(n)\}$ is defined as

$$F(z) = \sum_{n=0}^{\infty} f(n)z^{-n} \tag{7.6.14}$$

where $z = \alpha\gamma = |z|e^{j\beta}$ is a complex variable. Note that, in contrast to the Fourier transform of a sequence, the variable z is not restricted to the unit circle. If $\{f(n)\}$ represents the values of $f(t)$ [$f(t) = 0$ for

$t < 0]$ at the points $t = nh$ and if we set

$$z^{-1} = e^{-sh} \qquad s = \sigma + j\omega$$

then the definition of the z transform as given by Eq. (7.6.14) differs from the definition of the Laplace transform only in that the time function is replaced by a sequence and the integral by a summation.

Example 7.6.1: Determine the z transform of the two sequences

$$f_1(n) = \begin{cases} 0 & n < 0 \\ 1 & n > 0 \end{cases}$$

and $f_2(n) = nh$, $n = 1, 2, \ldots .$

Solution: By the direct application of Definition 7.6.1 we have

$$F_1(z) = \sum_{n=0}^{\infty} z^{-n} = 1 + z^{-1} + z^{-2} + \cdots$$

$$= \frac{1}{1 - z^{-1}} = \frac{z}{z - 1} \qquad \text{for } |z| > 1$$

and

$$F_2(z) = \sum_{n=0}^{\infty} hnz^{-n} = hz^{-1} + 2hz^{-2} + \cdots$$

$$= \frac{hz}{(z - 1)^2} \qquad \text{for } |z| > 1$$

As will become apparent in a later development, the class of functions in z of primary interest in the solution of discrete-state systems are the rational functions

$$F(z) = \frac{p(z)}{q(z)} z \tag{7.6.15}$$

where $p(z)$ is of lower degree than $q(z)$. The inverse transform can be evaluated by expanding $F(z)$ into partial fractions or by simply dividing the numerator by the denominator to generate a polynomial in z^{-1}. The partial-fraction expansion, in general, produces factors of the form

$$F(z) = \frac{A}{(z - \alpha)^k} \qquad k = 1, 2, 3, \ldots \tag{7.6.16}$$

By direct application of the definition of the z transform it can be verified that $zF(z)$ is the z transform of the sequence

$$f(n) = \begin{cases} AC_n^{k-1}a^{n-k+1} & \text{for } n \geq k - 1 \\ 0 & \text{for } n < k - 1 \end{cases} \tag{7.6.17}$$

where

$$C_n{}^{k-1} = \frac{n!}{(k-1)!(n-k+1)!} = \frac{n(n-1)(n-2)\cdots(n-k+2)}{(k-1)!}$$

Example 7.6.2: Evaluate the time sequence $f(n)$ corresponding to the z-domain function

$$F(z) = \frac{z^2}{(z-1)(z-2)^2} \tag{7.6.18}$$

Solution: Expanding $z/[(z-1)(z-2)^2]$ into partial fractions gives

$$\frac{z}{(z-1)(z-2)^2} = \frac{1}{z-1} + \frac{2}{(z-2)^2} - \frac{1}{z-2}$$

From Eqs. (7.6.16) and (7.6.17) the inverse z transform of each term in the expansion, after multiplication by z, gives

$$f(n) = 1 + n2^n - 2^n = 1 + (n-1)2^n \qquad n = 1, 2, \ldots$$

If the numerator of $F(z)$ as given in Eq. (7.6.18) is divided by the denominator, the first few terms are

$$F(z) = \frac{z^2}{z^3 - 5z^2 + 8z - 4} = z^{-1} + 5z^{-2} + 17z^{-3} + \cdots$$

But, from the definition of the z transform, it follows that the coefficients of z^{-n} represent the sequence; thus

$$f(0) = 0 \qquad f(1) = 1 \qquad f(2) = 5 \qquad f(3) = 17 \qquad \cdots$$

Two relatively simple but fundamental properties of the z transform of a sequence are given by the following two theorems.

Theorem 7.6.1 (initial value): If $F(z)$ represents the z transform of $\{f(n)\}$, then

$$f(0) = \lim_{z \to \infty} F(z)$$

Proof: From the definition of the z transform

$$F(z) = f(0) + f(1)z^{-1} + f(2)z^{-2} + \cdots$$

By taking the limit as $z \to \infty$ $(z^{-1} \to 0)$ there results

$$\lim_{z \to \infty} F(z) = f(0)$$

Theorem 7.6.2 (final value): If $f(n)$ is an asymptotically stable sequence then

$$\lim_{n \to \infty} f(n) = \lim_{z \to 1} (z-1)F(z)$$

Proof: Consider the z transform of $g(n) = f(n + 1) - f(n)$. Direct application of the definition shows that if the z transform of $f(n)$ is $f(z)$ then the z transform of $f(n + 1)$ is

$$\sum_{n=0}^{\infty} f(n + 1)z^{-1} = z[f(0) + f(1)z^{-1} + f(2)z^{-2} + \cdots] - zf(0)$$

$$= zf(z) - zf(0)$$

It follows, therefore, that the z transform of $g(n)$ is

$$G(z) = zF(z) - zf(0) - F(z) \tag{7.6.19}$$

But $G(z)$ can also be considered as the limit of a finite sum,

$$G(z) = \lim_{n \to \infty} \sum_{i=0}^{n} [f(i + 1) - f(i)]z^{-1}$$

Now, consider the limit of $G(z)$ as $z \to 1$. Since the sequence $f(n)$ is asymptotically stable, the order of the limits can be interchanged to give

$$G(z) = \lim_{n \to \infty} \sum_{i=0}^{n} \lim_{z \to 1} [f(i + 1) - f(i)]z^{-1}$$

$$= \lim_{n \to \infty} \sum_{i=0}^{\infty} [f(i + 1) - f(i)]$$

$$= \lim_{n \to \infty} [f(1) - f(0) + f(2) - f(1) + \cdots + f(n + 1) - f(n)]$$

$$= \lim_{n \to \infty} [-f(0) + f(n + 1)]$$

$$= -f(0) + \lim_{n \to \infty} f(n) \tag{7.6.20}$$

Equating Eqs. (7.6.19) and (7.6.20) establishes the theorem.

Theorem 7.6.3 (shifting theorem): If

$$u(n) = \begin{cases} 0 & n < 0 \\ 1 & n > 0 \end{cases}$$

then the z transform of $u(n - k)$ is given by

$$F[u(n - k)] = z^{-k}F[u(n)] = z^{-k}\frac{z}{z - 1}$$

Proof: From the definition of the z transform,

$$F[u(n - k)] = \sum_{n=0}^{\infty} u(n - k)z^{-n}$$

Now, if we let $n - k = m$, then

$$F[u(n - k)] = \sum_{m=-k}^{\infty} u(m)z^{-m}z^{-k}$$

Or since $u(n - k) = u(m) = 0$, for $m = n - k < 0$

$$F[u(n - k)] = \sum_{m=0}^{\infty} u(m)z^{-m}z^{-k}$$

$$= z^{-k}F[u(n)] = z^{-k}\frac{z}{z - 1}$$

7.7 COMPLEX-FREQUENCY EQUIVALENTS OF STATE MODELS

Consider the general linear state model

$$\frac{d}{dt}\mathbf{\Psi}(t) = \mathbf{P}\mathbf{\Psi}(t) + \mathbf{Q}\mathbf{E}(t) \tag{7.7.1}$$

$$\mathbf{R}(t) = \mathbf{M}\mathbf{\Psi}(t) + \mathbf{N}\mathbf{E}(t)$$

where, as previously, $\mathbf{E}(t)$ is a vector of known (input) time functions and $\mathbf{R}(t)$ is the response vector. The Laplace transform of $\mathbf{E}(t)$ is assumed to exist and is represented by the vector

$$\mathbf{E}(s) = \int_0^{\infty} e^{-st}\mathbf{E}(t)\, dt \tag{7.7.2}$$

This transform exists provided only that $\mathbf{E}(t)$ is finite and has at most a finite number of discontinuities for $t > 0$.

The state vector $\mathbf{\Psi}(t)$ is continuous in the entire interval $t > 0$ and therefore has a Laplace transform which will be indicated as

$$\mathbf{\Psi}(s) = \int_0^{\infty} e^{-st}\mathbf{\Psi}(t)\, dt$$

It is easy to show by integrating by parts that if $\mathbf{\Psi}(t)$ is defined and continuous then the Laplace transform of $(d/dt)\mathbf{\Psi}(t)$ exists and is given by

$$\int_0^{\infty} e^{-st}\frac{d}{dt}\mathbf{\Psi}(t)\, dt = s\int_0^{\infty} e^{-st}\mathbf{\Psi}(t)\, dt - \mathbf{\Psi}(0)$$

$$= s\mathbf{\Psi}(s) - \mathbf{\Psi}(0) \tag{7.7.3}$$

where $\mathbf{\Psi}(0) = \mathbf{\Psi}_0$ represents the initial state.

Since $\mathbf{R}(t)$ is a linear combination of $\mathbf{\Psi}(t)$ and $\mathbf{E}(t)$, it also has a Laplace transform. This vector is represented as $\mathbf{R}(s)$.

Taking the Laplace transform of Eqs. (7.7.1) and rearranging terms gives the equivalent complex-frequency-domain model

$$(s\mathbf{U} - \mathbf{P})\mathbf{\Psi}(s) = \mathbf{\Psi}(0) + \mathbf{Q}\mathbf{E}(s) \tag{7.7.4}$$

$$\mathbf{R}(s) = \mathbf{M}\mathbf{\Psi}(s) + \mathbf{N}\mathbf{E}(s)$$

Since these are linear algebraic equations, it is possible to solve the first set for the vector $\mathbf{\Psi}(s)$ and substitute the result into the second set, to obtain

$$\mathbf{R}(s) = \mathbf{M}(s\mathbf{U} - \mathbf{P})^{-1}[\mathbf{\Psi}(0) + \mathbf{Q}\mathbf{E}(s)] + \mathbf{N}\mathbf{E}(s) \qquad (7.7.5)$$

This expression shows the complex frequency spectrum of the response vector as an explicit function of the initial-state vector and the complex frequency spectrum of the input vector. The reader may have already observed the similarity between Eq. (7.7.5) and Eq. (7.2.17); for $\mathbf{\Psi}(0) = 0$ they differ only in that s and the complex frequency vectors $\mathbf{E}(s)$ and $\mathbf{R}(s)$ are replaced, respectively, by $\lambda = j\omega$ and the complex-number vectors $\mathbf{\bar{E}}$ and $\mathbf{\bar{R}}$ representing the magnitudes and phase angles of the sinusoidal excitation and response vectors. Consequently, when only sinusoidal response characteristics are required, the inverse and the associated matrix products in Eq. (7.7.5) can be evaluated in terms of the complex parameters involving $j\omega$ (rather than $s = \sigma + j\omega$). It should be evident then that complex impedance, admittance, and transfer matrices are obtained from corresponding s-domain matrices by simply replacing s by $j\omega$. The coefficient matrix relating the complex frequency spectrum of the response vector to the complex frequency spectrum of the excitation vector is also referred to as an *impedance, admittance,* or *transfer matrix.*

The time variation for the response vector for any given $\mathbf{E}(s)$ and $\mathbf{\Psi}(0)$ is obtained by taking the inverse Laplace transform of $\mathbf{R}(s)$ as expressed in Eq. (7.7.5). The coefficient matrix $s\mathbf{U} - \mathbf{P}$ is, of course, the characteristic matrix $\lambda\mathbf{U} - \mathbf{P}$ with λ replaced by s, and an algorithm has already been given in Sec. 6.3 for evaluating the inverse indicated in Eq. (7.7.5). In general, if $\mathbf{P}$ is of order n, this inverse is of the form

$$(s\mathbf{U} - \mathbf{P})^{-1} = \frac{1}{D(s)} \text{adj } (s\mathbf{U} - \mathbf{P}) = \frac{1}{D(s)} (\mathbf{U}s^{n-1} + \mathbf{C}_1 s^{n-2}$$
$$+ \cdots + \mathbf{C}_{n-1})$$

The inverse Laplace transform of $\mathbf{R}(s)$ is obtained by expanding the terms

$$\frac{1}{D(s)} \mathbf{M} \text{ adj } (s\mathbf{U} - \mathbf{P})\mathbf{\Psi}(0)$$

and

$$\left[\frac{1}{D(s)} \mathbf{M} \text{ adj } (s\mathbf{U} - \mathbf{P})\mathbf{Q} + \mathbf{N}\right] \mathbf{E}(s)$$

into partial fractions. If, for example, the roots of $D(s)$ are all distinct, then $D(s) = (s - s_1)(s - s_2) \cdots (s - s_n)$ and the first term expands into the form

$$\frac{1}{D(s)} \mathbf{M} \text{ adj } (s\mathbf{U} - \mathbf{P})\mathbf{\Psi}(0) = \frac{1}{s - s_1} \mathbf{R}_1 + \cdots + \frac{1}{s - s_n} \mathbf{R}_n$$

$$(7.7.6)$$

where $\mathbf{R}_i$ is the vector

$$\mathbf{R}_i = \lim_{s \to s_i} \frac{s - s_i}{D(s)} \mathbf{M} \text{ adj } (s\mathbf{U} - \mathbf{P})\mathbf{\Psi}(0) \qquad i = 1, 2, \ldots, n$$

The partial-fraction expansion of the second term, in general, will depend upon the vector $\mathbf{E}(s)$. If $\mathbf{E}(s)$ is a vector of rational functions of s with poles $s = s_a$, $s = s_b$, $\ldots$, $s = s_k$ and these poles are distinct from the zeros of $D(s)$, then the partial-fraction expression of the second term is of the general form†

$$\left[\frac{1}{D(s)} \mathbf{M} \text{ adj } (s\mathbf{U} - \mathbf{P})\mathbf{Q} + \mathbf{N} \right]\mathbf{E}(s) = \frac{1}{s - s_1} \mathbf{E}_1$$

$$+ \cdots + \frac{1}{s - s_n} \mathbf{E}_n + \frac{1}{s - s_a} \mathbf{E}_a + \cdots + \frac{1}{s - s_k} \mathbf{E}_k \quad (7.7.7)$$

where

$$\mathbf{E}_i = \lim_{s \to s_i} \frac{s - s_i}{D(s)} [\mathbf{M} \text{ adj } (s\mathbf{U} - \mathbf{P})\mathbf{Q} + \mathbf{N}]\mathbf{E}(s)$$

$$i = 1, 2, \ldots, n, a, b, \ldots, k$$

From Eqs. (7.7.6) and (7.7.7) it follows that the time response of $\mathbf{R}(t)$ as obtained from the inverse Laplace transform of each term is

$$\mathbf{R}(t) = \mathbf{R}_1 e^{s_1 t} + \cdots + \mathbf{R}_n e^{s_n t} + \mathbf{E}_a e^{s_a t} + \cdots + \mathbf{E}_k e^{s_k t} \qquad (7.7.8)$$

Example 7.7.1: By applying the Laplace transformation to the state equations, determine the time solution for the mechanical system shown in Fig. 7.7.1. This system is also considered in Example 6.1.2, where the state model is given as

$$\frac{d}{dt} \begin{bmatrix} f_1(t) \\ f_2(t) \\ \dot{\delta}_3(t) \\ \dot{\delta}_4(t) \end{bmatrix} = \begin{bmatrix} 0 & 0 & -K_1 & 0 \\ 0 & 0 & K_2 & -K_2 \\ 1/M_3 & -1/M_3 & 0 & 0 \\ 0 & 1/M_4 & 0 & 0 \end{bmatrix} \begin{bmatrix} f_1(t) \\ f_2(t) \\ \dot{\delta}_3(t) \\ \dot{\delta}_4(t) \end{bmatrix} + \begin{bmatrix} K_1 \\ 0 \\ 0 \\ 0 \end{bmatrix} \dot{\delta}_0(t) \qquad (7.7.9)$$

Solution: Since $\dot{\delta}_0(t)$ is unbounded at $t = t_1$, the excitation function does not have a complex frequency spectrum; i.e., the Laplace transform of $\dot{\delta}_0(t)$ does not exist. Also, it was shown in Example 6.1.2 that $f_1(t)$ is also discontinuous at $t = t_1$. Consequently, $(d/dt)f_1(t)$ is not defined at this point and does not have a complex frequency representation. However, by applying the transformation of variables

$$\psi_1(t) = f_1(t) - K_1 \delta_0(t)$$

† Some of the terms in this expression may vanish because of cancellation of certain poles with corresponding numerator terms.

as discussed in Example 6.1.2, the state model is transformed into the equivalent form

$$\frac{d}{dt}\begin{bmatrix} \psi_1(t) \\ f_2(t) \\ \dot{\delta}_3(t) \\ \dot{\delta}_4(t) \end{bmatrix} = \begin{bmatrix} 0 & 0 & -K_1 & 0 \\ 0 & 0 & K_2 & -K_2 \\ 1/M_3 & -1/M_3 & 0 & 0 \\ 0 & 1/M_4 & 0 & 0 \end{bmatrix} \begin{bmatrix} \psi_1(t) \\ f_2(t) \\ \dot{\delta}_3(t) \\ \dot{\delta}_4(t) \end{bmatrix} + \begin{bmatrix} 0 \\ 0 \\ K_1/M_3 \\ 0 \end{bmatrix} \delta_0(t)$$

$$(7.7.10)$$

where $\psi_1(t)$ is defined and continuous. The excitation function $\delta_0(t)$ is defined and sectionally continuous and can be represented as the sum

$$\delta_0(t) = \delta_0^{(1)}(t) + \delta_0^{(2)}(t) + \delta_0^{(3)}(t) + \cdots$$

where $\delta_0^{(i)}(t)$ has at most one discontinuity and is defined in Fig. 7.7.1b. The time solution to the system for the given periodic excitation function can be obtained as the sum of the solution for each of the functions $\delta_0^{(i)}(t)$. Consider first the complex frequency spectrum of the state vector for the excitation function $\delta_0^{(1)}(t)$. The s-domain state model as obtained by taking the Laplace transform of Eq. (7.7.10) with $\delta_0(t)$ replaced by $\delta_0^{(1)}(t)$ is

$$\begin{bmatrix} s & 0 & K_1 & 0 \\ 0 & s & -K_2 & K_2 \\ -1/M_3 & 1/M_3 & s & 0 \\ 0 & -1/M_4 & 0 & s \end{bmatrix} \begin{bmatrix} \psi_1^{(1)}(s) \\ f_2^{(1)}(s) \\ \dot{\delta}_3^{(1)}(s) \\ \dot{\delta}_4^{(1)}(s) \end{bmatrix} = \begin{bmatrix} 0 \\ 0 \\ K_1/M_3 \\ 0 \end{bmatrix} \delta_0^{(1)}(s) + \begin{bmatrix} \psi_1^{(1)}(0) \\ f_2^{(1)}(0) \\ \dot{\delta}_3^{(1)}(0) \\ \dot{\delta}_4^{(1)}(0) \end{bmatrix}$$

$$(7.7.11)$$

where

$$\delta_0^{(1)}(s) = \int_0^\infty \Delta\, t e^{-st}\, dt = \frac{\Delta}{s^2}$$

Upon multiplying by the inverse of the coefficient matrix in Eq. (7.7.11), the frequency spectrum of the state vector for $K_1 = K_2 = M_3 = M_4 = 1$ and zero

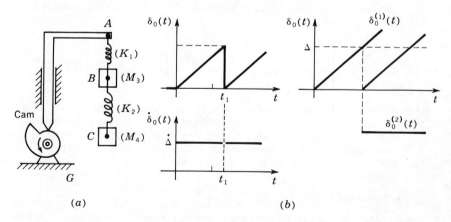

(a)   (b)

Fig. 7.7.1   (a) A mechanical system; (b) cam characteristics.

initial state is evaluated as

$$
\begin{bmatrix}
\psi_1^{(1)}(s) \\
f_2^{(1)}(s) \\
\dot{\delta}_3^{(1)}(s) \\
\dot{\delta}_4^{(1)}(s)
\end{bmatrix}
= \frac{\Delta}{s^2 D(s)}
\begin{bmatrix}
-(s^2 + 1) \\
s^2 \\
s(s^2 + 1) \\
s
\end{bmatrix}
\tag{7.7.12}
$$

where

$$D(s) = s^4 + 3s^2 + 1 = (1 + \tau_1 s)(1 + \hat{\tau}_1 s)(1 + \tau_2 s)(1 + \hat{\tau}_2 s)$$

with

$$\tau_1 \cong j0.623 \qquad \text{and} \qquad \tau_2 \cong j1.616$$

The component of the time solution corresponding to the excitation function

$$\delta_0^{(1)}(t) = \Delta t$$

is obtained by expanding each term in Eq. (7.7.12) into partial fractions and then taking the inverse transform of each term. The frequency spectrum $\psi_1^{(1)}(s)$, for example, expands into the form

$$
\psi_1^{(1)}(s) = \frac{-(s^2 + 1)}{s^2(s^4 + 3s^2 + 1)} = \frac{R_1}{1 + \tau_1 s} + \frac{\hat{R}_1}{1 + \hat{\tau}_1 s}
$$
$$
+ \frac{R_2}{1 + \tau_2 s} + \frac{\hat{R}_2}{1 + \hat{\tau}_2 s} + \frac{R_3}{s} + \frac{R_4}{s^2}
$$

The numerical values of the coefficients are $R_1 = -j0.0545$, $R_2 = j0.955$, $R_3 = 0$, and $R_4 = -1$.

Then, upon taking the inverse Laplace transform of each term, the corresponding component of the time response for the given excitation is

$$
\psi_1^{(1)}(t) = \frac{R_1}{\tau_1} e^{-t/\tau_1} + \frac{\hat{R}_1}{\hat{\tau}_1} e^{-t/\hat{\tau}_1} + \frac{R_2}{\tau_2} e^{-t/\tau_2} + \frac{\hat{R}_2}{\hat{\tau}_2} e^{-t/\hat{\tau}_2} + R_3 + R_4 t
$$
$$
= 2 \left| \frac{R_1}{\tau_1} \right| \cos\left(\frac{t}{|\tau_1|} + \theta_1 \right) + 2 \left| \frac{R_2}{\tau_2} \right| \cos\left(\frac{t}{|\tau_2|} + \theta_2 \right) + R_3 + R_4 t
$$

or, numerically,

$$
\psi_1^{(1)}(t) \cong 0.175 \cos\left(\frac{t}{0.623} + 90° \right) + 1.169 \cos\left(\frac{t}{1.616} + 90° \right) - t
$$

The second component of the excitation function $\delta_0^{(2)}(t)$ in Fig. 7.7.1b is described as a delayed step function of magnitude Δ. The frequency spectrum of this function is

$$
\delta_0^{(2)}(s) = \int_0^\infty \delta_0^{(2)}(t) e^{-st} \, dt = \int_0^{t_1} 0 e^{-st} \, dt + \int_{t_1}^\infty \Delta e^{-st} \, dt = \frac{\Delta}{s} e^{-st_1}
$$

It is easy to show that, in general, the complex frequency spectrum of a function delayed by an amount t_1 is equal to the frequency spectrum of the undelayed function multiplied by the factor e^{-st_1}. The frequency spectrum for the step-function component of the excitation is obtained by simply replacing the factor $\dot{\Delta}/s^2$ in Eq. (7.7.12) by $(\Delta/s)e^{-st_1}$, to obtain

$$
\begin{bmatrix} \psi_1{}^{(2)}(s) \\ f_2{}^{(2)}(s) \\ \dot{\delta}_3{}^{(2)}(s) \\ \delta_4{}^{(2)}(s) \end{bmatrix} = \frac{\Delta e^{-st}}{sD(s)} \begin{bmatrix} -(s^2+1) \\ s^2 \\ s(s^2+1) \\ s \end{bmatrix}
$$

The partial-fraction expansion of the rational fraction appearing in the expression for $\psi_1{}^2(s)$, for example, gives the form

$$
\psi_1{}^{(2)}(s) = \left(\frac{R_1'}{1+\tau_1 s} + \frac{\hat{R}_1'}{1+\hat{\tau}_1 s} + \frac{R_2'}{1+\tau_2 s} + \frac{\hat{R}_2'}{1+\hat{\tau}_2 s} + \frac{R_3'}{s} \right) e^{-st_1}
$$

The presence of the factor e^{-st_1} indicates that the inverse Laplace transform of each term in the expression is delayed in time by an amount t_1. That is,

$$
\psi_1{}^{(2)} = \begin{cases} 0 & \text{for } t < t_1 \\ \dfrac{R_1'}{\tau_1} e^{-(t-t_1)/\tau_1} + \dfrac{\hat{R}_1'}{\hat{\tau}_1} e^{-(t-t_1)/\hat{\tau}_1} + \dfrac{R_2'}{\tau_2} e^{-(t-t_1)/\tau_2} + \dfrac{\hat{R}_2'}{\hat{\tau}_2} e^{-(t-t_1)/\hat{\tau}_2} \\ \qquad\qquad\qquad\qquad\qquad\qquad + R_3' & \text{for } t > t_1 \end{cases}
$$

The components of the solutions resulting from the succeeding components in the excitation signal are obtained in exactly the same manner, and the complete solution is obtained as the sum of these solutions.

A similar development can be carried out for discrete-state systems, in terms of the z transform. That is, consider the general linear discrete-state system model

$$
\begin{aligned}
\Psi(n+1) &= \mathbf{P}\Psi(n) + \mathbf{Q}\mathbf{E}(n) \\
\mathbf{R}(n) &= \mathbf{M}\Psi(n) + \mathbf{N}\mathbf{E}(n)
\end{aligned}
\tag{7.7.13}
$$

Taking the z transform of Eqs. (7.7.13) transforms the difference equations to algebraic equations in z,

$$
\begin{aligned}
z\Psi(z) &= \mathbf{P}\Psi(z) + \mathbf{Q}\mathbf{E}(z) + z\Psi(0) \\
\mathbf{R}(z) &= \mathbf{M}\Psi(z) + \mathbf{N}\mathbf{E}(z)
\end{aligned}
\tag{7.7.14}
$$

or, solving for $\Psi(z)$,

$$
\begin{aligned}
\Psi(z) &= (z\mathbf{U} - \mathbf{P})^{-1}[\mathbf{Q}\mathbf{E}(z) + z\Psi(0)] \\
\mathbf{R}(z) &= [\mathbf{M}(z\mathbf{U} - \mathbf{P})^{-1}\mathbf{Q} + \mathbf{N}]\mathbf{E}(z) + \mathbf{M}(z\mathbf{U} - \mathbf{P})^{-1}z\Psi(0)
\end{aligned}
\tag{7.7.15}
$$

This result is identical in form to the Laplace transform of the continuous-state model given in Eq. (7.7.5), except that s is replaced by z and the initial conditions $\Psi(0)$ by $z\Psi(0)$. The coefficient matrix

$$
\mathbf{M}(z\mathbf{U} - \mathbf{P})^{-1}\mathbf{Q} + \mathbf{N}
$$

is called the *z-domain transfer matrix* relating the excitation and response functions, and, as in the case of s-domain models, it is common practice to specify the z-domain terminal characteristics of components in terms of zero initial state, that is, $\Psi(0) = 0$.

The time-sequence vector $\mathbf{R}(n)$ corresponding to $\mathbf{R}(z)$ in Eqs. (7.7.15) is, of course, obtained by taking the inverse z transform of the right-hand side. Since

$$(z\mathbf{U} - \mathbf{P})^{-1} = \frac{1}{D(z)} \text{ adj } (z\mathbf{U} - \mathbf{P})$$

it follows that the right-hand side of Eq. (7.7.15) is a matrix whose entries are rational functions of z and can be expanded into partial fractions. If, for example, $z = z_i$ is a zero of $D(z)$ of order r_i and $\psi(0) = 0$, then the expansion of $\mathbf{R}(z)$ contains r_i terms of the general form

$$\mathbf{R}_i(z) = \mathbf{Z}_j \frac{1}{(z - z_i)^j} \mathbf{E}(z) \qquad j = 1, 2, \ldots, r_i$$

where $\mathbf{Z}_j$ is the residue matrix corresponding to the factor $(z - z_i)^j$. The inverse transform of $\mathbf{R}_i(z)$ has already been given as Eq. (7.6.17).

Example 7.7.2: Obtain a solution to the following system of difference equations by means of the z transform,

$$\begin{bmatrix} \psi_1(n + 1) \\ \psi_2(n + 1) \end{bmatrix} = \begin{bmatrix} 0.2 & 1 \\ 0 & -0.5 \end{bmatrix} \begin{bmatrix} \psi_1(n) \\ \psi_2(n) \end{bmatrix} + \begin{bmatrix} 0 \\ 1 \end{bmatrix} e(n) \qquad (7.7.16)$$

where

$$e(n) = \begin{cases} 0 & \text{for } n < 0 \\ 1 & \text{for } n > 0 \end{cases}$$

and

$$\psi_1(0) = 1 \qquad \psi_2(0) = 0$$

Solution: Taking the z transform of the given equations gives

$$z \begin{bmatrix} \psi_1(z) \\ \psi_2(z) \end{bmatrix} = \begin{bmatrix} 0.2 & 1 \\ 0 & -0.5 \end{bmatrix} \begin{bmatrix} \psi_1(z) \\ \psi_2(z) \end{bmatrix} + \begin{bmatrix} 0 \\ 1 \end{bmatrix} \frac{z}{z - 1} + z \begin{bmatrix} \psi_1(0) \\ \psi_2(0) \end{bmatrix}$$

Solving for $\psi_1(z)$ and $\psi_2(z)$ gives

$$\begin{bmatrix} \psi_1(z) \\ \psi_2(z) \end{bmatrix} = \frac{z}{(z - 0.2)(z + 0.5)} \begin{bmatrix} z + 0.5 & 1 \\ 1 & z - 0.2 \end{bmatrix} \begin{bmatrix} \psi_1(0 \\ \psi_2(0) \end{bmatrix}$$

$$+ \frac{z}{(z - 1)(z - 0.2)(z + 0.5)} \begin{bmatrix} z + 0.5 & 1 \\ 0 & z - 0.2 \end{bmatrix} \begin{bmatrix} 0 \\ 1 \end{bmatrix}$$

Expanding into partial fractions gives

$$\begin{bmatrix} \psi_1(z) \\ \psi_2(z) \end{bmatrix} = \begin{bmatrix} \frac{20}{21} \\ -\frac{2}{3} \end{bmatrix} \frac{z}{z + 0.5} + \begin{bmatrix} -\frac{9}{14} \\ 0 \end{bmatrix} \frac{z}{z - 0.2} + \begin{bmatrix} \frac{5}{6} \\ \frac{2}{3} \end{bmatrix} \frac{z}{z - 1}$$

The corresponding sequences are

$$\begin{bmatrix} \psi_1(n) \\ \psi_2(n) \end{bmatrix} = \begin{bmatrix} \frac{20}{21} \\ -\frac{2}{3} \end{bmatrix} (-0.5)^n + \begin{bmatrix} -\frac{9}{14} \\ 0 \end{bmatrix} (0.2)^n + \begin{bmatrix} \frac{5}{6} \\ \frac{2}{3} \end{bmatrix}$$

Within the context of the above application, the complex frequency transformations can be regarded simply as alternative methods for obtaining solutions to linear time-invariant state models. However, if one applies the transformations to the component models before applying the constraint equations of the system graph, an alternative and sometimes more convenient model of the system can be generated for certain classes of systems.

7.8 SHORT-CIRCUIT PARAMETER MODELS (BRANCH EQUATIONS)

Let the system graph G contain p parts, $p \geq 1$. Let there exist a forest F in G such that (1) the edges for which the across variables are specified are included in F and (2) the edges for which the through variables are specified are included in the coforest of F. Let the complex-frequency terminal equations for all remaining edges in G be such that their direct sum can be written in short-circuit parameter form as

$$\begin{bmatrix} \mathbf{Y}_{b_2}(s) \\ \mathbf{Y}_{c_1}(s) \end{bmatrix} = \begin{bmatrix} \mathbf{W}_{11}(s) & \mathbf{W}_{12}(s) \\ \mathbf{W}_{21}(s) & \mathbf{W}_{22}(s) \end{bmatrix} \begin{bmatrix} \mathbf{X}_{b_2}(s) \\ \mathbf{X}_{c_1}(s) \end{bmatrix} \tag{7.8.1}$$

$$\mathbf{X}_{b_1}(s) = \text{specified frequency spectra} \tag{7.8.2}$$
$$\mathbf{Y}_{c_2}(s) = \text{specified frequency spectra} \tag{7.8.3}$$

where $\mathbf{X}_{b_1}(s)$, $\mathbf{X}_{b_2}(s)$ and $\mathbf{Y}_{b_1}(s)$, $\mathbf{Y}_{b_2}(s)$ are column matrices representing subsets of the branch across and through variables, respectively, and $\mathbf{X}_{c_1}(s)$, $\mathbf{X}_{c_2}(s)$ and $\mathbf{Y}_{c_1}(s)$, $\mathbf{Y}_{c_2}(s)$ are column matrices representing, respectively, subsets of the chord across and through variables. The entries in each submatrix $\mathbf{W}_{ij}(s)$ are rational functions of s. Since $\mathbf{Y}_{b_2}(s)$ and $\mathbf{Y}_{c_1}(s)$ appear as the dependent variables in the component terminal equations [Eq. (7.8.1)], let the fundamental cut-set equations for F be written in the form

$$\begin{bmatrix} \mathbf{U} & \mathbf{A}_{12} \\ \mathbf{0} & \mathbf{A}_{22} \end{bmatrix} \begin{bmatrix} \mathbf{Y}_{b_1}(s) \\ \mathbf{Y}_{c_2}(s) \end{bmatrix} + \begin{bmatrix} \mathbf{0} & \mathbf{A}_{11} \\ \mathbf{U} & \mathbf{A}_{21} \end{bmatrix} \begin{bmatrix} \mathbf{Y}_{b_2}(s) \\ \mathbf{Y}_{c_1}(s) \end{bmatrix} = \mathbf{0} \tag{7.8.4}$$

Substituting Eq. (7.8.1) into Eq. (7.8.4) gives

$$\begin{bmatrix} \mathbf{U} & \mathbf{A}_{12} \\ \mathbf{0} & \mathbf{A}_{22} \end{bmatrix} \begin{bmatrix} \mathbf{Y}_{b_1}(s) \\ \mathbf{Y}_{c_2}(s) \end{bmatrix} + \begin{bmatrix} \mathbf{0} & \mathbf{A}_{11} \\ \mathbf{U} & \mathbf{A}_{21} \end{bmatrix} \begin{bmatrix} \mathbf{W}_{11}(s) & \mathbf{W}_{12}(s) \\ \mathbf{W}_{21}(s) & \mathbf{W}_{22}(s) \end{bmatrix} \begin{bmatrix} \mathbf{X}_{b_2}(s) \\ \mathbf{X}_{c_1}(s) \end{bmatrix} = \mathbf{0} \tag{7.8.5}$$

The chord across variables $\mathbf{X}_{c_1}(s)$ in Eq. (7.8.5) can now be expressed as a function of the branch variables $\mathbf{X}_{b_1}(s)$ and $\mathbf{X}_{b_2}(s)$. The necessary information is available, of course, from the fundamental circuit equations for F,

$$\begin{bmatrix} \mathbf{B}_{11} & \mathbf{B}_{12} & \mathbf{U} & \mathbf{0} \\ \mathbf{B}_{21} & \mathbf{B}_{22} & \mathbf{0} & \mathbf{U} \end{bmatrix} \begin{bmatrix} \mathbf{X}_{b_1}(s) \\ \mathbf{X}_{b_2}(s) \\ \mathbf{X}_{c_1}(s) \\ \mathbf{X}_{c_2}(s) \end{bmatrix} = \mathbf{0}$$

From these circuit equations the required relation is

$$\mathbf{X}_{c_1}(s) = -[\mathbf{B}_{11} \quad \mathbf{B}_{12}]\begin{bmatrix}\mathbf{X}_{b_1}(s) \\ \mathbf{X}_{b_2}(s)\end{bmatrix} \tag{7.8.6}$$

Obviously, in any given problem, Eq. (7.8.6) can be written directly from the system graph, and it is expedient to do so. Alternatively, the circuit matrices can be obtained from the cut-set matrices by applying Theorem 4.6.2, which shows that

$$\mathbf{B}_{11} = -\mathbf{A}_{11}^T \quad \text{and} \quad \mathbf{B}_{12} = -\mathbf{A}_{21}^T \tag{7.8.7}$$

By substituting Eq. (7.8.7) into Eq. (7.8.6) and the result into Eq. (7.8.5), the general form of the short-circuit parameter model of the system is established as

$$\begin{bmatrix}\mathbf{U} & \mathbf{A}_{12} \\ \mathbf{0} & \mathbf{A}_{22}\end{bmatrix}\begin{bmatrix}\mathbf{Y}_{b_1}(s) \\ \mathbf{Y}_{c_2}(s)\end{bmatrix} + \begin{bmatrix}\mathbf{0} & \mathbf{A}_{11} \\ \mathbf{U} & \mathbf{A}_{21}\end{bmatrix}\begin{bmatrix}\mathbf{W}_{11}(s) & \mathbf{W}_{12}(s) \\ \mathbf{W}_{21}(s) & \mathbf{W}_{22}(s)\end{bmatrix}$$
$$\times \begin{bmatrix}\mathbf{0} & \mathbf{U} \\ \mathbf{A}_{11}^T & \mathbf{A}_{21}^T\end{bmatrix}\begin{bmatrix}\mathbf{X}_{b_1}(s) \\ \mathbf{X}_{b_2}(s)\end{bmatrix} = \mathbf{0} \tag{7.8.8}$$

The triple matrix product appearing in the above equations has an important implication. Once it is recognized that the matrix $\mathbf{W}(s)$ is premultiplied by a submatrix of the cut-set matrix and postmultiplied by its transpose, it is no longer necessary in the solution of a particular problem to write the fundamental circuit equations explicitly. Furthermore, if $\mathbf{W}(s)$ is symmetric, as is always the case in a system containing only two-terminal components, the triple matrix product is also symmetric. In fact, it is possible to give a simple algorithm for forming this triple matrix product when $\mathbf{W}(s)$ is diagonal.[3]

Equation (7.8.8) can be regarded as two sets of equations, the first set having the form

$$[\mathbf{U} \quad \mathbf{A}_{12}]\begin{bmatrix}\mathbf{Y}_{b_1}(s) \\ \mathbf{Y}_{c_2}(s)\end{bmatrix} + [\mathbf{0} \quad \mathbf{A}_{11}]\begin{bmatrix}\mathbf{W}_{11}(s) & \mathbf{W}_{12}(s) \\ \mathbf{W}_{21}(s) & \mathbf{W}_{22}(s)\end{bmatrix}$$
$$\times \begin{bmatrix}\mathbf{0} & \mathbf{U} \\ \mathbf{A}_{11}^T & \mathbf{A}_{21}^T\end{bmatrix}\begin{bmatrix}\mathbf{X}_{b_1}(s) \\ \mathbf{X}_{b_2}(s)\end{bmatrix} = \mathbf{0} \tag{7.8.9}$$

and since $\mathbf{X}_{b_1}(s)$ and $\mathbf{Y}_{c_2}(s)$ represent specified frequency spectra, it is convenient to write the second set in the form

$$\mathbf{A}_{22}\mathbf{Y}_{c_2}(s) + [\mathbf{U} \quad \mathbf{A}_{21}]\begin{bmatrix}\mathbf{W}_{11}(s) & \mathbf{W}_{12}(s) \\ \mathbf{W}_{21}(s) & \mathbf{W}_{22}(s)\end{bmatrix}\begin{bmatrix}\mathbf{U} \\ \mathbf{A}_{21}^T\end{bmatrix}\mathbf{X}_{b_2}(s)$$
$$+ [\mathbf{U} \quad \mathbf{A}_{21}]\begin{bmatrix}\mathbf{W}_{11}(s) & \mathbf{W}_{12}(s) \\ \mathbf{W}_{21}(s) & \mathbf{W}_{22}(s)\end{bmatrix}\begin{bmatrix}\mathbf{0} \\ \mathbf{A}_{11}^T\end{bmatrix}\mathbf{X}_{b_1}(s) = \mathbf{0} \tag{7.8.10}$$

A solution of the latter set of equations for $\mathbf{X}_{b_2}(s)$ establishes the frequency spectra of all the unknown across variables of the selected tree in the system graph. If the frequency spectra $\mathbf{Y}_{b_1}(s)$ are required, they are obtained by substituting the solution for $\mathbf{X}_{b_2}(s)$ into Eq. (7.8.9).

The order of the vector $\mathbf{X}_{b_2}(s)$ is always equal to the number of branches in the forest of the system graph less the number of across variables that have known frequency spectra. Consequently, if the number of specified branch across variables is n_x and the graph contains p parts and v vertices, then the order of the inverse required to establish the unknown frequency spectra is $v - p - n_x$.

The order of the coefficient matrix for this type of model may, in some cases, be lower than the order of the characteristic matrix $s\mathbf{U} - \mathbf{P}$ in a state model of the same system. However, in contrast to the characteristic matrix, the entries in the coefficient matrix on the vector $\mathbf{X}_{b_2}(s)$ in Eq. (7.8.10) are rational functions of s, and there is no general algorithm available for evaluating the required inverse on computing machines. If the order of the coefficient matrix is relatively low or if it contains only a few rational functions (all other entries being numbers), then the required inverse can be evaluated without much difficulty.

If only the steady-state response characteristic of a stable system to a sinusoidal excitation function of one frequency is required, then the substitution $s = j\omega_0$, where ω_0 is a known constant, can be made. In this case the rational functions in the coefficient matrix reduce to complex constants, and it is possible to realize the inverse on a computing machine. This important area of application of complex-frequency models is demonstrated in the following simple example.

Example 7.8.1: Determine the magnitude and phase angle of the steady-state component of the voltage v_3 across the "detector" of the bridge network of Fig. 7.8.1 as an explicit function of the parameters and excitation signal. Determine the magnitudes of the network parameters for which $i_3 = 0$ under steady-state conditions if the excitation signal is

$$v_1(t) = 10 \cos \omega_0 t$$

with $\omega_0 = 2\pi \times 400$.

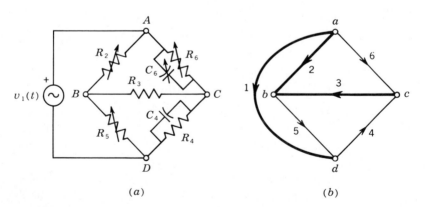

(a) (b)

Fig. 7.8.1 (a) A bridge circuit; (b) the system graph.

Solution: Since we are concerned only with steady-state characteristics, only the complex-frequency characteristics of the system with zero initial voltages on the capacitors are considered. The complex-frequency characteristics of the components are given in terms of the edges of the system graph in Fig. 7.8.1*b* by the equations

$$\mathbf{v}_1(s) \text{ specified}$$
$$\mathbf{i}_j(s) = w_j(s)\mathbf{v}_j(s) \qquad j = 2, 3, \ldots, 6 \tag{7.8.11}$$

where

$$w_j(s) = g_j \qquad \text{for } j = 2, 3, 5$$

and

$$w_j(s) = g_j + C_j s \qquad \text{for } j = 4, 6$$

Since the terminal equations are to be substituted into the cut-set equations, the latter are written in the form

$$\begin{bmatrix} \mathbf{i}_1(s) \\ 0 \\ 0 \end{bmatrix} + \begin{bmatrix} 0 & 0 & -1 & 1 & 0 \\ 1 & 0 & 1 & -1 & 1 \\ 0 & 1 & -1 & 0 & -1 \end{bmatrix} \begin{bmatrix} \mathbf{i}_2(s) \\ \mathbf{i}_3(s) \\ \mathbf{i}_4(s) \\ \mathbf{i}_5(s) \\ \mathbf{i}_6(s) \end{bmatrix} = \mathbf{0} \tag{7.8.12}$$

Upon substituting Eq. (7.8.11) into Eq. (7.8.12) and expressing the voltage variables in terms of the branch voltages, we have

$$\begin{bmatrix} \mathbf{i}_1(s) \\ 0 \\ 0 \end{bmatrix} + \begin{bmatrix} 0 & 0 & -1 & 1 & 0 \\ 1 & 0 & 1 & -1 & 1 \\ 0 & 1 & -1 & 0 & -1 \end{bmatrix} \begin{bmatrix} w_2(s) & 0 & 0 & 0 & 0 \\ 0 & w_3(s) & 0 & 0 & 0 \\ 0 & 0 & w_4(s) & 0 & 0 \\ 0 & 0 & 0 & w_5(s) & 0 \\ 0 & 0 & 0 & 0 & w_6(s) \end{bmatrix}$$

$$\times \begin{bmatrix} 0 & 1 & 0 \\ 0 & 0 & 1 \\ -1 & 1 & -1 \\ 1 & -1 & 0 \\ 0 & 1 & -1 \end{bmatrix} \begin{bmatrix} \mathbf{v}_1(s) \\ \mathbf{v}_2(s) \\ \mathbf{v}_3(s) \end{bmatrix} = \mathbf{0} \quad (7.8.13)$$

or

$$\begin{bmatrix} \mathbf{i}_1(s) \\ 0 \\ 0 \end{bmatrix}$$

$$+ \begin{bmatrix} w_4(s) + w_5(s) & -w_4(s) - w_5(s) & w_4(s) \\ -w_4(s) - w_5(s) & w_2(s) + w_4(s) + w_5(s) + w_6(s) & -w_4(s) - w_6(s) \\ w_4(s) & -w_4(s) - w_6(s) & w_3(s) + w_4(s) + w_6(s) \end{bmatrix}$$

$$\times \begin{bmatrix} \mathbf{v}_1(s) \\ \mathbf{v}_2(s) \\ \mathbf{v}_3(s) \end{bmatrix} = \mathbf{0} \quad (7.8.14)$$

Since $\mathbf{v}_1(s)$ is known, it follows that

$$\begin{bmatrix} \mathbf{v}_2(s) \\ \mathbf{v}_3(s) \end{bmatrix} = \frac{1}{D(s)} \begin{bmatrix} w_3(s) + w_4(s) + w_6(s) & w_4(s) + w_6(s) \\ w_4(s) + w_6(s) & w_2(s) + w_4(s) + w_5(s) + w_6(s) \end{bmatrix}$$

$$\times \begin{bmatrix} w_4(s) + w_5(s) \\ -w_4(s) \end{bmatrix} \mathbf{v}_1(s)$$

where

$$D(s) = [w_3(s) + w_4(s) + w_6(s)][w_2(s) + w_4(s) + w_5(s) + w_6(s)]$$
$$- [w_4(s) + w_6(s)]^2$$
$$= [g_3 + g_4 + g_6 + (C_4 + C_6)s][g_2 + g_4 + g_5 + g_6 + (C_4 + C_6)s]$$
$$- [g_4 + g_6 + (C_4 + C_6)s]^2$$

The complex frequency spectrum for $v_3(s)$ is specifically

$$v_3(s) = \frac{w_6(s)w_5(s) - w_4(s)w_2(s)}{D(s)} \, v_1(s) = [(g_6 + C_6s)g_5 - (g_4 + C_4s)g_2] \frac{v_1(s)}{D(s)}$$

If we let the magnitude and phase angle of the excitation voltage be represented by the complex number

$$\bar{V}_1 = V_1 e^{j\theta_1} = 10$$

then the magnitude and phase angle of the detector voltage are given by the complex number

$$\bar{V}_3 = |\bar{V}_3| e^{j\theta_3} = \frac{(g_6 + j\omega_0 C_6)g_5 - (g_4 + j\omega_0 C_4)g_2}{D(j\omega)} \, \bar{V}_1$$

The detector voltage $\bar{V}_3$ is zero when the coefficient of $\bar{V}_1$ vanishes, i.e., when

$$g_6 g_5 = g_4 g_2$$

and   (7.8.15)

$$C_6 g_5 = C_4 g_2$$

Equation (7.8.15), of course, can be used to evaluate the resistance and capacitance of an unknown RC component, given the values of the remaining parameters corresponding to the conditions $v_3 = 0$.

In the above example, where all components in the system have only two terminals, it is possible to define algorithms for writing the final system of equations directly from the electrical-network schematic diagram.[3] The analysis given here, however, is intended to demonstrate the properties of these models as they apply in general to systems of both two-terminal and multiterminal components.

7.9 OPEN-CIRCUIT PARAMETER MODELS (CHORD EQUATIONS)

Consider a system graph G containing p parts, $p \geq 1$. Let there exist a forest F in G such that (1) the edges corresponding to across drivers are included in F and (2) the edges corresponding to through drivers are included in the complement of F. Let the complex-frequency terminal equations for all remaining edges in G be such that their direct sum can be written in open-circuit parameter form

$$\begin{bmatrix} \mathbf{X}_{b_2}(s) \\ \mathbf{X}_{c_1}(s) \end{bmatrix} = \begin{bmatrix} \mathbf{Z}_{11}(s) & \mathbf{Z}_{12}(s) \\ \mathbf{Z}_{21}(s) & \mathbf{Z}_{22}(s) \end{bmatrix} \begin{bmatrix} \mathbf{Y}_{b_2}(s) \\ \mathbf{Y}_{c_1}(s) \end{bmatrix} \qquad (7.9.1)$$

$$\mathbf{X}_{b_1}(s) = \text{specified functions of time} \qquad (7.9.2)$$
$$\mathbf{Y}_{c_2}(s) = \text{specified functions of time} \qquad (7.9.3)$$

where the column matrices with subscripts b and c refer, respectively, to branches and chords.

Since $\mathbf{X}_{b_2}(s)$ and $\mathbf{X}_{c_1}(s)$ appear as independent variables in the component terminal equations [Eq. (7.9.1)], let the fundamental circuit equations be written in the form

$$\begin{bmatrix} \mathbf{B}_{11} & \mathbf{0} \\ \mathbf{B}_{21} & \mathbf{U} \end{bmatrix} \begin{bmatrix} \mathbf{X}_{b_1}(s) \\ \mathbf{X}_{c_2}(s) \end{bmatrix} + \begin{bmatrix} \mathbf{B}_{12} & \mathbf{U} \\ \mathbf{B}_{22} & \mathbf{0} \end{bmatrix} \begin{bmatrix} \mathbf{X}_{b_2}(s) \\ \mathbf{X}_{c_1}(s) \end{bmatrix} = 0 \qquad (7.9.3a)$$

Substituting Eq. (7.9.1) into Eq. (7.9.3a) gives

$$\begin{bmatrix} \mathbf{B}_{11} & \mathbf{0} \\ \mathbf{B}_{21} & \mathbf{U} \end{bmatrix} \begin{bmatrix} \mathbf{X}_{b_1}(s) \\ \mathbf{X}_{c_2}(s) \end{bmatrix} + \begin{bmatrix} \mathbf{B}_{12} & \mathbf{U} \\ \mathbf{B}_{22} & \mathbf{0} \end{bmatrix} \begin{bmatrix} \mathbf{Z}_{11}(s) & \mathbf{Z}_{12}(s) \\ \mathbf{Z}_{21}(s) & \mathbf{Z}_{22}(s) \end{bmatrix} \begin{bmatrix} \mathbf{Y}_{b_2}(s) \\ \mathbf{Y}_{c_1}(s) \end{bmatrix} = 0$$

$$(7.9.4)$$

From the fundamental cut-set equations of the system graph, the tree through variables $\mathbf{Y}_{b_2}(s)$ in Eq. (7.9.4) can be expressed as functions of the chord through variables $\mathbf{Y}_{c_1}(s)$ and $\mathbf{Y}_{c_2}(s)$, that is,

$$\begin{bmatrix} \mathbf{U} & \mathbf{0} & \mathbf{A}_{11} & \mathbf{A}_{12} \\ \mathbf{0} & \mathbf{U} & \mathbf{A}_{21} & \mathbf{A}_{22} \end{bmatrix} \begin{bmatrix} \mathbf{Y}_{b_1}(s) \\ \mathbf{Y}_{b_2}(s) \\ \mathbf{Y}_{c_1}(s) \\ \mathbf{Y}_{c_2}(s) \end{bmatrix} = 0 \qquad (7.9.5)$$

Since $\mathbf{A}_{21} = -\mathbf{B}_{12}^T$ and $\mathbf{A}_{22} = -\mathbf{B}_{22}^T$, the second set of cut-set equations can be written as

$$\mathbf{Y}_{b_2}(s) = -[\mathbf{B}_{12}^T \quad \mathbf{B}_{22}^T] \begin{bmatrix} \mathbf{Y}_{c_1}(s) \\ \mathbf{Y}_{c_2}(s) \end{bmatrix} \qquad (7.9.6)$$

The chord equations are obtained by substituting Eq. (7.9.6) into Eq. (7.9.4). The result is

$$\begin{bmatrix} \mathbf{B}_{11} & \mathbf{0} \\ \mathbf{B}_{21} & \mathbf{U} \end{bmatrix} \begin{bmatrix} \mathbf{X}_{b_1}(s) \\ \mathbf{X}_{c_2}(s) \end{bmatrix} + \begin{bmatrix} \mathbf{B}_{12} & \mathbf{U} \\ \mathbf{B}_{22} & \mathbf{0} \end{bmatrix} \begin{bmatrix} \mathbf{Z}_{11}(s) & \mathbf{Z}_{12}(s) \\ \mathbf{Z}_{21}(s) & \mathbf{Z}_{22}(s) \end{bmatrix}$$
$$\times \begin{bmatrix} \mathbf{B}_{12}^T & \mathbf{B}_{22}^T \\ \mathbf{U} & \mathbf{0} \end{bmatrix} \begin{bmatrix} \mathbf{Y}_{c_1}(s) \\ \mathbf{Y}_{c_2}(s) \end{bmatrix} = 0 \quad (7.9.7)$$

Equation (7.9.7) can be divided into the two sets of equations

$$\mathbf{B}_{11}\mathbf{X}_{b_1}(s) + [\mathbf{B}_{12} \quad \mathbf{U}] \begin{bmatrix} \mathbf{Z}_{11}(s) & \mathbf{Z}_{12}(s) \\ \mathbf{Z}_{21}(s) & \mathbf{Z}_{22}(s) \end{bmatrix} \begin{bmatrix} \mathbf{B}_{12}^T & \mathbf{B}_{22}^T \\ \mathbf{U} & \mathbf{0} \end{bmatrix} \begin{bmatrix} \mathbf{Y}_{c_1}(s) \\ \mathbf{Y}_{c_2}(s) \end{bmatrix} = 0$$

$$(7.9.8)$$

and

$$[\mathbf{B}_{21} \quad \mathbf{U}] \begin{bmatrix} \mathbf{X}_{b_1}(s) \\ \mathbf{X}_{c_2}(s) \end{bmatrix} + [\mathbf{B}_{22} \quad \mathbf{0}] \begin{bmatrix} \mathbf{Z}_{11}(s) & \mathbf{Z}_{12}(s) \\ \mathbf{Z}_{21}(s) & \mathbf{Z}_{22}(s) \end{bmatrix}$$
$$\times \begin{bmatrix} \mathbf{B}_{12}^T & \mathbf{B}_{22}^T \\ \mathbf{U} & \mathbf{0} \end{bmatrix} \begin{bmatrix} \mathbf{Y}_{c_1}(s) \\ \mathbf{Y}_{c_2}(s) \end{bmatrix} = 0 \quad (7.9.9)$$

Separating the known and unknown frequency spectra, Eq. (7.9.8) can be written as

$$[\mathbf{B}_{12} \quad \mathbf{U}] \begin{bmatrix} \mathbf{Z}_{11}(s) & \mathbf{Z}_{12}(s) \\ \mathbf{Z}_{21}(s) & \mathbf{Z}_{22}(s) \end{bmatrix} \begin{bmatrix} \mathbf{B}_{12}^T \\ \mathbf{U} \end{bmatrix} \mathbf{Y}_{c_1}(s) + [\mathbf{B}_{12} \quad \mathbf{U}]$$

$$\times \begin{bmatrix} \mathbf{Z}_{11}(s) & \mathbf{Z}_{12}(s) \\ \mathbf{Z}_{21}(s) & \mathbf{Z}_{22}(s) \end{bmatrix} \begin{bmatrix} \mathbf{B}_{22}^T \\ \mathbf{0} \end{bmatrix} \mathbf{Y}_{c_2}(s) + \mathbf{B}_{11}\mathbf{X}_{b_1}(s) = 0 \quad (7.9.10)$$

A solution of these equations for the vector $\mathbf{Y}_{c_1}(s)$ establishes the frequency spectra of all chord through variables. If the frequency spectra $\mathbf{X}_{c_2}(s)$ are required, they are obtained by substituting the solution for $\mathbf{Y}_{c_1}(s)$ into Eq. (7.9.9). All other frequency spectra are obtained as functions of $\mathbf{Y}_{c_1}(s)$ and $\mathbf{Y}_{c_2}(s)$ by applying either Eq. (7.9.1) or the cut-set equations of the system graph.

The number of equations in an open-circuit parameter model is always equal to the number of chords in the system graph. From Eq. (7.9.8) it can be seen that, if the number of specified chord through variables is n_y and the graph contains p parts and v vertices, then the order of the inverse to be evaluated is $e - v + p - n_y$. As in the case of the branch equations, this coefficient matrix, in general, has entries that are rational functions of s. In fact, except for the equation count, open-circuit parameter models have the same general properties as short-circuit parameter models. When the system contains only two-terminal components, the triple matrix product in Eq. (7.9.7) can again be evaluated by applying a simple algorithm.[3] For electrical networks of two-terminal components the final system of equations can also be written from inspection of the system schematic diagram following algorithms very similar to those defined in almost every book on electrical network theory.

Example 7.9.1: The mechanical structure shown in Fig. 7.9.1 is loaded at point H with a static load W, as indicated. For the purposes of design, determine (1) the forces in all members for the load indicated and (2) the forces in all members in the event that the base D of the supporting column settles into the soil by an amount $\delta_1(t) = \Delta_1$.

Each member of the system is considered to have a spring coefficient K, as indicated. The rate of change in $\delta_1(t)$ is very slow. Consequently, for the purposes of the required analysis, the mass and damping coefficients in the terminal equations of the cantilever beams can be neglected; i.e., the terminal characteristics of beam 1 are modeled in terms of the variables identified by edges 2 and 3 of the system graph and the algebraic equations

$$\begin{bmatrix} \delta_2(t) \\ \delta_3(t) \end{bmatrix} = \begin{bmatrix} k_{22} & k_{23} \\ k_{32} & k_{33} \end{bmatrix} \begin{bmatrix} f_2(t) \\ f_3(t) \end{bmatrix} \qquad (7.9.11)$$

The terminal characteristics of beam 2 are modeled in terms of measurements identified by edges 7 and 8 and the algebraic equations

$$\begin{bmatrix} \delta_7(t) \\ \delta_8(t) \end{bmatrix} = \begin{bmatrix} k_{77} & k_{78} \\ k_{87} & k_{88} \end{bmatrix} \begin{bmatrix} f_7(t) \\ f_8(t) \end{bmatrix} \qquad (7.9.12)$$

From elementary properties of materials, the stiffness coefficients k_{ij} $(i, j = 2,$ 3 and 7, 8) are related to the geometry of the beams and the mechanical characteristics of the material by

$$k_{22} = \frac{l_2{}^3}{3E_1I_1} \qquad k_{23} = k_{32} = \frac{l_1{}^2}{2E_1I_1}\left(l_2 - \frac{l_1}{3}\right) \qquad k_{33} = \frac{l_1{}^3}{3E_1I_1}$$

$$k_{77} = \frac{l_3{}^3}{3E_2I_2} \qquad k_{78} = k_{87} = \frac{l_3{}^2}{2E_2I_2}\left(l_4 - \frac{l_3}{3}\right) \qquad k_{88} = \frac{l_4{}^3}{3E_2I_2}$$

where

E_1 and E_2 represent the *moduli of elasticity*, or *Young's moduli*
I_1 and I_2 represent the *moments of inertia* of the cross sections of the beam
E_1I_1 and E_2I_2 represent *flexural rigidities*

Let the stiffness coefficients for the cantilever beams be given as $k_{22} = \frac{1}{3} \times 10^{-2}$, $k_{23} = k_{32} = \frac{8}{2}\frac{1}{} \times 10^{-5}$, $k_{33} = 9 \times 10^{-5}$, $k_{77} = 3 \times 10^{-6}$, $k_{78} = k_{87} = 16 \times 10^{-6}$, and $k_{88} = 72 \times 10^{-6}$.

Solution: A displacement driver $\delta_1(t)$ is included to represent the change in position of the base D of the supporting column, and the force driver $f_9(t) = w_9$ represents the static load. Select a tree T in the system graph so as to include the displacement driver (edge 1) and exclude the force driver (edge 9), and write the direct sum of the terminal equations for the components in the form

$$
\begin{bmatrix} \delta_2(t) \\ \delta_3(t) \\ \delta_4(t) \\ \delta_5(t) \\ \hline \delta_6(t) \\ \delta_7(t) \\ \delta_8(t) \end{bmatrix}
=
\left[\begin{array}{cccc|ccc}
k_{22} & k_{23} & 0 & 0 & 0 & 0 & 0 \\
k_{32} & k_{33} & 0 & 0 & 0 & 0 & 0 \\
0 & 0 & k_4 & 0 & 0 & 0 & 0 \\
0 & 0 & 0 & k & 0 & 0 & 0 \\
\hline
0 & 0 & 0 & 0 & k_6 & 0 & 0 \\
0 & 0 & 0 & 0 & 0 & k_{77} & k_{78} \\
0 & 0 & 0 & 0 & 0 & k_{87} & k_{88}
\end{array}\right]
\begin{bmatrix} f_2(t) \\ f_3(t) \\ f_4(t) \\ f_5(t) \\ \hline f_6(t) \\ f_7(t) \\ f_8(t) \end{bmatrix}
\begin{array}{l} \left.\rule{0pt}{30pt}\right\} \text{branches} \\[20pt] \left.\rule{0pt}{22pt}\right\} \text{chords} \end{array}
$$

(7.9.13)

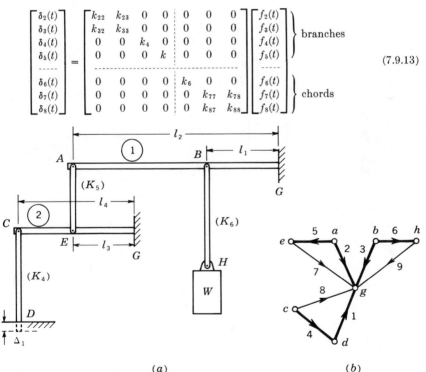

(a)

(b)

Fig. 7.9.1   (a) A mechanical system; (b) system graph.

The set of $e - v + 1 = 3$ fundamental circuit equations defined by the chords of the indicated tree are

$$
\begin{bmatrix} 0 \\ -\delta_1(t) \\ \delta_9(t) \end{bmatrix} +
\begin{bmatrix} -1 & 0 & 0 & 1 & 0 & 1 & 0 \\ 0 & 0 & -1 & 0 & 0 & 0 & 1 \\ 0 & -1 & 0 & 0 & 1 & 0 & 0 \end{bmatrix}
\begin{bmatrix} \delta_2(t) \\ \delta_3(t) \\ \delta_4(t) \\ \delta_5(t) \\ \delta_6(t) \\ \delta_7(t) \\ \delta_8(t) \end{bmatrix} = 0 \qquad (7.9.14)
$$

Substituting the terminal equations [Eq. (7.9.13)] into the circuit equations [Eq. (7.9.14)] gives

$$
\begin{bmatrix} 0 \\ -\delta_1(t) \\ \delta_9(t) \end{bmatrix} +
\begin{bmatrix} -1 & 0 & 0 & 1 & 0 & 1 & 0 \\ 0 & 0 & -1 & 0 & 0 & 0 & 1 \\ 0 & -1 & 0 & 0 & 1 & 0 & 0 \end{bmatrix}
$$

$$
\times
\begin{bmatrix}
k_{22} & k_{23} & 0 & 0 & 0 & 0 & 0 \\
k_{32} & k_{33} & 0 & 0 & 0 & 0 & 0 \\
0 & 0 & k_4 & 0 & 0 & 0 & 0 \\
0 & 0 & 0 & k_5 & 0 & 0 & 0 \\
0 & 0 & 0 & 0 & k_6 & 0 & 0 \\
0 & 0 & 0 & 0 & 0 & k_{77} & k_{78} \\
0 & 0 & 0 & 0 & 0 & k_{87} & k_{88}
\end{bmatrix}
\begin{bmatrix} f_2(t) \\ f_3(t) \\ f_4(t) \\ f_5(t) \\ f_6(t) \\ f_7(t) \\ f_8(t) \end{bmatrix} = 0 \qquad (7.9.15)
$$

From the cut-set equations, all the force variables in the above equation can be expressed in terms of the chord force variables, i.e.,

$$
\begin{bmatrix} f_2(t) \\ f_3(t) \\ f_4(t) \\ f_5(t) \\ f_6(t) \\ f_7(t) \\ f_8(t) \end{bmatrix} =
\begin{bmatrix} -1 & 0 & 0 \\ 0 & 0 & -1 \\ 0 & -1 & 0 \\ 1 & 0 & 0 \\ 0 & 0 & 1 \\ 1 & 0 & 0 \\ 0 & 1 & 0 \end{bmatrix}
\begin{bmatrix} f_7(t) \\ f_8(t) \\ f_9(t) \end{bmatrix} \qquad (7.9.16)
$$

Substituting Eq. (7.9.16) into Eq. (7.9.15) gives

$$
\begin{bmatrix} 0 \\ -\delta_1(t) \\ \delta_9(t) \end{bmatrix}
\begin{bmatrix} -1 & 0 & 0 & 1 & 0 & 1 & 0 \\ 0 & 0 & -1 & 0 & 0 & 0 & 1 \\ 0 & -1 & 0 & 0 & 1 & 0 & 0 \end{bmatrix}
$$

$$
\times
\begin{bmatrix}
k_{22} & k_{23} & 0 & 0 & 0 & 0 & 0 \\
k_{32} & k_{33} & 0 & 0 & 0 & 0 & 0 \\
0 & 0 & k_4 & 0 & 0 & 0 & 0 \\
0 & 0 & 0 & k_5 & 0 & 0 & 0 \\
0 & 0 & 0 & 0 & k_6 & 0 & 0 \\
0 & 0 & 0 & 0 & 0 & k_{77} & k_{78} \\
0 & 0 & 0 & 0 & 0 & k_{87} & k_{88}
\end{bmatrix}
\begin{bmatrix} -1 & 0 & 0 \\ 0 & 0 & -1 \\ 0 & -1 & 0 \\ 1 & 0 & 0 \\ 0 & 0 & 1 \\ 1 & 0 & 0 \\ 0 & 1 & 0 \end{bmatrix}
\begin{bmatrix} f_7(t) \\ f_8(t) \\ f_9(t) \end{bmatrix} = 0 \qquad (7.9.17)
$$

or

$$
\begin{bmatrix} 0 \\ -\delta_1(t) \\ \delta_9(t) \end{bmatrix} +
\begin{bmatrix} k_{22} + k_{77} + k_5 & k_{78} & k_{23} \\ k_{87} & k_{88} + k_4 & 0 \\ k_{32} & 0 & k_{33} + k_6 \end{bmatrix}
\begin{bmatrix} f_7(t) \\ f_8(t) \\ f_9(t) \end{bmatrix} = 0 \qquad (7.9.18)
$$

Since $f_9(t)$ is a specified function, the required solution is obtained by solving the first two equations simultaneously to determine $f_7(t)$ and $f_8(t)$ as explicit functions of $\delta_1(t)$ and $f_9(t)$. The result is

$$\begin{bmatrix} f_7(t) \\ f_8(t) \end{bmatrix} = \frac{1}{D} \begin{bmatrix} k_{88} + k_4 & -k_{78} \\ -k_{87} & k_{22} + k_{77} + k_5 \end{bmatrix} \begin{bmatrix} k_{23} f_9(t) \\ \delta_1(t) \end{bmatrix} \tag{7.9.19}$$

with

$$D = (k_{88} + k_4)(k_{22} + k_{77} + k_5) - k_{87} k_{78}$$

Substituting the numerical values of the stiffness coefficients given in the statement of the problem, taking $k_4 = k_5 = k_6 = 10^{-5}$, $f_9(t) = W_9 = 10^3$, and $\delta_1(t) = \Delta_1 = -10^{-2}$ gives

$$\begin{bmatrix} f_7(t) \\ f_8(t) \end{bmatrix} \cong \begin{bmatrix} 334 & 65 \\ 65 & 12{,}200 \end{bmatrix} \begin{bmatrix} \frac{3.1}{2} \times 10^{-5} W_9 \\ \Delta_1 \end{bmatrix} \tag{7.9.20}$$

From this solution all remaining forces in the system are determined from the cut-set equations of the system graph, i.e.,

$$f_4(t) = f_1(t) = -f_8(t) = 112$$
$$f_3(t) = -f_6(t) = -f_9(t) = -W_9$$
$$f_5(t) = -f_2(t) = f_7(t) = 51.12$$

Since $f_4(t) = -f_8(t)$, we find, using Eq. (7.9.20),

$$f_4(t) = 1{,}007.5 \times W_9 + 12{,}200\Delta_1 \tag{7.9.21}$$

If there is no settling, $\Delta_1 = 0$ and $f_4(t)$ is $1{,}007.5 W_9$. On the other hand, if load W_9 is removed from the system and the base of member CD moves down by an amount Δ_1 ($\Delta_1 < 0$), $f_4(t)$ is $-12{,}200\Delta_1$. If the base of CD moves down a distance

$$\Delta_1 = -\frac{1}{12.11} W_9$$

then $f_4(t) = 0$ and member CD can be removed without further effect on the system.

7.10 MIXED-PARAMETER SYSTEM MODELS (BRANCH-CHORD EQUATIONS)

As the names imply, open-circuit and short-circuit parameter system models are obtainable only if all components in the system can be modeled in terms of open-circuit and short-circuit parameters, respectively. In Chap. 3, however, there are included several examples of component models that cannot be presented in terms of either open-circuit or short-circuit parameters. For systems containing such components, the s-domain system model can be developed by a procedure very similar to that used in Chap. 5 to develop state models. The following theorem, stated here without proof, is fundamental to the formulation of mixed-parameter models. A complete proof of this theorem is included in Chap. 8.

Theorem 7.10.1: If a linear time-invariant system having a graph G with e edges has a complete and unique solution for all $2e$ variables corresponding to the edges of G, then there exist a tree (forest) T_1 and a tree (forest) T_2 (T_1 may be the same as T_2) in G such that the direct sum of the complex frequency models of the components can be written in the mixed-parameter form

$$\begin{bmatrix} \mathbf{X}_{b_1}(s) \\ \mathbf{Y}_{c_2}(s) \end{bmatrix} = \begin{bmatrix} \mathbf{H}_{11}(s) & \mathbf{H}_{12}(s) \\ \mathbf{H}_{21}(s) & \mathbf{H}_{22}(s) \end{bmatrix} \begin{bmatrix} \mathbf{Y}_{b_2}(s) \\ \mathbf{X}_{c_1}(s) \end{bmatrix} + \begin{bmatrix} \mathbf{F}_b(s) \\ \mathbf{F}_c(s) \end{bmatrix} \tag{7.10.1}$$

where the vectors $\mathbf{X}_{b_1}(s)$ and $\mathbf{X}_{c_1}(s)$ correspond, respectively, to edges of T_1 and its complement and the vectors $\mathbf{Y}_{b_2}(s)$ and $\mathbf{Y}_{c_2}(s)$ correspond, respectively, to the edges of T_2 and its complement.

Note that if edge k of the graph corresponds to a driver, then the corresponding row of the coefficient matrix has all zero entries.

Since it is always possible to write the direct sum of the component terminal equations explicitly in the primary variables for a pair of trees T_1 and T_2, let the fundamental circuit and cut-set equations also be written for T_1 and T_2, respectively, in the forms

$$\mathbf{X}_{c_1}(s) = -\mathbf{B}_1\mathbf{X}_{b_1}(s) \tag{7.10.2}$$
$$\mathbf{Y}_{b_2}(s) = -\mathbf{A}_2\mathbf{Y}_{c_2}(s) \tag{7.10.3}$$

The system model as obtained by simply substituting Eqs. (7.10.2) and (7.10.3) into Eq. (7.10.1) is of the general form

$$\begin{bmatrix} \mathbf{U} + \mathbf{H}_{12}(s)\mathbf{B}_1 & \mathbf{H}_{11}(s)\mathbf{A}_2 \\ \mathbf{H}_{22}(s)\mathbf{B}_1 & \mathbf{U} + \mathbf{H}_{21}(s)\mathbf{A}_2 \end{bmatrix} \begin{bmatrix} \mathbf{X}_{b_1}(s) \\ \mathbf{Y}_{c_2}(s) \end{bmatrix} = \begin{bmatrix} \mathbf{F}_1(s) \\ \mathbf{F}_2(s) \end{bmatrix} \tag{7.10.4}$$

In the cases where it is possible to take $T_1 = T_2$, then, of course,

$$\mathbf{B}_1 = -\mathbf{A}_2{}^T$$

In general, the coefficient matrix in Eq. (7.10.4) is of order $e \times e$ and is therefore always of a higher order than either open-circuit or short-circuit parameter models, when they exist. For this reason, a mixed-parameter model of the system is normally used only when other models do not exist.

Example 7.10.1: The lever system shown in Fig. 7.10.1 is driven at three terminals, with force and displacement drivers as indicated. Does the system have a solution when each lever is modeled as a perfect coupler?

Solution: The terminal graph for the three-terminal lever is represented as edges 3 and 4 in the system graph of Fig. 7.10.1*b*, and the terminal graph of the four-terminal lever is represented as edges 5, 6, and 7. Since the terminal equations for the two-terminal spring components (edges 8 and 9) can each be inverted, the corresponding edges can be in either a tree or its complement. Considering the fact that the displacement drivers must always be included in a tree, the problem reduces to that of finding a suitable tree from a combination of the following edges:

(a) Edges 1 and 2
(b) Edge 3 or 4
(c) Edges 5 and 6, or 5 and 7, or 6 and 7
(d) Edges 8 and/or 9

One such tree is shown by the heavy lines of Fig. 7.10.1b. The direct sum of the component terminal equations, written explicitly in the primary variables for this tree, is

$$
\begin{bmatrix} \delta_9(t) \\ \delta_3(t) \\ \delta_6(t) \\ \delta_7(t) \\ \hline f_4(t) \\ f_5(t) \\ f_8(t) \end{bmatrix} = \begin{bmatrix} k_9 & 0 & 0 & 0 & 0 & 0 & 0 \\ 0 & 0 & 0 & 0 & -n_{34} & 0 & 0 \\ 0 & 0 & 0 & 0 & 0 & n_{65} & 0 \\ 0 & 0 & 0 & 0 & 0 & -n_{75} & 0 \\ \hline 0 & n_{34} & 0 & 0 & 0 & 0 & 0 \\ 0 & 0 & -n_{65} & n_{75} & 0 & 0 & 0 \\ 0 & 0 & 0 & 0 & 0 & 0 & K_8 \end{bmatrix} \begin{bmatrix} f_9(t) \\ f_3(t) \\ f_6(t) \\ f_7(t) \\ \hline \delta_4(t) \\ \delta_5(t) \\ \delta_8(t) \end{bmatrix}
\tag{7.10.5}
$$

Upon applying the circuit and cut-set equations to eliminate the secondary variables from Eq. (7.10.5), the mixed-parameter model of the system is established as

$$
\begin{bmatrix} 1 & 0 & 0 & 0 & -k_9 & 0 & 0 \\ -n_{34} & 1 & n_{34} & 0 & 0 & 0 & 0 \\ 0 & -n_{65} & 1 & 0 & 0 & 0 & 0 \\ 0 & n_{75} & 0 & 1 & 0 & 0 & 0 \\ \hline 0 & 0 & 0 & 0 & 1 & n_{34} & n_{34} \\ 0 & 0 & 0 & 0 & -n_{65} & 1 & -n_{75} \\ 0 & -K_8 & 0 & K_8 & 0 & 0 & 0 \end{bmatrix} \begin{bmatrix} \delta_9(t) \\ \delta_3(t) \\ \delta_6(t) \\ \delta_7(t) \\ \hline f_4(t) \\ f_5(t) \\ f_8(t) \end{bmatrix} = \begin{bmatrix} 0 \\ 0 \\ n_{65}[\delta_2(t) - \delta_1(t)] \\ -n_{75}[\delta_2(t) - \delta_1(t)] \\ \hline n_{34}f_{10}(t) \\ n_{65}f_{10}(t) \\ 0 \end{bmatrix}
$$

The determinant of the coefficient matrix is

$$
D = (1 + n_{34}n_{65})^2 + k_9 K_8 n_{34}^2 (1 + n_{75})^2
\tag{7.10.6}
$$

where, from Fig. 7.10.1a, it is easy to show that $n_{75} = n_{34}n_{65}$. Since all parameters in Eq. (7.10.6) are nonnegative, $D > 0$ and the system has a unique solution.

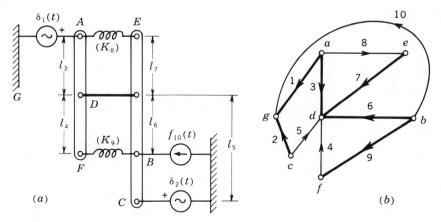

Fig. 7.10.1 (a) Typical lever system; (b) the system graph.

PROBLEMS

7.1   In the following state equations:

$$\frac{d}{dt}\begin{bmatrix} \psi_1(t) \\ \psi_2(t) \end{bmatrix} = \begin{bmatrix} 0 & 1 \\ -\omega_0{}^2 & -2\zeta\omega_0 \end{bmatrix}\begin{bmatrix} \psi_1(t) \\ \psi_2(t) \end{bmatrix} + \begin{bmatrix} 0 \\ 1 \end{bmatrix} e(t) \qquad \begin{bmatrix} \psi_1(0) \\ \psi_2(0) \end{bmatrix} = \begin{bmatrix} 0 \\ 0 \end{bmatrix}$$

ω_0 and ζ are positive parameters.

  (a)   Obtain the analytical expressions for $\psi_1(t)$ and $\psi_2(t)$ in terms of $e(t)$.
  (b)   Investigate the solution $\psi_1(t)$ when $e(t)$ is a unit step function.
  (c)   Sketch $\psi_1(t)$ for $\zeta = 0$, 0.1, 1, and 2.
  (d)   Sketch the trajectory of Ψ in the ψ_1-ψ_2 plane for $\zeta = 0$, 0.1, 1, and 2.

Note: The given state equations correspond to a typical second-order system. The parameters ω_0 and ζ are called the *natural frequency* and the *damping coefficient*, respectively.   When $\zeta = 1$, $\zeta < 1$, and $\zeta > 1$, the system is called *critically damped*, *underdamped*, and *overdamped*, respectively.

7.2   Derive the state equations for the mechanical system given in Fig. P7.2, and determine the velocity of the mass as the function of time.   The driving functions are given as

$$f(t) = 10u(t) \qquad u(t) = \text{unit step function} \qquad \dot{\delta}(t) = 10\sin\omega t$$

   Element values are $K_1 = K_2 = 1$, $M = 1$, $B = 1$, and all initial conditions are equal to zero.

  (a)   Assume that the velocity driver is removed from the system and that terminal A is connected to the ground G.   Obtain the solution for the velocity of the mass component in this operating condition.
  (b)   Assume now that only the force driver is removed from the system and that terminal B is left free.   In this case again determine the velocity of the mass component.
  (c)   Show that the solutions obtained in (a) and (b) when added give the same result obtained when both drivers exist in the system.   This is an example of the *superposition* property of linear systems.

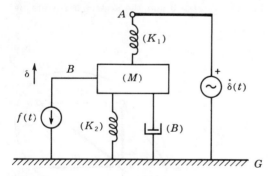

Fig. P7.2

7.3   Using the method introduced in Sec. 7.1, obtain the steady-state solution and the complete solution for the first-order state equation

$$\frac{d}{dt}\psi(t) = -2\psi(t) + e(t) \qquad \psi(0) = 1$$

when $e(t) = 3t^3$.

7.4   In Example 7.1.1, the numerical values of the solutions in parts b and c are not completed. Obtain these numerical solutions, and compare your answer with that in Eq. (7.1.13).

7.5   Justify the solutions given by Eqs. (7.1.34) to (7.1.36) which are developed from Eq. (7.1.33).

7.6   Assume that in Eq. (7.1.33) the square matrix $\mathbf{P}$ is singular. Determine the solutions of this equation when $e(t)$ is an impulse occurring at $t = 0$. Consider the impulse as the limit of a unit pulse. (*Hint:* Expand e^{Pt} in an infinite series before evaluating the integral.)

7.7   Repeat Example 7.1.4 if the inductor L is replaced by a capacitor C. Assume that the initial value of the capacitor voltage is equal to zero.

7.8   In Example 7.1.3, let the pulse-voltage driver be replaced by a rectangular-wave voltage driver for which

$$e(t) = \left\{ \begin{array}{ll} E & nT \leq t < nT + \dfrac{T}{2} \\ -E & nT + \dfrac{T}{2} \leq t < (n+1)T \end{array} \right\} \qquad n = 0, 1, 2, 3, \ldots$$

Obtain the expression for the current $i(t)$ through the inductor in the intervals $(0, T/2)$, $(T/2, T)$ and $(T, 3T/2)$. Sketch $i(t)$ in these intervals, and give exact values of $i(\ )$ at $t = T/2$, T, and $3T/2$.

7.9   The simple mechanical system in Fig. P7.9 is driven by a velocity driver $\phi_0(t) = E \cos \omega t$ at the terminals A and G. Calculate the steady-state solution for the velocity variable of the damper. Solve this problem (a) by determining the $\mathbf{W}$ matrix (which will have complex entries) in the transformation $\mathbf{\Xi} = \mathbf{\Psi} - \mathbf{WF}$ and (b) by application of Theorem 7.2.1.

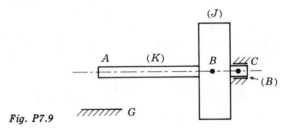

Fig. P7.9

7.10   Write the state equations for the simple RC network given in Fig. P7.10. Express the resistor current $i_R(t)$ in terms of the state variable and the driving function.

(a) Determine the steady-state and transient component of the state variables.

(b) From the expression for $i_R(t)$, how would you classify its steady-state and transient components?

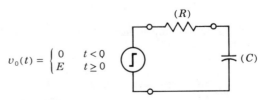

$$v_0(t) = \left\{ \begin{array}{ll} 0 & t < 0 \\ E & t \geq 0 \end{array} \right.$$

Fig. P7.10

7.11   Determine the expression for the sinusoidal steady-state component of the current variables in each resistor of the network given in Fig. P7.11.

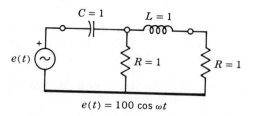

$$e(t) = 100 \cos \omega t$$

Fig. P7.11

7.12   Repeat Prob. 7.11 for the network given in Fig. P7.12.

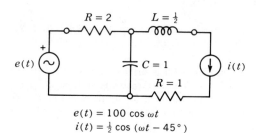

$$e(t) = 100 \cos \omega t$$
$$i(t) = \tfrac{1}{2} \cos (\omega t - 45°)$$

Fig. P7.12

7.13   Let the vector

$$\mathbf{X}(t) = \begin{bmatrix} X_1 \cos (\omega t + \theta_1) \\ X_2 \cos (\omega t + \theta_2) \\ \cdots\cdots\cdots \\ X_n \cos (\omega t + \theta_n) \end{bmatrix} = \bar{\mathbf{X}}e^{j\omega t} + \hat{\bar{\mathbf{X}}}e^{-j\omega t}$$

be given. Obtain expressions for $(d/dt)\mathbf{X}(t)$, $(d^2/dt^2)\mathbf{X}(t)$ of the form

$$\frac{d}{dt}\mathbf{X}(t) = \dot{\bar{\mathbf{X}}}e^{j\omega t} + \dot{\hat{\mathbf{X}}}e^{-j\omega t}$$

$$\frac{d^2}{dt^2}\mathbf{X}(t) = \ddot{\bar{\mathbf{X}}}e^{j\omega t} + \ddot{\hat{\mathbf{X}}}e^{-j\omega t}$$

and express the complex vectors $\dot{\bar{\mathbf{X}}}$ and $\ddot{\bar{\mathbf{X}}}$ in terms of the complex vector $\bar{\mathbf{X}}$. Generalize this relation to

$$\frac{d^n}{dt^n}\mathbf{X}(t) = \bar{\mathbf{X}}^{(n)}e^{j\omega t} + \hat{\bar{\mathbf{X}}}^{(n)}e^{-j\omega t}$$

7.14 For the system given in Fig. P7.14 write the state equations as in the form of Eqs. (7.2.1) and (7.2.2), where

$$\mathbf{R}(t) = \begin{bmatrix} i_1(t) \\ i_2(t) \\ v_3(t) \end{bmatrix} \text{ (resistor currents and voltage)}$$

Replacing the derivative operator d/dt by $j\omega$ and each vector by a complex vector, obtain a solution for $\mathbf{\bar{R}}$ in terms of $\mathbf{\bar{E}}$, and determine the transfer functions,

$$\frac{\bar{I}_1}{\bar{E}}, \frac{\bar{I}_2}{\bar{E}}, \text{ and } \frac{\bar{V}_3}{\bar{E}}$$

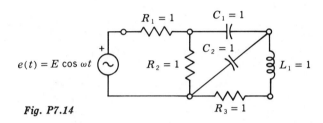

Fig. P7.14

7.15 Determine whether or not there would be any changes in the conclusions of the discussion on the sinusoidal steady-state solution of a linear system if the driving functions are taken in the form $E_k \sin(\omega t + \theta_k)$ rather than as $E_k \cos(\omega t + \theta_k)$.

7.16 Determine the driving-point impedance $\bar{Z}_m = -\bar{\phi}_0/\bar{\tau}_0$ seen between the terminals A and G of the mechanical system in Fig. P7.9.

7.17 Determine the resonance frequency and bandwidth of the mechanical system given in Fig. P7.17. Derive the expression for the driving-point impedance Z_m seen between the terminals A and G. What is the value of Z_m when resonance occurs?

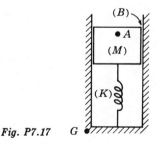

Fig. P7.17   G

7.18 In the electric circuit given in Fig. P7.18 the frequency of the voltage generator is kept constant at $f = 4$ kc. The variable capacitor is set to a value such that the a-c ammeter in the circuit indicates a maximum deflection. Calculate this value of capacitance. Also, calculate the voltages (magnitude and phase) across the terminals of the R, L, and C components.   What could you say about these voltages with reference to each other?

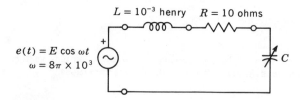

Fig. P7.18

7.19   For the RC network given in Fig. P7.19 calculate the transfer function

$$\frac{\bar{V}_0}{\bar{V}_i}$$

and sketch the corresponding Bode diagrams on a logarithmic paper.

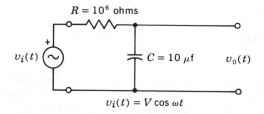

Fig. P7.19

7.20   Sketch the Bode diagram for the given transfer functions.   Note that in these functions $\lambda = j\omega$.

(a) $\dfrac{K(1 + \lambda/10)}{(1 + \lambda)(1 + \lambda/100)}$

(b) $\dfrac{\lambda}{1 + \lambda/2}$ and $\dfrac{K}{(\lambda + \frac{1}{2})(\lambda + 2)(\lambda + 3)}$

(c) $\dfrac{\lambda^2}{(1 + 10\lambda)(1 + \lambda)(1 + \lambda/10)(1 + \lambda/100)}$

(d) $\dfrac{K(\lambda + 3)}{\lambda(\lambda + 2)(\lambda^2 + 2\lambda + 5)}$

(e) $\dfrac{(1 + \lambda/10)(1 + \lambda/100)}{\lambda(1 + \lambda/10,000)}$

(f) $\dfrac{1 + \lambda/100}{1 - \lambda/100}$

7.21   For the system considered in Prob. 7.16 sketch the Bode diagrams for Z_m.   Take $M = 5$, $B = 5\sqrt{2}$, and $K = 10$, and calculate the parameters ω_0 and ζ, making use of the characteristics given in Fig. 7.3.8.

7.22 Determine the Fourier transform of the following functions:

(a) $f(t) = \begin{cases} F & -T \le t \le T \\ 0 & t < -T \text{ and } t > T \end{cases}$

(b) $f(t) = \begin{cases} \dfrac{F}{T} & -T \le t \le 0 \\ \dfrac{-F}{T} & 0 \le t \le T \\ 0 & t < -T \text{ and } t > T \end{cases}$

(c) $f(t) = \begin{cases} \cos \frac{1}{2}t & 0 \le t \le 2\pi \\ 0 & t < 0 \text{ and } t > 2\pi \end{cases}$

7.23 By means of partial-fraction expansions, calculate the inverse Fourier transform of the following functions, where $\lambda = j\omega$.

(a) $F(\lambda) = \dfrac{2\lambda - 1}{\lambda^2 + 3\lambda + 2}$

(b) $F(\lambda) = \dfrac{1}{(\lambda + \alpha)(\lambda + \beta)}$

7.24 Calculate the Laplace transform of the following functions:

(a) $u(t) = \begin{cases} 0 & t < 0 \\ 1 & t \ge 0 \end{cases}$

(b) $\cos \omega t$

(c) $\sin \omega t$

(d) $e^{-\alpha t} \sin \beta t$

(e) $e^{-\alpha t} \cos \beta t$

(f) $\sinh \alpha t$

(g) $\cosh \alpha t$

(h) t and t^n

(i) $te^{-\alpha t}$

7.25 Prove the following:

(a) $L\{f_1(t) + f_2(t)\} = L\{f_1(t)\} + L\{f_2(t)\}$

(b) $L\{f'(t)\} = sf(s) - f(0+)$

(c) $L\{f''(t)\} = s^2 f(s) - sf(0+) - f'(0+)$

(d) $L\{f^{(n)}(t)\} = s^n f(s) - s^{n-1}f(0+) - \cdots - f^{(n-1)}(0+)$

where

$$\mathbf{f}(s) = L\{f(t)\} = \int_0^\infty f(t)e^{-st}\, dt$$

7.26 Find the inverse Laplace transform of the following functions:

(a) $\dfrac{1}{s(s + a)(s + b)}$

(b) $\dfrac{1}{s^2 + \alpha^2}$

(c) $\dfrac{s}{s^2 - \alpha^2}$

(d) $\dfrac{s}{(s + a)^2 + b^2}$

(e) $\dfrac{n!}{s^{n+1}}$

7.27   Let $L\{f(t)\} = f(s)$; then show that

$$L\{f(t)u(t - a)\} = e^{-as}f(s)$$

7.28   Show that if $L\{f(t)\} = f(s)$ then

$$L\{e^{-at}f(t)\} = f(s + a)$$

7.29   Prove the following relation:

$$L\{f(\alpha t)\} = \frac{1}{\alpha} f\left(\frac{s}{\alpha}\right)$$

7.30   Let $f(t)$ be a periodic function of period T.   Prove that

$$L\{f(t)\} = \frac{1}{1 - e^{-st}} \int_0^T f(t)e^{-st}\, dt$$

7.31   For the network in Example 7.1.3 write the Laplace transform of the state equation, and solve the resulting algebraic equation for $i(s) = L\{i(t)\}$. From the partial-fraction expansion for $i(s)$, determine $i(t)$ by taking the inverse Laplace transform of $i(s)$.   Compare your result with that given in the discussion of Example 7.1.3.

7.32   Solve Prob. 7.8 by use of Laplace transform techniques.   The property given in Prob. 7.30 is to be used.

7.33   Consider the state equations for a linear time-invariant system of the form

$$\frac{d}{dt}\,\boldsymbol{\Psi}(t) = \mathbf{P}\boldsymbol{\Psi}(t) + \mathbf{Q}\mathbf{E}(t) + \mathbf{R}\frac{d}{dt}\,\mathbf{E}(t)$$

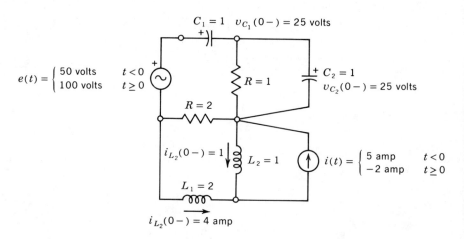

$$e(t) = \begin{cases} 50 \text{ volts} & t < 0 \\ 100 \text{ volts} & t \geq 0 \end{cases}$$

Fig. P7.33

After taking the Laplace transform of these equations one obtains

$$\tilde{\Psi}(s) = (sU - P)^{-1}[(Q + Rs)E(s) + \Psi(0+) - RE(0+)]$$

Use the relation in Eq. (6.1.2), and show that this expression can also be written as

$$\tilde{\Psi}(s) = (sU - P)^{-1}[(Q + Rs)E(s) + \Psi(0-) - RE(0-)]$$

It follows, therefore, that one might as well use $0-$ values instead of $0+$ values of the state variables, the latter of which are actually not specified.

For the network in Fig. P7.33 obtain the state model, and determine the state variables by using the Laplace transform technique, employing the given $0-$ initial values. Determine $0+$ values of the state variables from the relation in Eq. (6.1.2) and also from the solution in which t is taken equal to zero. Compare the results.

7.34 Investigate the solution of Prob. 7.1, using Laplace transform techniques.

7.35 Prove the following theorems:

(*a*) Final-value theorem: If the function $r(t)$ and its first derivative are Laplace-transformable, and if the rational function $sr(s)$ has poles only in the left-half s plane then

$$\lim_{s \to 0} sr(s) = \lim_{t \to \infty} r(t)$$

(*b*) Initial-value theorem: If the function $r(t)$ and its first derivative are Laplace-transformable and if $\lim_{s \to \infty} sr(s) = K$ exists, then

$$\lim_{t \to 0} r(t) = K$$

7.36 Apply the final- and initial-value theorems stated in Prob. 7.35 to the following response functions $r(t)$, and determine the values $r(0)$ and $r(\infty)$ without calculating the inverse Laplace transforms,

(*a*) $\mathbf{r}(s) = \dfrac{\mathbf{e}(s)}{s^2 + 2\zeta\omega s + \omega^2}$ $\zeta, \omega = $ constants

(*b*) $\mathbf{r}(s) = \dfrac{(s^2 + s + 1)\mathbf{e}(s)}{2s^4 + 3s^3 + 4s^2 + s + 1}$

where $\mathbf{e}(s)$ is the Laplace transform of a unit step function.

7.37 Let **A** be a nonsingular real matrix; then prove the relation

$$\int_0^\infty e^{-\mathbf{A}t}\mathbf{B}\, dt = \mathbf{A}^{-1}\mathbf{B}$$

by using Eq. (6.2.16) for $e^{-\mathbf{A}t}$.

7.38 For numerical evaluation of the sinusoidal steady-state response function develop a relation similar to that obtained in Sec. 7.5 such that the time-response curve is now approximated by the parabolic arcs indicated in Fig. P7.38. In this derivation the following relation is to be used,

$$\int_0^\infty f''(t)e^{-j\omega t}\, dt = -f'(0) - j\omega f(0) + (j\omega)^2 F(j\omega)$$

where $F(j\omega)$ represents the Fourier transform of $f(t)$ [$f(t) = 0$ for $t < 0$].

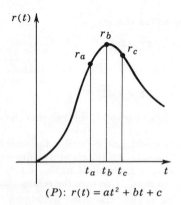

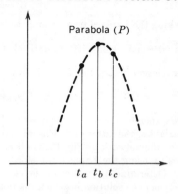

$$(P):\ r(t) = at^2 + bt + c$$

Fig. P7.38

7.39   Determine the z transform of the following sequences:

     (a) $f(n) = e^{-anh}$ $n = 0, 1, 2, \ldots$
     (b) $f(n) = Anh$ $n = 0, 1, 2, \ldots$
     (c) $f(n) = \sin \omega nh$ $n = 0, 1, 2, \ldots$

7.40   Determine the inverse z transform of the following rational functions:

     (a) $F(z) = \dfrac{z(3z^2 - 5z - 1)}{(z - 1)^2(z - 2)}$

     (b) $F(z) = \dfrac{z + 2}{(z - 1)^2}$

     (c) $F(z) = \dfrac{h^2}{2} \dfrac{z(z + 1)}{(z - 1)^3}$

7.41   Determine the expression for the displacement between the points A and G of the mechanical system given in Fig. P7.41. Use the branch formulation. The pulley and the spring together are to be considered as one three-terminal component, with a mathematical model as indicated.

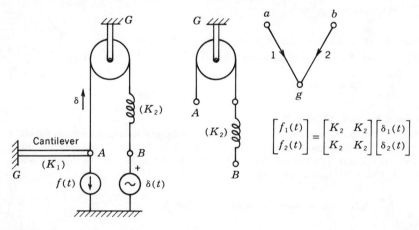

Fig. P7.41

7.42   For the system in Fig. P7.42a, using the branch formulation, express the voltage variables for the two-terminal inductor and capacitor in terms of the known functions $i(t)$ and $e(t)$. Use s-domain terminal equations. The terminal equations of the four-terminal R network in the system, corresponding to the terminal graph in Fig. 7.42b, are given as

$$\begin{bmatrix} i_1(t) \\ i_2(t) \\ i_3(t) \end{bmatrix} = \begin{bmatrix} 2 & -1 & 0 \\ -1 & 2 & 1 \\ 0 & 1 & 1 \end{bmatrix} \begin{bmatrix} v_1(t) \\ v_2(t) \\ v_3(t) \end{bmatrix}$$

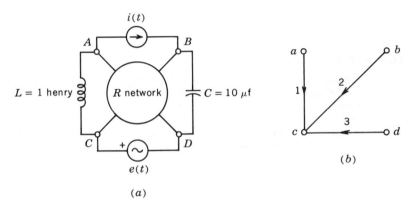

(a)

(b)

Fig. P7.42

7.43   Determine the current variable for the two-terminal resistor R_3 in the electrical network of Fig. P7.43a. Use the chord formulation. The terminal equations of the four-terminal RLC component corresponding to the terminal graph shown in Fig. P7.43b are given as

$$\begin{bmatrix} v_5(s) \\ v_6(s) \\ v_7(s) \end{bmatrix} = \begin{bmatrix} 1+s & s & 0 \\ s & s+1/s+1 & -1 \\ 0 & -1 & 1+1/s \end{bmatrix} \begin{bmatrix} i_5(s) \\ i_6(s) \\ i_7(s) \end{bmatrix}$$

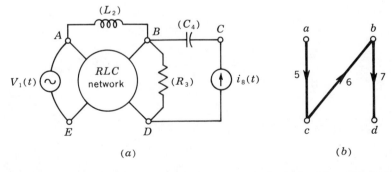

(a)   (b)

Fig. P7.43   (a) An electrical network; (b) terminal graph of four-terminal component in (a).

7.44   Formulate the mixed-parameter model for the transistor network given in Fig. P7.44.

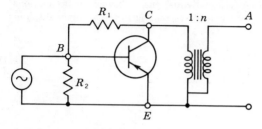

Fig. P7.44

FURTHER READING

1.   Gantmacher, F. R.: "The Theory of Matrices," vol. 1, chap. VIII, Chelsea Publishing Company, New York, 1959.

2.   Nyquist, H.: Regeneration Theory, *Bell System Tech. J.*, vol. 11, pp. 126–147, 1932.

3.   Koenig, H. E., and W. A. Blackwell: "Electromechanical System Theory," McGraw-Hill Book Company, New York, 1961.

8
Analysis of Large-scale Systems

Within the context of this book, a large-scale system is defined as any system that one chooses to analyze by the process of modeling identified subassemblies in the system and then recombining these models to form a model of the entire system. This procedure is also sometimes referred to as "tearing and reconstruction," and it may be used of necessity in the analysis of very complex systems or as an expedient in less complex systems.

The analysis of large-scale systems centers in the concept of mathematical models of multiterminal subassemblies and the procedures for deriving them as a function of their internal structural features. This chapter begins with a discussion of these analysis procedures as they apply to subassemblies of elementary components of the form discussed in Chaps. 2 and 3. Special-purpose procedures are then given for analyzing systems containing restricted classes of multiterminal components with restricted interconnection patterns. The chapter concludes with a fundamental theorem on the existence of both complex frequency and state models of systems of arbitrarily connected linear time-invariant multiterminal components of the most general form. This theorem, along with its proof, establishes an explicit procedure for (1) identifying an upper bound on the order of the system state vector, (2) identifying the components of the state vector, (3) generating the system model, and (4) developing state models of hierarchies of system components, i.e., the analysis of large-scale systems by tearing and reconstruction.

8.1 STATE MODELS OF SUBASSEMBLIES

Consider a system of components such as that shown in Fig. 8.1.1a having a graph $G_1 = 1, 2, 3, \ldots, 6$ as shown in Fig. 8.1.1c. If this collection of components is to be connected to other components at the four terminals A_1, A_2, A_3, and A_4, then this system, called a *subassembly*,

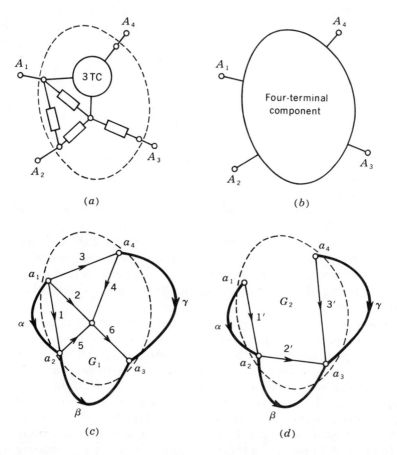

(a)

(b)

(c)

(d)

Fig. 8.1.1 (a) A subassembly of components viewed as a four-terminal component in (b). The corresponding graphs are indicated in (c) and (d), respectively.

or *module*, can be modeled as a four-terminal component in terms of a set of terminal equations corresponding to a terminal graph such as $G_2 = 1', 2', 3'$ in Fig. 8.1.1d; that is, it can be viewed externally as a four-terminal component shown in Fig. 8.1.1b. Further, if the system is linear, the model of the subassembly can always be developed systematically from the structural features of the assembly. The basic procedure represents a simple extension of the modeling procedures given in Chap. 5. Indeed, let the system graph G_1 of the subassembly and the terminal graph G_2 of the subassembly each be augmented by a tree T of "external edges" α, β, γ as indicated in Fig. 8.1.1c and d. Let the vectors Z_1 and Z_2, each of order 3, represent the six complementary variables identified by the edges of T. Suppose for the present that Z_1 can be selected in such a way that, given Z_1, the system represented by the graph $G_1 \cup T$ has a unique solution which can be written in the form

$$\mathbf{Z}_2(t) = \mathbf{F}(\mathbf{Z}_1, t) \tag{8.1.1}$$

From the graph $G_2 \cup T$ it follows that the components of the vector (Z_1, Z_2) are related to the complementary variables defined by the terminal graph G_2, by the simple relations

$$\begin{bmatrix} x_1' \\ x_2' \\ x_3' \end{bmatrix} = \begin{bmatrix} x_\alpha \\ x_\beta \\ x_\gamma \end{bmatrix} \quad \text{and} \quad \begin{bmatrix} y_\alpha \\ y_\beta \\ y_\gamma \end{bmatrix} = - \begin{bmatrix} y_1' \\ y_2' \\ y_3' \end{bmatrix} \tag{8.1.2}$$

Substituting Eqs. (8.1.2) into Eq. (8.1.1) establishes the required model of the subassembly.

It is, of course, possible that the system $G_1 \cup T$ has a solution only when the vector Z_1 is selected in a very special way, or it may not have a solution for any vector Z_1. These and other basic problems associated with the development of state models of arbitrary subassemblies are explored first in terms of specific examples.

Example 8.1.1: The assembly of mechanical components shown in Fig. 8.1.2a is to be connected to other components at points A, B, and G only. What are the forms of some of the time-domain models that might be developed to represent this subassembly as a three-terminal component?

Solution: Let the given system be considered as a three-terminal subassembly subjected to arbitrary forces $f_1(t)$ and $f_2(t)$ at the terminal pairs indicated by the terminal graph. The objective is to derive expressions showing the velocities between the corresponding pairs of terminals as functions of these forces.

The system graph, augmented by edges (1',2'), is shown in Fig. 8.1.2b. Since $f_1(t)$ and $f_2(t)$ are specified variables, regarded as corresponding to "force drivers," edges 1' and 2' are included in the complement of the formulation tree. Since the lever is assumed to be a perfect coupler, either edge 7 or edge 8 is included in the tree and the other in its complement. Consistent with the procedures given in Chap. 5, the tree is selected, as shown in Fig. 8.1.2b, so as to include a maximum number of edges corresponding to mass components as branches and a maximum number of edges corresponding to springs as chords. Such a tree has been designated as a *maximally selected tree*.

Let the direct sum of the component terminal equations be written as

$$\frac{d}{dt}\begin{bmatrix} \dot{\delta}_9(t) \\ f_5(t) \end{bmatrix} = \begin{bmatrix} 1/M_9 & 0 \\ 0 & K_5 \end{bmatrix}\begin{bmatrix} f_9(t) \\ \dot{\delta}_5(t) \end{bmatrix} \tag{8.1.3}$$

$$\begin{bmatrix} \dot{\delta}_3(t) \\ \dot{\delta}_4(t) \end{bmatrix} = \begin{bmatrix} 1/K_3 & 0 \\ 0 & 1/K_4 \end{bmatrix}\frac{d}{dt}\begin{bmatrix} f_3(t) \\ f_4(t) \end{bmatrix} \tag{8.1.4}$$

$$f_6(t) = B_6\dot{\delta}_6(t) \tag{8.1.5}$$

and

$$\begin{bmatrix} f_7(t) \\ \dot{\delta}_8(t) \end{bmatrix} = \begin{bmatrix} 0 & n \\ -n & 0 \end{bmatrix}\begin{bmatrix} \dot{\delta}_7(t) \\ f_8(t) \end{bmatrix} \tag{8.1.6}$$

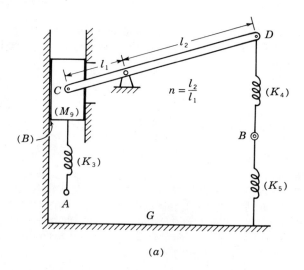

(a)

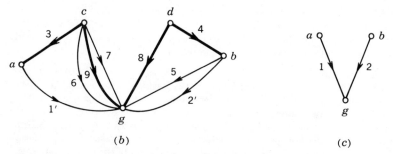

(b)   (c)

Fig. 8.1.2 (a) Mechanical system; (b) system graph, augmented by edges 1′ and 2′; (c) terminal graph for subassembly model.

Upon using the fundamental circuit and cut-set equations to eliminate the secondary variables, there results

$$\frac{d}{dt}\begin{bmatrix} \dot{\delta}_9(t) \\ f_5(t) \end{bmatrix} = \begin{bmatrix} -1/M_9 & -1/M_9 & 0 \\ 0 & 0 & K_5 \end{bmatrix}\begin{bmatrix} f_6 \\ f_7 \\ \dot{\delta}_8(t) \end{bmatrix} - \begin{bmatrix} (1/M_9)f_1'(t) \\ K_5\dot{\delta}_4(t) \end{bmatrix} \tag{8.1.7}$$

$$\begin{bmatrix} \dot{\delta}_3(t) \\ \dot{\delta}_4(t) \end{bmatrix} = \begin{bmatrix} (1/K_3)(d/dt)f_1'(t) \\ (1/K_4)(d/dt)[f_5(t) + f_2'(t)] \end{bmatrix} \tag{8.1.8}$$

$$f_6(t) = B_6\dot{\delta}_9(t) \tag{8.1.9}$$

and

$$\begin{bmatrix} f_7(t) \\ \dot{\delta}_8(t) \end{bmatrix} = \begin{bmatrix} 0 & -n \\ -n & 0 \end{bmatrix}\begin{bmatrix} \dot{\delta}_9(t) \\ f_5(t) \end{bmatrix} + \begin{bmatrix} -nf_2'(t) \\ 0 \end{bmatrix} \tag{8.1.10}$$

Substituting Eqs. (8.1.8) to (8.1.10) into Eq. (8.1.7) gives

$$\frac{d}{dt}\begin{bmatrix} \dot{\delta}_9(t) \\ f_5(t) \end{bmatrix} = \begin{bmatrix} -B_6/M_9 & n/M_9 \\ -nK_4K_5/(K_4 + K_5) & 0 \end{bmatrix}\begin{bmatrix} \dot{\delta}_9(t) \\ f_5(t) \end{bmatrix}$$
$$+ \begin{bmatrix} 1/M_9 & -n/M_9 \\ 0 & 0 \end{bmatrix}\begin{bmatrix} f_1(t) \\ f_2(t) \end{bmatrix}$$
$$+ \begin{bmatrix} 0 & 0 \\ 0 & K_5/(K_4 + K_5) \end{bmatrix}\frac{d}{dt}\begin{bmatrix} f_1(t) \\ f_2(t) \end{bmatrix} \tag{8.1.11}$$

where we have already made the substitution

$$f_1(t) = -f_1'(t)$$

and

$$f_2(t) = -f_2'(t)$$

From the circuit equations of the system graph the required terminal velocities are

$$\begin{bmatrix} \dot{\delta}_1(t) \\ \dot{\delta}_2(t) \end{bmatrix} = \begin{bmatrix} \dot{\delta}_1'(t) \\ \dot{\delta}_2'(t) \end{bmatrix} = \begin{bmatrix} -\dot{\delta}_3(t) + \dot{\delta}_9(t) \\ -\dot{\delta}_4(t) + \dot{\delta}_8(t) \end{bmatrix}$$

Substituting Eqs. (8.1.8) to (8.1.11) into these expressions gives

$$\begin{bmatrix} \dot{\delta}_1(t) \\ \dot{\delta}_2(t) \end{bmatrix} = \begin{bmatrix} 1 & 0 \\ -nK_4/(K_4 + K_5) & 0 \end{bmatrix}\begin{bmatrix} \dot{\delta}_9(t) \\ f_5(t) \end{bmatrix}$$
$$+ \begin{bmatrix} 1/K_3 & 0 \\ 0 & 1/(K_4 + K_5) \end{bmatrix}\frac{d}{dt}\begin{bmatrix} f_1(t) \\ f_2(t) \end{bmatrix} \tag{8.1.12}$$

Equations (8.1.11) and (8.1.12) together constitute a time-domain mathematical model of the assembly as a three-terminal component. This model is of the general form

$$\frac{d}{dt}\mathbf{\Psi}(t) = \mathbf{P}\mathbf{\Psi}(t) + \mathbf{Q}\mathbf{Z}_i(t) + \mathbf{R}\frac{d}{dt}\mathbf{Z}_i(t) \tag{8.1.13}$$

$$\mathbf{Z}_0(t) = \mathbf{M}\mathbf{\Psi}(t) + \mathbf{N}\mathbf{Z}_i(t) + \mathbf{L}\frac{d}{dt}\mathbf{Z}_i(t)$$

where vector $\mathbf{Z}_i(t)$ represents the arbitrary or independent terminal variables and the vector $\mathbf{Z}_0(t)$ represents the complementary terminal variables, i.e., the terminal variables not contained in $\mathbf{Z}_i(t)$. The coefficient matrix $\mathbf{N}$ is of course zero for the specific example given. If drivers exist internal to the terminals of the component, additional terms are included in the model, as shown in Sec. 8.11.

When the components in $Z_i(t)$ are through variables, as in the above example, the model is referred to as an *open-circuit parameter model*. If the components of $Z_i(t)$ are all across variables, the model is called a *short-circuit parameter model*, and if they are a mixed combination of through and across variables, the model is said to be of a *hybrid form*.

The general form of the model given in Eq. (8.1.13), however, is undesirable inasmuch as it involves the time derivative of the independent vector $Z_i(t)$, and for this reason it will *not* be referred to as a state model. The general analysis procedures discussed in the subsequent sections are based on time-domain models of the form resulting from Eq. (8.1.13) when $R \equiv 0$ and $L \equiv 0$. Such forms are called state models. We shall now demonstrate that such a state model of the system in Fig. 8.1.2 can be developed if the independent variables are properly selected.

Consider again the system in Fig. 8.1.2, but with the velocities $\dot{\delta}_1'(t)$ and $\dot{\delta}_2'(t)$ taken as the independent variables. Observe that the tree $(1',2',8,9)$ includes all edges corresponding to mass components as branches, and all spring components as chords. The time-domain model in this case is easily shown to be

$$\frac{d}{dt}\begin{bmatrix} f_3(t) \\ f_4(t) \\ f_5(t) \\ \dot{\delta}_9(t) \end{bmatrix} = \begin{bmatrix} 0 & 0 & 0 & K_3 \\ 0 & 0 & 0 & -nK_4 \\ 0 & 0 & 0 & 0 \\ -1/M_9 & n/M_9 & 0 & -B/M_9 \end{bmatrix}\begin{bmatrix} f_3(t) \\ f_4(t) \\ f_5(t) \\ \dot{\delta}_9(t) \end{bmatrix}$$
$$+ \begin{bmatrix} -K_3 & 0 \\ 0 & -K_4 \\ 0 & K_4 \\ 0 & 0 \end{bmatrix}\begin{bmatrix} \dot{\delta}_1(t) \\ \dot{\delta}_2(t) \end{bmatrix} \quad (8.1.14)$$

and

$$\begin{bmatrix} f_1(t) \\ f_2(t) \end{bmatrix} = \begin{bmatrix} -1 & 0 & 0 & 0 \\ 0 & -1 & 1 & 0 \end{bmatrix}\begin{bmatrix} f_3(t) \\ f_4(t) \\ f_5(t) \\ \dot{\delta}_9(t) \end{bmatrix} + \begin{bmatrix} 0 & 0 \\ 0 & 0 \end{bmatrix}\begin{bmatrix} \dot{\delta}_1(t) \\ \dot{\delta}_2(t) \end{bmatrix}$$

$$(8.1.15)$$

Equations (8.1.14) and (8.1.15) are in the form which will be used in later developments and together are referred to as a state model of the system. Although it may not at first appear obvious, Eqs. (8.1.14) and (8.1.15) can be derived from Eqs. (8.1.11) and (8.1.12). This derivation is left to the reader.

It is also left to the reader to satisfy himself that a hybrid parameter model of the system also involves the time derivative of the independent variables and that a state model as defined here exists only in short-circuit parameter form, for the given system. The following theorem establishes the fact that, at least for subassemblies of two-terminal components, a state model can always be developed by properly selecting the independent variables. Further, the proof of the theorem defines an operational procedure for selecting the independent variables, given the topology of the system and the component characteristics.

Theorem 8.1.1: Let a system having a graph G_s contain only two-terminal components each of which is modeled in terms of one of the following terminal equations,

$$x(t) = ay(t)$$

$$x(t) = b\frac{dy(t)}{dt}$$

$$y(t) = c\frac{dx(t)}{dt}$$

where $x(t)$ and $y(t)$ represent across and through variables, respectively, and a, b, and c are positive real constants. Let any set of n terminals in the system graph be taken as terminal vertices. Then, corresponding to any given terminal graph G_T on the n terminal vertices, there exists a state model of the form

$$\frac{d}{dt}\mathbf{\Psi}(t) = \mathbf{P}\mathbf{\Psi}(t) + \mathbf{Q}\mathbf{Z}_i(t) \tag{8.1.16}$$

$$\mathbf{Z}_0(t) = \mathbf{M}\mathbf{\Psi}(t) + \mathbf{N}\mathbf{Z}_i(t)$$

where $\mathbf{Z}_i(t)$ is a vector of $n - 1$ independent variables corresponding to the edges of the terminal graph G_T and $\mathbf{Z}_0(t)$ represents the terminal variables complementary to $\mathbf{Z}_i(t)$.

Proof: The proof of the theorem is based on the following three lemmas, stated here without proof. The proofs are either identical to or modified forms of those given for closely related theorems included in Chap. 4.

Lemma 8.1.1: Let T be a tree in a connected graph G, and let e_c be an edge in G not contained in T. Consider the circuit $(e_1, e_2, \ldots, e_k, e_c)$ where e_i $(i = 1, 2, \ldots, k)$ are edges in T. If any one of the edges e_i $(i = 1, 2, \ldots, k)$ is removed from $T \cup e_c$, the remaining subgraph T' of $T \cup e_c$ is a tree in G.

Lemma 8.1.2: If T is a tree in a connected graph G, then any cut set in G contains at least one edge of T.

Lemma 8.1.3: Let T be a tree in a connected graph G. Consider the cut set $(e_1, e_2, \ldots, e_s, e_t)$ defined by the branch e_t of T. Any one of the edges e_i ($i = 1, 2, \ldots, s$) of this cut set corresponds to a branch of some tree, T', which contains all elements of T except e_t.

To develop the proof of the main theorem, let the components in the system be referred to as types a, b, and c, and let $G = G_s \cup G_T$ represent the union of the system graph G_s and a tree of edges G_T on the n terminal vertices. Select a sequence of trees in subgraphs of G as follows:

(a) Let G_1 be a subgraph in G containing all edges corresponding to c-type components. Select a tree (forest) T_1 in G_1.

(b) Let G_2 represent the union of G_1 and G_T. Select a tree (forest) T_2 in G_2 such that $T_2 \supset T_1$.†

(c) Let G_3 represent the union of G_2 and all edges corresponding to a-type components. Select a tree (forest) T_3 in G_3 such that $T_3 \supset T_2$.

(d) Select a tree (forest) T in G such that $T \supset T_3$. Then, let the independent terminal variables be

   (i)   All across variables corresponding to edges of G_T which are included in T_2

   (ii) All through variables corresponding to the remaining edges of G_T

From Lemma 8.1.1 it follows that the edges corresponding to independent across variables form no circuits with the edges corresponding to c-type components. From Lemmas 8.1.2 and 8.1.3 it can be shown that edges corresponding to the independent through variables

---

† The symbol $\supset$ is to be read as "includes."

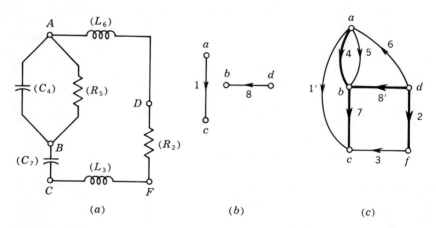

(a)   *(b)*   *(c)*

Fig. 8.1.3 *(a)* An electrical network; *(b)* two-port terminal graph; *(c)* system graph.

form no cut sets with edges corresponding to b-type components, and the theorem is proved.

Example 8.1.2:   Establish a two-port state model of the electrical network shown in Fig. 8.1.3a.

Solution: The system graph, augmented by edges representing the external variables, is shown in Fig. 8.1.3c.   The tree (8',4,7,2) includes all edges corresponding to capacitors as branches and all edges corresponding to inductors as chords. Consequently, a hybrid-parameter state model exists in which $v_8(t)$ and $i_1(t)$ are the independent variables.

In a formal application of Theorem 8.1.1, we have

(a) $G_1 = (4,7)$ and $T_1 = (4,7)$
(b) $G_2 = G_1 \cup G_T = (1',8',4,7)$ and $T_2 = (8',4,7)$
(c) $G_3 = (1',8',4,7,2,5)$ and $T_3 = (8',4,7,2)$
(d) $T = T_3$

Since edge 8' is the only edge in $G_T = (1',8')$ which is also in T_2, then $v_8'(t)$ and $i_1'(t)$ are taken as the independent variables in the state model.   In this particular example, the trees T_1, T_2, and $T_3 = T$ are all unique.   Consequently, a state model exists only in the indicated mixed-parameter form.

Example 8.1.3:   Derive a state model showing the input-output characteristics of the RLC network of Fig. 8.1.4 in h-parameter form.   What other forms are possible?

Solution: Since edges i' and $0'$, corresponding to external variables, form no circuits with capacitors or cut sets with inductors, it follows immediately that state models exist in the open-circuit, short-circuit, and mixed-parameter forms. By using the tree indicated by the heavy lines in Fig. 8.1.4b, the independent variables are $v_i(t)$ and $i_0(t)$, and the derived mixed-parameter state model is

$$\frac{d}{dt}\begin{bmatrix} i_2(t) \\ v_1(t) \end{bmatrix} = \begin{bmatrix} 0 & 1/L_1 \\ -1/C_1 & -G_3/C_1 \end{bmatrix}\begin{bmatrix} i_2(t) \\ v_1(t) \end{bmatrix} + \begin{bmatrix} 0 & 0 \\ G_3/C_1 & 1/C_1 \end{bmatrix}\begin{bmatrix} v_i(t) \\ i_0(t) \end{bmatrix} \quad (8.1.17)$$

$$\begin{bmatrix} i_i(t) \\ v_0(t) \end{bmatrix} = \begin{bmatrix} 0 & -G_3 \\ 0 & 1 \end{bmatrix}\begin{bmatrix} i_2(t) \\ v_1(t) \end{bmatrix} + \begin{bmatrix} G_3 & 0 \\ 0 & R_4 \end{bmatrix}\begin{bmatrix} v_i(t) \\ i_0(t) \end{bmatrix} \quad (8.1.18)$$

That state models in terms of other parameters also exist follows from the form of the coefficient matrix of the independent variables of Eq. (8.1.18).

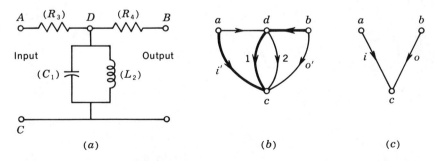

Fig. 8.1.4   (a) An RLC network; (b) augmented system graph; (c) terminal graph.

Since this matrix is nonsingular, the state equations can be inverted to obtain the form

$$\frac{d}{dt}\begin{bmatrix} i_2(t) \\ v_1(t) \end{bmatrix} = \begin{bmatrix} 0 & 1/L_2 \\ -1/C_1 & G_4/C_1 \end{bmatrix}\begin{bmatrix} i_2(t) \\ v_1(t) \end{bmatrix} + \begin{bmatrix} 0 & 0 \\ 1/C_1 & G_4/C_1 \end{bmatrix}\begin{bmatrix} i_i(t) \\ v_0(t) \end{bmatrix} \tag{8.1.19}$$

$$\begin{bmatrix} v_i(t) \\ i_0(t) \end{bmatrix} = -\begin{bmatrix} 0 & -1 \\ 0 & G_4 \end{bmatrix}\begin{bmatrix} i_2(t) \\ v_1(t) \end{bmatrix} + \begin{bmatrix} R_3 & 0 \\ 0 & G_4 \end{bmatrix}\begin{bmatrix} i_i(t) \\ v_0(t) \end{bmatrix} \tag{8.1.20}$$

In a similar manner, if the second expression in Eq. (8.1.18) is inverted, the result, combined with the first expression in that equation, yields a state model in the short-circuit parameter form. A state model in the cascade parameter form, however, does not exist, since the first expression in Eq. (8.1.18) does not have a solution for $v_0(t)$, nor does the second expression have a solution for $i_i(t)$.

8.2   TREE TRANSFORMATIONS

For effective exploitation of either s-domain or state models of subassemblies in the analysis of large-scale systems, it is frequently desirable to transform the model from one set of variables to another, i.e., to transform the equations for one terminal graph to the equations for another terminal graph. Such a transformation is called a *tree transformation* and is achieved by following the same general procedures used in deriving multiterminal representations. The procedure is demonstrated by the following simple example.

Example 8.2.1: The small-signal terminal characteristics of the triode in Fig. 8.2.1b can be given in terms of the variables defined by the terminal graph and the equations

$$\begin{bmatrix} i_1(t) \\ i_2(t) \end{bmatrix} = \begin{bmatrix} 0 & 0 \\ g_m & g_p \end{bmatrix}\begin{bmatrix} v_1(t) \\ v_2(t) \end{bmatrix} \tag{8.2.1}$$

These equations are said to represent a common-cathode model. To establish the equations corresponding to G_2, that is, a common-grid model, consider

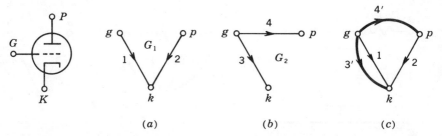

(a)   (b)   (c)

Fig. 8.2.1   (a) Terminal graph G_1 corresponding to a common-cathode model; (b) terminal graph G_2 corresponding to a common-grid model; (c) union of G_1 and an arbitrary tree $T' = (3',4')$.

first the union of G_1 and a tree $T = (3',4')$ shown in Fig. 8.2.1c. For the tree T, the circuit and cut-set equations show that

$$\begin{bmatrix} v_1(t) \\ v_2(t) \end{bmatrix} = \begin{bmatrix} 1 & 0 \\ 1 & -1 \end{bmatrix} \begin{bmatrix} v_{3'}(t) \\ v_{4'}(t) \end{bmatrix} \tag{8.2.2}$$

and

$$\begin{bmatrix} i_{3'}(t) \\ i_{4'}(t) \end{bmatrix} = - \begin{bmatrix} 1 & 1 \\ 0 & -1 \end{bmatrix} \begin{bmatrix} i_1(t) \\ i_2(t) \end{bmatrix}$$

But from the union of G_2 and $T = (3',4')$, we also have

$$\begin{bmatrix} i_{3'}(t) \\ i_{4'}(t) \end{bmatrix} = - \begin{bmatrix} i_3(t) \\ i_4(t) \end{bmatrix} \quad \text{and} \quad \begin{bmatrix} v_{3'}(t) \\ v_{4'}(t) \end{bmatrix} = \begin{bmatrix} v_3(t) \\ v_4(t) \end{bmatrix} \tag{8.2.3}$$

from which it follows that the required transformations are

$$\begin{bmatrix} v_1(t) \\ v_2(t) \end{bmatrix} = \begin{bmatrix} 1 & 0 \\ 1 & -1 \end{bmatrix} \begin{bmatrix} v_3(t) \\ v_4(t) \end{bmatrix} \quad \text{and} \quad \begin{bmatrix} i_3(t) \\ i_4(t) \end{bmatrix} = \begin{bmatrix} 1 & 1 \\ 0 & -1 \end{bmatrix} \begin{bmatrix} i_1(t) \\ i_2(t) \end{bmatrix}$$

Applying these transformations to Eq. (8.2.1) establishes the model for G_2,

$$\begin{bmatrix} i_3(t) \\ i_4(t) \end{bmatrix} = \begin{bmatrix} g_m + g_p & -g_p \\ -(g_m + g_p) & g_p \end{bmatrix} \begin{bmatrix} v_3(t) \\ v_4(t) \end{bmatrix} \tag{8.2.4}$$

While this new terminal representation is just an alternative representation of the vacuum tube (grounded-grid connection), it does not appear as simple as the previous one inasmuch as the coefficient matrix contains no zeros. The rank of the matrix, however, is still 1, as it should be, since the rank is unaltered by a nonsingular transformation.

It is a simple exercise in analysis to generalize the development given in the above example and establish the results summarized in the following theorem.

Theorem 8.2.1: Let the column matrices $X_1(s)$, $Y_1(s)$ and $X_2(s)$, $Y_2(s)$ represent, respectively, the across and through variables defined by two alternate terminal graphs G_1 and G_2 of a given component, and let $G = G_1 \cup G_2$ represent the union of G_1 and G_2.

(a) If the terminal equations for G_1 are given as

$$Y_1(s) = W_1(s)X_1(s)$$

then the terminal equations for G_2 are

$$Y_2(s) = [A_2 W_1(s) A_2{}^T] X_2(s) \tag{8.2.5}$$

where A_2 is the coefficient matrix in the cut-set equations

$$Y_2(s) - A_2 Y_1(s) = 0$$

for graph $G = G_1 \cup G_2$.

(b) If the terminal equations for G_1 are given as

$$X_1(s) = Z_1(s)Y_1(s)$$

then the terminal equations for G_2 are

$$\mathbf{X}_2(s) = [\mathbf{B}_1\mathbf{Z}_1(s)\mathbf{B}_1{}^T(s)]\mathbf{Y}_2(s) \tag{8.2.6}$$

where $\mathbf{B}_1$ is the coefficient matrix in the circuit equations

$$\mathbf{X}_2(s) + \mathbf{B}_1\mathbf{X}_1(s) = 0$$

for graph $G = G_1 \cup G_2$.

(c)   If the terminal equations for G_1 are given as

$$\mathbf{W}_1(s)\mathbf{X}_1(s) = \mathbf{Z}_1(s)\mathbf{Y}_1(s)$$

then the terminal equations for T_2 are

$$[\mathbf{W}_1(s)\mathbf{B}_2]\mathbf{X}_2(s) = [\mathbf{Z}_1(s)\mathbf{A}_1]\mathbf{Y}_2(s) \tag{8.2.7}$$

where $\mathbf{B}_2$ and $\mathbf{A}_1$ are the coefficient matrices in the circuit and cut-set equations

$$\mathbf{X}_1(s) + \mathbf{B}_2\mathbf{X}_2(s) = 0$$
$$\mathbf{Y}_1(s) - \mathbf{A}_1\mathbf{Y}_2(s) = 0$$

for graph $G = G_1 \cup G_2$.

Although Theorem 8.2.1 is stated for the s-domain models, it is also applicable to state models.   In fact, let the state model of a component, corresponding to the terminal graph G_1, be given as

$$\boldsymbol{\Psi}'(t) = \mathbf{P}\boldsymbol{\Psi}(t) + \mathbf{Q}\mathbf{Z}_i(t)$$
$$\mathbf{Z}_0(t) = \mathbf{M}\boldsymbol{\Psi}(t) + \mathbf{N}\mathbf{Z}_i(t) \tag{8.2.8}$$

If $\mathbf{Z}_i(t) \equiv \mathbf{X}_1(t)$ and $\mathbf{Z}_0(t) \equiv \mathbf{Y}_1(t)$, then the state model of the component, corresponding to another terminal graph G_2, is

$$\boldsymbol{\Psi}'(t) = \mathbf{P}\boldsymbol{\Psi}(t) + (-\mathbf{Q}\mathbf{A}_2)\mathbf{X}_2(t)$$
$$\mathbf{Y}_2(t) = (\mathbf{A}_2\mathbf{M})\boldsymbol{\Psi}(t) + (-\mathbf{A}_2\mathbf{N}\mathbf{A}_2)\mathbf{X}_2(t) \tag{8.2.9}$$

On the other hand, if $\mathbf{Z}_i(t) = \mathbf{Y}_1(t)$ and $\mathbf{Z}_0(t) = \mathbf{X}_1(t)$, then the state model, for G_2, is

$$\boldsymbol{\Psi}'(t) = \mathbf{P}\boldsymbol{\Psi}(t) + (-\mathbf{Q}\mathbf{B}_1{}^T)\mathbf{Y}_2(t)$$
$$\mathbf{X}_2(t) = (-\mathbf{B}_1\mathbf{M})\boldsymbol{\Psi}(t) + (\mathbf{B}_1\mathbf{Q}\mathbf{B}_1{}^T)\mathbf{Y}_2(t) \tag{8.2.10}$$

Note, however, that if $\mathbf{Z}_i$ and $\mathbf{Z}_0$ contain both components x_i and y_i, as in hybrid-parameter models, then the tree transformation, in general, may be difficult to apply, inasmuch as the number of through and across variables identified in each of the terminal vectors $\mathbf{Z}_i(t)$ and $\mathbf{Z}_0(t)$ depends on the terminal graph G_2 as well as the specific form of the given model. A theoretical basis for identifying the terminal variables and the more general form of the state model that might result from the transformation is contained in Theorem 8.11.1 in a later section of this chapter.

8.3 PARALLEL - CONNECTED n - TERMINAL COMPONENTS

When a large-scale system is analyzed by a process of tearing and reconstruction, i.e., by developing models of subassemblies which are in turn treated as multiterminal components, the state models of the multiterminal components may be of the form given in Eqs. (8.1.16) or even perhaps more general yet. Before considering the very general problem of analyzing arbitrary systems of linear multiterminal components, it is helpful to consider several special types of interconnection, starting first with what is perhaps the simplest.

Let the terminal characteristics of each of two component C_1 and C_2 be given in terms of terminal graphs G_1 and G_2, respectively, and let the terminal characteristics of the resulting component $C_1 \cup C_2$ be given in terms of a terminal graph G_3. The components are said to be united in parallel if all three graphs G_1, G_2, and G_3 are identical, i.e., if they have identical topological forms and labeling. If the s-domain models corresponding to G_1 and G_2 are, respectively,

$$\mathbf{Y}_1(s) = \mathbf{W}_1(s)\mathbf{X}_1(s) \tag{8.3.1}$$

and

$$\mathbf{Y}_2(s) = \mathbf{W}_2(s)\mathbf{X}_2(s) \tag{8.3.2}$$

then it follows immediately from the constraint equations of $G_1 \cup G_2 \cup G_3$ that the s-domain model for G_3, that is, the parallel-connected components C_1 and C_2, is

$$\mathbf{Y}_3(s) = [\mathbf{W}_1(s) + \mathbf{W}_2(s)]\mathbf{X}_3(s) \tag{8.3.3}$$

That is, the short-circuit coefficient matrix of the assembly is obtained as the sum of the short-circuit coefficient matrices of the components. Similarly, if the state models corresponding to G_1 and G_2 exist in the short-circuit parameter forms

$$\begin{aligned}
\dot{\mathbf{\Psi}}_1(t) &= \mathbf{P}_1\mathbf{\Psi}_1(t) + \mathbf{Q}_1\mathbf{X}_1(t) \\
\mathbf{Y}_2(t) &= \mathbf{M}_1\mathbf{\Psi}_1(t) + \mathbf{N}_1\mathbf{X}_1(t)
\end{aligned} \tag{8.3.4}$$

and

$$\begin{aligned}
\dot{\mathbf{\Psi}}_2(t) &= \mathbf{P}_2\mathbf{\Psi}_2(t) + \mathbf{Q}_2\mathbf{X}_2(t) \\
\mathbf{Y}_2(t) &= \mathbf{M}_2\mathbf{\Psi}_2(t) + \mathbf{N}_2\mathbf{X}_2(t)
\end{aligned} \tag{8.3.5}$$

then the state model of the parallel-connected assembly is

$$\begin{bmatrix} \dot{\Psi}_1(t) \\ \dot{\Psi}_2(t) \end{bmatrix} = \begin{bmatrix} P_1 & 0 \\ 0 & P_2 \end{bmatrix} \begin{bmatrix} \Psi_1(t) \\ \Psi_2(t) \end{bmatrix} + \begin{bmatrix} Q_1 \\ Q_2 \end{bmatrix} X_3(t)$$

$$Y_3(t) = [M_1 \quad M_2] \begin{bmatrix} \Psi_1(t) \\ \Psi_2(t) \end{bmatrix} + (N_1 + N_2)X_3(t) \tag{8.3.6}$$

The above algorithm can be extended to cover the "parallel" interconnection of an m-terminal and an n-terminal component $n > m$, by augmenting the terminal graph of the m-terminal graph with dummy vertices and edges corresponding to zero admittance. This procedure is demonstrated in the following example, taken from electronic circuits, where this particular technique finds extensive application.

Example 8.3.1: Determine the complex-frequency input-output characteristics of the amplifier in Fig. 8.3.1.

Solution: Consider the system as an assembly of three components or subsystems each having four terminals (the total number of points of union in the final system), with variables identified by the terminal graph in Fig. 8.3.1b and corresponding s-domain short-circuit admittance matrices as follows.

Capacitors:

$$W_1(s) = \begin{bmatrix} sC & -sC & 0 \\ -sC & sC & 0 \\ 0 & 0 & 0 \end{bmatrix}$$

Delta-connected resistors R_1, R_2, R_3 with

$$W_2(s) = \begin{bmatrix} 0 & 0 & 0 \\ 0 & g_1 + g_2 & -g_1 \\ 0 & -g_1 & g_1 + g_3 \end{bmatrix}$$

Vacuum tube:

$$W_3(s) = \begin{bmatrix} 0 & 0 & 0 \\ 0 & 0 & 0 \\ 0 & g_m & g_p \end{bmatrix}$$

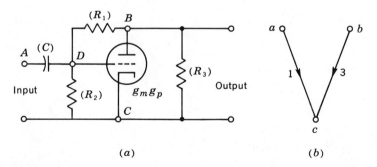

(a) (b)

Fig. 8.3.1 (a) A typical electronic amplifier, and (b) terminal graph identifying the variables used to model each of three subassemblies in the system.

The short-circuit matrix in a four-terminal representation of the given system is $\mathbf{W}(s) = \mathbf{W}_1(s) + \mathbf{W}_2(s) + \mathbf{W}_3(s)$, and the terminal equations of the assembly corresponding to the graph in Fig. 8.3.1b are

$$
\begin{bmatrix} \mathbf{i}_1(s) \\ \mathbf{i}_2(s) \\ \mathbf{i}_3(s) \end{bmatrix} \begin{bmatrix} sC & -sC & 0 \\ -sC & sC + (g_1 + g_2) & -g_1 \\ 0 & -g_1 + g_m & g_p + (g_1 + g_3) \end{bmatrix} \begin{bmatrix} \mathbf{v}_1(s) \\ \mathbf{v}_2(s) \\ \mathbf{v}_3(s) \end{bmatrix} \tag{8.3.7}
$$

The required input-output (three-terminal) representation is obtained by simply setting $i_2(s) = 0$ in Eq. (8.3.7) and eliminating $v_2(s)$. The result is

$$
\begin{bmatrix} \mathbf{i}_1(s) \\ \mathbf{i}_3(s) \end{bmatrix}
$$
$$
= \begin{bmatrix} [(g_1 + g_2)Cs]/[Cs + (g_1 + g_2)] & g_1Cs/[Cs + (g_1 + g_2)] \\ [(g_m - g_1)Cs]/[Cs + (g_1 + g_2)] & [(g_m - g_1)g_1]/[Cs + (g_1 + g_2)] + (g_p + g_1 + g_3) \end{bmatrix} \begin{bmatrix} \mathbf{v}_1(s) \\ \mathbf{v}_3(s) \end{bmatrix}
$$

8.4 CASCADED THREE-TERMINAL AND TWO-PORT COMPONENTS

One of the most frequently encountered types of subassembly interconnections found in practical application is the cascaded configuration shown in Fig. 8.4.1. The individual components may have either three or four terminals. However, the four-terminal components are actually used as *two-port* components; i.e., connections are made only between terminal pairs A-B and/or between terminals C-D as indicated in Fig. 8.4.2.

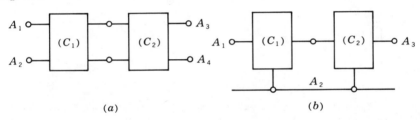

(a) (b)

Fig. 8.4.1 (a) Cascaded two-port components; (b) cascaded three-terminal components.

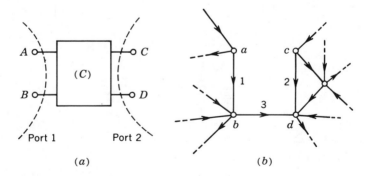

(a) (b)

Fig. 8.4.2 (a) Four-terminal component; (b) system graph containing a four-terminal component connected as a two-port component.

The graph G of any system containing a four-terminal component connected as a two-port component is of the general form shown in Fig. 8.4.2b, where edges 1, 2, and 3 correspond to the four-terminal component. Since edge 3 is contained in every tree in G, $y_3(t) \equiv 0$, and $x_3(t)$ is not included in any of the fundamental circuit equations, these variables and the corresponding edge 3 can be eliminated once and for all from the mathematical model of the component. That is, only a two-port model, rather than a full four-terminal model, is required to characterize a component operating under this restricted class of conditions. If the four-terminal model is given in terms of the open-circuit parameters, for example, then the two-port model is obtained by simply setting $y_3(s) = 0$ and deleting the corresponding equation.

A particularly effective procedure for applying the constraint equations of the cascade interconnection to s-domain models is demonstrated in the following example.

Example 8.4.1:   Figure 8.4.3 shows a diagram of a Ward-Leonard system used extensively as a subsystem in speed- and position-control systems. It consists of two d-c machines connected in cascade, one of which operates as a generator and the other as a motor. It is required to determine the complex-frequency transfer characteristics between the input and output ports of this system.

Solution: Let the direct sum of the complex-frequency models of the d-c generator and motor be taken as

$$\begin{bmatrix} v_1(s) \\ v_2(s) \\ \hline v_3(s) \\ \tau_4(s) \end{bmatrix} = \begin{bmatrix} R_1 + sL_1 & 0 & 0 & 0 \\ K_g & R_2 & 0 & 0 \\ \hline 0 & 0 & R_3 & K_m \\ 0 & 0 & -K_m & B_4 + sJ_4 \end{bmatrix} \begin{bmatrix} i_1(s) \\ i_2(s) \\ \hline i_3(s) \\ \dot{\phi}_4(s) \end{bmatrix} \qquad (8.4.1)$$

Since $v_2(s) - v_3(s) = 0$ and $i_3(s) = -i_2(s)$, add the negative of the third equation to the second and add the negative of the third column of the resulting 3×4 coefficient matrix to the second column, to obtain

$$\begin{bmatrix} v_1(s) \\ 0 \\ \tau_4(s) \end{bmatrix} = \begin{bmatrix} R_1 + sL_1 & 0 & 0 \\ K_g & R_2 + R_3 & -K_m \\ 0 & +K_m & B_4 + sJ_4 \end{bmatrix} \begin{bmatrix} i_1(s) \\ i_2(s) \\ \dot{\phi}_4(s) \end{bmatrix} \qquad (8.4.2)$$

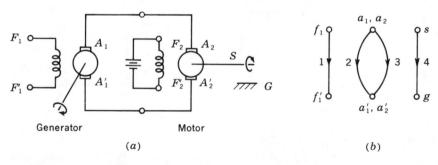

Generator   Motor

(a)   (b)

Fig. 8.4.3   (a) Ward-Leonard control system; (b) system graph.

Eliminating $i_2(s)$ from Eq. (8.4.2) establishes the input-output characteristics explicitly as

$$\begin{bmatrix} v_1(s) \\ \tau_4(s) \end{bmatrix} = \begin{bmatrix} R_1 + sL_1 & 0 \\ -K_m K_g/(R_2 + R_3) & K_m{}^2/(R_2 + R_3) + (B_4 + sJ_4) \end{bmatrix} \begin{bmatrix} i_1(s) \\ \dot{\phi}_4(s) \end{bmatrix}$$
(8.4.3)

State models of cascaded two-ports are easily developed if the state equations of each component in the cascaded assembly are first written explicitly in the primary variables of a tree in system graph.

Example 8.4.2:   Develop a state model for the system composed of the cascaded subassemblies C_1 and C_2 shown in Fig. 8.4.4.

Solution: For the tree indicated in Fig. 8.4.4b, the models of each component, written explicitly in the primary variables, are

$$\begin{bmatrix} i_1(t) \\ i_2(t) \end{bmatrix} = \begin{bmatrix} 1/R & -1/R \\ -1/R & 1/R \end{bmatrix} \begin{bmatrix} v_1(t) \\ v_2(t) \end{bmatrix} + \begin{bmatrix} 0 \\ C_1 \end{bmatrix} \frac{d}{dt} v_2(t)$$
(8.4.4)

and

$$\begin{bmatrix} v_3(t) \\ i_4(t) \end{bmatrix} = \begin{bmatrix} 0 & 1/C_2 \\ -1/L & 0 \end{bmatrix} \begin{bmatrix} v_3(t) \\ i_4(t) \end{bmatrix} + \begin{bmatrix} 1/C_2 & 0 \\ 0 & 1/L \end{bmatrix} \begin{bmatrix} i_3(t) \\ v_4(t) \end{bmatrix}$$
(8.4.5)

Setting $i_3(t) = -i_2(t)$ and $v_2(t) = v_3(t)$ and substituting the second expression in Eq. (8.4.4) into Eq. (8.4.5) gives

$$\begin{bmatrix} 1 + (C_1/C_2) & 0 \\ 0 & 1 \end{bmatrix} \frac{d}{dt} \begin{bmatrix} v_3(t) \\ i_4(t) \end{bmatrix} = \begin{bmatrix} -1/RC_2 & 1/C_2 \\ 1/L & 0 \end{bmatrix} \begin{bmatrix} v_3(t) \\ i_4(t) \end{bmatrix} + \begin{bmatrix} 1/RC_2 & 0 \\ 0 & 1/L \end{bmatrix} \begin{bmatrix} v_1(t) \\ v_4(t) \end{bmatrix}$$

or

$$\frac{d}{dt} \begin{bmatrix} v_3(t) \\ i_4(t) \end{bmatrix} = \begin{bmatrix} -1/R(C_1 + C_2) & 1/(C_1 + C_2) \\ 1/L & 0 \end{bmatrix} \begin{bmatrix} v_3(t) \\ i_4(t) \end{bmatrix} + \begin{bmatrix} 1/R(C_1 + C_2) & 0 \\ 0 & 1/L \end{bmatrix} \begin{bmatrix} v_1(t) \\ v_4(t) \end{bmatrix}$$
(8.4.6)

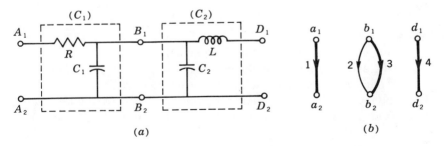

(a)   (b)

Fig. 8.4.4   (a) Cascaded subassemblies; (b) system graph.

Equation (8.4.6), along with the algebraic equations

$$\begin{bmatrix} i_1(t) \\ i_4(t) \end{bmatrix} = \begin{bmatrix} -1/R & 0 \\ 0 & 1 \end{bmatrix} \begin{bmatrix} v_3(t) \\ i_4(t) \end{bmatrix} + \begin{bmatrix} 1/R & 0 \\ 0 & 0 \end{bmatrix} \begin{bmatrix} v_1(t) \\ v_4(t) \end{bmatrix} \tag{8.4.7}$$

constitutes a state model of the cascaded system.

8.5 CASCADED UNILATERAL COMPONENTS

An ideal unilateral two-port component is defined as one having an s-domain model of the form

$$\begin{bmatrix} y_i(s) \\ x_0(s) \end{bmatrix} = \begin{bmatrix} 0 & 0 \\ \mu(s) & R_0(s) \end{bmatrix} \begin{bmatrix} x_i(s) \\ y_0(s) \end{bmatrix}$$

It is not difficult to show that a state model of such a component is of the general form

$$\frac{d}{dt} \mathbf{\Psi}(t) = \mathbf{P}\mathbf{\Psi}(t) + [\mathbf{Q} \quad \mathbf{Q}'] \begin{bmatrix} x_i(t) \\ y_0(t) \end{bmatrix}$$

$$\begin{bmatrix} y_i(t) \\ x_0(t) \end{bmatrix} = \begin{bmatrix} \mathbf{0} \\ \mathbf{M} \end{bmatrix} \mathbf{\Psi}(t) + \begin{bmatrix} 0 & 0 \\ n & R_0 \end{bmatrix} \begin{bmatrix} x_i(t) \\ y_0(t) \end{bmatrix} \tag{8.5.1}$$

where the constant n represents the "direct transmission," if any, between the output and input ports. When two such two-port components are connected in cascade, one component has no loading effect on the other and the terminal through variables do not, in any way, enter into the model of the *no-load* input-output characteristics of the assembly. This being the case, the through variable is usually omitted from the component models also. Thus, there is no loss in generality by taking the state equations of two cascaded unilateral components in the form

$$\frac{d}{dt} \mathbf{\Psi}_1(t) = \mathbf{P}_1\mathbf{\Psi}_1(t) + \mathbf{Q}_1 x_1(t)$$

$$x_2(t) = \mathbf{M}_1\mathbf{\Psi}_1(t) + n_1 x_1(t) \tag{8.5.2}$$

and

$$\frac{d}{dt} \mathbf{\Psi}_2(t) = \mathbf{P}_2\mathbf{\Psi}_2(t) + \mathbf{Q}_2 x_3(t)$$

$$x_4(t) = \mathbf{M}_2\mathbf{\Psi}_2(t) + n_2 x_3(t) \tag{8.5.3}$$

where

$x_1(t)$ and $x_3(t)$ represent the input signals
$x_2(t)$ and $x_4(t)$ represent the outputs
$\mathbf{M}_1$ and $\mathbf{M}_2$ represent row matrices each of rank 1

By applying nonsingular similarity transformations to the state vector, if necessary, it is always possible to reduce $\mathbf{M}_1$ and $\mathbf{M}_2$ to the forms

$$\mathbf{M}_1 = [1 \quad 0 \quad \cdots \quad 0]$$
$$\mathbf{M}_2 = [1 \quad 0 \quad \cdots \quad 0] \tag{8.5.4}$$

That is, the output can always be made one of the components in the state vector. In the following development it is assumed, without loss of generality, that this transformation has been made.

By applying the constraint equation $x_3(t) = x_2(t)$ to Eqs. (8.5.2) and (8.5.3), the no-load input-output state model of the assembly is

$$\frac{d}{dt}\begin{bmatrix} \mathbf{\Psi}_1(t) \\ \mathbf{\Psi}_2(t) \end{bmatrix} = \begin{bmatrix} \mathbf{P}_1 & 0 \\ \mathbf{Q}_2\mathbf{M}_1 & \mathbf{P}_2 \end{bmatrix}\begin{bmatrix} \mathbf{\Psi}_1(t) \\ \mathbf{\Psi}_2(t) \end{bmatrix} + \begin{bmatrix} \mathbf{Q}_1 \\ \mathbf{Q}_2 n_1 \end{bmatrix} x_1(t)$$

$$x_4(t) = \begin{bmatrix} n_2\mathbf{M}_1 & \mathbf{M}_2 \end{bmatrix}\begin{bmatrix} \mathbf{\Psi}_1(t) \\ \mathbf{\Psi}_2(t) \end{bmatrix} + n_1 n_2 x_1(t)$$

(8.5.5)

If the models for the components are given in the s domain in the form of the mixed parameters

$$\begin{bmatrix} \mathbf{y}_1(s) \\ \mathbf{x}_2(s) \end{bmatrix} = \begin{bmatrix} 0 & 0 \\ G_{21}(s) & Z_{22}(s) \end{bmatrix}\begin{bmatrix} \mathbf{x}_1(s) \\ \mathbf{y}_2(s) \end{bmatrix}$$

(8.5.6)

and

$$\begin{bmatrix} \mathbf{y}_3(s) \\ \mathbf{x}_4(s) \end{bmatrix} = \begin{bmatrix} 0 & 0 \\ G_{43}(s) & Z_{44}(s) \end{bmatrix}\begin{bmatrix} \mathbf{x}_3(s) \\ \mathbf{y}_4(s) \end{bmatrix}$$

(8.5.7)

then, of course, it follows upon setting $x_2(s) = x_3(s)$ that the complete input-output characteristics of the subassembly are given by the ideal unilateral form

$$\begin{bmatrix} \mathbf{y}_1(s) \\ \mathbf{x}_4(s) \end{bmatrix} = \begin{bmatrix} 0 & 0 \\ G_{43}(s)G_{21}(s) & Z_{44}(s) \end{bmatrix}\begin{bmatrix} \mathbf{x}_1(s) \\ \mathbf{y}_4(s) \end{bmatrix}$$

(8.5.8)

The important feature of both state models and s-domain models of cascaded unilateral two-ports is the fact that the characteristic polynomial of the cascaded assembly is given as *the product of the characteristic polynomials of the components.* In fact, from the state model in Eq. (8.5.5) it is evident that the characteristic polynomial of the cascaded system is

$$D(\lambda) = \det\begin{bmatrix} \lambda\mathbf{U} - \mathbf{P}_1 & 0 \\ -\mathbf{Q}_2\mathbf{M}_1 & \lambda\mathbf{U} - \mathbf{P}_2 \end{bmatrix} = \det(\lambda\mathbf{U} - \mathbf{P}_1)\det(\lambda\mathbf{U} - \mathbf{P}_2)$$

$$= D_1(\lambda)D_2(\lambda)$$

where $D_1(\lambda) = \det(\lambda\mathbf{U} - \mathbf{P}_1)$ and $D_2(\lambda) = \det(\lambda\mathbf{U} - \mathbf{P}_2)$ represent the characteristic polynomials of the respective components.

The fact that the no-load complex-frequency transfer function of cascaded unilateral components is given as the product of the corresponding transfer functions of the individual components makes the s-domain model of such components an almost indispensable tool in the analysis and design of linear systems. The following example demonstrates how this feature is exploited in a complete frequency-response analysis of typical cascaded unilateral components.

Example 8.5.1: Consider the grounded-cathode amplifier shown in Fig. 8.5.1. If the parameters of the tube and the values of R_k and R_l are selected as $\mu = 20$, $r_p = 7{,}000$ ohms, $R_k = 1{,}000$, and $R_l = 10{,}000$, determine the values of C_k, C_c, and R_g such that, for frequencies above $\omega = 200$, there is no appreciable phase shift between the input and output signals. For the high-frequency range, the grid-to-cathode and plate-to-cathode capacitors are to be taken as $C_{gk} = 100 \ \mu\mu\mathrm{f}$ and $C_{pk} = 2 \ \mu\mu\mathrm{f}$. Using these values for the component parameters, sketch the actual frequency-response characteristics.

Solution: Let the amplifier circuit first be divided into three cascaded three-terminal subassemblies according to their function, as indicated. Subassemblies A and C are simply basic plate-resistance amplifiers. The capacitor C_c is used to isolate the bias circuits of the two amplifiers, and the resistance R_g stabilizes the grid of the second stage.

The models to be used to characterize the functional subassemblies depend, of course, on the frequency range being considered. Consider first the low- and mid-band frequency range, where the interelectrode capacitances can be neglected. It is easy to see that functional subsystems A and C have identical unilateral characteristics, but subsystem B is bilateral. Consequently, we develop first a model of subassemblies A and B together as a unit. Following the techniques presented in Example 8.4.1, it is easy to show that the no-load transfer function from port A-G to port C-G is

$$G_{ac} = \frac{G_{ab}(s)R_g}{Z_a(s) + Z_3(s)} \tag{8.5.9}$$

$$G_{ab}(s) = \frac{-\mu R_l}{(R_l + r_p) + (1 + \mu)Z_k(s)} \tag{8.5.10}$$

$$Z_a(s) = \frac{R_p + (1 + \mu)Z_k(s)R_l}{(R_l + r_p) + (1 + \mu)Z_k(s)} \tag{8.5.11}$$

$$Z_3(s) = R_g + \frac{1}{C_c s} \tag{8.5.12}$$

with

$$Z_k(s) = \frac{R_k}{1 + R_k C_k s} = \left(\frac{1}{R_k} + C_k s\right)^{-1} \tag{8.5.13}$$

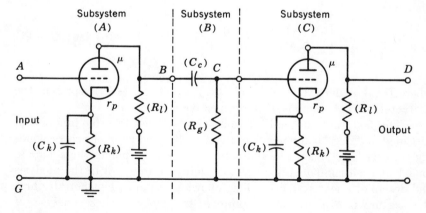

Fig. 8.5.1 A typical cascaded amplifier circuit.

The transfer function $G_{ab}(s)$ represents the no-load transfer function of subsystem A, and $Z_a(s)$ represents its output impedance. Since subsystem C is identical to A, it follows that the low- and mid-band no-load transfer function of the entire assembly from port A-G to D-G is given by

$$G_{ad} = G_{ac}(s)G_{cd}(s) = G_{ac}(s)G_{ab}(s) \tag{8.5.14}$$

and the output impedance of the assembly is

$$Z_0(s) = Z_a(s)$$

Upon setting $s = j\omega$ in the expressions for $G_{ab}(s)$ and $Z_a(s)$ given in Eqs. (8.5.10) and (8.5.11), it is evident that $Z_k(j\omega)$ is negligible if the frequency and the cathode bypass capacitor C_k are such that

$$\left| \frac{\mu + 1}{1/R_k + j\omega C_k} \right| \ll R_l + r_p$$

For the triode given, $\mu = 20$, $r_p = 7{,}000$ ohms, and the cathode and given plate resistors were selected as $R_k = 1{,}000$ and $R_l = 10{,}000$ ohms. The coefficient $Z_k(j\omega)$ can be neglected if

$$|10^{-3} + j\omega C_k| \gg \frac{21}{17 \times 10^3} = 1.235 \times 10^{-5}$$

or

$$\omega C_k \gg 0.725 \times 10^{-3} \tag{8.5.15}$$

This implies that, if there is to be no appreciable phase shift above $\omega = 145$ rps, the value of the cathode bypass capacitor must be such that

$$C_k \gg 5 \times 10^{-6}$$

This inequality is usually satisfied when C_k is taken as ten times the value indicated, that is, $C_k = 50$ μf.

From Eq. (8.5.12), it is apparent that if the coupling capacitance C_c is selected such that

$$\frac{1}{C_c \omega} \ll R_g \tag{8.5.16}$$

then any phase shift caused by this component can be neglected also. Consequently, for frequencies above $\omega = 200$ rps the overall transfer function of the network is

$$G_{ad}(j\omega) = \frac{\mu R_l R_g}{R_l + r_p} \frac{1}{R_l r_p/(R_l + r_p) + R_g + C_c \omega} \tag{8.5.17}$$

and the output impedance is

$$Z_2(s) = Z_2 = \frac{R_l R_p}{R_l + R_p}$$

For maximum mid-band gain, R_g should be selected as large as is practical. If $R_g = 0.5$ megohm, for example, then

$$\frac{R_l r_p}{R_g} \ll R_l + r_p$$

and the mid-band transfer function reduces to a constant

$$G_{ad} = \frac{\mu R_l}{R_l + r_p} = \frac{20 \times 10^4}{17 \times 10^3} = 11.75$$

If $C_c = 0.1$ μf, the inequality in Eq. (8.5.16) is satisfied as long as $\omega \gg 20$ rps; i.e., the coupling capacitor can be neglected for frequencies above about $\omega = 200$ rps. For the numerical values for the network parameters given above, the low and mid-band transfer functions of the two cascaded unilateral components are

$$\begin{aligned}
G_{ac}(s) &= \frac{(s + 20)s}{0.428s^2 + 27.78s + 380} \\
&= \frac{0.263(1 + s/20)s}{(1 + s/19.6)(1 + s/45.2)}
\end{aligned} \tag{8.5.18}$$

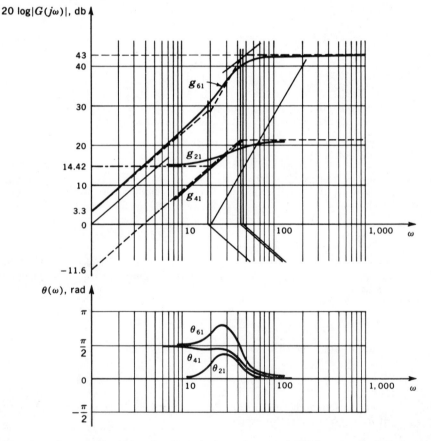

Fig. 8.5.2 Low- and mid-band gain and phase characteristics for transfer functions $G_{ac}(s)$, $G_{cd}(s)$, and $G_{ad}(s) = G_{ac}(s)G_{cd}(s)$ for the network in Fig. 8.5.1.

and

$$G_{cd}(s) = G_{ab}(s) = \frac{2(100 + 5s)}{38 + 0.85s}$$

$$= \frac{5.26(1 + s/20)}{1 + s/44.7} \tag{8.5.19}$$

The low- and mid-band decibel frequency-response characteristics of the system as obtained from the sum of the decibel frequency-response characteristics of the two stages are shown in Fig. 8.5.2.

The effects of the grid-to-cathode and plate-to-cathode capacitances of the triodes on the high-frequency characteristics are included when the short-circuit impedance matrices for the triodes are taken as

$$\begin{bmatrix} C_{gk}s & 0 \\ g_m & g_p + C_{pk}s \end{bmatrix} = \begin{bmatrix} C_{gk}s & 0 \\ 0 & 0 \end{bmatrix} + \begin{bmatrix} 0 & 0 \\ g_m & g_p \end{bmatrix} + \begin{bmatrix} 0 & 0 \\ 0 & C_{pk}s \end{bmatrix} \tag{8.5.20}$$

From the expanded form of this matrix it follows that each triode can be replaced by an equivalent ideal triode connected in parallel with two capacitors, as indicated in Fig. 8.5.3. The low- and mid-band transfer functions already developed are therefore extended into the high-frequency·range when R_g is replaced by

$$Z_g(s) = \left(\frac{1}{R_g} + C_{gk}s \right)^{-1}$$

and R_l is replaced by

$$Z_l(s) = \left(\frac{1}{R_l} + C_{gk}s \right)^{-1}$$

Capacitor C_{gk} in the first stage has no effect on the frequency characteristics, since $v_1(t)$ is a specified voltage.

The numerical values of the high-frequency transfer function so obtained are easily shown to be

$$G_{ac}(s) = \frac{3.448 \times 10^8}{s + 0.293 \times 10^8}$$

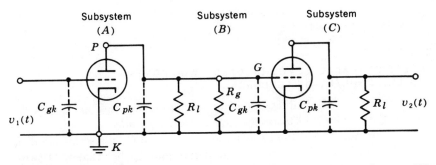

Fig. 8.5.3 Simplified circuit of two-stage amplifier in Example 8.5.1 for $\omega \gg 200$ rpms.

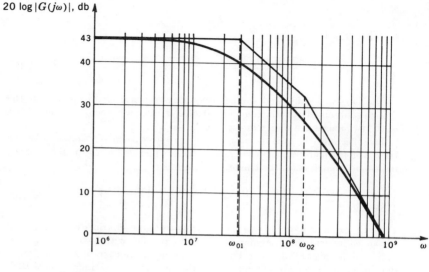

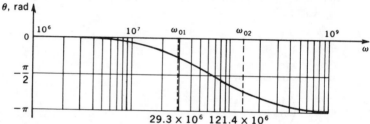

Fig. 8.5.4 High-frequency gain and phase characteristics for $G(s) = G_{ac}(s)G_{cd}(s)$ of network in Fig. 8.5.1.

and

$$G_{cd}(s) = G_{ab}(s) = \frac{14.3 \times 10^8}{s + 1.214 \times 10^8}$$

The high-frequency decibel input-output response characteristics of the network are shown in Fig. 8.5.4.

8.6 SERIES-PARALLEL-CONNECTED TWO-PORTS AND THE CONCEPT OF FEEDBACK

When two four-terminal components are interconnected as shown in Fig. 8.6.1, they are said to be *connected in series parallel*.

In general, each of the two components C_1 and C_2 in a series-parallel connection must be considered as a four-terminal (rather than as a two-port) component, since interconnections are made among all four terminals of each component. Suppose that component C_1 can be modeled by edges 1, 2, 3 and a mixed-parameter state model of the form

$$\frac{d}{dt}\,\mathbf{\Psi}_1(t) = \mathbf{P}_1\mathbf{\Psi}_1(t) + [\mathbf{Q}_1 \quad \mathbf{Q}_2 \quad \mathbf{Q}_3]\begin{bmatrix} y_1(t) \\ x_2(t) \\ x_3(t) \end{bmatrix}$$

$$\begin{bmatrix} x_1(t) \\ y_2(t) \\ y_3(t) \end{bmatrix} = \begin{bmatrix} \mathbf{M}_1 \\ \mathbf{M}_2 \\ \mathbf{M}_3 \end{bmatrix}\mathbf{\Psi}_1(t) + \begin{bmatrix} N_{11} & N_{12} & N_{13} \\ N_{21} & N_{22} & N_{23} \\ N_{31} & N_{32} & N_{33} \end{bmatrix}\begin{bmatrix} y_1(t) \\ x_2(t) \\ x_3(t) \end{bmatrix}$$

(8.6.1)

and component C_2 can be modeled by edges 4, 5, 6 and the mixed-parameter state model

$$\frac{d}{dt}\,\mathbf{\Psi}_2(t) = \mathbf{P}_2\mathbf{\Psi}_2(t) + [\mathbf{Q}_4 \quad \mathbf{Q}_5 \quad \mathbf{Q}_6]\begin{bmatrix} y_4(t) \\ x_5(t) \\ x_6(t) \end{bmatrix}$$

$$\begin{bmatrix} x_4(t) \\ y_5(t) \\ y_6(t) \end{bmatrix} = \begin{bmatrix} \mathbf{M}_4 \\ \mathbf{M}_5 \\ \mathbf{M}_6 \end{bmatrix}\mathbf{\Psi}_2(t) + \begin{bmatrix} N_{44} & N_{45} & N_{46} \\ N_{54} & N_{55} & N_{56} \\ N_{64} & N_{65} & N_{66} \end{bmatrix}\begin{bmatrix} y_4(t) \\ x_5(t) \\ x_6(t) \end{bmatrix}$$

(8.6.2)

Applying the constraint equations of the system graph, it is easy to see that the series-parallel system has a time-domain input-output model of the form

$$\frac{d}{dt}\begin{bmatrix} \mathbf{\Psi}_1(t) \\ \mathbf{\Psi}_2(t) \end{bmatrix} = \begin{bmatrix} \mathbf{P}_1 & 0 \\ 0 & \mathbf{P}_2 \end{bmatrix}\begin{bmatrix} \mathbf{\Psi}_1(t) \\ \mathbf{\Psi}_2(t) \end{bmatrix} + \begin{bmatrix} \mathbf{Q}_1 & \mathbf{Q}_2 & \mathbf{Q}_3 \\ \mathbf{Q}_4 & \mathbf{Q}_5 & \mathbf{Q}_6 \end{bmatrix}\begin{bmatrix} y_i(t) \\ x_0(t) \\ x_3(t) \end{bmatrix}$$

$$\begin{bmatrix} x_i(t) \\ y_0(t) \\ 0 \end{bmatrix} = \begin{bmatrix} \mathbf{M}_1 & \mathbf{M}_4 \\ \mathbf{M}_2 & \mathbf{M}_5 \\ \mathbf{M}_3 & \mathbf{M}_6 \end{bmatrix}\begin{bmatrix} \mathbf{\Psi}_1(t) \\ \mathbf{\Psi}_2(t) \end{bmatrix}$$

(8.6.3)

$$+ \begin{bmatrix} N_{11} + N_{44} & N_{12} + N_{45} & N_{13} + N_{46} \\ N_{21} + N_{54} & N_{22} + N_{55} & N_{23} + N_{56} \\ N_{31} + N_{64} & N_{32} + N_{65} & N_{33} + N_{66} \end{bmatrix}\begin{bmatrix} y_i(t) \\ x_0(t) \\ x_3(t) \end{bmatrix}$$

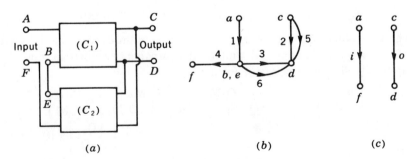

Fig. 8.6.1 (a) Series-parallel-connected four-terminal components; (b) system graph; (c) terminal graph used in modeling the characteristics of the assembly as a two-port component.

A state model of the system as a two-port assembly results when $x_3(t)$ is eliminated from Eqs. (8.6.3).

It is evident that under certain conditions the eigenvalues of the system are the direct sum of the eigenvalues of the components. It is also evident that the complex frequency parameters of the system are obtained as the sum of the s-domain parameter matrices corresponding to the hybrid state models given in Eqs. (8.6.1) and (8.6.2). However, it should be recognized that a subassembly may have a state model that cannot be put in the form given in Eqs. (8.6.1) or (8.6.2); yet it may be possible to arrange the s-domain model in the required h-parameter form. For example, if C_1 has an open-circuit parameter state model with no direct transmission, then it cannot be put into the form of Eqs. (8.6.2). But the required s-domain form can certainly exist.

If each of the two components in Fig. 8.6.1 contains only three terminals, then vertices b and d are one and the same and edges 3 and 6 and the corresponding variables are not present in the model. Given that only an input-output model of the assembly is required, it is evident from the system graph in Fig. 8.6.1b that two-port models (rather than complete four-terminal models) of each component are sufficient *only when* $y_3(t) + y_6(t) \equiv 0$. This condition is satisfied, in general, if at least one of the terminal graphs in a true four-terminal model of one component is in two parts, i.e., if one component is an "isolation type" component such as a two-winding transformer or a transducer. For this restricted class of system components, the system model is of the form given in Eqs. (8.6.3), with $x_3(t)$ and the corresponding last equation deleted.

In the subsequent development it is assumed that both components contain only three terminals or that at least one of the four-terminal components is of an isolation type.

If each two-port component is of the ideal unilateral type, with state equations of the type already given in the previous section as Eqs. (8.5.2) and (8.5.3), then upon applying the constraint equations

$$x_2(t) = x_3(t) = x_0(t) \qquad \text{and} \qquad x_1(t) = x_i(t) + x_4(t) \qquad (8.6.4)$$

the state equations characterizing the *no-load* input-output characteristics of series-parallel-connected unilateral components shown in Fig. 8.6.2 are easily shown to be of the form

$$\frac{d}{dt}\begin{bmatrix} \mathbf{\Psi}_1(t) \\ \mathbf{\Psi}_2(t) \end{bmatrix} = \begin{bmatrix} \mathbf{P}_1 + kn_2\mathbf{Q}_1\mathbf{M}_1 & k\mathbf{Q}_1\mathbf{M}_2 \\ k\mathbf{Q}_2\mathbf{M}_1 & \mathbf{P}_2 + n_1k\mathbf{Q}_2\mathbf{M}_2 \end{bmatrix}\begin{bmatrix} \mathbf{\Psi}_1(t) \\ \mathbf{\Psi}_2(t) \end{bmatrix}$$
$$+ \begin{bmatrix} k\mathbf{Q}_1 \\ kn_1\mathbf{Q}_2 \end{bmatrix} x_i(t) \quad (8.6.5)$$

$$x_0(t) = [k\mathbf{M}_1 \quad n_1k\mathbf{M}_2]\begin{bmatrix} \mathbf{\Psi}_1(t) \\ \mathbf{\Psi}_2(t) \end{bmatrix} + kn_1x_i(t)$$

where $k = 1/(1 - n_1n_2)$.

In a special, but frequently encountered, case, the direct transmission coefficient n_1 in the forward loop is zero, and the system state equations reduce to

$$\frac{d}{dt}\begin{bmatrix} \mathbf{\Psi}_1(t) \\ \hline \mathbf{\Psi}_2(t) \end{bmatrix} = \begin{bmatrix} \mathbf{P}_1 + n_2\mathbf{Q}_1\mathbf{M}_1 & \vdots & \mathbf{Q}_1\mathbf{M}_2 \\ \hline \mathbf{Q}_2\mathbf{M}_1 & \vdots & \mathbf{P}_2 \end{bmatrix} \begin{bmatrix} \mathbf{\Psi}_1(t) \\ \hline \mathbf{\Psi}_2(t) \end{bmatrix} + \begin{bmatrix} \mathbf{Q}_1 \\ \hline 0 \end{bmatrix} x_i(t)$$

(8.6.6)

$$x_0(t) = [\mathbf{M}_1 \quad 0]\begin{bmatrix} \mathbf{\Psi}_1(t) \\ \mathbf{\Psi}_2(t) \end{bmatrix}$$

In the interests of simplicity, subsequent developments are confined to this latter form, with the understanding that they can also be extended to the more general form.

If the characteristics of each component are given in the s-domain form shown as Eqs. (8.5.6) and (8.5.7), then upon applying the constraint equations in Eqs. (8.6.4) the s-domain input-output characteristics of the system are easily shown to be

$$\mathbf{x}_0(s) = \frac{G_{21}(s)\mathbf{x}_i(s)}{1 + G_{21}(s)G_{43}(s)} + \frac{Z_2(s)}{1 + G_{21}(s)G_{43}(s)}\,\mathbf{y}_0(s)$$

(8.6.7)

where the coefficient of $\mathbf{x}_i(s)$ is called the no-load transfer function and the coefficient of $\mathbf{y}_0(s)$ the output impedance.

By similar developments, the reader can show that if the terminal equations of C_2 are of the perfect-coupler form, then the resulting system models are of the same general unilateral form given above.

In general, any system for which the no-load input-output characteristics can be expressed in the general forms given above is called a *feedback system*—the output of the second stage is said to be fed back into the input of the first stage, *there being no other interaction between them*. The first important feature of feedback systems of this type is that it is possible to give an algorithm for the characteristic polynomial of the system as a function of the characteristic polynomials $p_1(\lambda)$ and $p_2(\lambda)$ of the components and certain other polynomials $h_1(\lambda)$ and $h_2(\lambda)$

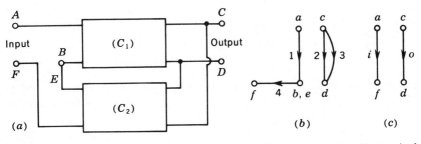

Fig. 8.6.2 (a) Parallel-series-connected system; (b) system graph; (c) terminal graph.

that depend only on the parameters of components C_1 and C_2, respectively, as shown next. Consider first the state model given as Eqs. (8.6.6). It follows that, since $\mathbf{Q}_1$ and $\mathbf{Q}_2$ are column matrices and $\mathbf{M}_1$ and $\mathbf{M}_2$ are row matrices, the vectors $\mathbf{\Psi}_1(t)$ and $\mathbf{\Psi}_2(t)$ can be partitioned so that one of the state variables is identified as the output $x_0(t)$ and so that state equations in the model shown as Eqs. (8.6.6) can be written in the form

$$
\frac{d}{dt}
\begin{bmatrix} x_0(t) \\ \mathbf{\Psi}_1'(t) \\ \psi_2(t) \\ \mathbf{\Psi}_2'(t) \end{bmatrix}
=
\left[
\begin{array}{cc:cc}
p_{11}+n_2 q_{11} & \mathbf{P}_{12} & q_{11} & 0 \\
\mathbf{P}_{12}+n_2\mathbf{Q}_{12} & \mathbf{P}_{22} & \mathbf{Q}_{12} & 0 \\
\hdashline
q_{21} & 0 & p_{22} & \mathbf{P}_{23} \\
\mathbf{Q}_{22} & 0 & \mathbf{P}_{32} & \mathbf{P}_{33}
\end{array}
\right]
\begin{bmatrix} x_0(t) \\ \mathbf{\Psi}_1'(t) \\ \psi_2(t) \\ \mathbf{\Psi}_2'(t) \end{bmatrix}
$$

$$
+
\begin{bmatrix} q_{11} \\ \mathbf{Q}_{12} \\ 0 \\ 0 \end{bmatrix}
x_i(t) \quad (8.6.8)
$$

where

$$
\begin{bmatrix} q_{11} \\ \mathbf{Q}_{12} \end{bmatrix} = \mathbf{Q}_1
\quad
\begin{bmatrix} q_{21} \\ \mathbf{Q}_{22} \end{bmatrix} = \mathbf{Q}_2
\quad
\mathbf{P}_1 = \begin{bmatrix} p_{11} & \mathbf{P}_{12} \\ \mathbf{P}_{21} & \mathbf{P}_{22} \end{bmatrix}
\quad
\mathbf{P}_2 = \begin{bmatrix} p_{22} & \mathbf{P}_{23} \\ \mathbf{P}_{32} & \mathbf{P}_{33} \end{bmatrix}
$$

By using the Laplace expansion about the first two row blocks of Eq. (8.6.8), the characteristic polynomial for the feedback system can be expressed as

$$
D(\lambda) = \det \begin{bmatrix} \lambda - p_{11} - n_2 q_{11} & -\mathbf{P}_{12} \\ -\mathbf{P}_2 - n_2\mathbf{Q}_{12} & \lambda\mathbf{U} - \mathbf{P}_{22} \end{bmatrix} \det \begin{bmatrix} \lambda - p_{22} & -\mathbf{P}_{23} \\ -\mathbf{P}_{32} & \lambda\mathbf{U} - \mathbf{P}_{33} \end{bmatrix}
$$
$$
+ \det \begin{bmatrix} -q_{11} & -\mathbf{P}_{12} \\ -\mathbf{Q}_{12} & \lambda\mathbf{U} - \mathbf{P}_{22} \end{bmatrix} \det \begin{bmatrix} -q_{21} & -\mathbf{P}_{23} \\ -\mathbf{Q}_{22} & \lambda\mathbf{U} - \mathbf{P}_{33} \end{bmatrix} \quad (8.6.9)
$$

If we let $\mathbf{P}_1'$ represent the forward-loop transition matrix with the column matrix $n_2\mathbf{Q}_1$ *added to the first column*, i.e.,

$$
\mathbf{P}_1' = \begin{bmatrix} p_{11}+n_2 q_{11} & \mathbf{P}_{12} \\ \mathbf{P}_{21}+n_2\mathbf{Q}_{12} & \mathbf{P}_{22} \end{bmatrix}
$$

then the characteristic polynomial in Eq. (8.6.9) can be written as

$$
D(\lambda) = \det (\lambda\mathbf{U} - \mathbf{P}_1') \det (\lambda\mathbf{U} - \mathbf{P}_2)
$$
$$
+ \det \mathbf{H}_1(\lambda) \det \mathbf{H}_2(\lambda) \quad (8.6.10)
$$

where $\mathbf{H}_1(\lambda)$ and $\mathbf{H}_2(\lambda)$ are, respectively, the characteristic matrices $\lambda\mathbf{U} - \mathbf{P}_1$ and $\lambda\mathbf{U} - \mathbf{P}_2$, with *the first columns replaced* by the respective column vectors $\mathbf{Q}_1$ and $\mathbf{Q}_2$.

If the return loop contains no direct transmission, then, of course, $n_2 = 0$ and $\mathbf{P}_1' = \mathbf{P}$ in Eq. (8.6.10). In this latter case, the characteristic polynomial of the system is equal to the product of the characteristic polynomials of the two components $p_1(\lambda)p_2(\lambda)$ plus an additional polynomial $h_1(\lambda)h_2(\lambda)$; that is, Eq. (8.6.10) is of the form

$$D(\lambda) = p_1(\lambda)p_2(\lambda) + h_1(\lambda)h_2(\lambda) \tag{8.6.11}$$

This result, of course, must be consistent with the characteristic polynomial as obtained from the s-domain transfer function given in Eq. (8.6.7). Indeed, if neither component has direct transmission, then $G_{21}(s)$ and $G_{43}(s)$ are both rational functions of s and, further,

$$G_{21}(s) = \frac{h_1(s)}{p_1(s)} \quad \text{and} \quad G_{43}(s) = \frac{h_2(s)}{p_2(s)}$$

where $h_1(s)$, $p_1(s)$, $h_2(s)$, and $p_2(s)$ correspond to the polynomials in Eq. (8.6.11), with λ replaced by s, and $h_1(s)$ and $h_2(s)$ are of lower degree than $p_1(s)$ and $p_2(s)$, respectively. It follows, therefore, that the transfer function can be written as

$$M(s) = \frac{G_{21}(s)}{1 + G_{21}(s)G_{43}(s)} = \frac{h_1(s)p_2(s)}{p_1(s)p_2(s) + h_1(s)h_2(s)} = \frac{h_1(s)p_2(s)}{D(s)}$$

where $D(s) = p_1(s)p_2(s) + h_1(s)h_2(s)$ represents the characteristic polynomial of the system.

If the return loop contains direct transmission without integration, as in the case of unity feedback, then, of course, Ψ_2 in Eq. (8.6.5) is an empty set and the corresponding characteristic polynomial is

$$
\begin{aligned}
D(\lambda) &= \det (\lambda\mathbf{U} - \mathbf{P}_1 - n_2\mathbf{Q}_1\mathbf{M}_1) \\
&= \det (\lambda\mathbf{U} - \mathbf{P}_1')
\end{aligned}
$$

where $\mathbf{P}_1' = \mathbf{P}_1 + n_2\mathbf{Q}_1\mathbf{M}_1$ is the forward-loop transition matrix, with the column vector $n_2\mathbf{Q}_1$ added to the first column. This determinant, also appearing as the first term in Eq. (8.6.9), can be written as the sum of two determinants, i.e.,

$$
\begin{aligned}
D(\lambda) &= \det (\lambda\mathbf{U} - \mathbf{P}_1') = \det (\lambda\mathbf{U} - \mathbf{P}_1) + \det \mathbf{H}_1(\lambda) \\
&= p_1(\lambda) + h_1(\lambda)
\end{aligned} \tag{8.6.12}
$$

where $\mathbf{H}_1(\lambda)$ represents the matrix $\lambda\mathbf{U} - \mathbf{P}_1$, with the first column replaced by the column matrix $n_2\mathbf{Q}_1$.

If the return loop contains direct transmission without integration, then $G_{43}(s) = 1$ in Eq. (8.6.7) and the characteristic polynomial as obtained from the s-domain transfer function is given by the denominator of

$$M(s) = \frac{G_{12}(s)}{1 + G_{12}(s)} = \frac{p_1(s)}{p_1(s) + h_1(s)}$$

The polynomial $D(s) = p_1(s) + h_1(s)$, of course, is identical to that given in Eq. (8.6.12).

8.7 STABILITY OF CONTINUOUS FEEDBACK SYSTEMS

Whether the characteristic polynomial of the feedback system is obtained from the state model or the s-domain model, it can always be written in the general form

$$D(\lambda) = p_1(\lambda)p_2(\lambda) + h_1(\lambda)h_2(\lambda) = [1 + \mu(\lambda)\beta(\lambda)]p_1(\lambda)p_2(\lambda) \quad (8.7.1)$$

where $\mu(\lambda) = h_1(\lambda)/p_1(\lambda)$ and $\beta(\lambda) = h_2(\lambda)/p_2(\lambda)$ are rational functions of λ and $p_1(\lambda)$ is assumed to be of equal or higher order than $h_1(\lambda)$ and similarly for $p_2(\lambda)$ and $h_2(\lambda)$.

If the characteristic polynomial has no zeros in the right half of the λ plane, then the system, of course, is stable. If $p_1(\lambda)$ and $p_2(\lambda)$ are known to be stable (zeros only in the left plane), then insofar as stability is concerned, the critical zeros of $D(\lambda)$ are the same as the critical zeros of

$$F(\lambda) = 1 + \mu(\lambda)\beta(\lambda) \quad (8.7.2)$$

Equation (8.7.2) forms the basis for an effective stability criterion given originally by Nyquist. The criterion makes use of one of the fundamental properties of functions of complex variables, as stated in the following theorem.

Theorem 8.7.1 (Cauchy): Let $F(\lambda)$ be a rational function of λ with real coefficients.† Consider a closed path C in the λ plane on which $F(\lambda)$ has no zeros and poles. When λ describes C in the positive direction only once, the increase in the angle of $F(\lambda)$ is equal to $2\pi(Z - P)$, where Z and P represent, respectively, the number of zeros and poles of $F(\lambda)$ in the interior of C.

Proof: Since $F(\lambda)$ is a rational function of λ with real coefficients, it can be written as

$$F(\lambda) = a_0 \frac{(\lambda - z_1)(\lambda - z_2) \cdots (\lambda - z_m)}{(\lambda - p_1)(\lambda - p_2) \cdots (\lambda - p_n)} \quad n \geq m \quad (8.7.3)$$

where a_0 is a real constant and it is assumed that $F(\lambda)$, in general, has m zeros and n poles.

If we let

$$\lambda - z_k = r_k e^{j\theta_k} \quad k = 1, 2, \ldots, m \quad (8.7.4)$$
$$\lambda - p_l = r_l' e^{j\theta'_k} \quad l = 1, 2, \ldots, n \quad (8.7.5)$$

then $F(\lambda)$ can be written as

$$F(\lambda) = Re^{j\theta} \quad (8.7.6)$$

---

† For discrete physical systems this is always the case. But the theorem is still true if these coefficients are complex constants.

where

$$R = \frac{r_1 r_2 \cdots r_m}{r'_1 r'_2 \cdots r'_n}$$

and

$$\phi = \sum_{k=1}^{m} \theta_k - \sum_{l=1}^{n} \theta'_l$$

are called the *modulus* and the *argument* of the complex function $F(\lambda)$, respectively.

The theorem states that, if $F(\lambda)$ is plotted for values of $\lambda = \lambda_1$, $\lambda_2, \ldots, \lambda_q, \lambda_1$ on the closed curve C in Fig. 8.7.1, then the argument ϕ of $F(\lambda)$ changes by the amount

$$2\pi(Z - P)$$

To show that this is the case, suppose that the zero z_k is inside the curve C as shown in Fig. 8.7.2a. Since the complex number $\lambda - z_k = r_k e^{j\theta_k}$ can be represented by a vector from the point z_k to the point s on the curve C, as indicated, it is evident that θ_k increases by an amount 2π as s assumes values on C for $\lambda = \lambda_1, \lambda_2, \ldots, \lambda_q, \lambda_1$.

On the other hand, if z_k is outside C, as shown in Fig. 8.7.2b, then the net change in θ_k is zero as s assumes values on C corresponding to one complete traverse of C. Therefore, we conclude that the argument ϕ

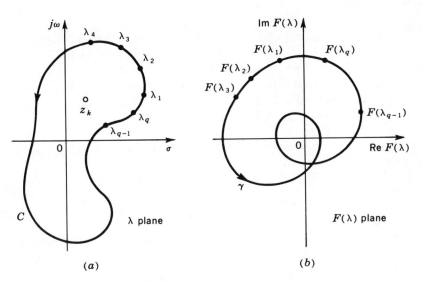

(a)   (b)

Fig. 8.7.1   Plot γ of $F(\lambda)$ for values of λ on a closed curve C in the s plane.

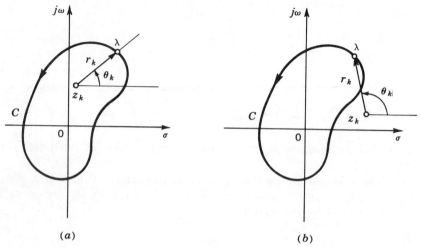

(a) (b)

Fig. 8.7.2   Position of a zero of $F(\lambda)$ with respect to simply closed curve C.

of $F(\lambda)$, as given in Eq. (8.7.6), increases by a factor of 2π for each zero contained in C and is unchanged by zeros outside C.

By exactly the same reasoning, we find that θ'_l increases by 2π if the pole p_l is inside C. From Eq. (8.7.6) it follows that the argument ϕ of $F(\lambda)$ is decreased by an amount 2π for each pole contained inside C as s assumes values on C corresponding to one complete traverse. Upon combining the results for the zeros and for the poles, the theorem is established.

In general, the plot of $F(\lambda) = Re^{j\phi}$ as a function of λ for values of λ on a given curve C is called the *mapping* of the curve C in the λ plane into the curve γ in the $F(\lambda)$ plane. Since an encirclement of the origin in the $F(\lambda)$ plane corresponds to an increase of 2π in the angle ϕ, it follows that the number of encirclements in the positive direction of the origin in the $F(\lambda)$ plane is equal to the number $Z - P$.

Example 8.7.1:   From the mapping of the curve C given in Fig. 8.7.3a show that the number of poles of

$$F(\lambda) = \frac{1 + 3\lambda}{(1 + \lambda)(1 + 2\lambda)}$$

inside C is equal to zero.

Solution: Consider first the region C_1 of the curve C extending over the imaginary axis from point $\lambda = j50$ to the point $\lambda = 0$. The mapping of this section of C is easily sketched by considering the points $\lambda = j50$, $\lambda = j5$, $\lambda = j2$, $\lambda = j1$, $\lambda = j0.5$, $\lambda = j0.2$, and $\lambda = 0$. At each of these points the values of $F(\lambda)$ are given in Table 8.7.1.

Table 8.7.1

λ	$|F(\lambda)|$	$arg\ F(\lambda),\ deg$
$j50$	0.30	-88.7
$j5$	0.293	-76.8
$j2$	0.660	-58.9
$j1$	1.000	-36.9
$j0.5$	1.140	-15.3
$j0.2$	1.060	-2.15
0	1.000	0

The mapping of the section C_1 of C is shown in Fig. 8.7.3b. The mapping of section C_2 of C is obtained as the conjugate of the mapping for C_1 and is shown dashed in Fig. 8.7.3b.

The mapping of the semicircular section C_3 of C is obtained by setting $\lambda = 50e^{j\alpha}$ and allowing α to vary from $-\pi/2$ to $\pi/2$. Thus

$$F(50e^{j\alpha}) = \frac{1 + 150e^{j\alpha}}{500e^{j2\alpha} + 150e^{j\alpha} + 1} \cong \tfrac{3}{100}e^{-j\alpha}$$

The mapping of C_3 is approximately a semicircle γ_3, as shown in Fig. 8.7.3b. Since the closed curve γ does not enclose the origin, we conclude that the argument of $F(\lambda)$ does not change and the difference between the numbers of zeros and poles of $F(\lambda)$ in C is therefore zero. To determine the number of poles of $F(\lambda)$ in C, it is, of course, necessary to know the number of zeros of $F(\lambda)$ in C. Since the given $F(\lambda)$ has no such zeros and $Z - P = 0$, it has no such poles.

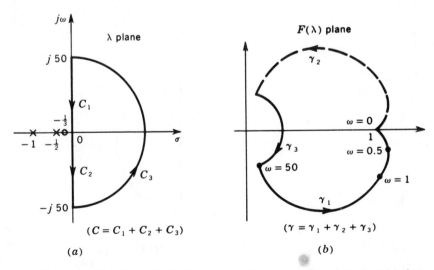

Fig. 8.7.3 (a) A Nyquist path C in the λ plane; (b) mapping C into γ in the $F(\lambda)$ plane.

The region of interest in stability studies is the entire right half of the λ plane. This region can be considered as the interior of the closed curve C shown in Fig. 8.7.4a. This closed path consists of the $j\omega$ axis and the large semicircle in the right half plane. If $F(\lambda)$ has poles or zeros on the $j\omega$ axis, these points are avoided by semicircles with very small radii, as shown in Fig. 8.7.4b. Such a path is referred to as a *Nyquist path*.

If the rational functions $\mu(\lambda)$ and $\beta(\lambda)$ have no poles in the right half plane, then $F(\lambda)$ [Eq. (8.7.2)] has no poles in this region. When such is the case, we conclude from Theorem 8.7.1 that, as λ describes the Nyquist path once in the direction indicated, the number of encirclements of the origin in the $F(\lambda)$ plane in the positive direction is equal to the number of zeros of $F(\lambda)$ which lie in the right half plane. In the limit, as the radius tends to infinity, C_1 reduces to the point at infinity of the λ plane and the curve C consists of the entire $j\omega$ axis. Thus, to investigate stability, it is necessary to consider the mapping of the $j\omega$ axis into the $F(\lambda)$ plane.

We note further that, since $F(\lambda) = 1 + \mu(\lambda)\beta(\lambda)$, it is convenient to consider the mapping of the $j\omega$ axis in the $\mu(\lambda)\beta(\lambda)$ plane, i.e., to consider first the function $F_1(\lambda) = \mu(\lambda)\beta(\lambda)$. The number of encirclements of $F(\lambda) = 1 + F_1(\lambda)$ about the origin in the $F(\lambda)$ plane is then the same as the number of encirclements of $F_1(\lambda)$ about the point $(-1, j0)$ in the $F_1(\lambda)$ plane. It is important to note that, since the Nyquist path is symmetrical with respect to the real axis, the mapped curve γ is also symmetrical with respect to the real axis in the $F_1(\lambda)$ plane.

For convenience, the above discussion is summarized by the following theorem.

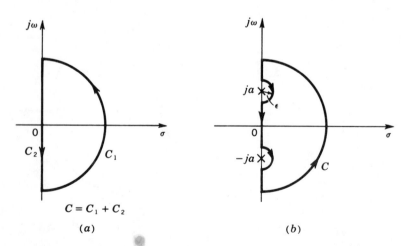

Fig. 8.7.4 (a) A Nyquist path; (b) Nyquist path for poles on $j\omega$ axis.

Theorem 8.7.2 (Nyquist stability criterion): Let the transfer function of a system be of the form

$$T(\lambda) = \frac{\mu(\lambda)}{1 + \mu(\lambda)\beta(\lambda)} \tag{8.7.7}$$

where $\mu(\lambda)$ and $\beta(\lambda)$ are rational functions of λ, with no poles in the right half plane. The solution represented by $T(\lambda)$ is stable if the mapping of the entire imaginary axis of the λ plane into the $\mu(\lambda)\beta(\lambda)$ plane does not encircle the point $(-1, j0)$ in the $\mu(\lambda)\beta(\lambda)$ plane.

Sometimes the characteristic polynomial of the feedback equation is written as

$$D(\lambda) = [1 - \mu(\lambda)\beta(\lambda)]p_1(\lambda)p_2(\lambda)$$

In this case, the number of encirclements of $\mu(\lambda)\beta(\lambda)$ about the point $(1, j0)$ determines stability.

Example 8.7.2: Consider the transfer function

$$T(\lambda) = \frac{\mu(\lambda)}{1 + \mu(\lambda)\beta(\lambda)} \tag{8.7.8}$$

with

$$\mu(\lambda)\beta(\lambda) = \frac{k}{\lambda + \alpha} \tag{8.7.9}$$

where k is a real number and $\alpha > 0$. Determine the range in values of k over which the solution is stable.

Solution: To map the $j\omega$ axis of the λ plane into the $\mu(\lambda)\beta(\lambda)$ plane, substitute $\lambda = j\omega$ in Eq. (8.7.9), to obtain

$$\mu(j\omega)\beta(j\omega) = \frac{k}{j\omega + \alpha} = \frac{k\alpha}{\omega^2 + \alpha^2} - j\frac{k\omega}{\omega^2 + \alpha^2} = x + iy \tag{8.7.10}$$

where ω varies from $+\infty$ to $-\infty$. Therefore, the parametric equations for the trace of γ in the $\mu(\lambda)\beta(\lambda)$ plane are

$$x = \frac{k\alpha}{\omega^2 + \alpha^2}$$
$$y = -\frac{k\omega}{\omega^2 + \alpha^2} \tag{8.7.11}$$

Upon eliminating the parameter ω between x and y in Eq. (8.7.11) we have

$$y^2 + \left(x - \frac{k}{2\alpha}\right)^2 = \left(\frac{k}{2\alpha}\right)^2 \tag{8.7.12}$$

which represents a circle, as shown in Fig. 8.7.5. If $k > 0$, the trace γ does not encircle the point $(-1, j0)$ and, from Theorem 8.7.2, the system is stable.

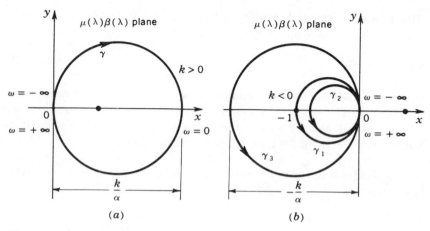

Fig. 8.7.5 Traces of $\mu(j\omega)\beta(j\omega) = k/(j\omega + \alpha)$ for (a) $k > 0$ and (b) $k < 0$.

But if $k < 0$, then the trace γ may or may not encircle the point $(-1, j0)$. In fact, if $|k|/\alpha < 1$, then no encirclements occur. Therefore, the system is stable for $k > -\alpha$ and unstable for $k < -\alpha$.

When the numerator and denominator in the rational function $\mu(\lambda)\beta(\lambda)$ are of degree greater than 1, the analytical procedure used in Example 8.7.2 above is not practical.

In Chap. 6, techniques for sketching Bode diagrams of rational functions given in *factored form* are discussed in detail. It is easy to see that the Nyquist plot of $\mu(j\omega)\beta(j\omega)$ is a polar plot of the Bode diagram showing magnitude and phase angle of $\mu(j\omega)\beta(j\omega)$ each as a function of ω. Consequently, the Nyquist plot can be obtained by simply plotting, point for point, the magnitude and phase angle as obtained from the Bode plots.

Example 8.7.3:   Consider the transfer function

$$T(\lambda) = \frac{\mu(\lambda)}{1 + \mu(\lambda)\beta(\lambda)}$$

with

$$\mu(\lambda)\beta(\lambda) = \frac{K}{(1 + \lambda)(1 + 0.1\lambda)(1 + \lambda/3)}$$

Determine the range of K for which the system is stable.

Solution: The Bode plots of the given function are shown in Fig. 8.7.6a. The corresponding Nyquist plots are shown in Fig. 8.7.6b and c for $K > 0$ and for $K < 0$. The solid lines in the Nyquist plots represent polar plots of the magnitude and phase angle as a function of ω and are taken directly from the Bode plots.

From the Nyquist diagrams it is evident that if $|K|$ is sufficiently large the system is unstable for both $K > 0$ and $K < 0$. The specific value of K at which the system becomes unstable is determined by the point at which the Nyquist plot crosses the real axis. For $K < 0$ we see from the Bode plot that zero phase angle occurs only below $\omega = 1$. Consequently, the system is stable only if the low-frequency end of the frequency-response curve falls below the zero-decibel line, i.e., provided that $20 \log |K| = 0$ or $|K| = 1$. If $K > 0$, then from the Bode plot we see that a 180° phase shift occurs at about $\omega = 4$. Consequently, the system is stable only if K is such that the frequency-response curve crosses the zero-decibel line at a frequency $\omega < 4$. Thus, in either case, the upper limit on the magnitude of the d-c gain coefficient K can be read directly from the Bode plot.

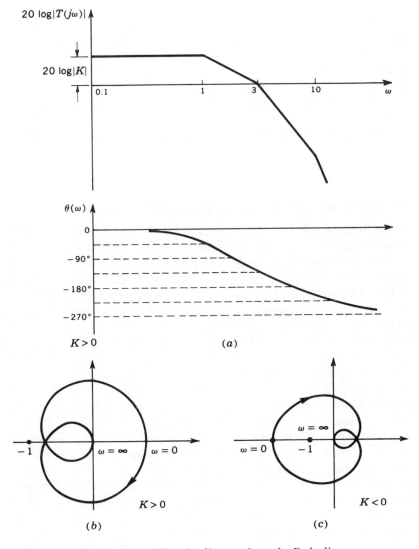

Fig. 8.7.6 Construction of Nyquist diagram from the Bode diagrams.

The precise range on K for which the system is stable can be found by use of Routh's theorem, for example. Indeed, the zeros of $1 + \mu(\lambda)\beta(\lambda)$ are the same as the zeros of the polynomial

$$(1 + \lambda)\left(1 + \frac{\lambda}{10}\right)\left(1 + \frac{\lambda}{3}\right) + K$$

or

$$\lambda^3 + 14\lambda^2 + 43\lambda + 30(1 + K)$$

Routh's algorithm gives the conditions for stability as $-1 < K < \frac{572}{30} \cong 19$.

From the above example, it is clear that it is not necessary to establish the Nyquist plot with any level of accuracy. In fact, it is not necessary to sketch it at all once the relationship between it and the frequency-response characteristics is established. All information can be determined directly from the latter.

It should be evident that, since the corner frequency technique for sketching Bode diagrams requires the rational function to be given in factored form, the Nyquist criterion is most useful as a stability criterion in system studies wherein the rational function $\mu(\lambda)\beta(\lambda)$ is in factored form.

8.8 BLOCK DIAGRAMS AND SIGNAL-FLOW GRAPHS

It has been established that when ideal unilateral components, or their equivalents, are connected in cascade or series parallel† the open-circuit transfer function of the system is a function only of the open-circuit transfer functions of the components and the no-load input-output state model of the assembly is a function only of the no-load input-output state models of the components. All input and output through variables under these conditions are identically zero and are of no concern in developing the system model. Although such systems represent a very special class, they nevertheless occur very frequently in contemporary engineering, particularly in the field of automatic controls, and there are special-purpose techniques or algorithms for formulating mathematical models of such systems. These special-purpose techniques are based on the same type of operational diagram discussed in Sec. 5.7 for the solution of state equations on analog computers. In fact, the operational amplifiers in an analog computer are all unilateral components of the same general type under consideration here. Consequently, if it is possible to construct, from a signal-flow graph of a system of equations, the corresponding system of unilateral components, then it seems reasonable to expect that the inverse construction might be possible. Consider, for example, the system shown in Fig. 8.8.1a.

† The component in the return loop of the series-parallel connection might also be a perfect coupler.

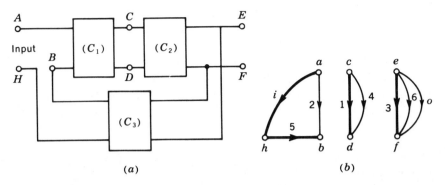

Fig. 8.8.1 (a) System of unilateral components; (b) the system graph.

Since, by hypothesis, the components are unilateral, the only parts of the terminal equations of the components involved in modeling the open-circuit transfer function of the system are the no-load input-output state models, which, for the present, are assumed to be of the form

$$\dot{\boldsymbol{\Psi}}_j(t) = \mathbf{P}_j\boldsymbol{\Psi}_j(t) + \mathbf{Q}_jx_{j+1}(t)$$
$$x_j(t) = \mathbf{M}_j\boldsymbol{\Psi}_j(t) + n_jx_{j+1}(t) \qquad j = 1, 3, 5 \tag{8.8.1}$$

or the equivalent s-domain no-load input-output transfer characteristic

$$x_j(s) = G_j(s)x_{j+1}(s) \qquad j = 1, 3, 5 \tag{8.8.2}$$

The constraint equations on the across variables in these equations are, of course, given by the circuit equations of the system graph in Fig. 8.8.1b. Using the mapping procedure discussed in Sec. 5.7, the three s-domain transfer characteristics in Eq. (8.8.2) and the algebraic constraint equations map into the signal-flow graph shown in Fig. 8.8.2a.

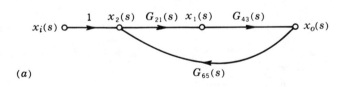

(a)

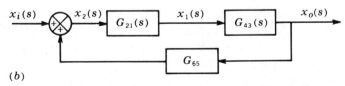

(b)

Fig. 8.8.2 (a) Signal-flow graph of the system; (b) block diagram of Fig. 8.8.1 as obtained from the system of equations given as Eq. (8.8.2).

Upon comparing this signal-flow diagram with the system schematic diagram in Fig. 8.8.1a, it is seen that the two diagrams are similar in appearance. This similarity is even more apparent when the slightly less abstract form of the signal-flow graph shown in Fig. 8.8.2b is used. The latter diagram is called a *block diagram* of the system and differs from the signal-flow graph only in the form of the operational diagram used in mapping the equations. The schemes used to represent the basic mathematical operations involved in characterizing the system are shown in Fig. 8.8.3. The circular-shaped junction point, containing plus and minus signs, is called a *summing point*, since it corresponds to the mathematical operation of addition (and subtraction).

A simple algorithm for drawing the block diagram can be stated as:

1.   Represent each two-port unilateral component as a "block" with a single line to represent each pair of terminals, the orientation of the line indicating the direction of transmission of the unilateral component.

2.   Represent a series connection by the summation symbol, using all $+$ signs when the edges of the system graph have the relative orientations indicated in Fig. 8.8.1b. If edge 6 in the system graph, for example, is reversed, then the corresponding sign in the summation symbol is changed.

3.   Represent a parallel connection by the intersection of the single lines corresponding to the terminal pairs connected in parallel.

When each of the three components in the system is modeled in terms of state models of the form given in Eqs. (8.8.1), each block in Fig. 8.8.2b or the equivalent edge in Fig. 8.8.2a can be replaced by the integral feed-

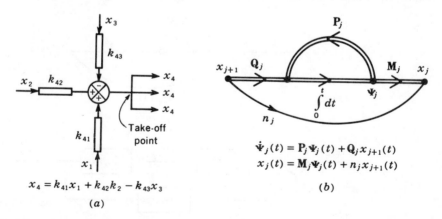

$$x_4 = k_{41}x_1 + k_{42}k_2 - k_{43}x_3$$

$$(a)$$

$$\dot{\Psi}_j(t) = P_j\Psi_j(t) + Q_j x_{j+1}(t)$$
$$x_j(t) = M_j\Psi_j(t) + n_j x_{j+1}(t)$$

$$(b)$$

Fig. 8.8.3 (*a*) Block-diagram representation of algebraic equations; (*b*) signal-flow representation of a component state model.

back diagram shown in Fig. 8.8.3b.   In this diagram, Ψ, of course, represents a vector.   In this example, x_j and x_{j+1} are taken as scalars, although,
in a multiple input-output representation, they can be taken as vectors
also.

It should be evident that in special cases, such as that given above,
where the block diagram or signal-flow graph can be established from the
system structure by an algorithm, it can be used as a basis of formulating
the system equations and it is not necessary to refer to a linear graph
of the system.   It can be said that, if it were possible to define, in general,
an operational procedure for drawing a signal-flow graph of any system
without reference to a linear graph and the associated circuit and cut-set
equations, then the signal-flow graph would serve as an alternative frame-
work for formulating system models.   It is only in special cases that
signal-flow diagrams can be drawn directly from the system.   For such
systems the block diagram or signal-flow graph can be a very effective
tool for formulating open-circuit input-output transfer relations, as the
following example demonstrates.

Example 8.8.1:   Using block-diagram techniques, formulate the open-circuit transfer
characteristics of the system shown in Fig. 8.8.4.

Solution: If the torque required to drive the tachometer is negligible or if the tachometer is included as part of the load, and if the two amplifiers are both considered as
unilateral components, then the no-load transfer function of the system is a
function only of the no-load transfer functions of the components C_1, C_2, C_3, and
C_4.   The block diagram for the system as obtained by the algorithm in a one-to-
one manner from the given physical system discussed in this section is given in
Fig. 8.8.5.   The orientations of both series connections are arbitrarily taken so
as to give positive signs in the summation symbol.

From the block diagram shown in Fig. 8.8.5a, the open-circuit transfer function of the system is formulated by first evaluating the transfer function of the
subassembly consisting of components C_3 and C_2; that is, the block diagram is

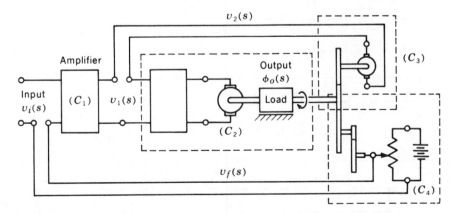

Fig. 8.8.4   Schematic diagram of an electromechanical position-control system.

reduced to the form shown in Fig. 8.8.5b.   For the subassembly of C_2 and C_3, we have

$$G_5(s) = \frac{\phi_0(s)}{v_1(s)} = \frac{G_{c_2}(s)}{1 - G_{c_3}(s)G_{c_2}(s)}$$

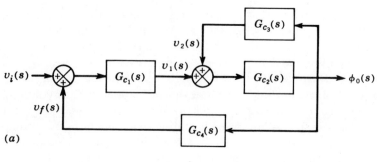

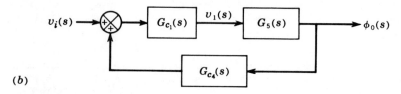

(b)

Fig. 8.8.5   (a) Block diagram for the system of Fig. 8.8.4; (b) reduced diagram.

Table 8.8.1

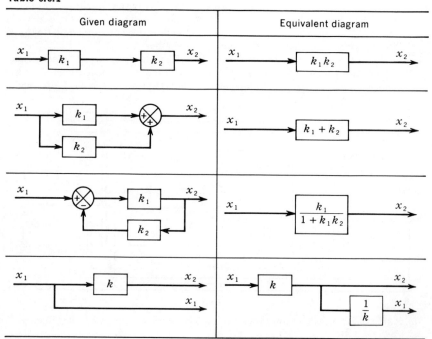

The transfer function for the entire system is, then,

$$\frac{\phi_0(s)}{v_i(s)} = \frac{G_{c_1}(s)G_5(s)}{1 - G_1(s)G_5(s)G_{c_4}(s)} \tag{8.8.3}$$

It should be noted that when, by algebraic substitution, some equations are eliminated, as in Eq. (8.8.3), the corresponding block diagram and signal-flow graphs are accordingly reduced. Therefore, it is possible to define a set of rules for operating on the signal-flow and block diagrams which are in a one-to-one correspondence with the various algebraic manipulations. Such a set of rules exists and some of the rules are given in Tables 8.8.1 and 8.8.2.

Table 8.8.2

Given diagram	Equivalent diagram
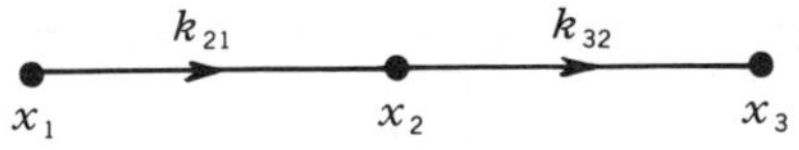 $x_1 \xrightarrow{k_{21}} x_2 \xrightarrow{k_{32}} x_3$	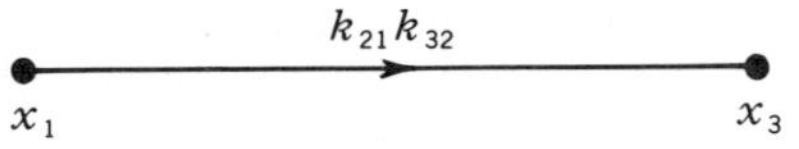 $x_1 \xrightarrow{k_{21}k_{32}} x_3$
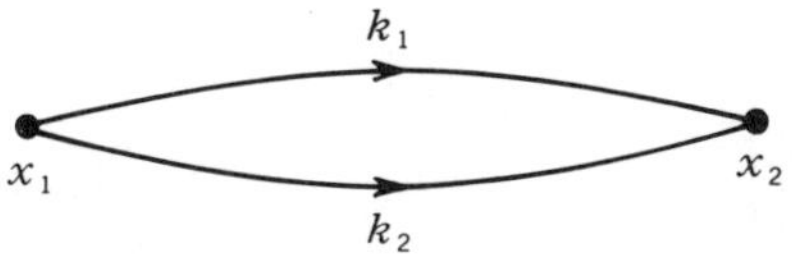 x_1 to x_2 via k_1 (upper path) and k_2 (lower path)	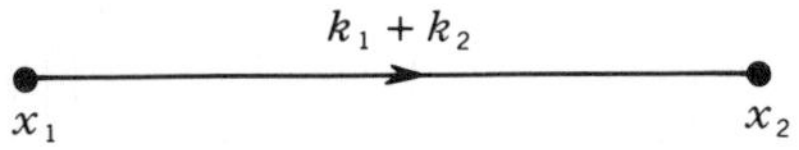 $x_1 \xrightarrow{k_1 + k_2} x_2$
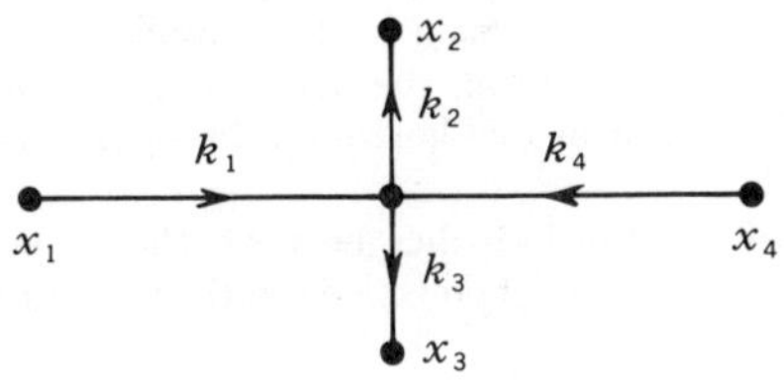 Node $x_1 \xrightarrow{k_1}$ center, with k_2 up to x_2, k_3 down to x_3, and k_4 to x_4	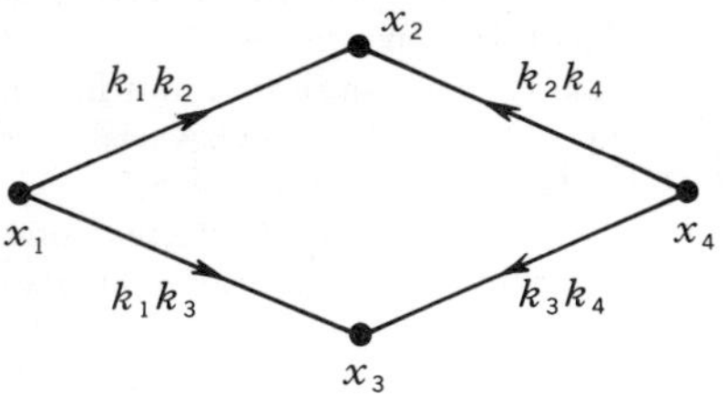 Diamond: $x_1 \xrightarrow{k_1 k_2} x_2 \xrightarrow{k_2 k_4} x_4$ and $x_1 \xrightarrow{k_1 k_3} x_3 \xrightarrow{k_3 k_4} x_4$
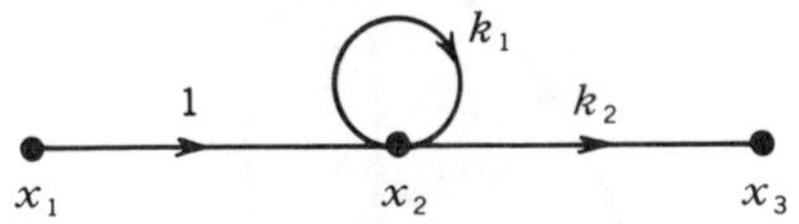 $x_1 \xrightarrow{1} x_2 \xrightarrow{k_2} x_3$ with self-loop k_1 at x_2	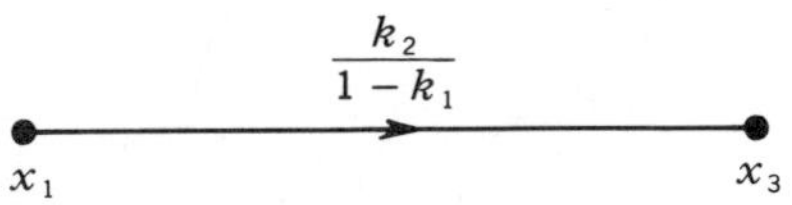 $x_1 \xrightarrow{\dfrac{k_2}{1 - k_1}} x_3$
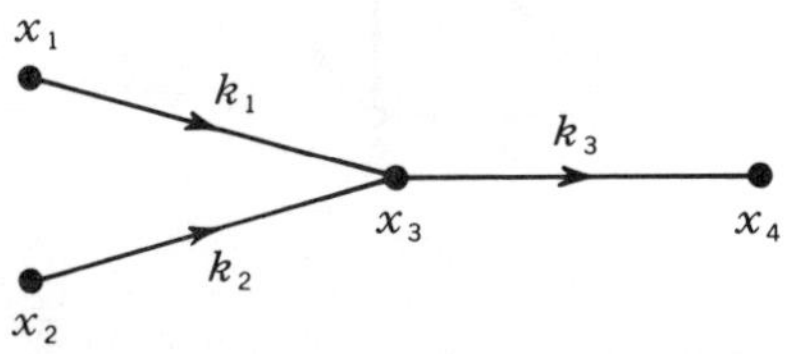 $x_1 \xrightarrow{k_1}$ and $x_2 \xrightarrow{k_2}$ into $x_3 \xrightarrow{k_3} x_4$	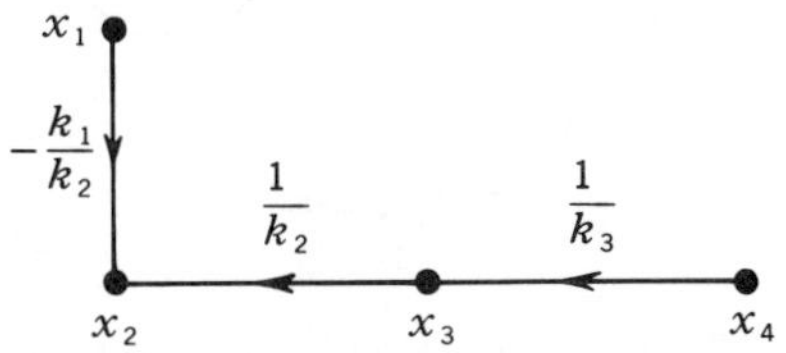 $x_1 \xrightarrow{-\dfrac{k_1}{k_2}} x_2$, $x_3 \xrightarrow{\dfrac{1}{k_2}} x_2$, $x_4 \xrightarrow{\dfrac{1}{k_3}} x_3$

For the reader interested in solving systems of algebraic equations by signal-flow-graph reduction rather than by standard algebraic means, the following procedure can always be used to systematically develop a signal-flow graph for any system from the given component terminal equations and the system graph.

Example 8.8.2: Develop a signal-flow graph corresponding to the system schematic diagram and corresponding system graph shown in Fig. 8.8.6.

Solution: Let the terminal equations for the tree indicated by the heavy lines in the system graph be written in the mixed form

$$\begin{bmatrix} x_1(s) \\ x_2(s) \\ x_3(s) \\ y_4(s) \\ y_5(s) \\ y_6(s) \end{bmatrix} = \begin{bmatrix} 0 & 0 & 0 & 0 & 0 & 0 \\ 0 & Z_{22}(s) & Z_{23}(s) & 0 & 0 & 0 \\ 0 & Z_{32}(s) & Z_{33}(s) & 0 & 0 & 0 \\ 0 & 0 & 0 & W_{44}(s) & 0 & W_{46}(s) \\ 0 & 0 & 0 & 0 & W_{55}(s) & 0 \\ 0 & 0 & 0 & W_{64}(s) & W_{65}(s) & W_{66}(s) \end{bmatrix} \begin{bmatrix} y_1(s) \\ y_2(s) \\ y_3(s) \\ x_4(s) \\ x_5(s) \\ x_6(s) \end{bmatrix} + \begin{bmatrix} f_1(s) \\ 0 \\ 0 \\ 0 \\ f_5(s) \\ 0 \end{bmatrix}$$

$$(8.8.4)$$

The fundamental circuit and cut-set equations of the system graph corresponding to the tree indicated in Fig. 8.8.6b are

$$\begin{bmatrix} x_4(s) \\ x_5(s) \\ x_6(s) \end{bmatrix} = \begin{bmatrix} 0 & 1 & -1 \\ 1 & -1 & 1 \\ -1 & 1 & 0 \end{bmatrix} \begin{bmatrix} x_1(s) \\ x_2(s) \\ x_3(s) \end{bmatrix} \qquad (8.8.5)$$

$$\begin{bmatrix} y_1(s) \\ y_2(s) \\ y_3(s) \end{bmatrix} = - \begin{bmatrix} 0 & 1 & -1 \\ 1 & -1 & 1 \\ -1 & 1 & 0 \end{bmatrix} \begin{bmatrix} y_4(s) \\ y_5(s) \\ y_6(s) \end{bmatrix} \qquad (8.8.6)$$

A signal-flow diagram for the system is established by simply drawing the algebraic diagram for Eqs. (8.8.4), (8.8.5), and (8.8.6). To establish this diagram systematically, and in a neat-appearing form, the nodes representing the across and through variables are arranged in two horizontal lines, respectively, as shown in Fig. 8.8.7.

The circuit equations are represented by the branches between the upper nodes representing the across variables and the cut-set equations by the branches

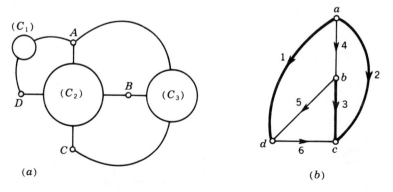

(a)   (b)

Fig. 8.8.6   (a) A system of multiterminal components; (b) system graph.

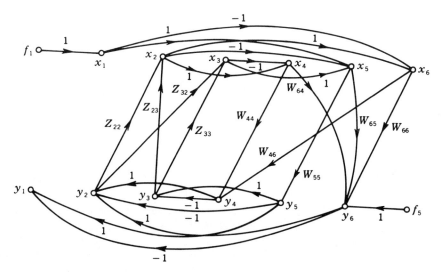

Fig. 8.8.7 Signal-flow graph for Eqs. (8.8.4) to (8.8.6).

between the lower nodes representing the through variables. Similarly, the terminal equations are represented by the branches between the nodes representing the through and across variables. Each driving function is represented by a separate node. It is interesting to note that the circuit, cut-set, and terminal equations can clearly be read from the signal-flow graph; i.e., by constructing the signal-flow graph in this fashion, one can detect the interconnection pattern of the components as well as their terminal equations.

All terminal variables $x_i(s)$ and $y_i(s)$ can be expressed in terms of driving functions $f_1(s)$ and $f_5(s)$ by using the rules given in Table 8.8.2.

8.9 LINEAR SAMPLED-DATA FEEDBACK SYSTEMS

In many feedback systems, the block in the return loop in the feedback connection is a special-purpose digital computer, called a *digital controller*. In its simplest form such a control system appears as in Fig. 8.9.1. The "switch" S in the schematic diagram is used to show that the output of the plant is "sampled and held" at uniformly spaced intervals of time ($t = 0, T, 2T, \ldots$) to produce a waveform $r_1^*(n) = e_2(n)$, as indicated. It is implied throughout the succeeding development that the two signals $e_1(n)$ and $r_2(n)$, corresponding, respectively, to the manual excitation (input signals to the plant) and output (response) of the digital controller, change in magnitude only at discrete points in time ($t = 0, T, 2T, \ldots$), as indicated in Fig. 8.9.1, and that these changes are synchronized in time with the sampling at the plant output.

The output $r(t)$ of the forward loop, called the *plant*, is usually a continuous function of time, as indicated, even though the excitation signals are discontinuous.   In this sense the system can be regarded as a mixed continuous-state and discrete-state system.   However, the two components are made compatible as discrete-state components by the sampling and hold mechanism.

To consider first the digital controller, the most general linear constant-coefficient equation relating the output sequence $r_2(n)$ to the input sequence $e_2(n)$ is the linear recursion formula

$$
\begin{aligned}
r_2(n) = a_0 e_2(n) + a_1 e_2(n-1) + \cdots + a_k e_2(n-k) \\
- b_1 r_2(n-1) - b_2 r_2(n-2) - \cdots - b_l r_2(n-l) \quad (8.9.1)
\end{aligned}
$$

which simply states that the output $r_2(n)$, at any time, is a linear combination of a previous set of k input and l output values.   Since the coefficients $a_0, a_1, a_2, \ldots, a_k$ and $b_1, b_2, \ldots, b_l$ are stored in the computer, the number of nonzero entries in Eq. (8.9.1) is a measure of the memory capacity of the controller.   Note that, if $a_0 = 0$, then the response at $t = nT$ is not affected by the input at the same time, and we say that the computer has a one-sampling-interval delay.   If $a_0, a_1 = 0$, then it has a two-interval delay, etc.   The magnitudes of the coefficients in the recursion formula are to be regarded as arbitrary at this point. They are established by design to realize a given performance specification, and the purpose of this analysis is to establish a basis of such design.

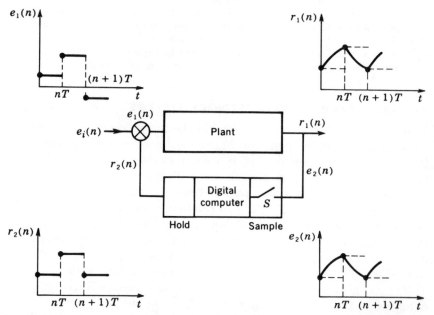

Fig. 8.9.1 Schematic diagram and signals in simple control system, with digital computer as controller.

The recursion formula for the controller given in Eq. (8.9.1) can be transformed to a discrete-state model by setting

$$r_2(n) = a_0\psi_1(n+1) + a_1\psi_1(n) + a_2\psi_2(n) + \cdots + a_k\psi_k(n)$$

(8.9.2)

where

$$\psi_2(n) = \psi_1(n-1) \qquad \psi_3(n) = \psi_2(n-1) \qquad \cdots$$
$$\psi_k(n) = \psi_{k-1}(n-1) \quad (8.9.3)$$

Substituting Eq. (8.9.2) into Eq. (8.9.1) and rearranging terms gives

$$[a_0 e_2(n) + a_1 e_2(n-1) + \cdots + a_k e_2(n-k)]$$
$$-a_0[\psi_1(n+1) + b_1\psi_1(n) + b_2\psi_1(n-1) + \cdots + b_l\psi_1(n-l+1)]$$
$$-a_1[\psi_1(n) + b_1\psi_1(n-1) + b_2\psi_1(n-2) + \cdots + b_l\psi_1(n-l)]$$
$$-a_2[\psi_2(n) + b_1\psi_2(n-1) + b_2\psi_2(n-2) + \cdots + b_l\psi_2(n-l)]$$
$$\cdot \cdot \cdot \cdot \cdot \cdot \cdot \cdot \cdot \cdot \cdot \cdot \cdot \cdot \cdot \cdot \cdot \cdot \cdot \cdot \cdot \cdot \cdot \cdot \cdot \cdot$$
$$-a_k[\psi_k(n) + b_1\psi_k(n-1) + b_2\psi_k(n-2) + \cdots$$
$$+ b_l\psi_k(n-l)] = 0 \quad (8.9.4)$$

Since Eq. (8.9.4) applies for all values of $n \geq 0$, it follows that the coefficients of a_i, $i = 0, 1, \ldots, k$, must vanish. In particular, the coefficient of a_0 is

$$e_2(n) - \psi_1(n+1) - b_1\psi_1(n) - b_2\psi_1(n-1)$$
$$+ \cdots + b_l\psi_1(n-l+1) = 0$$

or upon applying Eq. (8.9.3)

$$\psi_1(n+1) = -b_1\psi_1(n) - b_2\psi_2(n) - \cdots - b_l\psi_l(n) + e_2(n) \quad (8.9.5)$$

If $a_0 = 0$ and $l \geq k$, then Eqs. (8.9.2), (8.9.3), and (8.9.5) together take on the form of a state model,

$$\begin{bmatrix} \psi_1(n+1) \\ \psi_2(n+1) \\ \psi_3(n+1) \\ \cdots \\ \psi_l(n+1) \end{bmatrix} = \begin{bmatrix} -b_1 & -b_2 & -b_3 & \cdots & -b_l \\ 1 & 0 & 0 & \cdots & 0 \\ 0 & 1 & 0 & \cdots & 0 \\ \cdots & \cdots & \cdots & \cdots & \cdots \\ 0 & 0 & 0 & \cdots & 0 \end{bmatrix} \begin{bmatrix} \psi_1(n) \\ \psi_2(n) \\ \psi_3(n) \\ \cdots \\ \psi_l(n) \end{bmatrix}$$
$$+ \begin{bmatrix} 1 \\ 0 \\ 0 \\ \cdots \\ 0 \end{bmatrix} e_2(n) \quad (8.9.6)$$

$$r_2(n) = [a_1 \quad a_2 \quad \cdots \quad a_k] \begin{bmatrix} \psi_1(n) \\ \psi_2(n) \\ \cdot \\ \cdot \\ \cdot \\ \psi_k(n) \end{bmatrix}$$

If $a_0 \neq 0$, then the output $r_2(n)$ is related to the internal states $\psi_i(n)$ and the input by

$$r_2(n) = [(a_1 - a_0b_1)(a_2 - a_0b_2) \cdots (a_k - a_0b_k) \cdots -a_0b_l]$$

$$\times \begin{bmatrix} \psi_1(n) \\ \psi_2(n) \\ \cdot \\ \cdot \\ \cdot \\ \psi_k(n) \\ \cdot \\ \cdot \\ \cdot \\ \psi_l(n) \end{bmatrix} + e_2(n)$$

For the special case where $a_0 = 0$, there is, of course, at least a one-interval delay between input and output (no direct transmission) and the discrete-state model of the controller can be represented symbolically as

$$\Psi_2(n + 1) = P_2\Psi_2(n) + Q_2e_2(n)$$
$$r_2(n) = M_2\Psi_2(n) \tag{8.9.7}$$

Let the continuous no-load input-output characteristics of the plant be given in terms of a state model of the form

$$\frac{d}{dt}\Psi_1(t) = P_1\Psi_1(t) + Q_1e_1(t)$$
$$r_1(t) = M_1\Psi_1(t) + n_1e_1(t) \tag{8.9.8}$$

A discrete-state model of the plant showing the magnitude of the output at discrete points $t = nT$ as a function of the discrete-level input signal $e_1(t)$ over the interval $nT \leq t < (n + 1)T$ (see Fig. 8.9.1) is obtainable from the continuous-state model by procedures already given in Chaps. 5 and 6. It is of the form

$$\Psi_1(n + 1) = \bar{P}_1\Psi_1(n) + \bar{Q}_1e_1(n)$$
$$r_1(n) = M_1\Psi_1(n) + n_1e_1(n) \tag{8.9.9}$$

where

$$\bar{P}_1 = e^{P_1T} \quad \text{and} \quad \bar{Q}_1 = \int_0^T e^{P_1(T-t)}Q_1 \, dt$$

Applying the constraint equations indicated by the block diagram in Fig. 8.9.1, the discrete-state model of the system for the case where

$n_1 = 0$ is of the form

$$\begin{bmatrix} \mathbf{\Psi}_1(n+1) \\ \mathbf{\Psi}_2(n+1) \end{bmatrix} = \begin{bmatrix} \bar{\mathbf{P}}_1 & \bar{\mathbf{Q}}_1\mathbf{M}_2 \\ \bar{\mathbf{Q}}_2\mathbf{M}_1 & \mathbf{P}_2 \end{bmatrix} \begin{bmatrix} \mathbf{\Psi}_1(n) \\ \mathbf{\Psi}_2(n) \end{bmatrix} + \begin{bmatrix} \bar{\mathbf{Q}}_1 \\ 0 \end{bmatrix} e_1(n)$$

$$r_1(n) = \mathbf{M}_1\mathbf{\Psi}_1(n)$$

(8.9.10)

The characteristic polynomial for this discrete-state feedback system, of course, is of the same general form as that given in Eq. (8.6.10) for the continuous-feedback system. Again, as in the continuous case, it is always possible to reduce row vector $\mathbf{M}_2$ to the form

$$\mathbf{M}_2 = [1 \quad 0 \quad 0 \quad \cdots \quad 0]$$

by a similarity transformation on the state vector $\mathbf{\Psi}_2$ so that the characteristic polynomial in Eq. (8.9.10) can be written in the form of Eq. (8.6.11), namely

$$D(\lambda) = \bar{p}_1(\lambda)p_2(\lambda) + \bar{h}_1(\lambda)h_2(\lambda) = [1 + G(\lambda)H(\lambda)]\bar{p}_1(\lambda)p_2(\lambda)$$

where $\bar{p}_1(\lambda)$ and $p_2(\lambda)$ represent, respectively, the characteristic polynomials of $\bar{\mathbf{P}}_1$ and $\mathbf{P}_2$ and $\bar{h}_1(\lambda)$ and $h_2(\lambda)$ represent, respectively, the determinants of the characteristic matrices $\lambda\mathbf{U} - \bar{\mathbf{P}}_1$ and $\lambda\mathbf{U} - \mathbf{P}_2$ *with the first columns replaced* by the respective column vectors $\bar{\mathbf{Q}}_1\mathbf{M}_2$ and $\mathbf{Q}_2\mathbf{M}_1$.

It is also possible to represent the input-output characteristics of the controller by a z-domain transfer function, obtained by applying the z transform to Eqs. (8.9.7) or directly to the recursion formula given in Eq. (8.9.1). In either case the result, *for zero initial conditions*, is

$$(1 + b_1z + b_2z^2 + \cdots + b_lz^l)r_2(z)$$
$$= (a_0 + a_1z + \cdots + a_kz^k)e_2(z)$$

or

$$r_2(z) = \frac{a_0 + a_1z + a_2z^2 + \cdots a_kz^k}{1 + b_1z + b_2z^2 + \cdots b_kz^k}\, e_2(z)$$
$$= H(z)e_2(z)$$

(8.9.11)

Note the correspondence between the coefficients in the rational function $H(z)$ in Eq. (8.9.11) and the coefficients in the recursion formula in Eq. (8.9.1).

The z-domain no-load input-output transfer function of the plant as a discrete-state component can, of course, be obtained by taking the z transform of the plant model given in Eqs. (8.9.10). It can also be obtained directly from the s-domain model of the plant as a continuous-state component by applying the algorithm given in the following theorem.

Theorem 8.9.1:   Let the s-domain transfer function of a linear continuous-state stationary plant be given in the form

$$
\begin{aligned}
G(s) = {} & \zeta_{11}f(\lambda_1) + \zeta_{12}\frac{f^{(1)}(\lambda_1)}{1!} + \cdots + \zeta_{1r_1}\frac{f^{(r_1-1)}(\lambda_1)}{(r_1 - 1)!} \\
& + \zeta_{21}f(\lambda_2) + \zeta_{22}\frac{f^{(1)}(\lambda_2)}{1!} + \cdots + \zeta_{2r_2}\frac{f^{(r_2-1)}(\lambda_2)}{(r_2 - 1)!} \\
& + \cdots \cdots \cdots \cdots \cdots \cdots \cdots \cdots \\
& + \zeta_{k1}f(\lambda_k) + \zeta_{k2}\frac{f^{(1)}(\lambda_k)}{1!} + \cdots + \zeta_{kr_k}\frac{f^{(r_k-1)}(\lambda_k)}{(r_k - 1)!} \\
& + N
\end{aligned}
\tag{8.9.12}
$$

where $f(\lambda) = 1/(s - \lambda)$ and $\lambda_1, \lambda_2, \ldots, \lambda_k$ represent the k distinct zeros of the minimal polynomial of the plant, each of order r_i.

The corresponding z-domain transfer function $G(z)$ of the plant for a sampling period $h = T$ is given by Eq. (8.9.12), with the function

$$
f(\lambda) = \frac{1}{s - \lambda}
$$

replaced by

$$
\begin{aligned}
f^*(\lambda) &= \frac{1}{z - e^{\lambda h}} e^{\lambda h} \int_0^h e^{-\lambda \tau}\, d\tau \\
&= \frac{1}{z - e^{\lambda h}} \frac{e^{\lambda h} - 1}{\lambda} \qquad \text{for } \lambda \neq 0 \\
&= \frac{h}{z - 1} \qquad\qquad\quad \text{for } \lambda = 0
\end{aligned}
\tag{8.9.13}
$$

Proof: The given transfer function $G(s)$ represents the Laplace transform of some equivalent continuous-state model of the general form

$$
\begin{aligned}
\frac{d}{dt}\,\boldsymbol{\Psi}(t) &= \mathbf{P}\boldsymbol{\Psi}(t) + \mathbf{Q}e_1(t) \\
r_1(t) &= \mathbf{M}\boldsymbol{\Psi}(t) + Ne_1(t)
\end{aligned}
\tag{8.9.14}
$$

If $e_1(t)$ is constant and of magnitude $e_1(n)$ over the interval $nh < t < (n + 1)h$, then the solution at $t = (n + 1)h$ is given by

$$
\begin{aligned}
\boldsymbol{\Psi}(n + 1) &= e^{\mathbf{P}h}\boldsymbol{\Psi}(n) + \left(e^{\mathbf{P}h} \int_0^h e^{-\mathbf{P}\tau}\, d\tau\right) \mathbf{Q}e_1(n) \\
r_1(n) &= \mathbf{M}(n) + Ne_1(n)
\end{aligned}
\tag{8.9.15}
$$

Taking the Laplace transform of Eq. (8.9.14), with zero initial conditions, gives

$$
r_1(s) = G(s)e_1(s)
$$

where

$$
G(s) = \mathbf{M}(s\mathbf{U} - \mathbf{P})^{-1}\mathbf{Q} + N
\tag{8.9.16}
$$

The z transform of Eqs. (8.9.15) for zero initial conditions is

$$r_1(z) = G(z)e_1(z)$$

where

$$G(z) = \mathbf{M} \left[(z\mathbf{U} - e^{\mathbf{P}h})^{-1}e^{\mathbf{P}h} \int_0^h e^{-\mathbf{P}\tau}\, d\tau \right] \mathbf{Q} + N \qquad (8.9.17)$$

The matrix function

$$f_1(\mathbf{P}) = (s\mathbf{U} - \mathbf{P})^{-1}$$

in Eq. (8.9.16) has an expansion of the form given in Theorem 6.2.1, with

$$f(\lambda) = f_1(\lambda) = \frac{1}{s - \lambda}$$

The matrix function

$$f_2(\mathbf{P}) = (z\mathbf{U} - e^{\mathbf{P}h})^{-1}e^{\mathbf{P}h} \int_0^h e^{-\mathbf{P}\tau}\, d\tau$$

in Eq. (8.9.17) has the same form of expansion, but with

$$f(\lambda) = f_2(\lambda) = \frac{1}{z - e^{\lambda h}} e^{\lambda h} \int_0^h e^{-\lambda\tau}\, d\tau$$

Since $\mathbf{M}$ is a row matrix and $\mathbf{Q}$ is a column matrix, it follows that

$$G(s) = \mathbf{M}f_1(\mathbf{P})\mathbf{Q} + N$$

has an expansion of the form given in Eq. (8.9.12), with $f(\lambda) = f_1(\lambda)$. The scalar coefficient ζ_{ij} is given by the matrix product

$$\zeta_{ij} = \mathbf{M}Z_{ij}\mathbf{Q}$$

where Z_{ij} $(i, j = 1, 2, \ldots, k)$ represent the constituent matrices of $\mathbf{P}$. Since the constituent matrices depend only on the matrix $\mathbf{P}$, and not on the function of $\mathbf{P}$, it follows that the expansion for

$$G(z) = \mathbf{M}f_2(\mathbf{P})\mathbf{Q} + N$$

is also of the form given in Eq. (8.9.12), with $f(\lambda) = f_2(\lambda)$, and the theorem is proved.

To apply the algorithm given in Theorem 8.9.1, the coefficients ζ_{ij} in Eq. (8.9.12), of course, can be obtained by expanding the given rational function $G(s)$ in partial fractions.

Example 8.9.1:   Evaluate the z-domain transfer function for the discrete-state equivalent of a continuous-state system having the s-domain transfer function

$$G(s) = \frac{1}{s(s + 1)(s + 2)}$$

Solution: Expanding $G(s)$ in partial fractions gives

$$G(s) = 0.5\frac{1}{s} - \frac{1}{s+1} + 0.5\frac{1}{s+2}$$

Upon applying Theorem 8.9.1, the functions $1/s$, $1/(s+1)$, and $1/(s+2)$ in this expansion are replaced by the respective functions

$$f^*(\lambda_1) = f^*(0) = \frac{h}{z-1}$$

$$f^*(\lambda_2) = f^*(-1) = \frac{1}{z-e^{-h}}\frac{e^{-h}-1}{-1}$$

$$f^*(\lambda_3) = f^*(-2) = \frac{1}{z-e^{-2h}}\frac{e^{-2h}-1}{-2}$$

and the required z-domain transfer function is

$$G(z) = \frac{0.5h}{z-1} + \frac{e^{-h}-1}{z-e^{-h}} - \frac{e^{-2h}-1}{4(z-e^{-2h})}$$

Clearly, the numerical values of the coefficients in the rational function $G(z)$ and the poles of the function depend upon the size of the sampling period h. If $h = 1$, for example, then

$$G(z) = \frac{0.5}{z-1} + \frac{0.632}{z-0.368} - \frac{0.216}{z-0.135}$$

$$\cong \frac{1.35z^2 - 1.32z + 0.247}{(z-1)(z-0.368)(z-0.135)}$$

It is critical to recognize that Theorem 8.9.1 applies to *the s-domain model of the entire continuous plant as a multiport component.* The subassemblies are made compatible as discrete-state components only by the associated sampling and hold mechanisms on the input and output of the digital controller!

If the no-load discrete-state transfer function for the plant is taken as

$$r_1(z) = G_1(z)e_1(z) \qquad\qquad (8.9.18)$$

and if the corresponding transfer characteristics of the digital controller are given by Eq. (8.9.11), then from the block diagram in Fig. 8.9.1 it follows that the input-output characteristics of the system are given by

$$r_1(z) = \frac{G(z)}{1 + G(z)H(z)} e_i(z) \qquad\qquad (8.9.19)$$

The characteristic polynomial of the system as determined from the transfer function in Eq. (8.9.19) can be written in the same form as that given in Eq. (8.9.11). If the locations of the zeros of $p_1(\lambda)$ and $\bar{p}(\lambda)$ are known relative to the unit circle, then, of course, the stability of the system can be established in terms of the zeros of the rational function

$$F(z) = 1 + G(z)H(z)$$

The location of zeros of $1 + G(z)H(z)$ can be established by applying the Cauchy mapping theorem, as given in Theorem 8.7.1 for the rational function $F(\lambda)$. This region can be considered as the interior of the closed curve C, called a *Nyquist path*, shown in Fig. 8.9.2. This closed path consists of two concentric circles about the origin, one of unit radius, the other of radius $R > 1$, with a radial cut between them. Since the radial cut is traversed in opposite directions, it can usually be ignored in the plot of $F(z)$. If $F(z)$ has poles or zeros on the unit circle, they are avoided by semicircles with very small radii, ϵ, as indicated. As the radius $R \to \infty$, the circle C reduces to the point at infinity and the critical part of the contour is finally the unit circle. The counterpart of Theorem 8.7.2 for discrete-state systems is therefore as follows.

Theorem 8.9.2 (Nyquist stability criterion): Let the characteristic polynomial of a discrete-state system be given as

$$D(\lambda) = p_1(\lambda)p_2(\lambda) + h_1(\lambda)h_2(\lambda) = [1 + G(\lambda)H(\lambda)]p_1(\lambda)p_2(\lambda)$$

where $G(\lambda) = h_1(\lambda)/p_1(\lambda)$ and $H(\lambda) = h_2(\lambda)/p_2(\lambda)$. The system is stable if the mapping of the unit circle in the λ plane into the $G(\lambda)H(\lambda)$ plane does not encircle the point $(-1, j0)$ in the $G(\lambda)H(\lambda)$ plane.

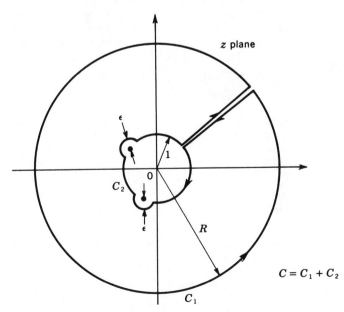

Fig. 8.9.2 Nyquist path in z plane.

Since the techniques for making Bode plots apply only to points on the imaginary axis rather than the unit circle, the Nyquist stability criterion is somewhat more difficult to apply directly to sampled-data systems than to continuous systems. However, as discussed in Sec. 6.6, the problem can be put into the realm of Bode-plot techniques by first applying the bilinear transformation

$$\lambda = \frac{1 + w}{1 - w}$$

to transform the unit circle in the λ plane into the imaginary axis of the w plane. This technique, along with the direct application of Theorem 8.9.2, is demonstrated in the following example.

Example 8.9.2: Investigate the stability of a sampled-data system with the characteristic polynomial

$$D(\lambda) = [1 + G(\lambda)H(\lambda)]p_1(\lambda)p_2(\lambda)$$

where

$$G(\lambda)H(\lambda) = \frac{k(-0.2 + 0.3\lambda)}{(\lambda - 1)(\lambda - 0.3)} \qquad k > 0 \tag{8.9.20}$$

Solution: Since $G(\lambda)H(\lambda)$ contains no poles outside the unit circle and one pole on the unit circle, the number of encirclements of $D(\lambda)$ about the point $(-1,j0)$, as λ takes on values along the Nyquist path C in Fig. 8.9.3a, establishes the number of zeros of the characteristic polynomial outside the unit circle. On the larger section of the unit circle from a to b, $\lambda = e^{j\theta}$, and θ takes on the values from $-\theta_0$ to $+\theta_0$, where θ_0 is an arbitrarily small angle. Consequently, we consider the function

$$F(\lambda) = \frac{k(-0.2 + 0.3e^{j\theta})}{(e^{j\theta} - 1)(e^{j\theta} - 0.3)} \qquad -\theta_0 < \theta < \theta_0$$

A sketch of this function from $\theta = -\theta_0$ (point a) to $\theta = +\theta_0$ (point b) is shown by the solid curve in Fig. 8.9.3b.

For that portion of the Nyquist path from b to a on the small semicircle around the point $\lambda = 1$ we take $\lambda = 1 + \epsilon e^{j\phi}$, where $-\pi/2 \leq \phi \leq \pi/2$ and ϵ is small. The corresponding function is

$$F(\lambda) \cong \frac{5k}{7\epsilon} e^{-j\phi} \qquad -\frac{\pi}{2} \leq \phi \leq \frac{\pi}{2}$$

The corresponding sketch of $F(\lambda)$ is shown dashed in Fig. 8.9.3b.

If k is such that the point c at which $\theta = \theta_1$ is to the right of $(-1,j0)$, as indicated in the sketch, then, of course, the system is stable. The system is unstable if the point c is to the left of $(-1,j0)$. This critical value of k can be determined as follows: Since $e^{j\theta} = \cos \theta + j \sin \theta$, Eq. (8.9.20) can be written as

$$G(\lambda)H(\lambda) = X(\theta) + jY(\theta)$$

where

$$X(\theta) =$$
$$\frac{(k/10)[(2 + 3\cos\theta)(\cos^2\theta - \sin^2\theta - 1.3\cos\theta + 0.3) + 3\sin^2\theta(2\cos\theta - 1.3)]}{(\cos^2\theta - \sin^2\theta - 1.3\cos\theta + 0.3)^2 + \sin^2\theta(2\cos\theta - 1.3)^2}$$

$$(8.9.21)$$

$$Y(\theta) = \frac{-(k/10)\sin\theta(4\cos\theta - 0.5)}{(\cos^2\theta - \sin^2\theta - 1.3\cos\theta + 0.3)^2 + \sin^2\theta(2\cos\theta - 1.3)^2}$$

Since, at the point c, $Y(\theta) = 0$, Eqs. (8.9.21) give $\sin\theta = 0$ and $4\cos\theta - 0.5 = 0$. The first of these relations corresponds to $\theta = 0$ (point e) and $\theta = \pi$ (point d) and the second relation, that is, $\cos\theta = \frac{1}{8}$, gives the desired value θ_1. Substituting $\cos\theta_1 = \frac{1}{8}$, $\sin\theta_1 = \sqrt{63/8}$, in Eqs. (8.9.21), we have

$$X(\theta_1) = G(\lambda)H(\lambda)\Big|_{\theta_1} \cong -0.286k$$

Therefore, the system is stable when

$$k < \frac{1}{0.286} = 3.495$$

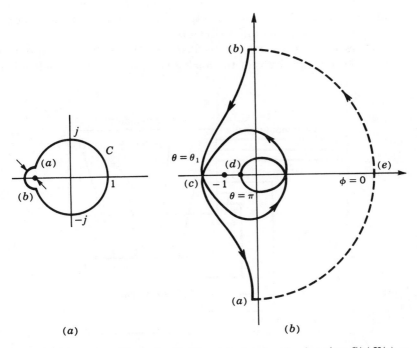

Fig. 8.9.3 (a) Nyquist path; (b) Nyquist plot for the function $G(\lambda)H(\lambda) = k(-0.2 + 0.3\lambda)/(\lambda - 1)(\lambda - 0.3)$.

If the Bode-plot technique is utilized, the expression $\lambda = (1 + w)/(1 - w)$ is first substituted into Eq. (8.9.20). The new transfer function is

$$D(w) = \frac{k(w - 1)(w + 5)}{2w(13w + 7)} \tag{8.9.22}$$

Using the methods described in Sec. 7.3, one can arrive at the same conclusion as given above.

8.10   MULTIVARIABLE FEEDBACK SYSTEMS

In automatic-control applications the two basic blocks in the feedback interconnection may have multiple inputs and outputs, as shown conceptually in Fig. 8.10.1. The block labeled "Plant" represents any continuous system or process such as a chemical plant or guidance system. A set of signals, called *outputs*, at selected points in the system serves as inputs to a unilateral *controller*, which activates corrective signals back into the plant. The controller may be an analog computer, a digital computer, or a simple feedback loop of passive components, depending upon the complexity of the system and the sophistication of the control requirements. The single input-output systems discussed in the previous section are special cases of this more general concept in that only one "plant" output is sensed and the output of the "controller" is connected in series with the manual input control.

To extend the concept of feedback to the multiple input-output case when the controller is of the analog type, let the state model of the

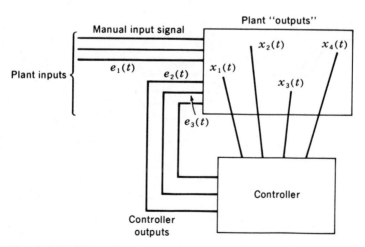

Fig. 8.10.1 Schematic of general process-control system using a controller to determine excitation signals.

plant be given in the form

$$\frac{d}{dt}\boldsymbol{\Psi}_1(t) = \mathbf{P}_1\boldsymbol{\Psi}_1(t) + \mathbf{Q}_1\mathbf{Z}_1(t)$$

$$\mathbf{Z}_2(t) = \mathbf{M}_1\boldsymbol{\Psi}_1(t) + \mathbf{N}_1\mathbf{Z}_1(t)$$

(8.10.1)

where the vectors $\mathbf{Z}_1(t)$ and $\mathbf{Z}_2(t)$ of order k_1 and k_2 represent, respectively, any set of k_1 input and k_2 output signals, of either the through type or the across type, or a combination thereof. The matrix $\mathbf{N}_1$ of order $k_2 \times k_1$ is called the *direct-transmission* matrix and in the interests of simplicity is assumed to be zero in the subsequent development.

If the controller is to be realized from linear time-invariant components, then the most general form of the input-output state model for this subsystem is

$$\frac{d}{dt}\boldsymbol{\Psi}_2(t) = \mathbf{P}_2\boldsymbol{\Psi}_2(t) + \mathbf{Q}_2\mathbf{Z}_3(t)$$

$$\mathbf{Z}_4(t) = \mathbf{M}_2\boldsymbol{\Psi}_2(t) + \mathbf{N}_2\mathbf{Z}_3(t)$$

(8.10.2)

where $\mathbf{Z}_3(t)$ and $\mathbf{Z}_4(t)$ represent, respectively, the input and output vectors of the controller.

Let the specific interconnections between the plant and controller shown schematically in Fig. 8.10.1 be such that the constraint equations are

$$\mathbf{Z}_0(t) = \mathbf{Z}_2(t) = \mathbf{Z}_3(t)$$

and

$$\mathbf{Z}_1(t) = \mathbf{Z}_i(t) + \mathbf{Z}_4(t)$$

where $\mathbf{Z}_0(t)$ is called the system output vector and $\mathbf{Z}_i(t)$ represents a vector of specified, or "manual," input signals. It is, of course, possible for some or all of the entries in $\mathbf{Z}_i(t)$ to be identically zero.

When the constraint equations are substituted into the component equations given as Eqs. (8.10.1) (with $\mathbf{N}_1 \equiv 0$) and (8.10.2), the resulting system model is

$$\frac{d}{dt}\begin{bmatrix} \boldsymbol{\Psi}_1(t) \\ \boldsymbol{\Psi}_2(t) \end{bmatrix} = \begin{bmatrix} \mathbf{P}_1 + \mathbf{Q}_1\mathbf{N}_2\mathbf{M}_1 & \mathbf{Q}_1\mathbf{M}_2 \\ \mathbf{Q}_2\mathbf{M}_1 & \mathbf{P}_2 \end{bmatrix} \begin{bmatrix} \boldsymbol{\Psi}_1(t) \\ \boldsymbol{\Psi}_2(t) \end{bmatrix} + \begin{bmatrix} \mathbf{Q}_1 \\ 0 \end{bmatrix} \mathbf{Z}_i(t)$$

(8.10.3)

$$\mathbf{Z}_0(t) = \mathbf{M}_1\boldsymbol{\Psi}_1(t)$$

When the controller contains only one feedback signal, $\mathbf{Z}_i(t)$ and $\mathbf{Z}_0(t)$ in Eq. (8.10.3) are scalars, $\mathbf{Q}_1$ and $\mathbf{Q}_2$ are column matrices, $\mathbf{M}_1$ and $\mathbf{M}_2$ are row matrices, $\mathbf{N}_2$ is a scalar, and Eqs. (8.10.3) reduce to Eqs. (8.6.6), for which the stability characteristics have already been considered in the previous section. The stability characteristics of this more general feedback system can be investigated by writing the characteristic polynomial in the form

$$D(\lambda) = \det \left[\begin{array}{c|c} \lambda\mathbf{U} - \mathbf{P}'_1 & -\mathbf{Q}_1\mathbf{M}_2 \\ \hline -\mathbf{Q}_2\mathbf{M}_1 & \lambda\mathbf{U} - \mathbf{P}_2 \end{array}\right] \tag{8.10.4}$$

where

$$\mathbf{P}'_1 = \mathbf{P}_1 + \mathbf{Q}_1\mathbf{N}_2\mathbf{M}_1$$

If each of the coefficient matrices $\mathbf{M}_1$ and $\mathbf{M}_2$ is of maximum row rank and the order of the plant and controller output vectors $\mathbf{Z}_1(t)$ and $\mathbf{Z}_2(t)$ is less than or equal to the order of the corresponding state vectors $\mathbf{\Psi}_1(t)$ and $\mathbf{\Psi}_2(t)$, then, by applying a nonsingular transformation on the state vectors, the coefficient matrices $\mathbf{M}_1$ and $\mathbf{M}_2$ can be reduced to normal form,

$$\mathbf{M}_1 = [\mathbf{U} \vdots \mathbf{0}] \quad \text{and} \quad \mathbf{M}_2 = [\mathbf{U} \vdots \mathbf{0}]$$

Under these conditions, the characteristic matrix in Eq. (8.10.4) can be partitioned in the form

$$D(\lambda) = \det \left[\begin{array}{cc|cc} \lambda\mathbf{U} - \mathbf{P}'_{11} & -\mathbf{P}'_{12} & -\mathbf{Q}_{11} & 0 \\ -\mathbf{P}'_{21} & \lambda\mathbf{U} - \mathbf{P}'_{22} & -\mathbf{Q}_{12} & 0 \\ \hline -\mathbf{Q}_{21} & 0 & \lambda\mathbf{U} - \mathbf{P}_{22} & -\mathbf{P}_{23} \\ -\mathbf{Q}_{22} & 0 & -\mathbf{P}_{32} & \lambda\mathbf{U} - \mathbf{P}_{33} \end{array}\right] \tag{8.10.5}$$

The expansion of the determinant in Eq. (8.10.5) by the first two row blocks can be written as

$$D(\lambda) = \det (\lambda\mathbf{U} - \mathbf{P}'_1) \det (\lambda\mathbf{U} - \mathbf{P}_2) + \det \mathbf{H}_1(\lambda) \det \mathbf{H}'_2(\lambda)$$
$$+ \cdots + \det \mathbf{H}_k(\lambda) \det \mathbf{H}'_k(\lambda) \tag{8.10.6}$$

where $\mathbf{H}_i(\lambda)$ and $\mathbf{H}'_i(\lambda)$ $(i = 1, 2, \ldots, k)$ represent, respectively, the remaining square minors of the first two blocks and their complements. If the controller, for example, contains two inputs and one output, then the matrices

$$\mathbf{Q}_1 = \left[\begin{array}{c} \mathbf{Q}_{11} \\ \mathbf{Q}_{12} \end{array}\right] \quad \text{and} \quad \mathbf{Q}_2 = \left[\begin{array}{c} \mathbf{Q}_{21} \\ \mathbf{Q}_{22} \end{array}\right]$$

contain two columns and one column, respectively, and the characteristic polynomial is of the form

$$D(\lambda) = \det (\lambda\mathbf{U} - \mathbf{P}'_1) \det (\lambda\mathbf{U} - \mathbf{P}_2) \mp \det \mathbf{H}_1(\lambda) \det \mathbf{H}'_2(\lambda)$$
$$\mp \det \mathbf{H}_2(\lambda) \det \mathbf{H}'_2(\lambda) \tag{8.10.7}$$

where $\mathbf{H}_1(\lambda)$ is the matrix $\lambda\mathbf{U} - \mathbf{P}'_1$, with the first column replaced by the first column of $\mathbf{Q}_1$, $\mathbf{H}'_1(\lambda)$ is $\lambda\mathbf{U} - \mathbf{P}_2$, with the first column replaced by the second column of $\mathbf{Q}_1$, and $\mathbf{H}'_2(\lambda)$ is $\lambda\mathbf{U} - \mathbf{P}_2$, with the second column replaced by $\mathbf{Q}_2$. From Eq. (8.10.7) it follows that the characteristic polynomial can be written in the form

$$
\begin{aligned}
D(\lambda) &= p_1'(\lambda)p_2(\lambda) + h_1(\lambda)h_1'(\lambda) + h_2(\lambda)h_2'(\lambda) \\
&= \left[1 + \frac{h_1(\lambda)}{p_1'(\lambda)} \frac{h_1'(\lambda)}{p_2(\lambda)} + \frac{h_2(\lambda)}{p_1'(\lambda)} \frac{h_2'(\lambda)}{p_2(\lambda)} \right] p_1'(\lambda)p_2(\lambda) \\
&= [1 + \mathbf{G}_1(\lambda)\mathbf{H}_1(\lambda) + \mathbf{G}_2(\lambda)\mathbf{H}_2(\lambda)]p_1'(\lambda)p_2(\lambda) \qquad (8.10.8)
\end{aligned}
$$

If the return loop contains no direct transmission, then $\mathbf{P}_1' = \mathbf{P}_1$ and $p_1(\lambda)p_2(\lambda)$ represents the product of the characteristic polynomials of the plant and controller. Each of the factors $\mathbf{G}_1(\lambda)\mathbf{H}_1(\lambda)$ and $\mathbf{G}_2(\lambda)\mathbf{H}_2(\lambda)$ can be regarded as transfer characteristics of the loops formed by the plant and each of the two return loops from the two inputs and the one output of the controller. If $p_1(\lambda)$ and $p_2(\lambda)$ are both stable polynomials, then, of course, stability of the system is determined by the rational function

$$
D(\lambda) = 1 + \mathbf{G}_1(\lambda)\mathbf{H}_1(\lambda) + \mathbf{G}_2(\lambda)\mathbf{H}_2(\lambda) \qquad (8.10.9)
$$

and it is possible to investigate the stability of this function by applying the Nyquist criterion to the rational function $\mathbf{G}_1(\lambda)\mathbf{H}_1(\lambda) + \mathbf{G}_2(\lambda)\mathbf{H}_2(\lambda)$. Since this rational function depends upon the magnitudes of the entries in the matrices $\mathbf{Q}_1$ and $\mathbf{Q}_2$, it follows that the response characteristics can be altered by adjusting the numerical values of the coefficients in these matrices.

It is not difficult to show that, if the controller contains k inputs and l outputs, then the characteristic polynomial is of the form

$$
\begin{aligned}
D(\lambda) = [1 + \mathbf{G}_1(\lambda)\mathbf{H}_1(\lambda) + \mathbf{G}_2(\lambda)\mathbf{H}_2(\lambda) \\
+ \cdots + \mathbf{G}_q(\lambda)\mathbf{H}_q(\lambda)]p_1'(\lambda)p_2(\lambda)
\end{aligned}
$$

where $q = kl$ and it is assumed that k is not greater than the order of the plant state vector and l is not larger than the order of the controller state vector.

When a digital controller is used as the control element, the selected plant outputs are measured at selected intervals of time called *sampling periods*. These signals are converted into binary-coded pulses and transmitted as inputs to a digital computer, wherein a set of binary-coded output signals is calculated consistent with a predesigned recursion formula within the digital computer. The actual output signals are then fed into a "digital-to-analog conversion unit," which converts the binary-coded pulses of the digital computer to magnitude-modulated signals of sufficient power level to drive the system. The levels of the excitation signals, as calculated by the computer at the point $t = nT$, are usually held constant until a new calculation is realized at $t = (n + 1)T$. In the following development it is assumed that the length of time T between successive calculations or changes in level of excitation is fixed.

Consider first the form of the discrete-state model of the plant showing, in particular, the magnitude of the outputs at the discrete points $t = nT$ as a function of the plant input signal $Z_i(t)$ over the interval $nT \leq t < (n + 1)T$.

The discrete-state equivalent of the continuous-state plant model given in Eqs. (8.10.1) is

$$\Psi_1[(n + 1)T] = \bar{P}_1\Psi_1(nT) + \bar{Q}_1Z_1(nT)$$
$$Z_2(nT) = M_1\Psi_1(nT) + N_1Z_1(nT) \tag{8.10.10}$$

where

$$\bar{P}_1 = e^{P_1 T}$$

is the discrete-state transition matrix and

$$\bar{Q}_1 = \int_0^T e^{P_1(T-t)}Q_1 \, dt \tag{8.10.11}$$

is the corresponding discrete-state coefficient matrix for the excitation vector.

If the time required to scan and sample the outputs of the plant is negligible, and if the time required for the computer to compute the output signals is either zero or equal to an integral number of sampling intervals, then a linear recursion formula describing the input-output characteristics of the computer is of the general form

$$\Psi_2[(n + 1)T] = P_2\Psi_2(nT) + Q_2Z_3(nT)$$
$$Z_4(nT) = M_2\Psi_2(nT) + N_2Z_3(nT) \tag{8.10.12}$$

As in the case of continuous control, the feedback interconnections are assumed to be such that

$$Z_0 = Z_2 = Z_3$$

and

$$Z_1 = Z_i + Z_4$$

If the plant model contains no direct transmission, then $N_1 = 0$ in Eqs. (8.10.10) and the component and constraint equations combine to give a system discrete-state model of the general form

$$\begin{bmatrix} \Psi_1(n + 1) \\ \Psi_2(n + 1) \end{bmatrix} = \begin{bmatrix} P_1 + Q_1N_2M_1 & Q_1M_2 \\ Q_2M_1 & P_2 \end{bmatrix} \begin{bmatrix} \Psi_1(n) \\ \Psi_2(n) \end{bmatrix} + \begin{bmatrix} Q_1 \\ 0 \end{bmatrix} Z_i(n)$$
$$\tag{8.10.13}$$

$$Z_0(n) = M_1\Psi_1(n)$$

where for convenience $\Psi(nT)$ is written simply as $\Psi(n)$. Since the transition matrix for the discrete-state system is of the same form as that for the continuous system given as Eqs. (8.10.3), it follows that the properties of the characteristic polynomial can be investigated in exactly the same manner.

8.11 SYSTEMS OF ARBITRARILY CONNECTED MULTITERMINAL COMPONENTS

We return now to the more general problem of analyzing the performance characteristics of an arbitrary system of n-terminal linear components. It should be emphasized that even for systems of parallel-connected, cascaded, and series-parallel-connected two-port components, it may not be possible to present the state model of the components in the forms required for the techniques presented in the previous section.

In the most general case, the state equations of each n-terminal component of a linear time-invariant system are of the form

$$\frac{d}{dt}\,\boldsymbol{\Psi}(t) = \mathbf{P}\boldsymbol{\Psi}(t) + \mathbf{Q}\mathbf{Z}_i(t) + \mathbf{F}_1(t)$$

$$\mathbf{Z}_0(t) = \mathbf{M}\boldsymbol{\Psi}(t) + \mathbf{N}\mathbf{Z}_i(t) + \mathbf{F}_2(t)$$

(8.11.1)

where

$$\mathbf{Z}_0(t) = (\mathbf{X}_0(t),\, \mathbf{Y}_0(t))$$

and

$$\mathbf{Z}_i(t) = (\mathbf{Y}_i(t),\, \mathbf{X}_i(t))$$

are complementary terminal-variable vectors whose entries correspond to the $n - 1$ edges of the terminal graph, $\boldsymbol{\Psi}(t)$ is the state vector of arbitrary order, and $\mathbf{F}_1(t)$ and $\mathbf{F}_2(t)$ are vectors of time functions accounting for active drivers, if any, internal to the component. In the examples of the previous section none of the subassemblies contain internal drivers, and so $\mathbf{F}_1(t)$ and $\mathbf{F}_2(t)$ are both zero. In the special case where $\boldsymbol{\Psi}(t)$ is of order 0, the component, of course, is characterized by algebraic equations only. On the other hand, when $\mathbf{N} \equiv 0$, $\mathbf{F}_2(t) = 0$, and $\mathbf{M} = \mathbf{U}$, then $\boldsymbol{\Psi}(t) = \mathbf{Z}_0(t)$ and Eqs. (8.11.1) reduce to a system of differential equations. In general, the matrix $\mathbf{N}$ is square, and $\mathbf{M}$ is rectangular, but neither need be of maximum rank.

We now inquire into the problems of developing state models of systems of subassemblies wherein each subassembly, as a multiterminal component, is characterized by a state model of the form given in Eqs. (8.11.1). The following theorem establishes a set of necessary conditions on the system structure under which a complete and unique solution exists. Since a unique solution exists if and only if the system has a state model, the theorem following also establishes a set of necessary conditions under which a subassembly of multiterminal components can be represented as an n-terminal component by a state model or an s-domain model.

Finally, it establishes a basis for actually developing state models of such systems.

Theorem 8.11.1:   Consider a system of K multiterminal components having a graph G with e edges and v vertices.   Let the direct sum of the component terminal equations be written in the form

$$\frac{d}{dt}\,\mathbf{\Psi}(t) = \mathbf{P}\mathbf{\Psi}(t) + \mathbf{Q}\mathbf{Z}_i(t) + \mathbf{F}_1(t)$$

$$\mathbf{Z}_0(t) = \mathbf{M}\mathbf{\Psi}(t) + \mathbf{N}\mathbf{Z}_i(t) + \mathbf{F}_2(t)$$

(8.11.2)

where $\mathbf{\Psi}(t)$ is a vector of order n and $\mathbf{Z}_0(t) = [\mathbf{X}_0(t),\, \mathbf{Y}_0(t)]$ and $\mathbf{Z}_i(t) = [\mathbf{Y}_i(t),\, \mathbf{X}_i(t)]$ are complementary vectors, each of order e, with one component corresponding to each edge of G.   The system has a complete and unique solution only if there exist a tree† T_1 and a tree† T_2 in G such that the $(n + e) \times (n + 2e)$ matrix

$$\begin{bmatrix} \lambda\mathbf{U} - \mathbf{P} & \mathbf{Q} & \mathbf{0} \\ \mathbf{M} & \mathbf{N} & -\mathbf{U} \end{bmatrix}$$

is of maximum rank.   Further, any set of linearly independent columns taken from the matrix

$$\begin{bmatrix} \mathbf{Q} & \mathbf{0} \\ \mathbf{N} & -\mathbf{U} \end{bmatrix}$$

corresponds to across variables in T_1 and through variables in the complement of T_2.

   Proof: The proof of the theorem is based on the following lemma.

Lemma 8.11.1:   The system of n first-order linear constant-coefficient differential equations

$$\mathbf{M}\dot{\mathbf{\Psi}}(t) = \mathbf{P}\mathbf{\Psi}(t) + \mathbf{F}(t)$$

(8.11.3)

has a unique solution for the vector $\mathbf{\Psi}(t)$ only if the matrix $\lambda\mathbf{M} - \mathbf{P}$ is nonsingular.

   Proof of lemma: A formal proof of this lemma can be found in Gantmacher.[5]   The validity can also be established by considering the Laplace transform of Eq. (8.11.3), which is

$$(s\mathbf{M} - \mathbf{P})\mathbf{\Psi}(s) = \mathbf{F}(s) + \mathbf{\Psi}(0)$$

A unique solution for the complex frequency spectra $\mathbf{\Psi}(s)$ exists only if $s\mathbf{M} - \mathbf{P}$ is nonsingular, and the lemma follows.

† Tree or forest.

Returning to the proof of the main theorem, let the direct sum of the component state models and the circuit and vertex equations of the system graph be written in the form†

n differential equations:
e algebraic equations:
$e - v + 1$ circuit equations:
$v - 1$ vertex equations:

$$\begin{bmatrix} \dot{\Psi}(t) \\ 0 \\ 0 \\ 0 \end{bmatrix} = \begin{bmatrix} P & Q & 0 \\ M & N & -U \\ 0 & B_1 & B_2 \\ 0 & A_1 & A_2 \end{bmatrix} \begin{bmatrix} \Psi(t) \\ Z_i(t) \\ Z_0(t) \end{bmatrix} + \begin{bmatrix} F_1(t) \\ F_2(t) \\ 0 \\ 0 \end{bmatrix}$$

By applying Lemma 8.11.1 or by direct application of the Laplace transformation, it follows that this system of equations has a unique solution for the vector (Ψ, Z_0, Z_i) only if the square matrix

$$\begin{array}{c} \\ (n) \\ R = \begin{array}{c} (n) \\ (e) \\ (e-v+1) \\ (v-1) \end{array} \end{array} \begin{array}{ccc} (n) & (e) & (e) \\ \begin{bmatrix} P - \lambda U & Q & 0 \\ M & N & -U \\ 0 & B_1 & B_2 \\ 0 & A_1 & A_2 \end{bmatrix} \end{array} \tag{8.11.4}$$

is nonsingular. Since the circuit and vertex equations involve mutually exclusive sets of variables, the columns of R can be rearranged so that Eq. (8.11.4) takes on the form

$$R' = \begin{array}{c} (n) \\ (e) \\ (e) \\ (e) \end{array} \begin{array}{ccc} (n) & (e) & (e) \\ \begin{bmatrix} P - \lambda U & Q_1 & Q_2 \\ M & K_1 & K_2 \\ 0 & B & 0 \\ 0 & 0 & A \end{bmatrix} \end{array} \tag{8.11.5}$$

Consider now the Laplace expansion of R' about the last e rows. A square matrix of order e taken from the last two row blocks is nonsingular if, and only if, it contains exactly $e - v + 1$ linearly independent columns from the circuit matrix and $v - 1$ linearly independent columns from the cut-set matrix. Therefore, the Laplace expansion gives a summation of the form

$$\det R' = \sum_{i,j} \pm \det \begin{bmatrix} B_i & 0 \\ 0 & A_j \end{bmatrix} \det [\Gamma_i \quad \Gamma_j]$$

where the columns of B_i and A_j correspond, respectively, to chords of some tree T_i and branches of some tree T_j in the system graph G. Since the columns Γ_i and Γ_j are complementary to the columns of B_i and A_j, respectively, it follows that any columns Γ_i and Γ_j correspond to a subset of branches of T_i and a subset of chords of T_j. It follows, therefore, that

† If the graph contains more than one part, the equation count is changed accordingly but the proof of the theorem is unchanged.

the matrix

$$
\begin{array}{c}
\quad\; (n) \quad\;\; (e) \;\; (e) \\
\begin{array}{c} (n) \\ (e) \end{array}
\left[\begin{array}{ccc}
\mathbf{P} - \lambda\mathbf{U} & \mathbf{Q} & \mathbf{0} \\
\mathbf{M} & \mathbf{N} & -\mathbf{U}
\end{array}\right]
\end{array}
\qquad (8.11.6)
$$

must be of maximum rank, with the linearly independent columns in the second and third column blocks corresponding to across variables of T_1 and through variables of the complement of T_2, and the theorem is proved.

An alternative statement of Theorem 8.11.1 can be developed if we let the terminal equations [Eqs. (8.11.2)] corresponding to the coefficient matrix (8.11.6) be partitioned and written in the form

$$
\begin{array}{c}
\qquad\qquad\quad (n) \\
\begin{array}{c} (n) \\ (e) \end{array}
\left[\begin{array}{cc}
\mathbf{P} - \mathbf{U}(d/dt) & \mathbf{L}_{11} \\
\mathbf{M} & \mathbf{L}_{21}
\end{array}\right]
\left[\begin{array}{c} \boldsymbol{\Psi}(t) \\ \mathbf{Z}_p(t) \end{array}\right]
+ \left[\begin{array}{c} \mathbf{L}_{12} \\ \mathbf{L}_{22} \end{array}\right] \mathbf{Z}_s(t)
+ \left[\begin{array}{c} \mathbf{F}_1(t) \\ \mathbf{F}_2(t) \end{array}\right] = \mathbf{0}
\end{array}
$$
$$
(8.11.7)
$$

where $\mathbf{Z}_p(t) = [\mathbf{X}_1(t),\, \mathbf{Y}_2(t)]$ is a vector of primary variables; i.e., the $v - 1$ entries of $\mathbf{X}_1(t)$ correspond to the edges of a tree T_1 and the $e - v + 1$ entries of $\mathbf{Y}_1(t)$ correspond to the edges of the complement of a tree T_2 in the system graph. If the coefficient matrix

$$
\left[\begin{array}{cc}
\mathbf{P} - \lambda\mathbf{U} & \mathbf{L}_{11} \\
\mathbf{M} & \mathbf{L}_{21}
\end{array}\right]
$$

is nonsingular, it can be reduced by elementary operations to the form

$$
\left[\begin{array}{cc}
\mathbf{P}' - \lambda\mathbf{C} & \mathbf{0} \\
\mathbf{M}' - \lambda\mathbf{D} & \mathbf{U}
\end{array}\right]
$$

where $\det\,[\mathbf{P}' - \lambda\mathbf{C}] \neq 0$. It follows, therefore, that for trees T_1 and T_2 the direct sum of the component-state equations can be reduced to the equivalent form

$$
\left[\begin{array}{cc}
\mathbf{P}' - \mathbf{C}(d/dt) & \mathbf{0} \\
\mathbf{M}' - \mathbf{D}(d/dt) & \mathbf{U}
\end{array}\right]
\left[\begin{array}{c} \boldsymbol{\Psi}(t) \\ \mathbf{Z}_p(t) \end{array}\right]
+ \left[\begin{array}{c} \mathbf{Q}' \\ \mathbf{N}' \end{array}\right] \mathbf{Z}_s(t)
+ \left[\begin{array}{c} \mathbf{F}_1'(t) \\ \mathbf{F}_2'(t) \end{array}\right] = \mathbf{0}
$$

and the alternative statement of Theorem 8.11.1 is as follows.

Theorem 8.11.1a:† Consider a system of $\mathbf{K}$ multiterminal components having a connected graph G with e edges and v vertices. If a unique solution exists for all system variables, then there exist a tree T_1 and a tree T_2 in the system graph for which the direct sum of the state equations for

---

† The authors are indebted to Henry Williams for the modified form of the theorem and its proof.

the K components can be written in the form

$$
\begin{aligned}
\mathbf{C}\dot{\boldsymbol{\Psi}}(t) &= \mathbf{P}\boldsymbol{\Psi}(t) + \mathbf{Q}'\mathbf{Z}_s(t) + \mathbf{F}_1(t) \\
\mathbf{Z}_p(t) &= \mathbf{D}\boldsymbol{\Psi}(t) + \mathbf{M}'\boldsymbol{\Psi}(t) + \mathbf{N}'\mathbf{Z}_s(t) + \mathbf{F}_2(t)
\end{aligned}
\tag{8.11.8}
$$

where

  (a)   The matrix $\lambda\mathbf{C} - \mathbf{P}$ is nonsingular.
  (b)   The components of the vectors $\mathbf{X}_1(t)$ and $\mathbf{Y}_2(t)$ of the vector $\mathbf{Z}_p(t) = [\mathbf{X}_1(t),\ \mathbf{Y}_2(t)]$ correspond, respectively, to edges in T_1 and edges in the complement of T_2.
  (c)   The vector $\mathbf{Z}_s(t) = [\mathbf{Y}_1(t),\ \mathbf{X}_2(t)]$ is the complement of $\mathbf{Z}_p(t)$.

It should be noted that the fact that $\lambda\mathbf{C} - \mathbf{P}$ is nonsingular does not imply that $\mathbf{C}$ or $\mathbf{P}$ is of maximum rank. If the rank r of $\mathbf{C}$ is less than n, then, by elementary row operations, $n - r$ rows of zeros can be introduced into the $\mathbf{C}$ matrix of Eqs. (8.11.8) and $n - r$ of the state equations degenerate to algebraic equations. Thus the theorem also establishes an upper bound on the order of the system state vector.

Still another form of the fundamental existence theorem is obtained by taking the Laplace transform of Eqs. (8.11.8). The result for zero initial conditions is

$$
\begin{aligned}
(s\mathbf{C} - \mathbf{P})\boldsymbol{\Psi}(s) &= \mathbf{Q}'\mathbf{Z}_s(s) + \mathbf{F}_1(s) \\
\mathbf{Z}_p(s) &= (s\mathbf{D} + \mathbf{M}')\boldsymbol{\Psi}(s) + \mathbf{N}'\mathbf{Z}_s(s) + \mathbf{F}_2(s)
\end{aligned}
\tag{8.11.9}
$$

If the determinant of the matrix $s\mathbf{C} - \mathbf{P}$ is not identically equal to zero as required in Theorem 8.11.1a, then the direct sum of the s-domain models (zero initial conditions) for the system components given in Eqs. (8.11.9) reduces to

$$
\mathbf{Z}_p(s) = [(s\mathbf{D} + \mathbf{M}')(s\mathbf{C} - \mathbf{P})^{-1}\mathbf{Q}' + \mathbf{N}']\mathbf{Z}_s(s) + \mathbf{F}(s)
$$

where

$$
\mathbf{F}(s) = (s\mathbf{D} + \mathbf{M}')(s\mathbf{C} - \mathbf{P})^{-1}\mathbf{F}_1(s) + \mathbf{F}_2(s)
$$

A third form of Theorem 8.11.1 can therefore be stated as follows.

Theorem 8.11.1b:[†]   If a linear time-invariant system having a graph G with e edges has a complete and unique solution for all $2e$ variables corresponding to the edges of the graph, then there exist a tree (forest) T_1 and a tree (forest) T_2 (T_1 may be the same as T_2) in G such that the direct sum of the s-domain component terminal equations can be written in the form

$$
\begin{bmatrix} \mathbf{X}_{b_1}(s) \\ \mathbf{Y}_{c_2}(s) \end{bmatrix} = \begin{bmatrix} \mathbf{H}_{11}(s) & \mathbf{H}_{12}(s) \\ \mathbf{H}_{21}(s) & \mathbf{H}_{22}(s) \end{bmatrix} \begin{bmatrix} \mathbf{Y}_{b_2}(s) \\ \mathbf{X}_{c_1}(s) \end{bmatrix} + \begin{bmatrix} \mathbf{F}_b(s) \\ \mathbf{F}_c(s) \end{bmatrix}
\tag{8.11.10}
$$

† This theorem was given originally by J. L. Wirth.[6]

where the vectors $\mathbf{X}_{b_1}(s)$ and $\mathbf{X}_{c_1}(s)$ correspond, respectively, to the edges of T_1 and its complement and the vectors $\mathbf{Y}_{b_2}(s)$ and $\mathbf{Y}_{c_2}(s)$ correspond, respectively, to the edges of T_2 and its complement.

To conclude from the above theorem that a given system has no solution, it is necessary to show that there are no two trees T_1 and T_2 for which the s-domain component equations can be written in the form of Eq. (8.11.10).

Example 8.11.1: Investigate the existence of a solution to the mechanical system shown in Fig. 8.11.1 when the two levers are considered as perfect couplers and $\delta_1(t) = \Delta_1$.

Solution: Let the direct sum of the terminal equations for the edges of the system graph indicated in Fig. 8.11.1b be written in the form

$$
\begin{bmatrix}
1 & 0 & 0 & & & & & & \\
0 & -K_2 & 0 & & & & & & \\
0 & 0 & -K_8 & & & & & & \\
& & & 1 & n_{34} & & & & \\
& & & 0 & 0 & & & & \\
& & & & & 0 & 0 & 0 & \\
& & & & & -n_{65} & 1 & 0 & \\
& & & & & n_{75} & 0 & 1 &
\end{bmatrix}
\begin{bmatrix}
\delta_1(t) \\
\delta_2(t) \\
\delta_8(t) \\
\hline
\delta_3(t) \\
\delta_4(t) \\
\hline
\delta_5(t) \\
\delta_6(t) \\
\delta_7(t)
\end{bmatrix}
$$

$$
+
\begin{bmatrix}
0 & 0 & 0 & & & & & & \\
0 & 1 & 0 & & & & & & \\
0 & 0 & 1 & & & & & & \\
& & & 0 & 0 & & & & \\
& & & -n_{34} & 1 & & & & \\
& & & & & 1 & n_{65} & -n_{76} & \\
& & & & & 0 & 0 & 0 & \\
& & & & & 0 & 0 & 0 &
\end{bmatrix}
\begin{bmatrix}
f_1(t) \\
f_2(t) \\
f_8(t) \\
\hline
f_3(t) \\
f_4(t) \\
\hline
f_5(t) \\
f_6(t) \\
f_7(t)
\end{bmatrix}
+
\begin{bmatrix}
-\Delta_1 \\
0 \\
0 \\
\hline
0 \\
0 \\
\hline
0 \\
0 \\
0
\end{bmatrix}
= 0 \quad (8.11.11)
$$

where the second row block corresponds to the three-terminal lever and the last row block to the four-terminal lever.

Since the system graph contains five vertices, eight edges, and one part, it follows from the above theorem that the system has a complete solution only if (1) $v - 1 = 4$ columns in the coefficient matrix of the displacement vector are linearly independent and correspond to a tree and (2) $e - v + 1 + 4$ columns in the coefficient matrix of the force vector are linearly independent and correspond to a cotree.

The rank of the first coefficient matrix is 6, and the columns corresponding to the tree $T_1 = (1,2,8,3)$ are linearly independent. The rank of the second coefficient matrix is 4, and the columns corresponding to the complement of the tree $T_2 = (1,4,6,7)$ are linearly independent.

There are in this example other trees and cotrees corresponding to linearly independent columns in the given coefficient matrices. In fact, the columns of the first coefficient matrix corresponding to $T_2 = (1,4,6,7)$ are also linearly independent; i.e., the existence theorem is satisfied for $T_1 = T_2$.

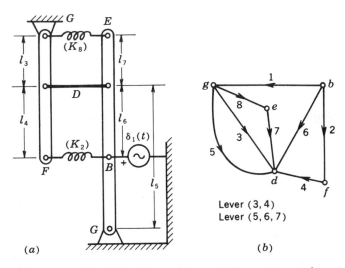

Fig. 8.11.1 (a) Typical lever system; (b) the system graph.

Practical application of one of the three forms of Theorem 8.11.1 depends critically on the procedure for identifying, in the graph, a tree (or possibly two trees) satisfying the hypothesis of the theorem. The following corollaries to the main theorem establish criteria for limiting the candidate trees to certain classes and thereby provide a practical basis for effective use of the existence theorem.

Corollary 8.11.1: A linear time-invariant system has a unique solution only if the edges of the system graph corresponding to across drivers and through drivers can be included as branches and chords, respectively, of a tree T in the system graph.

Proof: The proof follows directly from the fact that the coefficient matrix in Eq. (8.11.10) has a row of zeros for each across and through driver.

The properties of the coefficient matrix in Eq. (8.11.10) establish the following corollaries.

Corollary 8.11.2: If a system contains an N-port perfect coupler with terminal equations of the form

$$
\begin{bmatrix} x_1(t) \\ \cdots \\ x_{N-1}(t) \\ \hline y_N(t) \end{bmatrix} = \begin{bmatrix} 0 & \cdots & 0 & \vdots & k_1 \\ \cdots \cdots \cdots \cdots \cdots \cdots \\ 0 & \cdots & 0 & \vdots & k_{N-1} \\ \hline -k_1 & \cdots & -k_{N-1} & \vdots & 0 \end{bmatrix} \begin{bmatrix} y_1(t) \\ \cdots \\ y_{N-1}(t) \\ \hline x_N(t) \end{bmatrix}
$$

then a solution exists only if one set of $N - 1$ edges corresponding to the perfect coupler can be included in a tree T_1 (along with across drivers and certain other edges) and if the remaining edge can be included in the complement of a tree T_2 (with the specified through drivers and certain other edges). Further, there is no loss in generality by taking $T_1 = T_2$.

Corollary 8.11.3: If a system contains a two-port gyrator with terminal equations of the form

$$\begin{bmatrix} y_1(t) \\ y_2(t) \end{bmatrix} = \begin{bmatrix} 0 & k \\ -k & 0 \end{bmatrix} \begin{bmatrix} x_1(t) \\ x_2(t) \end{bmatrix}$$

then the system has a solution only if:

    (a) Both edges corresponding to the gyrator can be included in some tree T_1; or

    (b) Both edges can be included in the complement of a tree T_2; or

    (c) One edge is included in some tree T_1 and also in the complement of tree T_2.

The following example demonstrates the application of the preceding corollaries in developing a state model of subassemblies.

Example 8.11.2: The mechanical subassembly shown in Fig. 8.11.2a is to be connected to other components at terminals E, D, B and the inertia reference G. Develop a state model of this subassembly as a four-terminal component, and discuss the existence of a solution for an arbitrary set of terminal excitations.

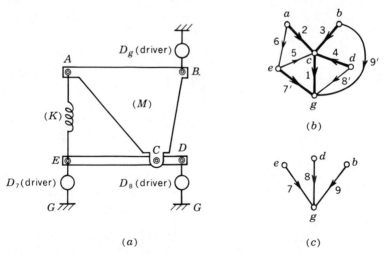

Fig. 8.11.2 *(a)* Mechanical subassembly; *(b)* system graph; *(c)* terminal graph of a four-terminal component.

Solution: The system graph, including the tree of edges corresponding to the external variables, is shown in Fig. 8.11.2b.   The mathematical models of the various components in the system are taken as follows:

Four-terminal rigid body: edges 1, 2, 3 and terminal equations

$$\begin{bmatrix} f_1(t) \\ f_2(t) \\ v_3(t) \end{bmatrix} = \begin{bmatrix} M_{11}(d/dt) & M_{12}(d/dt) & 0 \\ M_{12}(d/dt) & M_{22}(d/dt) & k_{23} \\ 0 & -k_{23} & 0 \end{bmatrix} \begin{bmatrix} v_1(t) \\ v_2(t) \\ f_3(t) \end{bmatrix}$$

or

$$\frac{d}{dt}\begin{bmatrix} \psi_1(t) \\ \psi_2(t) \end{bmatrix} = \begin{bmatrix} 0 & 0 \\ 0 & 0 \end{bmatrix}\begin{bmatrix} \psi_1(t) \\ \psi_2(t) \end{bmatrix} + \begin{bmatrix} \beta_{11} & \beta_{12} & \beta_{13} \\ \beta_{21} & \beta_{22} & \beta_{23} \end{bmatrix}\begin{bmatrix} f_1(t) \\ f_2(t) \\ f_3(t) \end{bmatrix}$$

$$\begin{bmatrix} \delta_1(t) \\ \delta_2(t) \\ \delta_3(t) \end{bmatrix} = \begin{bmatrix} 1 & 0 \\ 0 & 1 \\ 0 & -k_{23} \end{bmatrix}\begin{bmatrix} \psi_1(t) \\ \psi_2(t) \end{bmatrix} + \begin{bmatrix} 0 & 0 & 0 \\ 0 & 0 & 0 \\ 0 & 0 & 0 \end{bmatrix}\begin{bmatrix} f_1(t) \\ f_2(t) \\ f_3(t) \end{bmatrix}$$

(8.11.12)

Ideal lever: edges 4, 5 and terminal equations

$$\begin{bmatrix} \delta_4(t) \\ f_5(t) \end{bmatrix} = \begin{bmatrix} 0 & -k_{45} \\ k_{45} & 0 \end{bmatrix}\begin{bmatrix} f_4(t) \\ \delta_5(t) \end{bmatrix}$$

(8.11.13)

Two-terminal spring: edge 6 and terminal equation

$$\frac{d}{dt} f_6(t) = K\delta_6(t)$$

(8.11.14)

From Corollary 8.11.2 and the form of Eq. (8.11.13) it follows immediately that either edge 4 or edge 5, but not both, must be contained in some tree. From the form of Eqs. (8.11.12) to (8.11.14) it follows that the state vector of the system is of maximum order 3 if edges 1, 2, 3, and 4 *or* 5 can be included in some tree and edges 6 and 5 or 4 in a cotree.   Such a tree, called a *maximally selected tree,* is indicated by the heavy lines in Fig. 8.11.2b.   Since this tree includes edge 7′ as a branch and edges 8′ and 9′ as chords, the independent variables in the state model are $\dot{\delta}_{7'}(t)$ and $f_{8'}(t)$ and $f_{9'}(t)$.   It is also possible to select $\dot{\delta}_{8'}(t)$, $f_{7'}(t)$, and $f_{9'}(t)$ as the independent variables, since edges 1, 2, 3, 5, 8′ and edges 4, 6, 7′, 9′, respectively, represent a maximally selected tree and cotree.   There are, however, no other choices if *one* formulation tree is used.

After all secondary variables for the tree indicated in Fig. 8.11.2b are eliminated from the component terminal equations, their direct sum can be written as

$$\frac{d}{dt}\begin{bmatrix} \delta_1(t) \\ \delta_2(t) \\ f_6(t) \end{bmatrix} = \begin{bmatrix} 0 & 0 & -(\beta_{11}+\beta_{12}) \\ 0 & 0 & -(\beta_{21}+\beta_{22}) \\ K & K & 0 \end{bmatrix}\begin{bmatrix} \delta_1(t) \\ \delta_2(t) \\ f_6(t) \end{bmatrix} + \begin{bmatrix} 0 & -\beta_{11} & -(\beta_{11}+\beta_{13}) \\ 0 & -\beta_{21} & -(\beta_{21}+\beta_{23}) \\ -K & 0 & 0 \end{bmatrix}$$

$$\times \begin{bmatrix} \dot{\delta}_{7'}(t) \\ f_{8'}(t) \\ f_{9'}(t) \end{bmatrix} + \begin{bmatrix} \beta_{11} \\ \beta_{21} \\ 0 \end{bmatrix} f_5(t) \quad (8.11.15)$$

$$\begin{bmatrix} 0 & k_{23} & 1 & 0 & 0 \\ -k_{45} & 0 & 0 & 1 & 0 \\ 0 & 0 & 0 & 0 & 1 \end{bmatrix}\begin{bmatrix} \dot{\delta}_1(t) \\ \delta_2(t) \\ \delta_3(t) \\ \delta_4(t) \\ f_5(t) \end{bmatrix} = \begin{bmatrix} 0 & 0 & 0 \\ -k_{45} & 0 & 0 \\ 0 & -k_{45} & 0 \end{bmatrix}\begin{bmatrix} \dot{\delta}_{7'}(t) \\ f_{8'}(t) \\ f_{9'}(t) \end{bmatrix}$$

(8.11.16)

From the fundamental circuit and cut-set equations of the system graph, the complement of the excitation vector is related to the primary variables in Eqs. (8.11.15) and (8.11.16) by

$$
\begin{bmatrix} f_{7'}(t) \\ \dot{\delta}_{8'}(t) \\ \dot{\delta}_{9'}(t) \end{bmatrix} = \begin{bmatrix} 0 & 0 & 1 \\ 1 & 0 & 0 \\ 1 & 0 & 0 \end{bmatrix} \begin{bmatrix} \dot{\delta}_1(t) \\ \dot{\delta}_2(t) \\ f_6(t) \end{bmatrix} + \begin{bmatrix} 0 & 0 & -1 \\ 0 & 1 & 0 \\ 1 & 0 & 0 \end{bmatrix} \begin{bmatrix} \dot{\delta}_3(t) \\ \dot{\delta}_4(t) \\ f_5(t) \end{bmatrix}
\tag{8.11.17}
$$

The state model is obtained by simply solving Eq. (8.11.16) for the vector $(\dot{\delta}_3, \dot{\delta}_4, f_5)$ and substituting the result into Eqs. (8.11.15) and (8.11.17). The result is

$$
\frac{d}{dt} \begin{bmatrix} \dot{\delta}_1(t) \\ \dot{\delta}_2(t) \\ f_6(t) \end{bmatrix} = \begin{bmatrix} 0 & 0 & -(\beta_{11} + \beta_{12}) \\ 0 & 0 & -(\beta_{21} + \beta_{22}) \\ K & K & 0 \end{bmatrix} \begin{bmatrix} \dot{\delta}_1(t) \\ \dot{\delta}_2(t) \\ f_6(t) \end{bmatrix}
$$

$$
+ \begin{bmatrix} 0 & (1 + k_{45})\beta_{11} & \beta_{11} + \beta_{13} \\ 0 & (1 + k_{45})\beta_{21} & \beta_{21} + \beta_{23} \\ -K & 0 & 0 \end{bmatrix} \begin{bmatrix} \dot{\delta}_7(t) \\ f_8(t) \\ f_9(t) \end{bmatrix}
\tag{8.11.18}
$$

$$
\begin{bmatrix} f_7(t) \\ \dot{\delta}_8(t) \\ \dot{\delta}_9(t) \end{bmatrix} = \begin{bmatrix} 0 & 0 & -1 \\ 1 + k_{23} & 0 & 0 \\ -1 & -k_{23} & 0 \end{bmatrix} \begin{bmatrix} \dot{\delta}_1(t) \\ \dot{\delta}_2(t) \\ f_6(t) \end{bmatrix} + \begin{bmatrix} 0 & k_{45} & 0 \\ -k_{45} & 0 & 0 \\ 0 & 0 & 0 \end{bmatrix} \begin{bmatrix} \dot{\delta}_7(t) \\ f_8(t) \\ f_9(t) \end{bmatrix}
$$

$$
\tag{8.11.19}
$$

where the excitation and response vectors have been replaced by the terminal vectors, i.e.,

$$
\begin{bmatrix} \dot{\delta}_{7'}(t) \\ f_{8'}(t) \\ f_{9'}(t) \end{bmatrix} = \begin{bmatrix} \dot{\delta}_7(t) \\ -f_8(t) \\ -f_9(t) \end{bmatrix} \quad \text{and} \quad \begin{bmatrix} f_{7'}(t) \\ \dot{\delta}_{8'}(t) \\ \dot{\delta}_{9'}(t) \end{bmatrix} = \begin{bmatrix} -f_7(t) \\ \dot{\delta}_8(t) \\ \dot{\delta}_9(t) \end{bmatrix}
$$

Symbolically, the result is a state model of the form

$$
\frac{d}{dt} \boldsymbol{\Psi}(t) = \mathbf{P}\boldsymbol{\Psi}(t) + \mathbf{Q}\mathbf{Z}_i(t)
$$

$$
\mathbf{Z}_0(t) = \mathbf{C}\boldsymbol{\Psi}(t) + \mathbf{D}\mathbf{Z}_i(t)
$$

It is evident that the first two expressions in Eq. (8.11.19) can be inverted to establish a model in which the independent variables are $f_7(t)$, $\dot{\delta}_8(t)$, $f_9(t)$. This form is consistent with the form that would have resulted if the formulation tree had been taken as (1,2,3,5,8'). The other two possible forms include $\dot{\delta}_8(t)$, $f_8(t)$, $f_9(t)$ and $\dot{\delta}_7(t)$, $f_7(t)$, $f_9(t)$ as the independent variables. However, these latter two forms can be derived directly only by using one tree for writing the circuit equations and a second tree for writing the cut-set equations.

Finally, it should be noted that the above discussion does not imply that the system has no solution when $\dot{\delta}_7(t)$, $f_8(t)$, and $\dot{\delta}_9(t)$, for example, are specified functions of time. In fact, if $\dot{\delta}_9(t)$ is a known function of time, then from the last expression in Eq. (8.11.19)

$$\dot{\delta}_1(t) = -\dot{\delta}_9(t) - k_{23}\dot{\delta}_2(t) \tag{8.11.20}$$

and

$$\frac{d}{dt}\begin{bmatrix} -k_{23}\ \dot{\delta}_2(t) \\ 0 \quad \dot{\delta}_2(t) \\ 0 \quad f_6(t) \end{bmatrix} = \begin{bmatrix} 0 & -(\beta_{11}+\beta_{12}) \\ 0 & -(\beta_{12}+\beta_{22}) \\ K(1-k_{23}) & 0 \end{bmatrix}\begin{bmatrix} \dot{\delta}_2(t) \\ f_6(t) \end{bmatrix}$$

$$+ \begin{bmatrix} 0 & (1+k_{45})\beta_{11} & \beta_{11}+\beta_{13} \\ 0 & (1+k_{45})\beta_{21} & \beta_{21}+\beta_{23} \\ -K & 0 & 0 \end{bmatrix}\begin{bmatrix} \dot{\delta}_7(t) \\ f_8(t) \\ f_9(t) \end{bmatrix} + \begin{bmatrix} 0 \\ 0 \\ -K \end{bmatrix}\dot{\delta}_9(t) + \begin{bmatrix} 1 \\ 0 \\ 0 \end{bmatrix}\frac{d}{dt}\dot{\delta}_9(t)$$

$$\tag{8.11.21}$$

When the second row in Eq. (8.11.21) is multiplied by k_{23} and added to the first row, one of the differential equations reduces to an algebraic equation, which when solved for $f_9(t)$ gives a system model of the form

$$\begin{bmatrix} \dot{\delta}_2(t) \\ f_6(t) \end{bmatrix} = \begin{bmatrix} p_{11} & p_{12} \\ p_{21} & p_{22} \end{bmatrix}\begin{bmatrix} \dot{\delta}_2(t) \\ f_6(t) \end{bmatrix} + \begin{bmatrix} q_{11} & q_{12} & q_{13} \\ q_{21} & q_{22} & q_{23} \end{bmatrix}\begin{bmatrix} \dot{\delta}_7(t) \\ f_8(t) \\ \dot{\delta}_9(t) \end{bmatrix} + \begin{bmatrix} \alpha_1 \\ \alpha_2 \end{bmatrix}\frac{d}{dt}\dot{\delta}_9(t)$$

$$\tag{8.11.22}$$

$$\begin{bmatrix} f_7(t) \\ \dot{\delta}_8(t) \\ f_9(t) \end{bmatrix} = \begin{bmatrix} c_{11} & c_{12} \\ c_{21} & c_{22} \\ c_{31} & c_{32} \end{bmatrix}\begin{bmatrix} \dot{\delta}_2(t) \\ f_6(t) \end{bmatrix} + \begin{bmatrix} \tau_{11} & \tau_{12} & \tau_{13} \\ \tau_{21} & \tau_{22} & \tau_{23} \\ \tau_{31} & \tau_{32} & \tau_{33} \end{bmatrix}\begin{bmatrix} \dot{\delta}_7(t) \\ f_8(t) \\ \dot{\delta}_9(t) \end{bmatrix} + \begin{bmatrix} 0 \\ 0 \\ 0_3 \end{bmatrix}\frac{d}{dt}\dot{\delta}_9(t)$$

where the numerical values of the coefficients are functions of the coefficients in Eq. (8.11.21).

Clearly, if $\dot{\delta}_9(t)$, $f_8(t)$, and $\dot{\delta}_7(t)$ are given functions of time and $(d/dt)\dot{\delta}_9(t)$ is defined over some interval I, then Eqs. (8.11.22) have a solution in I. However, as already emphasized in this chapter, Eqs. (8.11.22) are not regarded as a state model of the subassembly, since it calls for the time derivative of one of the independent variables.

If $G = G_s \cup G_t$ represents the union of the system graph G_s and the terminal graph G_t, then, as the above example demonstrates, a suitable set of independent variables for a state model can be found as follows: Select, in G, trees T_1 and T_2 (take $T_1 = T_2$ if possible) for which the terminal equations for G_s are consistent with Theorem 8.11.1 or 8.11.1b and such that the order of the state vector in the direct sum of the component terminal equations is maximum. Such a pair of trees has already been referred to as being *maximally* selected. The across variables corresponding to those edges of G_2 that are contained in T_1 and the through variables corresponding to those edges of G_t contained in the complement of T_2 constitute an independent set of variables for a state model. If there are no trees T_1 and T_2 in G satisfying the hypothesis either of Theorem 8.11.1 or of Theorem 8.11.1b, then the subassembly cannot be represented by a state model or, equivalently, the system does not have a complete and unique solution for any mode of terminal excitation.

PROBLEMS

8.1   Derive the three-terminal model of the transistor amplifier shown in Fig. P8.1. The h parameters of the identical common-emitter transistors are to be taken as $h_{11} = h_{12} = h_{22} = 0$, $h_{21} = h$.

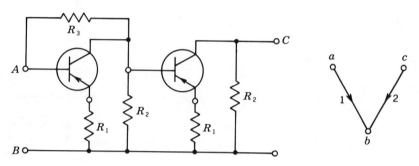

Fig. P8.1

8.2   Derive the two-terminal representation of the network containing a three-terminal gyrator shown in Fig. P8.2a. The terminal equations of the gyrator, corresponding to the terminal graph indicated in Fig. P8.2b, are given as

$$\begin{bmatrix} i_1(s) \\ i_2(s) \end{bmatrix} = \begin{bmatrix} 0 & -1 \\ 1 & 0 \end{bmatrix} \begin{bmatrix} v_1(s) \\ v_2(s) \end{bmatrix}$$

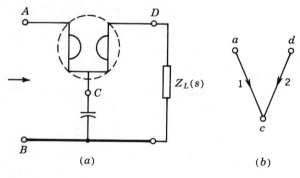

Fig. P8.2

8.3   Derive a three-terminal representation of the system in Fig. P8.3 having the terminals ABG. The terminal equations of the pistons are of the form

$$\begin{bmatrix} f(s) \\ g(s) \end{bmatrix} = \begin{bmatrix} Ms^2 + Bs & A \\ -A & 0 \end{bmatrix} \begin{bmatrix} \delta(s) \\ p(s) \end{bmatrix}$$

Observe that the three-terminal mechanical component is a lever. Indicate the fictitious pivotal point of this lever.

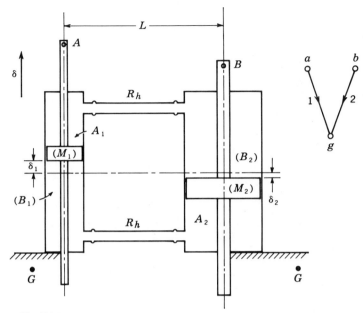

Fig. P8.3

8.4 Show that two four-terminal components are identical if their characteristics are given by the terminal graphs of Fig. P8.4a and b and the respective equations

$$\begin{bmatrix} y_1(t) \\ y_2(t) \\ y_3(t) \end{bmatrix} = \begin{bmatrix} 3 & 2 & -1 \\ 2 & 4 & -1 \\ -1 & -1 & 2 \end{bmatrix} \begin{bmatrix} x_1(t) \\ x_2(t) \\ x_3(t) \end{bmatrix}$$

and

$$\begin{bmatrix} y_1(t) \\ y_2(t) \\ y_3(t) \end{bmatrix} = \begin{bmatrix} 5 & 3 & 3 \\ 3 & 3 & 2 \\ 3 & 2 & 4 \end{bmatrix} \begin{bmatrix} x_1(t) \\ x_2(t) \\ x_3(t) \end{bmatrix}$$

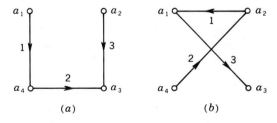

Fig. P8.4

8.5   Derive a three-terminal representation of the various combinations of two triodes.   The terminals are indicated in Fig. P8.5 by the small circles.

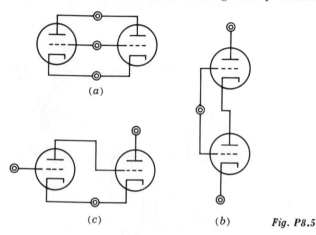

Fig. P8.5

8.6   The terminal equations of a transistor corresponding to the terminal graph (common-emitter connection) in Fig. P8.6a are given as

$$\begin{bmatrix} v_1(t) \\ v_2(t) \end{bmatrix} = \begin{bmatrix} r_{11} & r_{12} \\ r_{21} & r_{22} \end{bmatrix} \begin{bmatrix} i_1(t) \\ i_2(t) \end{bmatrix}$$

Obtain the terminal equations for the other representations of the transistor by the tree-transformation techniques.   These new equations will correspond to the terminal graphs indicated in Fig. P8.6b and c, which are called *common-base* and *common-collector connections*.

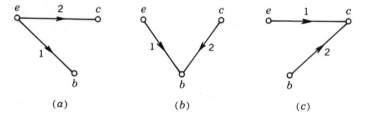

Fig. P8.6

8.7   The terminal equations of the gearbox in Fig. P8.7a corresponding to the Lagrangian terminal graph indicated in Fig. P8.7b are given as

$$\begin{bmatrix} \phi_1(s) \\ \phi_2(s) \\ \tau_3(s) \end{bmatrix} = \begin{bmatrix} 0 & 0 & -n_1 \\ 0 & 0 & -n_2 \\ n_1 & n_2 & Js^2 + Bs \end{bmatrix} \begin{bmatrix} \tau_1(s) \\ \tau_2(s) \\ \phi_3(s) \end{bmatrix}$$

By means of a tree transformation, obtain the terminal equations of the gearbox corresponding to the terminal graph in Fig. P8.7c.

8.8   Obtain a three-terminal representation of the electronic circuit shown in Fig. P8.8a corresponding to the terminal graph indicated in Fig. P8.8b.   Solve this problem in terms of the parallel-connected multiterminal components indicated in

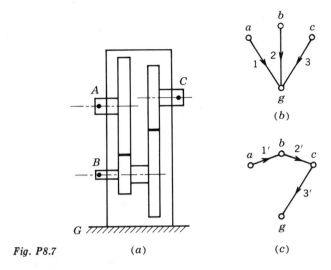

Fig. P8.7   (a)   (c)

Fig. P8.8c. (*Note:* First obtain a terminal representation of each component corresponding to an identical terminal graph, possibly taken as a Lagrangian tree; then proceed with the technique discussed in Example 8.3.1.)

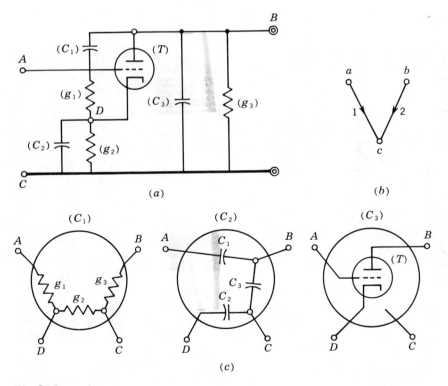

Fig. P8.8

8.9   Obtain the no-load transfer function $E_2(s)/E_1(s)$ of the amplifier circuit shown in Fig. P8.9.   First derive the cascade parameters for each of the three-terminal components which are connected in cascade to form the circuit.

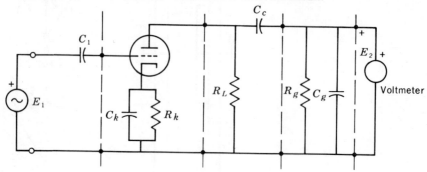

Fig. P8.9

8.10   The $\mu(s)\beta(s)$ functions for some physical systems are given as follows:

(a) $\mu(s)\beta(s) = \dfrac{K}{s^2(1 + \tau s)} \qquad \tau > 0$

(b) $\mu(s)\beta(s) = \dfrac{K(1 + \tau_1 s)}{(1 + \tau_2 s)(1 + \tau_3 s)} \qquad \tau_1 > \tau_2 > \tau_3 > 0$

(c) $\mu(s)\beta(s) = \dfrac{K(1 + \frac{10}{3}s)}{s(1 + s)(1 + s/20)(1 + s/50)}$

Investigate the stabilities of these systems in terms of the Nyquist stability criterion. (Show the sketch of the mapping of the Nyquist path for each case separately.)

8.11   Plot Nyquist diagrams for the following $\mu(s)\beta(s)$ functions:

(a) $\mu(s)\beta(s) = \dfrac{K(1 + s/5)(1 + s/40)}{s^3(1 + s/200)(1 + s/1{,}000)} \qquad K > 0$

(b) $\mu(s)\beta(s) = \dfrac{K}{s(1 + s)(1 + 2s)(1 + 3s)} \qquad K > 0$

8.12   Determine the gain margin for a feedback system characterized by the function

$$\mu(s)\beta(s) = \frac{K}{s(1 + \tau_1 s)(1 + \tau_2 s)}$$

[*Hint:* First, determine the frequency ω_c for which the imaginary part of $\mu(j\omega)\beta(j\omega)$ vanishes.]

8.13   (a)   Draw a block diagram and a signal-flow diagram for the system given in Fig. 8.8.4.

(b)   By using the rules given in Tables 8.8.1 and 8.8.2, reduce the diagrams of part a to their simplest form indicating the input-output relation.

8.14   By application of Theorem 8.11.1 to the two-port network given in Fig. P8.14 determine which forms of the state model are possible.   Determine your answer directly from the system graph before deriving the equations.

8.15   Derive a three-terminal state-model representation for the mechanical system shown in Fig. P8.15.   Assume that the pulley has inertia and damping coefficients.   The weights of the mass components M_1 and M_2 are also to be taken into consideration.

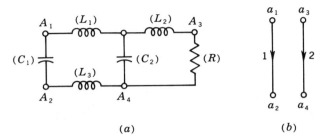

(a)   (b)

Fig. P8.14

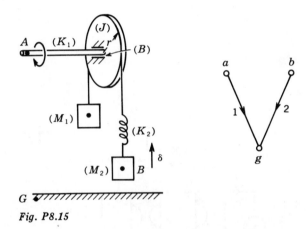

Fig. P8.15

8.16   The voltage-regulated d-c generator system in Fig. P8.16a is to be considered as two series-parallel-connected two-port components which are indicated by the dashed frames.   Write the state-model equations for each two-port component, and then obtain the two-port representation of this system corresponding to the indicated terminal graph in Fig. P8.16b.

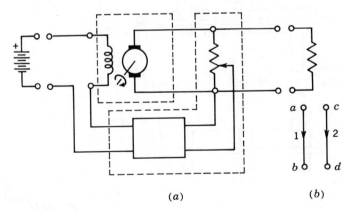

(a)   (b)

Fig. P8.16

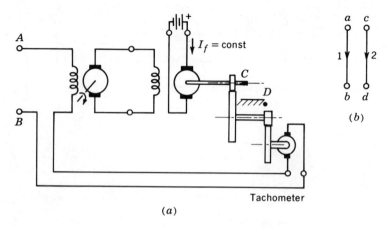

Fig. P8.17

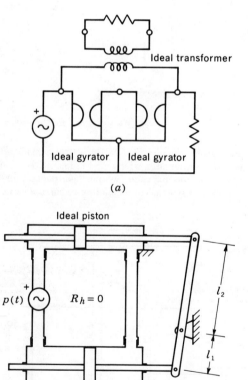

Fig. P8.18

8.17   Repeat Prob. 8.16 for the speed-control system given in Fig. P8.17a.

8.18   By using Corollaries 8.11.2 and 8.11.3, determine whether or not the systems in Fig. P8.18a and b satisfy the necessary conditions for a solution.   If the conditions are satisfied, obtain the solutions for the through variables associated with the across drivers.

8.19   Let the state-model equations of a system be given as

$$\frac{d}{dt}\begin{bmatrix} \psi_1(t) \\ \psi_2(t) \end{bmatrix} = \begin{bmatrix} 0 & -10 \\ 1 & -7 \end{bmatrix}\begin{bmatrix} \psi_1(t) \\ \psi_2(t) \end{bmatrix} + \begin{bmatrix} e_1(t) \\ 0 \end{bmatrix}$$

where the driving function $e(t)$ is given as $e(t) = 10 \sin \omega t$.   Taking $t = nh$, derive a recursion formula relating $\psi_1[(n + 1)h]$ and $\psi_2[(n + 1)h]$ to $\psi_1(nh)$ and $\psi_2(nh)$ and $e(nh)$.

FURTHER READING

1.   Koenig, H. E., and W. A. Blackwell: "Electromechanical System Theory," McGraw-Hill Book Company, New York, 1961.

2.   Truxal, J. G.: "Automatic Feedback Control System Synthesis," McGraw-Hill Book Company, New York, 1955.

3.   Gille, J. C., et al.: "Feedback Control Systems," McGraw-Hill Book Company, New York, 1959.

4.   Nyquist, H.: Regeneration Theory, *Bell System Tech. J.*, vol. 11, pp. 126–247, 1932.

5.   Gantmacher, F. R.: "The Theory of Matrices," vol. 2, Chelsea Publishing Company, New York, 1959.

6.   Wirth, J. L.: "Time-domain Models of Physical Systems and Existence of Solutions," Ph.D. dissertation, Michigan State University, East Lansing, Mich., 1962.

Appendix

A.1 POSITIVE DEFINITE MATRICES

Definition A.1.1 *Linear form:* Let x_1, x_2, . . . , x_n be a set of real variables, and let a_1, a_2, . . . , a_n, a_{n+1} be a set of real constants. The expression

$$a_1x_1 + a_2x_2 + \cdots + a_nx_n + a_{n+1} \tag{A.1.1}$$

is called a *linear form*. If $a_{n+1} = 0$, the linear form is said to be *homogeneous*, with *norm*

$$N = (a_1{}^2 + a_2{}^2 + \cdots + a_n{}^2)^{1/2}$$

From the above definition, every linear form can be regarded as a linear function (in fact a polynomial) in n variables. The nonhomogeneous form in Eq. (A.1.1) can always be reduced to the homogeneous linear form by selecting a new set of variables y_i each of which differs from x_i by an additive constant.

Definition A.1.2 *Billinear and quadratic forms:* Let $\mathbf{X} = [x_i]_n$ and $\mathbf{Y} = [y_i]_n$ be column matrices (vectors) with real entries x_i and y_i, and let $\mathbf{A} = [a_{ij}]_n$ be a square matrix of order n with real entries. The expression

$$\mathbf{X}^T\mathbf{A}\mathbf{Y} = [x_1 \quad x_2 \quad \cdots \quad x_n] \begin{bmatrix} a_{11} & a_{12} & \cdots & a_{1n} \\ a_{21} & a_{22} & \cdots & a_{2n} \\ \cdots\cdots\cdots\cdots\cdots\cdots \\ a_{n1} & a_{n2} & \cdots & a_{nn} \end{bmatrix} \begin{bmatrix} y_1 \\ y_2 \\ \cdots \\ y_n \end{bmatrix}$$

$$= \sum_{i=1}^{n} \sum_{j=1}^{n} a_{ij}x_i y_j \tag{A.1.2}$$

is called a *bilinear form*. If $\mathbf{A}$ is the unit matrix, then the bilinear form reduces to

$$\mathbf{X}^T\mathbf{Y} = [x_1 \quad x_2 \quad \cdots \quad x_n] \begin{bmatrix} y_1 \\ y_2 \\ \cdot \\ \cdot \\ \cdot \\ y_n \end{bmatrix} = \sum_{i=1}^{n} x_i y_i$$

and is called the *scalar product* of the vectors $\mathbf{X}$ and $\mathbf{Y}$. If $\mathbf{X} = \mathbf{Y}$, the bilinear form reduces to

$$\mathbf{X}^T\mathbf{A}\mathbf{X} = \sum_{i=1}^{n} \sum_{j=1}^{n} a_{ij}x_i x_j \tag{A.1.3}$$

and is called a *quadratic form*.

In Eq. (A.1.3) $\mathbf{A}$ is an arbitrary square matrix. Any such matrix can be regarded as the sum of two unique square matrices of the same order, one of which is symmetric and the other skew-symmetric, i.e.,

$$\mathbf{A} = \tfrac{1}{2}(\mathbf{A} + \mathbf{A}^T) + \tfrac{1}{2}(\mathbf{A} - \mathbf{A}^T)$$
$$= \mathbf{B} + \mathbf{C} \tag{A.1.4}$$

where $\mathbf{B}$ is a symmetric matrix and $\mathbf{C}$ is skew-symmetric.

If we now substitute the relation for $\mathbf{A}$ given in Eq. (A.1.4) into the quadratic form given in Eq. (A.1.3), we have

$$\mathbf{X}^T\mathbf{A}\mathbf{X} = \mathbf{X}^T(\mathbf{B} + \mathbf{C})\mathbf{X} = \mathbf{X}^T\mathbf{B}\mathbf{X} + \mathbf{X}^T\mathbf{C}\mathbf{X} \tag{A.1.5}$$

But since $\mathbf{C}$ is a skew-symmetric matrix ($c_{ij} = -c_{ji}$), the second quadratic form in Eq. (A.1.5) vanishes identically and the quadratic form reduces to

$$\mathbf{X}^T\mathbf{A}\mathbf{X} = \mathbf{X}^T\mathbf{B}\mathbf{X} \tag{A.1.6}$$

Therefore, we conclude that the square matrix in the definition of the quadratic form given in Eq. (A.1.3) can always be regarded as a symmetric matrix.

Definition A.1.3: A quadratic form $X^T AX$ is said to be *positive definite* if for all nonvanishing vectors X

$$X^T AX > 0$$

If for all nonvanishing vectors

$$X^T AX \geq 0$$

the quadratic form is said to be *positive semidefinite.*

Example A.1.1: Show that the quadratic form

$$q = [x_1 \quad x_2] \begin{bmatrix} 2 & 1 \\ 1 & 3 \end{bmatrix} \begin{bmatrix} x_1 \\ x_2 \end{bmatrix} = 2x_1{}^2 + 2x_1 x_2 + 3x_2{}^2$$

is positive for all nonzero real values of x_1 and x_2.

Solution: Upon factoring $x_1{}^2$ from each term, q can be written as

$$q = x_1{}^2 \left[2 + 2\frac{x_2}{x_1} + 3\left(\frac{x_2}{x_1}\right)^2 \right]$$
$$= x_1{}^2(3\lambda^2 + 2\lambda + 2) \tag{A.1.7}$$

where $\lambda = x_2/x_1$. The value of the polynomial in λ is positive for all real values of λ, and we conclude that $q > 0$ except for $x_1 = x_2 = 0$; that is, q is a positive definite quadratic form.

Example A.1.2: Using the procedure indicated in the solution of Example A.1.1, investigate the quadratic form

$$q = 4x_1{}^2 + 4x_1 x_2 + x_2{}^2$$

Solution: Setting $\lambda = x_2/x_1$, we have

$$q = x_1{}^2(\lambda^2 + 4\lambda + 4)$$

The polynomial in λ has a double zero at $\lambda = -2$. That is, if we take

$$x_2 = -2x_1$$

then $q = 0$. However, for all real λ except $\lambda = -2$, we have $q > 0$, and we conclude that q is a positive semidefinite quadratic form, that is, $q \geq 0$ for all x_1, x_2.

Consider the real quadratic form

$$q = X^T AX \tag{A.1.8}$$

where A is a real symmetric matrix, and let Y be a vector (column matrix) related to the vector X by a nonsingular transformation

$$X = BY \tag{A.1.9}$$

that is, $\mathbf{B}$ is a nonsingular matrix. Substituting Eq. (A.1.9) into Eq. (A.1.8), we have

$$q = \mathbf{Y}^T(\mathbf{B}^T\mathbf{A}\mathbf{B})\mathbf{Y}$$

Let us assume for the present that the transformation matrix $\mathbf{B}$ can be selected such that

$$\mathbf{B}^T\mathbf{A}\mathbf{B} = \mathbf{D} = [d_i]_n$$

where $\mathbf{D}$ is a diagonal matrix. If such a transformation can be found, any quadratic form can be reduced to the equivalent quadratic form involving only the sum of the squares, i.e.,

$$q = \mathbf{Y}^T\mathbf{D}\mathbf{Y} = d_1y_1{}^2 + d_2y_2{}^2 + \cdots + d_ny_n{}^2 \tag{A.1.10}$$

From Eq. (A.1.10) it is evident that the quadratic form

$$q = \mathbf{X}^T\mathbf{A}\mathbf{X} = \mathbf{Y}^T\mathbf{D}\mathbf{Y} \tag{A.1.11}$$

is positive definite if and only if all the coefficients d_i ($i = 1, 2, \ldots, n$) are positive numbers; that is, $d_i > 0$ is both necessary and sufficient to make $q > 0$. This observation suggests that the square matrix $\mathbf{A}$ in Eq. (A.1.11) be defined as being positive definite if $q > 0$. More formally we have the following definition.

Definition A.1.4: Let $\mathbf{X}$ be an arbitrary nth-order vector, and let $\mathbf{A}$ be a real square matrix of order n. The matrix $\mathbf{A}$ is said to be *positive definite* if and only if for all $\mathbf{X} \neq 0$ the quadratic form

$$q = \mathbf{X}^T\mathbf{A}\mathbf{X} > 0$$

If for all $\mathbf{X} \neq 0$

$$q = \mathbf{X}^T\mathbf{A}\mathbf{X} \geq 0$$

then $\mathbf{A}$ is said to be *positive semidefinite*.

One method for testing to determine whether or not a given matrix is positive definite is to reduce the given quadratic form

$$q = \mathbf{X}^T\mathbf{A}\mathbf{X}$$

to the equivalent form given in Eq. (A.1.10).

The following theorems establish several of the important properties of positive definite matrices.

Theorem A.1.1: Let $\mathbf{A}$ be a real, symmetric, and positive definite matrix of order n; then $\mathbf{A}$ is nonsingular. Further, $|\mathbf{A}| > 0$.

Proof: Consider the positive definite quadratic form

$$q = \mathbf{X}^T\mathbf{A}\mathbf{X} = [b_1 \quad b_2 \quad \cdots \quad b_n] \begin{bmatrix} x_1 \\ x_2 \\ . \\ . \\ . \\ x_n \end{bmatrix} > 0 \tag{A.1.12}$$

where

$$b_i = x_1a_{1i} + x_2a_{2i} + \cdots + x_na_{ni} \tag{A.1.13}$$

Since $q > 0$ for every value of x_i except for all $x_i = 0$, the entries in the matrix $[b_1 \quad b_2 \quad \cdots \quad b_n]$ cannot all become zero; i.e., at least one b_i is different from zero. From Eq. (A.1.13) $(i = 1, 2, \ldots, n)$ it follows then that any linear combination of the rows of matrix $\mathbf{A}$ cannot vanish; i.e., the rows of $\mathbf{A}$ are linearly independent. This establishes that $\mathbf{A}$ is nonsingular.

To show that the determinant of $\mathbf{A}$ is positive, consider the nonsingular matrix $\mathbf{B}$ such that

$$\mathbf{B}^T\mathbf{A}\mathbf{B} = \mathbf{D}$$

where $\mathbf{D}$ is diagonal with all positive entries. Since all the matrices are nonsingular, we have

$$|\mathbf{B}^T| \, |\mathbf{A}| \, |\mathbf{B}| = |\mathbf{D}|$$

$$|\mathbf{A}| = \frac{|\mathbf{D}|}{|\mathbf{B}|^2} > 0$$

Theorem A.1.2: A real symmetric matrix $\mathbf{A}$ of order n is positive definite only if each principal minor of the corresponding determinant is positive.

Proof: Consider the quadratic form

$$q = \mathbf{X}^T\mathbf{A}\mathbf{X}$$

and the particular expansion resulting by taking

$$x_{i+1} = x_{i+2} = \cdots = x_n = 0 \qquad i \geq 1$$

Since $\mathbf{A}$ is positive definite, we have

$$q = [\mathbf{X}_1^T \quad 0] \begin{bmatrix} \mathbf{A}_{11} & \mathbf{A}_{12} \\ \mathbf{A}_{21} & \mathbf{A}_{22} \end{bmatrix} \begin{bmatrix} \mathbf{X}_1 \\ 0 \end{bmatrix} = \mathbf{X}_1^T\mathbf{A}_{11}\mathbf{X}_1 > 0$$

which implies that the principal submatrix $\mathbf{A}_{11}$ of $\mathbf{A}$ is positive definite. From Theorem A.1.1 we have $|\mathbf{A}_{11}| > 0$. Since the order of $\mathbf{A}_{11}$ is i and i is taken as an arbitrary positive integer, all principal determinants $(i = 1, 2, \ldots, n)$ of $\mathbf{A}$ are positive.

Theorem A.1.3:   Let $\mathbf{A}$ be a real symmetric and positive definite matrix, and let $\mathbf{B}$ be real and nonsingular.   Then

$$\mathbf{BAB}^T$$

is also a real symmetric positive definite matrix.

Proof: Consider the quadratic form

$$q = \mathbf{X}^T(\mathbf{BAB}^T)\mathbf{X} = (\mathbf{X}^T\mathbf{B})\mathbf{A}(\mathbf{X}^T\mathbf{B})^T$$

Let $\mathbf{Y} = \mathbf{BX}$.   Since $\mathbf{B}$ is nonsingular, there is a one-to-one correspondence between the matrices $\mathbf{Y}$ and $\mathbf{X}$.   Hence, from Definition A.1.4,

$$q = \mathbf{Y}^T\mathbf{AY} > 0$$

That is, $\mathbf{BAB}^T$ is positive definite.

Corollary A.1.1:   Let $\mathbf{B}$ be a real nonsingular matrix.   Then the matrix $\mathbf{BB}^T$ is symmetric and positive definite.

Proof: Since the unit matrix is positive definite, it is sufficient to take $\mathbf{A} = \mathbf{U}$ in Theorem A.1.3.

Theorem A.1.4:   Let $\mathbf{B}$ be a real matrix of order $b \times m$ $(b < m)$ of rank $r = b$, and let $\mathbf{R}$ be a symmetric and positive definite matrix; then the matrix

$$\mathbf{BRB}^T$$

is nonsingular.

Proof: Let $\mathbf{K}$ be a nonsingular matrix such that

$$\mathbf{BK} = [\mathbf{B}_1 \quad \mathbf{0}]$$

where $\mathbf{B}_1$ is a nonsingular matrix.   Therefore,

$$\mathbf{BRB}^T = \mathbf{BKK}^{-1}\mathbf{R}(\mathbf{K}^{-1})^T\mathbf{K}^T\mathbf{B} = [\mathbf{B}_1 \quad \mathbf{0}][\mathbf{PRP}^T]\begin{bmatrix} \mathbf{B}_1{}^T \\ \mathbf{0} \end{bmatrix}$$

where $\mathbf{P} = \mathbf{K}^{-1}$.   From Theorem A.1.3, $\mathbf{A} = \mathbf{PRP}^T$ is positive definite and symmetric.   Hence

$$\mathbf{BRB}^T = [\mathbf{B}_1 \quad \mathbf{0}]\begin{bmatrix} \mathbf{A}_{11} & \mathbf{A}_{12} \\ \mathbf{A}_{12}^T & \mathbf{A}_{22} \end{bmatrix}\begin{bmatrix} \mathbf{B}_1{}^T \\ \mathbf{0} \end{bmatrix} = \mathbf{B}_1\mathbf{A}_{11}\mathbf{B}_1{}^T$$

Since $\mathbf{A}$ is positive definite, so is $\mathbf{A}_{11}$.   Therefore, from Theorem A.1.3, $\mathbf{B}_1\mathbf{A}_{11}\mathbf{B}_1{}^T$, and hence $\mathbf{BRB}^T$ is positive definite and nonsingular.

Theorem A.1.5:   Let $\mathbf{S}$ be a real symmetric and positive definite matrix of order m and $\mathbf{B}$ a real matrix of order $b \times m$ $(b \leq m)$ and rank $r < b$.

Then the matrix

$$P = BSB^T$$

is positive semidefinite.

Proof: Following a proof similar to that of Theorem A.1.4, there exist two nonsingular matrices K and L such that

$$LBK = \begin{bmatrix} B_1 & 0 \\ 0 & 0 \end{bmatrix}$$

where B_1 is a nonsingular matrix. Therefore,

$$LBSB^TL^T = L \begin{bmatrix} B_1 & 0 \\ 0 & 0 \end{bmatrix} \begin{bmatrix} A_{11} & A_{12} \\ A_{12} & A_{22} \end{bmatrix} \begin{bmatrix} B_1^T & 0 \\ 0 & 0 \end{bmatrix} L^T$$

$$= L \begin{bmatrix} B_1 A_{11} B_1^T & 0 \\ 0 & 0 \end{bmatrix} L^T = LPL^T$$

where $A = K^{-1}S(K^{-1})^T$ and $B_1 A_{11} B_1^T$ is positive definite but P is semidefinite.

Note that, if $r = b$, Theorem A.1.5 reduces to Theorem A.1.4.

Example A.1.3: Let A be a real symmetric and positive semidefinite (or positive definite) matrix of order n. Show that the quadratic form

$$X^*AX$$

where X is a column matrix with complex entries, $x_i = \alpha_i + j\beta_i$, and X^* indicates its transposed conjugate, is real and positive semidefinite (positive definite).

Solution: The quadratic form can be written as

$$X^*AX = \sum_{p,q=1}^{n} \hat{x}_p \bar{x}_q a_{pq}$$

Since

$$\hat{x}_p \bar{x}_q = (\alpha_p - j\beta_p)(\alpha_q + j\beta_q) = (\alpha_p\alpha_q + \beta_p\beta_q) + j(\alpha_p\beta_q - \alpha_q\beta_p)$$

we have

$$X^*AX = \sum_{p,q=1}^{n} a_{pq}(\alpha_p\alpha_q + \beta_p\beta_q) + j \sum_{p,q=1}^{n} a_{pq}(\alpha_p\beta_q - \alpha_q\beta_q)$$

In this expression the imaginary part vanishes, since A is a symmetric matrix. Therefore, we have

$$X^*AX = \sum_{p,q=1}^{n} a_{pq}\alpha_p\alpha_q + \sum_{p,q=1}^{n} a_{pq}\beta_p\beta_q$$

Since each summation represents a real positive semidefinite (positive definite) quadratic form, the property follows.

A.2 EIGENVALUES AND EIGENVECTORS

Definition A.2.1:   Let $\mathbf{A}$ be a real square matrix of order n.   Then the polynomial in λ,

$$D(\lambda) = |\lambda\mathbf{U} - \mathbf{A}| = \lambda^n - p_1\lambda^{n-1} + p_2\lambda^{n-2} - \cdots + (-1)^n p_n$$
$$= (\lambda - \lambda_1)^{r_1}(\lambda - \lambda_2)^{r_2} \cdots (\lambda - \lambda_k)^{r_k} \qquad (\text{A.2.1})$$

is called the characteristic polynomial of $\mathbf{A}$, and its zeros, $\lambda_1, \lambda_2, \ldots, \lambda_2$, are called the *characteristic values*, or *eigenvalues*, of $\mathbf{A}$.

From the expansion of the determinant in Eq. (A.2.1), it can be shown that the coefficient p_i of the characteristic polynomial is equal to the sum of the principal minors of order i of $\mathbf{A}$.   Therefore, in particular,

$$p_1 = a_{11} + a_{22} + \cdots + a_{nn} \text{ (trace of } \mathbf{A})$$

and

$$p_n = |\mathbf{A}|$$

On the other hand, p_i can also be expressed in terms of the eigenvalues. In fact, directly from Eq. (A.2.1), we see that p_i is equal to the sum of all possible products of eigenvalues (multiple eigenvalues are counted as many times as their multiplicities) taken i at a time.

Example A.2.1:   Determine the characteristic polynomial and the eigenvalues of the given matrix

$$\mathbf{A} = \begin{bmatrix} 1 & 0 & 0 \\ -1 & 2 & 1 \\ 0 & 0 & 2 \end{bmatrix}$$

Solution: Since

$$|\lambda\mathbf{U} - \mathbf{A}| = \begin{vmatrix} \lambda - 1 & 0 & 0 \\ 1 & \lambda - 2 & -1 \\ 0 & 0 & \lambda - 2 \end{vmatrix} = (\lambda - 1)(\lambda - 2)^2$$

the characteristic polynomial is

$$(\lambda - 1)(\lambda - 2)^2 = \lambda^3 - 5\lambda^2 + 8\lambda - 4$$

and the eigenvalues of $\mathbf{A}$ are $\lambda_1 = 1$ and $\lambda_2 = 2$, with λ_2 of multiplicity 2.

Note that the coefficient of the highest power of λ in the characteristic equation is always equal to unity.   A polynomial having this property is called a *monic* polynomial.

It is interesting to observe that there is no direct relation between a matrix and its eigenvalues; i.e., there can be infinitely many square matrices of the same order which all have the same eigenvalues.   Therefore, when a characteristic polynomial is given it is possible to find matrices which assume the given polynomial as their characteristic polynomial. In fact, let the polynomial

$$Q(\lambda) = \lambda^n + q_1\lambda^{n-1} + \cdots + q_n$$

be given. Then, for example, the matrix of order n,

$$\begin{bmatrix} 0 & 1 & 0 & \cdots & 0 \\ 0 & 0 & 1 & \cdots & 0 \\ \cdots & \cdots & \cdots & \cdots & \cdots \\ 0 & 0 & 0 & \cdots & 1 \\ -q_n & -q_{n-1} & -q_{n-2} & \cdots & -q_1 \end{bmatrix} \qquad (A.2.2)$$

will have the polynomial $Q(\lambda)$ as its characteristic polynomial. This becomes evident after forming the characteristic polynomial for the matrix in Eq. (A.2.2). The matrix in Eq. (A.2.2) has a special name. It is called the *companion matrix* associated with the given polynomial.

Now let us consider the following system of algebraic equations,

$$\mathbf{AX} = \lambda\mathbf{X} \qquad (A.2.3)$$

where

   $\mathbf{A}$ is a known real square matrix of order n
   $\mathbf{X}$ is an unknown column matrix (vector)
   λ is a scalar parameter

A nontrivial solution of Eq. (A.2.3) exists only if the scalar parameter λ has certain definite values. In fact, since Eq. (A.2.3) can be written as

$$(\lambda\mathbf{U} - \mathbf{A})\mathbf{X} = 0 \qquad (A.2.4)$$

this homogeneous equation can have nontrivial solutions if, and only if, the coefficient matrix $\lambda\mathbf{U} - \mathbf{A}$ is singular. Therefore, it is necessary that

$$|\lambda\mathbf{U} - \mathbf{A}| = 0$$

That is, λ must equal one of the eigenvalues of the matrix $\mathbf{A}$. Therefore, if λ_i is one of the eigenvalues, then, for $\lambda = \lambda_i$, Eq. (A.2.3), which now has a nontrivial solution, can be written as

$$\mathbf{AX} = \lambda_i\mathbf{X} \qquad (A.2.5)$$

The solution $\mathbf{X}_i$ to Eq. (A.2.5) be is called the *eigenvector* of $\mathbf{A}$ corresponding to the eigenvalue λ_i. It is evident that if $\mathbf{A}$ has k distinct eigenvalues then there can be calculated k eigenvectors.

If Eq. (A.2.3) is premultiplied on both sides by $\mathbf{A}$, we obtain

$$\mathbf{A}^2\mathbf{X} = \lambda\mathbf{AX} \qquad (A.2.6)$$

Substituting Eq. (A.2.3) into Eq. (A.2.6) yields

$$\mathbf{A}^2\mathbf{X} = \lambda^2\mathbf{X}$$

Repeating this procedure m times we have

$$\mathbf{A}^m\mathbf{X} = \lambda^m\mathbf{X}$$

or, for eigenvector $\mathbf{X}_i$ corresponding to the eigenvalue λ_i,

$$\mathbf{A}^m\mathbf{X}_i = \lambda_i{}^m\mathbf{X}_i \tag{A.2.7}$$

It follows, therefore, that the eigenvalues of $\mathbf{A}^m$ are the mth power of the eigenvalues of the matrix $\mathbf{A}$.

Theorem A.2.1: Let $\mathbf{X}_i$ $(i = 1, 2, \ldots, k)$ be the eigenvectors corresponding to the k distinct eigenvalues λ_i of a given matrix $\mathbf{A}$ of order n. Then the $\mathbf{X}_i$'s are linearly independent; i.e., any one of the eigenvectors cannot be expressed as a linear combination of the others.

Proof: Consider the linear relation between these eigenvectors,

$$\alpha_1\mathbf{X}_1 + \alpha_2\mathbf{X}_2 + \cdots + \alpha_k\mathbf{X}_k = 0 \tag{A.2.8}$$

where α_i is a real number. We shall show that in Eq. (A.2.8) all α_i's are equal to zero. Indeed, if at least one of the α_i's is not equal to zero then either (a) one of the eigenvectors can be expressed in terms of the others or (b) if only one α_i, say α_1, is different from zero, Eq. (A.2.8) gives $\mathbf{X}_1 = 0$, which is not true, since $\mathbf{X}_1$ is a nontrivial solution of Eq. (A.2.3). When Eq. (A.2.8) is satisfied only with all a_i's equal to zero, the $\mathbf{X}_i$'s then form a *linearly independent* set.

By premultiplying Eq. (A.2.8) by $\mathbf{A}$ repeatedly and using the relation in Eq. (A.2.7), the following set of equations can be obtained:

$$\begin{bmatrix} 1 & 1 & \cdots & 1 \\ \lambda_1 & \lambda_2 & \cdots & \lambda_k \\ \lambda_1{}^2 & \lambda_2{}^2 & \cdots & \lambda_k{}^2 \\ \cdots & \cdots & \cdots & \cdots \\ \lambda_1{}^{k-1} & \lambda_2{}^{k-1} & \cdots & \lambda_k \end{bmatrix} \begin{bmatrix} \alpha_1\mathbf{X}_1 \\ \alpha_2\mathbf{X}_2 \\ \alpha_3\mathbf{X}_3 \\ \cdots \\ \alpha_k\mathbf{X}_k \end{bmatrix} = 0 \tag{A.2.9}$$

Since the determinant of the coefficient matrix is nonsingular, Eq. (A.2.9) has the trivial solution, that is, $\alpha_i\mathbf{X}_i = 0$, and since $\mathbf{X}_i \neq 0$, then necessarily $\alpha_i = 0$ for $i = 1, 2, \ldots, k$. This implies that the eigenvectors are linearly independent.

Consider the square matrix $\mathbf{A}$ of order n, with distinct eigenvalues λ_i. The eigenvectors are given by

$$\mathbf{A}\mathbf{X}_i = \lambda_i\mathbf{X}_i \tag{A.2.10}$$

Equation (A.2.10), with $i = 1, 2, \ldots, n$, can be written in a matrix form as

$$A[\mathbf{X}_1 \quad \mathbf{X}_2 \quad \cdots \quad \mathbf{X}_n] = [\mathbf{X}_1 \quad \mathbf{X}_2 \quad \cdots \quad \mathbf{X}_n] \begin{bmatrix} \lambda_1 & & & & \\ & \lambda_2 & & & \\ & & \cdot & & \\ & & & \cdot & \\ & & & & \lambda_n \end{bmatrix}$$

(A.2.11)

where $\mathbf{P} = [\mathbf{X}_1 \quad \mathbf{X}_2 \quad \cdots \quad \mathbf{X}_n]$ is a square matrix, and since the eigenvectors are linearly independent $\mathbf{P}$ is nonsingular. Let us indicate the diagonal matrix containing the eigenvalues in Eq. (A.2.11) by $\mathbf{\Lambda}$; then Eq. (A.2.11) can be written as

$$\mathbf{AP} = \mathbf{P\Lambda}$$

or

(A.2.12)

$$\mathbf{A} = \mathbf{P\Lambda P}^{-1}$$

That is, if a matrix $\mathbf{A}$ has distinct eigenvalues, then it can be reduced to a diagonal matrix whose diagonal entries are equal to the eigenvalues of $\mathbf{A}$. The transformation in Eq. (A.2.12) is called a *similarity transformation*. In general, if $\mathbf{A}$ and $\mathbf{B}$ are square real matrices and if there exists a nonsingular matrix $\mathbf{P}$ such that

$$\mathbf{A} = \mathbf{PBP}^{-1} \qquad \text{or} \qquad \mathbf{PAP}^{-1} = \mathbf{A}$$

then $\mathbf{A}$ and $\mathbf{B}$ are called *similar matrices*. In Eq. (A.2.12), $\mathbf{A}$ is similar to a diagonal matrix and is assumed to have distinct eigenvalues. However, there exist matrices with repeated eigenvalues which also are similar to a diagonal matrix. In general, a square matrix may not be similar to a diagonal matrix, but by using a similarity transformation they can be reduced to a simpler form, called the *Jordan form*, which is defined as

$$\begin{bmatrix} \mathbf{J}_1 & & & & \\ & \mathbf{J}_2 & & & \\ & & \cdot & & \\ & & & \cdot & \\ & & & & \mathbf{J}_k \end{bmatrix}$$

where

$$\mathbf{J}_i = \begin{bmatrix} \lambda_i & 1 & 0 & & \cdots & 0 \\ 0 & \lambda_i & 1 & 0 & \cdots & 0 \\ \cdot & & \cdot & & \cdot & \\ \cdot & & & \cdot & & \\ \cdot & & & & \cdot & 1 \\ 0 & \cdots & & & & \lambda_i \end{bmatrix}$$

To develop other properties of the characteristic polynomial, consider the polynomials with real coefficients

$$f(\lambda) = a_0\lambda^n + a_1\lambda^{n-1} + \cdots + a_n$$

and

$$g(\lambda) = b_0\lambda^m + b_1\lambda^{m-1} + \cdots + b_m \tag{A.2.13}$$

where $n \geq m$. It is known from algebra that, by a long-division process, the following relation can be established:

$$f(\lambda) = q(\lambda)g(\lambda) + r(\lambda) \tag{A.2.14}$$

where the degree of $r(\lambda)$ is less than m. Under this condition the quotient polynomial $q(\lambda)$ and the remainder polynomial $r(\lambda)$ are uniquely determined. Further, if $r(\lambda) \equiv 0$, then $f(\lambda)$ is said to be divisible by $g(\lambda)$.

If, in Eqs. (A.2.13), λ is replaced by a square matrix $\mathbf{A}$, the relation in Eq. (A.2.14) is still valid, i.e.,

$$f(\mathbf{A}) = q(\mathbf{A})g(\mathbf{A}) + r(\mathbf{A}) \tag{A.2.15}$$

Consider now the polynomials in λ with square matrices as coefficients ($n \geq m$),

$$\begin{aligned}
\mathbf{F}(\lambda) &= \mathbf{A}_0\lambda^n + \mathbf{A}_1\lambda^{n-1} + \cdots + \mathbf{A}_n \\
\mathbf{G}(\lambda) &= \mathbf{B}_0\lambda^m + \mathbf{B}_1\lambda^{m-1} + \cdots + \mathbf{B}_m
\end{aligned} \tag{A.2.16}$$

It can be shown that there exist unique polynomials $\mathbf{Q}(\lambda)[\mathbf{Q}_1(\lambda)]$ and $\mathbf{R}(\lambda)[\mathbf{R}_1(\lambda)]$ where the degree of $\mathbf{R}(\lambda)[\mathbf{R}_1(\lambda)]$ is less than m, such that, similar to Eq. (A.2.14),

$$\mathbf{F}(\lambda) = \mathbf{Q}(\lambda)\mathbf{G}(\lambda) + \mathbf{R}(\lambda)$$

or

$$\mathbf{F}(\lambda) = \mathbf{G}(\lambda)\mathbf{Q}_1(\lambda) + \mathbf{R}_1(\lambda) \tag{A.2.17}$$

If $\mathbf{R}(\lambda)[\mathbf{R}_1(\lambda)]$ is a zero matrix, then $\mathbf{G}(\lambda)$ is said to be a right (left) divisor of $\mathbf{F}(\lambda)$.

In particular, let $\mathbf{G}(\lambda) = \lambda\mathbf{U} - \mathbf{A}$ in Eq. (A.2.17). Then it can be further shown that, when λ is replaced by the matrix $\mathbf{A}$, Eq. (A.2.17) gives

$$\mathbf{F}(\mathbf{A}) = \mathbf{R}(\mathbf{A}) = \mathbf{R}_1(\mathbf{A})$$

On the other hand, because of the relation

$$D(\lambda)\mathbf{U} = (\lambda\mathbf{U} - \mathbf{A})\ \mathrm{adj}\ (\lambda\mathbf{U} - \mathbf{A}) \tag{A.2.18}$$

it follows from Eqs. (A.2.17) that $\mathbf{R}_1(\lambda) \equiv \mathbf{0}$, that is,

$$D(\mathbf{A}) = 0 \tag{A.2.19}$$

This relation is called the *Cayley-Hamilton theorem*, and it can be stated formally as follows.

Theorem A.2.2: Every square matrix satisfies its own characteristic equation.

Any polynomial $d(\lambda)$ having the property that $d(\mathbf{A}) = 0$ is called an *annihilating polynomial*. The annihilating polynomial of least degree is called the *minimal polynomial* of $\mathbf{A}$ and is denoted by $m(\lambda)$.

Theorem A.2.3: The minimal polynomial of a square matrix is given by

$$m(\lambda) = \frac{D(\lambda)}{D_{n-1}(\lambda)} \tag{A.2.20}$$

where $D_{n-1}(\lambda)$ is the highest common factor of all the $(n-1)$-rowed minor determinants of $\lambda\mathbf{U} - \mathbf{A}$, which is assumed to be monic.

Proof: Since $D_{n-1}(\lambda)$ is a factor of all the $(n-1)$-rowed minor determinants of $\lambda\mathbf{U} - \mathbf{A}$, it is also contained in $D(\lambda)$ and therefore $m(\lambda)$ defined in Eq. (A.2.20) is a polynomial. On the other hand, every entry in the matrix

$$\frac{1}{D_{n-1}(\lambda)} \text{ adj } (\lambda\mathbf{U} - \mathbf{A})$$

is a polynomial, and we write

$$(\lambda\mathbf{U} - \mathbf{A}) \frac{1}{D_{n-1}(\lambda)} \text{ adj } (\lambda\mathbf{U} - \mathbf{A}) = m(\lambda)\mathbf{U} \tag{A.2.21}$$

Again from Eqs. (A.2.17), it follows that $m(\lambda)\mathbf{U}$ is divisible by $\lambda\mathbf{U} - \mathbf{A}$ and hence $m(\mathbf{A}) = 0$; that is, $m(\lambda)$ is an annihilating polynomial. To show that $m(\lambda)$ is the polynomial of lowest degree, let $d(\lambda)$ be an annihilating polynomial with the least degree. In this case, we have

$$m(\lambda) = q(\lambda)d(\lambda) + r(\lambda)$$

Since the degree of $r(\lambda)$ is less than that of $d(\lambda)$, if $r(\lambda) \neq 0$, then it is a contradiction to the assumption that $d(\lambda)$ is an annihilating polynomial of least degree. Hence

$$m(\lambda) = q(\lambda)d(\lambda) \tag{A.2.22}$$

and since $d(\mathbf{A}) = 0$, then $d(\lambda)\mathbf{U}$ must be divisible by $\lambda\mathbf{U} - \mathbf{A}$. That is,

$$d(\lambda)\mathbf{U} = (\lambda\mathbf{U} - \mathbf{A})\mathbf{H}(\lambda) \tag{A.2.23}$$

where $\mathbf{H}(\lambda)$ is a polynomial with matrix coefficients. From Eqs. (A.2.21) to (A.2.23) it follows that

$$(\lambda\mathbf{U} - \mathbf{A}) \frac{1}{D_{n-1}(\lambda)} \text{ adj } (\lambda\mathbf{U} - \mathbf{A}) = q(\lambda)d(\lambda)\mathbf{U}$$
$$= q(\lambda)(\lambda\mathbf{U} - \mathbf{A})\mathbf{H}(\lambda)$$

Since $\lambda\mathbf{U} - \mathbf{A}$ is nonsingular,

$$\frac{1}{D_{n-1}(\lambda)q(\lambda)} \text{ adj } (\lambda\mathbf{U} - \mathbf{A}) = \mathbf{H}(\lambda) \tag{A.2.24}$$

Since the left-hand side of Eq. (A.2.24) is a polynomial in λ, by necessity $q(\lambda) = 1$. Hence $m(\lambda) = d(\lambda)$, and the proof is complete.

A.3   ON THE CONVERGENCE OF MATRIX POWER SERIES

In Chap. 6 the power series

$$f(\mathbf{P}) = k_0\mathbf{U} + k_1\mathbf{P} + k_2\mathbf{P}^2 + \cdots + k_n\mathbf{P}^n + \cdots \tag{A.3.1}$$

is considered and the proof of the following theorem is postponed to this section.

Theorem A.3.1:   The power series in Eq. (A.3.1) is convergent if all eigenvalues of the matrix $\mathbf{P}$ lie within the circle of convergence in the complex plane of the corresponding series

$$f(\lambda) = k_0 + k_1\lambda + k_2\lambda^2 + \cdots + k_n\lambda^n + \cdots$$

Proof: The proof of this theorem can best be given by the use of the formula in Eq. (6.2.16). This is a valid procedure, since Eq. (6.2.16) was derived independently of the definition of the power series in Eq. (A.3.1). For ready reference Eq. (6.2.16) is repeated here as

$$\begin{aligned}
f(\mathbf{P}) = {} & \mathbf{Z}_{11}f(\lambda_1) + \mathbf{Z}_{12}\frac{f'(\lambda_1)}{1!} + \cdots + \mathbf{Z}_{1r_1}\frac{f^{(r_1-1)}(\lambda_1)}{(r_1 - 1)!} \\
& + \mathbf{Z}_{21}f(\lambda_2) + \mathbf{Z}_{22}\frac{f'(\lambda_2)}{1!} + \cdots + \mathbf{Z}_{2r_2}\frac{f^{(r_2-1)}(\lambda_2)}{(r_2 - 1)!} \\
& \cdots \cdots \cdots \cdots \cdots \cdots \cdots \cdots \cdots \\
& + \mathbf{Z}_{k1}f(\lambda_k) + \mathbf{Z}_{k2}\frac{f'(\lambda_k)}{1!} + \cdots + \mathbf{Z}_{kr_k}\frac{f^{(r_k-1)}(\lambda_k)}{(r_k - 1)!}
\end{aligned} \tag{A.3.2}$$

where, of course, it is assumed that $\mathbf{P}$ has k distinct eigenvalues, λ_1, λ_2, $\ldots$, λ_k, with multiplicities r_1, r_2, $\ldots$, r_k, respectively. Since the two expressions for $f(\mathbf{P})$ in Eqs. (A.3.1) and (A.3.2) are equivalent, for the convergence of the power series the expression on the right-hand side of Eq. (A.3.1) must be finite; i.e., corresponding to the power series in Eq. (A.3.1), the power series

$$f(\lambda) = k_0 + k_1\lambda + k_2\lambda^2 + \cdots + k_n\lambda^n + \cdots \tag{A.3.3}$$

and its derivatives must be convergent. This, of course, implies that the eigenvalues of the matrix $\mathbf{P}$ must lie within the circle of convergence, with radius R, of the series in Eq. (A.3.3). If some of the eigenvalues lie outside this circle, the power series in Eq. (A.3.1) is divergent. On the other hand, if $|\lambda_i| \leq R$, that is, if some of the eigenvalues lie on the circle, it is necessary and also sufficient for the convergence of $f(\mathbf{P})$ that $f(\lambda)$, $f'(\lambda), \ldots, f^{(r_1-1)}(\lambda)$ $[r_i = \max (r_1, r_2, \ldots, r_k)]$ are all convergent series.[1]

Example A.3.1: Determine the convergence conditions for

$$f(\mathbf{P}) = e^{\mathbf{P}} = \mathbf{U} + \frac{\mathbf{P}}{1!} + \frac{\mathbf{P}^2}{2!} + \cdots$$

Solution: Since the radius of convergence of the corresponding series

$$f(\lambda) = 1 + \frac{\lambda}{1!} + \frac{\lambda^2}{2!} + \cdots$$

is infinite, $f(\mathbf{P})$ converges absolutely for any square matrix $\mathbf{P}$.

A.4 LAGRANGE INTERPOLATION POLYNOMIAL

Consider a polynomial of degree n,

$$y(x) = a_0 x^n + a_1 x^{n-1} + \cdots + a_{n-1} x + a_n \tag{A.4.1}$$

Since, in general, $y(x)$ contains $n + 1$ arbitrary coefficients, one can impose $n + 1$ conditions on $y(x)$ to determine these coefficients. If we require that the plot of $y(x)$ pass through a given set of $n + 1$ distinct points (x_i, y_i) such that no two points lie on a vertical line, then one way to determine the polynomial in Eq. (A.4.1) is due to Lagrange. The idea in Lagrange's formula hinges on the determination of certain polynomials $K_j(x)$ which vanish when $x = x_i$ for $i \neq j$ and become unity when $x = x_i$ for $i = j$. The polynomial

$$L(x) = K_1(x)y_1 + K_2(x)y_2 + \cdots + K_{n+1}(x)y_{n+1} = \sum_{j=1}^{n+1} K_j(x)y_j \tag{A.4.2}$$

satisfies the imposed conditions; i.e., the plot of $L(x)$ will pass through all points (x_i, y_i) $(i = 1, 2, \ldots, n + 1)$. Since the degree of the polynomial to be constructed is n, if the polynomials $K_j(x)$ are selected in the form

$$K_j(x) = \frac{(x - x_1)(x - x_2) \cdots (x - x_{j-1})(x - x_{j+1}) \cdots (x - x_{n+1})}{(x_j - x_1)(x_j - x_2) \cdots (x_j - x_{j-1})(x_j - x_{j+1}) \cdots (x_j - x_{n+1})} \tag{A.4.3}$$

the degree of $L(x)$ becomes n and the desired polynomial is established.

The final form of the Lagrange interpolation formula is given as follows:

$$y(x) = \sum_{j=1}^{n+1} \left(\prod_{\substack{i=1 \\ i \neq j}}^{n+1} \frac{x - x_i}{x_j - x_i} \right) y(x_i) \tag{A.4.4}$$

A.5 PARTIAL - FRACTION EXPANSION

Consider the following rational function in the variable z,

$$R(z) = \frac{P_m(z)}{Q_n(z)} \tag{A.5.1}$$

where z is, in general, a complex variable and it is assumed that the coefficients of the polynomials $P_m(z)$ of degree m and $Q_n(z)$ of degree n are all real. If $m \geq n$, then by long division $R(z)$ can be written as

$$R(z) = A(z) + \frac{B(z)}{Q_n(z)} \tag{A.5.2}$$

where the polynomial $A(z)$ is called the *integral part* of $R(z)$ and the degree of $B(z)$ is less than the degree of $Q_n(z)$. Since all coefficients are real, $Q_n(z)$ can have zeros which are either real or complex. If $Q_n(z)$ has a complex zero, then the complex conjugate of this zero is also a zero of $Q_n(z)$. Furthermore, some of the complex zeros may occur on the imaginary axis. Therefore, $Q_n(z)$ can be written in the form

$$Q_n(z) = a_0(z - a_1)^{\lambda_1}(z - a_2)^{\lambda_2} \cdots (z - a_k)^{\lambda_k}(z^2 + \alpha_1 z + \beta_1)^{\mu_1}$$
$$\cdots (z^2 + \alpha_l z + \beta_l)^{\mu_l}$$
$$= a_0 \prod_{i=1}^{k} (z - a_i)^{\lambda_i} \prod_{j=1}^{l} (z^2 + \alpha_j z + \beta_j)^{\mu_i} \tag{A.5.3}$$

where the α_i represent real zeros of $Q_n(z)$ and the factors $z^2 + \alpha_j z + \beta_j$ correspond to the complex conjugate zeros of $Q_n(z)$ ($\alpha_j \geq 0$ and $\alpha_j^2 - 4\beta_j < 0$) and

$$\sum_{i=1}^{k} \lambda_i + \sum_{j=1}^{l} \mu_j = n$$

Since

$$z^2 + \alpha_j z + \beta_j = (z - b_j)(z - \hat{b}_j)$$

where b_j is complex, Eq. (A.5.3) can also be written as

$$Q_n(z) = a_0 \prod_{i=1}^{k} (z - a_i)^{\lambda_i} \prod_{j=1}^{l} (z - b_j)(z - \hat{b}_j) \tag{A.5.4}$$

After substituting the expression for $Q_n(z)$ from Eq. (A.5.3) into Eq. (A.5.2), we have the partial-fraction expansion for $R(z)$,

$$
\begin{aligned}
R(z) = A(z) &+ \frac{A_1{}^{(1)}}{(z-a_1)^{\lambda_1}} + \frac{A_2{}^{(1)}}{(z-a_1)^{\lambda_1-1}} + \cdots + \frac{A_{\lambda_1}^{(1)}}{z-a_1} \\
&+ \frac{A_1{}^{(2)}}{(z-a_2)^{\lambda_2}} + \frac{A_2{}^{(2)}}{(z-a_2)^{\lambda_2-1}} + \cdots + \frac{A_{\lambda_2}^{(2)}}{z-a_2} \\
&\cdots\cdots\cdots\cdots\cdots\cdots\cdots\cdots\cdots \\
&+ \frac{A_1{}^{(k)}}{(z-a_k)^{\lambda_k}} + \frac{A_2{}^{(k)}}{(z-a_k)^{\lambda_k-1}} + \cdots + \frac{A_{\lambda_k}^{(k)}}{z-a_k} \\
&+ \frac{B_1{}^{(1)}}{(z-b_1)^{\mu_1}} + \frac{B_2{}^{(1)}}{(z-b_1)^{\mu_1-1}} + \cdots + \frac{B_{\mu_1}^{(1)}}{z-b_1} \\
&\cdots\cdots\cdots\cdots\cdots\cdots\cdots\cdots\cdots \\
&+ \frac{B_1{}^{(l)}}{(z-b_l)^{\mu_l}} + \frac{B_2{}^{(l)}}{(z-b_l)^{\mu_l-1}} + \cdots + \frac{B_{\mu_l}^{(l)}}{z-b_l} \\
&+ \frac{\hat{B}_1{}^{(1)}}{(z-\hat{b}_1)^{\mu_1}} + \frac{\hat{B}_2{}^{(1)}}{(z-\hat{b}_1)^{\mu_1-1}} + \cdots + \frac{\hat{B}_{\mu_1}^{(1)}}{z-\hat{b}_1} \\
&\cdots\cdots\cdots\cdots\cdots\cdots\cdots\cdots\cdots \\
&+ \frac{\hat{B}_1{}^{(l)}}{(z-\hat{b}_l)^{\mu_l}} + \frac{\hat{B}_2{}^{(l)}}{(z-\hat{b}_l)^{\mu_l-1}} + \cdots + \frac{\hat{B}_{\mu_l}^{(l)}}{z-\hat{b}_l} \quad \text{(A.5.5)}
\end{aligned}
$$

where the $A_i{}^{(j)}$ are all real, while the $B_i{}^{(j)}$ are, in general, complex numbers.

The expression in Eq. (A.5.5) is unique and is actually an identity in z. Therefore, assigning various values for z, one establishes a sufficient number of linear algebraic equations to determine the unknown constants $A_i{}^{(j)}$ and $B_i{}^{(j)}$. However, to determine the coefficients $A_p{}^{(1)}$ ($1 \le p \le \lambda_1$) in Eq. (A.5.5), we can multiply both sides of the equation by the factor $(z-a_1)^{\lambda_1}$ and differentiate both sides $\lambda - p$ times. Since all terms to the right of this resulting equation except $A_p{}^{(1)}$ contain the factor $z - a_1$ at least once, all coefficients except those of $A_p{}^{(1)}$ vanish for $z = a_1$. These nonvanishing terms lead to the equation

$$
\begin{aligned}
\lim_{z \to a_1} &\left[\frac{d^{(\lambda_1-p)}}{dz^{(\lambda_1-p)}} (z-a_1)^{\lambda_1} R(z) \right] \\
&= \lim_{z \to a_1} \left[\frac{d^{(\lambda_1-p)}}{dz^{(\lambda_1-p)}} \frac{A_p{}^{(1)}(z-a_1)^{\lambda_1}}{(z-a_1)^p} \right] = (\lambda_1 - p)! A_p{}^{(1)}
\end{aligned}
$$

where the integer $(\lambda_1 - p)! = (\lambda_1 - p)(\lambda_1 - p - 1)(\lambda_1 - p - 2) \cdots 2 \cdot 1$ and is read as "$(\lambda_1 - p)$ factorial." If we now take the limit of both sides of Eq. (A.5.5) as z approaches a_1, we have

$$
A_p{}^{(1)} = \frac{1}{(\lambda_1 - p)!} \left[\frac{d^{(\lambda_1-p)}}{dz^{(\lambda_1-p)}} (z-a_1)^{\lambda_1} R(z) \right]_{z=a_1} \quad \text{(A.5.6)}
$$

Example A.5.1: Determine the partial-fraction expansion for

$$R(z) = \frac{-3z^2 + 10z - 6}{(z - 1)^3}$$

Solution: $R(z)$ can be written as

$$R(z) = \frac{A_1}{(z - 1)^3} + \frac{A_2}{(z - 1)^2} + \frac{A_3}{z - 1} \tag{A.5.7}$$

Multiplying both sides of Eq. (A.5.7) by $(z - 1)^3$, we have

$$(z - 1)^3 R(z) = -3z^2 + 10z - 6 = A_1 + A_2(z - 1) + A_3(z - 1)^2 \tag{A.5.8}$$

Therefore, from Eq. (A.5.6), we have

$$A_1 = (z - 1)^3 R(z) \Big|_{z=1} = 1$$

$$A_2 = \frac{1}{1!} \frac{d}{dz} (z - 1)^3 R(z) \Big|_{z=1} = -6z + 10 \Big|_{z=1} = 4$$

$$A_3 = \frac{1}{2!} \frac{d^2}{dz^2} (z - 1)^3 R(z) \Big|_{z=1} = \frac{1}{2}(-6) \Big|_{z=1} = -3$$

and the partial-fraction expansion is obtained as

$$R(z) = \frac{1}{(z - 1)^3} + \frac{4}{(z - 1)^2} - \frac{3}{z - 1}$$

FURTHER READING

1. Macduffee, C. C.: "Theory of Matrices," Chelsea Publishing Company, New York, 1946.

Index

Index